China-EU Law Series

Volume 7

More information about this series at http://www.springer.com/series/11933

Stephan Kuntner

China's Foreign-Invested Limited Partnership Enterprise

An Analysis of its Legal Personality, Limited Liability and Transferable Ownership Interest

Springer

Stephan Kuntner
Hamburg, Germany

ISSN 2198-2708 ISSN 2198-2716 (electronic)
China-EU Law Series
ISBN 978-3-030-54180-4 ISBN 978-3-030-54181-1 (eBook)
https://doi.org/10.1007/978-3-030-54181-1

This Springer imprint is published by the registered company Springer Nature Switzerland AG.
The registered company address is: Gewerbestrasse 11, 6330 Cham, Switzerland

In memory of my cousin
Sebastian Wiesler
*(*7.4.1995 †26.8.2014)*

Preface

The present book is an updated version of my PhD thesis, which was accepted by the University of Hamburg in June 2019 and defended with honours in December of the same year. The changes in legislation up to 30 April 2020 have been incorporated.

My passion for Chinese culture, history and law began in 2006 during my legal studies at the Institute of Law of the Chinese Academy of Social Sciences (中国社会科学院法学研究所) in Beijing. In the period between 2010 and 2014, I studied the Chinese language at Nanjing University (南京大学) and worked for an international law firm in Shanghai for over three years. Having had the chance to study and research but also practice law in China has been a great privilege, as it allowed me to take both an academic and a practical approach to my research question. The four years in China have been an unforgettable and rich experience, which has intensified my love for this fascinating culture.

I am very grateful to my supervisor Professor Dr. Hinrich Julius for his guidance, ongoing support and the academic freedom in conceptualising my research project. I am further indebted to Professor Dr. Rüdiger Veil for acting as a second supervisor and his encouragement throughout this project.

I would especially like to express gratitude to my friend Dr. Johanna Croon-Gestefeld for her invaluable scholarly advice, never-ending encouragement and strong support throughout my PhD studies. For fruitful theoretical discussions and helpful counsel, I would also like to acknowledge Anna Elshafei, Professor Dr. Dr. h.c. mult. Karsten Schmidt, Professor Dr. Knut Benjamin Pissler and Professor Dr. Carsten Jungmann. I am much obliged to Professor Fei Liu (刘飞), Professor Dr. Hinrich Julius and Ronald Monty Silley for including my book in the China-EU Law Series.

Writing this book over several years, on two different continents, would not have been possible without my friends. Their motivating encouragement, support and wonderful humour at all times have been invaluable. I would particularly like to recognise Martin Asseburg, Maximilian Neeb, Dr. Martin Hejma, Claire Proebstle, Dr. Alexander Stark, Dr. Tina Anderson, Conrad Wandt, Anouk Bender, Nina Marie Güttler, Dr. Jan Sturm, Mareile Paske and all my friends in Nanjing, Shanghai, Jork and Hamburg.

I thank my parents Anita and Johann Kuntner and my brother Christoph Kuntner and his family for their continuous assistance and encouragement during my entire legal studies and career. My entire family has always understood my passion for China and shown great support of my endeavours, even in times of sorrow. While I was writing this book, my cousin Sebastian Wiesler sadly passed away at a young age. I have dedicated this book to his memory.

Hamburg, Germany
May 2020

Stephan Kuntner 孔劭凡

Contents

Abbreviations[1]

AIC	Local Administration for Industry and Commerce
Art	Article
Arts	Articles
BGB	Bürgerliches Gesetzbuch
BGH	Bundesgerichtshof
BOT	Build–operate–transfer
CEPA	Closer Economic Partnership Arrangement
CBIRC	China Banking and Insurance Regulatory Commission
CJV	Sino-Foreign Cooperative Joint Venture
CJV Law	Sino-Foreign Cooperative Joint Venture Law
Constitution	PRC Constitution
CPC	Communist Party of China
CSRC	China Securities Regulatory Commission
eg	For example
ed	Editor
edn	Edition
eds	Editors
EJV	Sino-Foreign Equity Joint Venture
EJV Law	Sino-Foreign Equity Joint Venture Law
et al	And others
EU	European Union
f	Following (1 more page)
FDI	Foreign direct investment
ff	Following (2 or more following pages)
FICLS	Foreign-Invested Company Limited by Shares
FIE	Foreign-Invested Enterprise

[1]A list of all laws and regulations is provided in the Appendix. Included in this list are only abbreviations of laws and regulations that are used in the text.

FIE HoldCo	Foreign-Invested Enterprise Holding Company
FIGPE	Foreign-Invested General Partnership Enterprise
FIL	Foreign Investment Law
FILPE	Foreign-Invested Limited Partnership Enterprise
FIPE	Foreign-Invested Partnership Enterprise
FISGPE	Foreign-Invested Specialised General Partnership Enterprise
FIVCE	Foreign-Invested Venture Capital Enterprise
fn	Footnote
GAC	General Administration of Customs
GbR	Gesellschaft bürgerlichen Rechts
GmbH	Gesellschaft mit beschränkter Haftung
GPCL	General Principles of the Civil Law
GPE	General Partnership Enterprise
GRCL	General Rules of Civil Law
HGB	Handelsgesetzbuch
ie	That is
ibid	Ibidem
KG	Kommanditgesellschaft
KGaA	Kommanditgesellschaft auf Aktien
LLP	Limited liability partnership
LPE	Limited partnership enterprise
M&A	Mergers and acquisitions
MOF	Ministry of Finance
MOFCOM	Ministry of Commerce
MOFTEC	Ministry of Foreign Trade and Economic Cooperation
MOHRSS	Ministry of Human Resources and Social Security
NDRC	National Development and Reform Commission
no	Number
NPC	National People's Congress
p	Page
para	Paragraph
PE	Private equity
PEL	Partnership Enterprise Law
PRC	People's Republic of China
QFLP	Qualified foreign limited partnership
RMB	Renminbi
RQFLP	RMB-qualified foreign limited partnership
RUPA	Revised Uniform Partnership Act
SAFE	State Administration of Foreign Exchange
SAIC	State Administration for Industry and Commerce
SAMR	State Administration for Market Regulation
SASAC	State-Owned Assets Supervision and Administration Commission
SAT	State Administration of Taxation
SCNPC	Standing Committee of the National People's Congress

SFDA	State Food and Drugs Administration
SGPE	Specialised general partnership enterprise
Shanghai FTZ	China (Shanghai) Pilot Free Trade Zone
SOE	State-owned enterprise
SPC	Supreme People's Court
SPV	Special Purpose Vehicle
State Council	PRC State Council
UK	United Kingdom
ULPA	Uniform Limited Partnership Act
UPA	Uniform Partnership Act
US	United States
USD	US-Dollar
VC	Venture capital
VIE	Variable interest entity
vol	Volume
WFOE	Wholly Foreign-Owned Enterprise
WFOE Law	Wholly Foreign-Owned Enterprise Law
WTO	World Trade Organization

Chapter 1
Introduction and Concept

1.1 Framing the Task

'From bringing capital, technology, management experiences and export channels at the very beginning, to bringing the modern service models, new operation concepts [and] high-end talents nowadays, foreign-invested enterprises have become the major players in promoting economic and social development in China.'[1]

Foreign investors[2] who want to make a foreign direct investment[3] (FDI) in China[4] have to choose an enterprise form as their investment vehicle.[5] A number of factors and considerations influence the decision on the optimal enterprise form for a FDI project. The initial choice is between two different entry modes that interact with ownership strategies: (1) solely foreign-owned enterprises that are exclusively invested in and owned by foreign investors; (2) cooperative enterprises that are co-owned and co-invested by foreign investors and Chinese investors.[6] This book focuses on the latter entry mode of establishing a cooperative enterprise, and aims to be a contribution to the research and understanding of sino-foreign alliances and, in

---

[1]Para. 1 Explanatory Notes on the PRC Foreign Investment Law (Draft for Comments) (中华人民共和国外国投资法 (草案征求意见稿)的说明), promulgated by the Ministry of Commerce on 19 January 2015.

[2]In this book, 'Foreign investor' refers to companies, enterprises and other economic organisations that are incorporated outside the PRC, or individuals who are not PRC nationals.

[3]For a definition of FDI, see Chap. 2.

[4]For the purpose of this book, China refers to the People's Republic of China or PRC, excluding the Hong Kong Special Administrative Region, Macau Special Administrative Region and the territory of Taiwan.

[5]Jiao and Kasteleijn (2011), p. 50.

[6]In this book, 'Chinese investor' refers to companies, enterprises and other economic organisations that are incorporated in the PRC, excluding foreign-invested enterprises, or individuals who are PRC nationals.

S. Kuntner, *China's Foreign-Invested Limited Partnership Enterprise*, China-EU Law Series 7, https://doi.org/10.1007/978-3-030-54181-1_1

particular, the partnership enterprise law of the world's second largest economy. Up until now, under the highly regulated Chinese foreign investment regime,[7] the vast majority of sino-foreign alliances have been conducted in the form of an Equity Joint Venture (EJV).[8] More recently, another enterprise form—the limited partnership enterprise—has received more attention as a potential investment vehicle, from both foreign investors and the Chinese government.

For the purposes of this book, a limited partnership is defined as 'a form of business organisation in which one or more of the owners are general partners who are personally liable to the creditors of the business and who manage the business, and in which one or more of the owners are limited partners who are not personally liable to creditors of the business'.[9] Limited partnerships were historically among the first enterprise forms that were established.[10] Most jurisdictions today offer the limited partnership as an enterprise form and it is a common investment vehicle for investments in various industries.[11] The limited partnership enterprise itself can be understood as an organisation form which combines certain attributes of partnerships and corporations.[12]

> Conceptually, limited partners are passive investors with little or no control of the partnership or no authority to bind the partnership. In some ways, a limited partner is like a shareholder in a corporation. For example, a limited partner is liable for the partnership's liabilities only to the extent of its contribution. In other ways, however, the rights of limited partners are even more limited than those of a shareholder in a corporation and may resemble those of a creditor as much as a corporate shareholder. Nonetheless, under certain circumstances, a limited partner will be treated as a general partner for purposes of liability of the partnership if it exceeds statutory limitations on its management authority. At the most foundational level, however, limited partnerships are much more like partnerships than they are like corporations or debtor-creditor relationships because the governing structure borrows heavily from general partnership statutes.[13]

Legal practitioners have further developed the limited partnership enterprise by combining it with the legal form of a private limited company as its only general partner.[14] The result is the creation of the so-called limited partnership with a corporate general partner. The classic paradigm for this structure is the German

---

[7]'Foreign investment regime' refers to the legal regime that governs foreign investments in China, consisting of the specific laws and regulations governing foreign investments as well as any other rules and policies issued by the government on national, provincial or local levels.

[8]See Sect. 3.2 for other investment vehicles for sino-foreign alliances provided for by Chinese law, which have however been used significantly less in practice; see Sect. 3.1.5 for the impact of the new Foreign Investment Law.

[9]Ribstein (1988), p. 840.

[10]Bromberg and Ribstein (1994), pp. 11:19–11:23; Holdsworth (1925), pp. 195–199.

[11]Haase (2014), pp. 3, 4.

[12]Wu and Geu (2007–2008), p. 137.

[13]Ibid, p. 137.

[14]Schaper (2013), p. 80.

GmbH & Co. KG.[15] This is a combination of a German limited partnership (Kommanditgesellschaft/KG) and a German limited liability company (Gesellschaft mit beschränkter Haftung/GmbH) as its general partner. The GmbH & Co. KG was endorsed for the first time by a German Higher Regional court in 1912.[16] The original intention to combine the two legal forms was based on the desire to accumulate the advantages of partnership law and company law: in particular, the flexibility of the organisation of internal affairs and tax privileges in a partnership on the one hand, and the limited liability of corporations on the other.[17] Even though the limited partnership with a corporate general partner is now acknowledged as an independent type of legal structure, this kind of combination is regarded as a self-made hybrid form because it stems from creative legal practice, and not directly from the intentions of lawmakers.[18] Legal advisors took these combinations to the next level by forming transnational structures, with the limited partnership and the corporate general partner originating in different jurisdictions.[19] One of the most prominent examples of a cross-border combination is the (English) Limited & Co. KG, which, despite harsh criticism from some scholars, has been legally recognised by German courts.[20]

Over the years, lawmakers have observed the growing popularity of the combined partnership type of legal forms.[21] Beginning in the US, lawmakers have reacted by introducing statutory hybrid enterprise forms that effectively have the same features as a limited partnership with a corporate general partner.[22] Common examples in the US are the Limited Liability Company, the Limited Liability Partnership and the Limited Liability Limited Partnership.[23] Because these legal forms are readily available 'off the shelf', and do not require complex legal drafting, statutory hybrid enterprise forms have quickly gained popularity in the US, and to a large degree, have replaced the limited partnership with a corporate general partner.[24] In Europe, however, statutory hybrid legal forms have not developed to the same extent.[25] While the UK introduced a statutory hybrid legal form that is not limited to certain professions, similar legal forms in Germany and Italy do restrict access to particular professions, such as lawyers, accountants, architects, doctors etc.[26]

---

[15] Ibid, p. 91; Teichmann (2014), p. 220.

[16] *Bavarian Higher Regional Court (BayObLG)*, 16.02.1912, in: Deutsche Juristen-Zeitung vol 18 (1913), pp. 647–648.

[17] Schaper (2013), pp. 82, 91.

[18] Ibid, pp. 75, 83, 111; Fleischer and Wansleben (2017a), p. 169.

[19] Schaper (2013), p. 82.

[20] Ibid, pp. 91–92.

[21] Ibid, p. 89.

[22] Ibid, pp. 83–84.

[23] For an introduction to these hybrid forms, see Schaper (2013), pp. 84–87, 90.

[24] Schaper (2013), pp. 100–101.

[25] Ibid, pp. 101–103.

[26] Ibid, p. 101.

In 2010, the Chinese government finally opened the partnership enterprise form to foreign investors with the introduction of the Foreign-Invested Partnership Enterprise(外商投资合伙企业/ FIPE). This allowed foreign investors directly to establish limited partnership enterprises in China together with Chinese or foreign investors. The so-called Foreign-Invested Limited Partnership Enterprise (FILPE) provides a new option for FDI in sino-foreign alliances. Chinese lawmakers did not follow the trend in the US, opting against introducing statutory hybrid legal forms.[27] Instead, the FILPE can be combined with a corporate general partner, thus allowing for a structure that offers the flexibility and taxation conditions of a partnership while protecting its investors against personal liability like a company. Furthermore, the corporate general partner can be either a domestic or a foreign company, thus permitting the transnational combination of legal forms. The introduction of the FILPE can be regarded as a contribution to the liberalisation and deregulation of China's foreign investment regime. The limited choice of enterprise forms for sino-foreign alliances which had previously existed, no longer satisfied the requirements of different types of firms, sectors and industries, and failed to respond to firms' changing and evolving business needs.[28] Partnership enterprises typically allow more flexibility in terms of organisational structure, and in the definition of the rights and obligations of the investors than corporate enterprise forms.[29] Thus, with regard to the FILPE, the presumption is that foreign investors should have more latitude and flexibility in structuring their FDI. Unsurprisingly, more and more foreign investors are considering whether the FILPE might be a suitable enterprise form for their FDI project.[30] The particular investment structure of a FILPE with a foreign corporate general partner is the core object of analysis in this book.

However, in terms of factors and considerations that influence investment decisions, the FILPE as an enterprise form has to provide a legal framework that addresses investors' concerns and protects their interests. Various factors and diverse motives can lead to very different concerns and interests on the part of particular investors.[31] For the purpose of this book, the assumption is that, ultimately, the concern and interest of the investor is to maximise the financial return on his[32] investment. Among the vast number of factors that will influence the financial return of a particular investment, the legal framework within which an investment project

---

[27]Regarding the statutory hybrid elements in the Foreign-Invested Specialised General Partnership Enterprise, see Sect. 4.2.3.2.

[28]Lu (吕美昂) (2011), pp. 81–82; Yang (杨杰) and Qu (曲天明) (2010), p. 63.

[29]Yang (杨杰) and Qu (曲天明) (2010), p. 64; Werthwein (2010), p. 47; Wu and Geu (2007–2008), p. 137.

[30]The author himself, while working in the corporate law department of an international law firm in Shanghai, has been involved in FDI projects where foreign investors were considering to use a FILPE as investment vehicle.

[31]Haase (2014), pp. 3, 4.

[32]Throughout this book, all gender-specific terms are to be considered to refer to both the feminine and the masculine form.

operates, can be of critical importance.[33] Fundamentally, the needs and goals of enterprise forms are the same across national borders.[34] The organisational form of an enterprise determines the investors' relationships, their financial rights, their responsibilities for the enterprise's debts and their tax liabilities.[35] Investors are looking for an enterprise form that functions with low operational costs, which will not be impaired by conflicts of interest among its participants. Investors want to limit their potential liability while being entitled to their share of the profits. They want to be able to de-invest from an enterprise and sell their share of ownership. Therefore, it is vital for foreign investors that the FILPE as an investment vehicle sets the legal standards which protect their interests. Only if this is the case can the FILPE be an attractive alternative to other investment vehicles for foreign investors.

An academic analysis of the FILPE can provide fundamental insights for addressing the question: does the FILPE structure protect investors' interests? The introduction of a new legal form inevitably brings with it uncertainties for the legal community and market participants.[36] They cannot rely on their existing business experience to assess the new form, resulting in increased information costs for market participants trying to find the most suitable enterprise form for their investment project.[37] Initially, this requires skilled legal advice, and thereby entailing high legal costs for the establishment of a new enterprise form.[38] However, a systematic and fundamental academic analysis that puts the FILPE in perspective in its overall legal framework can provide structured information that may assist in establishing standards and model contracts for the new enterprise form.[39] While the FILPE has gained some attention from scholars and legal practitioners in China[40] and abroad,[41] articles typically focus only on a few selective legal issues of the FILPE. In the Chinese legal system for domestic commercial structures, a scattered variety of enterprise forms have evolved over the past few decades.[42] Not all forms have a (clear) legal basis or fulfil the characteristics that the name of the enterprise form promises.[43] Thus, it is important to comprehend how the FILPE actually functions in order to categorise it systematically in China's overall framework of enterprise

---

[33] Mahony (2015), pp. 173–174.

[34] Wu and Geu (2007–2008), p. 135.

[35] Chen (2014), p. 68.

[36] Schaper (2013), pp. 90–91.

[37] Ibid, pp. 112.

[38] Fleischer and Wansleben (2017a), pp. 177–178.

[39] Ibid, pp. 177–178.

[40] Exemplary, see Lu (吕美昂) (2011), pp. 81–82; Zhu (朱慈蕴) (2008), pp. 77–85; Du (杜瑞孔) (2006), pp. 69–70.

[41] For examples, see Shaddox (2013), pp. 469–490; Yu et al. (2012), pp. 10–13; Wu and Geu (2007–2008), pp. 133–178.

[42] Howson (2010), pp. 304–316.

[43] Ibid, pp. 304–316.

law.[44] Furthermore, through a comparison of enterprise organisation law between different jurisdictions, it is possible to identify an analytic framework of the key characteristics that define a standard corporate form.[45] Applying this analytic framework allows a comprehensive analysis of the FILPE in the light of investors' concerns. In addition, the comparison with other jurisdictions illustrates similarities and differences in legal developments between different national legal frameworks.[46] Particularly, the combination of legal forms, such as the FILPE with a foreign corporate general partner, can have important implications for the functioning of regulatory competition and, thereby, for the development of law.[47]

1.2 Research Question

The aim of this book is to contribute to the understanding of Chinese partnership enterprise law. Therefore, it analyses the FILPE from the perspective of a foreign investor. Analysing an enterprise form in its entirety, such as the FILPE with a corporate general partner, is an extensive undertaking. The complexity of the issues that arise during the lifecycle of an enterprise allows for its analysis from different perspectives, including, among others, organisational structure, agency problems, taxation, and creditor protection and treatment during insolvency. Each of these perspectives has its own special focus and raises important questions about the enterprise form. However, the limited scope of this book requires the research to focus on one particular perspective. This is found in the international and economically grounded analysis of the common structure of the law of business corporations developed by *Kraakman et al* in *The Anatomy of Corporate Law*.[48] *Kraakman et al* offer 'a common language and general analytic framework with which to understand the purposes that can potentially be served by corporate law, and with which to compare and evaluate the efficacy of different legal regimes in serving those purposes'.[49] The international comparison shows that business corporations in all jurisdictions 'have a fundamentally similar set of legal characteristics – and face a fundamentally similar set of legal problems'.[50] *The Anatomy of Corporate Law* identifies two immediate functions of corporate law. The first is to establish a structure of the corporate form that has common characteristics, the so called 'standard corporate form'.[51] The second principal function of corporate law is to

[44] Howson (2015), p. 410.

[45] Armour et al. (2017c), pp. 4, 22.

[46] Windbichler (2014), pp. 112–113.

[47] Schaper (2013), p. 80.

[48] Kraakman et al. (2017).

[49] Armour et al. (2017c), p. 4.

[50] Ibid, p. 1.

[51] Ibid, p. 2.

address and control the key agency problems[52] that arise in jointly-owned enterprises: conflicts between the enterprises' owners and its hired managers, conflicts between the owners themselves, and conflicts between the enterprise and third parties.[53] The present book focuses on the first of these two principal functions because the standard corporate form is the foundation for a subsequent analysis of the agency problems. The standard corporate form responds to the economic requirements of modern business enterprises and has been recognised as a common feature of corporate law in market economies.[54] By making the standard corporate form widely available, 'corporate law enables business participants to transact easily through the medium of the corporate entity, and thus lowers the costs of conducting business'.[55] FDI projects inherently contain an international element. Foreign investors have to adapt to circumstances and conditions in the target country that may differ fundamentally from the legal environment in their home jurisdictions. Therefore, foreign investors are looking for legal standards that they are familiar with, which they can rely on. Such a legal standard can be found in an enterprise form with the characteristics of a standard corporate form. Compliance with this standard is essential to control potential liabilities, to contain operational costs, and to integrate a Chinese subsidiary into the organisational structure of a multinational business organisation. For a FILPE to be an attractive option as an investment vehicle for sino-foreign alliances, it is of fundamental importance that the FILPE also complies with this standard. With a focus on the elements of a standard corporate form, the present book analyses the basic principles of Chinese partnership law and examines key issues in the lifecycle of a FILPE. While *Kraakman et al* focus on corporations, essentially, their analysis can be applied to other legal forms of jointly-owned enterprises, including the limited partnership enterprise.[56] The description of the function of corporate law can thus be read as a description of the function of enterprise form law in general. Therefore, in terms of terminology, whenever *The Anatomy of Corporate Law* refers to corporations, this could and should be understood in the present book as equally referring to limited partnership enterprises with a corporate general partner, unless expressly stated otherwise.[57]

---

[52]An 'agency problem' [or 'principal-agent problem']—in the most general sense of the term—arises whenever the welfare of one party, termed the 'principal', depends upon actions taken by another party, termed the 'agent'. The problem lies in motivating the agent to act in the principal's interest rather than simply in the agent's own interest. Viewed in these broad terms, agency problems arise in a broad range of contexts that go well beyond those that would formally be classified as agency relationships by lawyers. In particular, almost any contractual relationship, in which one party (the 'agent') promises performance to another (the 'principal'), is potentially subject to an agency problem. (Armour et al. 2017b, p. 29).

[53]Armour et al. (2017c), p. 2.

[54]Ibid, pp. 1–2.

[55]Ibid, p. 1.

[56]For more detail, see Sect. 1.3.1.3.2.

[57]Regarding the applicability of *The Anatomy of Corporate Law* to limited partnership enterprises, see Sect. 1.3.1.3.2.

The Anatomy of Corporate Law identifies five legal characteristics that constitute the standard corporate form: legal personality, limited liability, transferable ownership interest, delegated management under a board structure, and investor ownership.[58] The present book focuses on an in-depth analysis of the three elements of legal personality, limited liability and transferable ownership interest. Among the characteristics of the standard corporate form, these three are most strongly interconnected and interdependent. Legal personality is generally considered to be the single most important attribute of the corporate form. *The Anatomy of Corporate Law* has been given credit for clarifying its economic function.[59] One core element of legal personality is 'entity shielding', which ensures that the assets of the entity—the corporation—are shielded from the creditors of the entity's owners.[60] The opposite feature to entity shielding is the 'owner shielding' that is provided by limited liability.[61] This attribute shields the owners of the corporation from the claims of the corporation's creditors.[62] Together, legal personality and limited liability are essential prerequisites for the transferability of ownership interest.[63]

However, the focus on these three characteristics does not imply that the other two attributes—delegated management with a board structure and investor ownership—are irrelevant and should be ignored. Aspects of these features are included in the analysis. The feature of delegated management with a board structure,[64] for example, is addressed when the rules that specify the authority to represent the FILPE towards third parties are analysed under the attribute of legal personality.[65] The limited partnership enterprise is further characterised by rules that generally exclude limited partners from executing partnership affairs. These rules are analysed in detail together with the attribute of limited liability.[66] Furthermore, the element of investor ownership[67] is addressed with regard to the autonomy that is granted to

---

[58]Armour et al. (2017c), p. 1.

[59]Skeel (2003–2004), p. 1527; Enriques (2004), pp. 1012–1013.

[60]For more detail, see Sect. 7.1.

[61]Armour et al. (2017c), p. 9.

[62]For more detail, see Chap. 8.

[63]For more detail, see Chap. 9.

[64]The attribute of delegated management with a board structure has two key elements. Externally, it requires the existence of rules that specify to third parties the individuals who have the authority to enter into contracts that bind the firm and its assets (Armour et al. 2017c, p. 7). Internally, a corporation is defined by a governance structure in which all but the most fundamental decisions are generally delegated to a board of directors (Armour et al. 2017c, p. 12). This underscores the significance of the board of directors as an intermediary between the owners and managers. The owners ordinarily have the right to elect directors, but the directors choose and oversee the day-to-day managers (Skeel 2003–2004, p. 1525). This marks a deviation from general partnership forms that usually grant power to a majority of partners to directly manage the partnership in the ordinary course of business (Armour et al. 2017c, p. 11).

[65]See Sect. 7.2.

[66]See Sect. 8.3.2.1.

[67]Investor ownership highlights the fact that the owners (as opposed to employees, financial creditors, suppliers, and customers) have ultimate control over the firm, i.e. the right to choose its

parties when drafting the partnership agreement. It allows partners to separate the ratio of distributable profits and the exercise of control from the proportion of capital that each contributes to the partnership, and permits capital contributions to be made other than in cash, such as contributions of labour, tangible goods, intellectual property rights, land use rights, or other property rights.[68] The sections that deal with limited liability analyse limited partner's right to receive the profits without exercising any control over the FILPE.[69] In contrast, it must be taken into account that the attributes of delegated management with a board structure and investor ownership allow more flexibility with regard to modifications.[70] Therefore, corporate forms more often show deviations from these features than from the other three defining elements of a standard corporate form. That is the reason why the present book focuses on the analysis of the three selected attributes. While the term 'standard corporate form' conventionally refers to all five of the characteristics, throughout this book the term is—for convenience—used to refer to mainly the three elements of legal personality, limited liability, and transferable ownership interest.

Thus, the research question of this book is whether the FILPE with a foreign corporate general partner as an enterprise form fulfils legal personality, limited liability and transferable ownership interest as three important characteristics of a standard corporate form. This research question reflects the continuing international integration of enterprise form law which itself is a result of ongoing global economic integration.[71]

---

directors and the right to receive the firm's net earnings (Enriques 2004, p. 1017). This sets the corporation apart from enterprise types such as cooperatives, non-profit firms, and public benefit or community interest corporations (Armour et al. 2017c, pp. 13–14).

[68] See Sects. 3.2.1 and 4.1.9.3.

[69] See Sect. 8.3.2.1.

[70] The attribute of delegated management with a board structure is a default provision itself. In practice, the governance structure of corporations is often altered so that, *de facto*, the corporation will be managed directly by the owners (Enriques 2004, p. 1017). Furthermore, *The Anatomy of Corporate Law* recognises that many jurisdictions provide corporate forms that depart from delegated management by permitting the replacement of the board with direct management by the owners (Armour et al. 2017c, p. 15). This also applies to the EJV in China, the governance structure of which stipulates that shareholders have direct control over the management (Sect. 3.2.1). Therefore, the dogmatic function of delegated management with a board structure is restricted in the context of sino-foreign alliances. Regarding investor ownership, *The Anatomy of Corporate Law* recognises that, with sufficient special contracting, it is also possible to grant ownership of shares in a business corporation to contributors of labour or other factors of production, or in proportion to consumption of the firm's services. Such arrangements are especially common between entrepreneurs and investors in high-tech start-up firms (Armour et al. 2017c, p. 14).

[71] Armour et al. (2017c), p. 3.

1.3 Methodology

From a methodological perspective, this book utilises a broad approach based on several theoretical foundations. The reason for that choice is that no singular, generally accepted theory can be identified that would allow for an exclusive analysis and assessment of the limited partnership as an enterprise form in its entirety. Rather, this book can be viewed through a number of 'lenses', all of which provide valuable insights. The theoretical foundation of this book is the economic analysis of law and the comparative law approach. The cornerstone of this analysis is the underlying uniformity of the corporate form across jurisdictions as has been highlighted in *'The Anatomy of Corporate Law'* by *Kraakman et al.*[72] Their analysis, which combines an international comparison of law with the economic analysis of law, shows that 'business corporations have a fundamentally similar set of legal characteristics – and face a fundamentally similar set of legal problems – in all jurisdictions'.[73] In addition, this book will compare the FILPE with the EJV and other entity forms in Chinese corporate law with regard to selective aspects. This provides a broad, analytical framework that allows in-depth investigation of the research question. This chapter gives an overview of this book, and a brief introduction to the different theoretical foundations thereof. The methodologies will be described in more detail as they are applied in the later chapters.

1.3.1 Economic Analysis of Law

1.3.1.1 The Theory of Economic Analysis of Law

One of the key methodologies used in this book is the economic analysis of law.[74] 'Central to economic sciences is the question how a society can allocate its limited resources to maximise the "aggregated welfare" of society.'[75] The greater a society's welfare, the more efficient its economy is considered to be.[76] Welfare economics defines efficiency criteria with which instruments of economic policy and economic frameworks can be evaluated.[77] The economic analysis of law applies this approach to assess legal rules and legal concepts.[78] The purpose of the law is understood to be

[72]Kraakman et al. (2017).

[73]Armour et al. (2017c), p. 1.

[74]The theoretical cornerstone of the present book, The Anatomy of Corporate Law, is described by its authors as a *functional* analysis, and explicitly attributed to the economic analysis of law (Armour et al. 2017c, pp. 3–4).

[75]Schäfer and Ott (2012), p. XXXIII.

[76]Ibid, p. XXXIII.

[77]Towfigh (2017), p. 39.

[78]Schäfer and Ott (2012), p. XXXIII.

to stipulate a legal framework that provides for an efficient allocation of resources.[79] This focus on the principal of efficiency is, in general, subject to controversy in legal literature.[80] For the present book, efficiency is understood, as conventionally used in the application of the economic analysis of law, as *Kaldor-Hicks efficiency* within acceptable patterns of distribution.[81] In the context of corporate law, the goal of maximising aggregated social welfare can be reflected in ensuring that a corporation serves the best interests of its investors, or, more specifically, to maximise investors' financial return.[82] This efficiency criteria has been criticised for reducing the goal of corporate law to maximising investors' return.[83] However, 'in general, creditors, workers, and customers will consent to deal with a corporation only if they expect themselves to be better off as a result. Consequently, the corporation – and, in particular, its investors, as the firm's residual claimants and risk-bearers – have a direct pecuniary interest in making sure that corporate transactions are beneficial, not just to the investors, but to all parties who deal with the firm.'[84] This view is a convincing argument for investors' return to be the proper object of corporate law.[85] A further assumption essential to economic analysis of law is that of the rational choice of the *homo oeconomicus*: assuming that the human being is always a rational maximiser of his self-interest.[86] The rational choice theory has also been subject to manifold criticism from legal, economic, and social science scholars.[87] The critics are right insofar as human beings do not always behave rationally, and 'there are situations in which rational choice is precluded by uncertainty'.[88] Constraints of rationality therefore have to be considered when applying the rational choice theory.[89] Overall, however, it can be assumed that foreign investors will generally at least aim to maximise their financial return. In other words, it is unlikely that an investor will consciously act irrationally.

The economic analysis of law is the ideal theoretical framework within which to address the research question of this book. The assumption is that a foreign investor

---

[79]Posner (2014), p. 31.

[80]For an example on the discussion in Germany, see the overview in Kirstein (2000), p. 161; and also Posner (2014), p. 34.

[81]Conversely, *Pareto efficiency* occurs when one party benefits from a decision, but no one is made worse off. *Kaldor Hicks* states that a decision can be more efficient as long as—in theory—everyone can be compensated to offset any potential costs. A situation is regarded to be *Kaldor–Hicks efficient* if no potential *Kaldor–Hicks* improvement from that situation exists; Posner (2014), p. 34; Cooter and Ulen (2012), p. 42; Schäfer and Ott (2012), pp. 19–25.

[82]Armour et al. (2017c), p. 23.

[83]Ibid, p. 23.

[84]Ibid, p. 23.

[85]Ibid, p. 23.

[86]Schäfer and Ott (2012), pp. 12–13.

[87]For an example, see the overview in Ulen (2000), pp. 800–816; Schäfer and Ott (2012), pp. 103–110; Posner (2014), pp. 4–5, 17–18; Cooter and Ulen (2012), pp. 50–51.

[88]Posner (2014), pp. 4.

[89]Schäfer and Ott (2012), p. 116.

who plans to establish a sino-foreign alliance, will choose the enterprise form that offers him the legal framework which will achieve the biggest return on his investment. The investor is looking for the most *efficient* enterprise form. This book aims to analyse whether the FILPE as an enterprise form is efficient from the perspective of a foreign investor.

1.3.1.2 Economic Analysis of Law in the Context of Chinese Law

This book adopts an approach whereby conventional models of the economic analysis of law are applied directly to Chinese law. Economic analysis of law started to be developed in the US in the early 1960s, reaching other common law jurisdictions in the mid-1970s, and progressively gained importance in continental European civil law jurisdictions from the 1980s onward.[90] It is legitimate to question the extent to which the application of the economic analysis of law to developing economies like China is suitable.[91] 'A particular challenge (. . .) is the fact that many aspects of the Chinese legal system today do not correspond at all with what economists would advise as an efficient legal system.'[92] Various factors and peculiarities influence the Chinese legal context, including the well-known concept of informal and personal relations (关系 /guanxi) that play an important role within Chinese society, and its political and economic system.[93] Other examples of these factors are the speed of political, economic, and social developments in China, the strong involvement in and influence of the state over the economy, the sheer scale of the country and the resulting high complexity of interaction between various government authorities on different national, regional, and local levels, the vast number of political stakeholders and parallel structures of the Communist Party of China (CPC), the opaqueness of political decision-making processes and the often insufficient disclosure of relevant information by government authorities, the limited judicial independence, and the corruption in the political and economic system.[94] The presence of all these aspects could lead to the conclusion that the economic analysis of law with its focus on economic efficiency has no impact on this context. However, even within this unique environment, economic analysis of law can make a significant contribution to a better understanding of the Chinese legal system.[95] This view is supported by an extensive interest among Chinese scholars in the economic analysis of law. Presumably influenced by the gradual transition towards

[90]For a detailed account of the history of the economic analysis of law, see Mackaay (2000), pp. 65–94.

[91]Eger et al. (2007a), p. xiii.

[92]Ibid, p. xiv.

[93]Ibid, p. xiv. For an introduction to the concept of Guanxi, see Yang (2002), pp. 459–476; Spence (1990), pp. 638, 694, 737.

[94]For a general overview, see Chen (2016), pp. 172–228.

[95]Eger et al. (2007a), p. xiv.

a more market-oriented economy in China, leading foreign books on the economic analysis of law have been translated into Chinese since the late 1980s.[96] Starting from the mid-1990s, economic analysis of law has become a growing area of research and teaching in Chinese academia, leading to conferences, workshops, and publication of books and articles[97] by Chinese scholars.[98]

Certainly, traditional models of economic analysis of law have to be applied consciously and carefully in the context of a legal system like that of China, and with consideration of its special characteristics.

> One has to take into account the specific social and cultural constraints as perceived by the addressees of the formal legal rules and the specific problems of law enforcement via the courts. But this does not constitute an impediment to applying economic analysis of law in order to better understand the functioning of the Chinese economic and legal system. It is rather the normal way to apply economic analysis of law to the particular problems of a specific country.[99]

In this light, the authors of *The Anatomy of Corporate Law*, in its third edition, state that they aim to provide a conceptual analytic framework which can contribute to analysing the laws of large emerging market jurisdictions such as China.[100] Against this background, the economic analysis of law is a useful and suitable approach to analysing the FILPE and the legal environment surrounding it.

1.3.1.3 Relevant Efficiency Criteria

Evaluation of efficiency requires benchmarks. The criteria used in this book to analyse the efficiency of the FILPE concern whether the FILPE fulfils central elements of a standard corporate form. As outlined above, these efficiency criteria have been developed in *The Anatomy of Corporate Law*.[101] Before the criteria can be applied to the research subject, the ground-breaking contribution that *The Anatomy of Corporate Law* has made to the field of corporate law will be discussed, and the criteria will be explored in more detail. At the same time, the question has to be addressed of whether the findings of *The Anatomy of Corporate Law*, which evolve around the analysis of corporations, are suitable for the analysis of a limited partnership enterprise.

---

[96]Recent examples are Jiang (蒋兆康) (2012); Shi (史晋川) and Dong (董雪兵) (2012).

[97]Zhang (张乃根) (1995); Zhou (周林彬) (1998).

[98]Eger et al. (2007b), p. 308.

[99]Ibid, p. 308.

[100]Armour et al. (2017a), pp. 267–268.

[101]Kraakman et al. (2017).

1.3.1.3.1 The Anatomy of Corporate Law

The Anatomy of Corporate Law has been described as 'the first global and comprehensive comparative and functional analysis of corporate law',[102] and 'the most important corporate law book of the decade'[103] that 'will soon become the lingua franca of corporate law discourse'.[104] In 2019, a Chinese translation of *The Anatomy of Corporate Law* has been published.[105] In the first chapter of *The Anatomy of Corporate Law*, the basic features of a standard corporate form are described. In the second chapter, the authors analyse the three agency problems that typically arise in an enterprise, and develop their typology of strategies for how these agency problems can be addressed. In the remaining chapters, the authors apply the common language and analytic framework that they have developed to a series of key corporate law issues, covering most of the important problems in corporate law.[106] This structure illustrates how the features of the standard corporate form are connected with agency problems in business corporations. They can be the root of those problems, and simultaneously contribute to their solution.[107] 'The great virtue of *The Anatomy of Corporate Law* is that its typology of strategies provides a simple, user-friendly way to compare the corporate law regimes of a wide range of different countries.'[108]

Notwithstanding the contribution *The Anatomy of Corporate Law* has made to the understanding of corporate law, its first edition has also been subject to criticism from different directions. One central criticism has been that the analytic framework underestimates the importance of enforcement issues that stem from discrepancies between law 'in books' and 'law in action', and the impact that these enforcement issues have on corporate governance.[109] Notably, this criticism has been addressed in the second edition, in which more consideration was given to the relevance of enforcement issues. Commentators of the first edition have further pointed to the difficulties of applying the lessons of *The Anatomy of Corporate Law* to the distinctive problems of emerging jurisdictions of developing economies, such as China.[110] A key lesson from corporate governance reform projects in the past was 'that the strategies that are used in developed countries cannot simply be transplanted into a developing country with the expectation that they will function in a

[102]Enriques (2004), p. 1011 (*Luca Enriques* has not yet been an author of *The Anatomy of Corporate Law* when he published this book review).

[103]Skeel (2003–2004), p. 1577.

[104]Ibid, p. 1539.

[105]Lin (林建中) (2009).

[106]Armour et al. (2017c), p. 3.

[107]Enriques (2004), p. 1014; Armour et al. (2017c), p. 5.

[108]Skeel (2003–2004), p. 1521.

[109]Enriques (2004), p. 1019ff. For similar criticism, see Skeel (2003–2004), p. 1543.

[110]Skeel (2003–2004), p. 1571.

comparable way'.[111] Reforms often have a very different effect in a country where they are newly applied than in the jurisdiction from which they are borrowed or adapted.[112] Any corporate governance reform effort needs to take into account the limitations of the underlying enforcement systems.[113] This aspect has also been addressed in the latest revision of the book. In the first and second editions, the core jurisdictions on which the analysis of *The Anatomy of Corporate Law* was based, were all developed economies.[114] The third edition takes a broader perspective by including Brazil as a large emerging market economy among the core jurisdictions.[115] The authors of *The Anatomy of Corporate Law* are aware, and the inclusion of Brazil has shown, that their findings can only partially be applied to jurisdictions whose foundational legal institutions are lacking or compromised.[116] However, *The Anatomy of Corporate Law* provides an analytic framework for investigating corporate law across all jurisdictions to the extent that it provides an integrated analysis of the company laws of the core jurisdictions.[117] Because it offers a framework for understanding the issues that are inherent to corporations, a platform is provided for understanding corporate governance in emerging jurisdictions, and for rethinking possible future reforms.[118] This is especially appropriate for the present book, as several of the core jurisdictions of *The Anatomy of Corporate Law* have significantly influenced the development of partnership law in China.[119] The present book takes the perspective of a foreign investor who expects the FILPE to fulfil elements of a standard corporate form. By doing so, it does not ignore the practical deficiencies and restrictions of the emerging Chinese jurisdiction. Rather, in this context, this book aims to illustrate which options the FILPE offers for contractual arrangements in order to create an enterprise form that comes as close as possible to the 'standard' described in *The Anatomy of Corporate Law*.

1.3.1.3.2 The Analysed Features of a 'Standard Corporate Form'

The specific focus of the analysis of *The Anatomy of Corporate Law*—as indicated by the title—lies on the corporation. The authors have analysed seven core jurisdictions to determine the features that constitute a corporation.[120] These features address the practical problems that arise from organising and operating commercial

---

[111] Ibid, p. 1570.
[112] Ibid, pp. 1572–1573.
[113] Ibid, pp. 1572–1573.
[114] Kraakman (2009), p. vii.
[115] Kraakman (2017), p. vii.
[116] Armour et al. (2017a), pp. 268–269.
[117] Kraakman (2017), p. vii.
[118] Skeel (2003–2004), p. 1574.
[119] See Sect. 4.1.1.2.
[120] Armour et al. (2017c), pp. 5–15.

activity in developed market economies throughout the world.[121] The three defining elements—legal personality, limited liability and transferable shares—that build the core of this analysis will be described in detail in Part II of this book, as they are applied to the FILPE.

The approach of listing central corporate attributes is not a new concept, but rather builds on comparable classifications that have been used in corporate law before.[122] The authors still manage to add a new perspective by reshaping the characteristics instead of just recycling the traditional description of these parameters.[123] In *The Anatomy of Corporate Law*, the features of the standard corporate form only take up a rather small part of the analysis because it primarily serves as a starting point for the typology of strategies to address agency problems.[124] The analysis of the FILPE, however, requires a more in-depth application of the three features of the standard corporate form. This stems from the nature of the FILPE as a partnership enterprise, and relates to the question of whether the findings of *The Anatomy of Corporate Law* are suitable for an analysis of a limited partnership enterprise. In scholarship, the corporation is most commonly characterised as a 'nexus of contracts',[125] meaning that a corporation consists of a set of long-term relationships between investors, management, creditors, workforce, and other contractual partners.[126] Thus, it is important to consider the contractual nature of the characteristics, and 'the fact that most are (just) default deviations from default terms under general contract law'.[127] The authors of *The Anatomy of Corporate Law* recognise the different variations of the corporate form. The core subject of their analysis is the standard corporate form that can be found in all well-developed market economies.[128] This corporate form is particularly designed to enable the formation of corporations with freely tradable shares, so called 'open' or 'public' corporations.[129] Another corporate form that is common in major jurisdictions is the 'closed' or 'private' corporation.[130] These corporate forms typically[131] fulfil the attributes of the standard corporate form, but 'differ from open companies chiefly because their shares, though transferable at least in principle, are presumed – and in some cases required – not to trade freely in a public market'.[132] In addition, some

---

[121] Ibid, pp. 3–4.

[122] For an example, see Eisenberg (2000), p. 100; Skeel (2003–2004), p. 1525.

[123] Skeel (2003–2004), p. 1525; Enriques (2004), pp. 1012–1013.

[124] Skeel (2003–2004), p. 1525.

[125] Armour et al. (2017c), p. 5, with further references in footnote 11; Enriques (2004), p. 1014.

[126] Schaper (2013), p. 80.

[127] Enriques (2004), p. 1014.

[128] Armour et al. (2017c), p. 15.

[129] Ibid, p. 15.

[130] Ibid, p. 15.

[131] Regarding possible deviations from the feature 'delegated management under a board structure', see Armour et al. (2017c), p. 15.

[132] Armour et al. (2017c), p. 15.

jurisdictions have adopted '*quasi*-corporate statutory forms' that in principle can be used to form enterprises with all of the features of a corporation, though some of the attributes have to be added by contractual agreement.[133] Examples of this include certain statutory hybrid legal forms, originating in the US, that contain elements of both corporations and partnerships.[134] This development is the result of the softening of the once strict demarcation between corporations and partnerships that has evolved over recent decades.[135] *The Anatomy of Corporate Law* recognises this trend towards greater organisational choice which extends to the basic elements and governance structure of any particular type of enterprise, enabling investors to replicate the essential features of the corporate form by contract.[136] Consequently, the authors widen the scope for the application of their analytic framework:

> [I]nsofar as these entities contain the five basic elements of the corporate form, they qualify as '*de facto*' corporations for our purposes. Even if these organisational forms lack one or more of the key elements of the corporate form, our framework can shed light on the agency problems generated by the remaining characteristics and how the law addresses them.[137]

Since the FILPE with a foreign corporate general partner is such a type of hybrid legal form, the analytic framework of *The Anatomy of Corporate Law* is a very suitable methodology for the present book. In Part II, a detailed analysis is undertaken of which contractual provisions must be included in a partnership agreement in order to establish a FILPE with a foreign corporate general partner so that it satisfies the features of a standard corporate form.

1.3.1.3.3 The Role of Statutory Law in Governing Enterprises

To an important degree, the relationships among the participants in an enterprise are contractual.[138] In the FILPE, the principal contract that binds them is the corporation's charter, termed 'partnership agreement'.[139] 'The charter sets out the basic terms of the relationship among the firm's shareholders, and between the shareholders and the firm's directors and other managers. By explicit or implicit reference, the charter can also become part of the contract between the firm and its employees or creditors.'[140] At the same time, enterprise forms across all jurisdictions are subject to a large body of statutory law.[141] Accordingly, the laws and regulations that govern the FILPE in China are the principal focus of this book. Before examining the details

---

[133] Ibid, p. 15.

[134] See Sect. 1.1.

[135] Ribstein (2004), pp. 153 ff; McCahery and Vermeulen (2004), pp. 191–195.

[136] Armour et al. (2017a), p. 269.

[137] Ibid, p. 269.

[138] Ibid, p. 17.

[139] Ibid, p. 17. See Sect. 4.1.9.

[140] Ibid, p. 17.

[141] Ibid, p. 17.

of this legislation, it is important to address the question of what role statutory law plays in the organisation and governance of enterprises.[142] The authors of *The Anatomy of Corporate Law* have shown that, with few exceptions, the defining elements of the standard corporate form could, in theory, be established by contractual arrangements.[143] In general, the limited partnership is described as a standard form contract that attempts to anticipate the contractual preferences of the parties to this specific type of enterprise form.[144] Given the possibility of creating the structure of an enterprise by means of contract, why does every advanced economy have elaborate statutes providing numerous detailed rules for the internal governance of enterprises?[145] In analysing the benefit of enterprises being governed by statutory legal frameworks, a distinction must be made between default provisions and mandatory rules.[146]

1.3.1.3.3.1 Default Provisions and Mandatory Rules

Default provisions are legal provisions that govern an enterprise only if the parties do not explicitly provide for something different, that is, they apply 'in default' of the parties stipulating something else.[147] The enterprise law basically offers a standard form contract that the parties can adopt, at will, in whole or in part.[148] A key advantage of such a legally provided standard form is that it saves on transaction costs.[149] 'It simplifies contracting among the parties involved by requiring that they specify only those elements of their relationship that deviate from the standard terms.'[150] This function is best served by default provisions if they are majoritarian, i.e., if they reflect the terms that the majority of well-informed parties would most commonly choose.[151] Another function that default provisions can serve is to encourage the disclosure of superior information that one contracting party has over the other.[152] The default provisions may impose a burden or a penalty on the informed party, in the sense that the default provisions will only be waived by the other party if the relevant information is disclosed.[153] The purpose of such a provision is to encourage parties to reveal their private information, initiating

---

[142] Ibid, p. 17.

[143] Ibid, p. 17.

[144] Ribstein (1988), p. 895.

[145] Armour et al. (2017c), pp. 17–18; Schäfer and Ott (2012), p. 728.

[146] Armour et al. (2017c), p. 18.

[147] Ibid, p. 18.

[148] Ibid, p. 18.

[149] Armour et al. (2017c), p. 18; Posner (2014), p. 543. Transaction costs: the costs involved in organising economic activity through voluntary exchange (Posner 2014, p. 533).

[150] Armour et al. (2017c), p. 18.

[151] Ibid, p. 18.

[152] Armour et al. (2009), p. 20.

[153] Ibid, p. 20.

explicit bargaining between the parties that will lead to an outcome superior to that which would otherwise be expected.[154]

Default provisions can be supplied in a variety of techniques.[155] The choice of technique affects the ease and means of contracting around it, which in return will affect the way the default provision operates.[156] A common form of default provision is a statutory enterprise law provision that will govern unless the parties explicitly provide a different regulation.[157] Alternatively, the law itself can specify the rule that will govern if the default provision is not chosen, making it an either-or provision.[158] Furthermore, the law may even provide a menu of more than two specified rules from which the parties can choose.[159] 'The law may also impose special procedures for altering a default rule, such as by requiring minority approval to alter default rules that protect their interests.'[160]

Then again, certain important provisions of enterprise organisation law are also mandatory.[161]

> The rational for mandatory terms (. . .) is usually based on some form of 'contracting failure': some parties might otherwise be exploited because they are not well informed; the interests of third parties might be affected; or collective action problems might otherwise lead to contractual provisions that are inefficient or unfair. Mandatory terms may also serve as a useful standardising function in circumstances (such as with accounting rules) where the benefits of compliance increase if everyone adheres to the same provision.[162]

Mandatory rules also allow lawmakers to impose certain policies, such as restricting the rights of foreign investors in relation to their domestic counterparts, for example.[163] From a broader perspective, mandatory rules can also perform an enabling function similar to that of default rules, particularly where mandatory rules are used in conjunction with a choice of enterprise form.[164] If the law provides enterprise forms that are subject to mandatory rules, thus to some degree inflexible, but at the same time permits a choice among different enterprise forms, then mandatory rules actually facilitate freedom of contract.[165] Among the standard form legal entities from which investors may choose in structuring an organisation,

[154]Ibid, pp. 20–21.

[155]Armour et al. (2017c), p. 18.

[156]Ibid, p. 18.

[157]Ibid, p. 18.

[158]Ibid, p. 18.

[159]Ibid, p. 18.

[160]Ibid, p. 18.

[161]Ibid, p. 19.

[162]Ibid, p. 19.

[163]Regarding the discriminatory investment restrictions that affect a FILPE in China, see Sect. 4.1.7.

[164]Armour et al. (2017c), p. 19.

[165]Ibid, p. 19.

each is subject to a specific set of mandatory and default rules.[166] This enables the investor to signal, via the choice of enterprise form, the terms that the enterprise offers to other contracting parties, and to make credible the investor's commitment not to change those terms.[167] In this regard, the addition of the FILPE to the limited menu of enterprise forms for sino-foreign alliances in China is an expansion of the contractual freedom of investors.[168] Besides offering choices between different forms of enterprises within one jurisdiction, the investors can also be given, for a single type of enterprise form, the choice between different jurisdictions' laws.[169] To a degree, the Chinese lawmaker is granting this freedom by permitting the use of a foreign enterprise as a corporate general partner in a FILPE.[170]

1.3.1.3.3.2 The Benefit of Legal Rules

In addition to providing convenient standard terms, encouraging disclosure of information, and facilitating choice of the most efficient among several alternative rules, default rules also enable adaptation to developments that occur over time, but cannot easily be foreseen at the outset.[171] An enterprise's charter is a contract that must govern complex relationships over a long period of time, and, as such, is necessarily 'incomplete'.[172]

> Situations will arise for which the contract fails to provide clear guidance, either because the situation was not foreseeable at the time the contract was drafted or because the situation, though foreseeable, seemed too unlikely to justify the costs of making clear provision for it in the contract. Statutory amendments, administrative rulings, and judicial decisions can provide for such situations as they arise, by either altering or interpreting existing rules. This is the *gap-filling* role of corporation law.[173]

An enterprise will get the greatest advantage from this effect if it adopts standard charter terms used by many other firms, since those standard terms are likely to be subject to repeated interpretation by courts and administrative rulings.[174] The most widely used standard charter terms are usually the default rules provided by the statutory enterprise organisation law.[175] Furthermore, these standard provisions are also more familiar to analysts and investors, and thus can reduce their costs of

---

[166] Ibid, p. 19.

[167] Ibid, p. 19.

[168] Regarding the strictly regulated foreign investment regime in China, see Sect. 3.1.2.

[169] Armour et al. (2017c), p. 19.

[170] See Sect. 8.2.2.2.

[171] Armour et al. (2017c), p. 19.

[172] Ibid, p. 19.

[173] Ibid, pp. 19–20.

[174] Ibid, p. 20.

[175] Ibid, p. 20.

evaluating the firm as an investment.[176] The problem of contractual incompleteness, however, reaches beyond mere gap-filling.[177]

Given the long lifespan of many corporations, it is likely that some of a firm's initial charter terms, no matter how carefully chosen, will become obsolete with the passage of time owing to changes in the economic and legal environment. Default rules of law have the feature that they are altered over time—by statutory amendments and by judicial interpretation—to adapt them to such changing circumstances. Consequently, by adopting statutory default rules, a firm has a degree of assurance that its provisions will not become anachronistic.[178]

In contrast, a charter provision that was individually drafted for the enterprise, can only be changed by the enterprise itself,[179] thus taking the potential risk that the firm's own mechanisms for charter amendments may be vetoed or hijacked by particular constituencies in order to enforce their partial interests.[180] For many enterprises, there may often be little practical difference between mandatory and default rules, and they eventually adopt both types of rules in their charter.[181] The most important choice, as has been pointed out above, is that between different forms of enterprises.[182] This conclusion affirms the usefulness of this book.

Throughout the subsequent chapters, it will be analysed whether the provisions that govern the FILPE are mandatory or default rules, whether the latter are majoritarian in nature, and how easy it can be to contract around them.

1.3.2 Comparative Law Approach

The second methodological cornerstone of this book is the comparative law approach. The purpose of comparative law, as described by Zweigert and Kötz, is to establish an international dialogue about problems of jurisprudence.[183] Thus, the comparison of legal systems can contribute to legal science and legal practice by informing national lawmakers, assisting judges in the resolution of difficult questions, extending awareness in legal education, and, perhaps most importantly, by providing a basis for global legal unification or harmonisation.[184] The process of legal reform that began in China at the end of the 1970s has been fundamentally

[176]Ibid, p. 20 fn. 76.

[177]Ibid, p. 20.

[178]Ibid, p. 20.

[179]Ibid, p. 20.

[180]Ibid, p. 20.

[181]Ibid, p. 20.

[182]Ibid, p. 20.

[183]Zweigert and Kötz (1996), p. 3.

[184]Ibid, p. 14.

influenced by comparative law.[185] The majority of Chinese scholars considered the comparative law approach as a great opportunity and a necessity for rebuilding the Chinese legal system.[186] Thus, the laws of other jurisdictions have been studied in detail by lawmakers and law institutes established at universities throughout China.[187] Presumably, not many other countries in the world have used the methodology of comparative law to build their own legal system as extensively as China has done over the past few decades.[188] Foreign legal experts have even been involved in the drafting of several laws,[189] including the revision of the Chinese partnership enterprise law.[190] Chinese lawmakers have not simply westernised China's legal system, but selectively adopted foreign laws or provisions when those have been considered most suitable.[191] The result is a mixed legal system 'with the traditional law as basis, primed with socialistic law and legal principles and covered with dots of different colours from various foreign jurisdictions'.[192] Against this specific background of China's legal history and development, the comparative law approach is particularly suitable for this book.

In the comparison of different legal systems, a distinction has been developed between macro comparison and micro comparison.[193] Macro comparison considers the entire legal system, whereas micro comparison focuses on specific institutions or specific legal problems.[194] These two models cannot be clearly distinguished as they tend to overlap, and very often one model must refer to the other.[195] This also holds true for this book: while the detailed analysis of the various aspects of Chinese partnership law merits micro comparison, the Chinese legal system as a whole has to be taken into account at the same time in order to fully understand the functioning and background of certain regulations, and therefore also requires macro comparison. The comparative law approach will help to analyse and understand the structure and nature of the FILPE. It can contribute to filling gaps or loop-holes within current regulations, and provide recommendations on how these can be resolved. 'Similarly, China's fresh look at limited partnership law may provide new perspectives and

[185] Chen (2009), p. 101ff.

[186] Mi (2009), pp. 803–804; Huang (黄毅诚) (1997), p. 13.

[187] Senger (2006) p. 56.

[188] Mi (2009), p. 806. For the importance and development of the field of comparative law in China during the past decades, see Pan (潘汉典) (1992); or the Journal of Comparative Law (比较法研究) that is published by the Institute of Comparative Law of the Chinese University of Political Science and Law (中国政法大学比较法学研究院) in Beijing since 1987.

[189] Ibid, p. 807.

[190] Zhu (朱少平) and Gebhardt (葛毅) (2004), p.

[191] Julius (2008), p. 68.

[192] Zinser (2012), p. 75.

[193] Zweigert and Kötz (1996), p. 4.

[194] Ibid, pp. 4–5.

[195] Ibid, p. 5.

insights unencumbered by long accustomed limited partnership practices and less constrained by legal path dependencies.'[196]

A comparative law analysis requires the identification of jurisdictions to serve as comparisons to Chinese law. One meta-reference for this analysis is provided by *The Anatomy of Corporate Law*, which itself is based on a comparative law analysis.[197] The authors hail from disparate jurisdictions. To develop their analytic framework, they chose six core jurisdictions from developed market economies—France, Germany, Italy, Japan, the UK and the USA—, plus Brazil as a jurisdiction from a large emerging market.[198] They have identified that commercial activity and organisation cause problems that are roughly similar across these core jurisdictions. Furthermore, they analysed how these problems are addressed in different jurisdictions.[199] Therefore, they show that 'the features of a standard corporate form shape the agency problems that corporate law must address, and they create the domain in which a functional framework for comparative corporate law makes sense'.[200] This methodological approach of *The Anatomy of Corporate Law* allows it to compare the corporate law regimes of a wide range of different countries, thereby offering an extensive and well-grounded frame of reference.[201] In addition, a particular focus is placed in this book on the comparison of the FILPE with the German partnership law. While Germany is already one of the seven core jurisdictions of *The Anatomy of Corporate Law*, this special focus stems from two causes. One aspect is the fundamental role that the German GmbH & Co. KG has played in the overall development of limited partnership enterprises with a corporate general partner.[202] When it was legally recognised in 1912, the GmbH & Co. KG was the first combined legal form of its kind.[203] Over the years, it spread across continental Europe, and the limited partnership enterprise with a corporate general partner was included in the corporate landscape of most European jurisdictions.[204] The second aspect is the substantial influence that German legal theory and legal thinking has had on the development of the legal system in China over the past decades. Historically, German law, together with Japanese law, was analysed and implemented in China from the end of the Qing-dynasty[205] until the foundation of the PRC in 1949.[206] German law was a driving factor in the establishment of the civil law system in

[196] Wu and Geu (2007–2008), p. 135.

[197] Kraakman (2017), p. vii.

[198] Ibid, p. vii.

[199] Armour et al. (2017c), p. 3.

[200] Davies et al. (2009), p. 305.

[201] Skeel (2003–2004), p. 1521.

[202] Fleischer and Wansleben (2017b), p. 634.

[203] Ibid, p. 639.

[204] Ibid, p. 639.

[205] 1644–1912.

[206] Mi (2009), p. 791.

China at that time.[207] When comparative law began to flourish again with the policy of 'Reform and Opening up' in the late 1970s, the main reference for Chinese law reforms were the Anglo-American common law systems of the USA and UK.[208] Towards the end of the 1980s, however, Chinese scholars shifted their focus back towards an implementation of European Civil Law, with Germany as the core jurisdiction.[209] Numerous German laws and major law books have been translated into Chinese and studied by Chinese scholars and lawmakers,[210] including the 'German Commercial Code' (Handelsgesetzbuch/HGB)[211] that governs partnership enterprises.[212] The German theory and taxonomy of corporate and economic law have therefore had, and continue to have, much influence over the structure of China's commercial and corporate laws.[213] Even though Chinese partnership law bears similarities to US partnership law, the latter follows the common law tradition, while Chinese law is generally based on the civil law tradition.[214] Because of the different approaches under the common law and civil law systems, such legal transplants are always precarious.[215] Comparison with the German civil law system can help to analyse the implementation of the partnership law into the overall Chinese civil law system, thus adding an additional perspective. This is why Chinese scholars have always also turned to German partnership law for their comparative analyses.[216] The distinct impact that German law has had on the development of China's legal system, and on the origin of the limited partnership enterprise with a corporate general partner, is the basis for the special focus that this book places on the comparison with German law. However, when it is relevant to the overall analysis, considerable attention is also paid to the partnership laws of other jurisdictions.

Within comparative law theory, two main methods and approaches can be identified: functional comparison and cultural legal comparison. Functional comparison starts from the premise that the function of law lies in responding to social problems, and that all societies essentially face the same problems.[217]

> This makes it possible to compare legal institutions, even if they display different doctrinal structures, as long as they fulfil the same function, because they are deemed to be functionally equivalent. (...) Cultural comparison in contrast rejects the reduction of law to its

[207]Mi (2007), p. 132.

[208]Mi (2009), pp. 787–788, 791.

[209]Ibid, p. 791; Yu (1997), p. 61 fn. 151.

[210]Mi (2009), pp. 794–795.

[211]German Commercial Code (Handelsgesetzbuch), adopted by the German Reichstag on 10 May 1897; last amended by the German Bundestag on 12 December 2019.

[212]Du (杜景林) and Lu (卢谌) (1999); Yang (杨继) (2006).

[213]Mi (2009), p. 787.

[214]Wu and Geu (2007–2008), p. 136.

[215]Ibid, p. 136.

[216]For example, see Yuantao et al. (1989), p. 60.

[217]For a detailed introduction to functionalism, see Zweigert and Kötz (1996), p. 33ff.

> function and instead understands national law as an expression and development of the culture of a society. The focus here lies on the mentality expressed through a legal system, which is not considered fully comprehensible to outsiders and can only be fully experienced by participants in that legal system.[218]

Thus, cultural comparison opposes comparative evaluation and legal unification as both impossible and undesirable.[219] This is a position that has been shared by some Chinese scholars who have opposed the idea of adapting foreign laws, and advocated the development of the Chinese legal system from within.[220] *Von Senger* advocates an explicit cultural comparative approach for the analysis and understanding of Chinese law, as comparatists would often force the Chinese legal system and the structure of Chinese society into categories appropriate to foreign jurisdictions, thereby drawing incomplete conclusions and failing to gain a full understanding of the functionality of law and society in China.[221] However, commentators consider discrepancies between functional and cultural legal comparison to be much less drastic than that, as both approaches reject the limitation of comparative law to the analysis of black letter law. Instead, both approaches seek to identify the role of law in society while valuing and accepting the differences between legal systems.[222] Regarding Chinese comparative law, *PAN* has stated that it must result in failure if legal systems of other countries are blindly copied and adopted without taking into account the country's own specific situation.[223] Therefore, foreign law, especially from countries with different social systems, must be analysed with a strictly scientific and objective attitude.[224] 'While national chauvinism has to be avoided, blind imitation of foreign jurisdictions equally has to be prevented.'[225]

The comparative law analysis in this book will therefore take into account the specific social, cultural, and economic conditions in China.[226] The authors of *The Anatomy of Corporate Law* have also given great attention to this aspect in their efforts to ensure the neutrality of their analysis, in the sense that they avoid evaluative comparisons among the corporate law systems of the seven core jurisdictions.[227] Thus, they offer an analytic framework that is sufficiently open to include views of both sides of a controversial issue of legal policy, and that can incorporate circumstances which are specific to a country or culture.[228]

---

[218]Michaels (2012), pp. 297–298.

[219]Ibid, pp. 297–298.

[220]Mi (2009), pp. 803–804.

[221]Senger (2006), pp. 52–59.

[222]Michaels (2012), pp. 297–298.

[223]Pan (潘汉典) (1990), pp. 10–11.

[224]Ibid, p. 11.

[225]Ibid, p. 11.

[226]For a similar discussion with regard to the application of the economic analysis of law to developing countries, see Sect. 1.3.1.2.

[227]Kraakman (2017), pp. viii–ix.

[228]Ibid, pp. vii, viii–ix.

1.3.3 Comparison with the Equity Joint Venture

The third element of the methodical approach is a comparison of the FILPE with the EJV. Since the attractiveness of the limited partnership enterprise to a large degree depends on how much more contractual freedom it offers in comparison with a jurisdiction's corporation,[229] the starting point of this book is the foreign investor who needs to make a choice between different investment vehicles for the establishment of a sino-foreign alliance.[230] In recent decades, the EJV has been the most commonly adopted enterprise form for this purpose, and as such sets a certain 'standard'.[231] With the newly promulgated Foreign Investment Law[232] having entered into force on 1 January 2020, the EJV Law has been annulled.[233] A newly established sino-foreign joint venture will no longer take on the enterprise form of an EJV. Instead, a sino-foreign joint venture in the form of a corporation will be established as a limited liability company under the 'PRC Company Law'. The impact of the new Foreign Investment Law on the FDI legal regime will be analysed in detail below.[234]

An analysis of a sino-foreign alliance directly governed by the PRC Company Law should be the subject of a separate research project, and is not included in the scope of the current one. However, at the time of writing of this book, the provisions in the Foreign Investment Law are rather broad and general, primarily setting out an overall framework for the governance of FDI with detailed regulations lacking for many issues.[235] Many of the special provisions that govern EJVs are regulated in rules and regulations not included in the EJV Law.[236] At the time of writing of this book, it is not clear to what extend these provisions will also be repealed, or whether they will be recast in other regulations.[237] This leaves a degree of uncertainty and many open questions in regard to the legal framework that governs a corporate type joint venture under the Company Law.

Regarding the EJV, however, a wide range of writings by academics and practitioners has been published over the years, and considerable practical experience has been accumulated. At the same time, the legal framework that still governs existing EJVs at the time of writing of this book, provides context and important insights to understand the functioning and innovative aspects of the FIPE. While reference will be made to the Foreign Investment Law, where relevant, this book continues to draw valuable insights from a comparison of the FILPE with the well-established EJV.

---

[229] Fleischer and Wansleben (2017b), p. 641.

[230] See Sect. 1.1.

[231] Kroymann (2009), p. 385. For more details, see Sect. 3.2.1.

[232] See Sect. 3.1.5.3.

[233] Art. 42 Para. 1 Foreign Investment Law.

[234] See Sect. 3.1.5.

[235] McGinty et al. (2020), p. 10; Zhang and Tsoi (2019); Clifford Chance LLP (2019).

[236] See Sect. 3.1.3.

[237] McGinty et al. (2020), p. 10; McGinty et al. (2019).

Yet, this book does not provide an in-depth analysis of the EJV, or a detailed comparison of the EJV with the FILPE. Instead, a comparison with the EJV will be drawn on selectively where it assists in the understanding of the FILPE. At its core, this book provides an analysis of the FILPE independent from the nature or status of the EJV as a separate enterprise form under Chinese law.

1.4 Course of the Investigation

Can the FILPE with a foreign corporate general partner fulfil the defining features of the standard corporate form? This research question and analytic framework has been established within this first chapter.

A FILPE operates in the particular legal framework for foreign investments that has been established in China. For reasons of systematisation and clarity, the description of the legal history and the basic legal framework of China's FDI regime in general, and the partnership enterprise law in particular, are outlined in Part I. In order to better understand the special characteristics of the FILPE, Part I includes an overview of the alternative enterprise forms which have been available for sino-foreign alliances with a special focus on the EJV. An introduction is provided to the historical development of partnership enterprises and their governing laws and regulations in China. Fundamental elements of a FILPE, including the partnership agreement and its tax treatment, are likewise analysed. Part I closes with an outlook on the role that partnership enterprises play in China's economy, and an overview of the possible ownership and governance structures of a FILPE. Part II provides an in-depth analysis of the characteristics of the standard corporate form, and aims to determine which contractual arrangements might be necessary to fulfil the features of legal personality (Chap. 7), limited liability (Chap. 8), and transferable ownership interest (Chap. 9). The findings of all chapters are summarised in the conclusion set out in Part III.

References

Armour J, Hansmann H, Kraakman R (2009) What is corporate law? In: Kraakman R et al (eds) The anatomy of corporate law, 2nd edn. Oxford University Press, Oxford, pp 1–34

Armour J, Enriques L, Pargendler M, Ringe W-G (2017a) Beyond the anatomy. In: Kraakman R et al (eds) The anatomy of corporate law, 3rd edn. Oxford University Press, Oxford, pp 267–272

Armour J, Hansmann H, Kraakman R (2017b) Agency problems and legal strategies. In: Kraakman R et al (eds) The anatomy of corporate law, 3rd edn. Oxford University Press, Oxford, pp 29–47

Armour J, Hansmann H, Kraakman R, Pargendler M (2017c) What is corporate law? In: Kraakman R et al (eds) The anatomy of corporate law, 3rd edn. Oxford University Press, Oxford, pp 1–28

Bromberg AR, Ribstein LE (1994) Bromberg and Ribstein on Partnership, vol 3 limited partnership. Wolters Kluwer, Boston

Chen J (2009) Modernisation, westernisation, and globalisation: legal transplant in China. In: Oliveira JC, Cardinal C (eds) One country, two systems, three legal orders – perspectives of

evolution: essays on Macau's autonomy after the resumption of sovereignty by China. Springer, Berlin, pp 91–114
Chen K (2014) Corporations and partnerships in China. Kluwer Law, Alphen aan den Rijn
Chen J (2016) Chinese law: context and transformation, revised and expanded edition. Brill, Leiden
Clifford Chance LLP (2019) China's New Foreign Investment Law – What Does This Mean for Foreign Investors in China? https://www.cliffordchance.com/briefings/2019/03/china_s_new_foreigninvestmentlawwhatdoe.html. Accessed 15 May 2020
Cooter R, Ulen T (2012) Law & economics, 6th edn. Pearson Education International, Boston
Davies P, Enriques L, Hertig G, Hopt K, Kraakman R (2009) Beyond the anatomy. In: Kraakman R et al (eds) The anatomy of corporate law, 2nd edn. Oxford University Press, Oxford, pp 305–315
Du J (杜景林), Lu C (卢谌) (1999) German commercial code (德国商法典). Law Press China (法律出版社), Beijing.
Du R (杜瑞孔) (2006) On the advantages of partnership enterprises over limited liability companies (论合伙企业相对有限责任公司的比较优势). Theoret Observ (理论观察) 2006/6:69-70.
Eger T, Faure M, Zhang N (2007a) Economic analysis of law in China. Edward Elgar, Cheltenham, pp xiii–xix
Eger T, Faure M, Zhang N (2007b) Conclusions. In: Eger T, Faure M, Zhang N (eds) Economic analysis of law in China. Edward Elgar, Cheltenham, pp 307–309
Eisenberg MA (2000) Corporations and other business organizations: cases and materials, 8th edn Unabridged. Foundation Press, New York
Enriques L (2004) Book review: the comparative anatomy of corporate law. Am J Comp Law 52:1011–1036
Fleischer H, Wansleben T (2017a) Die GmbH & Co. KG als kautelarjuristische Erfolgsgeschichte. GmbH-Rundschau 106:169–180
Fleischer H, Wansleben T (2017b) Die GmbH & Co. KG in den Auslandsrechten - Zirkulation eines gesellschaftsrechtlichen Regelungsmodells. GmbH-Rundschau 106:633–643
Haase F (2014) Introduction. In: Haase F (ed) Taxation of international partnerships – 15 years OECD partnership report: past, present and future. IBFD, Amsterdam, pp 3–11
Holdsworth WS (1925) A history of English law, vol 8. Methuen, London
Howson NC (2010) Corporate law in the Shanghai People's Courts, 1992-2008: judicial autonomy in a contemporary authoritarian state. East Asia Law Rev 5:303–442
Howson NC (2015) Return of the prodigal form? Partnerships and partnership law in the People's Republic of China. In: Hillman RW, Loewenstein MJ (eds) Research handbook on partnerships, LLCs and alternative forms of business organizations. Edward Elgar, Cheltenham, pp 390–411
Huang Y (黄毅诚) (1997) Explanations on the Draft PRC Partnership Enterprise Law – delivered on 23 October 1996 to the 22nd Session of the Standing Committee of the 8th National People's Congress (关于《中华人民共和国合伙企业法(草案)》的说明—1996年10月23日在第八届全国人民代表大会常务委员会第二十二次会议上). Gazette of the Standing Committee of the National People's Congress 1997 No 1 (中华人民共和国全国人民代表大会常务委员会公报1997年1号), pp 12–16
Jiang Z (蒋兆康) (2012) Translation of Richard A Posner: economic analysis of law (理查德•波斯纳 法律的经济分析), 2nd edn. Law Press China (法律出版社), Beijing
Jiao L, Kasteleijn B (2011) Foreign acquisitions and joint ventures in China. In: Campbell D (ed) Mergers and acquisitions in North America, Latin America, Asia and the Pacific: selected issues and jurisdictions. Wolters Kluwer Law & Business, Alphen aan den Rijn, pp 29–62
Julius H (2008) Institutionalisierte rechtliche Zusammenarbeit: Die Erfahrungen der GTZ in China. Rabels Zeitschrift für ausländisches und internationales Privatrecht 72:55–87
Kirstein R (2000) Law and economics in Germany. In: Bouckaert B, De Geest G (eds) Encyclopedia of law and economics volume I – the history and methodology of law and economics. Edward Elgar, Cheltenham, pp 160–227
Kraakman R (2009) Preface. In: Kraakman R et al (eds) The anatomy of corporate law, 2nd edn. Oxford University Press, Oxford, pp vii–ix

Kraakman R (2017) Preface to the third edition. In: Kraakman R et al (eds) The anatomy of corporate law, 3rd edn. Oxford University Press, Oxford, pp vii–x

Kraakman R, Armour J, Davies P, Enriques L, Hansmann H, Hertig G, Hopt K, Kanda H, Pargendler M, Ringe W-G, Rock E (2017) The anatomy of corporate law, 3rd edn. Oxford University Press, Oxford

Kroymann B (2009) Das Kapitalgesellschaftsrecht der VR China – Analyse der Rahmenbedingungen für ausländische Investoren. Mohr Siebeck, Tübingen

Lin J (林建中) (2009) The anatomy of corporate law (解構公司法 比較與功能取徑) – translation of vol. 3 of Kraakman R et al. Xin xue lin (新學林), Taibei

Lu M (吕美昂) (2011) A comparison of the nature of foreign-invested enterprises in China (我国外商投资企业性质的比较). Legal Syst Soc (法制与社会) 8:81–82.

Mackaay E (2000) History of law and economics. In: Boudewijn B, De Geest G (eds) Encyclopedia of law and economics volume i – the history and methodology of law and economics. Edward Elgar, Cheltenham, pp 65–117

Mahony T (2015) Foreign investment law in China: regulation, practice and context. Tsinghua University Press, Beijing

McCahery JA, Vermeulen EPM (2004) The evolution of closely held business forms in Europe. In: McCahery JA, Raaijmakers T, Vermeulen EPM (eds) The governance of close corporations and partnerships: US and European perspectives. Oxford University Press, Oxford, pp 191–239

McGinty A, Xu L, Li J (2019) The foreign investment law: a new chapter opens for foreign direct investment in China. https://f.datasrvr.com/fr1/819/48729/Hogan_Lovells_New_FDL_opens_new_door.PD. Accessed 15 May 2020

McGinty A, Sun W, Wei J, Feng K, Xu L, Zhou L (2020) The Foreign Investment Law Implementation Regulations come into force: but why all the last minute changes? https://www.hoganlovells.com/en/publications/the-foreign-investment-law-implementation-regulations-come-into-force. Accessed 15 May 2020

Mi J (2007) Deutsches Recht in China seit der Politik der Reform und Öffnung. Zeitschrift für Chinesisches Recht 14:132–139

Mi J (2009) Die Vergleichende Rechtswissenschaft Chinas in den letzten 30 Jahren. In: Altmeppen H, Reichard I, Schermaier MJ (eds) Festschrift für Rolf Knütel zum 70. Geburtstag. C. F. Müller, Heidelberg, pp 787–812

Michaels R (2012) Comparative law. In: Basedow J et al (eds) The Max Planck Encyclopedia of European private law, vol 1. Oxford University Press, Oxford, pp 297–301

Pan H (潘汉典) (1990) Comparative law in China: retrospect and prospect (比较法在中国:回顾与展望). J Comp Law (比较法研究) 1990/2:1–13.

Pan H (潘汉典) (1992) Translation of Konrad Zweigert and Hein Kötz: Einführung in die Rechtsvergleichung (茨威格特•克茨比较法总论). China Legal Publishing House (中国法制出版社), Beijing

Posner RA (2014) Economic analysis of law, 9th edn. Wolters Kluwer Law & Business, New York

Ribstein LE (1988) An applied theory of limited partnership. Emory Law J 37:835–895

Ribstein LE (2004) The evolving partnership. In: McCahery JA, Raaijmakers T, Vermeulen EPM (eds) The Governance of close corporations and partnerships: US and European perspectives. Oxford University Press, Oxford, pp 153–190

Schäfer H-B, Ott C (2012) Lehrbuch der ökonomischen Analyse des Zivilrechts, 5th edn. Springer, Berlin

Schaper M (2013) hybrid legal forms at the gates – the transition from combined legal forms to hybrid corporations and its consequences for creditor protection. Eur Comp Financ Law Rev 10:75–112

Senger HV (2006) Von der Vergleichung des Rechts zur Vergleichung der Gesellschaftsführung. Zeitschrift für Europarecht, internationales Privatrecht und Rechtsvergleichung 47:43–62

Shaddox SH (2013) China's foreign invested partnership enterprise law: the lifeless or sleeping dragon? Pacific Rim Law Policy J 22:469–490

Shi J (史晋川), Dong X (董雪兵) (2012) Translation of Robert Cooter and Thomas Ulen: law & economics (罗伯特•考特, 托马斯•尤伦 法和经济学), 6th edn. Gezhi Press (格致出版社), Shanghai

Skeel DA (2003–2004) Book review: corporate anatomy lessons. Yale Law J 113:1519–1577

Spence JD (1990) The search for modern China. Norton, New York

Teichmann C (2014) Die Auslandsgesellschaft & Co. Zeitschrift für Unternehmens- und Gesellschaftsrecht 43:220–251

Towfigh EV (2017) Das ökonomische Paradigma. In: Towfigh EV, Petersen N (eds) Ökonomische Methoden im Recht, 2nd edn. Mohr Siebeck, Tübingen, pp 25–44

Ulen TS (2000) Rational choice theory in law and economics. In: Bouckaert B, De Geest G (eds) Encyclopedia of law and economics volume i – the history and methodology of law and economics. Edward Elgar, Cheltenham, pp 790–818

Werthwein S (2010) Corporations and partnerships. In: Bu Y (ed) Chinese business law. C. H. Beck/Hart/Nomos, Munich/Oxford, pp 15–54

Windbichler C (2014) Eine internationale Landkarte der Personengesellschaften (einschließlich juristische Personen und Gesamthand). Zeitschrift für Unternehmens- und Gesellschaftsrecht 43:110–138

Wu Y, Geu TE (2007–2008) The new PRC limited partnership enterprise law and the limited partnership law of the United States: a selective analytical comparison. UCLA Pacific Basin Law J 25:133–178

Yang J (杨继) (2006) Translation of Claus Wilhelm Canaris: Handelsrecht, 23rd edn (卡纳里斯德国商法). Law Press China (法律出版社), Beijing

Yang J (杨杰), Qu T (曲天明) (2010) A study on the application of foreign-invested partnership enterprise law – comment on the FIPE measures (外商合伙企业的法律适用问题研究—兼评《外国企业或者个人在中国境内设立合伙企业管理办法》). Sci Manage (科学与管理) 2010/3:63–66.

Yang MM (2002) The Resilience of Guanxi and Its new deployments: a critique of some New Guanxi Scholarship Rebuttal. China Q 170:459–476

Yu D, Feng S, Wei J (2012) Foreign invested partnerships: a new vehicle for investments? China Law Pract 26(8):10–13

Yu G (1997) The emerging framework of China's business organizations law. Transnl Lawyer 10:39–76

Yuantao X, Binxue S, Zhang D (1989) Translation of Liufang Fang: Chinese partnership. Law Contemp Probl 52:43–67

Zhang N (张乃根) (1995) Economic analysis of law: comments and comparison (经济学分析法学—评介及其比较). Shanghai Sanlian Publishin House (上海三联书店), Shanghai

Zhang ZA, Tsoi V (2019) China Adopts New Foreign Investment Law. https://www.whitecase.com/publications/alert/china-adopts-new-foreign-investment-law. Accessed 15 May 2020

Zhou L (周林彬) (1998) On law and economics (法律经济学论纲). Beijing University Press (北京大学出版社), Beijing

Zhu C (朱慈蕴) (2008) The problem resulting from a corporation participating in a partnership as a general partner (公司作为普通合伙人投资合伙企业引发的法律思考). Mod Law Sci (现代法学) 30/5:77–85.

Zhu S (朱少平), Gebhardt I (葛毅) (eds) (2004) The Amendment of the Partnership Enterprise Law of the PRC – Materials on the Drafting Process 2001–2002 (中华人民共和国合伙企业法的修订- 立法进程资料汇编 2001–2002年). CITC, Beijing.

Zinser R (2012) Die Entstehung des chinesischen Sachenrechtsgesetzes: Eine Analyse des Diskurses innerhalb der chinesischen Rechtswissenschaft. Lang, Frankfurt a. M

Zweigert K, Kötz H (1996) Einführung in die Rechtsvergleichung, 3rd edn. Mohr Siebeck, Tübingen

Part I
Basic Principles of Chinese Partnership Law

While this book focuses on the characteristics of the standard corporate form in a FILPE, such an analysis can only be undertaken against the background of China's overall legal framework. Two areas of law are of particular relevance: the legal regime that governs foreign direct investments, and the legal framework for partnership enterprises in China. This part therefore begins by analysing the concept of FDI in China in Chap. 2. It continues in Chap. 3 with a more general introduction to China's foreign investment regime, with an emphasis on joint venture law. Joint ventures have played a significant role in the evolution of FDI in China, and the development of the legal framework for sino-foreign alliances. Many features of the FILPE can only be fully appreciated in the context of the history of joint venture law, the types of joint ventures that are available in China, the legal and administrative framework that surrounds them, and the most recent reforms in the FDI regime. Chapter 4 provides a comprehensive analysis of the historical development and legal framework that governs partnership enterprises in China in general, and the FILPE in particular. Certain basic aspects of the FILPE are analysed in Part I, as they are helpful for the general understanding of the subsequent Part II. Those aspects include the registration process for the FILPE, its partnership agreement, how partnership enterprises are dealt with in Chinese courts, and how the FILPE is taxed. Further, an overview of the different types of partnerships that are available in China, is provided. This Part I concludes in Chap. 5 with an overview of the role that partnership enterprises play in China's modern economy, and a discussion of different structuring options for the utilisation of a FILPE in an actual foreign investment project.

Chapter 2
The Concept of Foreign Direct Investment in China

The development of China's foreign investment laws, and the enormous influx of FDI in recent decades, have largely complemented and enhanced each other.[1] One would not have been possible without the other. Thereby, FDI has made a decisive contribution to the rebuilding of China's legal system as a whole.[2] This part therefore starts with a definition and analysis of the concept of FDI in China. Based upon the OECD Benchmark Definition, FDI is defined as

> a category of cross-border investment made by a resident in one economy (the direct investor) with the objective of establishing a lasting interest in an enterprise (the direct investment enterprise) that is resident in an economy other than that of the direct investor. The motivation of the direct investor is a strategic long-term relationship with the direct investment enterprise to ensure a significant degree of influence by the direct investor in the management of the direct investment enterprise.[3]

The nature of FDI is an ownership arrangement instead of a mere contractual arrangement.[4] Quantitatively, the OECD definition acknowledges a 'lasting interest' when the direct investor owns at least 10% of the voting power of the direct investment enterprise.[5] Conversely, for a long time, Chinese law required the foreign investor to contribute at least 25% of the capital of a Foreign-Invested Enterprise

[1]Wei (2010), pp. 55–56; Mahony (2015), pp. 1–2.

[2]Wei (2010), p. 56; Mahony (2015), pp. 1–2. Recognising the important role of FDI in China: Para. 1 Explanatory Notes on the PRC Foreign Investment Law (Draft for Comments) (中华人民共和国外国投资法（草案征求意见稿)的说明), promulgated by the Ministry of Commerce on 19 January 2015.

[3]OECD (2008), Para. 11, p. 17.

[4]Yu (2006), p. 423.

[5]OECD (2008), Para. 11, p. 17.

S. Kuntner, *China's Foreign-Invested Limited Partnership Enterprise*, China-EU Law Series 7, https://doi.org/10.1007/978-3-030-54181-1_2

(FIE).[6] In 2003, this restrictive policy was softened.[7] The authorities now have the power to approve an FIE with less than 25% foreign ownership.[8] Unlike the OECD definition, Chinese law does not establish a specific threshold for when the foreign investor is deemed to have reached a 'lasting interest'.[9] In practice, the threshold of 25% has been drawn on as a general point of reference, notwithstanding that a 'lasting interest' could, in certain cases, be established with an investment below this threshold.[10] In the new Foreign Investment Law, a FIE is defined as 'an enterprise registered and established in China in accordance with the Chinese laws, which is wholly or partly invested by foreign investors.'[11] This broader definition thus makes no reference to a threshold to establish a 'lasting interest'. FDI can be categorised, according to the purpose of the investment, into types, such as the purchase or sale of existing equity in the form of mergers and acquisitions (M&A), greenfield investments, and the extension of capital.[12]

> While M&A transactions imply the purchase or sale of existing equity, greenfield investments refer to altogether new investments (*ex nihilo* investments). Extension of capital relates to additional new investments as an expansion of an established business; conceptually and in terms of economic impact, it is similar to greenfield investments.[13]

Regarding the effect that FDI has on the receiving economy, it is generally conceived that greenfield investment and extension of capital have the potential of exerting more influence over employment, business performance, and economic growth.[14] The analysis in this part follows these OECD definitions, but focuses mainly on greenfield investments by adopting the perspective of a foreign investor who intends to establish a new sino-foreign alliance in China.

---

[6]For example, see Article 4 Paragraph 2 EJV Law (see Sect. 3.1.2 fn. 18) and Article 18 Paragraph 3 CJV Implementing Regulations (see Sect. 3.1.3. fn. 49).

[7]Art. 2 Circular on Issues Related to Strengthening the Administration over the Approval, Registration, Foreign Exchange, and Taxation Pertaining to Foreign-Invested Enterprises (关于加强外商投资企业审批、登记、外汇及税收管理有关问题的通知), promulgated jointly by the State Administration for Industry and Commerce; State Administration of Foreign Exchange; Ministry of Foreign Trade and Economic Cooperation and State Administration of Taxation on 30 December 2002 and effective as of 1 January 2003.

[8]OECD (2003), p. 28; Liu (2008), p. 27.

[9]Hübner (2014), p. 12.

[10]ibid, p. 12.

[11]Art. 2 Para. 3 FIL. Regarding the broader scope of application of the Foreign Investment Law, see Sect. 3.1.5.2.

[12]OECD (2008), Para. 272, pp. 86–87.

[13]OECD (2008), Para. 273, p. 87.

[14]Wei (2010), p. 55.

References

Hübner PA (2014) Rechtsschutz ausländischer Investoren vor chinesischen Gerichten. De Gruyter, Berlin

Liu C (2008) Chinese company and securities law: investment vehicles, mergers and acquisitions and corporate finance in China. Kluwer Law, Alphen aan den Rijn

Mahony T (2015) Foreign investment law in China: regulation, practice and context. Tsinghua University Press, Beijing

OECD (Organisation for Economic Co-operation and Development) (2003) Investment policy reviews China – progress and reform challenges. OECD, Paris

OECD (Organisation for Economic Co-operation and Development) (2008) Benchmark definition of foreign direct investment, 4th edn. OECD, Paris

Wei W (2010) Foreign investment law. In: Bu Y (ed) Chinese business law. C. H. Beck, Hart and Nomos, Munich/Oxford, pp 55–79

Yu Y (2006) The experience of FDI recipients: the case of China. In: Urata S, Yue CS, Kimura F (eds) Multinationals and economic growth in East Asia – foreign direct investment, corporate strategies and national economic development. Routledge, New York, pp 423–451

Chapter 3
Joint Venture Enterprises as Sino-Foreign Alliances

3.1 History and Framework of Foreign Direct Investments and Joint Venture Law

3.1.1 *Early Forms of FDI in China*

Early forms of FDI in China can be traced back to as far as the late Qing-dynasty (1644–1911).[1] Very little written Chinese law addressed the regulation of private economic activity[2] until China's first 'Company Law' was issued on 21 January 1904 (the 1904 Company Law).[3] Said Law established the corporation as an enterprise form, basing it on the 'modern' western corporate structures of that time.[4] With the 1904 Company Law, the Qing government aimed to modernise the economy, and restore economic sovereignty.[5] However, the new law did not lay a foundation for a foreign investment regime. In fact, most foreign enterprises in China at that time were exempt from Chinese laws because of the privilege of extraterritoriality.[6] They registered in their home country or with the respective consulate in China, and remained subject to their home jurisdiction.[7] Circumstances suddenly changed for foreign enterprises, when extraterritoriality came to an end in

[1]Spence (1990), p. 158ff.

[2]Notwithstanding the absence of codified law, a well-established system of commercial law existed at that time in China. On the history of partnership law in China, see Sect. 4.1.1.1.

[3]Kirby (1995), pp. 43–44. For more details on the 1904 Company Law, see Sect. 4.1.1.2.

[4]Jiang (江平) and Li (李固光) (2005), p. 24; Kirby (1995), p. 47.

[5]For a detailed account of the history of the corporation and Company Law in China, see Jiang (江平) and Li (李固光) (2005), pp. 24–29; Kirby (1995), pp. 43–63.

[6]Kirby (1995), p. 53; Teesdale (1932), p. 248.

[7]Kirby (1995), p. 53.

S. Kuntner, *China's Foreign-Invested Limited Partnership Enterprise*, China-EU Law Series 7, https://doi.org/10.1007/978-3-030-54181-1_3

1943–1944.[8] The Nationalist Government of the time undertook a revision of the '1929 Company Law',[9] and the question of how to address foreign enterprises became one of the key issues in the drafting of the new law.[10] While attracting FDI was essential for the development of the industrial sector in China, the Nationalist Government was nonetheless determined to exert control over foreign investments.[11] The conflict of interest between these two objectives has dominated the development of foreign investment laws ever since, and continues to do so today. The revised 'Company Law' was promulgated on 12 April 1946 (the 1946 Company Law). For the first time, it defined a 'foreign company' as a legal basis upon which foreign enterprises could operate in post-extraterritoriality China.[12] With the promulgation of the 1946 Company Law, the Nationalist Government left 'no doubt that it would now determine the nature and terms of the foreign business presence in China'.[13] However, with the establishment of the PRC in 1949, and the abolition of the entire Republican legal system, the 1946 Company Law was repealed, and a political process initiated that eventually led to the nationalisation or collectivisation of all enterprises and organisations in China.[14]

3.1.2 The 'Opening up' of China: Introducing Joint Ventures and Foreign Investment Laws

China's legal system was in a state of virtual non-existence[15] when the policy of 'Reform and Opening up'—led by Deng Xiaoping—was initiated in December 1978.[16] 'The mounting task was for China's legislators and administrators to lay down a legal framework that would adequately protect the interests of foreign investors.'[17] The promulgation of the 'Sino-Foreign Equity Joint Venture Law'[18] (EJV Law) in 1979 constituted the first step in the re-creation of a Chinese legal

[8]ibid, pp. 53–54.

[9]The 1904 Company Law was replaced by the 1914 Company Law, which itself was superseded by the 1929 Company Law, which entered into force in 1931. See Kirby (1995), pp. 49, 51.

[10]Kirby (1995), p. 54; Teesdale (1932), p. 248.

[11]Kirby (1995), p. 55.

[12]ibid, p. 55.

[13]ibid, p. 56.

[14]ibid, p. 56.

[15]Mahony (2015), p. 1.

[16]Spence (1990), pp. 656–659.

[17]Wei (2010), pp. 56–57.

[18]PRC Sino-Foreign Equity Joint Venture Law (中华人民共和国中外合资经营企业法), adopted by the 2nd Session of the 5th National People's Congress on 1 July 1979; amended at the 3rd Session of the 7th National People's Congress on 4 April 1990, amended at the 4th Session of the 9th National People's Congress on 15 March 2001, amended at the 22nd Session of the Standing Committee of the 12th National People's Congress on 3 September 2016 and repealed on 01 January

system.[19] The EJV Law provided a set of rudimental rules for foreign investors to establish an enterprise together with Chinese investors.[20] The law defines an EJV as a limited liability company,[21] guarantees government protection of lawfully established EJVs,[22] and permits foreign investors to remit lawfully-generated profits out of China.[23] Beyond introducing the EJV, the EJV Law was also significant because it symbolised China's commitment to encouraging FDI, and recognising the legal status of foreign interests in China.[24] Throughout the 1980s, the inflow of FDI steadily increased but also developed into more diverse investment projects, which brought with them new requirements and problems that demanded further FDI-related legislation.[25] In response to criticism that the governance structure of the EJV did not allow enough flexibility for establishing sino-foreign alliances for certain types of investments,[26] the cooperative joint venture[27] (CJV) was introduced in 1988 with the promulgation of the 'Sino-Foreign Cooperative Joint Venture Law'[28] (CJV Law). Two years before that, in 1986, the Wholly Foreign-Owned Enterprise (WFOE) had been established with the promulgation of the 'Wholly Foreign-Owned Enterprise Law'[29] (WFOE Law), which allowed foreign investors to incorporate an enterprise in China in the form of a limited liability company without a Chinese partner.[30] The EJV, CJV, and WFOE together form the basic triumvirate of FIEs in China: the so-called 三资企业—'three investment enterprises'.[31] The 1990s saw a new round of rapid inflow of FDI, necessitating further reform of the foreign investment regime, and the creation of two new enterprise

2020. Unless otherwise indicated, citations of legislation in this book always refer to its latest amended version.

[19]Bath (2007), p. 774.

[20]Wei (2010), p. 57; Mahony (2015), p. 4.

[21]Art. 4 Para. 1 EJV Law.

[22]Art. 2 Para. 1 EJV Law.

[23]Art. 11 Para. 1 EJV Law.

[24]Wei (2010), p. 57.

[25]ibid, pp. 56–57.

[26]Mahony (2015), p. 8; Wei (2010), p. 57.

[27]Regarding the two different forms of CJVs that have been codified, see Sect. 3.2.2.

[28]PRC Sino-Foreign Cooperative Joint Venture Law (中华人民共和国中外合作经营企业法), adopted at the 1st Session of the 7th National People's Congress on 13 April 1988; amended at the 18th Session of the Standing Committee of the 9th National People's Congress on 31 October 2000, amended at the 22nd Session of the Standing Committee of the 12th National People's Congress on 3 September 2016, amended at the 30th Session of the Standing Committee of the 12th National People's Congress on 4 November 2017 and repealed on 01 January 2020.

[29]PRC Wholly Foreign-Owned Enterprise Law (中华人民共和国外资企业法), adopted at the 4th Session of the 6th National People's Congress on 12 April 1986; amended at the 18th Session of the Standing Committee of the 9th National People's Congress on 31 October 2000, amended at the 22nd Session of the Standing Committee of the 12th National People's Congress on 3 September 2016 and repealed on 01 January 2020.

[30]Mahony (2015), p. 10.

[31]ibid, p. 11; Chen (2016), p. 847.

forms for foreign investors.[32] In 1995, the Foreign-Invested Company Limited by Shares (FICLS) was introduced with the promulgation of the 'FICLS Provisions'.[33] The FICLS is a sino-foreign alliance with limited liability that—in theory—can be listed on China's stock markets.[34] In the same year, the Foreign-Invested Enterprise Holding Company (FIE HoldCo) was introduced with the promulgation of the 'FIE HoldCo Provisions'.[35] Strictly speaking, the FIE HoldCo is not a separate type of investment vehicle, but a special-feature limited liability company in the form of an EJV or WFOE that is available to foreign investors who have already made significant investments in China.[36]

3.1.3 *The Dual Structure of Domestic and Foreign Investment Laws*

The EJV, CJV, and WFOE played a pioneering role in the early 1980s, as they have been the front-runners in the development of corporate law in China. The three associated laws introduced corporate forms with limited liability, even though no general legal framework for dealing with corporations had yet been established in China at that time.[37] In 1982, the new 'PRC Constitution'[38] (Constitution) for the first time contained a clause recognising and protecting the lawful rights and interests of foreign investors under Chinese law.[39] However, it took 7 years from the issuance of the EJV Law before a minimal legal basis for private Chinese companies, and a simple understanding of certain *quasi* corporate law concepts, was provided with the

[32] Wei (2010), pp. 55–56; Mahony (2015), p. 36.

[33] Interim Provisions on Certain Issues Concerning the Establishment of Foreign-invested Companies Limited by Shares (关于设立外商投资股份有限公司若干问题的暂行规定), promulgated by the Ministry of Foreign Trade and Economic Cooperation on 1 October 1995, amended on 28 October 2015 and repealed on 01 January 2020.

[34] Mahony (2015), p. 32.

[35] Interim Provisions on Foreign Investor's Establishment of Companies with Investment Nature (关于外商投资举办投资性公司的暂行规定), promulgated by the Ministry of Foreign Trade and Economic Cooperation on 4 April 1995 and repealed by the Provisions on the Establishment of Investment Companies by Foreign Investors (关于外商投资举办投资性公司的规定), promulgated by the Ministry of Commerce on 17 November 2004, amended on 26 May 2006 and amended on 28 October 2015 with effect as of the same date.

[36] Mahony (2015), pp. 206–207.

[37] Bath (2007), p. 774.

[38] Constitution of the PRC (中华人民共和国宪法), adopted at the 5th Session of the 5th National People's Congress on 4 December 1982, amended at the 1st Session of the 7th National People's Congress on 12 April 1988, amended at the 1st Session of the 8th National People's Congress on 29 March 1993, amended at the 2nd Session of the 9th National People's Congress on 15 March 1999, amended at the 2nd Session of the 10th National People's Congress on 14 March 2004, and amended at the 1st Session of the 13th National People's Congress on 11 March 2018.

[39] Art. 18 Constitution.

promulgation of the 'PRC General Principles of the Civil Law'[40] (GPCL) in 1986, and the 'Interim Regulations on Private Enterprises'[41] in 1988.[42] Yet, the legal basis for privately held limited liability companies was not provided until 1993, when the 'PRC Company Law'[43] (Company Law) was promulgated.

Both the EJV Law and CJV Law were rather cryptic and provisional, which is quite symptomatic of the difficulty of filling the legal vacuum that existed at that time.[44] Since then, supplementing laws with further legislation has become a common pattern and defining characteristic of China's legislation in the area of FDI.[45] Legal reform in China is not proceeding in accordance with a detailed master plan, but rather involves a great deal of experimentation.[46] 'In any given field there are frequent cycles of laissez-faire—creating a policy laboratory in which the government can study the effects of unbridled activity—followed by a tightening of regulation.'[47] Hence, 4 years after the issuance of the EJV Law, in 1983, the 'EJV Implementing Regulations'[48] were promulgated, and were followed by the 'CJV Implementing Regulations'[49] in 1995, 7 years after the CJV Law came into effect. It is quite common for Chinese implementing regulations in certain respects to go

[40]PRC General Principles of the Civil Law (中华人民共和国民法通则), adopted at the 4th Session of the 6th National People's Congress on 12 April 1986, amended at the 10th Session of the Standing Committee of the 11th National People's Congress on August 27, 2009 and effective from the same date; starting from 1 October 2017, the new General Rules of Civil Law (GRCL) (Sect. 4.2.1.1 fn. 600) will eventually replace the GPCL. Since it has not yet been clarified for all provisions of the GPCL how long these will stay effective (see discussion in Sect. 4.2.1.1), provisions from both the GPCL and GRCL will be cited throughout this book, whenever relevant.

[41]PRC Interim Regulations on Private Enterprises (中华人民共和国私营企业暂行条例), promulgated by the State Council on 26 June 1988 and repealed on 19 March 2018.

[42]Mahony (2015), pp. 4–5; Kirby (1995), p. 56.

[43]PRC Company Law (中华人民共和国公司法), adopted at the 5th Session of the Standing Committee of the 8th National People's Congress on 29 December 1993; amended at the 13th Session of the Standing Committee of the 9th National People's Congress on 25 December 1999; amended at the 11th Session of the Standing Committee of the 10th National People's Congress on 28 August 2004; amended at the 18th Session of the Standing Committee of the 10th National People's Congress on 27 October 2005; amended at the 6th Session of the Standing Committee of the 12th National People's Congress on 28 December 2013; and amended at the 6th Session of the Standing Committee of the 13th National People's Congress on 26 October 2018 and effective as of the same date.

[44]Lubman (2006–2007), p. 11.

[45]ibid, p. 11; Mahony (2015), p. 5.

[46]Cohen and Lange (1997), pp. 345–348.

[47]ibid, pp. 345–348.

[48]PRC Sino-Foreign Equity Joint Venture Law Implementing Regulations (中华人民共和国中外合资经营企业法实施条例), promulgated by the State Council on 20 September 1983; amended on 21 December 1987; amended on 22 July 2001; amended on 29 February 2014; amended on 2 March 2019 and repealed on 01 January 2020.

[49]PRC Sino-Foreign Cooperative Joint Venture Law Detailed Implementing Regulations (中华人民共和国中外合作经营企业法实施细则), promulgated by the State Council on 4 September 1995, amended on 19 February 2014, amended on 01 March 2017 and repealed on 01 January 2020.

beyond the specific scope of the legislation which they purportedly implement.[50] The EJV Implementing Regulations are much more detailed than the EJV Law, providing additional statutory guidance for areas such as the contribution of capital,[51] the establishment and operation of the board of directors,[52] finance and accounting,[53] and the dissolution and liquidation of the EJV.[54] The EJV Implementing Regulations therefore complement the EJV Law as the legal basis for the EJV. The legal framework governing the EJV further contains numerous rules, notices, and circulars that have been enacted by various authorities at different levels.[55] These regulations have often been issued in response to specific questions that arose in the course of approving a specific EJV. Therefore, they address very detailed aspects, such as the permissibility of establishing joint ventures with unlimited terms of operation, or the legality of using leased equipment as capital contribution.[56] 'In this way the government authorities were able to gradually fill in many of the gaps in the regulatory framework, intentionally left open by the broad general provisions of the basic law and, to a lesser extent, by the implementing regulations.'[57] The foreign investment laws and regulations gradually established a legal regime that is separate from the general domestic legal system.[58] The differentiation between domestic-invested Chinese enterprises on the one hand, and FIEs on the other hand created a parallel structure of corporate law with two diverse and unequal sub-systems.[59] This policy of differing treatment can be understood as an expression of the conflict between attracting more FDI while trying to retain control over it.[60] On the one hand, China's authorities desired to prevent foreign influence at the level of society, culture, and politics. On the other hand, they wanted to gain the benefit of foreign capital, technology, and management expertise.[61] The foreign investment regime thus reflected the constantly changing perceptions of the need for and usefulness of FDI.[62] In many cases, FIEs operated in paradoxical legal spaces that were simultaneously more restrictive and more liberal than the laws which applied to domestic enterprises.[63] 'The foreign investment policy at the early stage

[50]Bath (2007), p. 779.

[51]Chap 4, Arts. 22-29 EJV Implementing Regulations.

[52]Chap 5, Arts. 30-39 EJV Implementing Regulations.

[53]Chap 11, Arts. 69-79 EJV Implementing Regulations.

[54]Chap 14, Arts. 89-96 EJV Implementing Regulations.

[55]Shen (2015), p. 34.

[56]Mahony (2015), p. 11.

[57]ibid, p. 12.

[58]Chen (2016), pp. 645, 844; Bath (2007), p. 774; Lu (吕美昂) (2011), p. 81; Wei (2010), p. 58.

[59]Mahony (2015), pp. 76, 80; Bath (2007), pp. 774–775; Nägeli (2003), p. 57. For a fundamental analysis and comparison to German law, see Stursberg (2014).

[60]Mahony (2015), p. 76; Wei (2010), p. 58.

[61]Mahony (2015), p. 76; Wang (2015), pp. 202–203; Wei (2010), p. 58; Pearson (1991), p. 3.

[62]Chen (2016), pp. 847–848.

[63]Mahony (2015), p. 76; Yang (2015), pp. 96–97.

was primitive and inconsistent, moving between two extremes of openness and restriction. A widespread lack of uniformity, inconsistency and self-contradiction occasionally endangered the foreign investment community's confidence in China.'[64] With the further development of FDI, the Chinese authorities partially began to relax this sharp divide. The promulgation of the 'PRC Contract Law'[65] (Contract Law) in 1999 was the first fundamental legislation in which one unified regulation was applied to both foreign and domestic investments, replacing separate laws for each.[66]

However, the dual structure of the legal system continued to present a challenge for foreign investors. This is illustrated in the question of to what extent the Company Law applies to FIEs. Most types of FIEs are organised as limited liability companies, which are generally regulated in the Company Law. At the same time, the laws and regulations governing the EJV and the CJV[67] can be understood as creating their own regulatory regime with distinctive corporate structure and governance rules.[68] The Company Law stipulates in Article 217—per *lex specialis derogate lex generalis*—that the laws (法) governing FIEs shall prevail over the provisions of the Company Law.[69] The Company Law thus functions as a background law, and applies to joint ventures to the extent that the EJV Law and CJV Law are silent.[70] However, it is less clear whether rules (规章) and administrative regulations (行政法规)—including the EJV Implementing Regulations and CJV Implementing Regulations—have the same prevailing effect over the Company Law.[71] In general, the hierarchy and primacy of Chinese laws, regulations, and rules is regulated by the 'Legislation Law'.[72] Furthermore, the 'Opinions on Applying the Company Law',[73] which were issued in 2006 in relation to the approval and registration of FIEs, clarify in Article 1 that the Company Law stipulates in Article

[64]Shen (2015), p. 5.

[65]PRC Contract Law (中华人民共和国合同法), adopted at the 2nd Session of the 9th National People's Congress on 15 March 1999 and effective as of 1 October 1999.

[66]Prior to the PRC Contract Law, separate laws were applied to contractual disputes depending upon whether a foreign entity was party to the contract. For further references, see Mahony (2015), pp. 46–49, 77.

[67]For the WFOE, this is the case only to a lesser degree.

[68]Shen (2015), p. 6; Lu (吕美昂) (2011), p. 81.

[69]Shen (2015), p. 6; Hübner (2014), p. 19.

[70]Shen (2015), p. 5.

[71]Wei (2010), p. 70.

[72]PRC Legislation Law (中华人民共和国立法法), adopted at the 3rd Session of the 9th National People's Congress on 15 March 2000; amended at the 3rd Session of the 12th National People's Congress on 15 March 2015.

[73]Implementing Opinions on Certain Issues Concerning the Application of the Law in the Administration of the Examination, Approval and Registration of Foreign-Invested Enterprises (关于外商投资的公司审批登记管理法律适用若干问题的执行意见), promulgated jointly by the State Administration for Industry and Commerce; Ministry of Commerce; General Administration of Customs and State Administration of Foreign Exchange on 24 April 2006.

217 a prevailing effect only for FIE *laws*[74] in the narrow sense (法).[75] Administrative regulations and rules shall only be applicable to matters regarding the approval and registration of FIEs when these are not covered in the Company Law, the 'Regulations on the Administration of Company Registration',[76] or the FIE laws.[77] Therefore, when applying FIE related administrative regulations and rules, it is important to check whether the Company Law contains contrary provisions.[78] However, an exception is recognised in respect of the EJV Implementing Regulations and the CJV Implementing Regulations. Despite their nature as administrative regulations, in practice, they are regarded as being on the same level as FIE laws on the grounds that it is the sole purpose of the regulations to implement FIE laws,[79] and that the implementing regulations would otherwise exist without any substance.[80] It is further pointed out that, in practice, the government authorities are used to applying more specific FIE regulations, and are thus likely to continue to apply rules and regulations in the drafting and implementation of which they have been involved.[81]

Over the years, numerous opinions and circulars have been issued by government authorities[82] that touch upon particular areas of conflict between the Company Law and the FIE regulations. In addition, the PRC Supreme People's Court (Supreme People's Court/ SPC), which is granted the power to issue binding interpretations of concrete (i.e., non-theoretical) problems arising from the implementation of laws and regulations in specific cases,[83] has issued a number of interpretations on this issue.[84] This inconsistent application of the Company Law to FIEs has created a complicated corporate legal regime for FDI in China.[85] Therefore, the application of the governing laws and regulations for the establishment of an FIE needs to be confirmed for each case, project, and location.[86]

Starting from 1 January 2020, with the effectiveness of the Foreign Investment Law, this dual legislative structure has been eliminated, meaning that the

---

[74]Pursuant to Article 7 Legislation Law, laws can only be enacted and amended by the National People's Congress or the Standing Committee of the National People's Congress.

[75]Wei (2010), p. 71; Hübner (2014), pp. 19–20.

[76]Regulations on the Administration of Company Registration (中华人民共和国公司登记管理条例), promulgated by the State Council on 24 June 1994, amended on 18 December 2005, amended on 19 February 2014 and amended on 6 February 2016.

[77]Art. 1 Opinions on Applying the Company Law.

[78]Hübner (2014), p. 20.

[79]Wei (2010), p. 71.

[80]Hübner (2014), p. 20.

[81]Shen (2015), p. 7.

[82]See the compilation in Bath (2007), p. 778; Mahony (2015), p. 86.

[83]Art. 104 Legislation Law. For a detailed analysis of the role of the SPC, see Tang et al. (2016), pp. 25–27.

[84]See the compilation in Shen (2015), pp. 5–7.

[85]Wei (2010), p. 71.

[86]Shen (2015), p. 7; Kroymann (2009), p. 35.

organisational structure, governance and operating rules of FIEs are now the same as that of domestic invested enterprises.[87] However, it remains to be seen if and how fast the legal framework that governs FIEs, which is scattered among so many laws and regulations, can be transformed into a unified legal framework that governs all enterprise forms equally.[88]

3.1.4 China's Accession to the WTO: Initiating Liberalisation of the Foreign Investment Regime

Efforts to reform and liberalise the foreign investment regime towards the end of the 1990s were primarily driven by China's aim to gain access to the World Trade Organisation (WTO).[89] China formally became a member of the WTO on 21 December 2001,[90] marking one of the most significant events in the history of China's process of Reform and Opening up.[91] In order to meet the general requirements of the WTO, and to fulfil the specific commitments that China had agreed to, a substantial number of non-conforming provisions and practices were abolished before and after the accession, resulting in amendments to the EJV Law, CJV Law, and WFOE Law.[92] China's commitments range from making the legal system more transparent, predictable, and fair for foreign investors to providing greater market access to FIEs in numerous industries and sectors, and granting them full trading and distribution rights.[93] Thus, China's WTO accession 'has greatly enlarged the market access for FDI and the general liberalisation of China's economy'.[94] Beside the preparation for the WTO accession, the late 1990s also saw a wave of consolidation among FIEs in China, partly as a result of large global mergers that affected the China operations of the merging companies, and partly due to a large number of failed FIEs that the original investors wanted to de-invest from.[95] In order to address these developments, new regulations were issued that 'shared a common feature in that they were intended to either bring more investment into China or to

[87]For a detailed analysis of the Foreign Investment Law, and the abolishment of the dual legislative structure, see Sect. 3.1.5.

[88]McGinty et al. (2020), p. 10; Xu et al. (2020).

[89]For a detailed account of China's accession to the WTO, see for example Esplugues Mota (2010), pp. 1–13.

[90]All official documents relating to China's accession are available at https://www.wto.org/english/thewto_e/countries_e/china_e.htm, accessed 15 May 2020.

[91]Mahony (2015), pp. 49–50.

[92]Wei (2010), p. 60; Mahony (2015), p. 50.

[93]Wei (2010), p. 60; Mahony (2015), p. 50.

[94]Wei (2010), p. 61.

[95]Mahony (2015), pp. 37, 43.

keep already invested funds in the country'.[96] Each of the new regulations governs a different type of transaction. The 'FIE Changes in Equity Provisions'[97] were issued in 1997 as a legal foundation for the transfer of equity interest in an incorporated FIE from an existing foreign investor to a new foreign investor.[98] The 'FIE Merger and Division Provisions'[99] were promulgated in 1999 to address situations in which foreign investors wish to merge or divide existing FIEs.[100] In 2000, the 'FIE Reinvestment Provisions'[101] were issued, which govern and restrict subsidiary investments within China by existing FIEs (with the exception of investments by FIE HoldCos).[102] However, these provisions did generally not permit direct mergers with, or acquisition of, entirely domestic Chinese companies.[103] This only changed with the promulgation of the 'M&A Provisions'[104] in 2003, which permitted FIEs to directly purchase equity in, and assets of, Chinese domestic companies.[105] 'These provisions ushered in a new era in foreign investment in China and were eagerly greeted by foreign lawyers and business people alike.'[106]

[96]ibid, p. 37.

[97]Certain Provisions on Change of the Equity Interests of the Investors of a Foreign-Invested Enterprise (外商投资企业投资者股权变更的若干规定), promulgated by the Ministry of Foreign Trade and Economic Cooperation and the State Administration for Industry and Commerce on 28 May 1997 and repealed on 01 January 2020.

[98]Mahony (2015), p. 345.

[99]Provisions on Merger and Division of Foreign-Invested Enterprises (关于外商投资企业合并与分立的规定), promulgated by the Ministry of Foreign Trade and Economic Cooperation and the State Administration for Industry and Commerce on 23 September 1999, amended on 22 September 2001 and amended on 28 October 2015.

[100]Mahony (2015), p. 352.

[101]Interim Provisions on Investment Made by Foreign-Invested Enterprises in China (关于外商投资企业境内投资的暂行规定), promulgated by the Ministry of Foreign Trade and Economic Cooperation and the State Administration for Industry and Commerce on 25 July 2000, amended on 26 May 2006 and amended on 28 October 2015.

[102]Mahony (2015), p. 341.

[103]ibid, pp. 356–357.

[104]Interim Provisions on Mergers with and Acquisitions of Domestic Enterprises by Foreign Investors (关于外国投资者并购境内企业暂行规定), promulgated jointly by the Ministry of Foreign Trade and Economic Cooperation, the State Taxation Administration, the State Administration for Industry and Commerce, and the State Administration of Foreign Exchange on 2 January 2003; later repealed by the Provisions on Mergers with and Acquisitions of Domestic Enterprises by Foreign Investors (关于外国投资者并购境内企业的规定), promulgated jointly by the Ministry of Commerce, State-Owned Assets Supervision and Administration Commission of the State Council, State Administration of Taxation, State Administration of Industry and Commerce, China Securities Regulatory Commission and State Administration of Foreign Exchange on 8 August 2006 and amended on 22 June 2009.

[105]Mahony (2015), p. 357.

[106]ibid, p. 357.

3.1.5 *The Mark of a New Era: The New Foreign Investment Law*

On 15 March 2019, the NPC promulgated the long-awaited 'PRC Foreign Investment Law' (FIL), which came into effect on 1 January 2020.[107] The FIL brings China's FDI regime into a new era by granting 'national treatment' to FIEs. One of the most striking reform measures of the new law is the unification of the legal framework that governs FIEs and domestic enterprises. This reform marks a major turning point in China's foreign investment policy. The fundamental impact that the FIL has on existing and future foreign investment projects in China is discussed in this section. A further analysis of the relevance of the FIL to the FILPE follows below.[108]

3.1.5.1 Motives and Legislative Timeline for the Foreign Investment Law

Economic and legal development in China has reached unprecedented levels over the three decades from the beginning of the policy of Reform and Opening up.[109] Economically, FDI in China totalled a negligible 80,000 USD when the reforms began in 1979.[110] From there, foreign direct investments increased rapidly and steadily with an annual growth rate of 10% during most of the 1980–2010 period.[111] Even though China was confronted with an economic slow-down over the years following, it remained an attractive destination for FDI. In 2014, it outperformed the US as the top destination for FDI.[112] In 2018, FDI in China grew by only 3%, which is a slowdown compared to the 7.9% growth in 2017, but still amounts to a total investment amount of 134.9 billion USD.[113] In 2019, FDI inflows to China remained stable at 140 billion USD.[114] While foreign-invested enterprises comprised less than 3% of the total firms operating in China in 2017, they contributed around a quarter of the country's manufacturing business profits, and one-fifth of China's tax revenue.[115] Legally, Chinese lawmakers and administrators have achieved a great accomplishment in creating a vast body of FDI regulations from the ground up in

[107]PRC Foreign Investment Law (中华人民共和国外商投资法), adopted at the 2nd Session of the 13th National People's Congress on 15 March 2019 and with effect as of 1 January 2020.

[108]See Sect. 4.1.6.

[109]Chen (2016), pp. 844–846.

[110]Yu (2006), pp. 423–424.

[111]World Bank Group (2010).

[112]BBC (2015).

[113]China Daily (2019).

[114]United Nations Conference on Trade and Development (2020).

[115]ibid.

a relatively short period.[116] 'China has been transformed from a closed and impoverished country into a nation with a flourishing private sector and increasingly open to influences from the outside world. Foreign investment had become an integral part of the national economic system.'[117] The decade following WTO accession saw further signs of liberalisation and consolidation with Chinese legislation that governed both Chinese and foreign enterprises under a common set of rules.[118] The strict and complex approval process has already been relaxed in certain areas in favour of a more streamlined and liberal approval and record-filing regime.[119]

However, despite these substantial achievements and the progressive but hesitant signs of reform and liberalisation, China's foreign investment regime still retained some distinctive features of the legacy of the pre-WTO era.[120] The parallel structure of the legal system was persistently criticised for subjecting foreign and domestic investments to separate sets of regulations.[121]

> FDI-related regulations are essentially a bundle of corporate organisational instruments tailored respectively to relevant industry or service sectors. They are in fact industry-specific company laws for foreign-invested enterprises. (...) As a result, China's FDI regulation continues being piecemeal, departmental, and sector specific. This leads to inconsistency and repetitiveness among the provisions in the FDI regulations.[122]

Therefore, foreign commentators and investors have been eagerly awaiting the unification and further liberalisation of the foreign investment regime for a long time.[123] Among Chinese commentators, the picture was more diverse. While some called for a unification of the legal framework for foreign and domestic investors,[124] others expressed themselves in favour of upholding the dual structure of foreign investment law and domestic company law.[125] Some argued that it was still too early to grant unreserved national treatment to foreign investors, as the emerging Chinese economy was not yet sufficiently prepared for such a far-reaching liberalisation.[126] However, in 2013, the Chinese government has opened a testing ground in the form of the Shanghai FTZ to study a new administrative mode of foreign investment

---

[116] Wei (2010), p. 59.

[117] Mahony (2015), p. 51.

[118] Wei (2010), p. 61.

[119] For an analysis of the gradual relaxation of the foreign investment approval and registration process, see Sect. 3.1.6.3.

[120] ibid, p. 61.

[121] Wei (2010), p. 61.

[122] ibid, p. 61.

[123] Mahony (2015), p. 140; Wei (2010), p. 72; Bath (2007), p. 785; Nägeli (2003), p. 57.

[124] Lu (吕美昂) (2011), pp. 81, 82.

[125] Zhang (张宇轩) (2011), p. 215; Zhao (赵旭东) (2005), p. 18.

[126] Mei (2014), pp. 38–39.

regulation, and then initiated further reform measures with a CPC policy decision of November 2013.[127]

A new chapter of reforms opened in January 2015 when MOFCOM issued the 'Draft Foreign Investment Law',[128] (2015 Draft FIL) together with 'Explanatory Notes on the 2015 Draft Foreign Investment Law'.[129] The latter outlines some of the reasoning and principles applied by MOFCOM in preparing the innovative draft. The 2015 Draft FIL was welcomed as the most significant and comprehensive reform of China's foreign investment regime since 1978, as it announced to replace the fragmentary and sometimes contradictory regulations that have been promulgated over the years with the first unified law for foreign investments.[130] At the same time, the draft law was highly controversial as it introduced new and far-reaching administrative and regulatory measures, and was regarded as having a rather hostile tone towards FDI.[131] Following this first draft, uncertainty existed about when (and if) further progress on the FIL reform project would be visible. In late 2018, the reform gained noticeable momentum—most likely as a reaction to the trade conflict with the US and to the emerging slowdown in domestic economic growth.[132] On 6 December 2018, the NPC issued the 'Revised Draft Foreign Investment Law'[133] (2018 Draft FIL). Compared to the 2015 Draft FIL, which contained 11 Chapters with 170 Articles and very detailed provisions, the 2018 has been significantly simplified and drafted in a far more generic style, comprising only 6 Chapters and 39 Articles. The public was given about 2 months to submit their comments, the deadline was 24 February 2019.[134] The 2018 draft was credited for taking a more permissive, welcoming approach to FDI, compared to the existing legal framework and the 2015 Draft FIL.[135] Only 3 months after the second draft was issued, the NPC promulgated the FIL on 15 March 2019. The final law contains six Chapters with 42 Articles, and is largely based on the 2018 Draft FIL. Thus, it is more simplified and high-level than the first draft of 2015. The law lacks detailed regulations for many issues, and the FIL itself provides for a subsequent promulgation of implementing regulations.[136] On 1 November 2019, the 'Draft FIL Implementing

[127] Yang (2015), p. 112. For an analysis of the FTZ reform process, see Sect. 3.1.6.2.

[128] PRC Foreign Investment Law (Draft for Comments) 中华人民共和国外国投资法 (草案征求意见稿), promulgated by the Ministry of Commerce on 19 January 2015.

[129] Explanatory Notes on the PRC Foreign Investment Law (Draft for Comments) (中华人民共和国外国投资法 (草案征求意见稿)的说明), promulgated by the Ministry of Commerce on 19 January 2015.

[130] Zhang (2016), p. 61; Luttermann (2015), p. 185; McGinty et al. (2015), p. 12.

[131] McGinty et al. (2019c).

[132] Fu (2019).

[133] Notice on Soliciting Public Opinions on the Foreign Investment Law (Draft) (外商投资法(草案)征求意见), issued by the Standing Committee of the National People's Congress on 21 December 2018.

[134] Preamble to the 2018 Draft FIL.

[135] McGinty et al. (2019c).

[136] Art. 42 Para. 2 Foreign Investment Law.

Regulations'[137] have been released to solicit public comments.[138] Only a few weeks later, the State Council promulgated the 'FIL Implementing Regulations.'[139] The final regulations contain 49 Articles and in a surprise move, the regulators made rather substantial changes in the final version as compared to the draft.[140] Before the FIL and FIL Implementing Regulations took effect, MOFCOM and SAMR issued several new rules and circulars, some of which are touched upon in the further analysis, in an apparent effort to reconcile the vast number of existing rules that regulate and govern foreign investments and FIEs in China with the FIL and the FIL Implementing Regulations.[141] Underlining the significance of this reform, the Supreme People's Court has promulgated its first set of judicial interpretations, the 'SPC Interpretation of the Foreign Investment Law',[142] even before the FIL took effect. The SPC interpretation addresses issues as to the validity of investment contracts in relation to foreign investments.

3.1.5.2 Scope of Application and Definition of Foreign Investment

The FIL governs foreign investments in China.[143] The term 'foreign investment' includes all direct and indirect investment activities carried out by foreign investors.[144] However, the law does not clarify which investment activities will be regarded as indirect investments. A 'foreign investor' is defined as foreign natural person, foreign enterprise or other foreign organisation.[145] Investment activities include (1) greenfield investments, (2) M&A transactions, (3) project investments and (4) investments in China 'by other means specified by laws, administrative regulations or provisions of the State Council'.[146]

This definition of foreign investment removes four other activities that were regarded as investments in the 2015 Draft FIL. The first draft introduced a new 'control concept' to define foreign investments, which was criticised for being too broad in its application, and was one of the most controversial aspects of the 2015

[137]PRC Foreign Investment Law Implementing Regulations (Draft for Comments) (中华人民共和国外商投资法实施条例(征求意见稿)), promulgated by the Ministry of Justice on 01 November 2019.

[138]For an alaysis of these draft provision, see: McGinty et al. (2019a).

[139]PRC Foreign Investment Law Implementing Regulations (中华人民共和国外商投资法实施条例), promulgated by the State Council on 26 December 2019 and effective as of 01 January 2020.

[140]McGinty et al. (2020), p. 1.

[141]ibid, p. 1.

[142]Interpretation of Certain Issues Concerning the Application of the "PRC Foreign Investment Law" (适用《中华人民共和国外商投资法》若干问题的解释), promulgated by the Supreme People's Court on 26 December 2019 and with effect as of 1 January 2020.

[143]Art. 2 Para. 1 FIL.

[144]Art. 2 Para. 2 FIL.

[145]Art. 2 Para. 2 FIL.

[146]Art. 2 Para. 2 No 1-4 FIL.

Draft FIL.[147] At the time, the control concept was 'seen as an expression of the legislative intent of the Chinese government to expand its jurisdiction over investment activities involving foreign players and their attempt to address the legal status of investments involving 'control through contract', of which the most prominent example is the variable interest entity (VIE) structure.'[148] VIEs are designed to allow foreign investors to invest in Chinese enterprises without becoming a shareholder of the enterprise, thereby making an investment in a sector that actually prohibits foreign investments.[149] Even though VIEs are essentially a circumvention of investment restrictions and operate in a legal grey area, they have become a frequent investment structure in the technology, telecommunications, and internet sector.[150] In a VIE structure, the foreign investor does not directly own the Chinese target enterprise, but rather controls it through a set of Special Purpose Vehicles (SPV), and a number of interconnecting contractual arrangements.[151] Under the now final definition, the fourth type of investment serves as a catch-all that covers any other type of investment in China. Commentators have pointed out that this catch-all leaves room for implementing rules later to address the issue of VIEs.[152] However, the implemented FIL Implementing Regulations fail to provide clarity and still leave the VIE structure in the grey area.[153]

3.1.5.3 Domestic Enterprise Forms Opened to Foreign Investors

One of the breakthrough innovations of the proposed law is the opening of China's domestic enterprise forms to foreign investors. To a large extent, this means giving up the separate regime of special enterprise forms for foreign investments. With the FIL taking effect, the EJV Law, CJV Law, and WFOE Law have been annulled immediately.[154] Starting from 1 January 2020, the organisational form, governance structure and business operation of an FIE are governed directly by the Company Law, the Partnership Enterprise Law and other relevant laws.[155] A sino-foreign alliance in the form of a corporation will thus be established and governed under the Company Law instead of the EJV Law. Existing FIEs established before the FIL came into effect, are granted a 5 year grace period to change their corporate form and governance structure to comply with the FIL, and accordingly with the Company

[147] McGinty et al. (2019c); Feuerstein (2016), p. 191.

[148] McGinty et al. (2019c); Feuerstein (2016), p. 191.

[149] For a detailed discussion of the VIE structure, see Mahony (2015), pp. 234–244; Wei (2010), p. 73; Shu (2012), pp. 13–15.

[150] Mahony (2015), p. 235.

[151] ibid, pp. 236–239.

[152] McGinty et al. (2019b).

[153] McGinty et al. (2020), p. 1.

[154] Art. 42 Para. 1 FIL.

[155] Art. 31 FIL.

Law or the Partnership Enterprise Law.[156] The FIL Implementing Regulations further clarify that an existing FIE, which would fail to make the transition before 1 January 2025, will be banned from making other changes that require registration with SAMR.[157] The transition of existing FIEs is expected to be the trickiest aspect of the FIL.[158] While a WFOE is already a limited liability company with a governance structure similar to that under the Company Law, the transition of EJVs and CJVs requires substantial modifications of their governance structure.[159] In an EJV, the highest governance authority is the board of directors, while the shareholder meeting is the highest authority under the Company Law.[160] This illustrates that the transition of enterprise forms will usually lead to a re-negotiation of the joint venture contract and the articles of association. However, the FIL Implementing Regulations stipulate an agreement-over-statute carve-out for certain aspects that were contained in an existing FIE. After an EJV or CJV has made the transition under the governance structure of the Company Law or Partnership Law, provisions on the transfer of equity interest/rights, the method for distribution of profits and the method of residual property distribution may continue to be valid, even though they may technically be inconsistent with the provisions of these laws.[161] This regulation reflects the party autonomy which is granted under the Partnership Law and Company Law.[162] Regarding the vast number of administrative regulations, provisions, measures, rules, circulars and notices which were promulgated, adopted and enforced by the NDRC, SAMR/SAIC, MOFCOM, and other ministries and departments to micro-manage every aspect of FDI over the past decades, the FIL Implementing Regulations end with a clarifying statement.[163] In the event of any inconsistency between the FIL and FIL Implementing Regulations on the one hand, and any FDI related regulation which was promulgated before 1 January 2020 on the other, the FIL and FIL Implementing Regulations shall prevail.[164]

---

[156] Art. 42 Para. 2 FIL.

[157] Art. 44 Para. 2 FIL Implementing Regulations.

[158] Zhang and Tsoi (2019).

[159] McGinty et al. (2019b).

[160] ibid.

[161] Art. 46 FIL Implementing Regulations.

[162] Hong and Liu (2020).

[163] McGinty et al. (2020), p. 10.

[164] See Sect. 3.1.5.2.

3.1.5.4 Promoting and Protecting FDI

In January 2017, 'State Council Circular No 5'[165] was issued. This has been regarded as the blueprint for China's policies for attracting FDI in the upcoming years by calling on various ministries to take concrete steps to liberalise foreign investment.[166] In June 2018, the first circular was supplemented by 'State Council Circular No 19',[167] which promised additional reform measures. Among the various envisaged measures, one stood out in particular: a new set of industries to be opened up to FDI, including the service sectors like the financial industry, investment fund management, and digital services.[168] Many of these changes are already reflected in the new Negative List System.[169] Efforts are made to create a level playing field for foreign and domestic investors. Local governments are expressly prohibited from imposing any additional, unauthorised restrictions on FIEs.[170] Government agencies are urged to handle FIEs' applications for permits and licences according to the same standards, and within the same time-frame, as domestic enterprises.[171] FIEs are eligible for favourable policies designed for the Made in China 2025 policy.[172] Greater autonomy is granted to local governments to offer local incentives for foreign investment.[173] FIEs in encouraged industries continue to benefit from lower land use costs.[174] Commentators have welcomed the announced reforms, but pointed out that only a gradual implementation could be expected, as neither circular provides any specific indication of the extent or time-line for implementing their liberalisation measures.[175]

The FIL and its implementing regulations now confirm that China will continue with the national policy of opening-up and lays down a number of principles designed to promote and encourage foreign investments into China. These measures include the equal application of all national policies for investment promotion to domestic and foreign invested enterprises;[176] seeking the views of FIEs when

[165]Circular on Several Measures for the Active Use of Foreign Capital in Opening Up to the Outside World (扩大对外开放积极利用外资若干措施的通知), promulgated by the State Council on 12 January 2017 and effective as of the same date.

[166]Tam and Guo (2017).

[167]Circular on Several Measures for the Active and Effective Use of Foreign Capital to Promote Quality Economic Development (积极有效利用外资推动经济高质量发展若干措施的通知), promulgated by the State Council on 10 June 2018 and effective as of the same date.

[168]Art. 1 (2) State Council Circular No 19; Art. 1 Para. 2 State Council Circular No 5.

[169]Art. 1 (2) State Council Circular No 19; Art. 2 (8) State Council Circular No 5.

[170]Art. 1 (2) State Council Circular No 19; Art. 2 (8) State Council Circular No 5.

[171]Art. 2 (9) State Council Circular No 5.

[172]Art. 1 (4) State Council Circular No 5.

[173]Art. 3 (15) State Council Circular No 5.

[174]Art. 3 (17) State Council Circular No 5.

[175]Lin and Harris (2017) and Tam and Guo (2017).

[176]Art. 9 FIL, Art. 6 FIL Implementing Regulations.

formulating FDI-related legislation;[177] allowing FIEs to participate in government procurement projects through fair competition;[178] permitting FIEs to raise financing in China through the public offering of shares or issuance of corporate bonds.[179] At the same time, the FIL provides for an improved level of FDI protection. Allowing free transfer of RMB or foreign currency into and out of China, for returns of capital, profits, capital gains and royalty payments;[180] protection of intellectual property rights of FIEs and foreign investors;[181] prohibiting government authorities from forcing technology transfer of foreign investors by administrative means.[182]

While commentators welcome all of these improvements, the actual implementation and enforcement of these measures will show whether the FIL does *de facto* lead to a stronger protection of foreign investors and their FDI projects.[183]

3.1.5.5 National Security Review

The FIL reiterates that foreign investment 'which affects or may affect the national security' will be subject to review under a national security review system.[184] It is unclear whether this rather sketchy provision refers to the existing security review system that was implemented in 2011.[185] Notably, the 2015 Draft FIL dedicated an entire chapter to the introduction of a comprehensive and unified national security review system for foreign investments.[186] While the current national security review is limited by transaction type and sector, the scope of the proposed approach has been significantly expanded to include any foreign investment, regardless of sector, transaction type, or control rights.[187] Commentators have noted that this would allow the Chinese government to block more foreign investments in the future.[188] However, the FIL Implementing Regulations merely reiterate the provision in the FIL and do not elaborate on this topic. Therefore it remains to be seen whether the Chinese government will create separate legislation on foreign investment national security review in the future.

[177] Art. 10 FIL, Art. 13 FIL Implementing Regulations.

[178] Art. 16 FIL, Art. 15 FIL Implementing Regulations.

[179] Art. 17 FIL, Art. 18 FIL Implementing Regulations.

[180] Art. 21 FIL, Art. 22 FIL Implementing Regulations.

[181] Art. 22 Para. 1 FIL, Art. 23 FIL Implementing Regulations.

[182] Art. 22 Para. 2 FIL, Art. 24 FIL Implementing Regulations.

[183] McGinty et al. (2019b).

[184] Art. 35 Para. 1 FIL.

[185] Clifford Chance LLP (2019).

[186] Art. 48 2015 Draft FIL.

[187] McGinty et al. (2015), p. 7.

[188] Yang (2015), p. 120.

3.1.6 The Administrative Framework: Guidance, Approval and Registration of Foreign Investment Projects

FDI projects in China generally require registration with, or approval from the government.[189] This regulatory hurdle is used by the Chinese government to direct FDI into certain industries, and to exclude it from others. The underlying regulations on encouraging and directing foreign investments express the somewhat paradoxical nature of China's foreign investment policy, wanting to attract FDI while maintaining control over it.[190] This has led to a foreign investment regime that differentiates FDI from domestic investment in a variety of industry categories, and applies different treatments in terms of levels of approval, permitted ratios of foreign to domestic investment, the limited choice of legally available investment vehicles, and tax concessions.[191] Over the past few years, the original framework of stringent government guidelines and close supervision by authorities has undergone some significant deregulating reforms. Nevertheless, the pre-existing principles of FDI administration are still partially applicable. The functioning of the administrative framework and the significance of the latest reforms is therefore best illustrated by a concise analysis of its evolution over the past decades, starting with a description of longstanding administrative practices, followed by an introduction to experiments carried out in a new special testing zone, and concluding with an analysis of the latest substantial reform measures which were implemented with the Foreign Investment Law and its implementing regulations.

3.1.6.1 The Longstanding Benchmark: Restrictive Government Supervision of FDI

3.1.6.1.1 Directing and Restricting FDI: The Guidance Catalogue

It was an early strategy of the policy of Reform and Opening up to guide FDI by restricting it to designated geographical areas: the Special Economic Zones.[192] At that time, foreign investment in China was often a frustrating and difficult endeavour involving nebulous, unclear procedures. There were only very limited publicly accessible regulations with many principles applicable to FDI being kept as internal departmental rules or guarded secrets.[193] The underlying objective of the Chinese government was to attract foreign capital, technology, and expertise, while at the

[189]Regarding the examination and verification process for FDI projects, see Sects. 3.1.6.1.4 and 3.1.6.3.1.

[190]Wei (2010), p. 58; Mahony (2015), p. 15.

[191]Wei (2010), p. 62.

[192]The initial Special Economic Zones were established in 1979-1980 in Shenzhen, Zhuhai, Shantou, and Xiamen. See Mahony (2015), p. 100; Nägeli (2003), pp. 15–18, 78.

[193]Wei (2010), p. 62; Mahony (2015), p. 100.

same time limiting the perceived negative social and ideological impact of FDI as much as possible.[194] By the mid-1990s, the Chinese government recognised the benefit of establishing an overall plan and system for guiding FDI, and expanded the emphasis of its foreign investment policy to the development of the national economy as a whole.[195] In 1995, with the promulgation of the 'Guidance Provisions'[196] and the 'Guidance Catalogue',[197] a comprehensive legal framework was introduced that directs the examination and approval of FDI projects in accordance with national government priorities and macroeconomic planning needs.[198] The Guidance Provisions provide that all foreign investment projects are to be divided into four categories: encouraged, permitted, restricted, and prohibited.[199] The Guidance Catalogue provides a very detailed related list of specific industries that fall under the encouraged, restricted, and prohibited categories.[200] Foreign investment projects that are not listed in the Guidance Catalogue all fall under the permitted category.[201] Despite the latest reforms of the Guidance Catalogue—analysed in detail below—, these four categories are still utilised, forming a core element of the foreign investment guidance policy.[202] The Guidance Catalogue can be seen as the practical implementation of the central government's general policy objectives as expressed in its 'Five-Year Plans'.[203] In accordance with the policy objective of advancing China's economy by promoting high-technology industries, the Guidance Catalogue is supplemented by the 'Catalogue of Encouraged Hi-tech

[194]Mahony (2015), p. 100; Nägeli (2003), p. 78.

[195]Mahony (2015), p. 101; Nägeli (2003), p. 78.

[196]Interim Provisions Guiding Foreign Investment (指导外商投资方向暂行规定), promulgated jointly by the State Planning Commission; State Economic and Trade Commission and Ministry of Foreign Trade and Economic Cooperation on 20 June 1995; subsequently repealed by the Provisions on Guiding the Direction of Foreign Investment (指导外商投资方向规定), promulgated by the State Council on 11 February 2002 and effective as of 1 April 2002.

[197]Catalogue of Industries for Guiding Foreign Investment (外商投资产业指导目录), promulgated jointly by the National Development and Reform Commission and Ministry of Commerce on 20 June 1995, amended on 31 December 1997, amended on 3 November 2002, amended on 30 November 2004, amended on 31 October 2007, amended on 24 December 2011, amended on 10 March 2015, amended on 28 June 2017, amended on 28 June 2018 and most recently amended on 30 June 2019 with effect as of 30 July 2019.

[198]Art. 3 Para. 2 Guidance Provisions; Mahony (2015), p. 101; Nägeli (2003), p. 78; Wei (2010), p. 62.

[199]Art. 4 Para. 1 Guidance Provisions.

[200]Art. 4 Para. 2 Guidance Provisions.

[201]Art. 4 Para. 2 Guidance Provisions.

[202]See detailed analysis in Sect. 3.1.6.3.3.

[203]The current 13th Five-Year Plan for National Economic and Social Development (国民经济和社会发展第十三个五年规划纲要) was adopted at the 4th Session of the 12th National People's Congress on 16 March 2016. The plan sets out the guiding principles for China's economic and social development for the 5 years from 2016 to 2020.

Products for Foreign Investment'.[204] Considering the nebulous nature of the early attempts to guide FDI, the Guidance Provisions and Guidance Catalogue significantly improved the level of legal transparency and certainty.[205] The different versions of the Guidance Catalogue over the years also reflect the gradual relaxation of China's policy towards FDI.[206] Meanwhile, it still imposes significant limitations on many foreign investment projects. The foreign investment community therefore continually requests further liberalisations and material reform of the restrictive policies governing foreign investments in China.[207]

3.1.6.1.2 Limited Scope of Business Operation

The category that an investment project falls under is not only relevant for the approval of the establishment of an FIE, but also for its business operation.[208] Differing from many jurisdictions that permit a properly-established company to engage in 'any lawful activity', foreign-invested companies established in China are required to have a specific and limited 'scope of business' that is defined in the company's articles of association, registered with the authorities, and included in the company's business licence.[209] The FIE may only legally engage in business activities that fall within its approved scope of business.[210] The authorities will not approve an unlimited business scope such as conducting 'any lawful business' for FIEs, even though this is possible for Chinese domestic enterprises.[211] The type of business activity that an FIE will conduct has to be defined with a high degree of specification.[212] The business scope of the FIE is the direct link between a proposed investment project and the Guidance Catalogue.[213] When the authorities review an application for the establishment of an FIE, it is the proposed scope of business that indicates what type of business activity the FIE will engage in, and, therefore, which category of the Guidance Catalogue the project falls under.[214] Likewise, the specified business scope ensures that the incorporated FIE adheres to the field of business

---

[204]Catalogue of Encouraged Hi-tech Products for Foreign Investment (鼓励外商投资高新技术产品目录), promulgated jointly by the Ministry of Commerce and Ministry of Science and Technology on 2 June 2003 and amended on 31 December 2006.

[205]Wei (2010), p. 64.

[206]Nägeli (2003), p. 80.

[207]Regarding the latest reforms, see Sect. 3.1.6.3.3.

[208]Wei (2010), p. 72.

[209]Mahony (2015), p. 114.

[210]ibid, pp. 114–115.

[211]Wei (2010), p. 72.

[212]Mahony (2015), p. 115.

[213]ibid, p. 115; Wei (2010), p. 72.

[214]Mahony (2015), p. 115.

it is categorised in, because an FIE that conducts any business outside the registered business scope risks significant fines or other penalties.[215]

3.1.6.1.3 Offering Preferential Treatment

Another principle of early foreign investment policy was to provide incentives to foreign investors that were not available to domestic enterprises, which were predominantly State-Owned Enterprises (SOEs) at that time.[216] The 'FDI Encouragement Provisions'[217] that were promulgated in 1986, are the legal grounds for preferential treatments such as tax benefits,[218] granting permissions to import and export certain goods that are otherwise prohibited for import,[219] and allowing more leeway in the operation and management of enterprises.[220]

> Various other provisions granting preferential treatment exceeding those introduced under the FDI Encouragement Provisions were promulgated on the national, provincial and local level. In order to generate as much foreign investment as possible while competing with each other, the different provinces and municipalities aimed to offer the most attractive preferential treatment.[221]

Especially during the early years of Reform and Opening up, FIEs that operated in particular industries or locations, profited from a specially reduced corporate income tax rate, or could even enjoy a temporary exemption from corporate income tax altogether.[222] These benefits were offered to foreign investors to outweigh the disadvantages of the restricted FIE structures and foreign investment regime.[223] However, these privileges have gradually been reduced over time, and no longer have the same significance. For example, the tax benefits have been replaced by a now largely unified tax regime for FIEs and domestic owned enterprises.[224]

[215] ibid, pp. 115–116; Wei (2010), p. 64.

[216] Nägeli (2003), p. 74; Shen (2015), pp. 13–15.

[217] Provisions of the State Council for the Encouragement of Foreign Investment (国务院关于鼓励外商投资的规定), promulgated by the State Council on 11 October 1986.

[218] Arts. 10 and 11 FDI Encouragement Provisions.

[219] Arts. 12 and 13 FDI Encouragement Provisions.

[220] Art. 15 FDI Encouragement Provisions.

[221] Nägeli (2003), p. 77.

[222] Mahony (2015), pp. 15–17; Ting and Ge (2014), pp. 673, 674; Wei (2010), p. 75.

[223] Bath (2007), p. 776.

[224] ibid, pp. 774–775; Wei (2010), pp. 61, 75.

3.1.6.1.4 FDI Approval Process and Authorities

One of the basic and longstanding pillars of the foreign investment regime in China was the requirement that almost all[225] foreign investment projects had to obtain approval for their establishment from various government authorities.[226] These approval requirements applied to not only greenfield EJV or CJV investment projects, but also to M&A transactions.[227] Despite the latest reforms of the FDI regulations, elements of this administrative regime are still in place. To illustrate the development of the latest reforms, the approval requirements that have defined FDI to China for decades, are outlined in this section. The length and complexity of the verification process depended on various factors, including the category of the Guidance Provisions that the investment fell under, or the specific industry.[228] On a general level, three government entities played a key role in the foreign investment approval process, as each was responsible for a separate, essential stage of the process.[229] The first stage was the project verification by the National Development and Reform Commission[230] (NDRC). The NDRC is one of the major agencies of the Chinese government. It is responsible for macroeconomic planning, industrial policy, and the overall reform and development of the Chinese economy, thus making it one of the most important agencies for foreign investors to understand.[231] The project verification was regulated by the '2014 Foreign Investment Measures',[232] in conjunction with the '2016 Government Verification Catalogue'.[233] Based on a

[225]For the exception that applies to the FILPE, see Sect. 4.1.8.1.

[226]Mahony (2015), p. 118; Zhang (2016), p. 55; Wei (2010), p. 58.

[227]Hübner (2014), p. 17.

[228]For a detailed description of the examination and verification process, see Mahony (2015), pp. 118–145; Faßbender (2014), pp. 344–351.

[229]Mahony (2015), p. 119.

[230]The NDRC has been established in March 2003 with the transformation of the former 'State Development and Planning Commission' (Nägeli 2003, p. 68).

[231]A detailed description of NDRC's responsibilities is provided in Mahony (2015), pp. 121–122.

[232]Administrative Measures for the Verification and Record-filing of Foreign Investment Projects (外商投资项目核准和备案管理办法), promulgated by the National Development and Reform Commission on 17 May 2014 and amended on 27 December 2014; substituting the Interim Administrative Measures for the Verification of Foreign Investment Projects (外商投资项目核准暂行管理办法), promulgated by the National Development and Reform Commission on 9 October 2004.

[233]Catalogue of Investment Projects Subject to Government Verification—2016 Version (政府核准的投资项目目录—2016年本), promulgated by the State Council on 12 December 2016, substituting the Catalogue of Investment Projects Subject to Government Verification—2014 Version (政府核准的投资项目目录—2014年本), promulgated by the State Council on 31 October 2014; the Catalogue of Investment Projects Subject to Government Verification—2013 Version (政府核准的投资项目目录—2013年本), promulgated by the State Council on 2 December 2013 and the Catalogue of Investment Projects Subject to Government Verification—2004 Version (政府核准的投资项目目录—2004年本), promulgated by the State Council on 16 July 2004.

detailed project proposal,[234] and accompanying documents[235] submitted by the foreign investor, NDRC examined the investment project for conformity with the Guidance Catalogue, national economic and development plans, environmental protection, national interests, and for various other measures.[236] While all FDI projects previously had to undergo this examination and verification by NDRC, the 2014 Foreign Investment Measures introduced a new approach which divided investment projects into those that had to obtain prior verification from NDRC, and those that needed only to file certain information for the record.[237] That certain categories of foreign investment projects no longer required prior planning approval from NDRC, was welcomed by commentators as a significant development in the evolution of China's foreign investment approval regime.[238] Whether NDRC was responsible for the approval of a project at the national level or at the provincial government level depended on the amount of the proposed total investment (its total investment amount), and the nature of the project.[239] Those projects that only needed to be registered could be filed with the relevant department of the local government.[240] Upon approval of a project, the appropriate level of NDRC would issue a written verification and approval document.[241]

The next major stage of the approval process was the review of the articles of association and the joint venture contract (if any) by the Ministry of Commerce[242] (MOFCOM). This is the government authority most directly concerned with FDI, and the agency with which foreign investors were most likely to have direct contact and interaction.[243] MOFCOM was directly responsible for examining and verifying the establishment of most FIEs, and for M&A activities involving foreign investors.[244] For the formation of a joint venture, MOFCOM had to review and approve the joint venture contract and the articles of association, as well as further documents, before the enterprise approval certificate could be issued.[245] Whether the approval of a specific FIE was handled by MOFCOM at the national level, or by one of its branches at the provincial or municipal level (a Commerce Bureau), depended

[234] Art. 8 2014 Foreign Investment Measures.

[235] Art. 10 2014 Foreign Investment Measures.

[236] Art. 16 2014 Foreign Investment Measures.

[237] Art. 3 2014 Foreign Investment Measures.

[238] Mahony (2015), p. 124.

[239] Art. 4 2014 Foreign Investment Measures in conjunction with the 2016 Government Verification Catalogue.

[240] Art. 5 2014 Foreign Investment Measures.

[241] Art. 17 2014 Foreign Investment Measures.

[242] MOFCOM is the result of the consolidation in 2004 of the State Economic Trade Commission, focused on domestic PRC trade issues, and the Ministry of Foreign Trade and Economic Cooperation (MOFTEC), responsible for foreign trade affairs (Mahony 2015, p. 132).

[243] Mahony (2015), pp. 130–131.

[244] ibid, p. 132.

[245] For the EJV, Articles 6-15 EJV Law; for the CJV, Articles 6-13, 24-25 CJV Law.

on its total investment amount.[246] Over the years, the total investment amount threshold for national level MOFCOM approval had been increased, thus allowing more projects to obtain approval from the provincial or local Commerce Bureau, which involved a comparatively simplified and more expeditious examination and verification process.[247]

The concluding key stage was registration with the State Administration of Industry and Commerce (SAIC). After obtaining verification from NDRC and approval from MOFCOM, registration with SAIC was considered a matter of formality.[248] SAIC functioned as China's national corporate registry, and it was responsible for the registration and administrative oversight of both FIEs and domestic-invested enterprises.[249] Following registration with SAIC or a local Administration of Industry and Commerce (AIC),[250] the FIE would receive its business licence. This marked an important moment, as the legal establishment of an FIE takes effect on the date that the business licence is issued, and an FIE is prohibited from conducting business before that date.[251] In March 2018, the NPC issued the 'Institutional Reform Plan',[252] which is generally considered to be the most comprehensive government restructuring which China has undertaken since the country implemented its policy of Reform and Opening up.[253] As part of the new plan, China has established the State Administration for Market Regulation (SAMR). SAMR is a consolidation of different authorities, including SAIC. The responsibilities which had been carried out by SAIC so far were transferred to SAMR, and SAIC has been abolished.[254] However, existing rules and regulations promulgated by SAIC will remain in effect until SAMR, or any higher government authority, issues new laws, rules, and regulations in conflict with them.[255]

'These three entities, while central to the approval process for the majority of foreign investments, are not the only government agencies involved. Depending upon the nature of the investment, the approval of or registration with other

[246]Mahony (2015), p. 139.

[247]ibid, p. 140.

[248]Wei (2010), p. 65.

[249]Art. 5, Art. 6 Para. 2 Regulations on the Administration of Company Registration.

[250]The allocation of competences between SAIC and local AIC is regulated in Articles 3–4 of the Administrative Measures on the Authorisation over the Registration of Foreign-Invested Enterprises (外商投资企业授权登记管理办法), promulgated by the State Administration of Industry and Commerce on 12 December and amended on 29 April 2016.

[251]Art. 3 Regulations on the Administration of Company Registration.

[252]Decision on the Institutional Reform Plan of the State Council (关于国务院机构改革方案的决定), adopted at the 1st Session of the 13th National People's Congress on 17 March 2018 and effective as of the same day.

[253]Wang et al. (2018).

[254]Ibid. For responsibilities previously carried out by SAIC and AIC, reference is now made SAMR throughout this book, unless otherwise specified.

[255]ibid.

ministries and departments may also be required.'[256] There are various post-registration procedures with different authorities that a FIE must complete before it may officially commence its operations.[257] They include registration at the national or local level with the State Administration of Taxation (SAT) in respect of tax matters, the State Administration of Foreign Exchange (SAFE) for the foreign currency exchange issues, the General Administration of Customs (GAC) for export and import and customs duties, agencies of the Ministry of Finance (MOF) for accounting matters, and the Ministry of Human Resources and Social Security (MOHRSS) and its local labour bureaus regarding labour matters.[258] The nature of the investment project may necessitate additional approval or registration requirements.[259] Should a foreign investment project involve a state-owned enterprise or state-owned assets, an additional approval and appraisal procedure with the State-Owned Assets Supervision and Administration Commission (SASAC) should be initiated.[260] With the introduction of the 'Anti-monopoly Law',[261] a comprehensive competition law regime emerged in China that can make foreign investments under certain circumstances subject to an anti-monopoly review.[262] Among the types of economic conduct that the Anti-monopoly Law primarily regulates, the 'concentration of business operations with a possible negative effect on competition'[263] can be particularly relevant for the establishment of a sino-foreign alliance. The legal definition of circumstances that constitute a 'concentration of business operations' goes beyond mergers and acquisitions, also referring to obtaining control or a decisive influence over other business operators through contractual arrangements.[264] MOFCOM had taken the view that the latter category also included the establishment of entirely new joint ventures, even though it can be argued that in a joint venture, no party takes control over the other.[265] With the concentration of all anti-monopoly agencies under the newly established SAMR, it remains to be seen whether SAMR the latter will continue with this approach taken by MOFCOM.[266] Therefore, investors have to consider whether the establishment of their joint venture exceeds the relevant thresholds,[267] and hence prompts an anti-monopoly review

[256]Mahony (2015), p. 120.

[257]Wei (2010), p. 66.

[258]ibid, p. 66; Liu (2008), p. 4; Nägeli (2003), pp. 71–72.

[259]Liu (2008), p. 5.

[260]For more details, see Mahony (2015), pp. 59–61.

[261]PRC Anti-monopoly Law (中华人民共和国反垄断法), adopted at the 29th Session of the Standing Committee of the 10th National People's Congress on 30 August 2007 and effective as of 1 August 2008.

[262]For more details, see Mahony (2015), pp. 65–67; 389–406; Harris Jr et al. (2011).

[263]Art. 3 Para. 3 Anti-monopoly Law.

[264]Art. 20 Para. 3 Anti-monopoly Law.

[265]Harris Jr et al. (2011), pp. 129–130.

[266]Brumfield et al. (2018).

[267]Harris Jr et al. (2011), pp. 138–141.

process. In addition, a foreign-invested M&A transaction may be required to undergo a national security review, conducted under the joint supervision of NDRC, MOFCOM, and the PRC State Council (State Council).[268] The acquisition of a company that is listed on China's stock exchange requires the involvement of the China Securities Regulatory Commission (CSRC).[269] In particular sectors, prior approval of an industry-specific regulator may also be necessary, e.g., the State Food and Drugs Administration (SFDA) for investments in the pharmaceutical industry.[270] It is not uncommon for the different ministries and agencies involved to reach conflicting conclusions, or demand diverging requirements for the approval of a foreign investment project.[271] The implementation of rules and regulations in relatively more developed regions, or by higher-level authorities, is often much more consistent and transparent than in remote regions or by lower level authorities.[272] Balancing these conflicts and contradictions between authorities causes additional transaction costs for foreign investors.[273]

Foreign investors that have been denied approval for their FDI project, or are otherwise dissatisfied with the decision of an agency, can theoretically apply for administrative reconsideration,[274] and subsequently file a lawsuit with the People's Court.[275] However, in practice, aspiring foreign investors rarely appeal against administrative decisions as they are conscious of the lack of independence and transparency of the judiciary, and do not want to risk damaging their relationships with government authorities.[276] On a positive note, the overall process of obtaining approval for FDI projects has been steadily refined, simplified, and improved over the years, especially around China's accession to the WTO.[277] However, the

[268]For more details, see Mahony (2015), pp. 73–76, 406–415.

[269]Liu (2008), p. 5.

[270]ibid, p. 5; Mahony (2015), p. 120.

[271]Bath (2007), p. 778; Clarke (2005–2006), pp. 66–67; McGinty et al. (2015), p. 4.

[272]Wei (2010), p. 66.

[273]ibid, p. 66.

[274]Art. 38 PRC Administrative Licensing Law (中华人民共和国行政许可法), adopted at the 4th Session of the Standing Committee of the 10th National People's Congress on 27 August 2003 and amended at the 10th Session of the Standing Committee of the 13th National People's Congress on 23 April 2019 and effective as of the same date; in conjunction with Art. 6 Para. 8 PRC Administrative Reconsideration Law (中华人民共和国行政复议法), adopted at the 9th Session of the Standing Committee of the 9th National People's Congress on 29 April 1999, amended at the 10th Session of the Standing Committee of the 11th National People's Congress on 27 August 2009 and amended at the 29th Session of the Standing Committee of the 12th National People's Congress on 01 September 2017 and with effect as of 01 January 2018.

[275]Art. 12 Para. 3 PRC Administrative Procedure Law (中华人民共和国行政诉讼法), adopted at the 2nd Session of the 7th National People's Congress on 4 April 1989, amended at the 11th Session of the Standing Committee of the 12th National People's Congress on 01 November 2014 and amended at the 28th Session of the 12th National People's Congress on 27 June 2017 and effective as of 01 July 2017.

[276]US Chamber of Commerce (2012); Wei (2010), p. 65; McGinty et al. (2015), p. 8.

[277]Mahony (2015), p. 140.

administrative examination and verification process, outlined above, still presented a significant hurdle for foreign investors, who have been demanding reform for many years.[278]

3.1.6.2 Experimenting with Reforms: The Shanghai Free Trade Zone

After decades of adhering to the strict verification system, and allowing only for small and selective reforms, a conglomeration of factors urged the Chinese government to venture towards more profound reforms of the foreign investment regime during the past years. As a consequence of the global financial crisis, the international environment for attracting foreign capital has become significantly more competitive.[279] At the same time, raising costs of doing business in China lead to government concern about China's attractiveness as a destination for FDI.[280] In addition, foreign investors already present in China have become increasingly pessimistic about their business opportunities in China, but indicated that they would likely increase their investments if they were given greater market access.[281] The Chinese government further acknowledged that its approach of directing and restricting foreign investments through the Guidance Catalogue was a hindrance in negotiating bilateral and multilateral treaties that required foreign investors to be granted equal market access.[282]

Against this background, the China (Shanghai) Pilot Free Trade Zone (Shanghai FTZ) was established by the Chinese government on 30 September 2013 as a testing ground for substantial reform of the foreign investment administrative regime.[283] Geographically, the Shanghai FTZ was originally composed of four existing bonded zones in the municipality of Shanghai, which was further expanded in April 2015.[284] Among the large number of regulations that have been promulgated in relation to the Shanghai FTZ, of particular importance are the 'Shanghai FTZ Authorisation

---

[278]Wei (2010), p. 62; Mahony (2015), pp. 140–141.

[279]Mahony (2015), p. 87; Zhang (2016), p. 53.

[280]Mahony (2015), p. 81.

[281]European Union Chamber of Commerce in China (2016).

[282]Yang (2015), p. 127.

[283]ibid, p. 105; Mahony (2015), p. 84.

[284]Zhang (2016), p. 53.

Decision',[285] the 'Shanghai FTZ General Plan',[286] and the 'FTZ Negative List'.[287] The significance of the Shanghai FTZ lies in the introduction of the FTZ Negative List, which reverses the restrictive approval process that applies to almost all FIEs in the rest of China. Under the negative list approach, the establishment of foreign investment projects is only subject to record-filing requirements; prior examination and verification is no longer required, unless the investment project falls under one of the categories on the FTZ Negative List.[288] Furthermore, a special focus of the Shanghai FTZ is the liberalisation and promotion of the service sector.[289] To that effect, limitations with regard to the qualifications of foreign investors, the percentage of foreign shareholding, and the scope of a business are to be suspended or repealed, aiming to offer equal treatment to foreign and domestic investors in the Shanghai FTZ.[290] However, while initial expectations of foreign investors were high, the first FTZ Negative List issued in 2013 was surprisingly long. Critics complained that it merely replicated the 'prohibited' category of the Guidance Catalogue.[291] While subsequent versions of the FTZ Negative List in 2014, 2015, 2017, 2018 and 2019 have gradually shortened, they still fall short of providing foreign investors with equal market opportunities to those enjoyed by their domestic counterparts.[292] Accordingly, commentators have expressed disappointment about the lack of any breakthrough in the liberalisation of the foreign investment regime, stating that the Shanghai FTZ has not had the impact that foreign investors expected

---

[285]Decision Authorising the State Council to Temporarily Adjust Administrative Approvals Under Relevant Laws Within the China (Shanghai) Pilot Free Trade Zone (授权国务院在中国(上海)自由贸易试验区暂时调整有关法律规定的行政审批的决定), adopted at the 4th Session of the Standing Committee of the 12th National People's Congress on 30 August 2013, effective as of 1 October 2013 and repealed with effect as of 1 October 2016 by Art. 4 Para. 3 of the Decision to Revise FIE Laws (see Sect. 3.1.6.3.1 fn. 306).

[286]General Plan for the China (Shanghai) Pilot Free Trade Zone (中国(上海)自由贸易试验区总体方案), promulgated by the State Council on 18 September 2013.

[287]Special Management Measures on the Entry of Foreign Investment into the China (Shanghai) Pilot Free Trade Zone (2013 Negative List) (中国(上海)自由贸易试验区外商投资准入特别管理措施(负面清单)(2013年修订)), promulgated by the Shanghai Municipal People's Government on 29 September 2013, repealed by the Special Management Measures on the Entry of Foreign Investment into the China (Shanghai) Pilot Free Trade Zone (2014 Negative List) (中国(上海)自由贸易试验区外商投资准入特别管理措施(负面清单)(2014年修订)), promulgated by the Shanghai Municipal People's Government on 30 June 2014, and substituted by the Special Management Measures for the Market Entry of Foreign Investment into Pilot Free Trade Zones (Negative List) (自由贸易试验区外商投资准入特别管理措施(负面清单)), promulgated by the General Office of the State Council on 8 April 2015, amended on 5 June 2017; amended jointly by the National Development and Reform Commission and the Ministry of Commerce on 30 June 2018 and amended on 30 June 2019 with effect as of 30 July 2019.

[288]Para. 1 Shanghai FTZ Authorisation Decision; Art. 2 Para. 2c Shanghai FTZ General Plan.

[289]Art. 2 Para. 2b Shanghai FTZ General Plan in conjunction with the Appendix to the Shanghai FTZ General Plan.

[290]Art. 2 Para. 2b Shanghai FTZ General Plan.

[291]Mahony (2015), pp. 83, 147; Yang (2015), p. 117.

[292]Zhang (2016), p. 61; Yang (2015), p. 117.

it to have.[293] In March 2017, the State Council reacted by issuing the 'Shanghai FTZ Confirmation Plan'[294] to further develop and expand the reforms already introduced in the Shanghai FTZ.[295]

In accordance with its function as a testing ground,[296] the concept of the Shanghai FTZ was expanded to other regions of China in 2014. This led to the establishment of similar pilots of free trade zones in Guangdong, Tianjin, and Fujian.[297] Effective as of 1 April 2017, the State Council further established seven more pilot free trade zones in the provinces of Liaoning, Zhejiang, Henan, Hubei, Sichuan, and Shaanxi, as well as in the Chongqing Municipality.[298] The establishment of a free trade zone has been announced for Hainan in 2020.[299] For the Chinese government, the adaptation and expansion of the negative list approach is an important step in gradually forming a foreign investment administration system in line with international standards, and in reaching bilateral and multilateral treaty agreements.[300] Despite the fact that the initial testing period of the Shanghai FTZ was limited to 3 years, the establishment of additional FTZs in April of 2017, the promulgation of the Shanghai FTZ Confirmation Plan, and the nature of the FTZs as R&D centres and pilot regions for other reforms, indicate that FTZs will continue to exist in the medium to long term. This is reiterated in the newly promulgated FIL, which provides a legal basis for further expanding FTZs.[301] For foreign investors, the establishment of the Shanghai FTZ, and the introduction of the negative list approach, clearly marked a step towards a more liberalised foreign investment regime in China. However, it is the length of the FTZ Negative List that determines how significant the reforms are in practice. The Chinese government should be encouraged to further shorten the FTZ Negative List, and implement the negative list approach in a way that would allow it to fulfil its real purpose.

3.1.6.3 Approaching a New Normal: Registration Instead of Approval and Guidance by Negative List System

Not long after the establishment of the Shanghai FTZ, in November 2013, the Central Committee of the CPC made a fundamental policy decision to initiate

---

[293] See the overview of comments in Zhang (2016), pp. 56–57.

[294] Plan for the Comprehensive Deepening of the Reform and Liberalisation of the China (Shanghai) Pilot Free Trade Zone (全面深化中国(上海)自由贸易试验区改革开放方案的通知), promulgated by the State Council on 30 March 2017 with effect as of the same day.

[295] For an overview of this expanded plan, see Chan et al. (2017).

[296] Art. 2 Shanghai FTZ General Plan.

[297] Yang (2015), pp. 94–95.

[298] China Central Government (2017).

[299] Reuters (2018).

[300] Yang (2015), p. 127; Zhang (2016), p. 62; Luttermann (2015), p. 186.

[301] Art. 13 FIL, Art. 10 FIL Implementing Regulations.

substantial reform of the foreign investment regime.[302] These proposed far-reaching measures included: the implementation of a nationwide negative list and unified market entry system that would be based on simple enterprise record-filing instead of approval requirements; reform of the capital contribution system and SAMR-registration; unification of laws and regulations for domestic enterprises and FIEs; expansion of the pilot FTZs.[303] These reforms were driven by a number of factors. First, there was a need to maintain economic growth through a long-term strategic shift towards a service industry and high-tech manufacturing—the so-called 'Made in China 2025' Strategy.[304] 'Second, increasing inbound investment [would] attenuate China's imbalanced investment flows and thereby help alleviate the Renminbi's (RMB) depreciation. Third, these reforms [would] help quell growing resentment in Europe and the United States about lack of investment access to China's most lucrative sectors.'[305] However, the implementation of the announced reforms took some time, until they finally manifested in the promulgation of the FIL and FIL Implementing Regulations.

3.1.6.3.1 The Interim Reform: Allowing Record-Filing for Certain Investments

Beginning in September 2016, reforms of the administration of FIEs were rolled out. The Standing Committee of the National People's Congress (SCNPC) promulgated the 'Decision to Revise FIE Laws',[306] which prescribed significant amendments to the WFOE Law, EJV Law, and CJV Law effective from 1 October 2016.[307] The longstanding approval requirement for FIEs was abolished, and replaced with a simple record-filing procedure for the establishment of, and changes to, FIEs.[308] However, this relaxation did not apply to all foreign investment projects. Two different administrative procedures have been maintained. One was the longstanding approval process, and the other was the revised registration process. The latter only applied to FIEs that were not restricted by any special market entry management measures, meaning that they were not included in a negative list.[309] This marked the

[302]Xinhua News Agency (2013).

[303]ibid.

[304]See exemplarily Articles 3 (9) and 4 (7) of the Circular on the publication of 'Made in China 2025' (印发《中国制造2025》的通知), promulgated by the State Council on 8 May 2015.

[305]Lin and Harris (2017).

[306]Decision to Revise Four Laws including the PRC Wholly Foreign-Owned Enterprise Law (修改《中华人民共和国外资企业法》等四部法律的决定), adopted at the 22nd Session of the Standing Committee of the 12th National People's Congress on 3 September 2016 and effective as of 1 October 2016.

[307]Last Paragraph of the Decision to Revise FIE Laws.

[308]Arts. 1-3 Decision to Revise FIE Laws.

[309]Arts. 1-3 Decision to Revise FIE Laws.

nationwide roll-out of the negative list approach that had been tested in the FTZs.[310] Analogous, MOFCOM issued 'Draft FIE Administration Measures'[311] for public comment, which provided an initial outline of the essential features of the new filing regime. SAIC followed shortly after with the 'Record-Filing Administration Circular',[312] which outlined how the registration authorities should implement the new procedures. On 8 October 2016, NDRC and MOFCOM jointly promulgated 'Notice No 22'[313] to specify the cases in which the pre-existing approval mechanism would continue to apply. Contrary to general expectations, legislators did not issue a new negative list for this purpose, but rather converted parts of the existing Guidance Catalogue into a *quasi*-negative list.[314] According to Notice No 22, the traditional approval process still applied to the following cases: foreign investment projects that fall under the restricted or prohibited categories of the Guidance Catalogue; projects that fall under the encouraged category, but are subject to requirements on shareholding or senior management;[315] cross-border M&A projects by foreign investors. Simultaneously, MOFCOM promulgated the finalised 'FIE Administration Measures',[316] after more than 530 comments on the earlier draft version had been received.[317] The FIE Administration Measures provided guidance for the administration of the establishment of, and major changes[318] to, all investment projects that were subject to the newly-introduced record-filing system.[319] They primarily addressed the scope of filing, procedure, supervision, and liability in case of violations. Furthermore, they raised a number of notable points. Previously, MOFCOM approval always had to be obtained prior to the registration with SAMR. The filing process was designed to be purely procedural in nature, for information purposes, instead of the substantial review conducted under the previous approval regime.[320]

---

[310]Hezel and Vinck (2016).

[311]Interim Measures for the Administration of the Establishment and Change of Foreign-invested Enterprises (Draft for Comments) (《外商投资企业设立及变更备案管理暂行办法》(征求意见稿)), promulgated by the Ministry of Commerce on 3 September 2016.

[312]Circular on Proper Registration for Foreign-Invested Enterprises after the Implementation of Record-Filing Administration (关于做好外商投资企业实行备案管理后有关登记注册工作的通知), promulgated by the State Administration of Industry and Commerce on 30 September 2016 and effective as of 1 October 2016.

[313]Notice No 22 of 2016 (公告2016年第22号), promulgated jointly by the National Development and Reform Commission and the Ministry of Commerce on 8 October 2016 and effective as of the same date.

[314]Koppitz and Meng (2016).

[315]For a definition thereof, see Sect. 3.1.6.3.3.

[316]Interim Measures for the Administration of the Establishment and Change of Foreign-invested Enterprises (外商投资企业设立及变更备案管理暂行办法), promulgated by the Ministry of Commerce on 8 October 2016, revised on 30 July 2017, revised on 29 June 2018 and repealed on 01 January 2020.

[317]Koppitz and Meng (2016).

[318]What constitutes a 'major change' is defined in Article 6 Administration Measures.

[319]Art. 2 FIE Administration Measures.

[320]Art. 12 Para. 1 FIE Administration Measures.

The record-filing should be completed by MOFCOM within 3 days after the online submission of application documents.[321] This was expected to significantly speed up the establishment of FIEs.[322] On 16 May 2018, the State Council decided to simplify business registration procedures for foreign-invested enterprises further by introducing an online 'one-stop shop' procedure.[323] Under the new policy, filing with MOFCOM and registration with SAMR was combined into one step.[324] Regional governments were instructed to set up the new registration process by 30 June 2018. Accordingly, an online platform was launched in Shanghai on that date.[325] In January 2017, 'NDRC Circular No 111'[326] was issued to clarify that the previously established benchmarks for project approval or filing with NDRC would continue to apply under the new nationwide record-filing regime.

With the 2017 revision of the FIE Administration Measures, the scope of the new record-filing system was expanded to include many cross-border mergers and acquisitions, where foreign investors purchased the shares or assets of domestic-invested Chinese enterprises.[327] This reform was meant to encourage FDI. Commentators regarded it as a reaction to the reduced inflow of foreign investment in the first half of 2017.[328]

3.1.6.3.2 The New Unified Registration and Reporting System

When the FIL and FIL Implementing Regulations took effect on 1 January 2020, the regulatory and administrative landscape for foreign investments has changed once more. Most significantly, MOFCOM's power to review the establishment of FIEs has been taken away. No approval of, or record-filing with MOFCOM is required for the incorporation of an FIE and joint venture contracts are no longer subject to MOFCOM review or approval. 'MOFCOM – the long-time watchdog for foreign investment – will only take the back seat in monitoring foreign investment through the information reporting system.'[329] Instead, the responsibility for the registration of all foreign invested enterprises is now vested with SAMR.[330]

---

[321] Art. 12 Para. 1 FIE Administration Measures.

[322] Linklaters LLP (2016b) and Koppitz and Meng (2016).

[323] State Council (2018).

[324] ibid.

[325] Koty (2018).

[326] Circular on Proper Implementation of the Catalogue of Investment Projects Subject to Government Verification—2016 Version—Regarding Foreign Investments (做好贯彻落实《政府核准的投资项目目录(2016年本)》有关外资工作的通知), promulgated by the National Development and Reform Commission on 14 January 2017 and effective as of the same date.

[327] Art. 5 Para. 2 FIE Administration Measures.

[328] Koppitz and Wu (2017).

[329] Xu et al. (2020).

[330] Art. 37 FIL Implementing Regulations.

Under the new system, a foreign investment project will be subject to three major regulatory procedures. (1) Project approval by, or filing with, the NDRC, when applicable.[331] The FIL Implementing Regulations have clarified that NDRC retains this function to approve or maintain record-filing of foreign investment projects.[332] (2) Approval by industry-specific regulators, to the extent applicable.[333] 'In practice, a number of industry specific rules and regulations impose various restrictions on foreign investment. These restrictions are often broader than those enumerated in the Negative List, including special requirements applicable to foreign investors in shareholder qualification, industry experience, and registered capital.'[334] The FIL Implementing Regulations stipulate that industry specific licensing requirements may not discriminate against foreign investors, unless this is stipulated in law or administrative measures issued by the NPC or State Council.[335] (3) Registration with SAMR, which provides detailed information on how it will handle the registration of incorporation of, and changes to FIEs in the 'Notice on Registration of FIEs'.[336]

The central role that SAMR is now taking in the administration of FIEs is complemented by a reform of the administrative information reporting system. Previously, FIEs had to submit information through two channels, MOFCOM's foreign investment information system as well as SAMR's company registration system and enterprise credit information disclosure database.[337] The FIL stipulates a unified foreign investment information reporting system that consolidates the two previous channels to avoid duplicated reporting.[338] SAMR and MOFCOM have since issued the 'Reporting Measures'[339] and the 'Reporting Notice'.[340] The two regulations provide detailed practical guidance and specific content on the information that FIEs need to report in regard to the establishment, changes and fulfilment of annual reporting obligations of FIEs and their branches. SAMR will then share the

[331] See Sect. 3.1.6.1.4.

[332] Art. 36 FIL Implementing Regulations.

[333] See Sect. 3.1.6.1.4.

[334] Xu et al. (2020).

[335] Art. 35 FIL Implementing Regulations.

[336] Notice on Effectively Completing the Registration of Foreign Invested Enterprises for the Implementation of the Foreign Investment Law (贯彻落实《外商投资法》做好外商投资企业登记注册工作的通知), promulgated by the State Administration for Market Regulation on 31 December 2019 and effective as of 01 January 2020.

[337] Xu et al. (2020).

[338] Art. 34 FIL, Arts. 38-39 FIL Implementing Regulations.

[339] Foreign Investment Information Reporting Measures (外商投资信息报告办法), jointly promulgated by the Ministry of Commerce and the State Administration for Market Regulation on 30 December 2019 and effective as of 01 January 2020.

[340] Notice No. 62 on Matters Relating to Foreign Investment Information Reporting (公告2019年第62号——关于外商投资信息报告有关事项的公告), promulgated by the Ministry of Commerce on 31 December 2019 and effective as of 01 January 2020.

information with MOFCOM and other authorities. Noncompliance with the information reporting system makes FIEs subject to penalties.[341]

3.1.6.3.3 The New Comprehensive Negative List System

On 7 December 2016, NDRC and MOFCOM issued the '2016 Draft Guidance Catalogue'[342] for public consultation. This consultation period lasted until 6 January 2017.[343] Around half a year later, in June 2017, the seventh version of the Guidance Catalogue[344] was promulgated, which accepted all changes proposed by the draft.[345] The 2017 version of the Guidance Catalogue repealed the 2015 version, and effectively replaced the *quasi*-negative list that was established by Notice No 22.[346] The 2017 version was replaced 1 year later by the 2018 version of the Guidance Catalogue, which has been replaced by the current 2019 version on 30 July 2019. The structure of the 2017 version of the Guidance Catalogue differed substantially from previous versions. The 2017 Guidance Catalogue consisted of two parts: the first part listed all the industries in which foreign investment is encouraged; the second part contained the special market entry management measures for foreign investors, referred to as the 'FDI Negative List'. The FDI Negative List comprised explanatory notes and two sub-categories of industries which had been already known from previous versions of the Guidance Catalogue: industries that were restricted, and industries that were prohibited for foreign investors. The structure in the 2018 and 2019 version has been different again. The 2019 version of the Guidance Catalogue consists of the explanatory notes, and the FDI Negative List. The FDI Negative List is organised by industry, and stipulates the special management measures for each industry, in the form of investment restrictions or prohibitions. The 2019 version does not contain a list of all the industries in which foreign investment is encouraged. Instead, NDRC and MOFCOM issued a separate regulation, the 'Catalogue of Encouraged Industries for Foreign Investment',[347] which has replaced the list of encouraged industries set out in the 2017 version of the Guidance Catalogue and the 'Catalogue for Guiding FDI to Central and Western

---

[341] Art. 25 Reporting Measures.

[342] Notice on Soliciting Public Opinions on the Revised Draft Catalogue of Industries for Guiding Foreign Investment (《外商投资产业指导目录》修订稿公开征求意见的公告), promulgated jointly by the National Development and Reform Commission and the Ministry of Commerce on 7 December 2016.

[343] Foreword to the 2016 Draft Guidance Catalogue.

[344] See Sect. 3.1.6.1.1. fn. 197.

[345] Koppitz and Wu (2017).

[346] Preamble, Guidance Catalogue.

[347] Catalogue of Industries for Encouraging Foreign Investment (2019 Version) (鼓励外商投资产业目录(2019年版)), promulgated jointly by the National Development and Reform Commission and the Ministry of Commerce on 30 June 2019 with effect as of 30 July 2019.

China'.[348] This new catalogue consists of two sub-catalogues, one applies to the entire country and one is applicable to 22 provinces in China's central, western, and northeaster regions. Nationwide, the number of encouraged industries has increased from 348 to 415, with 67 items added and 45 items revised, compared to the 2017 list of encouraged industries.

The novelty of the FDI Negative List is that only foreign investment projects that fall under one of the categories on the FDI Negative List, are subject to restrictions. That is, a project that belongs to a prohibited industry, is excluded from foreign investment; an investment project that falls under a restricted industry is subject to specific investment restrictions. The Guidance Provisions set out a wide variety of restrictions that can be imposed on a restricted FDI project. For example, in certain industries and sectors, a FIE can only be established as a sino-foreign joint venture.[349]

In addition, the Guidance Catalogue can require that a Chinese party will be the 'controlling shareholder',[350] or will hold 'the relative majority of shares',[351] that the enterprise must be 'led by the Chinese party',[352] that the legal representative must be a Chinese citizen,[353] or that the foreign investment may not exceed a specific

[348]Catalogue of Priority Industries for Foreign Investment in Central and Western China (中西部地区外商投资优势产业目录), promulgated jointly by the National Development and Reform Commission and the Ministry of Commerce on 16 June 2000; amended on 23 December 2008, amended on 9 May 2013 and amended on 17 February 2017 and effective as of 20 March 2017.

[349]Art. 8 Guidance Provisions. The 2019 Negative List in the Guidance Catalogue stipulates two types of foreign investment projects that are limited to EJVs, one type that is limited to CJVs, and two types that are limited to EJVs or CJVs. Notably, the wording in the 2019 Negative List still referred to EJV and CJV, even though these special types of enterprises were to be abolished with the FIL on 1 January 2020. The requirement for an EJV will most likely have to be understood as the requirement of establishing a sino-foreign joint venture in the form of a limited liability company under the Company Law. Regarding the CJV, however, it remains to be seen if these industries will be opened to foreign invested partnership enterprises or if they also will require the establishment of a sino-foreign joint venture in the form of a limited liability company under the Company Law.

[350]Chinese controlling shareholding (中方控股) is defined in Article 8, Para. 2 Guidance Provisions as the aggregated investment of the Chinese party accumulating to at least 51% of the investment project. The 2019 Negative List in the Guidance Catalogue requires Chinese controlling shareholding for nine foreign investment projects.

[351]Chinese relative controlling shareholding (中方相对控股) is defined (in Art. 8 Para. 2 Guidance Provisions) as the aggregated ratio of the Chinese investors is more than the investment of any individual foreign investor. The 2019 Negative List in the Guidance Catalogue requires Chinese relative controlling shareholding for only one foreign investment projects.

[352]The term 'Chinese leading party' (中方主导) has been newly introduced with the 2015 version of the Guidance Catalogue. The 2019 Negative List in the Guidance catalogue requires a Chinese leading party for one type of foreign investment project in the field of education. It is defined in Item No 31 of the FDI Negative List as 'the principals or principal administrative officers shall be Chinese citizens and Chinese members shall not be less than half of all members of their councils, boards of directors or joint management committees'.

[353]Regarding the significance of the role of the legal representative, see Sect. 7.2.2. The 2019 Negative List in the Guidance catalogue requires a Chinese legal representative for two industries.

proportion of the shares.[354] From the 2018 FDI Negative List version, a timetable is provided for certain sectors on when some of the restrictions and prohibitions will be lifted over the course of the next few years.[355]

A project in the encouraged category can benefit from a lower level of approval—by local authorities, rather than central authorities in Beijing—, and possibly from certain tax concessions and other preferential treatment.[356] In practice, foreign investors and their Chinese partners occasionally create dubious legal investment structures to circumvent the investment restrictions of the Guidance Catalogue to invest in restricted or prohibited industries.[357] These endeavours carry a high risk, as they can lead to the total loss of the investment. An FIE that has been approved in violation of the Guidance Provisions or Guidance Catalogue is subject to the cancellation of its approvals and all related contracts, and articles of association may be declared void.[358] The new FDI Negative List consolidates the restrictions that were scattered across the different categories of previous Guidance Catalogues and thus provides easier reference and clearer guidance to foreign investors.[359] The FDI Negative List is mainly a reorganisation of the existing categories, but it does also open up some additional industries to foreign investment.[360] The total number of foreign investment restrictions was reduced from 93 in the 2015 version of the catalogue to 63 in the 2017 FDI Negative List, and was further reduced to 48 restrictions in the 2018 version and 40 restrictions in the 2019 FDI Negative List.

Regarding the relationship between the FDI Negative List and the FTZ Negative List, MOFCOM has clarified that the FTZ Negative List continues to be in effect in the FTZs, as these zones do not fall under the scope of application of the FDI Negative List.[361] The introduction of the FDI Negative List was part of the preparations for the new overall Negative List System that the Chinese government has prepared to establish over the past years. This new Negative List System consists of a so called 'Master Negative List', which is a nationwide market access list that applies to all investors, domestic and foreign alike. In 2015, the State Council issued

[354] This limitation is not expressly grounded in the Guidance Provisions, but is utilised in the 2019 Negative List in the Guidance Catalogue for two types of foreign investment projects.

[355] A promise was made, for example, for the manufacturing of automobiles to lift the restriction on the proportion of shares held by foreign investors (currently at a maximum of 50%) for commercial vehicles in 2020, and for passenger cars in 2022, Item No 9 2019 FDI Negative List in the Guidance Catalogue.

[356] Art. 9 Guidance Provisions. Approvals from local authorities are considered advantageous as they leave more room for local support and flexibility (Wei 2010, pp. 62, 66; Mahony 2015, p. 110).

[357] Hübner (2014), pp. 23, 47–63.

[358] Art. 13 Guidance Provisions.

[359] Linklaters LLP (2016a) and Tam and Qi (2016).

[360] For a detailed account, see Koppitz and Wu (2017). For the 2016 Draft Guidance Catalogue, see Tam and Qi (2016).

[361] Koppitz and Wu (2017).

a respective 'Market Access Negative List Opinion',[362] which provided for the Master Negative List to be rolled out nationwide starting from 2018. NDRC and MOFCOM issued an initial version of the list with their 'Pilot Master Negative List Circular'[363] in 2016. The Master Negative List was first tested in four pilot areas in Tianjin, Shanghai, Fujian, and Guangdong—which pilot areas are different from the FTZs in these municipalities.[364] In 2017, the pilot area was expanded to cover a total of 15 provinces.[365] The pilot version of the Master Negative List contains 327 items, of which 96 prohibit access to specific industries, and 231 stipulate investment restrictions.[366] The pilot programme for testing the Master Negative List was set to last until 31 December 2017.[367]

On 21 December 2018, the finalised '2018 Master Negative List'[368] was promulgated by NDRC and MOFCOM, and took effect as of the same day. For the first time, licensing and procedural requirements in China came to be applied to both foreign and domestic enterprises nationwide. The 2018 version of the list differed significantly from the earlier version, as 177 items and 288 specific management measures were removed from the pilot list. On 24 October 2019, an updated version of the Master Negative List has been promulgated. The 2019 version still imposes limitations on 145 business activities, compared to 151 in the previous version. These are grouped in two categories: (1) the 'prohibited' category of industries in which investment is completely prohibited, and (2) the '"licensed" category in which investments are subject to specific procedures, standards and approval requirements. Industries not mentioned on the list are open to all businesses for investment without the need for additional approval. The prohibited category consists of four sub-categories, namely (1) business activities expressly prohibited by laws or other market access regulations issued by the State Council; (2) investment projects explicitly banned under the 'Catalogue for Guiding Industry Restructuring';[369] (3) unlawful financial activities; (4) unlawful internet-related business activities.

[362]Opinions on Implementing the System of Negative List for Market Access (实行市场准入负面清单制度的意见), promulgated by the State Council on 2 October 2015 and effective as of the same date.

[363]Circular on the publication of the Draft Market Access Negative List (Pilot Edition) (印发市场准入负面清单草案(试点版)的通知), promulgated jointly by the National Development and Reform Commission and the Ministry of Commerce on 2 March 2016.

[364]Para. 4 Pilot Master Negative List Circular.

[365]Chan et al. (2019).

[366]Para. 1 Pilot Master Negative List Circular.

[367]Art. 1 Para. 11 Market Access Negative List Opinion.

[368]Circular on the publication of the Market Access Negative List (2018 Version) (印发市场准入负面清单草案(试点版)的通知), promulgated jointly by the National Development and Reform Commission and the Ministry of Commerce on 21 December 2018 and effective as of the same date.

[369]Catalogue for Guiding Industrial Restructuring (产业结构调整指导目录), promulgated by the National Development and Reform Commission on 27 March 2011, amended on 16 February 2013 and amended on 30 October 2019 with effect as of 01 January 2020.

From its introduction, the Master Negative List has been credited for not only being a more transparent list of restrictions, but also abolishing existing restrictions in certain industries, such as the relaxation of access restrictions to certain resource-related industries like coal and nonferrous metals.[370] The 2019 version has further opened up services, agriculture, mining, and manufacturing sectors. Some critics take a dimmer view on the new list, contending that the impact of new provisions on the list might be inhibited by the actual reality of industry-specific laws, regulations and administrative approvals that continue to apply despite the unified Master Negative List.[371]

The FDI Negative List and the Master Negative List differ insofar that the former stipulates equity or management requirements which apply only to foreign investors, whereas the latter stipulates market conditions and formalities necessary for market access for all investors alike, including SOEs, private domestic companies and foreign investors.[372] Notably, some of the investment restrictions on foreign investors that have been deleted from the FDI Negative List, have actually simply been 'moved' to the Master Negative List, because these restrictions also apply to domestic investment projects, such as casinos, theme parks, and golf courses.[373]

In summary, the newly established comprehensive Negative List System is now the first point of reference for a foreign investor. Up to three different lists—the Master Negative List, the FDI Negative, List and the FTZ Negative List—might have to be considered to determine whether a FDI project is (a) prohibited; (b) subject to restrictions; or (c) unrestricted and subject to direct registration with SAMR. In case of any discrepancy between the FTZ Negative List and the FDI Negative List, the former is regarded as prevailing because it would be more specific to foreign investment.[374] Likewise, the FDI Negative List would prevail over the Master Negative List.[375] However, should an FDI project be subject to any bilateral or multilateral trade agreement, such a treaty would have prevailing effect over the Negative List System.[376]

[370] Chan et al. (2019).

[371] Wong (2019).

[372] ibid.

[373] Tam and Qi (2016).

[374] Note No 4 FTZ Negative List.

[375] Ranft and Meng (2016).

[376] Art. 2 Para. 8 Market Access Negative List Opinion; Note No 6 to the FDI Negative List in the 2016 Draft Guidance Catalogue.

3.1.7 Assessing the Foreign Investment Law and Latest Reforms

The implementation of the FIL is regarded as the 'biggest change to the FDI regime in China since the 1980s.'[377] The pre-existing, multi-layered and lengthy verification process, involving numerous government agencies, represented a complex and costly entry threshold for FDI that left room for discrimination against foreign investors, and in favour of domestic enterprises.[378] Establishing a sino-foreign alliance under this framework in China required not only an agreement with a Chinese business partner, but, equally important, negotiation with representatives of the Chinese government in its various administrative authorities.[379] Against this background, the unified registration with SAMR and the introduction of the FDI Negative List are welcomed by foreign investors as substantial breakthroughs. However, it should be noted that the FIL Implementing Regulations provide less detail in certain regards than what could be expected from a typical set of Chinese implementing rules.[380] They remain silent on a number of sensitive topics closely watched by the business community. 'This demonstrates the Chinese government's commitment to improve overall environment for foreign investment while remaining prudent when facing complicated issues regarding foreign investment regulation, all against the bigger picture of the ever-changing landscape of international relations.'[381] Therefore, commentators call for more detailed rules to be put in place and expect that the commencement of this new era will require great efforts in further clearing up existing legislation which conflicts with the FIL and its implementing regulations.[382]

Regarding the FDI Negative List, in a more detailed analysis, commentators have criticised it as a reform more in form than in substance, stating that too many industries and sectors are still restricted and prohibited for foreign investors.[383] The expectation is that it will still be a long time before the FDI Negative List is substantially shortened in a true commitment to the implementation of same treatment for foreign investors and nationals.[384]

---

[377] McGinty et al. (2019a), p. 12.

[378] Wei (2010), p. 62; Mahony (2015), pp. 140–141.

[379] Nägeli (2003), p. 66.

[380] McGinty et al. (2020), p. 10.

[381] Xu et al. (2020).

[382] Hong and Liu (2020).

[383] Baker & McKenzie International (2017).

[384] ibid.

3.2 Forms of Joint Ventures as Sino-Foreign Alliances

As noted above, the EJV was the first enterprise form that allowed foreign investors to establish a sino-foreign alliance after the process of Reform and Opening up was initiated. Several years later, the EJV was supplemented by the CJV. Gradually, special variations of both joint venture types were developed. This section provides a brief introduction to the various types of joint venture enterprises. This overview is provided to illustrate the alternative investment vehicles that were available to foreign investors in contrast to the FILPE. Certain aspects of the EJV will be discussed in more detail in the analysis of the FILPE below. However, for a comprehensive analysis of the joint venture enterprise forms, reference is made to respective specialised literature.[385] Even though the EJV and CJV are no longer available as stand-alone enterprise forms after the FIL came into effect, the different forms of joint ventures still provide context and important insights to understand the functioning and innovative aspects of China's foreign investment laws.[386] Furthermore, existing joint ventures remain in force for up to 5 years from the date that the FIL came into effect.[387]

3.2.1 Equity Joint Venture 中外合资经营企业

The EJV was the first, and for many years also the most favoured, enterprise form for foreign investment in China.[388] Later, the WFOE, an FIE that could be established by foreign investors without a Chinese partner, gradually became the enterprise form most commonly used by foreign investors.[389] By way of illustration, in 2017, 27,007 WFOEs were established, compared to 8364 EJVs.[390] In 2018, the ratio was similar with 50,106 new WFOEs and 10,170 new EJVs.[391] For the period of January to November 2019, the statistics show a ratio of 27,592 WFOEs to 8913 EJVs.[392] However, the EJV still remains the most popular enterprise form by far for sino-foreign alliances. For certain projects, it was the only available option, as the

[385] Mahony (2015), Shen (2015), Pang (2014) and Kroymann (2009).

[386] See Sect. 1.3.3.

[387] See Sect. 3.1.5.3.

[388] Nägeli (2003), p. 88; Pearson (1991), pp. 3–4.

[389] Shen (2015), p. 35; Mahony (2015), pp. 11, 174–176.

[390] National Bureau of Statistics of China (中华人民共和国国家统计局) (2019), Chapter 11–15.

[391] National Bureau of Statistics of China (中华人民共和国国家统计局) (2019), Chapter 11–15.

[392] Foreign Investment Department of the Ministry of Commerce (中华人民共和国商务部外国投资管理司) (2019); at the time of writing of this book, no statistic for the entire year 2019 has been published yet.

Guidance Catalogue explicitly required that foreign investments in specific sectors could only be made in the form of the EJV.[393]

The EJV is probably the most comprehensively regulated type of investment vehicle in China.[394] The formation, operation, and dissolution of EJVs is governed by the EJV Law,[395] the EJV Implementing Regulations,[396] and numerous rules enacted by various authorities at different levels. An EJV is a limited liability company,[397] with the status of a Chinese legal person.[398] It was formed by at least one Chinese and one foreign investor.[399] While the foreign party could also be a natural person, the Chinese party had to be a Chinese company, enterprise, or other economic organisation.[400] The EJV was established on the basis of a joint venture contract and articles of association, which both had to fulfil specific legal requirements, and had to be registered with or approved by MOFCOM.[401] The lifespan of the EJV was not perpetual, but would only be granted for a specific term, which could be renewed upon registration with, or approval of, the relevant authorities.[402]

A distinctive feature that sets the EJV apart from similar corporate forms in Western jurisdictions is that its parties share the profits, risks, and losses on a mandatory *pro rata* basis to their respective contributions to the registered capital of the EJV.[403] EJVs do not issue shares like limited liability companies in other jurisdictions.[404] Instead, the two essential concepts in its financial structure are 'registered capital' and 'total investment amount'.[405] 'Registered capital' refers to the equity contributed by an investor in local or foreign currency to provide capital to the company.[406] The parties in an EJV subscribed for a ratio of the equity interest in the form of registered capital.[407] 'Total investment amount' refers to the total sum of registered capital plus any debt that was required to finance the EJV.[408] As a general

[393]See for example manufacturing of automobiles, Item No 9 of the 2019 FDI Negative List in the Guidance Catalogue. For other specific sectors, investors are given a choice between the EJV and CJV. See for example medical institutions, Item No 33 of the 2019 FDI Negative List in the Guidance Catalogue.

[394]Shen (2015), p. 34; Kroymann (2009), p. 83.

[395]See Sect. 3.1.2. fn. 18.

[396]See Sect. 3.1.3. fn. 48.

[397]Art. 4 Para. 1 EJV Law, Art. 16 Para. 1 EJV Implementing Regulations.

[398]Art. 2 EJV Implementing Regulations.

[399]Art. 1 EJV Law.

[400]Art. 1 EJV Law.

[401]Arts. 10-13 EJV Implementing Regulations.

[402]For industrial manufacturing EJVs, it is typical to have a term of 30–50 years. In the service sector, the term is usually shorter (Mahony 2015, p. 181).

[403]Art. 4 Para. 3 EJV Law.

[404]Shen (2015), p. 35.

[405]ibid; Mahony (2015), pp. 181–182.

[406]Art. 18 EJV Implementing Regulations.

[407]Shen (2015), p. 36.

[408]Art. 17 EJV Implementing Regulations.

rule, the EJV Law stipulates that the foreign parties' total contribution to the registered capital should not be lower than 25%,[409] but exceptions to this rule were possible.[410]

The highest governing organ of the EJV is not a shareholders' meeting, but the board of directors.[411] The members of the board of directors were appointed by both parties in proportion to their respective equity interest.[412] This governance structure does not provide for a legislatively mandated separation between the investors as shareholders and the directors as independent managers of the company.[413] All major decisions must be passed by a resolution of the board of directors.[414] By law, certain decisions require a unanimous resolution, thus giving the minority party *de facto* a veto on those decisions.[415] The chairman of the board of directors serves as the legal representative, who has the statutory power to represent the EJV in its business operation.[416] The daily operation of the EJV's business is usually run by a management team that is appointed by the board of directors, and lead by the general manager.[417] Since 2006, a newly established EJV was further required to establish a supervisory system that consisted either of a board of supervisors or one or two individual supervisors.[418] The implementation of a supervisory system in the governance structure of the joint venture enterprises has produced obstacles, and has been subject to criticism.[419]

3.2.2 Cooperative Joint Venture 中外合作经营企业

In response to foreign investors' dissatisfaction with the inflexible governance structure of the EJV, initial forms of contractual joint ventures began to evolve in

[409] Art. 4 Para. 2 EJV Law.

[410] See Section 2.

[411] Art. 6 Para. 1 EJV Law, Art. 30 EJV Implementing Regulations.

[412] Art. 6 Para. 1 EJV Law, Art. 31 EJV Implementing Regulations.

[413] Bath (2007), p. 782.

[414] Mahony (2015), p. 180.

[415] Art. 33 EJV Implementing Regulations.

[416] Art. 34 EJV Implementing Regulations.

[417] Art. 6 Paras. 2–3 EJV Law, Arts. 35–38 EJV Implementing Regulations.

[418] Art. 51 Para. 1 Company Law in conjunction with Art. 2 Para. 2 of the Interpretation of Key Provisions of the 'Implementing Opinions on Certain Issues Concerning the Application of the Law in the Administration of the Examination, Approval and Registration of Foreign-Invested Enterprises' (《关于外商投资的公司审批登记管理法律适用若干问题的执行意见》重点条款解读), promulgated by the State Administration for Industry and Commerce on 22 September 2006 (Interpretation of the Opinions on Applying the Company Law).

[419] For a detailed discussion of the problems associated therewith, see Bath (2007), pp. 782–784; Kroymann (2009), pp. 183–192.

the early 1980s, and enjoyed great popularity.[420] However, it was not until 1988 that the CJV became available with the promulgation of the CJV Law,[421] which was later supplemented by the CJV Implementing Regulations,[422] and various other rules and regulations. In practice, EJV-related regulations are also often applied to CJVs by government authorities.[423] Two different forms of CJVs have been introduced: one with legal person status (Legal Person CJV), often referred to as Cooperative Joint Venture, and one without legal person status (Non-Legal Person CJV), also known as a Contractual Joint Venture.[424] This chapter describes the common features of both types of the CJV, and analyses how they differ.

For reasons discussed below, the practical relevance of both types of CJVs has been very limited during the past years. This is reflected in low numbers of newly established CJVs: only 124 in 2017,[425] and 107 in 2018,[426] compared to 1343 newly established CJVs in 2004.[427] In the period January to November 2019, 64 new CJVs were established.[428] However, a comparison of the amount of invested capital in the different FIEs shows interesting results. In 2018, the average amount of invested capital for a WFOE was 1.8 million USD, for an EJV 3.4 million USD, but for a CJV 7.2 million USD.[429] These numbers suggest that CJVs were utilised for more capital-intensive investment projects. Despite the limited popularity of the CJV, the Guidance Catalogue has provided that certain foreign investment projects could only be carried out in the form of the CJV.[430]

A CJV was formed by at least one Chinese and one foreign investor.[431] It was established on the basis of a joint venture contract and articles of association, both of which required registration with or approval from MOFCOM.[432] The key feature that distinguishes the CJV from an EJV is the less rigid and more flexible structure of

---

[420] Mahony (2015), pp. 8–9; Kroymann (2009), pp. 84–85; Pearson (1991), p. 232.

[421] See Sect. 3.1.2 fn. 28.

[422] See Sect. 3.1.3 fn. 49.

[423] Shen (2015), p. 35.

[424] Art. 2 Para. 2 CJV Law; Art. 4 CJV Implementing Regulations.

[425] National Bureau of Statistics of China (中华人民共和国国家统计局) (2019), Chapter 11–15.

[426] National Bureau of Statistics of China (中华人民共和国国家统计局) (2019), Chapter 11–15.

[427] National Bureau of Statistics of China (中华人民共和国国家统计局) (2005), Chapter 18–14.

[428] Foreign Investment Department of the Ministry of Commerce (中华人民共和国商务部外国投资管理司) (2019). At the time of writing of this book, no statistic for the entire year 2019 has been published yet.

[429] Calculation by the author, based on data from National Bureau of Statistics of China (中华人民共和国国家统计局) (2019), Chapter 11–15.

[430] See exemplary higher learning institutions, Item No 31 of the 2019 FDI Negative List in the Guidance Catalogue. For other specific sectors, investors are given a choice between the EJV and CJV. See exemplary medical institutions, Item No 33 of the 2019 FDI Negative List in the Guidance Catalogue.

[431] Art. 1 CJV Law. Like in the EJV, the Chinese party can only be a Chinese company, enterprise or other economic organisation, while the foreign party can also be a natural person.

[432] Arts. 10–13 CJV Implementing Regulations.

the CJV.[433] In an EJV, the parties were bound to share the profits and losses on a strict *pro rata* basis to their respective contributions to the registered capital.[434] In a CJV, the parties could freely determine the ratio of the allocation of profits and losses in the joint venture contract, independently from their capital contributions.[435] In addition, the parties to a CJV could agree in the joint venture contract that the foreign party may recover its investment on a priority basis before the term of the joint venture has ended.[436] This differs from the EJV, in which investors are generally not permitted to decrease the registered capital during the life of the company.[437] In return, the Chinese party to the CJV receives, upon expiration of the term of the CJV, all net assets of the enterprise free of charge.[438] This sort of arrangement is especially common in Build-Operate-Transfer (BOT) projects that are frequently utilised for infrastructure investments, and the exploitation of natural resources.[439] ‘This, in fact, is the main reason that investors choose this type of vehicle for certain types of capital-intensive projects such as power plants, toll roads, oil exploration projects, water treatment plants etc., that require large initial capital investments and which generate a relatively stable and predictable income stream over the life of the project.’[440] The foreign investor can get his investment back on a priority basis, but has no long-term commitment to the development of the project.[441]

The CJV did not only offer more freedom in relation to the ratio of the capital contributions, but also in determining the forms of capital contributions. In addition to the cash and non-cash contributions that were permitted for the EJV,[442] a party to a CJV could also provide ‘cooperative conditions’ in exchange for an agreed share of the profits.[443] Cooperative conditions is a rather broad concept that could include access to or use of certain assets or rights that were not formally assigned to the CJV.[444] According to a MOFCOM regulation, cooperative conditions could be granted with regard to real estate and other property rights, including land use rights, usage rights of buildings, and the right to use the fixed attachments to a building and auxiliary equipment.[445] In practice, however, features like ‘guanxi’ (personal relationships), government relations, obtaining required approvals, market access rights,

[433] Mahony (2015), p. 187; Shen (2015), p. 35; Wei (2010), p. 68.

[434] Art. 4 Para. 3 EJV Law.

[435] Art. 21 Para. 1 CJV Law, Art. 43 Para. 1 CJV Implementing Regulations.

[436] Art. 21 Para. 2 CJV Law, Art. 44 CJV Implementing Regulations.

[437] Wei (2010), p. 68.

[438] Art. 21 Para. 2 CJV Law, Art. 44 CJV Implementing Regulations.

[439] Mahony (2015), p. 189; Kroymann (2009), p. 87.

[440] Mahony (2015), p. 188.

[441] ibid, p. 189.

[442] Art. 5 Para. 1 EJV Law, Art. 22 EJV Implementing Regulations.

[443] Art. 8 CJV Law, Art. 18 Para. 1 CJV Implementing Regulations.

[444] Liu (2008), p. 20; Kroymann (2009), p. 142.

[445] Art. 2 Explanatory Notes on the Implementation of the ‘PRC Sino-Foreign Cooperative Joint Venture Law Detailed Implementing Regulations’ (关于执行《中华人民共和国中外合作经营企

and supplying certain services that could promote the business prospects of the CJV, have also been agreed as cooperative conditions in joint venture contracts.[446] While contributing non-monetary assets usually triggered a rather complex and lengthy appraisal process that could provoke conflicts between the parties over the actual value of such assets, the rather vague category of cooperative conditions allowed more flexibility in this regard.[447] Usually, the Chinese party to the CJV would provide the non-equity cooperative conditions and the foreign party contributed most or all of the real registered capital in the form of cash or other permitted in-kind contributions.[448]

3.2.2.1 Legal Person CJV法人资格的合作企业

A CJV that fulfilled the relevant legal requirements could obtain the status of a Chinese legal person,[449] and take the legal form of a limited liability company.[450] In its legal nature and operational structure, the Legal Person CJV therefore largely resembles an EJV.[451] Regarding the governance structure, the investors of a CJV could choose to implement either a board of directors or a joint management committee as the company's highest governing organ.[452] Legal Person CJVs commonly have a board of directors and a management structure similar to that of an EJV.[453] The composition of the board of directors or joint management committee had to be agreed by the Chinese and foreign party with reference to their respective contributions of capital or cooperative conditions.[454] The chairman of the board of directors or the head of the joint management committee, as appropriate, serves as the legal representative of the CJV.[455] As in the case for the EJV, the Legal Person CJV was generally required to establish a supervisory system comprised of a board of supervisors, or one or two individual supervisors.[456] The daily operation of a CJV's business is run by a management team that is appointed by the board of

业法实施细则》若干条款的说明), promulgated by the Ministry of Foreign Trade and Economic Cooperation on 22 October 1996.

446 Interview with a partner of a foreign law firm in Shanghai that the author has conducted in October 2015; Liu (2008), p. 20.

447 Kroymann (2009), p. 143.

448 Liu (2008), pp. 20–21.

449 Art. 2 Para. 2 CJV Law; Art. 4 CJV Implementing Regulations.

450 Art. 14 Para. 1 CJV Implementing Regulations.

451 Mahony (2015), p. 187.

452 Art. 12 CJV Law.

453 Wei (2010), p. 68.

454 Art. 25 CJV Implementing Regulations.

455 Art. 31 CJV Implementing Regulations.

456 Art. 51 Para. 1 Company Law in connection with Art. 2 Para. 2 Interpretation of the Opinions on Applying the Company Law.

directors or joint management committee, and lead by the general manager.[457] Another expression of the more flexible structure of the CJV is the option to assign the management of the daily operation to a third party.[458] This requires a unanimous decision by the board of directors or joint management committee, and approval by SAMR.[459] In practice, such an assignment of management is rare, but it can be observed in hotels, where a specialised third party management company is entrusted with the daily operations of the CJV.[460]

3.2.2.2 Non-legal Person CJV 不具有法人资格的合作企业

The CJV Implementing Regulations contained specific provisions for the Non-Legal Person CJV.[461] With its establishment, no separate legal person was created.[462] The parties to a Non-Legal Person CJV bear civil responsibilities according to China's civil law.[463] The parties therefore assumed unlimited liability for the debts of the Non-Legal Person CJV, regardless of the amount of their capital contribution. In its legal nature, the Non-Legal Person CJV therefore resembles a general partnership enterprise.[464] Unlike the Legal Person CJV, its contributed capital or cooperative conditions needed to be registered with SAMR.[465] Ownership of the contributed assets or cooperative conditions remained with the investor that contributed them, or, subject to the agreement in the joint venture contract, became the jointly owned or partly jointly owned property of all parties.[466] Regardless of whether the parties opted for individual or joint ownership, the contributed capital and cooperative conditions had to be put under the unified management of the joint venture. None of the parties can dispose of the capital or cooperative conditions without the agreement of the other parties.[467] New assets accumulated as a result of the operation of the CJV are jointly owned by all parties.[468] The Non-Legal Person CJV is required to keep unified accounting books at the site of the enterprise, while the parties must also maintain their respective individual accounting books.[469]

---

457 Art. 12 Para. 1 CJV Law, Arts. 32–34 CJV Implementing Regulations.

458 Art. 12 Para. 2 CJV Law, Art. 35 Para. 1 CJV Implementing Regulations.

459 Art. 12 Para. 2 CJV Law.

460 Mahony (2015), p. 195; Kroymann (2009), p. 181.

461 Art. 4 Para. 2, Arts. 50-54 CJV Implementing Regulations.

462 Art. 2 Para. 2 CJV Law, Art. 4 Para. 1 CJV Implementing Regulations.

463 Art. 50 CJV Implementing Regulations.

464 Mahony (2015), pp. 174, fn. 44, 196; Lu (吕美昂) (2011), p. 81; Yang (杨杰) and Qu (曲天明) (2010), pp. 64–65.

465 Art. 51 CJV Implementing Regulations.

466 Art. 52 Para. 1 CJV Implementing Regulations.

467 Art. 52 Para. 2 CJV Implementing Regulations.

468 Art. 52 Para. 1 CJV Implementing Regulations.

469 Art. 54 CJV Implementing Regulations.

Regarding its governance structure, the parties could not elect to have a board of directors because the Non-Legal Person CJV was required to establish a joint management committee as its highest governing organ.[470] It is difficult to determine the extent to which the board of directors and the joint management committee differ, as neither the CJV Law nor the CJV Implementing Regulations indicate specific structural differences between the two organs.[471] The joint management committee must comprise at least three members, who are appointed by the joint venture parties with reference to their respective contributions of capital or cooperative conditions as specified in the joint venture contract.[472] The joint management committee is responsible for deciding all major matters concerning the Non-Legal Person CJV.[473] In practice, it differs from the board of directors in-so-far as, where any regulatory gaps exist in the CJV Implementing Regulations with regard to the board of directors, these are filled by provisions in the Company Law, which apply as a background law.[474] For the joint management committee, authorities have more leeway in addressing such regulatory gaps.[475]

Unlike the Legal Person CJV, the Non-Legal Person CJV did not require the establishment of a supervisory board, as this was only stipulated for limited liability companies.[476] The function of the legal representative was assigned to the head of the joint management committee.[477] In a joint venture with legal person status, the legal representative acts as an organ of the enterprise in relation to third parties.[478] For the Non-Legal Person CJV, conversely, the legal representative acts as representative of the investors.[479] Similar to the Legal Person CJV, the daily operation is either run by the general manager and a management team,[480] or assigned to a third party.[481]

[470] Art. 53 CJV Implementing Regulations.

[471] Kroymann (2009), p. 167.

[472] Art. 25, Art. 53 Para. 1 CJV Implementing Regulations.

[473] Art. 53 Para. 2 CJV Implementing Regulations.

[474] Kroymann (2009), p. 168. On the relationship between the CJV Implementing Regulations and the Company Law, see also Sect. 3.1.3.

[475] Kroymann (2009), p. 168.

[476] Argumentum a contrario to Article 51, Paragraph 1 Company Law in connection with Article 2, Paragraph 2 Interpretation of the Opinions on Applying the Company Law.

[477] Art. 31 CJV Implementing Regulations.

[478] Kroymann (2009), p. 170.

[479] ibid, p. 170.

[480] Art. 12 Para. 1 CJV Law, Arts. 32-34 CJV Implementing Regulations.

[481] Art. 12 Para. 2 CJV Law, Art. 35 Para. 1 CJV Implementing Regulations.

3.2.2.3 Decline in Practical Relevance of CJVs

The numbers of newly registered CJVs in recent years stated above show that foreign investors have been reluctant to opt for these enterprise forms when establishing a sino-foreign alliance. The reasons why CJVs were not commonly chosen, are manifold. Some commentators considered the CJV as generally not appropriate for an enterprise which was intended to develop a business over time, such as manufacturing or retail projects.[482] Rather, because of its 'early return on investment' feature, the CJV was seen as best suited for projects that would have relatively high up-front capital construction costs, and a generally fixed economically-productive lifetime, as in large infrastructure projects.[483] However, projects which operated on a BOT model were very common in the 1990s, but became relatively rarer over time.[484]

While CJVs offered more flexibility in investment and management structure, establishing a CJV required parties to describe their respective rights and obligations in great detail in the underlying joint venture contract.[485] Negotiating the terms of a CJV could therefore take a considerable amount of time. Furthermore, Chinese parties generally seemed more familiar with the standard EJV model, whereby the forms of capital contribution, distribution of profits, and apportionment of directors were relatively straightforward.[486] Practitioners have further reported that approval authorities tended to review the terms of a CJV more carefully and critically, and sometimes were even reluctant to approve the use of such an enterprise form at all.[487] While CJVs were uncommon in general, the Non-Legal Person CJV was particularly rare in practice. An often-provided explanation is the unlimited liability that the parties have to bear.[488] Moreover, with the introduction of the FIPE in 2010, Chinese law began to provide a much more developed and comprehensive legal structure to achieve the same advantages as the Non-Legal Person CJV provided.[489] Given the similarity in nature of the Non-Legal Person CJV to a partnership enterprise, at first, it might have seemed obvious to use this enterprise form as a key reference for a comparison with the FILPE. However, the little practical relevance and the rudimentary legal framework that was provided in the CJV Law and CJV Implementing Regulations make such a comparison unattractive. The CJV was born out of the

[482]Mahony (2015), p. 189.

[483]ibid, p. 189.

[484]Interview with a partner of a foreign law firm in Shanghai that the author has conducted in October 2015.

[485]Wei (2010), p. 68.

[486]Interview with a partner of a foreign law firm in Shanghai that the author has conducted in October 2015.

[487]Yang (杨杰) and Qu (曲天明) (2010), p. 63; Marsh et al. (2008).

[488]Interview with a partner of a foreign law firm in Shanghai that the author has conducted in October 2015.

[489]Mahony (2015), p. 198.

practical need for a more flexible enterprise form during an era in which legal developments had to catch up with fundamental changes caused by China's rapid economic growth, ground-breaking political reforms, and constant ambiguity. The CJV served an important purpose during that time, but a foreign investor became unlikely to even consider establishing a Non-Legal Person CJV in previous years. Likewise, the analysis of the Non-Legal Person CJV in China-related legal research has been much less extensive than the analysis of the EJV. The emphasis of the present research question is therefore better placed on a comparison with the EJV in particular. On selective issues, however, reference will also be made to the Non-Legal Person CJV.

3.2.3 Special Variations of Joint Venture Enterprises

Besides the EJV and CJV as primary forms, a number of special variations of the joint venture enterprise to address the need for more complex and specialised enterprise forms have been established by China's lawmakers over time in the light of the evolving Chinese economy. These special variations can be categorised under the two primary forms, but still show distinctive characteristics and deviations.[490] In the sections below, the special variations are briefly described.

3.2.3.1 Foreign-Invested Enterprise Holding Company 外商投资举办性公司

The FIE HoldCo was introduced in 1995 with the promulgation of the 'FIE HoldCo Provisions'.[491] The FIE HoldCo is an umbrella-structure arrangement that enables a foreign investor to hold all of its FIE subsidiaries in China and to provide integrated inter-group services to its group affiliates.[492] While in many jurisdictions a holding company serves as a relatively simple structure that can be used as an initial investment vehicle or even be established prior to making any specific investments, the FIE HoldCo is only available to investors who have already made significant investments in China.[493] Foreign investors wishing to establish an FIE HoldCo are required to have total assets of no less than 400 million USD, and to have established at least one FIE in China with a minimum paid-in capital contribution of at least 10 million USD; or alternatively to have established at least 10 FIEs in China with a minimum of 30 million USD paid-in registered capital.[494] Because of these stringent

490 Kroymann (2009), p. 80.

491 See Sect. 3.1.2 fn. 35.

492 Shen (2015), p. 43; Wei (2010), pp. 69–70.

493 Mahony (2015), p. 38.

494 Art. 3 Para. 1 FIE HoldCo Provisions.

requirements, the list of the now more than 300 FIE HoldCos mirrors the list of Fortune 500 companies.[495]

With regard to its legal structure, an FIE HoldCo is a limited liability company or a joint stock company that was previously established as either a WFOE or an EJV, and now can be established as an enterprise form under the Company Law.[496] For an FIE HoldCo in EJV form, the Chinese joint venture party was required to have assets of at least 100 million RMB.[497] However, in practice, virtually all FIE HoldCos were established as WFOEs, ie, a foreign investor without a Chinese partner.[498] Given the marginal practical relevance of the EJV structure for the FIE HoldCo, reference is made to specific literature for further analysis.[499]

3.2.3.2 Foreign-Invested Venture Capital Enterprise 外商投资创业投资企业

The Foreign-Invested Venture Capital Enterprise (FIVCE) form was created by the 'FIVCE Provisions'.[500] The purpose of the FIVCE was to provide foreign investors with a vehicle for raising and managing onshore investment funds in China.[501] The primary business of a FIVCE is to invest in unlisted high or new technology enterprises, and to provide managerial skills.[502] A FIVCE may be formed by foreign investors alone, or by foreign and Chinese investors together.[503] It can be established as a limited liability company—previously in the form of a WFOE, EJV, or Legal Person CJV, and now under the Company Law—, or in an unincorporated form without legal person status, very similar to the Non-Legal Person CJV which fell under the Foreign Invested Partnership Enterprise category.[504] The majority of existing FIVCE are established in the unincorporated form, because this form was afforded more beneficial tax treatment in the past.[505] The Non-Legal Person FIVCE can be structured in a very similar way to a limited partnership, which is the common

[495]Mahony (2015), p. 39.

[496]Art. 2 FIE HoldCo Provisions.

[497]Art. 3 Para. 2 FIE HoldCo Provisions.

[498]Mahony (2015), p. 208.

[499]Shen (2015), pp. 43–46; Mahony (2015), pp. 206–213; Kroymann (2009), pp. 310–382.

[500]Interim Provisions on Establishing Foreign Venture Capital Investment Enterprises (设立外商投资创业投资企业的暂行规定), promulgated jointly by the Ministry of Foreign Trade and Economic Cooperation, the Ministry of Science and Technology and the State Administration of Industry and Commerce on 28 August 2001; later replaced by the Administrative Provisions for Foreign-Invested Venture Capital Investment Enterprises (外商投资创业投资企业管理规定), promulgated on 30 January 2003 and amended on 28 October 2015.

[501]Zhang and Du (2014), p. II-5.1.2.

[502]Art. 3 FIVCE Provisions.

[503]Art. 2 FIVCE Provisions.

[504]Art. 4 Para. 1 FIVCE Provisions.

[505]Zhang and Du (2014), p. II-5.1.10.

and familiar form to most venture capital funds.[506] The investors in a Non-Legal Person FIVCE can either all share joint and several liability for the debts of the FIVCE, or select one investor, the 'requisite investor', who bears unlimited liability (similar to a general partner), while the remaining investors enjoy limited liability to the extent of their respective capital contributions (similar to limited partners).[507] The requisite investor in this scenario must contribute at least 1% of the total subscribed capital of the Non-Legal Person FIVCE.[508] Therefore, the provisions on the Non-Legal Person FIVCE are sometimes regarded as experimental regulations implemented to pave the way for the official recognition of the limited partnership enterprise.[509] In a Legal Person FIVCE, the liability of each investor is limited to its respective contribution to the company's registered capital.[510] The Legal Person FIVCE also has to have a requisite investor who must contribute at least 30% of the total subscribed capital.[511]

The establishment of a FIVCE is regarded as cumbersome and time-consuming.[512] The threshold for qualification as a requisite investor is high, requiring *inter alia* extensive fund management experience, and an accumulated amount of managed capital of 100 million USD, of which at least 50 million USD must have been invested in venture capital projects.[513] Following the introduction of the FILPE, special pilot programmes have been initiated to facilitate equity investments through FILPEs.[514] At the same time, tax regulations have been changed, and it is not clear whether the FIVCE still can be utilised in a tax beneficial investment structure.[515] As a result, the FIVCE is now used much less in practice, and is no longer the favourite choice of foreign investors for establishing private equity funds.[516] Against this background, the FIVCE will not be analysed in more detail, but reference is made to relevant literature.[517] The role of the FILPE in the private equity and venture capital industry will be analysed further below.[518]

---

[506] Shen (2015), p. 47; Zhang and Du (2014), p. II-5.1.10. See Sect. 5.3.3 on the utilisation of the Foreign Invested Limited Partnership Enterprise for a venture capital fund.

[507] Art. 4 Para. 2 FIVCE Provisions.

[508] Art. 7 Para. 6 FIVCE Provisions.

[509] Zhang (2017), p. 237.

[510] Art. 4 Para. 3 FIVCE Provisions.

[511] Art. 7 Para. 6 FIVCE Provisions.

[512] Lin (2017), p. 185; Zhang and Du (2014), p. II-5.1.14.

[513] Art. 7 FIVCE Provisions.

[514] Zhang and Du (2014), p. II-5.1.3.

[515] Zhang and Du (2014), p. II-5.1.19-20.

[516] Lin (2017), p. 185; Zhang and Du (2014), p. II-5.1.3.

[517] Shen (2015), pp. 46–49; Zhang and Du (2014).

[518] See Sect. 5.3.3.

3.2.3.3 Foreign-Invested Company Limited by Shares 外商投资股份有限公司

The FICLS was introduced in 1995 with the promulgation of the FICLS Provisions.[519] The FICLS was not a special variation of the joint venture enterprises, but rather a separate type of investment vehicle.[520] Nevertheless, it is briefly introduced at this point to complete the overview of sino-foreign alliances.

The FICLS is an enterprise with legal person status and with limited liability, formed by foreign and Chinese investors.[521] As indicated in the name, a FICLS issues shares,[522] thereby bearing great resemblance to Western-style corporations.[523] It was based on the domestic company limited by shares, which is regulated by the Company Law,[524] and is the basic vehicle for listing purely domestic-invested corporations on China's stock markets. The FICLS was the only type of FIE that could be listed on Chinese or overseas stock exchanges, and thus was often referred to as a 'foreign-invested joint-stock company'.[525] With the FIL taking effect, the FICLS Provisions have been repealed. Foreign investors now can establish a domestic company limited by shares, which is explicitly encouraged in the FIL and its implementing regulations.[526]

The FICLS was to have a minimum registered capital of 30 million RMB, of which the foreign investor had to hold at least 25%.[527] The FICLS never developed to gain substantial practical relevance as a legal vehicle for FDI.[528] Newly established FICLS amounted to only 125 enterprises in 2017,[529] and 129 in 2018.[530] In the period from January to November 2019, 101 FICLS were established.[531] Reasons for this unpopularity include the relatively high minimum registered capital requirements, and the very complex and expensive process for incorporating a FICLS.[532] Application requirements for FICLS were stricter than for EJVs, CJVs, or WFOEs, and more often than not, authorities have denied

[519] See Sect. 3.1.2 fn. 33.

[520] Shen (2015), p. 39.

[521] Arts. 1-2 FICLS Provisions.

[522] Art. 2 FICLS Provisions.

[523] Shen (2015), p. 33.

[524] Arts. 76-145 Company Law.

[525] Shen (2015), p. 39; Mahony (2015), pp. 214–215.

[526] Art. 17 FIL, Art. 18 FIL Implementing Regulations.

[527] Art. 7 FICLS Provisions.

[528] Wei (2010), p. 69; Kroymann (2009), pp. 250–251.

[529] National Bureau of Statistics of China (中华人民共和国国家统计局) (2019), Chapter 11–15.

[530] National Bureau of Statistics of China (中华人民共和国国家统计局) (2019), Chapter 11–15.

[531] Foreign Investment Department of the Ministry of Commerce (中华人民共和国商务部外国投资管理司) (2019). At the time of writing of this book, no statistic for the entire year 2019 has been published yet.

[532] Mahony (2015), p. 214.

applications for their establishment.[533] Consequently, only a very small number of incorporated FICLS have actually been listed on China's stock exchanges.[534] Given the high capital requirements, it is no surprise that the average amount of invested capital of FICLS amounted to 64.3 million USD in 2018.[535] For a more detailed analysis of FICLS, reference is made to relevant literature.[536]

References

Baker & McKenzie International (2017) Draft 2016 Foreign investment catalogue - China continues opening sectors to foreign investors. http://www.bakermckenzie.com/en/insight/publications/2017/01/draft-2016-foreign-investment-catalogue. Accessed 15 May 2020

Bath V (2007) The company law and foreign investment enterprises in the PRC – parallel systems of Chinese-foreign regulation. Univ New South Wales Law J 30:774–785

BBC (2015) China overtakes US for foreign direct investment. https://www.bbc.com/news/business-31052566. Accessed 15 May 2020

Brumfield NA, Gidley JM, Zhang ZA, Ying Y (2018) China merges antitrust enforcement agencies into one, as its anti-monopoly law approaches 10th anniversary. https://www.whitecase.com/publications/alert/china-merges-antitrust-enforcement-agencies-one-its-anti-monopoly-law-approaches. Accessed 15 May 2020

Chan BC, Roberts A, Yan A, Gu M (2017) China kicks off free trade zone momentum in second quarter of 2017. http://www.linklaters.com/Insights/AsiaNews/LinkstoChina/Pages/China-Kicks-Off-Free-Trade-Zone-Momentum-Second-Quarter-2017.aspx. Accessed 15 May 2020

Chan JK, Lange JE, Liu XG, Shortell JN, Yap B, Hermann H-G (2019) China issues market-entry negative list and publishes draft foreign investment law for public comment. https://www.paulweiss.com/practices/transactional/corporate/publications/china-issues-market-entry-negative-list-and-publishes-draft-foreign-investment-law-for-public-comment?id=28118. Accessed 15 May 2020

Chen J (2016) Chinese law: context and transformation, Revised and Expanded Edition. Brill, Leiden

China Central Government (2017) State Council Publishes Masterplans for the China (Liaoning), (Zhejiang), (Henan), (Hubei), (Chongqing), (Sichuan) and (Shaanxi) Pilot Free Trade Zones (press release) (国务院印发《中国(辽宁、浙江、河南、湖北、重庆、四川、陕西)自由贸易试验区总体方案》). http://www.gov.cn/xinwen/2017-03/31/content_5182442.htm. Accessed 15 May 2020

China Daily (2019) China to attract more foreign investment. http://www.chinadaily.com.cn/a/201904/16/WS5cb519a9a3104842260b6593.html. Accessed 15 May 2020

Clarke DC (2005–2006) How do we know when an enterprise exists? Unanswerable questions and legal polycentricity in China. Columb J Asian Law 19:50–71

Clifford Chance LLP (2019) China's new foreign investment law – what does this mean for foreign investors in China? https://www.cliffordchance.com/briefings/2019/03/china_s_new_foreigninvestmentlawwhatdoe.html. Accessed 15 May 2020

[533]Shen (2015), p. 41.

[534]Mahony (2015), p. 218.

[535]Calculation by the author, based on data from the National Bureau of Statistics of China (中华人民共和国国家统计局) (2019), Chapter 11–15.

[536]Shen (2015), pp. 39–43; Mahony (2015), pp. 214–219; Kroymann (2009), pp. 248–309.

Cohen JA, Lange JE (1997) The Chinese legal system: a primer for investors. N Y Law School J Int Comp Law 17:345–377

Esplugues Mota C (2010) China's accession to WTO. In: Bu Y (ed) Chinese business law. C. H. Beck/Hart/Nomos, Munich/Oxford, pp 1–13

European Union Chamber of Commerce in China (2016) European business in China – business confidence survey 2016. http://www.europeanchamber.com.cn/en/publications-business-confidence-survey. Accessed 15 May 2020

Faßbender S (2014) Ein Überblick über den Genehmigungsprozess für Unternehmensgründungen in China: Behörden, Verfahren, Hindernisse. Zeitschrift für Chinesisches Recht 21:344–351

Feuerstein M (2016) Die geplante Gesetzesnovilierung zum Recht der ausländischen Investitionen. In: Binding J, Pissler KB (eds) Chinesisches Zivil- und Wirtschaftsrecht Band 2 – Schwerpunkt Wirtschaftsrecht. R&W, Frankfurt a.M., pp 186–200

Foreign Investment Department of the Ministry of Commerce (中华人民共和国商务部外国投资管理司) (2019) Statistics about utilisation of foreign investment in China from Jan to Nov 2019 (2019年1-11月利用外资统计简表). http://www.fdi.gov.cn/1800000121_49_5014_0_7.html. Accessed 15 May 2020

Fu X (2019) China: new foreign investment law adopted. https://www.roedl.com/insights/china-law-investments-foreign-fil-equal-treatment. Accessed 15 May 2020

Harris HS Jr, Wang PJ, Zhang Y, Cohen MA, Evrard SJ (2011) Anti-monopoly law and practice in China. Oxford University Press, Oxford

Hezel C, Vinck I (2016) China opens up the regulatory framework for foreign direct investment. https://china.taylorwessing.com/en/china-opens-up-the-regulatory-framework-for-foreign-direct-investment. Accessed 15 May 2020

Hong S, Liu J (2020) China's State Council issues implementation regulations for Foreign Investment Law. https://www.nortonrosefulbright.com/en/knowledge/publications/cc526837/chinas-state-council-issues-implementation-regulations-for-foreign-investment. Accessed 15 May 2020

Hübner PA (2014) Rechtsschutz ausländischer Investoren vor chinesischen Gerichten. De Gruyter, Berlin

Jiang P (江平), Li G (李固光) (2005) The new company law training course (最新公司法培训教程). People's Court Publishing House (人民法院出版社), Beijing

Kirby WC (1995) China unincorporated: company law and business enterprise in twentieth-century China. J Asian Stud 54:43–63

Koppitz R, Meng C (2016) A new era - from approval to filing - China streamlines foreign direct investment process. https://china.taylorwessing.com/en/a-new-era-from-approval-to-filing-china-streamlines-foreign-direct-investment-process. Accessed 15 May 2020

Koppitz R, Wu S (2017) From July 28, 2017: opening the market? China's 2017 negative list for foreign investment. https://china.taylorwessing.com/en/updates-to-from-july-28-2017-opening-the-market-china-s-2017-negative-list-for-foreign-investment?from=timeline&isappinstalled=0. Accessed 15 May 2020

Koty AC (2018) Shanghai business registration: online platform for foreign invested enterprises launched. http://www.china-briefing.com/news/shanghai-business-registration-online-platform-foreign-invested-enterprises-launched. Accessed 15 May 2020

Kroymann B (2009) Das Kapitalgesellschaftsrecht der VR China – Analyse der Rahmenbedingungen für ausländische Investoren. Mohr Siebeck, Tübingen

Lin L (2017) Engineering a venture capital market: lessons from China. Columb J Asian Law 30:160–220

Lin E, Harris G (2017) China introduces new regulations to encourage foreign investment. http://www.elexica.com/en/legal-topics/mergers-and-acquisitions/08%2D%2Dchina-introduces-new-regulations-to-encourage-foreign-investment. Accessed 15 May 2020

Linklaters LLP (2016a) China advances foreign investment and negative list reform with seventh draft catalogue. http://www.linklaters.com/Insights/AsiaNews/LinkstoChina/

Pages/China-advances-foreign-investment-negative-list-reform-seventh-draft-catalogue.aspx. Accessed 15 May 2020

Linklaters LLP (2016b) Incremental reform under China's latest foreign investment rule changes. http://www.linklaters.com/Insights/AsiaNews/Pages/Incremental-reform-under-Chinas-latest-foreign-investment-rule-changes.aspx. Accessed 15 May 2020

Liu C (2008) Chinese company and securities law: investment vehicles, mergers and acquisitions and corporate finance in China. Kluwer Law, Alphen aan den Rijn

Lu M (吕美昂) (2011) A comparison of the nature of foreign-invested enterprises in China (我国外商投资企业性质的比较). Legal Syst Soc (法制与社会) 8:81–82

Lubman S (2006–2007) Looking for law in China. Columb J Asian Law 20:1–92

Luttermann C (2015) Rechtsreform für ausländische Investitionen in China. Auf dem Weg zum einheitlichen 'Foreign Investment Law'. Zeitschrift für Internationales Steuer- und Wirtschaftsrecht 2015:185–192

Mahony T (2015) Foreign investment law in China: regulation, practice and context. Tsinghua University Press, Beijing

Marsh N, Kadet J, Ye B, Wang G (2008) Partnerships in China: the new frontier. http://www2.deloitte.com/cn/en/pages/real-estate/articles/partnerships-in-china-new-frontier.htm. Accessed 15 May 2020

McGinty A, Jun W, Emch A, Robinson SN, Parsons M (2015) China to unify inbound foreign investment laws – but will it create a true level playing field with domestic investors? https://www.hoganlovells.com/en/publications/china-to-unify-inbound-foreign-investment-laws-but-will-it-create-a-true-level-playing-field-with-domestic-investors. Accessed 15 May 2020

McGinty A, Sun W, Wei J, Feng K, Xu L, Zhou L (2019a) The foreign investment law gets wings: draft implementation regulations released for public consultation. https://www.hoganlovells.com/en/publications/the-foreign-investment-law-gets-wings. Accessed 15 May 2020

McGinty A, Xu L, Li J (2019b) The foreign investment law: a new chapter opens for foreign direct investment in China. https://f.datasrvr.com/fr1/819/48729/Hogan_Lovells_New_FDL_opens_new_door.PD. Accessed 15 May 2020

McGinty A, Xu L, Wang S, Li J (2019c) New draft of the Foreign Investment Law takes a more 'stripped-down' approach, but defers discussion on the 'elephant in the room'. https://f.datasrvr.com/fr1/119/93499/New_draft_of_the_Foreign_Investment_Law_takes_a_more__strippeddown__approach.pdf. Accessed 15 May 2020

McGinty A, Sun W, Wei J, Feng K, Xu L, Zhou L (2020) The foreign investment law implementation regulations come into force: but why all the last minute changes? https://www.hoganlovells.com/en/publications/the-foreign-investment-law-implementation-regulations-come-into-force. Accessed 15 May 2020

Mei X (2014) Beware the pitfalls – the negative-list approach is not without its flaws and caution is advised. Beijing Rev July 2014:38–39

Nägeli E (2003) Alternative investment forms to joint ventures in China. Schulthess, Zürich

National Bureau of Statistics of China (中华人民共和国国家统计局) (2005) China Statistical Yearbook 2005 (中国统计年鉴2005). China Statistics Publishing House (中国统计出版社), Beijing, Chapter 18–14

National Bureau of Statistics of China (中华人民共和国国家统计局) (2019) China Statistical Yearbook 2019 (中国统计年鉴2019). China Statistics Publishing House (中国统计出版社), Beijing, Chapter 11–15

Pang P (2014) Forms of investment and business in China. In: Moser MJ, Yu F (eds) Doing business in China, vol 1. Juris Publishing, Huntington, p II-2.1

Pearson MM (1991) Joint ventures in the People's Republic of China – the control of foreign direct investment under socialism. Princeton University Press, Princeton

Ranft MF, Meng C (2016) A more structured World - the birth of FIE negative list. https://china.taylorwessing.com/en/a-more-structured-world-the-birth-of-fie-negative-list. Accessed 15 May 2020

Reuters (2018) China to set up Hainan free trade zone by 2020, port by 2025. https://www.reuters.com/article/us-china-economy-hainan/china-to-set-up-hainan-free-trade-zone-by-2020-port-by-2025-xinhua-idUSKBN1HL0RZ. Accessed 15 May 2020

Shen W (2015) Corporate law in China – structure, governance and regulation. Sweet&Maxwell, Hong Kong

Shu B (2012) How to invest in restricted or prohibited categories. In: Tring D, Mok S (eds) The legal guide to FDI in China. China Law & Practice, Hong Kong, pp 13–15

Spence JD (1990) The search for modern China. Norton, New York

State Council (2018) China will further cut red tape to spur foreign investment. http://english.gov.cn/premier/news/2018/05/16/content_281476149589926.htm?mc_cid=c5f6185f21&mc_eid=509661d30c. Accessed 15 May 2020

Stursberg C (2014) Der Dualismus des chinesischen Kapitalgesellschaftsrechts: Eine Untersuchung des Verhältnisses des Gesellschaftsrechts und der kapitalgesellschaftsrechtlichen Bestimmungen des Rechts der ausländisch investierten Unternehmen der VR China. LIT Verlag, Berlin

Tam B, Guo G (2017) China issues guidelines to attract foreign investment. https://m.mayerbrown.com/china-issues-guidelines-to-attract-foreign-investment-01-24-2017. Accessed 15 May 2020

Tam B, Qi F (2016) China plans to revise the foreign investment catalogue. https://m.mayerbrown.com/china-plans-to-revise-the-foreign-investment-catalogue-12-12-2016. Accessed 15 May 2020

Tang ZS, Xiao Y, Huo Z (2016) Conflict of laws in the People's Republic of China. Edward Elgar, Cheltenham

Teesdale JH (1932) A short analysis of the new Chinese company and partnership law. J Comp Legis Int Law 14:247–254

Ting A, Ge X (2014) The current state of play of foreign investment vehicles in China: is partnership a rising star? Bull Int Tax 68:669–677

United Nations Conference on Trade and Development (2020) Global Investment Trend Monitor No. 33. https://unctad.org/en/PublicationsLibrary/diaeiainf2020d1_en.pdf. Accessed 15 May 2020

US Chamber of Commerce (2012) China's approval process for inbound foreign direct investment: impact on market access, National Treatment and Transparency. https://www.uschamber.com/sites/default/files/documents/files/020021_China_InboundInvestment_Cvr.pdf. Accessed 15 May 2020

Wang G (2015) International investment law: a Chinese perspective. Routledge, Oxfordshire

Wang K, Yang M, Zhang D (2018) China's new state administration for market regulation: what to know and what to expect. https://www.ropesgray.com/en/newsroom/alerts/2018/04/Chinas-New-State-Market-Regulatory-Administration-What-to-Know-and-What-to-Expect. Accessed 15 May 2020

Wei W (2010) Foreign investment law. In: Bu Y (ed) Chinese business law. C. H. Beck/Hart/Nomos, Munich/Oxford, pp 55–79

Wong D (2019) China issues market-entry negative list and publishes draft foreign investment law for public comment. https://www.china-briefing.com/news/chinas-new-negative-list-targets-unified-market-access. Accessed 15 May 2020

World Bank Group (2010) Foreign direct investment – the China story. http://www.worldbank.org/en/news/feature/2010/07/16/foreign-direct-investment-china-story. Accessed 15 May 2020

Xinhua News Agency (2013) CPC: China to further open up its economy. http://english.cntv.cn/20131116/100735.shtml. Accessed 15 May 2020

Xu P, Yao L Feng C, Yao P, Zhu J (2020) Implementing regulation for foreign investment law heralding a new era of foreign investment regime in China. https://www.kwm.com/en/cn/knowledge/insights/implementing-regulation-for-foreign-investment-20200108. Accessed 15 May 2020

Yang S (2015) China's administrative mode for foreign investment: from positive list to negative list. Singapore Law Rev 33:93–127

Yang J (杨杰), Qu T (曲天明) (2010) A study on the application of foreign-invested partnership enterprise law – comment on the FIPE measures (外商合伙企业的法律适用问题研究—兼评《外国企业或者个人在中国境内设立合伙企业管理办法》). Sci Manag (科学与管理) 2010(3):63–66

Yu Y (2006) The experience of FDI recipients: the case of China. In: Urata S, Yue CS, Kimura F (eds) Multinationals and economic growth in East Asia – foreign direct investment, corporate strategies and national economic development. Routledge, New York, pp 423–451

Zhang Y (张宇轩) (2011) The relationship between foreign invested and non-foreign invested enterprises (外商投资与非外商投资企业法的关系). Academia Bimestrie (学海) 2011/2:213–216.

Zhang X (2016) Further disapplying differentiated treatment of foreign investment in China: is this the only way out for the Shanghai Free Trade Zone? Int Bus Law J 2016:53–71

Zhang C (2017) The distorted Governance model of venture capital limited partnerships in China: a political perspective. Bus Law Rev 38:234–240

Zhang Y, Du A (2014) Private equity funds in China. In: Moser MJ, Yu F (eds) Doing business in China, vol 1. Juris Publishing, Huntington, p II-5.1.2

Zhang ZA, Tsoi V (2019) China adopts new foreign investment law. https://www.whitecase.com/publications/alert/china-adopts-new-foreign-investment-law. Accessed 15 May 2020

Zhao X (赵旭东) (2005) Integrated or parallel – the legislative choice between foreign invested enterprise law and company law (融合还是并行—外商投资企业法与公司法的立法选择). J Law Appl (法律适用) 2005(3):15–18

Chapter 4
Partnership Enterprises as Sino-Foreign Alliances

4.1 History and Framework of Partnership Law in China

This section analyses the historical development and legal framework of both domestic and foreign-invested partnership enterprises in China. Certain legal aspects of the FIPE are also analysed, such as the partnership agreement, taxation of the FIPE, dispute resolution mechanisms, and the judiciary practice in China with regard to partnership enterprises. These aspects are important legal pillars for understanding the fundaments of the FIPE, and the analysis of them fits better in this part than in Part II.

4.1.1 Early Forms of Partnerships in China

4.1.1.1 Ancient Forms of Partnerships

The partnership enterprise is the form of business organisation with the longest history in human society.[1] In Europe, the evolution of partnership enterprises can be traced back to the Roman Empire (100 BC-400).[2] In China, the partnership has been the dominant form of business organisation throughout the country's long history.[3] The partnership was developed as a response to changing business needs in different eras, and played a crucial role in China's vibrant economy.[4] Earliest forms of

[1]Mao (茆荣华) and Zhao (赵超) (2007), p. 58; Jaeger (1961–1962), p. 138.

[2]Hansmann et al. (2005), p. 6; Kaser and Knütel (2014), pp. 267–270.

[3]For a detailed account of the history of partnership enterprise law in ancient China, see Lin (2013b), pp. 219, 221–237; Yuantao et al. (1989), pp. 43–46.

[4]Lin (2013b), p. 219.

S. Kuntner, *China's Foreign-Invested Limited Partnership Enterprise*, China-EU Law Series 7, https://doi.org/10.1007/978-3-030-54181-1_4

partnerships in China can be traced back as far as the Spring and Autumn Period (approximately 770-476 BC).[5] Partnerships in this era had only little in common with a modern partnership enterprise. Partnerships were not yet regulated by law. The term 'partnership' in ancient Chinese documents referred not to a distinct legal concept, but rather to a relationship or a general category of relationships that shared common characteristics.[6] They were temporary relationships or joint projects between two or more persons for an economic purpose or to achieve a similar objective, such as providing social, cultural, or political benefits for their family members.[7] During the Song Dynasty (960–1279), China's economy was the most prosperous and advanced in the medieval world.[8] This was partly due to the development of partnerships into more advanced business forms that were extensively used in various business areas like maritime trading, transportation, tea trading, and commercial lending.[9] However, the governance structure of these partnerships remained very basic, and they were not yet governed by any written partnership law.[10]

During the Ming Dynasty (1368–1644) and early Qing Dynasty (1644–1911), China continued to be the world's largest economy.[11] This period saw the establishment of many large, capital-intensive partnerships with dozens of partners.[12] Research conducted in a suburb of Beijing identified 137 written partnership contracts from the Ming and Qing Dynasties.[13] The Ming and Qing partnerships were more advanced than their Song ancestors in that formal, written partnership agreements were widely used, which already contained differentiated liability provisions, and specified in detail the transfer of shares and distribution of profits.[14] This period also saw the evolution of the first forms of limited partnership enterprises, in which one partner contributed capital while the other partners ran the business.[15] The partner who contributed capital acted as the 'silent' or 'dormant' partner, who did not participate in the operation of daily business.[16] However, for the most part, partnership law was still not codified.[17] 'Partnerships were mainly governed by customs, various business rules (e.g. guild rules, well rules and mining rules) and

[5]Yuantao et al. (1989), p. 43.
[6]Lin (2013b), p. 223.
[7]Ibid, p. 223.
[8]Ibid, p. 225.
[9]Ibid, p. 226.
[10]Ibid, p. 227.
[11]Ibid, p. 230.
[12]Ibid, p. 230.
[13]Yuantao et al. (1989), pp. 43–44.
[14]Lin (2013b), pp. 230–231.
[15]Yuantao et al. (1989), pp. 43–44.
[16]Ibid, pp. 43–44.
[17]Lin (2013b), p. 236.

partnership agreements.'[18] At that time, written Chinese law only addressed the regulation of private economic activity very little.[19] There was no separate civil or commercial code in ancient China, and—unlike in Europe—no merchant court existed in China.[20]

> To be sure, the limited scope of formal law did not mean that there were no systems for resolving disputes relating to commerce. 'Law' was not limited to [codified law]. Late-Qing China had a highly commercialised society, and dispute resolution by guild, lineage, or local notables, based on the detailed regulations of guilds and families as well as on longstanding custom, was commonplace.[21]

Hence, the absence of codified law and institutionalised conflict resolution may be explained by different ideologies, social and legal traditions, and levels of development of commodity markets in ancient China and Europe.[22]

4.1.1.2 Evolving Partnership Law at the Dawn of the Qing Dynasty

The first written partnership law was introduced in China with the promulgation of the 1904 Company Law (公司律).[23] The law consists of 131 Articles, and codifies the partnership enterprise and the limited partnership enterprise—besides the joint-stock company and the company limited by shares.[24] In 1907, a draft was prepared of the first Chinese Civil Law (大清明律草案) with 1569 Articles, adopting German, Japanese, and Swiss civil law codifications.[25] The draft law contained regulations for the individual partnership and the silent or dormant partnership in Chapter II, Sections 14 and 15.[26] Furthermore, a Draft Commercial Law (大清商律草案) with 334 Articles was promulgated in 1910.[27] Due to the collapse of the imperial Qing Dynasty in 1911, neither of the two draft laws ever came into effect in China.[28]

Following the foundation of the Republic of China in 1912, the Company Ordinance (公司条例) was promulgated in 1914.[29] Its 251 Articles contained regulations for the company limited by shares (股份有限公司), and also for the general partnership enterprise (无限公司), the commandite company (联合公司)—

[18]Ibid, p. 238.

[19]Kirby (1995), pp. 43–44.

[20]Lin (2013b), pp. 238–239; Kirby (1995), p. 44.

[21]Kirby (1995), p. 45.

[22]Lin (2013b), p. 248.

[23]Also the first Company Law in China, see Sect. 3.1.1.

[24]Jiang (江平) and Li (李固光) (2005), pp. 24–25; Kirby (1995), p. 48.

[25]Ye (2002), pp. 1–2.

[26]Ibid, p. 2.

[27]Jiang (江平) and Li (李固光) (2005), p. 25.

[28]Ibid, p. 25; Ye (2002), p. 2.

[29]Jiang (江平) and Li (李固光) (2005), p. 25.

a type of limited partnership–, and the partnership limited by shares (股份联合公司).[30] Borrowing more directly from German commercial law, the Company Ordinance was more detailed and comprehensive than its predecessor, and also more clear in its basic regulations, e.g., how companies were to be organised and dissolved.[31] The Nationalist Government, which gained power in 1927, continued the codification process that was initiated during the Qing Dynasty.[32] In 1929, a Civil Code (民法) as well as a Company Law (公司法) were promulgated.[33] The Civil Code was strongly influenced by Japanese, German, and Swiss civil laws, and reached the standard of a modern civil law codification.[34] The law regulated the individual partnership in Articles 667 to 699, and the silent or dormant partnership in Articles 700 to 709.[35] The Company Law was likewise a very modern codification that borrowed mainly from English company law. It was revised in 1946.[36] This law contained regulations for the limited liability company and the joint stock company, and also provisions on the general partnership, the limited partnership, and the partnership limited by shares.[37] Notwithstanding the influx of Western-type limited liability companies in the early twentieth century, partnerships did not disappear from China's business landscape.[38] On the contrary, 'according to survey statistics produced in 1933 by the Resources Committee of the Nationalist Government, out of 2400 factories in seventeen provinces, 994 (40.82%) were partnerships, 682 (28.21%) were companies, 561 (20.21%) were sole proprietorships, and 163 (8.12%) were government owned and administered.'[39] However, foreign invasions, internal rebellions, and civil wars caused Chinese business activities to experience piecemeal development, and made China receptive to Western legal enterprise forms.[40] These factors prevented Chinese partnerships from developing logically or naturally out of traditional Chinese concepts and ancient Chinese law.[41] Opinions therefore differ about the role that ancient forms of partnerships played in the development of modern Chinese partnership law. On the one hand, an argument is made that today's partnership enterprises do not succeed the legal tradition and legacy of their Chinese ancestors.[42] On the other hand, the period of the Republic of

[30]Ibid, p. 25; Lin (2013b), p. 239.

[31]Kirby (1995), p. 49.

[32]Ibid, p. 51.

[33]Ye (2002), p. 3; Lin (2013b), p. 239.

[34]Ye (2002), pp. 2–3.

[35]These provisions regarding partnerships are still valid in Taiwan today (Ye 2002, p. 3).

[36]Teesdale (1932), p. 248; regarding the 1946 Company Law, see Sect. 3.1.1.

[37]Ye (2002), p. 3; Teesdale (1932), p. 249.

[38]Lin (2013b), pp. 219–220.

[39]Yuantao et al. (1989), p. 46.

[40]Lin (2013b), pp. 220–221.

[41]Ibid, p. 220.

[42]Ibid, p. 220 fn. 10, 240.

China is credited with being a significant influence on the development of China's partnership law scholarship.[43]

4.1.1.3 Partnerships After the Foundation of the PRC

Following the foundation of the PRC in 1949, all laws that had been enacted by the Nationalist Government, were repealed.[44] The PRC Government inherited 1.3 million private industrial and commercial businesses, of which 99% were individual businesses and partnerships, and only 1% were registered companies.[45] The government had to address this legislative vacuum. The 'Interim Provisions on Private Enterprises' were enacted in 1950.[46] These provisions recognised three types of organisational forms for private enterprises: sole proprietorship, company and general partnership.[47] One year later, the 'Implementing Measures for Interim Regulations on Private Enterprises'[48] were promulgated. This contained more detailed regulations for the establishment, registration, governance, and liability of the general partnership.[49] In 1954, the policy of socialist transition of privately owned enterprises was initiated with the promulgation of the 'Interim Provisions on the Merger of State-Owned and Private-Owned Industrial Enterprises'.[50] The government required almost all privately owned companies to either merge with state-owned enterprises or to close down their business by 1956.[51] At that time, according to a 1956 survey by the State Statistical Commission, 53.8% of enterprises that were managed by private shareholders were partnerships, 38% were sole proprietorships, and only 8.2% were limited liability companies.[52] The Interim Provisions on Private Enterprises and their implementing measures were no longer valid.[53] Partnership enterprises, together with other business vehicles, were abandoned because they were considered 'for profit' vehicles, deemed expressions of capitalism.[54] Instead,

---

[43] Ye (2002), p. 3.

[44] Lin (2013b), p. 220 fn. 10; Ye (2002), p. 3.

[45] Kirby (1995), p. 56.

[46] Interim Provisions on Private Enterprises (私营企业暂行条例), promulgated by the Administrative Council on 30 December 1950 and repealed on 25 July 1986.

[47] Art. 3 Interim Provisions on Private Enterprises.

[48] Measures for Implementing the Interim Regulations on Private Enterprises (私营企业暂行条例施行办法), promulgated by the Finance and Economic Commission of the Administrative Council on 30 March 1951 and repealed on 25 July 1986.

[49] Arts. 31–39 Implementing Measures for Interim Regulations on Private Enterprises.

[50] Interim Provisions on the Merger of State-Owned and Private-Owned Industrial Enterprises (公私合营工业企业暂行条例), promulgated by the Administrative Council on 5 September 1954 and and repealed on 25 July 1986.

[51] Chen (2014a), p. 21; Ye (2002), p. 4.

[52] Yuantao et al. (1989), p. 47.

[53] Ye (2002), p. 4; Kirby (1995), p. 56.

[54] Lin (2013b), p. 220 fn. 10; Ye (2002), p. 5.

socialist state economy and state run organisations became the dominant forms for almost all economic-social activities.[55] Enterprises were no longer categorised by form of investment and method of liability, but instead by form of ownership (state-owned or collectively-owned) and by trade classification (e.g., industrial, trading, foreign trading, or transportation).[56] Codifications for enterprises were all drafted in accordance with these classifications.[57] No new laws or regulations with regard to partnership enterprises were promulgated during this entire period.[58]

4.1.2 'Opening Up' of China and Reintroduction of Partnerships

The 1978 policy of 'Reform and Opening up' initiated a gradual expansion of economic reform that lead to the re-introduction of partnerships as enterprise forms in urban and rural China.[59]

> Although the resurgence of partnership began in the early 1980s, in most cases people still avoided using the term 'partnership' because the word had been connected with the private ownership economy. People instead tried to invent terms with socialist characteristics, such as 'cooperative operation organisation' [合作经营组织], 'new economic association' [新经济联合体], 'commune members' joint enterprise' [社员联营企业], and 'joint household business' [联户企业].[60]

Each of these terms for partnership-type entities was connected to a certain economic regulation.[61] Wording and terms used in later partnership legislation often refer to these early economic policies and regulations.[62]

The first codification of partnerships in a national law followed in 1986 with the promulgation of the GPCL.[63] The law introduced two[64] kinds of partnership entities:

---

[55]Chen (2014a), p. 21.

[56]Chen (2016), p. 650; Ye (2002), p. 5.

[57]Ye (2002), p. 5.

[58]Ibid, p. 5.

[59]Ibid, p. 5; Yuantao et al. (1989), p. 47.

[60]Yuantao et al. (1989), p. 47.

[61]Ibid, pp. 47–48.

[62]Ibid, p. 48.

[63]See Sect. 3.1.3 fn. 40.

[64]The Individual Industrial and Commercial Household (个体工商户) and Rural Contracting Household (农村承包经营户), regulated in Articles 26–29 GPCL/ 54–56 GRCL, also resemble characteristics of a partnership, when run by an entire family. However, Chinese scholars point out that these two households are regulated under the section for Citizen (Natural Person), and categorise them as 'special subjects of civil law' (Chen (2016), pp. 633–634, 654; Epstein and Shen (2009), p. I-6.1.34). Even scholars who consider them as partnerships under certain circumstances, recognise that they only meet the partnership criteria in very few cases (Yuantao et al. 1989, p. 52). Therefore, both households are not further analysed in this book.

(1) the Individual Partnership (个人合伙);[65] and (2) the Joint Operation (联营).[66] The creation of these two different types is directly related to the socialist model of categorising enterprises by form of ownership and trade.[67] The Individual Partnership is the most basic model for a partnership, consisting of two or more natural persons[68] associated in a business and working together, with each providing funds, material objects, and techniques according to an agreement.[69] The Joint Operation refers to an economic association between enterprises or between an enterprise and an institution (e.g., social organisations, such as hospitals, schools, or research institutions).[70] However, a Joint Operation could not be formed by private businesses or individuals, but only by state-owned or collectively owned enterprises or institutions.[71] Many of the partnership type entities formed during the early reform-era were absorbed or channeled into the concept of the Joint Operation.[72] A Joint Operation can be established as a company type legal person,[73] a bilateral contractual arrangement,[74] or—relevant for this book—a partnership type entity.[75]

In practice, a natural person and a legal person were already able to form a partnership together, although this type of partnership was not formally permitted under the GPCL.[76] This reflects the inconsistency of various government agencies at that time when having to address the question of whether or not to acknowledge the existence of a particular business entity.[77] 1988 was a turning point for the recognition of private economy in China with the implementation of two legislative milestones. The Constitution[78] was amended with a new paragraph that 'permits the private sector of the economy to exist and develop within the limits prescribed by law'.[79] Previously, under the 1982 Constitution, the protection of foreign investment had been stipulated, but the basis of the socialist economic system had still been seen to be socialist public ownership, which included ownership by the people as a whole

[65] Arts. 30–35 GPCL.

[66] Arts. 51–53 GPCL.

[67] Ye (2002), p. 6.

[68] The GPCL actually use the term citizen (公民) instead of natural person. However, since the usage of the term citizen has primarily historical and ideological reasons (Chen 2016, pp. 471–475), and the new General Rules of Civil Law (see Sect. 4.2.1.1 fn. 600) replace the term citizen with the term natural person, the term natural person will be utilised in this book.

[69] Art. 30 GPCL. For a more detailed analysis, see Sect. 4.2.1.2.

[70] Art. 52 GPCL. For a more detailed analysis, see Sect. 4.2.1.3.

[71] Epstein and Shen (2009), p. I-6.1.31; Yuantao et al. (1989), p. 54; Zheng (1986), p. 681.

[72] Howson (2015), p. 394.

[73] Art. 51 GPCL.

[74] Art. 53 GPCL.

[75] Art. 52 GPCL; Yuantao et al. (1989), p. 57.

[76] Yuantao et al. (1989), p. 63.

[77] Clarke (2005–2006), p. 64.

[78] See Sect. 3.1.3 fn. 38.

[79] Art. 11 Para. 2 Constitution in the version of 1988.

and collective ownership by the working people.[80] The only other form of business allowed by the Constitution at that time was 'individual economy' (个体经济), referring primarily to self-employment, including small-scale, privately-owned industrial, commercial, catering, transport and service businesses, operated mainly by individuals or households with a strictly limited number of employees.[81] The newly added term 'private economy' (私营经济) in the 1988 amendment refers to the economy in the form of private enterprises as 'defined by law'.[82] Such a definition was provided with the promulgation of the 'Interim Regulations on Private Enterprises',[83] which was later supplemented by the 'Implementing Measures for Interim Regulations on Private Enterprises'.[84] A 'private enterprise' is defined as 'a privately funded economic entity which employs at least eight persons'.[85] The threshold of eight employees was adopted to distinguish private enterprises from small businesses and households of the individual economy.[86] Three types of private enterprises are recognised: (1) sole proprietorship enterprises; (2) partnership enterprises; (3) limited liability companies.[87] A partnership enterprise is defined as an enterprise that is jointly funded and managed by two or more persons who assume joint and several liability for the obligations of the enterprise.[88] Notably, the partnership is recognised as an enterprise (企业) in this definition, while not having been granted enterprise status under the GPCL. The reason is that the GPCL were promulgated before the private economy was legally recognised with the amendment of the Constitution in 1988.[89] The GPCL therefore could not contain any provisions on private enterprises.[90] Further deviating from the Individual Partnership under the GPCL, the Interim Regulations on Private Enterprises no longer required that the partners to a partnership must be natural persons.[91] The amended Constitution[92] and the Interim Regulations on Private Enterprises therefore legalised the new category of business entity—private enterprise—that had already existed for

[80]Chen (2016), pp. 629–630.

[81]Hershkovitz (1985), p. 427.

[82]Chen (2016), p. 630.

[83]See Sect. 3.1.3 fn. 41.

[84]Implementing Measures for PRC Interim Regulations on Private Enterprises (中华人民共和国私营企业暂行条例施行办法), promulgated by the State Administration of Industry and Commerce on 16 January 1989; amended on 17 December 1996 and amended on 3 December 1998.

[85]Art. 2 Interim Regulations on Private Enterprises.

[86]For more details, see Chen (2016), pp. 635–637; Heuser (2002), pp. 384–386.

[87]Art. 6 Interim Regulations on Private Enterprises.

[88]Art. 8 Interim Regulations on Private Enterprises.

[89]Chen (2016), p. 636; Ye (2002), p. 6.

[90]Ibid, p. 6.

[91]Heuser (2002), pp. 388–389.

[92]The further amendment of the Constitution in 1999 no longer considered the individual and private economies as a complement to the socialist public economy, but rather defined it as 'an important component of the country's socialist market economy'. (Art. 11 1999 Constitution). The latest revision of the Constitution of 2004 recognises the ongoing development of the private sector in different new business forms and structures by adding the phrase 'other non-public economy' in

many years outside the law.[93] *Clarke* has pointed out that this approach is typical of the Chinese legal system.[94] The primary purpose of legal rules in China is to regulate activities and organisations that already exist in practice, rather than initiating new developments or creating new enterprise organisations.[95] With a view to further supporting the development of domestic partnership enterprises, the State Council and SAIC issued a number of regulations governing partnership enterprises in the late 1980s and early 1990s.[96]

For foreign investors, partnership enterprises were made available only in the 1990s. The CJV Implementing Regulations[97] laid the groundwork for the Non-Legal Person CJV in 1995, which resembles a general partnership enterprise and has been discussed in detail above.[98] Already in 1990, the 'WFOE Implementing Regulations'[99] were promulgated to supplement the WFOE Law. The regulations stipulated in Article 18 that a WFOE may also be established in a form other than a limited liability company. Commentators consider this to be a reference to the provisions on sole proprietorships and partnership enterprises.[100] However, this theoretical option is not utilised in practice.[101] The partnership-type WFOE will therefore not be further analysed in this book. Nevertheless, these two regulations can be credited with laying the groundwork for foreign-invested partnership enterprises in China.[102] With the Foreign-Invested Venture Capital Enterprise, another partnership-type enterprise was added, since its unincorporated form resembles a limited partnership, as analysed above.[103]

The above outline of the development of partnership law shows that laws and regulations already had a practical significance during the time of economic awakening of China, but it also illustrates the fact that the legal framework for partnership enterprises during this era lacked both systematisation and coherence.[104]

addition to the individual and private economies (Art. 11 of the 2004 Constitution). Shen (2015), p. 27; Chen (2016), p. 630.

[93]Chen (2016), p. 630.

[94]Clarke (2005–2006), p. 66.

[95]Ibid, p. 66.

[96]Ye (2002), p. 7.

[97]See Sect. 3.1.3 fn. 49.

[98]See Sect. 3.2.2.2.

[99]PRC Wholly Foreign-Owned Enterprise Law Detailed Implementing Regulations (中华人民共和国外资企业法实施细则), approved by the State Council on 28 October 1990 and promulgated by the Ministry of Foreign Economic Relations and Trade on 12 December 1990; amended on 12 April 2001, amended on 19 February 2014 and repealed on 01 January 2020.

[100]Yang (杨杰) and Qu (曲天明) (2010), p. 65; Ye (2002), pp. 6–7, with further references.

[101]Glatter (2016), p. 135.

[102]Ye (2002), p. 7.

[103]See Sect. 3.2.3.2.

[104]Ye (2002), p. 7.

4.1.3 The First Partnership Enterprise Law in 1997

4.1.3.1 Legislative History

In 1992, the 14th National Congress of the CPC established the new policy of a socialist market economy in China.[105] Among the instruments employed to implement the new policy was the drafting of new laws to govern enterprises. Therefore, the drafting of a Company Law and Partnership Law were placed on the agenda of the NPC's legislative plan.[106] These new laws were no longer to follow the ideological method of classification by forms of ownership and trade, marking a turning point and a shift towards a modern corporate law system categorised by form of investment and method of liability.[107] The first Company Law[108] of the PRC was accordingly promulgated in 1993. The Company Law regulated the limited liability company and the company limited by shares, but did not contain any provisions governing partnership enterprises.

About four months after the Company Law, the 'Shenzhen Partnership Regulations'[109] were promulgated. Even though their scope of application was geographically limited to partnerships established in the Shenzhen Special Economic Zone, these regulations have attracted much attention, being the first legislation specific to partnership enterprises in modern China.[110] Most Chinese scholars took the position that the GPCL did not prohibit provinces from enacting local partnership regulations.[111] The Shenzhen Partnership Regulations consist of 73 Articles, and is divided in four chapters. The regulations provided for the establishment of a general partnership,[112] with partners bearing unlimited joint and several liability, and limited partnership,[113] with the general partner bearing unlimited liability, while limited partners were not liable beyond their respective investments.[114] The provisions on general partnerships equally applied to limited partnerships except where they would conflict with provisions specific to limited partnerships.[115] The general partnership was to be established by two partners at a minimum, who had to be natural persons or

---

[105]Ibid, p. 7.

[106]Huang (黄毅诚) (1997), pp. 12–13.

[107]Chen (2016), p. 628; Ye (2002), p. 8; Heuser (2002), pp. 385–386.

[108]See Sect. 3.1.3 fn. 43.

[109]Regulations of the Shenzhen Special Economic Zone on Partnerships (深圳经济特区合伙条例), promulgated by the Standing Committee of the Shenzhen Municipal People's Congress on 20 April 1994 and effective as of 1 May 1994; repealed on 27 April 2012.

[110]For a detailed analysis, see Heuser (2002), pp. 389–292 and Martinek (2018), pp. 200–201.

[111]Wu and Geu (2007–2008), pp. 138–139.

[112]Chap 2, Arts. 9–52 Shenzhen Partnership Regulations.

[113]Chap 3, Arts. 53–69 Shenzhen Partnership Regulations.

[114]Art. 2 Shenzhen Partnership Regulations.

[115]Art. 53 Shenzhen Partnership Regulations.

non-legal person economic organisations.[116] A limited partnership could be established by at least two but no more than twenty partners.[117] The general partner had to be a natural person or non-legal person business organisation, while limited partners could be any legal person.[118] Thus, the Shenzhen Partnership Regulations adopted a rather modern approach to partnership legislation, and have generally been considered a pragmatic addition to the national regulations for partnerships at that time.[119]

On a national level, the Economic and Financial Commission of the NPC established a group to draft the first partnership law in May 1994, which presented a first draft in early 1995.[120] Notably, at that time, 120,000 partnership enterprises already existed in China.[121] It was clear that 'the sketchy provisions in the GPCL were not adequate for dealing with partnerships as an emerging and rapidly developing enterprise form'.[122] The draft law underwent a process of extensive consultation for 3 years before it was formally submitted to the SCNPC in October 1996.[123] The draft further underwent substantial revision by the Law Commission of the NPC and the SCNPC in the following months, until the first 'Partnership Enterprise Law'[124] (1997 PEL) was finally adopted in February 1997.[125] The law was supplemented with the '1997 Partnership Enterprise Registration Measures' in the same year,[126] the latter of which specified when a partnership would be qualified to lawfully operate, and standardise its registration process.[127]

4.1.3.2 Scope of Application

The 1997 PEL consisted of 9 Chapters and 78 Articles. Similar to provisions on limited liability companies and companies limited by shares in the Company Law,

[116]Art. 10 Shenzhen Partnership Regulations.

[117]Art. 54 Shenzhen Partnership Regulations.

[118]Art. 57 Shenzhen Partnership Regulations.

[119]Ye (2002), p. 9.

[120]Huang (黄毅诚) (1997), p. 12.; Ye (2002), p. 9.

[121]Huang (黄毅诚) (1997), p. 12.

[122]Chen (2016), p. 654.

[123]ibid, p. 655.

[124]PRC Partnership Enterprise Law (中华人民共和国合伙企业法), adopted at the 24th Session of the Standing Committee of the 8th National People's Congress on 23 February 1997 and effective from 1 August 1997.

[125]Li (厉以宁) (1997), pp. 17–20; Xue (薛驹) (1997), pp. 21–22.

[126]PRC Administrative Measures for Partnership Enterprise Registration (中华人民共和国合伙企业登记管理办法), promulgated by the State Council on 19 November 1997 and effective as of the same date.

[127]Art. 1 1997 Partnership Enterprise Registration Measures.

the Chapters of the 1997 PEL regulated the lifecycle of a partnership enterprise from its establishment to the relationship with third parties and its dissolution.[128]

Deviating from the GPCL, partnerships were granted the status of an 'enterprise' (企业) in the PEL. However, Chinese law does not provide a clear definition of what constitutes an enterprise.[129] The prevailing perception in literature is that an enterprise is a profit-making organisation that produces and/or trades goods and/or services, acts independently, and has been established legally.[130] The PEL took a pragmatic stance and recognised as an enterprise anything that can be legally registered as enterprise.[131] Certainly, this definition is merely circular.[132] Therefore, in academia and legal practice, the term 'enterprise' is commonly used as a general term to refer to any type of business organisation.[133] The term 'company', however, has a much more narrow meaning. Commonly, 'company' is understood as a generic term covering, *inter alia*, corporations and partnerships.[134] In the context of Chinese law, the scope is even more restricted as the term company (公司) is defined in Article 2 Company Law as exclusively referring to limited liability companies and joint stock companies.[135]

In the 1997 PEL, a 'partnership enterprise' was defined as a profit-making organisation, established by partners who conclude a partnership agreement, make joint capital contributions, conduct business jointly, share incomes and risks, and bear unlimited joint and several liability for the debts of the partnership enterprise.[136] Unlike the Shenzhen Partnership Regulations, the 1997 PEL only allowed the formation of a General Partnership Enterprise (GPE).[137] While an early draft of the law also provided for the establishment of limited partnerships, those provisions were not included in the promulgated law.[138] The 1997 PEL exclusively applied to partnership enterprises that were established for the purposes of making profit.[139] Notably, the objective of profit-making can be traced back to as early as ancient Chinese partnership law.[140] Nowadays, the purpose of making profit is the differentiating characteristic between the individual partnership in the GPCL and the

[128]Epstein and Shen (2009), p. I-6.1.38.

[129]Münzel (2006a), p. 405.

[130]Instructive with a comparative law approach, see: Gan (干勾) (2003).

[131]This can be concluded from Article 107 of the 2006 version of the PEL, which stipulates that the regulations on the SGPE are also applicable for organisations from service sectors that do not allow registration as enterprise (e.g. law firms). See also Wang (王翔) (2006), item 4.

[132]Münzel (2006a), pp. 405–406.

[133]Bu (2017b), p. 191.

[134]Garner (2009), p. 318.

[135]Du (2014), p. 335; Werthwein (2010), p. 17; Bu (2017b), p. 191.

[136]Art. 2 Partnership Law 1997.

[137]Arts. 2 and 3 1997 PEL.

[138]Ye (2002), p. 10.

[139]Art. 2 1997 PEL.

[140]Yuantao et al. (1989), p. 44.

commercial general partnership enterprise in the 1997 PEL. This attribute is favoured by Chinese scholars because it allows a clear differentiation between the two forms of partnerships.[141] German scholars have instead noted that the criteria of profit-making may widen the scope of application for commercial partnerships beyond the intention of the lawmaker, e.g., when a married couple is selling their jointly-owned house as a one-off occurrence.[142] According to the German HGB, a commercial partnership exists where the activities of a partnership require 'a commercially organised business operation'.[143] This criterion has been criticised by Chinese scholars as too vague to provide clear and reliable guidance in practice.[144]

A very controversial point in the law-making process was whether only natural persons or also legal persons could become a partner in a partnership enterprise.[145] The 1997 PEL required that a partner must be 'a person who has the full capacity to perform civil acts'.[146] The term 'person' was not explicitly defined in the 1997 PEL, but the content of this provision in conjunction with the GPCL provides more clarity.[147] A differentiation between limited, full, and no capacity to perform civil acts was only provided for natural persons,[148] while legal persons were always given full capacity to perform civil acts.[149] In addition, the term 'legal person' was not mentioned at all in the 1997 PEL. Hence, the 1997 PEL provided only for individual partnerships, allowing only natural persons, no corporate legal persons, to act as partners in the GPEs.[150]

The question of whether a foreign investor could become a partner was not clearly answered in the 1997 PEL. *Ye*[151] argues that a foreign natural person could not become a partner because the required 'full capacity to perform civil acts' was only granted to Chinese citizens.[152] This argument overlooks the stipulation in the GPCL that 'citizen' should apply to foreigners as well as Chinese nationals, except as otherwise provided for by law.[153] The 1997 PEL and its registration measures were silent with regard to foreign partners. This implies that a foreign individual could indeed establish a partnership enterprise. However, under Chinese law, the fact that a

[141] Julius and Bitter (2005), p. 62.

[142] ibid, pp. 62–63.

[143] Art. 1 Para. 2 HGB.

[144] Julius and Bitter (2005), p. 62.

[145] For a detailed discussion, see Sect. 8.2.2.1.

[146] Art. 9 1997 PEL.

[147] Ye (2002), p. 25.

[148] Arts. 11–13 GPCL/ Arts. 18–22 GRCL.

[149] Art. 36 GPCL/ Art. 57 GRCL.

[150] Wang (王翔) (2006), item 1.

[151] Ye (2002), pp. 25–26.

[152] Article 9 GPCL, using the term citizen (公民). For a discussion on why the term citizen is used in Chinese law instead of natural person, see also Chen (2016), pp. 470–477.

[153] Art. 8 Para. 2 GPCL. Notably, Article 12 GRCL no longer differentiates between foreigners and Chinese nationals.

law does not prohibit a certain act does not mean that said act is automatically permitted, and, as the later development of partnership law has proven, the participation of foreign investors in partnerships required the enactment of special administrative regulations. Accordingly, other scholars have concluded that the 1997 PEL was not applicable to foreign individuals.[154] In addition, the very narrow scope of potential partners would have made the GPE a rather unattractive investment vehicle under the 1997 PEL. Foreign corporations were excluded from becoming a partner for the same reasons as domestic corporations.[155] Accordingly, a foreign natural person would eventually have had to bear unlimited liability for the debts of the GPE.

4.1.3.3 Relationship to Other Laws and Regulations

The 1997 PEL was transplanted into a scattered legal framework for partnerships. This requires an analysis of the relationships between the different laws and regulations that were applicable at that time.

4.1.3.3.1 General Principles of Civil Law

The GPCL are the most important codification of civil law regulations in China, and are often referred to as its 'civil law constitution'.[156] The provisions of the 1997 PEL therefore had to conform to the GPCL.[157] Regarding partnership enterprises, however, the 1997 PEL was *lex specialis* to the GPCL.[158] With its comprehensive legal framework for partnership enterprises, this special statute left no gaps that could be filled by the rather sketchy provisions on partnerships in the GPCL.[159] However, the provisions of the GPCL certainly also apply to partnership enterprises with respect to general issues of civil law, e.g. competence of a natural person to perform civil acts; conclusion and validity of the partnership agreement.[160]

---

[154] Chen (2016), p. 654; Liu (2014), p. 183.

[155] Ye (2002), p. 26.

[156] Ibid, p. 12.

[157] Ibid, p. 12.

[158] Ibid, p. 12.

[159] Werthwein (2010), p. 45. Regarding the abolishment of the provisions on the Individual Partnership in the new General Rules of Civil Law, see discussion in Sect. 4.2.1.1.

[160] Ye (2002), p. 12.

4.1.3.3.2 Interim Regulations on Private Enterprises

The 1988 Interim Regulations on Private Enterprises and their implementing regulations were important developments in laying the groundwork for the recognition of private enterprises in China. The 1997 PEL fully integrated the provisions about partnership enterprises from the Interim Regulations on Private Enterprises, thus adopting their regulatory content and replacing them in governing the establishment of partnership enterprises.[161]

4.1.3.3.3 Shenzhen Partnership Regulations

The scope of application of the Shenzhen Partnership Regulations was geographically limited to partnerships established in the Shenzhen Special Economic Zone, and the 1997 PEL remained applicable to partnership enterprises as a background law. In cases where the two regulations have conflicted, the Shenzhen Partnership Regulations have prevailed.[162] Following their revocation on 27 April 2012, the Shenzhen Partnership Regulations were no longer applicable.

4.1.3.3.4 CJV Implementing Regulations

With regard to a partnership-type Non-Legal Person CJV, commentators have stated that the principle of *lex specialis derogate legi generali* should be applied, with the PEL serving as the *lex generalis* to the respective CJV Law and CJV Implementing Regulations.[163] This would mean that the CJV Implementing Regulations would only be applied to issues that are not regulated by the PEL. However, it is doubtful that the CJV Implementing Regulations do, in practice, prevail only in cases of conflicting regulations.[164] The CJV Implementing Regulations have been promulgated under a foreign investment regime that is characterised by the largely separate legal treatment of foreign investment vehicles and domestic enterprises. Against this background, the Non-Legal Person CJV would in fact not be affected by the provisions of the 1997 PEL.[165]

---

[161] Ibid, p. 13; Heuser (2002), p. 389.

[162] Art. 2 Regulations on Special Economic Zones in Guangdong Province (广东省经济特区条例), promulgated by the Standing Committee of the Guangdong Province People's Congress on 15 April 1980, approved at the 15th Session of the Standing Committee of the 5th National People's Congress on 26 August 1980, and effective as of the same date.

[163] Xiao (晓富) (1997), p. 108.

[164] Ye (2002), p. 13.

[165] See also Sect. 4.1.5.4, with a clarifying statement that was issued by SAIC in the similar discussion with regard to the FIPE.

4.1.3.4 Perception of the First Partnership Enterprise Law

The promulgation of the 1997 PEL was credited as an important effort to rationalise the fragmented and rudimentary Chinese enterprise law.[166] The law was recognised for playing a positive role in constituting a new legal form of enterprise structure, standardising its establishment and operation, and protecting the lawful rights and interests of the partnership and its partners.[167] However, the 1997 PEL was also criticised by commentators for being not business-friendly.[168] Significant defects were seen in the very narrow scope of application of the law, the lack of provisions on limited partnerships, tax liabilities, foreign partners in partnerships, and bankruptcy of partnership enterprises.[169] Commentators pointed out that the 1997 PEL was not able to properly address the practical problems and new challenges resulting from the rapid development of the socialist market economic system.[170] The law restricted the usage of the partnership enterprise mainly to smaller private enterprises, but did not recognise the potential that the partnership enterprise would offer for large corporations in cooperating with small and medium-sized enterprises.[171] The primarily mandatory or immutable provisions of the 1997 PEL left little room for what is generally considered the essence of the partnership form—contractual self-ordering, or contracting out of statutory default rules, via the partnership agreement.[172] In summary, the 1997 PEL was a very specialised enterprise organisation law with its scope of application limited to general partnerships established by individuals with a view to making profits.[173] All these factors resulted in rather low numbers of newly established partnership enterprises, 'as of early 2006 only some 60,000 partnerships had been formed since the law came into effect in August 1997',[174] amounting to only 127,804 partnership enterprises in total nationwide.[175]

> The need for private investment, the increasing importance of encouraging venture capital investment in the push for high tech development, and the rapid expansion of professional services (e.g. accountancy, law firms etc.) further highlightened the defects of the 1997 [PEL] in practice and demanded an urgent revision of the law.[176]

---

166 Chen (2016), p. 653.

167 Cao (曹德斌) and Zhang (张小奕) (2017), foreword p. 1; Yan (严义埙) (2006), p. 595.

168 Clarke (2007), p. 573.

169 Yang (杨杰) and Qu (曲天明) (2010), p. 63; Chen (2016), p. 654; Epstein and Shen (2009), p. I-6.1.38-39; McKenzie and Mendel (2007), p. 32.

170 Yan (严义埙) (2006), pp. 595–596; Wang (王翔) (2006), first paragraph.

171 Yan (严义埙) (2006), pp. 595–596.

172 Howson (2015), p. 395.

173 Ye (2002), p. 11.

174 Clarke (2007), p. 573.

175 Howson (2015), p. 396.

176 Chen (2016), pp. 654–655.

4.1.4 The 2006 Revision of the Partnership Enterprise Law

In response to its obvious shortcomings and the market's lack of enthusiasm towards the partnership enterprise, the PEL was substantially revised in August 2006.[177]

4.1.4.1 Legislative History

The revision of the 1997 PEL was officially initiated with its inclusion in the legislative plan of the Standing Committee of the 10th NPC.[178] In February 2004, the Financial and Economic Committee of the NPC was entrusted with composing a first draft of a revised partnership enterprise law together with the relevant departments of the State Council.[179] Based on this draft, further opinions from other ministries, departments, enterprises, institutions, scholars and foreign experts were solicited.[180] The process took more than 2 years. The Financial and Economic Committee submitted a consolidated draft of the new partnership enterprise law to the SCNPC in April 2006.[181] Deliberation on the draft in the SCNPC was performed in three sessions in April, June, and August 2006.[182] During all sessions, deliberations on the draft law were overwhelmingly positive, with critical remarks being limited to the timing of the revision and technical details of the draft's provisions.[183] On 27 August 2006, the revised 'PRC Partnership Enterprise Law'[184] (PEL) was adopted by the SCNPC, and took effect on 1 June 2007.

Shortly after, the revised PEL was complemented by a revision of the 'Partnership Enterprise Registration Measures'.[185] Already in May 2007, SAIC issued the 'Partnership Enterprise Administrative Circular'[186] to ensure a unified implementation of the revised partnership provisions. Various other laws and regulations further contributed to the legal framework that now governs partnership enterprises in

[177] Clarke (2007), p. 573.

[178] Yan (严义埙) (2006), p. 595.

[179] Ibid, p. 595.

[180] Ibid, p. 595.

[181] Cao (曹德斌) and Zhang (张小奕) (2017), foreword p. 1.

[182] Hong (洪虎) (2006b), p. 602.

[183] Chen (2016), p. 655 fn. 114.

[184] PRC Partnership Enterprise Law (中华人民共和国合伙企业法), adopted at the 24th Session of the Standing Committee of the 8th National People's Congress on 23 February 1997; amended at the 23rd Session of the Standing Committee of the 10th National People's Congress on 27 August 2006 and effective from 1 June 2007.

[185] PRC Administrative Measures for Partnership Enterprise Registration (中华人民共和国合伙企业登记管理办法), promulgated by the State Council on 19 November 1997, amended on 9 May 2007, amended on 19 February 2014 and amended on 2 March 2019.

[186] Circular on Proper Registration of Partnership Enterprise (做好合伙企业登记管理工作的通知), promulgated by the State Administration for Industry and Commerce on 29 May 2007 and effective as of the same date.

China.[187] Regarding potential conflicts between the PEL and other laws and regulations, the above analysis of the 1997 PEL applies.[188]

In China, it is common practice to provide guidance for the application of a law after its promulgation, or when judicial or legislative interpretations of a law are issued. The SPC is responsible for issuing binding judicial interpretations of concrete problems arising from the implementation of laws and regulations in specific cases.[189] A judicial interpretation of the PEL has not yet been issued. Legislative interpretations (法律解释), however, fall under the authority of the lawmaker itself, in the form of the SCNPC. The SCNPC shall issue an interpretation 'if the specific meaning of a provision needs to be further defined; or after its enactment, new developments make it necessary to define the basis on which to apply the law'.[190] Such a legal interpretation adopted by the SCNPC would have the same legal effect as the law it relates to.[191] Regarding the PEL, the SCNPC has not yet issued a legally binding interpretation. However, it is also common practice in China for an interpretation of a new law to be edited and compiled by the Legislative Committee of the SCNPC. Such an interpretation of the PEL was issued in 2006 under *LI Fei*, at the time Vice-President of the Legal Committee of the SCNP, as chief editor.[192] This sort of interpretation (释义) does not have the same binding effect as an official legislative interpretation by the SCNPC. The purpose of these interpretations is to accurately reflect the legislative aim, and to provide a valid and authoritative interpretation of the content of the legal provisions.[193] Experts, scholars and legislators who had participated in the drafting of the law, were therefore invited to compile this interpretation.[194] Comparative law research shows that legislative materials are utilised for the interpretation of laws across jurisdictions, although this remains subject to occasional criticism.[195] Legislative materials record discussions among legislators and express motivations and explanations for why the lawmaker has chosen a specific phrasing in a regulation over alternative wording. The interpretation edited by *LI* differs insofar that it is not a collection of official records, but a compendium of opinions of people who actively participated in the legislative process. Nevertheless, these kinds of interpretations are attributed a high

[187] A comprehensive account of the relevant laws and regulations is provided in Cao (曹德斌) and Zhang (张小奕) (2017).

[188] See Sect. 4.1.3.3.1.

[189] Regarding SPC interpretations of laws, see Sect. 3.1.3.

[190] Art. 45 Legislation Law.

[191] Art. 50 Legislation Law.

[192] Li (李飞) (ed) (2006).

[193] Ibid, p. 1.

[194] Besides *LI Fei (李飞)*, authors are *YUAN Jie (袁杰)*, *WANG Qing (王清)*, *LI Jianguo (李建国)*, *WANG Xiang (王翔)* and *CHEN Yangyue (陈扬跃)*.

[195] Fleischer (2011), pp. 347–348.

degree of authority among Chinese legal scholars and practitioners.[196] They are regarded as directly expressing the intention and understanding of the lawmaker. Within this book, the interpretation edited by *LI* is referred to as the opinion of 'the lawmaker'.

4.1.4.2 Scope of Application

While the 1997 PEL had 78 Articles, the revised PEL contains 109 Articles. In addition to the newly added Articles, many existing ones have been amended or extended.[197] Most revisions fill regulatory gaps or address problems that emerged during the implementation of the 1997 PEL.[198] Three improvements of the law are most significant: the expansion of the scope of application by permitting legal persons to become partners; the introduction of the specialised general partnership enterprise; the introduction of the limited partnership enterprise. Given their importance, these reforms will be further analysed in the following sections. In addition, the revised PEL provides more comprehensive provisions on partnership bankruptcy.[199]

The revised PEL contains a new, circular definition of partnership enterprises,[200] defining them as 'general partnership enterprises and limited partnership enterprises established by natural persons, legal persons or other organisations within the territory of China'.[201] The defect of a circular definition is remedied, however, by further provisions defining both forms of liabilities in the general and limited partnership enterprise.[202] The new definition no longer expressly requires a partnership enterprise to be a 'profit-making organisation'.[203] This leads to the question of for what purposes—non-profit and/or profit-making—a partnership enterprise can be formed under the PEL. An international comparison of partnership laws shows a wide range of permitted purposes, from forming partnerships for any purpose to rather narrow definitions of pursuing a commercially organised business operation.[204] Regarding the PEL, the new definition is likely related to the discussion on the nature of the new Specialised General Partnership Enterprise.[205] However, the

---

[196]This has been unequivocally expressed during interviews with Chinese scholars and practitioners by the author.

[197]Münzel (2006a), p. 405.

[198]Wang (王翔) (2006), first paragraph.

[199]Cao (曹德斌) and Zhang (张小奕) (2017), foreword p. 2.

[200]Chen (2016), p. 655.

[201]Art. 2 Para. 1 PEL.

[202]See Sects. 8.2.1 and 8.3.1; Chen (2016), pp. 655–656.

[203]See the discussion in Sect. 4.1.3.2.

[204]For an overview of UK, US, French and German law, see Windbichler (2014), pp. 116–118. Regarding the German HGB, also see Sect. 3.1.1.

[205]See the discussion in Sect. 4.1.4.4.

PEL still makes an implicit reference to the purpose of profit-making by stipulating the mandatory requirement that the partnership agreement must include provisions on the profit distribution among the partners.[206] In addition, the partnership agreement must specify a business scope for the operation of the partnership enterprise.[207] This indicates that the PEL requires the partners of a partnership enterprise to pursue a common business objective.[208] While this term is not further defined, it follows from the statutory reference that only those objectives qualify a partnership to be registered with the relevant authorities that can be included in the partnership enterprise's business scope.[209]

The revised PEL governs the entire lifecycle of a partnership enterprise. Provisions regulate the establishment of a partnership enterprise,[210] its property,[211] the management of routine affairs,[212] and the relationships between the partnership enterprise and third parties.[213] The law further contains provisions on joining and withdrawing from the partnership enterprise,[214] dissolution and liquidation,[215] as well as the legal liability of the partnership enterprise.[216]

4.1.4.3 Permitting Corporate General Partners

The revised PEL introduces the eligibility of legal persons, such as limited liability companies and other organisations, to become partners in partnership enterprises.[217] Since the 1997 PEL only permitted natural persons to become partners, this reform offers many new options for investors to use partnership enterprises, and it was welcomed as a major step towards modernising Chinese partnership enterprise law.[218] Using a limited liability legal person as a general partner in a partnership can address what might be considered the major disadvantage of being a general partner, which is the unlimited liability that the general partner is required to bear. Even though he acts as general partner, utilising a corporate general partner allows the investor to ultimately limit his liability for the partnership's debts. The

[206] Art. 18 No 5 PEL.

[207] Art. 18 No 2 PEL.

[208] Li (李飞) (ed) (2006), p. 4.

[209] Regarding the concept of business scope in Chinese law, see Sect. 3.1.6.1.2.

[210] Arts. 14–19, 56, 61–66 PEL.

[211] Arts. 20–25, 72–74 PEL.

[212] Arts. 26–36, 67–68 PEL.

[213] Arts. 37–42, 57–59, 76 PEL.

[214] Arts. 43–54, 77–81 PEL.

[215] Arts. 75, 85–92 PEL.

[216] Arts. 93–106 PEL.

[217] Art. 2 Para. 1 PEL.

[218] Zhu (朱慈蕴) (2008), p. 77; Zhu (朱少平) (2006), item 3.

motivation of the Chinese lawmaker for introducing this reform, its international context, and the legal questions that arise from it, will be analysed in more detail below.[219]

4.1.4.4 Introducing the Specialised General Partnership Enterprise

The Specialised General Partnership Enterprise (SGPE) resembles the Limited Liability Partnership (LLP) that was created by US legislation in the early 1990s in response to the rising malpractice claims against accountancy and law firms.[220] The SGPE shields partners of professional service firms from liabilities arising from the misconduct or negligence of their co-partners.[221] The introduction of the SGPE is in line with international trends, as, in recent years, the LLP enterprise form has been adopted in many jurisdictions, such as the UK, Singapore, India, Japan, and Germany.[222] However, the Chinese SGPE bears unique characteristics in essential aspects.[223]

For the 1997 PEL, provisions on the SGPE were proposed in the first drafts, but were subsequently removed.[224] During the revision of the PEL, the necessity for the SGPE to meet the demands of local professional service firms, was widely recognised.[225] The firms were facing severe pressure in the shape of competition from foreign firms, and therefore needed to be able to control the liability risks associated with an increasing number of their partners.[226] Chinese lawmakers discussed whether the SGPE constitutes its own category of partnership enterprises, but decided to treat it as a sub-type of the general partnership enterprise.[227] This is also reflected in the codification of the SGPE under the same chapter as the provisions on the general partnership enterprise in a section of the PEL.[228] The PEL further clarifies that any matters which are not regulated in the special provisions on the SGPE, shall be governed by the general provisions of the PEL on general partnership enterprises.[229]

Initially, the draft law proposed to name the new partnership vehicle LLP.[230] Commentators raised the concern that a Limited Liability Partnership Enterprise

[219]See Sect. 8.2.2.1.

[220]Lin (2010), p. 259.

[221]Art. 57 PEL.

[222]Lin (2010), p. 259.

[223]For further analysis, see Sect. 4.2.2.2.

[224]Huang (黄毅诚) (1997), pp. 12–13.

[225]Cao (曹德斌) and Zhang (张小奕) (2017), foreword p. 2.

[226]Yan (严义埙) (2006), pp. 596–597; Wang (王翔) (2006), item 4.

[227]Hong (洪虎) (2006b), pp. 354–355.

[228]Arts. 55–59 PEL.

[229]Article 55 Para. 3 PEL, making reference to Sections 1 to 5 of Chapter 2 of the PEL.

[230]Hong (洪虎) (2006a), pp. 602–603.

(有限责任合伙企业) could too easily be confused with the Limited Partnership Enterprise (有限合伙企业). The legislator eventually choose the name SGPE (特殊普通合伙企业).[231] *Lin* rightly points out that 'unlike the term "Limited Liability Partnership", which makes it clear that the partner's liability is "limited", the term "Specialised General Partnership", either in English or Chinese, fails to indicate the limited liability protection of the partners'.[232] As a result, the term SGPE could actually lead to less clarity and transparency, and thereby undermine the intended protection of third parties that a different name of an enterprise form might provide.[233]

A much debated question since the drafting of the 1997 PEL has been about which professional service firms can form an SGPE.[234] While the LLP is available to all types of businesses in the UK and US (Delaware),[235] the Chinese approach resembles the 'German Partnership Enterprise Law',[236] with the SGPE being restricted to a specific group of professions, namely 'professional services firms that provide paid services to their clients on the basis of professional knowledge and specialised skills'.[237] The reasoning behind this approach is the nature of the SGPE as an enterprise. The core question is whether professional service firms like law firms, accountancy firms, and architecture firms can be regarded as enterprises.[238] The discussion in China—and likewise in Germany—stems from the perception that professional service firms, while they are clearly aimed at making profits, do not consider profit-making their primary purpose.[239] The primary function of a law firm is for example considered to be serving the legal system, and they have therefore been subject to a special treatment historically.[240] Hence, during the legislative process, views have differed about which specific professions could establish an enterprise.[241] Some commentators from China and Germany argued a modern view: all these professions operate profit-oriented organisations, and special treatment for them is therefore no longer justified.[242] Accordingly, a provision has been included in Article 107 PEL, providing that even in the case of non-enterprise type professional service firms, the liability of the partners may be guided by the rules on the

[231]Ibid, pp. 602–603.

[232]Lin (2010), p. 262.

[233]Ibid, p. 262.

[234]Huang (黄毅诚) (1997), p. 12–13.

[235]Lin (2010), pp. 259–260.

[236]Art. 1 German Partnership Enterprise Law (Partnerschaftsgesellschaftsgesetz), promulgated on 30 July 1994; last amended on 22 December 2015.

[237]Art. 55 Para. 1 PEL.

[238]Werthwein (2010), p. 46.

[239]Julius and Bitter (2005), p. 62.

[240]Ibid, p. 62.

[241]Hong (洪虎) (2006b), pp. 354, 356; Werthwein (2010), p. 46.

[242]Julius and Bitter (2005), p. 62.

liability of partners in the SGPE.[243] In addition, sector specific regulations like the 'Lawyers Law'[244] have clarified that professional service firms can be established in the form of the SGPE. Overall, the introduction of the SGPE has been considered a milestone in the development of partnership law, and the professional services market in China.[245]

4.1.4.5 Introducing the Limited Partnership Enterprise

Another major improvement of the revised PEL is the introduction of the limited partnership as an additional type of partnership structure. A Limited Partnership Enterprise (LPE) is composed of one or more general partners, who bear unlimited joint and several liability, and one or more limited partners, who bear liability for the debts of the partnership only to the extent of the capital contribution to the partnership to which they have subscribed.[246]

Recognising a practical business need for a limited partnership form, and the important role it has played in the economic development of other countries, the draft of the 1997 PEL already contained special provisions on the LPE.[247] However, the Law Commission of the NPC argued that insufficient experience existed in China in dealing with limited partnerships, and recommended that the provisions on the LPE be deleted.[248] The 1997 PEL thus provided only for the establishment of general partnerships. In subsequent years, the State Council adopted a policy of fostering the development of advanced technology by encouraging scientific innovation.[249] The Chinese government also recognised that such innovative research and development requires capital.[250] In response to this policy, local authorities in Beijing and more than ten other municipalities and provinces issued their own regulations on limited partnerships.[251] Limited partnerships allow for, and are primarily aimed at, more flexibility in structuring the enterprise by permitting the

---

[243]For the discussion, see Hong (洪虎) (2006b), pp. 354, 356.

[244]Art. 15 Para. 2 PRC Law on Lawyers (中华人民共和国律师法), adopted at the 19th Session of the Standing Committee of the 9th National People's Congress on 15 May 1996; amended at the 25th Session of the Standing Committee of the 9th National People's Congress on 29 December 2001, amended at the 30th Session of the Standing Committee of the 10th National People's Congress on 28 October 2007, amended at the 29th Session of the Standing Committee of the 11th National People's Congress on 26 October 2012, and amended at the 29th Session of the Standing Committee of the 12th National People's Congress on 01 September 2017 and with effect as of 01 January 2018.

[245]Lin (2010), p. 265.

[246]Art. 2 Para. 3, Arts. 60–84 PEL.

[247]Huang (黄毅诚) (1997), p. 15.

[248]Li (厉以宁) (1997), pp. 17–18.

[249]Wu and Geu (2007–2008), p. 140.

[250]Ibid, p. 140.

[251]Chen (2016), p. 658 fn. 125; Wu and Geu (2007–2008), p. 140 fn. 20.

combination of institutions or individuals who have management experience or special technical know-how with those who have capital, i.e. venture capital investors.[252] Taking the Beijing 'Regulations on the Zhongguancun Science and Technology Park'[253] as an example, a single Article[254] established the limited partnership form, and regulated its governance and liability.[255] Notably, this local regulation has nullified creditor's rights under the national 1997 PEL, which stipulated that all partners of the partnership were liable for the debts of the partnership.[256] This reflects the pressure that local authorities were facing to attract private capital investments in order to facilitate high technology development, and it underlines the absence of a national legal framework for limited partnerships.[257] Accordingly, the reintroduction of the LPE under the revised PEL was backed by wide support from different government agencies that all recognised the importance of the LPE for the development of venture capital driven innovation and high-tech enterprises.[258] In addition, the introduction of the LPE in China was in line with international practice at that time.[259]

Notably, the provisions in the PEL on the LPE closely derive many of the limited partnership provisions from the Shenzhen Partnership Regulations.[260] The 25 Articles that govern the LPE are regulated separately in Chapter III of the PEL. For any matters that are not regulated in Chapter III, the PEL stipulates a fall-back regulation whereby the relevant provisions on general partnership enterprises and general partners will become applicable.[261] The Chinese lawmakers thus follow the approach of most jurisdictions, in which the law of limited partnerships simply 'supplements' the existing law of general partnerships.[262] In German law, the provisions on the limited partnership enterprise consist of only 18 Articles, and also make reference to the provisions on the general partnership enterprise.[263] Legislation takes a different approach in the UK and US,[264] providing for separate specific

[252] Werthwein (2010), p. 46.

[253] Regulations on the Zhongguancun Science and Technology Park (中关村科技园区条例), promulgated by the Standing Committee of the Beijing Municipal People's Congress on 8 December 2000 and repealed on 23 December 2010.

[254] Art. 25 Regulations on the Zhongguancun Science and Technology Park.

[255] Clarke (2005–2006), p. 59.

[256] Ibid, p. 60.

[257] Chen (2016), pp. 657–658.

[258] Yan (严义埙) (2006), p. 596.

[259] Lin and Yeo (2010), p. 104.

[260] Wu and Geu (2007–2008), p. 139.

[261] Article 60 PEL, making reference to Sections 1 to 5 of Chapter 2 of the PEL.

[262] Wu and Geu (2007–2008), p. 137.

[263] Arts. 161-177a, Art. 161 Para. 2 HGB.

[264] The term 'US law' is used because the majority of the States have, albeit with deviations in details, adopted the Uniform Acts, Uniform Limited Partnership Act (fn. 266 below) and Revised Uniform Partnership Act (see Sect. 4.2.2.2 fn. 663).

limited partnership enterprise acts.[265] The US lawmaker consciously decided to draft the 2001 version of the 'Uniform Limited Partnership Act'[266] (ULPA) as a fully self-contained organisational statute without relying on partnership law outside the act itself.[267]

4.1.4.6 Perception of the Revised Law

The revised PEL follows the principles of liberalisation and deregulation, and expands investors' options when establishing enterprises.[268] It has therefore been considered a positive contribution to the modernisation of China's enterprise law system, and a recognition of the needs of the national and global economy.[269] While the revised law did not result in an immediate increase in number of formal partnership enterprise formations, it did enable a clear increase of the amount of capital that has been invested in partnership enterprises.[270]

On a more general level, *Lin* points out:

> [T]he PEL is not developed naturally out of traditional Chinese law, but is a part of the state's economic and legal reforms in the transitional period of 1990s. Today's partnership enterprise, regulated by the PEL, does not succeed to the legal tradition and legacy of its Chinese ancestors. It is simply a creation of law that has less than a two-decade history.[271]

This non-generic development of the partnership law in China will be of relevance for different aspects of this book. For instance, in the basic provisions of the PEL, a degree of incoherence is shown on the LPE structure and the fragmented regulations on the implementation of legal mechanisms that protect partners' rights.[272] On a more positive note, the partnership enterprise form—dating back to ancient times and first codified in 1904—has now been resurrected in China's law.[273]

For foreign investors, conversely, the revised PEL has initially been a disappointment, as the law postponed the opening of the partnership enterprise to foreign investors until administrative measures were issued by the State Council.[274] While

---

265 Lin (2013a), p. 212.

266 Uniform Limited Partnership Act (2001), promulgated by the National Conference of Commissioners on Uniform State Laws in 2001, amended in 2011 and 2013.

267 2001 Prefatory Note to the ULPA. For a detailed account on the legislative history of the ULPA, see Wu and Geu (2007–2008), pp. 141–142.

268 Bu (2017b), p. 192.

269 Zhang (2011), pp. 868–869; Julius and Bitter (2005), p. 63; Chen (2016), p. 661; Li (李飞) (ed) (2006), pp. 1–2.

270 Howson (2015), pp. 396–397.

271 Lin (2013b), p. 220 fn. 10.

272 Lin and Yeo (2010), p. 107.

273 Howson (2015), p. 410.

274 Art. 108 PEL.

no regulations were included that expressly prohibited foreign investors from establishing a partnership, in practice, they were unable to establish partnership enterprises under the PEL before specific guidelines were promulgated for government authorities with regard to the approval and registration of a foreign-invested partnership enterprise.[275] Foreign investors thus remained restricted to the Non-Legal Person CJV and the FIVCE if they directly wanted to establish partnership-like entities.[276] For the special scenario in which a foreign investor would intend to use an existing FIE—other than an FIE HoldCo—to act as general partner or limited partner in a domestic partnership enterprise, SAIC issued special provisions that refer to the FIE Reinvestment Provisions.[277]

4.1.5 The Introduction of Foreign-Invested Partnerships Enterprises

4.1.5.1 Legislative History

Foreign investors' interest in and demand for utilising partnership enterprises was already recognised by Chinese lawmakers in 2004 at the start of the revision of the PEL.[278] In addition, the inclusion of foreign investors under the scope of the PEL was regarded as an acknowledgment of China's WTO commitment to open its domestic market to foreign professional service firms, which are often organised in the form of partnership enterprises.[279] An early draft of the revised PEL therefore expressly included foreign investors by stating that 'foreign enterprises or foreign individuals establishing or joining a partnership enterprise and becoming a general partner shall comply with the relevant legal provisions of the State'.[280] However, commentators and authorities considered that the protection of creditors would be endangered whenever the unlimited-liable general partner was a foreign investor with no actual commercial presence or property in China.[281] The suggestion was made that more practical experience should be gained and further research carried out into legal means to regulate and control foreign investors in partnership

---

[275]Werthwein (2010), p. 48; Liu (2008), p. 83.

[276]See Sects. 3.1.5 and 3.2.3.2.

[277]Art. 4 Partnership Enterprise Administrative Circular. However, this construction of an FIE investing in a domestic partnership raises various questions, e.g. the FIE Reinvestment Provisions provide in Article 4 that FIEs can only establish new enterprises that take the form of a limited liability company or joint stock company. The lawfulness of such an FIE-partnership investment structure therefore requires further analysis which falls outside of the scope of the research question at hand.

[278]Hong (洪虎) (2006a), pp. 602, 604.

[279]Ibid, p. 604.

[280]Hong (洪虎) (2006b), p. 357.

[281]Wang (王翔) (2006), item 6.

enterprises.[282] The revised PEL therefore only contained a provision entrusting the State Council with promulgating further regulations for foreign-invested partnerships.[283]

Shortly after the revised PEL was promulgated, on 28 September 2006, the Law Office of the State Council sent a letter to MOFCOM with the instruction to draft administrative measures for the establishment of foreign-invested partnership enterprises.[284] MOFCOM conducted comprehensive research and collected opinions from relevant government authorities.[285] In January 2007, it published the first 'Draft FIPE Measures',[286] inviting the public to submit comments. Introducing the foreign-invested partnership thereby presented a challenge for the Chinese government on how to balance its FDI policies.[287] Reinforcing the flexibility and liberalisation that defines the nature of a partnership enterprise would grant a degree of freedom to the foreign-invested partnership that is not available to other FIEs, and could thus cause a large-scale abandonment of other FIE-types.[288] Keeping the foreign-invested partnership in parity with traditional FIEs instead, would deprive it of the attractiveness of the partnership form, and essentially defeat the purpose of forming a partnership enterprise.[289] At the same time, pressure increased on the Chinese government gradually to reform the FIE regime, as FDI significantly slowed down during that time.[290] China, as most other major economies, felt the impact of the global economic and financial crisis that began in the US in 2008.[291] The Chinese government responded, in addition to implementing its own domestic economic stimulus plan, by seeking to make the process for attracting foreign investments simpler and more effective.[292] The rather detailed and restrictive first draft was therefore further deliberated on and revised during a relatively lengthy legislative process, until the State Council finally promulgated the 'FIPE

[282] Hong (洪虎) (2006b), p. 357.

[283] Art. 108 PEL.

[284] Explanations on the Draft Administrative Measures for Foreign-Invested Partnership Enterprises (外商投资合伙企业管理办法(送审稿)起草说明), promulgated by the Ministry of Commerce on 23 January 2007, <http://www.mofcom.gov.cn/aarticle/bh/200703/20070304413077.html>, accessed 15 May 2020.

[285] Ibid.

[286] Draft Administrative Measures for Foreign-Invested Partnership Enterprises (外商投资合伙企业管理办法(送审稿)), promulgated by the Ministry of Commerce on 23 January 2007, <http://www.mofcom.gov.cn/aarticle/bh/200703/20070304413083.html>, accessed 15 May 2020; for an analysis of the Draft FIPE Measures see: Liu (2008), pp. 83–100.

[287] Fu (傅明) (2008), p. 74.

[288] Cui (2008), p. 30.

[289] Ibid, p. 30.

[290] Shaddox (2013), p. 470.

[291] Mahony (2015), p. 68.

[292] Ibid, pp. 68–73.

Measures'[293] in November 2009. The latter were further complemented by the 'FIPE Provisions' in January 2010,[294] issued by SAIC. The FIPE Measures and FIPE Provisions, collectively referred to as 'FIPE Legislation', both became effective on 1 March 2010. In October 2010, SAIC additionally issued the—later repealed—'FIPE Implementation Circular'[295] to instruct and guide all its local branches on the unified implementation of the FIPE Legislation.

4.1.5.2 Scope of Application

In the typical style of State Council regulations, the FIPE Measures are rather brief with only 16 Articles.[296] They are significantly shorter than the original Draft FIPE Measures, and only set out the fundamental principles of regulating the FIPE.[297] The FIPE Provisions are however much more comprehensive in their guidance for the implementation of the FIPE. The 68 Articles provide very detailed rules on the establishment, registration, changes to registration, and dissolution of the FIPE.[298] Together, these regulations set out the prerequisites for foreign investors directly to establish partnership enterprises in China together with other foreign investors or Chinese legal entities or natural persons.[299] In that respect, the FIPE Legislation is also applicable to investors from Hong Kong, Macao and Taiwan wishing to set up a partnership enterprise in China.[300]

The FIPE Legislation follows the structure of the revised PEL, allowing investors to establish partnership enterprises in the form of the Foreign-Invested General Partnership Enterprise (FIGPE) (外商投资普通合伙企业), the Foreign-Invested Specialised General Partnership Enterprise (FISGPE) (外商投资特殊普通合伙企业)

[293]Measures for the Administration of the Establishment of Partnership Enterprises by Foreign Enterprises or Individuals in the Territory of China (外国企业或者个人在中国境内设立合伙企业管理办法), promulgated by the State Council on 25 November 2009 and effective as of 1 March 2010.

[294]Administrative Provisions for the Registration of Foreign-Invested Partnership Enterprises (外商投资合伙企业登记管理规定), promulgated by the State Administration of Industry and Commerce on 29 January 2010 with effect from 1 March 2010, amended on 20 February 2014 and amended on 8 August 2019.

[295]Circular on Implementing the Measures for the Administration of the Establishment of Partnership Enterprises by Foreign Enterprises or Individuals in China (《外国企业或者个人在中国境内设立合伙企业管理办法》贯彻实施工作的通知), promulgated by the State Administration for Industry and Commerce on 10 February 2010 and repealed on 31 May 2016.

[296]Wang and Yong (2010), p. 15.

[297]Jiao and Kasteleijn (2011), p. 58.

[298]Art. 2 Para. 2 FIPE Provisions.

[299]Art. 2 FIPE Measures; Art. 2 Para. 1 FIPE Provisions.

[300]Art. 15 FIPE Measures.

and the Foreign-Invested Limited Partnership Enterprise (FILPE) (外商投资有限合伙企业).[301]

The FIPE seems to have primarily been designed for foreign private equity and venture capital investors, but the FIPE Provisions also expressly encourage foreign investors with advanced technology and management experience to set up FIPEs in order to promote the modern services industry.[302] In principle, the FIPE enterprise form is open to all industries.[303] For seasoned foreign investors, the promulgation of the FIPE Legislation brought significant innovations to the foreign investment regime.[304] An investment in a FIPE does not require a minimum capital contribution, but, where applicable, such a contribution can be made in foreign currency or RMB.[305] Unlike in respect to EJVs at that time, MOFCOM did not have any continuing role in the establishment and operation of a FIPE,[306] and investors have great flexibility in determining the inner organisational structure of the FIPE.[307] An investor can exercise a degree of control over the FIPE that need not reflect the proportion of capital he contributed to it.[308]

4.1.5.3 Relationship to the Partnership Enterprise Law and the Partnership Registration Measures

Both the FIPE Measures and the FIPE Provisions were promulgated pursuant the overarching law in this field—the PEL. The legal legitimacy of the FIPE is directly established in the PEL.[309] The provision in Article 108 PEL merely stipulates the requirement that administrative measures for the establishment of the FIPE have to be promulgated beforehand. The FIPE Measures and FIPE Provisions make direct references to the PEL.[310] In addition, it follows from the hierarchy of Chinese legislation that the PEL—a law enacted by the NPC—ranks higher than measures and provisions that were promulgated by the State Council and SAIC/SAMR.[311] This means that, for any matter that is not governed in the FIPE Legislation but is addressed in the PEL, PEL provisions will apply.[312] Consequently, many legal problems that arise from the domestic partnership enterprise are also relevant with

[301] Art. 11 FIPE Provisions.

[302] Art. 3 Para. 2 FIPE Provisions.

[303] Regarding the limitations, see Sect. 4.1.7.

[304] Howson (2015), p. 399.

[305] Art. 4 FIPE Measures, Art. 14 FIPE Provisions.

[306] Art. 5 FIPE Provisions. Additionally, see Sect. 4.1.8.

[307] See Sect. 4.1.9.3.

[308] See Sect. 4.1.9.3.

[309] Münzel (2006b), p. 425 fn. 13.

[310] Art. 3 Para. 1 FIPE Measures; Art. 3 Para. 1, Art. 6 Para. 1, Art. 31 FIPE Provisions.

[311] Art. 88 Para. 1 Legislation Law.

[312] Yang (杨杰) and Qu (曲天明) (2010), pp. 63–64.

regard to the FIPE. Where the FIPE Legislation regulates the administration of the establishment of FIPEs, these provisions have precedence over the relevant provisions in the PEL, as Article 108 PEL specifically delegates the competence to formulate administrative provisions tailored to foreign-invested partnerships to the State Council and its departments.[313] The legal framework of the FIPE was a novelty in China's FIE legislation.[314] As has been pointed out above, the legal frameworks for the EJV, CJV, and WFOE were developed as a legal regime that was separate from the general domestic legal system, e.g. only allowing the sporadic application of the Company Law.[315] However, the FIPE was regulated by the same law as the domestic partnership enterprise from the beginning, and governed by administrative legislation that also fell under that same law. To a large extent, the same provisions therefore apply to domestic and foreign-invested partnership enterprises. In this regard, the legal framework that governs the FIPE can be seen as a blueprint for the fundamental reform of unifying the application of the Company Law and PEL, as was implemented by the FIL.

With regard to the FIPE Provisions, their relationship to the Partnership Registration Measures also deserves further analysis. Formally, the State Council is the highest executive organ in China, and thus its promulgated Partnership Registration Measures rank higher than the FIPE Provisions, which were issued by SAIC.[316] However, the Partnership Registration Measures explicitly provide that 'where laws and administrative regulations have otherwise provided for the registration of a partnership enterprise, such provisions shall prevail'.[317] Therefore, this leaves room for the FIPE Provisions, which in return state that a FIPE has to comply with the Partnership Registration Measures.[318] In substance, the structure and content of the FIPE Provisions largely reflect the provisions of the Partnership Registration Measures. Deviations and supplements primarily relate to the involvement of foreign parties,[319] or the usage of foreign currency.[320] Most significantly, the FIPE Provisions stipulate that, in certain industries, investments cannot be conducted in the form of the FIPE.[321] For domestic partnerships, a corresponding

[313]Formulating administrative regulations for the implementation of laws is one of the core responsibilities of the State Council (Art. 65 Para. 1 (1) Legislation Law); Yang (杨杰) and Qu (曲天明) (2010), pp. 63–64.

[314]Stursberg (2014), p. 14.

[315]See Sect. 3.1.3.

[316]Art. 85 Constitution.

[317]Art. 4 Para. 5 Partnership Registration Measures.

[318]Art. 1 FIPE Provisions. A similar reference is found in the FIPE Measures, which stipulate in Article 10 that the establishment of a FIPE has to be in accordance with the Partnership Registration Measures and other relevant national regulations.

[319]For example, notarisation and legalisation requirements for foreign documents, Article 12, Para. 4 FIPE Provisions, or the impact of the Guidance Catalogue, Article 42, Para. 3 FIPE Provisions.

[320]For instance, Article 14 FIPE Provisions.

[321]Art. 3 Para. 3 FIPE Provision. Also, see analysis in Sect. 4.1.7.

provision does not exist. The FIPE Provisions run to 66 Articles, while the Partnership Registration Measures only consist of 49 Articles.

4.1.5.4 Relationship to the CJV Implementing Regulations

As explained above, the Non-Legal Person CJV, which was regulated in the CJV Implementing Regulations, could essentially be regarded as a partnership enterprise established by foreign investors.[322] Commentators have pointed out inconsistencies between the legal framework that governs the FIPE and the CJV Implementing Regulations, regarding the governance structure, establishment procedure, and the means of capital contributions.[323] This raised the question of the relationship between the sets of regulations.

The FIPE Measures and CJV Implementing Regulations have both been promulgated by the State Council, and thus share the same legislative rank. The CJV Implementing Regulations could however be regarded as the more specific legislation, and thereby prevail where there is inconsistency between the regulations.[324] Conversely, the FIPE Measures could also be said to have the prevailing effect as they are the newer regulation.[325] The FIPE Provisions have been issued by SAIC in turn, and thus ranked below the CJV Implementing Regulations.[326] In addition, the CJV Implementing Regulations were promulgated under a foreign investment regime that was characterised by the separate legal treatment of foreign investment vehicles and domestic enterprises.[327] To resolve the complex relationship between the different regulations, the Draft FIPE Measures clarified that 'the establishment of the Non-Legal Person CJV shall be handled according to the CJV Law and CJV Implementing Provisions'.[328] Later, SAIC further emphasised this position in a clarifying statement.[329] At heart, the FIPE Legislation did not affect the CJV, which remained subject to its own, separate legal regime.[330] However, as has been mentioned before, the CJV as a stand-alone enterprise form has been abolished and

---

322 See Sect. 3.2.2.2.

323 Yang (杨杰) and Qu (曲天明) (2010), pp. 64–65; Fu (傅明) (2008), p. 74; Werthwein (2010), pp. 48–49.

324 Art. 92 Legislation Law.

325 Art. 92 Legislation Law.

326 Art. 88 Para. 2 Legislation Law.

327 See Sect. 3.1.3.

328 Art. 36 Draft FIPE Measures.

329 Art. 3 Para. 1 FIPE Implementation Circular. In a strict sense, however, it would have been the role of the State Council to resolve this conflict. See Art. 94 Para. 1 Legislation Law.

330 Yang (杨杰) and Qu (曲天明) (2010), pp. 64–65; Fu (傅明) (2008), p. 74; Xu (徐春雷) and Cao (曹秀峰) (2007), p. 29. Regarding the impact of the Draft Foreign Investment Law on the CJV, see Sect. 3.1.5.3.

the CJV Implementing Regulations have been repealed when the FIL took effect on 1 January 2020.[331]

4.1.6 The Impact of the Foreign Investment Law

The enactment of the FIL is a fundamental reform of China's foreign investment legal regime.[332] While the consequences for the FIPE are less substantial than for the EJV and CJV, the reform also has an impact on the legal framework that governs the FIPE.

Foreign investments in partnership enterprises clearly fall under the scope of application of the FIL. The definition of 'foreign investment' comprises the establishment of domestic enterprises, without stipulating an exception for the establishment of partnership enterprises.[333] Furthermore, the acquisition of 'shares of property' (财产份额) of a domestic enterprise is included in the definition of foreign investments.[334] The term shares of property is a clear reference to partnership enterprises.[335] Hence, the establishment of a FIPE and the purchase of shares of property of an existing partnership enterprise by a foreign investor are generally subject to the FIL.

A ground-breaking reform of the FIL was the abolishment of the EJV, CJV, and WFOE as special investment vehicles for FDI, and opening China's domestic enterprise forms to foreign investors.[336] This raised the question whether the FIL would have a similar effect on the existence of the FIPE. So far, the literature is silent on this aspect. As has been analysed above, the FIPE differs insofar from the other FIEs that it pierces the dual legislative structure that characterised most other FIEs.[337] Major aspects of the inner organisation, establishment and liability of the FIPE are governed directly by the PEL. The FIPE Legislation only stipulates where the FIPE deviates from its purely domestic-invested counterpart. Commentators expect that regulations will likewise be promulgated by the Chinese lawmaker, which will provide certain adjustments to the Company Law for FIEs. The legislative framework that governs the FIPE—with the PEL as the fundamental law and the FIPE Legislation with implementing regulations—, which already came into effect in 2010, can therefore be seen as a testing ground and blueprint for the reforms that are now being carried out for the other types of FIEs. A substantial amendment to the FIPE Legislation due to the FIL is not necessary. The 2019 amendment to the FIPE

[331] See Sect. 3.2.2.

[332] See Sect. 3.1.5.

[333] Art. 2 Para. 2 No 1 FIL.

[334] Art. 2 Para. 2 No 2 FIL.

[335] See Sect. 9.1.

[336] Art. 31 FIL. See also Sect. 3.1.5.3.

[337] See Sect. 4.1.5.3.

Provisions merely replaced SAIC with SAMR as the new authority in charge of the establishment of a FIE. However, should the Chinese lawmaker decide to repeal the FIPE Legislation and grant full national treatment to foreign investors that establish a partnership enterprise, the FIPE Measures and FIPE Provisions could simply be repealed by an administrative regulation. Because they have been promulgated by the State Council and SAIC respectively, a hypothetical abolishment of the FIPE legislation would not have to be stipulated in a formal law, like the FIL.

Against this background, it is not surprising that the FIL and its implementing regulations make very limited reference to partnership enterprise law. The word PEL appears only once, in Article 31 FIL, which stipulates that FIEs shall be governed by the provisions of the Company Law, the PEL or other relevant laws. In addition, Article 42, Paragraph 2 FIL provides that existing FIEs have a 5-year grace period to change their organisational form into an enterprise form under one of these laws.[338] Especially a non-legal person CJV is likely to be converted into a partnership enterprise under the PEL, given the similarity in nature of the non-legal person CJV and partnership enterprises.

However, other reforms of the FIL and FIL Implementing Regulations are directly applicable to the FIPE. This includes the measurements for promoting and protecting foreign investments,[339] the national security review,[340] and new reporting obligations.[341] It further remains to be seen to what degree subsequent regulations will provide additional changes to the legal framework that governs FIPEs.

4.1.7 Directing and Restricting Investments in FIPEs

China's overarching policy objective of maintaining government control over foreign investments through imposed guidance and restrictions affects the entire scope of FDI, with no exception in respect of the FIPE.[342] The provisions of the Guidance Catalogue and the FDI Negative List apply to the FIPE in the same manner that they apply to other types of FDI.[343] Essentially, the FIPE is even more restricted than EJVs or CJVs were. In addition to being forbidden in industries that are prohibited to all foreign investors, Article 3, Paragraph 3 FIPE Provisions stipulates that a FIPE cannot be established either in (1) any industry that is open to only EJVs and CJVs; (2) any industry that is only open to a project with either relative or absolute controlling Chinese shareholders; (3) any industry for which is determined a specific (maximum) shareholding ratio of the foreign investment. These limitations are

[338] This stipulation is reiterated in Art. 44 Para. 1 FIL Implementing Regulations.

[339] See Sect. 3.1.5.4.

[340] See Sect. 3.1.5.5.

[341] See Sect. 3.1.6.3.2.

[342] For an analysis of the guidance and restrictions on FIEs in general, see Sect. 3.1.6.

[343] Art. 13 FIPE Measures; Art. 3 Para. 3 FIPE Provisions.

further underlined in a special provision of the FDI Negative List, stipulating that FIPEs cannot be established in industries that are subject to equity requirements.[344] These investment restrictions not only apply when a new FIPE is established, but likewise when a foreign investor becomes a partner of an existing domestic partnership enterprise.[345] From its outset, the FIPE has been restricted to the same investment limitations as WFOEs. It shows that the Chinese government did not want to provide a level playing field for the FIPE in comparison to the EJV and CJV.[346] In contrast, the Draft FIPE Measures still provided more opportunities to use the FIPE. For an industry that was limited to EJVs or CJVs in the Guidance Catalogue, a FIPE would have been required to have more than one Chinese general partner, but would not have been banned from such an industry.[347]

Under the FDI Negative List in the 2019 version of the Guidance Catalogue, these additional limitations affect the vast majority of the listed industries,[348] including value-added telecommunications services,[349] security companies,[350] and medical institutions.[351] As a result, only one industry under the 2019 FDI Negative List is currently available for investment in the form of the FIPE.[352] However, according to the timetable in the FDI Negative List, more industries will be freed from restrictions over the next few years.[353] While investors might be tempted to find ways to circumvent these investment restrictions by developing creative business structures, violations of the provisions of the Guidance Catalogue are expressly sanctioned in Article 51, para 2 FIPE Provisions. In addition, the new nationwide Master Negative List applies to investments in FIPEs as it does to any other domestic or foreign investment.[354]

Like all other enterprises in China,[355] a FIPE is limited in its operation to a specific business scope, as registered with the relevant authorities.[356] Apart from the investment restrictions discussed in the Guidance Catalogue, there are no general statutory limitations on the business scope of a FIPE, and it can be used as investment vehicle for all permitted industries and lines of business.[357] Following

[344]Note No 4 to the FDI Negative List in the Guidance Catalogue.

[345]Art. 63 in conjunction with Art. 3 Para. 3 FIPE Provisions.

[346]Shaddox (2013), p. 473; Pissler (2010), pp. 125–131.

[347]Art. 7 Para. 2 Draft FIPE Measures.

[348]For a detailed account, see Sect. 3.1.6.3.3 fn. 348–353.

[349]Item 20 2019 FDI Negative List in the Guidance Catalogue.

[350]Item 22 2019 FDI Negative List in the Guidance Catalogue.

[351]Item 33 2019 FDI Negative List in the Guidance Catalogue.

[352]Item 10 2019 FDI Negative List in the Guidance Catalogue: production of satellite, television and radio ground receiving facilities and key parts.

[353]See Sect. 3.1.6.3.3.

[354]See Sect. 3.1.6.3.3.

[355]See Sect. 3.1.6.1.2.

[356]Art. 7 Para. 4 FIPE Provisions.

[357]Mahony (2015), p. 231.

the implementation of the FIPE, SAIC issued the 'FIPE Business Licence Circular'[358] to determine the specifics of its business licence.

4.1.8 Registration of FIPE and Relevant Authorities

4.1.8.1 Pioneer for Simplified Administration with SAMR

When the FIPE was introduced, one of its most significant features was considered to be that the establishment and subsequent changes of a FIPE would not be subject to the rigid two-tier administrative procedure for FIEs, requiring a foreign investor to first obtain approval from MOFCOM before registering with SAMR. Instead, the establishment or changes of a FIPE become effective through direct registration with SAMR.[359] While SAMR is the authority in charge of administering the FIPE registration nationwide, the actual registration of a FIPE will usually be conducted with its local counterpart.[360] From the introduction of the FIPE, the same registration authority has therefore been responsible for FIPEs and domestic partnership enterprises.[361] Making the FIPE only subject to the registration procedure with SAMR marked a major distinction to the examination and verification process with MOFCOM that all other FIEs at that time had to undergo.[362] Notably, the Draft FIPE Measures still provided for such examination and verification of the FIPE establishment under the supervision of MOFCOM.[363] In an official explanation of this policy shift, the government acknowledged the new approach to the nature of partnership enterprises to be easier to establish and more flexible to manage, and stated the intention of the government to attract more foreign investments.[364] Commentators welcomed the new registration procedure for the FIPE, and considered it a possible indication for upcoming reforms of the approval regime that had governed FDI for the preceding 30 years.[365] These expectations have been fulfilled with the introduction of the FTZ, the overall reform of the verification process in late

[358]Circular on Usage of Business Licence for Foreign Investment Partnership Enterprise and Business Licence for Branches of Foreign Investment Partnership Enterprise (启用《外商投资合伙企业营业执照》和《外商投资合伙企业分支机构营业执照》的通知), promulgated by the State Administration for Industry and Commerce on 12 February 2010 and repealed on 14 July 2014.

[359]Art. 5 Para. 1, Art. 6 FIPE Measures; Arts. 4 and 5 FIPE Provisions.

[360]Art. 5 Para. 2 FIPE Provisions. For a FIPE mainly engaged in investments (PE and VC funds), the provincial level department of SAMR is the responsible authority (Art. 5 Para. 3 FIPE Provisions).

[361]Art. 4 Para. 3 Partnership Registration Measures.

[362]Mahony (2015), p. 231.

[363]Arts. 9, 20 Draft FIPE Measures.

[364]Art. 1 Para. 2 FIPE Implementation Circular.

[365]Yu (虞亚光) (2010), p. 43; Wang and Yong (2010), p. 15; Liu (2010), pp. 37–38.

2016, and the unified registration of all FIEs with SAMR as implemented with the FIL.[366]

However, this transfer of authority from MOFCOM to SAMR has also been regarded with scepticism. Together with the FIPE registration, a foreign investor has to submit a statement regarding his compliance with foreign investment industrial policy, including the Guidance Catalogue for instance.[367] Since SAMR has not undertaken detailed reviews of foreign investment in the past, as this was the duty of MOFCOM, it was questioned how well SAMR would be suited to implement this assessment in practice.[368] Following the registration of a FIPE, SAMR is also required to notify the local branch of MOFCOM about the establishment of the enterprise.[369] The necessary inter-departmental coordination between the relevant branches was regarded as giving MOFCOM a greater ability to continue to impose its views on the establishment of a FIPE.[370] However, SAMR has addressed these concerns and has proven capable of carrying out this administrative task in practice.[371] In the light of the 2016 administrative reforms, which have reconfirmed MOFCOM's role in administrating FIEs,[372] no amendment or repeal of the FIPE Provisions has been promulgated, thereby restating the central function of SAMR in the administration of FIPEs.

In hindsight, this streamlined procedure can be regarded as the blueprint for the newly introduced 'one-stop shop' procedure for the registration of all FIEs with SAMR.[373] The new administrative information reporting system, which was introduced with the FIL and its implementing regulations, likewise applies to FIPEs.[374]

4.1.8.2 Documents for SAMR Registration

The FIPE Provisions stipulate in Article 7 what information has to be registered with SAMR: (1) the name of the FIPE; (2) its principal business premise;[375] (3) the name of the managing partner; (4) the FIPE's business scope; (5) the type of partnership enterprise; (6) names or titles of all partners, their nationality and address, the type of

[366] See Sect. 3.1.6.3.

[367] Art. 12 Para. 2 No 7 FIPE Provisions.

[368] Lu (吕美昂) (2011), p. 82; Wang and Yong (2010), p. 16.

[369] Art. 44 FIPE Provisions.

[370] Wang and Yong (2010), p. 16; Liu (2010), pp. 37–38.

[371] Art. 1 Para. 3 FIPE Implementation Circular.

[372] See Sect. 3.1.6.3.1.

[373] See Sect. 3.1.6.3.1.

[374] Art. 1 Reporting Notice.

[375] A lease contract or equivalent of the principal business premise must be submitted. The principal business premise is the place where the administrative headquarter of the partnership enterprise is located. See Gao (高富平) et al. (1997), p. 151. The principal business premise must be located within the geographic area of its responsible SAMR (Art. 9 FIPE Provisions).

liability they are assuming, the amount of subscribed or paid-in capital contributions, the capital contribution schedule, the method for making capital contributions, and the valuation method. Should the term of the partnership be limited on establishment, such a term must be registered as well. Should a foreign enterprise, Chinese legal person, or other organisation act as the managing partner, its appointed representative must likewise be registered.

The type of partnership enterprise must be a part of the enterprise name to indicate the organisational structure of the FIPE.[376] The characters '普通合伙' (general partnership), '特殊普通合伙' (specialised general partnership) or '有限合伙' (limited partnership) have to be included between brackets in the enterprise name.[377] Notably, the enterprise name does not have to contain the prefix 'Foreign-invested' (外商投资),[378] but it has to comply with the general stipulations of the 'Enterprise Name Administrative Provisions'.[379] German law provides a special regulation for partnership enterprises in which no natural person is personally liable as general partner. The name of such a partnership must indicate that the liability of the corporate general partner is limited.[380] The rationale is to inform and warn the market participants about the overall limited liability of the partnership enterprise with a corporate general partner.[381] The organisational form of the corporate general partner is therefore included in the limited partnership's name, leading to the most prominent example of the suffix 'GmbH & Co. KG', with the 'GmbH' indicating that the general partner is a German limited liability company.[382] Nowadays, more and more foreign corporate general partners are being integrated in German limited partnership enterprises. Because not all market participants are familiar with the foreign corporate types that act as general partner, a discussion is ongoing in scholarship if a unified suffix should be used instead, which would clarify the liability of the partnership enterprise.[383] Chinese law lacks an equivalent provision. The Enterprise Name Administrative Provisions in Article 12 only require that the enterprise name indicates its organisational form. In this regard, the term 'limited partnership' (有限合伙) expresses that some partners only bear liability to the extent of their capital contribution, but it is silent on the ultimate liability of the general partner. Instead, a supplement to the enterprise name that informs about the form of

376 Art. 54 FIPE Provisions; Art. 8 FIPE Provisions in conjunction with Art. 7 Partnership Enterprise Registration Measures.

377 Art. 8 FIPE Provisions in conjunction with Art. 2 Partnership Enterprise Administrative Circular.

378 Art. 54 FIPE Provisions.

379 Administrative Provisions for the Enterprise Name Registration (企业名称登记管理规定), promulgated on 22 July 1991 and amended on 9 November 2012 with effect as of 01 January 2013. This requirement is stipulated in Art. 8 FIPE Provisions.

380 Art. 19 Para. 2 HGB.

381 Heidinger (2016), p. 499.

382 Ibid, pp. 378, 499.

383 Regarding the discussion in Germany, see Heidinger (2016), p. 499; Raiser and Veil (2015), p. 657; Teichmann (2014), pp. 238–239.

liability which the partnership enterprise has effectively taken on, would much better protect creditors and other market participants.

The application for establishment of the FIPE must be submitted to SAMR by a representative appointed by all partners.[384] In Article 12, Paragraph 2, the FIPE Provisions further contain a non-exhaustive list of the documents that have to be filed for the enterprise registration. Certain documents of a foreign partner need to be notarised and legalised by the competent authorities in his home jurisdiction and legalised by the Chinese consulate.[385] Moreover, a letter has to be submitted, authorising a person in China to receive legal documents on behalf of the foreign partner.[386] These requirements are deviations from the respective provisions for domestic partnership enterprise registration.[387]

4.1.8.3 Effect of Registration

The registration with SAMR is of material significance. The establishment of the FIPE takes effect on the date on which the business licence for the FIPE is issued by SAMR.[388] The FIPE is not permitted to conduct any business activities prior to this.[389] The issuance of the business licence hence has a constitutive effect. US law recognises a similar registration requirement for limited partnerships. One of the prerequisites for the establishment of a limited partnership is the effectiveness of a 'certificate of limited partnership' that must be filed with government authorities.[390] Under German law, the registration of a limited partnership usually has a merely declaratory effect.[391] However, the registration does take on constitutive effect when the activities of a limited partnership do not yet require a commercially organised business operation.[392]

4.1.8.4 Timeline of Registration

Regarding the timeline of the registration, SAMR is obliged to register the FIPE immediately, and issue the business licence on site if the application materials are

[384] Art. 12 Para. 1 FIPE Provisions.

[385] Art. 12 Para. 4 FIPE Provisions.

[386] Art. 12 Para. 5 FIPE Provisions.

[387] Art. 11 Para. 2 Partnership Enterprise Registration Measures.

[388] Art. 17 FIPE Provisions.

[389] Art. 4 FIPE Provisions. Regarding the liability of partners before legal establishment of the FIPE, see Sect. 8.4.1.

[390] Art. 201 ULPA.

[391] Grunewald (2019), p. 10. For more detail, see also Sect. 8.4.1.

[392] Ibid, p. 10.

complete and meet the statutory requirements.[393] Otherwise, SAMR has to make a decision whether or not to grant registration within twenty days of the application for registration having been accepted.[394] Should SAMR deny the registration of a FIPE, it must issue a written statement providing the reasons for the refusal.[395] In practice, registration of a FIPE in Shanghai normally takes between 5 to 10 business days, but can also take longer in individual cases depending on the scope of the documents that SAMR needs to verify.[396] A different timeline applies for FIPEs that fall under the restricted category of the Guidance Catalogue, but are not required to obtain pre-approval, and FIPEs that relate to areas for which other authorities or departments bear a special responsibility.[397] In such cases, SAMR formally has to solicit the opinion of the relevant authorities within five days of the application being accepted. After SAMR receives that written opinion, it has another five days to make the decision whether to grant or deny registration for the FIPE. In case of denial, a written statement has to be issued. This often affects investments in industries that are under the special supervisions of an authority, such as the finance and insurance industry, which would trigger the requirement to solicit the opinion of the CSRC or the China Banking and Insurance Regulatory Commission (CBIRC).[398]

Where a FIPE involves investments that are subject to government examination and verification, such procedures have to be carried out in addition to the FIPE registration.[399] A timeline for this extended procedure is not stipulated. However, as has been pointed out above, SAMR tis the competent authority to carry out such an examination and verification in accordance with the relevant provisions.[400] It is not clear however if this understanding also applied to the approval process with NDRC, as the respective 2014 Foreign Investment Measures make an explicit reference to FIPEs.[401] However, the practical relevance of this question is very limited. Because of the special investment restrictions of the FIPE and the reform of the NDRC approval regime, the only FIPEs that would be subject to NDRC pre-approval are investments of more than 50 million USD in the one industry in the restrictive category of the FDI Negative List that is open to FIPEs.[402]

[393] Art. 42 Para. 1 FIPE Provisions.

[394] Art. 42 Para. 2 FIPE Provisions.

[395] Art. 42 Para. 2 FIPE Provisions.

[396] Interview with a partner of a foreign law firm in Shanghai that the author has conducted in April 2020.

[397] Art. 42 Para. 3 FIPE Provisions.

[398] Pissler (2010), p. 128.

[399] Art. 43 FIPE Provisions.

[400] Art. 3 Para. 2 FIPE Implementation Circular.

[401] Art. 2 2014 Foreign Investment Measures.

[402] Art. 4 Para. 1 2014 Foreign Investment Measures. Regarding the limited use of FIPEs in the restricted category of the FDI Negative List in the Guidance Catalogue, see Sect. 4.1.7.

4.1.8.5 Subsequent Registration Obligations

Following the registration with SAMR, the FIPE has to undergo the same post-registration procedures as other FIEs, i.e., with SAFE for foreign exchange issues, SAT for taxes, and GAC for customs registration.[403] As all enterprises in China, FIPEs used to be subject to an annual inspection process by various government authorities.[404] This was first replaced by a more simplified annual reporting and disclosure procedure in 2014 that required the upload of specific information about the FIPE to SAMR's online enterprise credit information disclosure system.[405] This procedure now has further been reformed under the new unified administrative information reporting system with SAMR.[406]

The aforementioned registration process does not only apply to the establishment of a greenfield FIPE, but also when a foreign investor becomes partner of a domestic partnership enterprise, as such transforming the domestic-invested partnership into a FIPE.[407] In addition, registration with SAMR is required for any change of the registered items of the FIPE, including changes to the partnership agreement, information regarding the partners, or the FIPE's business scope.[408] Commentators have criticised this strict registration requirement as throwing the essence of a partnership 'out of the window' by making the government an indispensable 'partner', and giving the latter the final decision making power in any major partnership decision.[409]

4.1.9 The Partnership Agreement

The partnership agreement is the corporate charter of a partnership enterprise. It plays a central role in giving a FILPE the structure that is necessary to fulfil the defining elements of the standard corporate form. Therefore, a more detailed survey is undertaken of the partnership agreement under Chinese law.

[403] Art. 66 FIPE Provisions.

[404] Mahony (2015), p. 317.

[405] Arts. 8–9 Interim Regulations on the Disclosure of Enterprise Information (企业信息公示暂行条例), promulgated by the State Council 7 August 2014 and effective as of 1 October 2014, (Enterprise Information Regulations).

[406] Art. 1 Reporting Notice.

[407] Art. 12 FIPE Measures; Art. 63 FIPE Measures.

[408] Arts. 18–30 FIPE Provisions.

[409] Shaddox (2013), p. 472; Cui (2008), p. 30.

4.1.9.1 Nature of the Partnership Agreement

The formation of any type of civil law enterprise requires an underlying civil juristic act.[410] The PEL stipulates that the partnership agreement, concluded by all partners with the goal to establish a partnership enterprise, is the respective civil juristic act for the partnership enterprise.[411] Under German law, the legal nature of the partnership agreement is subject to long-lasting controversy.[412] The debate culminates in the question of whether the partnership agreement is a mere contractual agreement or stipulates something 'more' or something 'different' than a contract.[413] The question is rather relevant because it relates to the controversy around the legal nature of the partnership enterprise, and the legal nature of the partner's share of the partnership property.[414] In Germany, the prevailing opinion now regards the nature of the partnership agreement as simultaneously contractual, for its conclusion, and normative, for stipulating governing rules for the operation of the partnership enterprise that come close to the effect of normative laws.[415]

Under Chinese law, a dual function of the partnership agreement is likewise recognised. It creates a legal relationship between the parties that are involved in the partnership enterprise, and stipulates their rights and obligations.[416] At the same time, it forms the legal foundation (charter) for the establishment and operation of the partnership enterprise.[417] On the one hand, a partnership agreement contains regular contractual elements.[418] It is subject to the principles of voluntariness, equality, fairness, and good faith,[419] which are also the basic principles of the GPCL/GRCL for all civil activities.[420] Furthermore, the conclusion of the partnership agreement has to comply with the general requirements of the GPCL/GRCL[421] and the Contract Law[422] on the formation and validity of a contractual agreement.[423]

410Schmidt (2002), p. 75.

411Arts. 4–5 PEL.

412Instructive: Schmidt (2002), pp. 75–80; Wiedemann (2004), pp. 89–95.

413Wiedemann (2004), p. 90.

414Westermann (2017), § 5 No 132; Schmidt (2002), p. 547. For the detailed discussion, see Sect. 7.1.2.1.

415Schmidt (2002), p. 77.

416Zhang (张桂龙) and Liu (刘淑强) (1997), p. 41.

417Ibid, p. 41.

418Ibid, p. 41.

419Art. 5 PEL. For a more detailed analysis of these principles in respect to the partnership enterprise, see Zhang (张桂龙) and Liu (刘淑强) (1997), p. 42.

420Art. 4 GPCL/Arts. 5–7 GRCL.

421Especially Article 55 GPCL/Article 143 GRCL.

422For example, Articles 9–43 Contract Law.

423Li (李飞) (ed) (2006), p. 7. At the time of writing of this book, the comprehensive Civil Code has not yet been promulgated by the NPC. For respective provisions on partnership agreements, see Art. 751 of the PRC Civil Code (Draft) (中华人民共和国民法典 (草案)), issued by the NPC in November and December 2019.

On the other hand, the partnership agreement has an effect that reaches beyond a contract for the mutual exchange of specific performances.[424] The capital contributions of the partners have the purpose to constitute a material basis for the operation of the partnership enterprise. As such, they are obligations owed to the partnership enterprise, not among the partners.[425] The partnership agreement stipulates and defines different types of legal relationships at the same time: reciprocal legal relationships between all partners, as well as legal relationships between each partner and the partnership enterprise. Should a general partner violate the prohibition in Article 32 PEL to enter into competition with the partnership enterprise, either the partnership enterprise or another partner can file a direct claim for compensation against that general partner, depending on who suffers the loss.[426] Because of this dual function, Chinese scholars regard the partnership agreement as a special type of contract.[427] Thus, the understanding of the Chinese partnership law is similar to the conception of the German partnership law in this regard. The distinction between a common contractual relationship, and the special nature of the partnership agreement, is further reflected in the terminology of the PEL. The Chinese lawmaker has purposefully termed the charter of the partnership enterprise 'partnership agreement' (合伙协议) instead of 'partnership contract' (合伙合同).[428]

4.1.9.2 Written Form of the Partnership Agreement

According to Article 4 PEL, the partnership agreement must be put in writing. This formal requirement was already stipulated in the GPCL for the establishment of an Individual Partnership.[429] However, in practice, partners have often neglected to record the partnership agreement, resulting in numerous partnership disputes.[430] Despite the written form being a mandatory requirement, the SPC has decided, in an interpretation of the GPCL in 1988, that a partnership relationship can also be established by an oral agreement under certain circumstances.[431] In the absence of a written partnership agreement, and without the certification and registration from SAMR having been obtained, the People's Court can recognise a partnership relationship if the parties have satisfied all the other requirements for a partnership,

[424]Zhang (张桂龙) and Liu (刘淑强) (1997), pp. 41–42.

[425]Art. 20 PEL; Zhang (张桂龙) and Liu (刘淑强) (1997), pp. 41–42.

[426]Art. 32 PEL; Li (李飞) (ed) (2006), p. 156.

[427]Su (苏号朋) and Wang (王斌来) (1997), pp. 28–29.

[428]Gao (高富平) et al. (1997), p. 140.

[429]Art. 31 GPCL.

[430]Huang (黄毅诚) (1997), p. 14.

[431]Item 50 Opinions on Certain Issues Concerning the Implementation of the 'General Principles of Civil Law of the PRC' (Trial) (贯彻执行《中华人民共和国法通则》若干问题的意见 (试行)), promulgated by the Supreme People's Court on 26 January 1988 and revised on 18 December 2008 with effect as of 24 December 2008 (Opinion of the SPC on the Implementation of the GPCL).

and if two or more persons without any direct interests thereto prove that an oral partnership agreement had been concluded.[432] No clarification has been offered on whether this interpretation of the SPC also applies to partnership enterprises under the new PEL. This is of particular interest as it is closely related to the question of what type of legal entity (if any) is established if all criteria of the foundation of a partnership enterprise are met, except the written partnership agreement. *Münzel* assumes that the SPC would apply the same doctrine to a partnership enterprise today as it did in 1988, even if that could lead to unfair consequences for some 'partners' if they had no intention to act as a (general) partner of a partnership enterprise.[433] *Chen* seems to share this opinion, as he emphasises the civil contractual nature of the relationship and liabilities between the partners and the partnership enterprise, and between the partnership enterprise and third parties, that otherwise would disappear, leaving partners or third parties unprotected.[434] This assessment is further supported by the approach taken by courts in dealing with *de facto* partnerships, as is analysed in more detail below.[435] Under certain circumstances, it seems possible that a Chinese court would recognise a FILPE despite no written partnership agreement having been concluded. This can pose a risk to foreign investors if they are drawn into a partnership enterprise that they did not want to be a part of. Investors therefore need to be cautious if a close collaboration with a (Chinese) partner may have evolved from a mere contractual relationship to the *de facto* establishment of a partnership enterprise.

4.1.9.3 Mandatory and Default Content of the Partnership Agreement

The PEL stipulates in Article 18 a statutory minimum of ten items that have to be regulated in the partnership agreement. Because of the special characteristics of a limited partnership enterprise, Article 63 PEL alters some of the content from Article 18, adding further items that need to be regulated in a partnership agreement of a limited partnership enterprise.[436] The minimum content to be regulated in the partnership agreement of a FILPE is: (1) the name of the partnership enterprise,[437] and location of its principal business premises;[438] (2) the objective[439] of the

[432]Item 50 Opinion of the SPC on the Implementation of the GPCL.

[433]Münzel (2006a), pp. 405–406.

[434]Chen (2014a), p. 68.

[435]See Sect. 4.1.10.

[436]Li (李飞) (ed) (2006), p. 102.

[437]Art. 18 No 1 PEL. See Sect. 4.1.8.2.

[438]Art. 18 No 1 PEL. See Sect. 4.1.8.2 fn. 375.

[439]The objective of the partnership enterprise describes the goal that it aims to pursue. It is not necessarily identical to the individual objective of each partner. Rather, the partners must combine their respective objectives to identify a common objective that the partnership enterprise shall pursue (Li (李飞) (ed) (2006), p. 27.

partnership enterprise and its business scope;[440] (3) names and domiciles of the partners, and their status as general partner or limited partner;[441] (4) the amount, time limit, and form of capital contribution;[442] (5) the method of profit distribution and loss sharing among the partners;[443] (6) the execution and management of partnership affairs, including the requirements and procedures for selecting a managing partner, the scope of power of the managing partner, and the conditions under which a managing partner can be expelled;[444] (7) joining and retiring from the partnership;[445] (8) methods of dispute settlement;[446] (9) dissolution and liquidation of the partnership;[447] (10) liabilities of the partners for breach of contract;[448] (11) the procedure for a limited partner to convert to a general partner and vice versa.[449]

Regarding the specific configuration of these items, the partners have a significant degree of discretion as the PEL does not prescribe detailed compulsory stipulations on the organisational structure and operation of partnership enterprises.[450] In contrast to the 1997 PEL, and most of China's FDI legislation, the revised PEL proclaims the freedom of partners to contract into their own arrangements, and thus formulates many more of the statute's rules as default, rather than mandatory, provisions.[451] The detailed analysis in the subsequent chapters will show that, in many provisions of the PEL, partners are authorised to agree on their own disposition of an issue, or that default rules are accompanied by an explicit invitation to contract out of them.[452] In addition, Article 19, Paragraph 3 PEL, stipulates a general default provision.[453] Any matter that is not—or not clearly—specified in the partnership agreement shall be resolved through consultation between the partners. Should consultation fail, the matter is subject to the provisions of the PEL or other relevant laws and administrative regulations. While the philosophy embodied in these structures may not appear surprising from the perspective of jurisdictions of developed market economies, they constitute a very significant shift of profound importance in the Chinese political, commercial, and legal environment.[454]

---

[440] Art. 18 No 2 PEL. See Sect. 4.1.7.

[441] Art. 18 No 3, Art. 63 No 1 PEL.

[442] Art. 18 No 4 PEL.

[443] Art. 18 No 5 PEL.

[444] Art. 18 No 6, Art. 63 No 2–4 PEL.

[445] Art. 18 No 7, Art. 63 No 5 PEL. For a further analysis, see Sect. 9.3.

[446] Art. 18 No 8 PEL. For a further analysis, see Sect. 4.1.9.5.

[447] Art. 18 No 9 PEL. For a further analysis, see Sect. 9.2.2.

[448] Art. 18 No 10 PEL. For a further analysis, see Sect. 8.4.5.

[449] Art. 63 No 6 PEL. For a further analysis, see Sect. 9.3.5.

[450] Werthwein (2010), p. 49.

[451] Howson (2015), p. 402.

[452] Ibid, p. 402.

[453] Li (李飞) (ed) (2006), pp. 30–31.

[454] Howson (2015), p. 402.

In addition to the eleven mandatory items listed above, the partnership agreement can contain further provisions tailored to the actual business needs of the partners.[455] Defining a specific term of the partnership enterprise is a rather common provision.[456] The reason is that the circumstances under which a partner may withdraw from a partnership enterprise differ depending on whether a term has been specified.[457] For FILPEs, detailed specifications of the duties and responsibilities of the managing partners are common.[458] For a partnership enterprise with the purpose to make private equity investments, a provision might be added that specifies the types of investment that shall be made.[459] In the light of the diverse market practices and economic conditions within the large geographical territory, the commercial terms in the partnership agreement vary from investment fund to investment fund in China.[460] Notwithstanding the contractual freedom and flexibility that is granted to the partners, the mandatory provisions of the PEL and FIPE Legislation mark a firm boundary for the principle of party autonomy.[461]

This section illustrates that partners can tailor a partnership enterprise towards their individual needs and preferences to a large degree. This becomes particularly clear when comparing it with the minimal degree of autonomy that investors had in drafting the articles of association of an EJV.[462] However, this requires a significant amount of negotiations among the partners, and sophisticated contract drafting skills. Against the background of limited experience and lack of awareness of Chinese investors, commentators have raised concerns that smaller partnership enterprises might not be equipped with a well-tailored partnership agreement that specifies existing or potential issues of the enterprise.[463]

4.1.9.4 Governing Law

It has been noted above that two distinct dimensions of flexibility can be identified in enterprise organisation law. The first is the ability to select, within one jurisdiction, from different statutory forms of enterprises, and from different default rules.[464] The second dimension is the ability of an investor to choose the governing law for an enterprise from among different jurisdictions.[465] This choice of the jurisdiction in

[455] Li (李飞) (ed) (2006), pp. 29–30.
[456] Ibid, p. 30.
[457] Arts. 45–46 PEL. Additionally, see Sect. 9.3.2.
[458] Yu et al. (2012b), p. 13.
[459] Lin (2013a), p. 206.
[460] Ibid, p. 206.
[461] Li (李飞) (ed) (2006), p. 31.
[462] Kroymann (2009), pp. 126–127.
[463] Lin (2013a), p. 212; Lin (2011), p. 213.
[464] Armour et al. (2017), p. 21.
[465] Ibid, pp. 20–21.

which an enterprise will be incorporated relates to the principle of party autonomy, and to conflict of laws rules. 'In the U.S., for example, the prevailing choice of law rule for corporate law is the "place of incorporation" rule, which permits a business corporation to be incorporated under—and hence governed by—the law of any of the 50 individual states (or any foreign country).'[466] Following European Court of Justice Decisions,[467] the same principle now applies throughout the European Union, providing for domestic recognition of corporations that were formed in other member states.[468] This abolished the 'real seat' doctrine according to which, in many European countries, firms had formerly been required to incorporate under the law of the state where the enterprise had its principal place of business.[469]

From the investor's perspective, a non-Chinese party will typically prefer a non-Chinese law to govern his legal relationships, as he will generally be more familiar with the laws of his home jurisdiction or those of a third country, and feel that these laws offer greater certainty.[470] This leads to the question whether Chinese law permits the establishment of a FILPE under the governance of the law of a foreign jurisdiction. Neither this question nor how to determine the applicable law for a partnership enterprise in China has yet been analysed in legal literature.[471]

The rules on conflict of laws in China have materially been modernised and systemised in 2010 with the promulgation of the 'Foreign-Related Civil Relations Law'.[472] The law stipulates that the conflict of law provisions, and the option for a choice of law only apply to 'foreign-related' civil relations.[473] Under what circumstances civil relations are regarded as 'foreign-related', has been further defined in a judicial interpretation of the SPC.[474] A FILPE, by definition, requires the involvement of at least one foreign enterprise or foreign individual. This is explicitly recognised by the SPC as establishing the foreign relationship, and the application

---

466 Ibid, p. 21.

467 *European Court of Justice*, Case C-212/97, *Centros* [1999], ECR 1999 I-1459; *European Court of Justice*, Case C-20/00, *Überseering* [2002], ECR 2002 I-9919; *European Court of Justice*, Case C-167/01, *Inspire Art.* [2003], ECR 2003 I-10155.

468 Armour et al. (2017), p. 21.

469 Ibid, p. 21.

470 Herbert Smith Freehills LLP (2016), p. 7.

471 The later analysis will show that the determination of the applicable law in a FILPE with a foreign corporate general partner reaches an additional level of complexity. See Sects. 8.2.2.2.1 and 8.2.2.2.3.

472 PRC Law on the Application of Laws to Foreign-Related Civil Relations (中华人民共和国涉外民事关系法律适用法), adopted at the 17th Session of the Standing Committee of the 11th National People's Congress on 28 October 2010 and effective as of 1 April 2011.

473 Art. 2 Para. 1 Foreign-Related Civil Relations Law.

474 Art. 1 First Interpretation of Certain Issues Concerning the Application of the 'PRC Law on the Application of Laws to Foreign-Related Civil Relations' (适用《中华人民共和国涉外民事关系法律适用法》若干问题的解释(一)), promulgated by the Supreme People's Court on 28 December 2012 and with effect as of 7 January 2013 (SPC Interpretation of the Foreign-Related Civil Relations Law).

of the conflict of law provisions.[475] The Foreign-Related Civil Relations Law strongly emphasises the principle of party autonomy.[476] According to Article 3, the parties may freely choose the applicable law by express agreement, as long as this is in accordance with the Foreign-Related Civil Relations Law and other Chinese statutes.[477] Regarding the EJV, CJV, and WFOE, choice of a foreign governing law is expressly prohibited in the respective implementing regulations and the Contract Law.[478] Notably, the FIPE Measures and FIPE Provisions do not contain any similar provisions with regard to the governing law. While this could lead to the conclusion that the investors are free to choose the governing law of a FILPE, the SPC interpretation has also restricted the party autonomy granted by the Foreign-Related Civil Relations Law. The parties may only select the applicable law, when a law explicitly permits a choice of law.[479] Due to the absence of such a positive codification in the FIPE Legislation, investors may not pick a foreign law to govern a FILPE.

This leads to the specific Chinese conflict of laws rules. For legal persons, the rules contain an explicit regulation to determine the governing law in Article 14 Foreign-Related Civil Relations Law. The Chinese lawmaker choose a middle ground between the place of incorporation and the real seat doctrine.[480] The governing law of a legal person is generally the law of the place of incorporation, but if it differs from the location of the place of the principal business, the law of the latter may be the governing law.[481] This provision is criticised for leaving too much discretionary power to judges.[482] The law that is deemed applicable shall govern the issues of legal capacity, the capacity to act, the organisational structure, shareholders' rights and obligations, and other related matters of a legal person.[483]

For enterprises that are non-legal persons, like partnership enterprises,[484] no corresponding special provision has been included. This is somewhat surprising, as the FIPE Legislation was already in effect at the time that the Foreign-Related Civil Relations Law was promulgated. It is not clear why the Chinese lawmaker has not provided an explicit conflict of laws regulation for partnership enterprises, or for non-legal person enterprises in general. Under German conflict of laws' provisions, one rule applies to all enterprise forms.[485] Legal persons and partnership enterprises

[475] Art. 1 No 1 SPC Interpretation of the Foreign-Related Civil Relations Law.

[476] Chen (2014b), pp. 53–54.

[477] Ibid, p. 54.

[478] Art. 126 Para. 2 Contract Law; Art. 12 EJV Implementing Regulations; Art. 55 CJV Implementing Regulations; Art. 2 Para. 1 WFOE Implementing Regulations.

[479] Art. 6 SPC Interpretation of the Foreign-Related Civil Relations Law.

[480] Du (2014), p. 341.

[481] Art. 14 Foreign-Related Civil Relations Law.

[482] Du (2014), p. 348.

[483] Art. 14 Para. 1 Foreign-Related Civil Relations Law.

[484] Regarding the legal nature of the FILPE, see Sect. 7.1.1.1.

[485] Kindler (2018), p. 1682.

are treated equally, because they have comparable characteristics and fulfil similar functions within corporate law.[486] In addition, applying one conflict of laws rule to all enterprise forms avoids the problems that can arise in the absence of a clear line between similar types of enterprises.[487] Under Chinese law, the express wording of 'legal person' in Article 14 Foreign-Related Civil Relations Law makes it difficult to expand the scope of this provisions to non-legal person enterprise forms. Article 2, Paragraph 2 Foreign-Related Civil Relations Law provides that the principle of the closest connection shall apply as a supplementary principle to a foreign-related civil relation that is not governed by the special provisions of the Foreign-Related Civil Relations Law or any other law. This leads to the question whether a conflict of law rule for partnership enterprises is provided in any other Chinese law. Aside from the Foreign-Related Civil Relations Law, a substantial number of conflict of law provisions are scattered among various laws enacted by the NPC and its Standing Committee.[488] The provisions of the Foreign-Related Civil Relations Law are generally multilateral choice of law rules that stipulate which law—of all the laws that have a connection to the specific matter—shall be applicable.[489] In contrast, conflict of laws' provisions in other laws are often unilateral choice of law rules that merely define the international reach of the respective law.[490] Such a provision determines when Chinese law is applicable, but it makes no reference to what shall be the governing law if Chinese law does not apply. An example of a unilateral choice of law provisions is found in Article 2 WFOE Law, which states that 'for the purposes of this law, a WFOE refers to an enterprise established in China under the relevant laws of China with its capital fully invested by foreign investors'.[491] For partnership enterprises, Article 2, Paragraph 1 PEL states in a very similar manner that 'for the purposes of this law, partnership enterprises shall mean general partnership enterprises and limited partnership enterprises established in accordance with this law and within the territory of China'. For foreign investors, Article 3 FIPE Measures makes reference to Article 2, Paragraph 1 PEL when stating that a foreign-invested partnership enterprise can be established in the territory of China only in compliance with the PEL. This means that a FILPE in China may only be established under the provisions of the PEL, and thus under the governance of Chinese law.[492] Since the Foreign-Related Civil Relations Law does not provide specific conflict of law rules for partnership enterprises, this unilateral rule in the

[486]Ibid, pp. 1682–1683.

[487]Ibid, p. 1683.

[488]Huang (2014), p. 6.

[489]Cuniberti (2017), p. 4.

[490]Ibid, p. 16.

[491]Du (2014), p. 334.

[492]Leibküchler ultimately reaches the same conclusion by stating that all types of FIEs are subject to Chinese law as governing law (Leibküchler 2017, p. 122).

PEL shall thus have prevailing effect.[493] The role of bilateral (investment) treaties that China has entered into will be analysed further below.[494]

4.1.9.5 Conflict Resolution

The establishment and operation of a FILPE involves multiple parties, thereby carrying the risk of conflicts and disputes between the involved partners.[495] This is recognised by the PEL, which requires the partners to determine the methods for settling disputes in the partnership agreement.[496] Article 103 PEL further stipulates a three-stage procedure for dispute resolution. In the initial stage, partners are encouraged to settle disputes through friendly consultation and mediation.[497] Advised is to include in the partnership agreement an escalation clause that specifies how such mediation shall be carried out and provides a clear time limit for friendly consultations.[498] However, parties can also opt to rule out mediation and consultation, and proceed directly to the second stage: arbitration.[499] For emerging market economies like China, the reliability of formal institutions can be limited.[500] Judges do not enjoy complete independence in China, and can be subject to political influence.[501] Against this background, arbitration is the most common and most recommended method of dispute resolution for foreign-related disputes in China.[502] The details of the arbitration proceeding, tribunal and enforcement are regulated in the 'Arbitration Law'.[503] The field of China-related arbitration is subject to in depth analysis by scholars and practitioners. Regarding the formulation of a valid and unambiguous arbitration clause, the choice of the right arbitration institution, differences between onshore and offshore arbitration, and etcetera, reference is made to respective specialised literature.[504] An important point with regard to the enforcement is that

---

[493] Art. 3 SPC Interpretation of the Foreign-Related Civil Relations Law.

[494] See Sect. 8.2.

[495] Li (李飞) (ed) (2006), p. 28.

[496] Art. 18 No 8 PEL.

[497] Art. 103 Para. 2 PEL.

[498] Li (李飞) (ed) (2006), p. 29.

[499] Herbert Smith Freehills LLP (2016), p. 33.

[500] Kroymann (2009), pp. 17–19.

[501] Ibid, p. 18; Cohen and Lange (1997), p. 351.

[502] Yang (杨杰) and Qu (曲天明) (2010), pp. 63–66; Li (李飞) (ed) (2006), p. 164; Roos and Steinberg (2012), 27; Herbert Smith Freehills LLP (2016), p. 15.

[503] PRC Arbitration Law (中华人民共和国仲裁法), adopted at the 9th Session of the Standing Committee of the 8th National People's Congress on 31 August 1994, amended on 27 August 2009 and effective as of the same date.

[504] Exemplary, see Trakman (2015), pp. 131–194; Lianbin et al. (2016), pp. 1–51; Herbert Smith Freehills LLP (2016), pp. 13–37; Li (李飞) (ed) (2006), p. 163.

China is a member of the 'New York Convention'.[505] An offshore commercial arbitral awards issued in another New York Convention country will therefore be recognised and enforced by Chinese courts.[506] An equivalent regime is in place that ensures recognition and enforcement of arbitral awards issued in Hong Kong.[507] If arbitration is not stipulated in the partnership agreement, partners may still opt for arbitration in a written agreement after a dispute arises.[508] Should the partners avoid arbitration altogether, a dispute is subject to litigation in Chinese courts.[509] Partnership disputes are regarded as contractual disputes, and thus fall to the People's Court (人民法官).[510] Regarding details of litigation in China, reference is made to respective literature.[511]

4.1.9.6 Language of the Partnership Agreement

In international agreements, the language of a contract is a critical aspect in ensuring that all parties fully understand the contractual provisions, and in safeguarding that the intended meaning of the agreement is accentuated in a possible dispute. China's Contract Law provides in Article 125, Paragraph 2 that, in general, contracts can be written in Chinese or any other language. However, certain types of contracts are required to be in the Chinese language, including the articles of association of an EJV, CJV, and WFOE.[512] For the FILPE, a comparable stipulation does not exist. However, it can still be advisable to make the partnership agreement bilingual, in Chinese and the language of the foreign party. Often, the Chinese party to the FILPE would insist on a Chinese language version of the agreement. In addition, during the registration of the FILPE, SAMR will check if the application materials are complete and meet the statutory requirements.[513] A partnership agreement that is not written in Chinese, could cause problems or delays during the registration process.

When a partnership agreement is written in Chinese and another language, the question arises on how to deal with differences between both versions. The Contract Law stipulates that generally both language version shall be equally valid.[514] In case

505 Convention on the Recognition and Enforcement of Foreign Arbitral Awards, promulgated by the Secretary-General of the United Nations and effective as of 7 June 1959.

506 'Commercial' excludes, for example, sports arbitral awards between a private person and the Chinese government; Herbert Smith Freehills LLP (2016), pp. 23–24.

507 Herbert Smith Freehills LLP (2016), p. 23.

508 Art. 103 Para. 2 PEL.

509 Art. 103 Para. 3 PEL.

510 Li (李飞) (ed) (2006), p. 28.

511 Hübner (2014); Peerenboom (2010).

512 Art. 7 Para. 2 EJV Implementing Regulations; Art. 7 Para. 2 CJV Implementing Regulations; Art. 10 Para. 2 WFOE Implementing Regulations.

513 Art. 42 Para. 1 FIPE Provisions.

514 Art. 125 Para. 2 Contract Law.

of deviation between the versions, in practice, a determination will be made which wording best reflects the intention and the purpose of the overall agreement.[515] Because this approach is subject to unpredictable interpretations and ambiguity, practitioners recommend to specify in the partnership agreement one official language that prevails in case of a dispute.[516] This also shows the critical importance of ensuring through correct translations that multiple language versions of the partnership agreement—as any other contract with regard to the FILPE—are consistent.[517]

4.1.9.7 Effectiveness of the Partnership Agreement

The partnership agreement becomes effective after all partners have signed it or affixed their seals thereto.[518] However, the FILPE as a partnership enterprise is established and takes effect towards third parties only when it is registered with SAMR.[519] Article 19, Paragraph 1 PEL clarifies that the partners are internally bound to their obligations once the partnership agreement is in force, regardless of the completion of registration.[520] Partners are also responsible for bearing all costs that are incurred between the taking effect of the partnership agreement and registration of the FILPE.[521]

4.1.10 Partnership Enterprises in Chinese Courts: The Treatment of De Facto Partnerships

An extensive review by *Howson* of more than 2000 corporate and partnership law related disputes shows that partnerships do not figure as prominently in Chinese courts as companies.[522] However, partnership law or the partnership form do play a central rôle in a significant number of case decisions, including final rehearing by the Supreme People's Court.[523] In the overwhelming majority of cases, they are not partnerships that have been established as such *ex ante*, but rather that have been identified as a partnership or partnership relationship *ex post* by a judicial institution.[524] Courts are confronted with entities established and registered within the

[515]Chow (2002), p. 68.

[516]Harris (2009).

[517]Mahony (2015), p. 332; Chow (2002), p. 68.

[518]Art. 19 Para. 1 PEL.

[519]Art. 5 Para. 1, Art. 6 FIPE Measures; Arts. 4–5 FIPE Provisions.

[520]Li (李飞) (ed) (2006), p. 30.

[521]ibid, p. 30.

[522]Howson (2015), p. 406.

[523]ibid, p. 406.

[524]ibid, pp. 406–407.

framework of the Company Law but that actually constitute partnership enterprises.[525] Refusing to apply substantive corporate law to these entities, Chinese courts instead apply universal partnership law principles to what are formally called corporations—making them *de facto* partnerships.[526]

The reason for this lies in the unique and rapid development of the corporate law regime in China since the late 1970s.[527] Investments and commercial activities were undertaken through special arrangements so that even when registered with SAIC, the resulting enterprise would often have no legal basis in Company Law or the broader corporate law framework.[528] Some enterprises had a prior legal basis, as is the case with certain 'collectively-owned enterprises'. Others were based on regulations promulgated by local governments, deviating from national laws. A rather large number of enterprises in China was directly established by government departments at national and local levels.[529] In addition, the rather sketchy and vaguely drafted laws and regulations did not always specify the distinctions that set a partnership apart from a corporation. The task of identifying the actual nature of an enterprise was therefore left to the courts.[530] Before the LPE was introduced in 2006, *de facto* LPEs have been formed under the formal umbrella of the Company Law.[531] Courts refused to miss-apply Company Law doctrines to these enterprises, and made them subject to partnership law principles instead.[532] In a 2014 opinion on a dispute between investors of a coal mine, the Supreme People's Court decided that the mine was a partnership by operation of law, based on the reading of the original agreement between the investors, notwithstanding that it was formally registered with SAIC as a different type of enterprise.[533] The SPC granted the plaintiff a property right in the enterprise according to the principles of a GPE.[534] The fact that the courts apply partnership principles to *de facto* partnerships is regarded as a demonstration of judicial autonomy and competence of the involved judges by *Howson*.[535]

Regarding FIEs in general, or Non-Legal Person CJVs in particular, however, there seems to be no evidence of any litigation where foreign-invested partnership

[525]ibid, p, 356.

[526]ibid, p. 356; Clarke (2005–2006), p. 55.

[527]Howson (2010), p. 356.

[528]ibid, pp. 356–357.

[529]ibid, pp. 357–358.

[530]ibid, p. 361.

[531]ibid, p. 362.

[532]ibid, p. 362.

[533]Su Qi et al v Li Zhanfei et al, application for retrial of civil ruling on dispute over recognition of equity interest and profit distribution (苏琪与府谷县老高川乡恒益煤矿、李占飞、李维斌、李旺荣股权确认及分配利润纠纷申请再审民事裁定书), Supreme People's Court of the PRC, Case No 2014/20 (最高人民法院(2014)民申字第20号) , judgment date: 26 January 2014, available at <http://www.court.gov.cn/wenshu/xiangqing-2539.html>, accessed 15 May 2020.

[534]Ibid.

[535]Howson (2010), p. 362.

type enterprises were made subject to the PEL or partnership law principles.[536] Reasons for this can be the infrequency of partnership type FIEs or the strong preference among foreign investors to select arbitration for dispute resolution instead of Chinese courts.[537]

4.1.11 Taxation of Income from Partnership Enterprises

The following analysis of partnership enterprise taxation in China is limited to its basic principles. The reasoning for this limitation is twofold. Firstly, tax analysis is very complex. A limited partnership enterprise can be structured very flexibly with regard to its ownership structure and profit distribution. In addition, a FILPE, by its very nature, involves a cross-border scenario which affects the tax regimes of a minimum of two jurisdictions, and—a possibility—of at least one double taxation treaty. This results in a large number of potential scenarios, each with different consequences and indications for taxation that need to be analysed.

> Apart from the problems under the national tax law of many jurisdictions, this is particularly due to two conflicting principles: some countries treat partnerships as taxable entities, while others treat them as transparent and only see the partners as taxpayers for tax purposes. This situation can lead to double taxation or double non-taxation. Particular problems can furthermore arise in triangular situations.[538]

Thus, 'the taxation of partnerships in cross-border situations has proved to be exceptionally complicated and is perhaps one of the most difficult issues in the application of rules on international tax law'.[539] As such, this aspect requires its own research project of the FILPE with a singular tax law focus.[540] Secondly, the scholarship has advocated that an excessively strong focus on the taxation of limited partnership enterprises can lead to an inefficient choice of enterprise form. Substantial non-tax related elements of an enterprise determine the functionality and efficiency of an enterprise form. The importance of these non-tax factors can be underestimated and misunderstood if they are suppressed by tax considerations. 'Many businesses probably have adopted this form because the tax advantages of partnership offset agency and other organisational costs'.[541] Even if the cost of operating the business in the partnership form is higher than in other enterprise forms, the partnership will remain an attractive option as long as the tax benefit is substantial enough.[542] From the perspective of an investor, understandably, a

[536] Howson (2015), p. 409.

[537] Ibid, p. 409.

[538] Haase (2014), pp. 3, 8.

[539] Essers and Meussen (2004), p. 415.

[540] Respective examples are Liu (2014), pp. 183–215; Meyer (2016), pp. 203–222.

[541] Ribstein (1988), p. 871.

[542] ibid, p. 873.

business form is considered efficient as long as the tax advantage outweighs the operation and agency costs. However, for an academic analysis whether the FILPE fulfils the requirements of a standard corporate form, it is important to take a broader approach, and choose a perspective that is not compromised by particular tax law considerations. The German GmbH & Co. KG, which has evolved beyond merely offering tax advantages, can serve as an example. While this combined form of a limited partnership initially gained popularity because it allowed avoiding double taxation, this benefit was later abolished by a tax reform.[543] Meanwhile, the GmbH & Co. KG is still being chosen as an investment vehicle because it can offer advantages from the perspective of enterprise organisation law.[544] Therefore, this book only outlines the fundamentals of the tax treatment of partnership enterprises in China. For a more detailed discussion, reference is made to specialised literature.[545]

4.1.11.1 Taxation of Purely Domestic-Invested Partnership Enterprises

Originally, partnership enterprises in China were regarded as taxable entities and subject to double taxation: the partnership enterprise itself was taxed as an enterprise and the partners were subject to individual income tax on the profits obtained from the partnership.[546] This practice was already abolished in 2000, pursuant to Article 4 of 'Tax Circular 91'.[547] Article 6 of the revised PEL and the subsequently issued 'Tax Circular 159',[548] provided further clarity. Under these regulations, a partnership enterprise is in principle treated as a flow-through entity in China.[549] The first unified 'Enterprise Income Tax Law',[550] promulgated in 2008, emphasises this general principle, and excludes Chinese partnership enterprises from its scope.[551] Income tax is only imposed at the partner level, instead of at the level of the

[543]Fleischer and Wansleben (2017), pp. 176–177; Raiser and Veil (2015), p. 658.

[544]Fleischer and Wansleben (2017), pp. 176–177.

[545]Liu (2014), pp. 183–215; Meyer (2016), pp. 203–222.

[546]Werthwein (2010), p. 47; Li (李飞) (ed) (2006), p. 9.

[547]Circular Concerning Collecting Individual Income Tax from Investors of Sole Proprietorship Enterprises and Partnership Enterprises (关于个人独资企业和合伙企业投资者征收个人所得税的规定的通知), jointly promulgated by the Ministry of Finance and State Administration of Taxation on 19 September 2000, amended on 10 April 2006, amended on 3 June 2008 and amended on 29 July 2011.

[548]Circular on Issues Concerning Income Tax for Partners of Partnership Enterprises (关于合伙企业合伙人所得税问题的通知), promulgated jointly by the Ministry of Finance and State Administration of Taxation on 23 December 2008 and effective as of 1 January 2008.

[549]Art. 3 Tax Circular 159, Art. 6 PEL.

[550]PRC Law on Enterprise Income Tax (中华人民共和国企业所得税法), adopted at the 5th Session of the 10th National People's Congress on 16 March 2007, amended at the 26th session of the Standing Committee of the 12th National People's Congress on 24 February 2017, amended at the 7th Session of the Standing Committee of the 13th National People's Congress on 29 December 2018 with effect as of the same day.

[551]Art. 2 Enterprise Income Tax Law.

partnership enterprise, thereby making each partner of a partnership enterprise a taxpayer.[552] In principle, a legal person partner is subject to Enterprise Income Tax at the standard rate of 25%,[553] and a natural person partner is subject to Individual Income Tax at progressive rates from 5 to 35%[554] at the national level.[555]

However, several local tax authorities have issued conflicting local tax policies to promote the establishment of partnership enterprises.[556] Instead of applying the progressive tax rates, these local regulations have deemed natural person's income from partnerships to be dividend, making them subject to a flat rate of 20% Individual Income Tax. Some only applied this special tax treatment to limited partners, others also extended it to general partners under certain circumstances.[557] While it is a legitimate discussion whether limited and general partners should be treated differently in respect to the applicable rate of Individual Income Tax,[558] these local tax policies are violating national tax regulations.[559] However, in December 2018, the State Council announced a special tax program that allows individual partners of venture capital enterprises to choose between a flat rate of 20% income tax on their income from equity transfers and dividends, or to pay the progressive rates of 5% to 35%.[560] This preferential treatment is granted for a 5 year period from 1 January 2019 to 31 December 2023, and aims to enhance economic development and technological innovation through larger venture capital investments.[561]

Remarkably, a legal person partner cannot use losses incurred by the partnership enterprise to offset other income.[562] The loss from a partnership enterprise will only be allowed to be offset against future profits from said partnership enterprise.[563] This

---

[552] Art. 2 Tax Circular 159; Art. 6 PEL.

[553] Art. 4 Enterprise Income Tax Law.

[554] Art. 3 Para. 2 PRC Law on Individual Income Tax (中华人民共和国个人所得税法), adopted at the 3rd Session of the 5th National People's Congress on 10 September 1980, amended at the 4th Session of the Standing Committee of the 8th National People's Congress on 31 October 1993, amended at the 11th Session of the Standing Committee of the 9th National People's Congress on 30 August 1999, amended at the 18th Session of the Standing Committee of the 10th National People's Congress on 27 October 2005, amended at the 28th Session of the Standing Committee of the 10th National People's Congress on 29 June 2007, amended at the 31st Session of the Standing Committee of the 10th National People's Congress on 29 December 2007, amended at the 21st Session of the Standing Committee of the 11th National People's Congress on 30 June 2011 and amended at the 5th Session of the Standing Committee of the 13th National People's Congress on 31 August 2018 and with effect as of 01 January 2019 (Individual Income Tax Law).

[555] Liu (2014), p. 186.

[556] Ibid, p. 186; Chen and Chen (2009), p. 34.

[557] Liu (2014), pp. 186–187; Chen and Chen (2009), p. 34.

[558] See exemplary the discussions in Ting and Ge (2014), pp. 675–676; Chen and Chen (2009), p. 34.

[559] Art. 6 Tax Circular 159.

[560] State Council (2018).

[561] State Council (2018).

[562] Art. 5 Tax Circular 159.

[563] For a detailed discussion, see Ting and Ge (2014), p. 675.

limitation on the tax use of losses reduces the benefit of the flow-through character of partnership enterprises.[564]

4.1.11.2 Taxation of FIPEs

The Chinese lawmaker and foreign investors all regarded the taxation of income derived from FIPEs as a key element for the practical success of the FIPE as an enterprise form.[565] The FIPE itself, like it's purely domestic-invested equivalent, is regarding as a flow-through entity.[566] Its Chinese partners will be taxed according to the conditions outlined above. In principle, a FIPE can thus enjoy substantially more tax advantages in comparison to a corporation, which is generally subject to double taxation under the classical system of China's Enterprise Income Tax.[567]

However, no clarifying tax regulations have been issued so far on how foreign partners of the FIPE will be taxed in China exactly.[568] Regarding a foreign legal person partner, the Enterprise Income Tax Law stipulates an initial differentiation between 'tax resident enterprises' and 'non-resident enterprises'.[569] If the foreign legal person partner is established under the law of a foreign jurisdiction, but with its place of effective management located in China, it should be regarded as a tax resident enterprise, and hence be subject to 25% Enterprise Income Tax on its income generated in China.[570] Otherwise, the foreign legal person partner is considered a non-resident enterprise, and as such subject to a 'Permanent Establishment' test for determination of its Enterprise Income Tax liabilities.[571] Should a foreign non-resident enterprise be regarded as having a Permanent Establishment in China, its income derived therefrom is likewise subject to Enterprise Income Tax at 25%.[572] Should the Permanent Establishment test be negative, income sourced in China is subject to a lower withholding tax of—generally—10%.[573] Permanent Establishment is defined as 'an organisation or place in China where business is carried

[564] Cao (2011), p. 17.

[565] Yang (杨杰) and Qu (曲天明) (2010), pp. 65–66; Mahony (2015), p. 233; Yu et al. (2012b), p. 12.

[566] Art. 11 FIPE Measures in conjunction with Art. 6 PEL.

[567] Ting and Ge (2014), p. 672; Yu et al. (2012b), p. 12.

[568] Liu (2014), p. 186.

[569] Arts. 3–4 Enterprise Income Tax Law.

[570] Liu (2014), p. 187.

[571] Ibid, p. 187.

[572] Art. 3 Para. 2 Enterprise Income Tax Law.

[573] Arts. 4 and 27 Para. 5 Enterprise Income Tax Law in conjunction with Art. 91 of the PRC Law on Enterprise Income Tax Implementing Regulations (中华人民共和国企业所得税法实施条例), promulgated by the State Council on 6 December 2007, amended on 23 April 2019 with effect as of the same day (Enterprise Income Tax Law Implementing Regulations).

on'.[574] Particularly relevant for the FILPE, a non-resident enterprise which 'entrusts an agent to carry out business operation in China, including an agent who executes contracts on behalf of the non-resident enterprise on a regular basis, handles warehouses or delivers goods etc.' may be regarded as constituting a Permanent Establishment in China.[575] However, the Chinese tax authorities have not yet specified how these provisions are applied to foreign legal person partners of a FILPE.[576] A comparison with the tax treatment of foreign investors in a non-legal person CJV also does not provide more clarity, as no express regulations with regard to their taxation are available. In the absence of unified national regulations, the tax treatment that is applied to earnings from FIPEs, can vary substantially between different local tax authorities.[577] This is particularly critical as the mere existence of a FILPE could be regarded as a Permanent Establishment of its foreign partner.[578] Alternatively, tax authorities could take a differentiated approach. A foreign general partner of a FILPE could be deemed as having a Permanent Establishment, while a foreign limited partner—who is not permitted to get involved in the business operation of the FILPE—could be exempt from constituting a Permanent Establishment.[579] In addition, China has concluded Double Taxation Agreements with more than 90 countries, which may reduce the tax burden of the foreign investor.[580] This requires a case-by-case analysis of the specific tax treatment for each foreign partner under consideration of his home jurisdiction.[581]

Should the foreign partner be a natural person, his income from the FILPE is subject to Individual Income Tax, notwithstanding if the natural person has its domicile in China.[582] Whether the progressive tax rate from 5 to 35% applies, or at a flat tax rate of 20%, the same discussion as outlined above is relevant for domestic natural persons.[583] In addition, Double Taxation Agreements may also apply with regard to Individual Income Tax.

Notably, the preceding analysis does not apply to a partnership enterprise that has been established under the law of a foreign jurisdiction, as it is not exempt from the application of the Enterprise Income Tax Law.[584] Hence, Partnerships established

---

[574] Art. 5 Para. 1 Enterprise Income Tax Law Implementing Regulations. A detailed discussion of the concept of Permanent Establishment goes beyond the scope of this book. See exemplary Qiu (2014), pp. 274–306.

[575] Art. 5 Para. 2 Enterprise Income Tax Law Implementing Regulations.

[576] Liu (2014), p. 187.

[577] Meyer (2016), pp. 204–205.

[578] Liu (2014), pp. 187–188.

[579] Meyer (2016), p. 204; Ting and Ge (2014), p. 676; Liu (2014), p. 188.

[580] Liu (2014), p. 190.

[581] In respect to the German-Chinese Double Taxation Agreement, see Meyer (2016), pp. 203–222; 229–234.

[582] Art. 1 Individual Income Tax Law.

[583] Liu (2014), p. 188.

[584] Art. 1 Enterprise Income Tax Law in conjunction with Art. 2 Enterprise Income Tax Law Implementing Regulations.

outside of China would be subject to double taxation on their income generated in China.[585] This has been justified by Chinese tax authorities by mentioning their concern of not being able to collect tax revenue from foreign partners, if the foreign partnership also enjoys the flow-through treatment.[586] In this scenario, the partnership enterprise as well as the partners are situated abroad. In the FIPE investment scenario, however, the FIPE is established in China, and thus tangible for the local authorities.

4.1.12 Perception of the FIPE

The introduction of the FIPE was eagerly anticipated by foreign investors and the legal community alike.[587] Commentators expect it to become a popular choice for foreign investors who appreciate the ease of establishment and operation, and the flexible organisation structure.[588] Shortly after its implementation, the first registered FIPE has been formed in Jiangsu Province by a Chinese natural person and a US company, establishing a garden centre.[589] This was followed soon afterwards by the formation of two FIPEs in the private equity and real estate investment sector.[590] Foreign investors have quickly become more confident in using FILPEs in the establishment of private equity funds, but likewise utilise the FIPE as investment vehicle to carry out actual business operations.[591] The new enterprise form developed rapidly, and over 2,000 FIPEs had been established in China by the end of 2013.[592]

The FIPE Legislation has been credited for providing an alternative investment vehicle for FDI that reflects the principle of 'national treatment' for foreign investors, thus contributing to the further opening of China's economic and legal system.[593] Conversely, the FIPE Legislation has been criticised for lacking detailed implementing regulations, and for making the FIPE subject to excessively strict investment limitations.[594] This has been associated with the question whether the FIPE receives the appropriate government support.[595] This criticism underlines the importance of the functional analysis that is undertaken in this book. If the FILPE

585 Ting and Ge (2014), p. 674; Liu (2014), p. 188.

586 Ting and Ge (2014), p. 674.

587 Qiu (2014), p. 301; Zhang (2011), p. 872; Wang and Yong (2010), p. 15.

588 Mahony (2015), p. 233.

589 Jiao and Kasteleijn (2011), p. 60.

590 Williams (2012), p. 11.

591 Yu et al. (2012a), p. 10.

592 Qiu (2014), p. 301.

593 Liu (2014), p. 185; Yang (杨杰) and Qu (曲天明) (2010), p. 66.

594 Shaddox (2013), pp. 473–474, 476.

595 Ibid, p. 477.

can be structured so that it fulfils features of a standard corporate form, foreign investors can mitigate their risk when using this enterprise form. However, regarding the taxation of FIPEs, a conclusion can already be disclosed that more clarifying regulations on cross-border taxation of profits gained from FIPEs are crucial to provide more legal certainty for foreign investors.[596]

4.2 Forms of Partnerships Under Chinese Law

The analysis of the development and framework of partnership law touched upon the different types of partnerships that have gradually evolved in China. This section provides a concise description of the types of partnerships and their special variations that are available in China today. Merely an overview is provided, as many aspects of partnership enterprise law will be analysed in more detail in the subsequent chapters. This overview addresses purely domestic-invested as well as foreign-invested partnership enterprises to emphasise the structural interrelationship between the PEL and the FIPE Legislation. To complete the picture, the starting point is the partnership types under the GPCL. Because of its partnership-type nature, the Non-Legal Person CJV could also be included in this overview. Since it has already been analysed under the forms of joint ventures above, reference is made to the respective chapter.[597]

4.2.1 Partnership Types Under the General Principles of Civil Law

4.2.1.1 The Effect of the 2017 General Rules of Civil Law

The Individual Partnership and the Joint Operation were the first legally codified partnerships after the Opening up of China was initiated.[598] Both have been regulated in the GPCL of 1986.[599] However, the future status of these two types of partnerships is not clear. In March 2017, the 'General Rules of Civil Law' (GRCL)[600] have been promulgated by the NPC. China's lawmakers have worked on the GRCL for over a decade. It shall serve as the general section of China's first

[596] Meyer (2016), p. 213; Shen (2015), p. 56.

[597] See Sect. 3.2.2.1.

[598] See Sect. 4.1.2.

[599] Arts. 30–35, 51–53 GPCL.

[600] PRC General Rules of Civil Law (中华人民共和国民法总则), adopted at the 5th Session of the 12th National People's Congress 15 on March 2017 and with effect as 1 October 2017.

comprehensive Civil Code that is expected to be enacted in 2020.[601] The GRCL contain general provisions on civil subjects, civil relations, personal rights, and property rights that are applicable, among others, to contract law, tort law, family law, and—for some parts—to commercial law.[602] As such, the new law strongly resembles the subject matter of the GPCL. However, the GRCL neither contains respective regulations on the Individual Partnership and the Joint Operation, nor does the law mention them explicitly in any other provision. This raises the question whether the promulgation of the GRCL entails the abolishment of these two partnership types. The GRCL themselves neither repeal the GPCL in their entirety nor make any statements about which provisions shall no longer be in effect. Shortly before the GRCL were adopted, the Vice Chairman of the Standing Committee of the NPC, *LI Jianguo*, had issued the 'Explanatory Notes on the Draft GRCL'[603] that provide some guidance on the relationship between both laws. *LI* stated that the GRCL only codify the basic principles and general rules of civil law, while the GPCL still address issues that go beyond this scope. Those issues will only be considered and improved in the future, when the other parts of the Civil Code are to be issued.[604] Should there be inconsistencies between the laws, the new GRCL shall prevail over the GPCL.[605]

The Individual Partnership is regulated in Chapter II, Section 5 of the GPCL, which addresses Natural Persons. In the new GRCL, the chapter on Natural Persons overall contains the same sections as the GPCL, including the fourth section on the Individual Industrial and Commercial Household and the Rural Contracting Household, but no longer contains a fifth section on the Individual Partnership. The Joint Operation is regulated under Chapter III, Section 4 on Legal Persons, in the GPCL. The respective chapter on Legal Persons in the GRCL has been restructured in respect of sections, and does no longer contain a section on the Joint Operation either. The fact that the structure and other content of the chapters largely remain the same suggests that these omissions were a conscious decision by the lawmaker. In Chapter IV, the GRCL introduce a new category of civil subjects, the Non-Legal Person Organisations.[606] A list of examples for Non-Legal Person Organisations is provided in Article 102, Paragraph 2 GRCL, and explicitly includes partnership enterprises, while making no reference to non-enterprise type partnerships like the Individual Partnership. Should these omissions constitute an inconsistency for which the GRCL prevails over the former GPCL, it would have the effect of the abolishment of both types of partnerships. However, Article 11 GRCL states that 'where other laws provide specific stipulations on civil relations, such stipulations shall

---

[601] Li (2018), pp. 17–50. At the time of writing of this book, the comprehensive Civil Code had not yet been promulgated by the NPC.

[602] Bu (2017a), p. 185.

[603] Li (李建国) (2017).

[604] Ibid, item 3.5.

[605] Ibid, item 3.5.

[606] For an analysis of this new category, see Sect. 7.1.1.1.

apply'. The provision in the GPCL on the Individual Partnership and Joint Operation constitutes such specific stipulations. This suggests that these provisions in the GPCL remain in effect until they are repealed. An instant abolishment of these partnership types would deprive Chinese law of a legal framework that governs relationships that go beyond a mere contractual nature, but do not yet fit within the concept of a partnership enterprise. Taking Germany as an example, the most basic type of a partnership, and equivalent to the Individual Partnership, is codified in the 'German Civil Code' (Bürgerliches Gesetzbuch/BGB).[607] The so-called Gesellschaft bürgerlichen Rechts (GbR) plays an important role in German society and economy up until today.[608] Commentators expect that the Individual Partnership will be regulated as a special type of contract in a different part of the Civil Code that will be promulgated subsequently.[609] This would be a deviation from the German BGB, which serves as a model for the planned Chinese Civil Code.[610] The provisions on the GbR are regulated in the general section of the BGB.[611] From a dogmatic standpoint, the codification of a partnership as a specific type of contract is questionable, as a partnership constitutes more than a mere contractual relationship.[612] However, there should be general agreement that the rudimentary provisions on the Individual Partnership in the GPCL no longer meet the needs of modern business organisations.[613] They only provide a basic legal framework that is too vague to be practical, and carries the risk of evoking disputes among the partners.[614] While both the Individual Partnership and the Joint Operation fulfilled important roles during the early phases of the economic modernisation in China, today, the PEL provides a far more modern and sophisticated legal framework. Therefore, reforms of the provisions that govern Individual Partnerships are necessary. Drafts of the book on contracts for the comprehensive Civil Code propose respective provisions.[615] However, until such new regulations are promulgated, the provisions on the Individual Partnership and Joint Operation in the GPCL remain in effect, and are therefore analysed briefly.

---

[607]German Civil Code (Bürgerliches Gestzbuch), adopted by the German Reichstag on 18 August 1896; last amended by the German Bundestag on 19 March 2020.

[608]*Carsten Schäfer*, Gesellschaft, in: Schäfer (2017), pp. 16–17; Windbichler (2014), p. 137.

[609]Wang (2017), p. 156.

[610]Bu (2017a), p. 186; at time of writing of this book, the new Civil Code has not yet been promulgated by the NPC.

[611]Binding and Zhang (2015), p. 53; Wang (2014), p. 62.

[612]See the discussion in Sect. 4.1.9.1.

[613]Yu (余文唐) (2017).

[614]Ibid.

[615]See Arts. 751–762 of the PRC Civil Code (Draft) (中华人民共和国民法典 (草案)), issued by the NPC in November and December 2019.

4.2.1.2 Individual Partnership个人合伙

The Individual Partnership is the most basic type of a partnership in China, consisting of two or more natural persons associated in a business and working together, with each providing funds, material objects, or techniques according to an agreement.[616] For the establishment and operation of an Individual Partnership, this means that only natural persons, no legal persons or other types of business organisations, can become a partner in an Individual Partnership. In principle, natural persons are not limited to Chinese nationals, but also include foreigners.[617] Differing from the commercial partnerships under the PEL, an Individual Partnership does not have to pursue the purpose of making profit.[618] Correspondingly, it is not termed partnership 'enterprise' under the GPCL, but simply partnership.

An Individual Partnership is established on the basis of consensus among the partners, evidenced by a written partnership agreement.[619] The law gives great discretion to the partners, leaving most substantive issues to be decided by the partnership agreement, such as capital contribution, distribution of profits, responsibility for debts, entry into and withdrawal from the partnership, and operation and termination of the partnership.[620] The capital of the Individual Partnership is jointly contributed by all partners, and the law requires all partners to take part in the joint operation of the partnership.[621] This strict requirement has later been relaxed by the SPC, thus permitting investments by silent partners who contribute capital and participate in the share of profit, but do not engage in the management of the partnership.[622]

The establishment of an Individual Partnership must be registered with SAMR.[623] However, the registration process is simpler than for the partnership enterprises under the PEL.[624] The property obtained through the operation of the Individual Partnership is co-owned by all partners.[625] Partners bear unlimited joint and several liability towards third parties for the debts of the Individual Partnership with their personal property.[626] However, partners can internally claim compensation if they pay more than they are obliged to under the partnership agreement or their respective

[616] Art. 30 GPCL.

[617] Art. 8 Para. 2 GPCL/ Art. 4 GRCL; Binding and Zhang (2015), p. 54; Yuantao et al. (1989), p. 62.

[618] See Sects. 4.1.3.2 and 4.1.4.4.

[619] Art. 31 GPCL. Regarding the relaxation of the statutory requirement of a partnership agreement in writing, see Sect. 4.1.9.2.

[620] Art. 31 GPCL.

[621] Art. 34 GPCL, allowing partners to elect a managing partner in Paragraph 2.

[622] Art. 46 Opinion of the SPC on the Implementation of the GPCL.

[623] For exceptions, see Article 50 Opinion of the SPC on the Implementation of the GPCL.

[624] Ye (2002), p. 19.

[625] Art. 32 Para. 2 GPCL.

[626] Art. 35 GPCL.

share of the contributed capital.[627] These liability provisions are a crucial disadvantage of the Individual Partnership.[628] Under the PEL, debts are primarily paid from the property of the partnership enterprise, and only secondarily from the partner's individual property.[629] Under the GPCL, third parties can directly claim payments from the personal property of the partners. The Individual Partnership can be given a trade name, but partners are not obliged to do so.[630] In a civil action, the trade name is regarded as a party to the civil action, and the managing partner acts as representative for all other partners.[631] Where the Individual Partnership does not carry a trade name, all partners are co-litigants in the civil action.[632]

4.2.1.3 Joint Operation 联营

A Joint Operation is a horizontal economic association between enterprises, or between an enterprise and an institution.[633] The term enterprise here refers to state-owned enterprises or collectively-owned enterprises with legal person status.[634] The term institution refers to a state-owned or collectively-owned social organisation—such as a hospital, school, or research institution—with legal person status, the main goal of which is not profit-making, and which has no direct connection to commodity production and exchange.[635] A privately-owned enterprise or individual cannot establish a Joint Operation.[636] In the prevailing opinion, foreign enterprises are also excluded from forming a Joint Operation, as the EJV was created as their extraordinary investment vehicle.[637]

The legal status of the Joint Operation depends on the stipulations in the constituting agreement.[638] If the latter meet the qualifications of a legal person, the Joint Operation can be established as a company type legal person.[639] Otherwise, SAMR will register it as a partnership type enterprise without legal person status.[640] In this case, the parties can choose between proportional liability or joint and several

627 Art. 35 Para. 2 GPCL.

628 Binding and Zhang (2015), p. 54.

629 Art. 38 PEL, see also Sect. 8.1.

630 Art. 33 GPCL.

631 Art. 45 Para. 1 Opinion of the SPC on the Implementation of the GPCL.

632 Art. 45 Para. 2 Opinion of the SPC on the Implementation of the GPCL.

633 Art. 52 GPCL.

634 Yuantao et al. (1989), p. 54.

635 Ibid, p. 54.

636 Epstein and Shen (2009), p. I-6.1.31; Yuantao et al. (1989), p. 54; Zheng (1986), p. 681.

637 Epstein and Shen (2009), p. I-6.1.31; Zheng (1986), p. 681. For a differing opinion, see Yuantao et al. (1989), p. 62.

638 Binding and Zhang (2015), p. 60.

639 Art. 51 GPCL.

640 Art. 52 GPCL.

liability.[641] Should the Joint Operation be operated by each party independently, it can be regarded as a bilateral contractual arrangement for which the parties bear liability separately.[642] By placing the provisions on the Joint Operation in the Chapter on Legal Persons, the lawmaker has emphasised that it is more a form of business than a contractual arrangement.[643] However, in the one Article that the GPCL contains on the partnership type Joint Operation, no further guidance is provided for its establishment, operation and dissolution.[644] Immediately after the GPCL was promulgated, the use of the Joint Operation form rapidly developed throughout China.[645] Once the Company Law came into effect, however, the practical relevance of the Joint Operation was drastically reduced.[646]

4.2.2 *Domestic-Invested Partnership Enterprises*

The enterprise-status of partnerships was only recognised with the promulgation of the 1997 PEL. The PEL—together with the Partnership Enterprise Registration Measures—is the principle and overarching law for all types of partnership enterprises in China.[647] The PEL itself codifies three types of partnership enterprises: the GPE, the SGPE, and the LPE.

4.2.2.1 General Partnership Enterprise普通合伙企业

The GPE is the basic type of partnership enterprise. It serves as a model and referential framework for the SGPE and LPE. The chapter on the GPE is comprised of 40 Articles, out of the total 109 provisions of the PEL. A GPE is exclusively formed by general partners. Each general partner bears unlimited joint and several liability with his personal property for the debts of the partnership enterprise.[648] Since the reform of the PEL in 2006, natural persons as well as enterprises can act as general partner.[649] The management of a GPE shall jointly be decided by all partners, and each partner will have equal rights in the execution thereof.[650] Nonetheless, the partners may elect a managing partner, who will run the management

---

[641] Art. 52 GPCL.

[642] Art. 53 GPCL.

[643] Zheng (1986), p. 681.

[644] Chen (2016), pp. 653–654.

[645] Yuantao et al. (1989), pp. 60–61; Zheng (1986), p. 681.

[646] Epstein and Shen (2009), p. I-6.1.31.

[647] See Sect. 4.1.5.3.

[648] Art. 2 Para. 2 PEL.

[649] See the detailed analysis in Sects. 8.2.2.1 and 9.2.1.2.2.

[650] Art. 26 Para. 1 PEL.

affairs and represent the partnership enterprise towards third parties.[651] As has been pointed out above, the PEL leaves a significant degree of discretion to the partners in tailoring major issues of the inner organisation of a partnership enterprise to their specific requirements in the partnership agreement.[652] This flexibility is a decisive advantage of the GPE, while the unlimited liability of all partners marks the greatest disadvantage.

4.2.2.2 Specialised General Partnership Enterprise特殊普通合伙企业

The definition of the GPE in Article 2, Paragraph 2 PEL provides that 'special provisions on the liability of general partners shall have prevailing effect. This is a reference to the five provisions that regulate the SGPE in Articles 55–59 PEL. They have been added to the chapter on General Partnership Enterprises with the revision of the PEL in 2006, in a new Section 6. Matters not regulated in these five special provisions are subject to the general provisions that govern the GPE.[653] Essentially, the SGPE is a special form of the GPE.[654] All partners of the SGPE are general partners.[655] However, the distinct objective of the SGPE is providing paid services to clients with specialised knowledge and skills, such as lawyers, accountants, and other professional service firms.[656] The SGPE shields partners of professional service firms from liabilities due to the misconduct or negligence of their co-partners.[657] Two special conditions characterise the SGPE: (1) forms of liability of the partners; (2) the requirement to purchase insurance and to establish an occupational risk fund.[658]

The key liability provision of the SGPE is Article 57 PEL. The special liability regulation only applies to debts that are incurred by partners while performing their professional services. Partners whose intentional or gross negligent acts have caused such debts shall bear unlimited joint and several liability, while other partners will bear limited liability to the extent of their shares in the partnership only.[659] However, for debts incurred by the SGPE for any other reason, all partners shall bear unlimited joint and several liability.[660] Hence, the Chinese SGPE only provides a partial liability shield for its partners.[661] This resembles the situation under the German

[651] Art. 26 Para. 2 PEL.
[652] See Sect. 4.1.9.3.
[653] Art. 55 Para. 3 PEL.
[654] Lin (2010), p. 260.
[655] Art. 55 Para. 2 PEL.
[656] Art. 55 Para. 1 PEL.
[657] Art. 57 PEL.
[658] Chen (2016), p. 657.
[659] Art. 57 Para. 1 PEL.
[660] Art. 57 Para. 2 PEL.
[661] Lin (2010), p. 261.

Partnership Enterprise Law before 2013.[662] Under the US 'Revised Uniform Partnership Act'[663] (RUPA), on the other hand, partners are granted full-shield protection by limiting their liability in general to their capital contributions.[664] Remarks have been made that the lack of a full-shield protection under the PEL may undermine the advantages of the SGPE, and reduce its practical appeal as an investment vehicle for professional service firms.[665] In addition, the fact that the liability provisions contain several uncertainties has been criticised.[666] The terms 'intentional' and 'gross negligent' are essential elements in stipulating the shielded liability, but the PEL does not provide any further definition of these terms.[667] The liability of innocent partners is limited to 'the extent of their share in the partnership.' *Lin* argues that it can be difficult to quantify each partner's share in the SGPE in practice, and thus suggest that the PEL should instead follow the international practice of granting the innocent partner a liability shield to the extent of his capital contribution.[668]

Creditor protection shall be ensured through (1) disclosure provisions; (2) the requirement of professional liability insurance; and (3) the establishment of a separate risk fund by the SGPE. Disclosure of the limited liability status shall be ensured by the obligation to add the words Specialised General Partnership (特殊普通合伙) to the name of the SGPE.[669] However, it has been pointed out above that the name Specialised General Partnership can hardly serve this purpose.[670] The SGPE is required to purchase professional liability insurance.[671] However, unlike respective laws in some states of the US, the PEL does not stipulate a minimum capital requirement and duration requirement for such insurance.[672] Under German law, similar requirements are laid out in the industry-specific regulations that govern each

---

[662]Following the reform in 2013, partners can opt between a partial shielding and a full liability shield in connection to a professional liability insurance. See Article 8 German Partnership Enterprise Law.

[663]Revised Uniform Partnership Act, promulgated by the National Conference of Commissioners on Uniform State Laws in 1997 as a replacement for the 1914 Uniform Partnership Act (UPA), later amended in 2011 and 2013.

[664]Section 306 (c) RUPA.

[665]Lin (2010), p. 261.

[666]Ibid, p. 261.

[667]Ibid, p. 261.

[668]Ibid, pp. 261–262.

[669]Art. 56 PEL.

[670]See Sect. 4.1.4.3.

[671]Art. 59 Para. 1 PEL.

[672]Lin (2010), p. 262.

profession, e.g. the regulations on law firms.[673] China's 'Law Firm Measures'[674] only stipulate that specific provisions on professional liability insurance for lawyers shall be formulated separately, without providing any standards or minimum requirements.[675] To offset its operational debt, the SGP is further required to allocate a portion of its revenue in a separate bank account to establish an occupational risk fund.[676] However, commentators lament that no further details are provided on the establishment, management, taxation, and supervision of the risk fund.[677]

To encourage the use of the SGPE in China, several laws and policies have been promulgated, including the Law Firm Measures.[678] However, these regulations often set a high threshold for the establishment of a SGPE. Taking a law firm as example, among other requirements, it would need to have at least twenty partners and assets of at least 10 million RMB to form a SGPE.[679] An argument is made that these requirements are out of reach for smaller law firms.[680] Conversely, a law firm in the form of a GPE only demands a minimum of three partners and assets of 300,000 RMB.[681] The conversion of an existing professional service firm into a SGPE is not regulated in the PEL. Instead, sector specific regulations make some stipulations. For law firms, the conversion into a SGPE requires approval from at least two authorities but no further details are provided on the transfer of an existing firm's business, management, assets and liabilities to the SGPE.[682] *Lin* suggests that general regulations for the conversion should be stipulated that apply to any existing professional service firm.[683]

4.2.2.3 Limited Partnership Enterprise有限合伙企业

The LPE is regulated in 25 separate Articles in Chapter III of the PEL.[684] In addition, the provisions that govern the GPE are applicable supplementary.[685] Chapter III thus

---

[673] For law firms, the minimum amount of the professional liability insurance must be 2.5 million Euros per claim, and at least 10 million Euros per year. See Schäfer (2017), p. 647.

[674] Measures for the Administration of Law Firms (律师事务所管理办法), promulgated by the Ministry of Justice on 18 July 2008, amended on 30 November 2012, amended on 6 September 2016, and amended on 5 December 2018 with effect as of 15 January 2019.

[675] Art. 52 Para. 2 Law Firm Measures.

[676] Art. 59 Para. 2 PEL.

[677] Lin (2010), p. 263.

[678] ibid, p. 260.

[679] Art. 10 No 2 and 4 Law Firm Measures.

[680] Lin (2010), p. 260.

[681] Art. 9 No 2 and 4 Law Firm Measures.

[682] Art. 26 Para. 1 in conjunction with Art. 29 Law Firm Measures.

[683] Lin (2010), p. 264.

[684] Arts. 60–84 PEL.

[685] Art. 60 PEL.

mainly regulates the rights, obligations and conduct of the limited partners in a LPE.[686] A LPE is composed of one or more general partners, who bear unlimited joint and several liability, and one or more limited partners, who bear liability for the debts of the partnership only to the extent of the capital contribution to the partnership to which they have subscribed.[687] It has at least one general partner and one limited partner, but the total number of partners cannot exceed fifty.[688] The LPE is managed by the general partner, who bears the unlimited liability.[689] However, it is possible to structure the LPE so that the general partner is a legal person with limited liability.[690] This allows the investor to limit his liability eventually, even though he acts as the general partner. The limited partnership with a limited liability company as a general partner offers a suitable mechanism for the combination of capital and expertise. However, the limited partner is generally excluded from the management of the LPE.[691] Further differentiating it from the general partner, special terms apply to the capital contribution of a limited partner.[692]

4.2.3 Foreign-Invested Partnership Enterprises

It has been pointed out above that the FIPE Legislation has evolved from the PEL and the Partnership Registration Measures.[693] Consequently, the variations of foreign-invested partnership enterprises reflect the types of partnership enterprises that are available under the PEL.[694]

4.2.3.1 Foreign-Invested General Partnership Enterprise外商投资普通合伙企业

The FIGPE serves as the basic type of partnership enterprise for foreign investors, with all the general partners bearing unlimited joint and several liability. Formation of a FIGPE requires a minimum of two general partners, of whom at least one must be a foreign enterprise or individual. The other partner(s) can either be foreign

[686]Chen (2016), p. 658.
[687]Art. 2 Para. 3 PEL.
[688]Art. 61 PEL. Additionally, see Sect. 9.2.1.2.1.
[689]Art. 67 PEL.
[690]For a detailed analysis, and complete discussion of this structure, see Sect. 8.2.2.
[691]For a detailed analysis, see Sect. 8.3.2.1.
[692]Art. 64 PEL.
[693]See Sect. 4.1.5.3.
[694]Art. 11 FIPE Provisions.

enterprises or individuals, or Chinese natural or legal persons or other organisations.[695]

4.2.3.2 Foreign-Invested Specialised General Partnership Enterprise 外商投资特殊普通合伙企业

The FISGPE is included in the canon of foreign-invested partnership enterprises, thus permitting foreign investors to set up professional service firms as a FIPE.[696] The SGPE having been made available for foreign investors especially relates to China's WTO commitment to develop and open the professional service sector.[697] However, in practice, the use of the FISGPE by foreign investors is likely to face several obstacles. In addition to having to satisfy the conditions for a SGPE that are stipulated in the PEL, a FISGPE is also subject to the special restrictions of foreign investments.[698] Under the FDI Negative List, certain sectors are still prohibited to professional service firms, including the business of foreign law firms.[699] In addition, numerous local professional licensing limitations that are placed on non-Chinese individuals, are regarded as a significant obstacle for the FISGPE to become a viable investment vehicle for foreign professional service firms.[700] Therefore, the FISGPE is not analysed in more detail in this book.[701]

4.2.3.3 Foreign-Invested Limited Partnership Enterprise 外商投资有限合伙企业

The FILPE follows the same structure as the LPE. A foreign enterprise or individual can act as the general partner, or as the limited partner, or both types of partner can be formed by a foreign party.[702] The FILPE is the core subject of this book, and will therefore be analysed in more detail in the following chapters.

---

[695] Art. 2 Para. 1 FIPE Provisions. See also further analysis in Sect. 9.2.1.2.

[696] Art. 11 FIPE Provisions.

[697] Lin (2010), p. 259.

[698] See Sect. 4.1.7.

[699] Foreign investor are prohibited from investing in 'Chinese legal matters', according to Item 30 of the 2018 FDI Negative List in the Guidance Catalogue. Foreign law firms are only permitted to provide advice on 'the impact of China's legal environment', and may only be organised in the form of a Representative Office. For a detailed overview, see Mahony (2015), pp. 164–173.

[700] Liu (2014), p. 184; Ting and Ge (2014), p. 672.

[701] For an in-depth analysis of the Specialised Partnership Enterprise, see Xia (夏凤英) and Dong (董书萍) (2011), pp. 125–128; Liu (刘新民) (2011), pp. 78–82.

[702] Art. 2 FIPE Provisions.

4.2.4 Special Variations of Foreign-Invested Partnership Enterprises

To complement the overview of foreign-invested partnership enterprises, two special variations of the FIPE are briefly described. While these special variations can be categorised under the aforementioned forms of FIPEs, they play a special role for FDI, showing distinctive characteristics.

4.2.4.1 Qualified Foreign Limited Partnership Program 合格境外有限合伙企业

Article 14 FIPE Measures makes an important reference by stating that, to the extent that there are 'provisions governing partnership enterprises established by foreign enterprises whose main business is making investments, such provisions shall take precedence'. Commentators have identified the FIVCE-Provisions as one set of rules under which the establishment of onshore limited partnership funds with foreign participation would potentially be possible.[703] The FIVCE has already been analysed above.[704]

Another set of rules, more specifically based on the FIPE, are sub-national regulations on the Qualified Foreign Limited Partnership (QFLP). A QFLP fund structure refers to a foreign-invested equity investment fund established in the form of a FILPE under local QFLP pilot programs.[705] The 'QFLP Shanghai Pilot Measures'[706] were the first regulations to facilitate QFLP funds in Shanghai, starting from January 2011. Further QFLP programs followed in Beijing, Tianjin, and Chongqing that same year.[707]

The impact of the QFLP becomes clear in the light of the stringent capital control regime in China and the—now repealed—'SAFE Circular 142',[708] which was formerly the major rule regulating the conversion and use of foreign currency by

---

[703] Wang and Yong (2010), p. 16; Pissler (2010), p. 129.

[704] See Sect. 3.2.3.2.

[705] Zhang and Du (2014), p. II-5.1.8; Zhang (2011), pp. 875–876.

[706] Implementation Measures on Pilot Program of Foreign-Invested Equity Investment Enterprises in Shanghai (本市开展外商投资股权投资企业试点工作的实施办法), jointly promulgated by the Shanghai Financial Services Office, Shanghai Municipal Commission of Commerce and Shanghai Administration for Industry and Commerce on 24 December 2010 with effect as of 24 January 2011.

[707] Howson (2015), p. 399.

[708] Circular on the Relevant Operating Issues concerning the Improvement of the Administration of Payment and Settlement of Foreign Currency Capital of Foreign-Invested Enterprises (完善外商投资企业外汇资本金支付结汇管理有关业务操作问题的通知), promulgated by the General Affairs Department of the State Administration of Foreign Exchange on 29 August 2008 and repealed with effect as of 1 June 2015.

FIEs.[709] For transactions involving a cross border element, China distinguishes between current account transactions—which refer to trade and other recurring business transactions—, and capital account transactions—which comprise equity investments and loans/debts.[710] FIEs are required to maintain separate current and capital accounts. While foreign currency in the current account is fully convertible, the capital account has been subject to numerous limitations with the aim to control the amount of foreign currency that flows into China.[711] Under SAFE Circular 142, FIEs were generally not allowed to convert foreign currency in their capital account into RMB for the purpose of making domestic equity investments,[712] with the exception of FIE HoldCos and FIVCEs.[713] The QFLP provides an exception to these limitations. Under the QFLP pilot program, a qualified foreign investor can apply for a quota to convert foreign currency into RMB and then make multiple domestic equity investments within the quota limit.[714] However, a foreign investor needs to meet several thresholds to qualify under the QFLP program. Taking Shanghai as an example, the pilot program is mainly aimed at large foreign sovereign wealth funds, pensions funds, insurance companies, banks and securities companies that own assets of over 500 million USD, or manage assets of no less than 1 billion USD, and have a track record of investment experience of at least 5 years.[715] While foreign investors regard the QFLP program as more attractive than the FIVCE, it is still an investment structure that is only open to a very limited number of foreign investors in practice.[716]

Initially, authorities in Shanghai aimed to provide an additional benefit for the QFLP. If no more than 5% of the partnership capital were contributed in foreign currency (immediately converted into RMB), the equity fund would neither be regarded 'foreign' nor 'foreign-invested', and thus not subject to the general FDI restrictions.[717] The prospect of such 'national treatment' was perceived as one of the biggest incentives for foreign fund managers.[718] However, NDRC clarified in April 2012 that any investment of a QFLP is regarded as a foreign investment, subject to the Guidance Catalogue and the foreign investment approval process.[719] The portfolio companies are respectively regarded as FIEs.[720]

---

[709]For a detailed discussion, see Zhang (2011), pp. 881–882.

[710]McGinty et al. (2017), p. 1.

[711]Zhang (2011), p. 881.

[712]Art. 3 Para. 2 SAFE Circular 142.

[713]See Sect. 3.2.3.1.

[714]McGinty and Jun (2015), p. 3; Zhang (2011), p. 881.

[715]Art. 20 QFLP Shanghai Pilot Measures.

[716]Zhang and Du (2014), p. II-5.1.3.

[717]Art. 24 QFLP Shanghai Pilot Measures; Howson (2015), p. 399.

[718]Howson (2015), pp. 399–400.

[719]Ibid, p. 400.

[720]Zhang and Du (2014), p. II-5.1.17.

4.2.4.2 RMB Qualified Foreign Limited Partnership Program 人民币合格境外有限合伙企业

In reaction to the NDRC decision, RMB-QFLP (RQFLP) funds have been set up that use RMB available offshore (i.e. in Hong Kong) instead of converting foreign currency into RMB.[721] However, a RQFLP is also treated as a foreign investment under current regulations.[722]

In June 2015, the stringent capital control regime in China has been significantly relaxed with the abolishment of SAFE Circular 142, and the promulgation of 'SAFE Circular 19'.[723] Under the latter, all FIEs are allowed to convert any amount of foreign currency in their capital account into RMB at any time.[724] It further allows FIEs to use their converted RMB to make equity investments in China.[725] While this expressly applies to FIEs with the business scope of making investments, it appears that even non-investment FIEs are granted more discretion in making equity investments by certain local branches of SAFE.[726] This reform allows foreign investors to set up investment funds in the form of a FIPE without obtaining a QFLP quota. However, it remains to be seen how SAFE Circular 19 will be applied by the authorities in practice.[727]

References

Armour J, Hansmann H, Kraakman R, Pargendler M (2017) What is corporate law? In: Kraakman R et al (eds) The anatomy of corporate law, 3rd edn. Oxford University Press, Oxford, pp 1–28

Binding J, Zhang H (2015) Die Allgemeinen Grundsätze des Zivilrechts. In: Binding J, Pissler KB und Xu L (eds) Chinesisches Zivil- und Wirtschaftsrecht. R&W, Frankfurt a.M., pp 27–92

Bu Y (2017a) Die Kodifikation des chinesischen Zivilgesetzbuches. Zeitschrift für Chinesisches Recht 24:183–202

Bu Y (2017b) Einführung in das Recht Chinas, 2nd edn. C. H. Beck, Munich

Cao D (曹德斌), Zhang X (张小奕) (2017) A practical guide to the new partnership enterprise law (新合伙企业法实用手册). China Industry and Commerce Press (中国工商出版社), Beijing

Cao F (2011) Corporate income tax law and practice in the People's Republic of China. Oxford University Press, Oxford

Chen J (2016) Chinese law: context and transformation, revised and expanded edition. Brill, Leiden

Chen K (2014a) Corporations and partnerships in China. Kluwer Law, Alphen aan den Rijn

---

[721] For more details on the RQFLP, see Howson (2015), p. 400.

[722] Zhang and Du (2014), p. II-5.1.16–17.

[723] Circular on Reforming the Administrative Approach Regarding the Settlement of the Foreign Exchange Capitals of Foreign-Invested Enterprises (改革外商投资企业外汇资本金结汇管理方式的通知), promulgated by the State Administration of Foreign Exchange on 30 March 2015 and amended on 30 December 2019.

[724] Art. 1 SAFE Circular 19.

[725] Art. 4 SAFE Circular 19.

[726] McGinty and Jun (2015), p. 3.

[727] Ibid, p. 3.

Chen W (2014b) Selected problems of general provisions in private international law: the PRC perspective. In: Basedow J, Pissler KB (eds) Private international law in Mainland China, Taiwan and Europe. Mohr Siebeck, Tübingen, pp 51–63

Chen W, Chen P (2009) Limited partnership tax circular eases investor concerns. China Law Pract 23:34

Chow DCK (2002) A primer on foreign investment enterprises and protection of intellectual property in China. Kluwer Law, The Hague

Clarke DC (2005–2006) How do we know when an enterprise exists? Unanswerable questions and legal polycentricity in China. Columbia J Asian Law 19:50–71

Clarke DC (2007) Legislating for a market economy in China. China Q 191:567–585

Cohen JA, Lange JE (1997) The Chinese legal system: a primer for investors. N Y Law School J Int Comp Law 17:345–377

Cui W (2008) Will partnership law be worth it? Int Financ Law Rev 27(9):30–32

Cuniberti G (2017) Conflict of laws: a comparative approach; text and cases. Edward Elgar, Cheltenham/Northampton

Du T (2014) The new Chinese conflict-of-law rules for legal persons: is the middle way feasible? In: Basedow J, Pissler KB (eds) Private international law in Mainland China, Taiwan and Europe. Mohr Siebeck, Tübingen, pp 331–348

Epstein E, Shen WW (2009) Chinese civil law. In: Moser MJ, Yu F (eds) Doing business in China, Vol 1. Juris Publishing, Huntington, pp I-6.1.20

Essers P, Meussen GTK (2004) Taxation of partnerships/hybrid entities. In: McCahery JA, Raaijmakers T, Vermeulen EPM (eds) The Governance of close corporations and partnerships: US and European perspectives. Oxford University Press, Oxford, pp 415–426

Fleischer H (2011) Rechtsvergleichende Beobachtungen zur Rolle der Gesetzesmaterialien bei der Gesetzesauslegung. Archiv für die civilistische Praxis 211:317–351

Fleischer H, Wansleben T (2017) Die GmbH & Co. KG als kautelarjuristische Erfolgsgeschichte. GmbH-Rundschau 106:169–180

Fu M (傅明) (2008) Legal impediments to foreign-invested partnership enterprises (外商投资合伙企业的法律障碍). Capital Shanghai (上海国资) 2008/2:74

Gan G (干勾) (2003) Concept and nature of the enterprise (企业的概念和性质). http://lawsky.org/detail.asp?id=2394. Accessed 15 May 2020

Gao F (高富平), Su H (苏号朋), Li Z (刘智慧) (1997) Principles and practice of partnership enterprise law (合伙企业法原理与实务). China Legal Publishing House (中国法制出版社), Beijing

Garner B (ed) (2009) Black's law dictionary, 9th edn. St. Paul-Minn, Thomson West

Glatter J (2016) Form der Präsenz ausländischer Unternehmen in China. In: Binding J und Pissler KB (eds) Chinesisches Zivil- und Wirtschaftsrecht Band 2 – Schwerpunkt Wirtschaftsrecht. R&W, Frankfurt a.M., pp 108–162

Grunewald B (2019) Kommanditgesellschaft. In: Schmidt K (ed) Münchener Kommentar zum Handelsgesetzbuch, vol 3, 4th edn. C. H. Beck, Munich, pp 1–142

Haase F (2014) Introduction. In: Haase F (ed) Taxation of international partnerships – 15 years OECD partnership report: past, present and future. IBFD, Amsterdam, pp 3–11

Hansmann H, Kraakman R, Squire R (2005) The new business entities in evolutionary perspective. Univ Ill Law Rev 2005:5–14

Harris D (2009) China OEM agreements. Why Ours Are In Chinese. Flat Out. http://www.chinalawblog.com/2009/07/china_oem_agreements_we_like_o.html. Accessed 15 May 2020

Heidinger A (2016) Handelsfirma. In: Schmidt K (ed) Münchener Kommentar zum Handelsgesetzbuch, vol 1, 4th edn. C. H. Beck, Munich, pp 378–561

Herbert Smith Freehills LLP (2016) Dispute resolution and governing law clauses in China-related commercial contracts. HSF, Hong Kong

Hershkovitz L (1985) The fruits of ambivalence: China's Urban individual economy. Pac Aff 58:427–450

Heuser R (2002) Einführung in die chinesische Rechtskultur. IFA, Hamburg

Hong H (洪虎) (2006a) Examination Report on the Draft Revision of the PRC Partnership Enterprise Law – delivered on 22 August 2006 to the 23rd Session of the Standing Committee of the 10th National People's Congress (关于《中华人民共和国合伙企业法(修订草案)》审议结果的报告—2006年8月22日在第十届全国人民代表大会常务委员会第二十三次会议上). Gazette of the Standing Committee of the National People's Congress 2006 No 7 (中华人民共和国全国人民代表大会常务委员会公报2006年7号), pp 602–604

Hong H (洪虎) (2006b) Report on the Circumstances of the Revision of the Amended Draft of the PRC Partnership Enterprise Law – delivered on 24 June 2006 to the 22nd Session of the Standing Committee of the 10th National People's Congress (关于《中华人民共和国合伙企业法(修订草案)》修改情况的汇报—2006年6月24日在第十届全国人民代表大会常务委员会第二十二次会议上). Yearbook of the National People's Congress 2006: (全国人民代表大会年鉴2 0 0 6 年卷), pp 354–357

Howson NC (2010) Corporate law in the Shanghai People's Courts, 1992–2008: Judicial autonomy in a contemporary authoritarian state. East Asia Law Rev 5:303–442

Howson NC (2015) Return of the prodigal form? Partnerships and partnership law in the People's Republic of China. In: Hillman RW, Loewenstein MJ (eds) Research handbook on partnerships, LLCs and alternative forms of business organizations. Edward Elgar, Cheltenham, pp 390–411

Huang J (2014) New perspectives on private international law in the People's Republic of China. In: Basedow J, Pissler KB (eds) Private international law in Mainland China, Taiwan and Europe. Mohr Siebeck, Tübingen, pp 3–15

Huang Y (黄毅诚) (1997) Explanations on the Draft PRC Partnership Enterprise Law – delivered on 23 October 1996 to the 22nd Session of the Standing Committee of the 8th National People's Congress (关于《中华人民共和国合伙企业法(草案)》的说明—1996年10月23日在第八届全国人民代表大会常务委员会第二十二次会议上). Gazette of the Standing Committee of the National People's Congress 1997 No 1 (中华人民共和国全国人民代表大会常务委员会公报1997年1号), pp 12–16

Hübner PA (2014) Rechtsschutz ausländischer Investoren vor chinesischen Gerichten. De Gruyter, Berlin

Jaeger WHE (1961–1962) Partnership or joint venture. Notre Dame Lawyer 37:138–159

Jiang P (江平), Li G (李固光) (2005) The new company law training course (最新公司法培训教程). People's Court Publishing House (人民法院出版社), Beijing

Jiao L, Kasteleijn B (2011) Foreign acquisitions and joint ventures in China. In: Campbell D (ed) Mergers and acquisitions in North America, Latin America, Asia and the Pacific: selected issues and jurisdictions. Wolters Kluwer Law & Business, Alphen aan den Rijn, pp 29–62

Julius H, Bitter M (2005) Symposium zum chinesischen Personenhandelsgesellschaftsrecht. Zeitschrift für Chinesisches Recht 12:62–63

Kaser M, Knütel R (2014) Römisches Privatrecht, 20th edn. C. H. Beck, Munich

Kindler P (2018) Internationales Handels- und Gesellschaftsrecht. In: Säcker FJ et al (eds) Münchener Kommentar zum Bürgerlichen Gesetzbuch, vol 12, 7th edn. C. H. Beck, Munich, pp 1565–1929

Kirby WC (1995) China unincorporated: company law and business enterprise in twentieth-century China. J Asian Stud 54:43–63

Kroymann B (2009) Das Kapitalgesellschaftsrecht der VR China – Analyse der Rahmenbedingungen für ausländische Investoren. Mohr Siebeck, Tübingen

Leibküchler P (2017) Die Parteiautonomie im chinesischen internationalen Privatrecht – Das Recht der Volksrepublik China im Lichte eines Vergleichs mit deutschem und europäischem Kollisionsrecht. Mohr Siebeck, Tübingen

Li F (李飞) (ed) (2006) Interpretation of the PRC Partnership Enterprise Law (中华人民共和国合伙企业法释义). Law Press China (法律出版社), Beijing

Li H (2018) The codification of Chinese civil law: innovations and controversies. In: Möllers TMJ, Li H (eds) The general rules of Chinese civil law – history, Reform and Perspective, Baden-Baden, pp 17–50.

Li J (李建国) (2017) Explanatory Notes on the PRC General Rules of Civil Law (Draft) – delivered on 8 March 2017 to the 5th Session of the 12th National People's Congress (《中华人民共和国民法总则(草案)》的说明—2017年3月8日在第十二届全国人民代表大会第五次会议上). http://www.npc.gov.cn/npc/xinwen/2017-03/09/content_2013899.htm. Accessed 15 May 2020. (Explanatory Notes on the Draft GRCL)

Li Y (厉以宁) (1997) Examination Report of the Law Commission of the National People's Congress on the Draft PRC Partnership Enterprise Law, delivered to the 24th Session of the Standing Committee of the 8th National People's Congress on 19 February 1997, (全国人大法律委员会关于《中华人民共和国合伙企业法(草案)》审议结果的报告—1997年2月19日在第八届全国人民代表大会常务委员会第二十四次会议上). Gazette of the Standing Committee of the National People's Congress 1997 No 1 (中华人民共和国全国人民代表大会常务委员会公报1997年1号), pp 17–20

Lianbin S, Chen HHC, Fu P (2016) Annual review on commercial arbitration in China (2016). In: Beijing arbitration commission, commercial dispute resolution in China: an annual review and preview (2016). Lexis Nexis, Beijing, pp 1–51

Lin L (2010) The limited liability partnership in China: a long way ahead. Int Comp Commer Law Rev 21:259–265

Lin L (2011) The limited partner's derivative action: problems and prospects in the private equity market of China. Hong Kong Law J 41:201–230

Lin L (2013a) The private equity limited partnership in China: a critical evaluation of active limited partners. J Corp Law Stud 13:185–217

Lin L (2013b) The evolution of partnerships in China from the perspective of asset partitioning. Stanford J Law 18:215–249

Lin L, Yeo HY (2010) Limited partnership – the new business vehicle in China. Butterworth J Int Bank Financ Law 25:104–108

Liu C (2008) Chinese company and securities law: investment vehicles, mergers and acquisitions and corporate finance in China. Kluwer Law, Alphen aan den Rijn

Liu J (2014) China. In: Haase F (ed) Taxation of international partnerships – 15 years OECD partnership report: past, present and future. IBFD, Amsterdam, pp 183–215

Liu X (2010) Partnerschaftsunternehmen als neues Vehikel für Auslandsinvestitionen in China. Zeitschrift für Chinesisches Recht 17:37–40

Liu X (刘新民) (2011) Research on the system of creditor protection of special general partnership enterprises (特殊的普通合伙企业债权人保护法律制度研究). Soc Sci Res (社会科学研究) 2011/4:78-82.

Lu M (吕美昂) (2011) A comparison of the nature of foreign-invested enterprises in China (我国外商投资企业性质的比较). Leg Syst Soc (法制与社会) 8:81-82.

Mahony T (2015) Foreign investment law in China: regulation, practice and context. Tsinghua University Press, Beijing

Mao R (茆荣华), Zhao C (赵超) (2007) Judicial response regarding the revised partnership enterprise law (《合伙企业法》修改的司法应对). J Law Appl (法律适用) 2007/3:58

Martinek M (2018) Experimental legislation in China between efficiency and legality - the delegated legislative power of the Shenzhen special economic zone. Springer, Berlin

McGinty A, Jun W (2015) China liberalises settlement of foreign exchange capital through SAFE Circular 19: a game-changer for the foreign investment fund industry? https://www.hoganlovells.com/en/publications/china-liberalises-settlement-of-foreign-exchange-capital-through-safe-circular-19-a-gamechanger-for-the-foreign-investment-fund-industry. Accessed 15 May 2020

McGinty A, Jun W, Xu L (2017) China's new foreign exchange controls create fresh concerns. https://www.hoganlovells.com/en/publications/chinas-new-foreign-exchange-controls-create-fresh-concerns. Accessed 15 May 2020

McKenzie P, Mendel F (2007) China's partnership enterprise law revised. China Law Pract 2007 (3):32–33

Meyer P (2016) Besteuerung und steuerliche Gestaltung deutscher Direktinvestitionen in China. Springer Gabler, Wiesbaden
Münzel F (2006a) Einige Anmerkungen zur Revision des Partnerschaftsunternehmensgesetzes. Zeitschrift für Chinesisches Recht 13:405–406
Münzel F (2006b) Gesetz der Volksrepublik China über Partnerschaftsunternehmen (Übersetzung). Zeitschrift für Chinesisches Recht 13:407–425
Peerenboom R (ed) (2010) Judicial independence in China: lessons for global rule of law promotion. Cambridge University Press, Cambridge
Pissler KB (2010) Die Gründung ausländischer Partnerschaftsunternehmen nach den neuen Registrierungsbestimmungen: Konkretisierungen, Antworten, Einschränkungen und neue Fragen. Zeitschrift für Chinesisches Recht 17:125–131
Qiu D (2014) Permanent establishment: an evolving concept under China's tax treaties (1983–2013). Br Tax Rev 2014:274–306
Raiser T, Veil R (2015) Recht der Kapitalgesellschaften, 6th edn. Verlag Franz Vahlen, Munich
Ribstein LE (1988) An applied theory of limited partnership. Emory Law J 37:835–895
Roos M, Steinberg L (2012) When to use a joint venture. In: Tring D, Mok S (eds) The legal guide to FDI in China. China Law & Practice, Hong Kong, pp 24–27
Schäfer C (2017) Gesellschaft. In: Säcker FJ et al (eds) Münchener Kommentar zum Bürgerlichen Gesetzbuch, vol 6, 7th edn. C. H. Beck, Munich, pp 3–667
Schmidt K (2002) Gesellschaftsrecht, 4th edn. Heymanns, Cologne
Shaddox SH (2013) China's foreign invested partnership enterprise law: the lifeless or sleeping dragon? Pac Rim Law Policy J 22:469–490
Shen W (2015) Corporate law in China – structure, governance and regulation. Sweet & Maxwell, Hong Kong
State Council (2018) China to support venture capital firms with new tax incentives. http://english.gov.cn/premier/news/2018/12/12/content_281476430832924.htm. Accessed 15 May 2020
Stursberg C (2014) Der Dualismus des chinesischen Kapitalgesellschaftsrechts: Eine Untersuchung des Verhältnisses des Gesellschaftsrechts und der kapitalgesellschaftsrechtlichen Bestimmungen des Rechts der ausländisch investierten Unternehmen der VR China. LIT Verlag, Berlin
Su H (苏号朋), Wang B (王斌来) (1997) On the partnership enterprise's partnership agreement (论合伙企业中的合伙协议). J Gansu Polit Sci Law Inst (甘肃政法学院学报) 1997/3:28-32.
Teesdale JH (1932) A short analysis of the new Chinese company and partnership law. J Comp Legis Int Law 14:247–254
Teichmann C (2014) Die Auslandsgesellschaft & Co. Zeitschrift für Unternehmens- und Gesellschaftsrecht 43:220–251
Ting A, Ge X (2014) The current state of play of foreign investment vehicles in China: is partnership a rising star? Bull Int Tax 68:669–677
Trakman LE (2015) China and foreign direct investment: looking ahead. In: Liu Q, Shan W, Ren X (eds) China and international commercial dispute resolution. Brill, Leiden, pp 131–194
Wang A, Yong C (2010) Radical reform or unmet expectations? China Law Pract 24:15–17
Wang J (2014) Company law in China: regulation of business organizations in a socialist market economy. Edward Elgar, Cheltenham
Wang X (王翔) (2006) Introduction to the Circumstances of the Revisions of the Partnership Enterprise Law (合伙企业法修改情况介绍). http://www.npc.gov.cn/npc/xinwen/lfgz/lfdt/2006-08/28/content_352015.htm. Accessed 15 May 2020
Wang Z (2017) Big data analysis on whether several rules in the general rules of civil law (draft) should be kept or not. J Sichuan Univ (Philos Soc Sci Ed) 2017/1:151–162
Werthwein S (2010) Corporations and partnerships. In: Bu Y (ed) Chinese business law. C. H. Beck, Hart and Nomos, Munich/Oxford, pp 15–54
Westermann HP (2017) Entstehung der Personengesellschaft. In: Westermann HP, Wertenbruch J, Handbuch Personengesellschaften. Schmidt, Cologne, update 68, § 5
Wiedemann H (2004) Gesellschaftsrecht – Ein Lehrbuch des Unternehmens- und Verbandsrechts, Band II, Recht der Personengesellschaften. C. H. Beck, Munich
Williams A (2012) Flexible finance. China-Britain Business Focus 2012/19:11

Windbichler C (2014) Eine internationale Landkarte der Personengesellschaften (einschließlich juristische Personen und Gesamthand). Zeitschrift für Unternehmens- und Gesellschaftsrecht 43:110–138

Wu Y, Geu TE (2007–2008) The new PRC limited partnership enterprise law and the limited partnership law of the United States: a selective analytical comparison. UCLA Pac Basin Law J 25:133–178

Xia F (夏凤英), Dong S (董书萍) (2011) Research on certain issues regarding special general partnership enterprises (特殊的普通合伙企业若干问题研究). Shandong Soc Sci (山东社会科学) 2011/7:125-128.

Xiao F (晓富) (1997) Central issues in the partnership enterprise law (有关合伙企业法中的几个问题). Chinese Foreign Leg Sci (中外法学) 1997/4:107-111.

Xu C (徐春雷), Cao X (曹秀峰) (2007) A study on the administrative registration of foreign-invested partnership enterprises (外商投资合伙企业登记管理问题研究). Study China's Adm Ind Commer (中国工商管理研究) 2007/12:29-31.

Xue J (薛驹) (1997) Written Report on the Revision of the Draft Partnership Enterprise Law (关于合伙企业法(草案修改稿)修改意见的汇报(书面)). Gazette of the Standing Committee of the National People's Congress 1997 No 1 (中华人民共和国全国人民代表大会常务委员会公报1997年1号), pp 21–22

Yan Y (严义埙) (2006) Explanations on the Revised Draft of the PRC Partnership Enterprise Law – delivered on 25 April 2006 to the 21st Session of the Standing Committee of the 10th National People's Congress (关于《中华人民共和国合伙企业法(修订草案)》的说明—2006年4月25日在第十届全国人民代表大会常务委员会第二十一次会议上). Gazette of the Standing Committee of the National People's Congress 2006 No 7 (中华人民共和国全国人民代表大会常务委员会公报2006年7号), pp 595–597

Yang J (杨杰), Qu T (曲天明) (2010) A study on the application of foreign-invested partnership enterprise law – comment on the FIPE measures (外商合伙企业的法律适用问题研究—兼评《外国企业或者个人在中国境内设立合伙企业管理办法》). Sci Manag (科学与管理) 2010/3:63-66.

Ye F (2002) Das chinesische Gesetz über Partnerschaftsunternehmen: Im Vergleich zum deutschen Recht. Lang, Frankfurt a.M

Yu D, Feng S, Wei J (2012a) FIPs as the new investment vehicle. In: Tring D, Mok S (eds) The legal guide to FDI in China. China Law & Practice, Hong Kong, pp 9–12

Yu D, Feng S, Wei J (2012b) Foreign invested partnerships: a new vehicle for investments? China Law Pract 26(8):10–13

Yu W (余文唐) (2017) Do the general rules of civil law mark the death of the individual partnership? (《民法总则》给个人合伙判了死刑?). http://www.360doc.com/content/17/0331/11/819919_641651757.shtm. Accessed 15 May 2020

Yu Y (虞亚光) (2010) Three highlights of the FIPE measures (外商投资合伙企业管理办法的三个亮点). Adm Ind Commer (工商行政管理) 2010/5:43

Yuantao X, Binxue S, Zhang D (1989) Translation of Liufang Fang: Chinese partnership. Law Contemp Probl 52:43–67

Zhang G (张桂龙), Liu S (刘淑强) (1997) Guidebook on the PRC partnership enterprise law (《中华人民共和国合伙企业法》指南). China City Press (中国城市出版社), Beijing

Zhang LZ (2011) The legal environment for foreign private equity firms in China. Fordham J Corp Financ Law 16:839–889

Zhang Y, Du A (2014) Private equity funds in China. In: Moser MJ, Yu F (eds) Doing business in China, vol 1. Juris Publishing, Huntington, p II-5.1

Zheng HR (1986) China's new civil law. Am J Comp Law 34:669–704

Zhu C (朱慈蕴) (2008) The problem resulting from a corporation participating in a partnership as a general partner (公司作为普通合伙人投资合伙企业引发的法律思考). Mod Law Sci (现代法学) 30/5:77-85.

Zhu S (朱少平) (2006) Discussion of the Revised Partnership Enterprise Law (谈合伙企业法修改). http://www.npc.gov.cn/npc/xinwen/rdlt/fzjs/2006-04/26/content_348775.htm. Accessed 15 May 2020

Chapter 5
The Use of FIPE as Business Organisation in China

This book does not aim to provide a glossary of all legal questions that arise in the lifecycle of a FILPE. Instead, this book aims to provide the foundation for finding answers to particular legal issues that occur during the establishment, operation, or termination of a FILPE by answering the research question, and addressing the functionality of the law underlying the FILPE. However, the objective of this book is to explore whether the FIPE as an investment vehicle fulfils the legal standards that are necessary to protect foreign investor's interests. The FIPE can only be an attractive alternative for foreign investors to other types of sino-foreign alliances if this is the case. This chapter therefore focuses on the practical use of the FIPE as an investment vehicle. A brief account of the current practical relevance of partnership enterprises in China, especially the FIPE, is provided. To understand the business conditions under which foreign investors operate, an analysis of the ownership structure of China's economy follows. In addition, a number of potential options are introduced for structuring an investment through a FIPE.

5.1 The Role of Partnership Enterprises in China's Economy

'The history of legal forms of partnerships is undoubtedly a success story. In many jurisdictions, partnerships nowadays play a vital economic role.'[1] Partnerships are traditionally used in specific industries and for specific aims, with the variety of intended purposes being almost endless, in theory as well as in practice.[2] The extensive contractual freedom and less formal framework that govern the law of

[1]Haase (2014), p. 3.
[2]Ibid, p. 5.

S. Kuntner, *China's Foreign-Invested Limited Partnership Enterprise*, China-EU Law Series 7, https://doi.org/10.1007/978-3-030-54181-1_5

partnerships is interesting not only for commercial entrepreneurs, family-owned businesses, ship owners, and start-ups, but also for private equity or venture capital investors.[3] For instance, the classic German limited partnership with a corporate general partner—the GmbH & Co. KG—was developed in order to combine legal and tax benefits, but still plays an important role in Germany's corporate landscape.[4] Exact numbers of the utilisation of the GmbH & Co. KG are not available.[5] However, estimates indicate that seven out of eight limited partnerships in Germany are formed with a corporate general partner.[6] A statistic on the revenue of turnover tax in Germany lists 148,574 GmbH & Co. KGs in 2017.[7] While this accounts for only 4.33 per cent of all businesses, the GmbH & Co. KGs generate 25.40 per cent of Germany's turnover tax revenue.[8] In the US, the role of limited partnerships has fluctuated over the years due to changes in the tax laws, first favouring, then restricting, partnerships as tax shelters.[9] The use of the limited partnership enterprise in the US—especially in the real estate industry—saw its peak in the 1970s and 1980s, until this boom was ended by a tax reform in 1986.[10] Later, the newly introduced hybrid forms of the LLC and LLP became very popular investment vehicles, and are currently being used far more often than the limited partnership with a corporate general partner.[11] There are only very few reliable statistics on the number and size of limited partnerships in the US that can be drawn on.[12] However, they still seem to serve as investment vehicle for particular industries and sectors.[13] Limited partnerships are utilised for venture capital investments, in the oil and gas industries, for real estate development, the entertainment industry, research and development ventures, and family businesses.[14]

In the Chinese economy, partnerships are widely used by Chinese investors.[15] From a legal and regulatory perspective, the partnership enterprise is regarded as a 'convenient' enterprise form.[16] The flexibility in the organisation structure and capital contribution methods, the lighter tax burden, and the strong links between partners are perceived as great advantages of the partnership enterprise.[17] *Kirby*

---

[3]Ibid, p. 5.

[4]Ibid, pp. 5–6.

[5]Mueller-Thuns (2016), para. 1.9.

[6]Fleischer and Wansleben (2017), p. 640.

[7]Federal Statistical Office (2017).

[8]Calculation by the author, based on data from Federal Statistical Office (2017).

[9]Bromberg and Ribstein (1994b), pp. 1:11–1:12.

[10]Bromberg and Ribstein (1994b), pp. 11:16–11:17.

[11]Schaper (2013), p. 85.

[12]Bromberg and Ribstein (1994b/2000), pp. 11:9–11:10.

[13]Fleischer and Wansleben (2017), p. 641.

[14]Schaper (2013), p. 89; Wu and Geu (2007–2008), p. 141.

[15]Yu (1997), p. 52.

[16]Shen (2015), p. 55.

[17]Zhu (朱慈蕴) (2008), p. 80: Du (杜瑞孔) (2006), pp. 69, 70.

identifies an explanation for its popularity in the general desire for trust and predictability.[18] In the light of the political and economic events of twentieth-century Chinese history, it is not irrational for investors to be focused on the safety of assets, and the maintenance of personal and family control.[19]

> Partnerships are the expression of an intimate, non-owner-alienated, business association, where the relatively few partners will participate in the running of the business and have confidence in the trustworthiness and technical competence of their co-venturers – a confidence based on knowledge about the other partners, their past performance in business, their skill-sets, etc.[20]

The LPE with a corporate general partner is recognised in China as providing a wide range of investment opportunities and chances for in-depth cooperation and mutual knowledge exchange between business partners.[21] Corporate general partners can exploit the potential of their own technology by utilising the skill and knowledge of other partners in the flexible and diversified business models that LPEs can provide.[22] In China's private equity sector, the LPE has become the most popular and common enterprise form in this industry since it was adopted with the revised PEL in 2007.[23] Following the international practice, the domestic private equity investors utilise the LPE to combine the professional knowledge and skills of the general partner with the capital of the limited partners.[24] The combination of limited liability of the investors and personal liability of the fund managers is attractive to passive investors who prefer to entrust their capital to skilled fund managers.[25] In addition to the tax benefits, the terms of the partnership agreement can be negotiated very flexibly, and the LPE offers the investors more privacy than corporations in the sense that the accounts of a partnership enterprise and the partnership agreement are generally not disclosed publicly.[26] Official statistics from SAMR account for 138,375 newly established partnership enterprises in 2011 with a registered capital of 14,631,555 RMB.[27] While SAMR does not consistently publish a nationwide break down of the newly established LPEs, data from 2010 and 2011 shows a significant increase in LPE establishments with

[18]Kirby (1995), p. 58.

[19]Ibid, p. 58.

[20]Howson (2010), p. 361 fn. 195.

[21]Zhu (朱慈蕴) (2008), p. 80.

[22]Ibid, p. 80.

[23]Lin (2011), p. 201.

[24]Wang (王翔) (2006), item 3.

[25]Lin (2013), p. 190.

[26]Ibid, pp. 190–191.

[27]Howson (2015), p. 397.

numbers increasing from 3132 to 10,165 newly established LPEs.[28] This would account for 7.34 per cent of the newly established partnership enterprises.[29]

Regarding the FIPE, an analysis was provided above that it was welcomed by foreign investors and quickly utilised as investment vehicle for private equity and real estate investments, and likewise for actual business operations.[30] Regarding the actual utilisation of the FIPE, it has proven difficult to identify reliable data. For the end of 2013, the establishment of more than 2000 FIPEs had been reported.[31] The official breakdown of FDI by enterprise forms in China's Statistical Yearbook only began to provide information on the FIPE in 2018. In 2017, a total of thirty FIPEs were approved,[32] while the number for 2018 decreased to twenty.[33] Notably, for the period of January to November 2019, 77 new FIPEs have been established, marking a strong increase.[34] For all of these statistics, it remains unclear how many of the FIPEs have been FILPEs, FIGPEs and FISGPEs respectively. While the numbers in the Statistical Yearbook are exceptionally low, an analysis of the invested capital in the FIPEs is of great interest. With an average amount of invested capital of 40.6 million USD in 2018, the average invested capital in a FIPE exceeds that of an EJV by almost twelve times, and that of an CJV by more than five times.[35] This can be explained by the important role that the FILPE plays in private equity and venture capital investments.[36]

[28]Ibid, pp. 397–398.

[29]A World Bank Group Enterprise survey from 2012 differs strongly from these numbers, claiming that 30.3 per cent of all enterprises in China are organised in the form of an LPE, while only 3.4 per cent are formed as a limited liability company. In comparison, the percentage of LPEs for all countries is stated to be 7.1 per cent. This deviation is so significant that it obviously does not reflect the business reality in China. The deviation possibly relates to misinterpretations or translation errors of the underlying Chinese statistics. See World Bank Group (2012).

[30]See Sect. 4.1.12.

[31]Qiu (2014), p. 301.

[32]National Bureau of Statistics of China (中华人民共和国国家统计局) (2019), Chapter 11–15.

[33]National Bureau of Statistics of China (中华人民共和国国家统计局) (2019), Chapter 11–15.

[34]Foreign Investment Department of the Ministry of Commerce (中华人民共和国商务部外国投资管理司) (2019). At the time of writing of this book, no statistic for the entire year 2019 has been published yet.

[35]Calculation by the author, based on data from the National Bureau of Statistics of China (中华人民共和国国家统计局) (2019), Chapter 11–15.

[36]See Sect. 5.3.3.

5.2 The Ownership Structure in China and its Effect on Corporate Law

'The correlation between ownership structure and corporate law has been a common theme in academic literature for the past three decades.'[37] To a greater or lesser degree, all developed market economies have self-consciously shaped their law to enhance the efficiency with which corporations can be financed and managed in the context of the country's particular pattern of ownership.[38] The ownership structure can significantly influence the interest group dynamics that govern changes in the enterprise law framework.[39] The ownership structure can therefore help to explain differences between various systems of enterprise organisation law.[40]

Two main ownership structures can be distinguished. In a 'dispersed' ownership structure, no single shareholder, investor or affiliated group of shareholders is capable of exercising control over most large enterprises,[41] a structure that is characteristic for publicly traded corporations in the US, UK, and Japan.[42] In contrast, in a 'controlled' ownership structure, the majority of the largest enterprises, and almost all small listed companies, traditionally had a controlling shareholder in the form of individuals, families, the state or a bank at the top of a closely coordinated group of other firms.[43] Such traditional blockholder jurisdictions are Germany, France, and Italy.[44] However, these rather stereotype patterns have changed in recent years. While there is a certain degree of convergence in the ownership structure of a jurisdiction, there is also great variety in the ownership patterns of different firms within any given jurisdiction.[45]

As a sino-foreign alliance, the FIPE will usually be formed by foreign and Chinese partners. Foreign investors are generally in a disadvantaged position in forming an effective interest group on account of their non-national status, and hence have only limited influence in shaping enterprise organisation laws in the target country of their investment.[46]

This leads to the analysis which ownership structure dominates China's economy. For decades, China has been a state-owned economy with SOEs being the central vehicle for implementing socialist economic policies and controlling China's

[37]Davies et al. (2009), pp. 305, 306.

[38]Armour et al. (2017b), p. 27.

[39]Ibid, p. 25.

[40]Armour et al. (2017a), p. 267.

[41]Armour et al. (2017b), pp. 25–26.

[42]Ibid, pp. 25–26.

[43]Ibid, p. 26.

[44]Ibid, p. 26.

[45]Ibid, p. 26.

[46]Armour et al. (2017a), p. 270.

economy.[47] Despite the policy of Reform and Opening up, this economic structure continues to have an enduring effect today.[48] The state still takes a dominant position in controlling listed and unlisted enterprises—both on a central and local level.[49] Common are also joint public-private ownership structures of enterprises.[50] 'China still has more than 150,000 SOEs. Their share of industrial assets hovers stubbornly near 40%.'[51] This accounts for a highly concentrated state-owned ownership structure in China.[52] While the Chinese government aims to improve the efficiency of SOEs, plans for reforms strongly focus on consolidating the market by merging SOEs to form even larger, globally-competitive industrial groups.[53] In addition, local governments have further increased ownership in enterprises in recent years.[54] Turning around the general trajectory towards a greater role for market forces, investments by SOEs have outpaced those by private investors since 2015.[55] These developments give not much reason to anticipate that the current ownership structure will likely change in the near future. Local governments, state-owned securities companies and state-owned banking groups further play a dominant role as investors in China's private equity and venture capital industry.[56] Since the limited partnership enterprise is a common investment vehicle in this industry, this raises the question how these investments by the Chinese state influence the functioning of the legal framework that governs the FILPE.

State ownership as a large blockholder influences enterprise organisation law in two ways.[57] 'First, the interests of the state as a shareholder may continue to play a role in the political economy of corporate law reforms. Second, the very content of "optimal" corporate law may be different when the interests of shareholders are highly heterogenous, which is usually the case in the presence of state ownership.'[58] Consistent with these general observations, *Shen* has identified non-profit centred motives of the Chinese state that may not be in line with the principle of shareholder wealth maximisation, such as maintaining urban employment levels, directing control over pillar industries, controlling prices in a given sector, and extracting profits for politically-oriented purposes.[59] From the perspective of the state, ideal private investment decisions are in sync with the national targets and development

[47]Goetzmann and Köll (2005), p. 149.

[48]Zhang (2011), p. 866.

[49]Shen (2015), p. 199; Zhang (2015), p. 63; Lin (2013–2014), p. 230.

[50]Goetzmann and Köll (2005), p. 149.

[51]The Economist (2017).

[52]Shen (2015), p. 199; Lin (2013–2014), p. 230.

[53]Reuters (2015).

[54]Zhang (2015), p. 63.

[55]The Economist (2017).

[56]Zhang (2017), p. 235.

[57]Armour et al. (2017a), p. 271.

[58]Ibid, p. 271.

[59]Shen (2015), p. 199.

plans of the government and the CPC.[60] *Zhang* even implies that the political impact of China's private equity and venture capital industry may significantly influence the development of the legal framework of limited partnership enterprises in China.[61] This may provoke severe conflicts between majority and minority shareholders, and could even cause the exploitation of the latter.[62] In addition, this ownership structure can influence the allocation of power between shareholders and management, with the state as omnipresent controlling shareholder bypassing the board of directors, and getting directly involved in the daily decision-making process.[63] Some FIEs reportedly have been pressured to revise the terms of their joint ventures with state-owned partners to allow the CPC a final say over business operations and investment decisions.[64] Dominant state ownership can also culminate in the abuse of political power and connections to affect decisions made by the judiciary in a dispute between majority and minority shareholders.[65] Therefore, the overall influence of China's concentrated ownership structure should always be considered when analysing the legal framework for FDI in China.

5.3 Structuring a FIPE as an Investment Vehicle for Foreign Investors

Despite having been in existence for ten years, and being favoured by an increasing number of investors, the FIPE structure is still not as widely known and recognised as the EJV and CJV.[66] This seems particularly remiss as the different variations of the FIPE offer great liberty and flexibility in structuring a foreign investment into China. A limited partnership enterprise can be set up as a closely held enterprise—e.g., a FILPE to conduct manufacturing—or as a more publicly held enterprise—e.g., a FILPE in an investment fund structure.[67] Based on rather standard models, this section aims to outline structuring options for the utilisation of the FILPE in practice. However, foreign investor's creativity may produce far more complex and advanced structures in an actual investment scenario. It is important to note that the legal questions in relation to a FILPE that is established to carry out active business operations may differ from the legal issues that arise in a FILPE that is designed to make passive investments, such as private equity funds. In addition, limited partnerships differ from other business associations in that they are often designed to

[60]South China Morning Post (2017).

[61]Zhang (2017), p. 235.

[62]Shen (2015), p. 199.

[63]Ibid, p. 199.

[64]Reuters (2017).

[65]Shen (2015), p. 199; Perkins (2005), p. 183.

[66]Yu et al. (2012), p. 9.

[67]Ribstein (1988), p. 866.

economise on a specific commercial transaction.[68] Considering the complexity of the potential structures of a FILPE, the analysis in the subsequent chapters is focused on the general principles of a FILPE, but specialties that arise in a particular investment scenario will be sporadically indicated. The focus of this book lies on the FILPE, because international practice shows that the limited partnership variation of the FIPE can be expected to be utilised significantly more in business practice than the general partnership type. However, many aspects that are discussed, can likewise be applied to a FIGPE. This section therefore begins with a brief consideration of how the FIGPE can be utilised by foreign investors in practice and then turns to different options of structuring a FILPE.

5.3.1 General Partnership Enterprise as Project Company

The FIGPE can serve an important function in the realisation of investments where foreign and Chinese investors collaborate in a specifically tailored project for a rather short duration of time. This relates to BOT projects in the form of infrastructure investments and the exploitation of natural resources, such as power plants, toll roads, oil exploration projects, water treatment plants, and etcetera. Other examples are the construction of large real estate projects. Previously, sino-foreign collaborations in these fields have been carried out in the form of the CJV.[69] Characteristic for these investments is that the parties do not intent to develop a long-term business together. They only want to cooperate for the completion of a specific project. Comparison with the US and Germany shows that it is likewise common for enterprises to form a new project company for this kind of investment projects. In both jurisdictions, such project companies are usually established in the most basic form of the general partnership.[70] Reasons for the formation of a project company are manifold: each partner may have different skills and specialties that only in their combination enables them to carry out the project, or the project in its entirety is too large to be carried out by only one of the partners.[71] From the perspective of the customer, the advantage is to have only one contractual partner who is coordinating the project, and who is bearing the joint liability of the participating enterprises.[72]

The FIGPE is an attractive investment vehicle because of its less bureaucratic and more streamlined establishment process, its flexible organisation structure, and its tax transparency. By acting as general partners, the foreign and Chinese investor are permitted to actively engage in the management and daily operation of the FIGPE.[73]

[68]Raaijmakers (2004), pp. 408–409.

[69]Mahony (2015), pp. 188–189.

[70]For US Law: Bromberg and Ribstein (1994a), p. 1:9; for German law: Schäfer (2017), pp. 20–22.

[71]Schäfer (2017), p. 21.

[72]Ibid, p. 21.

[73]For a comparison with the role of the limited partners, see Sect. 8.3.2.1.

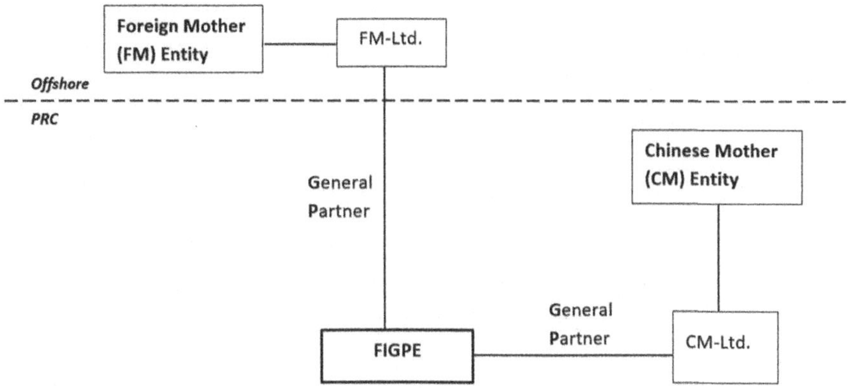

Fig. 5.1 Investment structure of FIGPE as project company

The major disadvantage would be the unlimited liability that follows from acting as general partner. However, this can be controlled by utilising a limited liability company as an intermediary investment vehicle, as shown in Fig. 5.1.[74] A problem with regard to the Chinese partner can result from the regulation in the PEL that excludes SOEs from acting as general partner.[75] Especially for infrastructure projects in China, a SOE would likely be involved as one project partner.

In theory, a FIGPE can also be formed by foreign partners exclusively, without the involvement of a Chinese partner. However, comparison with the WFOE, which could also be jointly established by several foreign investors, shows that this is rarely has been utilised in practice.[76] Instead, foreign investors will usually jointly establish an offshore investment vehicle that subsequently sets up a subsidiary in the form of a WFOE/limited liability company in China.[77] However, the FIGPE may still be a possible option should the foreign investors want to establish an FIE that can be opened to investments by Chinese partners at a later date.

5.3.2 *FILPE for Greenfield Investments in Business Operations*

The FILPE is an attractive and not uncommon investment vehicle to carry out actual business operation in China.[78] Object of the analysis in subsequent chapters is a FILPE with a foreign corporate general partner, a structure that shields all investors

[74]Regarding the risk of piercing the corporate veil of a corporate general partner, see Sect. 8.2.2.3.

[75]Art. 3 PEL. For further analysis, see Sect. 8.2.2.1.

[76]Mahony (2015), p. 200.

[77]Ibid, pp. 183–184.

[78]Yu et al. (2012), pp. 9–10.

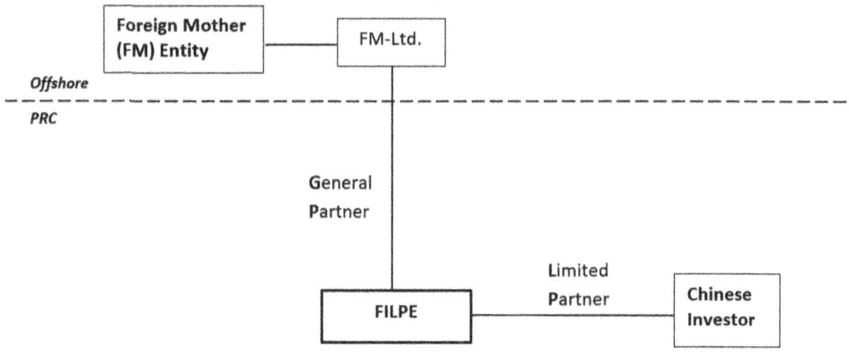

Fig. 5.2 Principle investment structure of a FILPE

from unlimited liability.[79] The distinctive feature of this investment vehicle is that the basic structure of both enterprise forms—the limited partnership enterprise and the corporate limited liability company—continue to exist, even though these enterprises are intertwined.[80] Naturally, some of the difficulties that are studied throughout this book arise from this specific conjunction.[81] However, the complexity of the legal relationships in each FILPE vary depending on the particular investment structure. For the German equivalent of a limited partnership with a corporate general partner, the GmbH & Co. KG, scholarship has identified three different types of structures that are utilised in greenfield investments in business operations.[82]

5.3.2.1 FILPE with Separate Owners of General Partner and Limited Partner

The first type, and also the principal structure of the FILPE that is analysed in this book, is one with a corporation as the only general partner, and the owner of the corporate general partner being different from the limited partner, as shown in Fig. 5.2. The investor who serves as the general partner, e.g. the foreign party, may provide technology and managerial experience, while the investor who serves as limited partner provides capital to the FILPE. In this scenario, the roles are clearly divided between the different investors.

Naturally, the investment structure could also be the reverse in the sense that the Chinese party serves as general partner, whereas the limited partners are foreign investors or both foreign and Chinese investors.

[79] See detailed analysis in Sect. 8.2.2.

[80] Wiedemann (2004), p. 842.

[81] Freudenberg (2014), p. 207.

[82] Ibid, p. 207.

5.3.2.2 FILPE with Overlapping Ownership Structure of General Partner and Limited Partner

Often, both investors want to engage in the management of the limited partnership enterprise, while likewise benefitting directly from the pass-through tax treatment. Therefore, more complex structures have been developed in the international practice that allow each investor to take a dual role as general partner and limited partner. They are categorised as the second type, which can be further distinguished in different investment scenarios, with each posing distinctive difficulties in the light of Chinese law.

5.3.2.2.1 Identical Ownership of Corporate General Partner and Limited Partner

The aforementioned objective can be realised if the limited partners are also the owners of the sole corporate general partner, with each limited partner holding the same share of ownership in the corporate general partner as he holds in the FILPE. The partnership agreement would stipulate that all profits are to be distributed among the limited partners, leaving the general partners with a mere managerial function. This scenario allows both investors to directly benefit from the pass-through tax treatment as a limited partner, while the role of general partner allows them to co-manage the FILPE.

This investment scenario is the most common structure chosen for the German GmbH & Co. KG,[83] and likewise a popular investment structure in the US.[84] To ensure the consistency of this investment scheme, the articles of association of the corporate general partner and the partnership agreement should contain stipulations that guarantee the identity of the shareholders and partners to prevent the ownership of both entities from falling into separate hands.[85] A critical issue under German law became the strict distinction between the capitalisation of the corporate general partner, and the capital contribution that it has to make as general partner to the partnership enterprise.[86] Failing that, the investor can be subject to subsequent capital contributions in the event of the insolvency of the partnership enterprise.[87] In the US, the legitimacy of this investment structure as a whole has also been questioned. Limited liability is extended to limited partners in exchange for their renunciation of control over the partnership enterprise. An argument is made that this doctrine is bypassed when the limited partner simultaneously takes control through

[83] Ibid, p. 207.

[84] Ratigan (1983), p. 950.

[85] Freudenberg (2014), pp. 207–208.

[86] Wenzel (2016), para. 5.106–5.121.

[87] Ibid, para. 5.106–5.121.

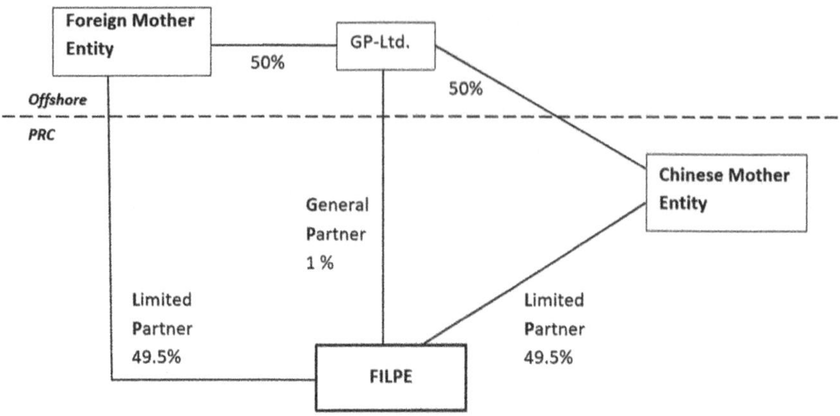

Fig. 5.3 Investment structure of identical ownership with offshore corporate general partner

the general partner, and suggested that such limited partners should be subject to unlimited liability by piercing the corporate veil.[88]

Under Chinese law, an additional issue arises, which is related to the place of incorporation of the corporate general partner. One option would be to incorporate the corporate general partner of the FILPE as an offshore entity outside of China, as shown in Fig. 5.3. This would add an additional layer of government regulation, as the Chinese investor needs to obtain the proper permits to make an outbound investment in the offshore corporate general partner.[89] In addition, the Chinese investor could be subject to the regulations on 'Round-Trip Investments'. In 2014, 'SAFE Circular 37'[90] has introduced a broader definition of Round-Trip Investments that refers to 'direct domestic investment activities conducted by domestic residents directly or indirectly through SPVs, by virtue of setting up new foreign-invested enterprises or projects in China, mergers and acquisitions, and obtaining ownership, controlling rights or management rights in the enterprises or projects'.[91] Since it is the purpose of the offshore corporate general partner to make an equity investment in the FILPE and to exercise control over it, the Chinese investor may have to undergo special registration or obtain permission from authorities to carry out the investment in the corporate general partner legally.[92] The corporate general partner would also be governed by a foreign law, which can make it more complex to ensure the

[88] Instructive on the discussion under US law, Ratigan (1983), pp. 949–985; for the FILPE, see Sect. 8.3.2.2.

[89] Instructive on China's outbound investment regime, Wolff (ed) (2011).

[90] Circular on the Administration of Foreign Exchange Involved in Offshore Investment, Financing and Round-Trip Investment Conducted by Domestic Residents Through Special Purpose Vehicles (境内居民通过境外特殊目的公司融资及返程投资外汇管理有关问题的通知), promulgated by the State Administration of Foreign Exchange on 4 July 2014 with effect as of the same day.

[91] Art. 1 Para. 2 SAFE Circular 37.

[92] Art. 3 SAFE Circular 37.

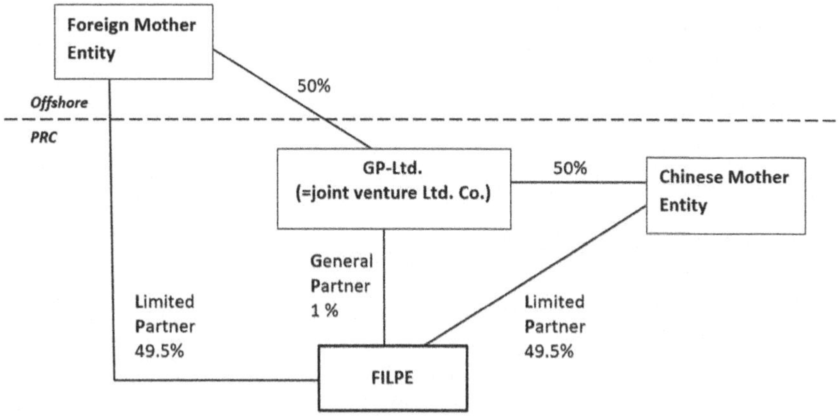

Fig. 5.4 Investment structure of identical ownership with onshore corporate general partner

synchronised structure between the domestic limited partner, the offshore general partner, and the FILPE.[93]

The alternative option would be to establish the corporate general partner as an onshore entity in China, as shown in Fig. 5.4. Such a domestic corporate general partner, co-invested by a foreign and Chinese investor, previously could only be established in the form of the EJV, which would create a number of issues. The Chinese investor could not be a natural person, as only Chinese companies, enterprises, or other economic organisations were permitted to invest in an EJV.[94] Since the FIL took effect on 1 January 2020, such a domestic corporate general partner would be established as a joint venture governed under the Company Law, which allows direct investments of Chinese individuals.[95] However, this structure also touches upon the question whether an FIE is permitted to make an equity investment in an enterprise form without limited liability.[96] Above all, the foreign investor would have to bear significant transaction costs by going through the cumbersome establishment process of a foreign invested joint venture, only to establish a FILPE thereafter.

5.3.2.2.2 Parallel Ownership Structure of General Partners and Limited Partners

To avoid the problems that arise with the establishment of a jointly owned offshore or onshore corporate general partner, the FILPE could be structured to have the same

[93]Teichmann (2014), p. 240.

[94]Art. 1 EJV Law.

[95]See Sect. 9.2.1.2.2.

[96]See discussion in Sect. 4.1.4.6 fn. 277.

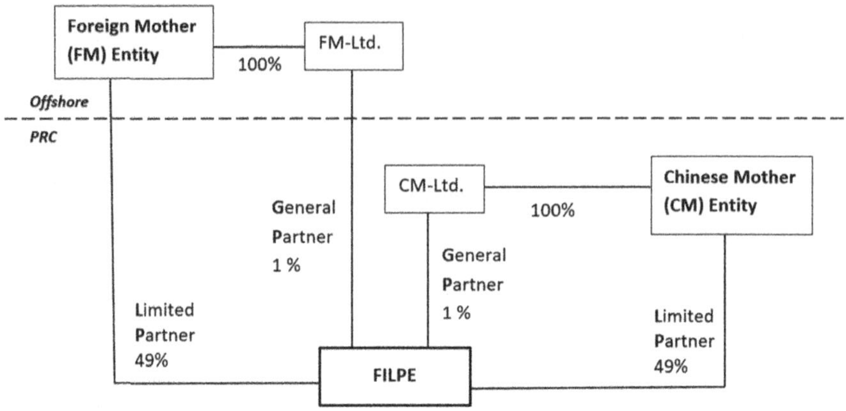

Fig. 5.5 Investment structure of parallel ownership of general partner and limited partner

number of general partners as it has limited partners. This structure is illustrated in Fig. 5.5. Each investor would own one hundred per cent of a corporate general partner. For the foreign investor, this would be realised in the form of an offshore SPV, and for the Chinese investor in the form of an onshore SPV. At the same time, each investor would also act as limited partner. The share of ownership of each investor would accumulate to the sum of his investment as general partner and as limited partner. However, the existence of several corporate general partners who are all engaged in the management of the FILPE poses the greatest disadvantage of this structure. The necessary coordination between the different general partner entities would impose additional transaction costs and increase the potential for agency problems between the investors.

5.3.2.3 FILPE Owning the Corporate General Partner

The third type is named 'Einheits-GmbH & Co. KG' in Germany.[97] This structure is regarded as a legal masterpiece combining two distinct legal entities into one business unit in order to alleviate friction caused by the interaction of corporation and partnership enterprise law.[98] Transferring this structure, the FILPE itself is the sole shareholder of the corporate general partner, while the investors only act as limited partners. The corporate general partner is the unlimited joint and several liable partner of the FILPE while—at the same time—a one hundred per cent subsidiary of the FILPE. This investment structure precludes the risk, which is still inherent in the identical ownership structure analysed above, that the ownership of the corporate general partner may be dissociated from the limited partners in the

[97] Freudenberg (2014), p. 208.
[98] Schaper (2013), p. 91.

course of transfers of ownership or inheritance.[99] The legitimacy of this legal construct has been subject to debate in German scholarship, but it was eventually approved by Germany's Bundesgerichtshof (BGH)—the Federal Court of Justice.[100] Two of the main issues that are discussed in Germany with regard to this investment structure, are creditor protection and decision making.[101] Generally, creditors of the limited partnership enterprise can resort to the registered capital of the partnership enterprise, and the registered capital of the corporate general partner. Both liable capitals must be maintained independently from each other.[102] German law therefore provides that the registered capital of the partnership enterprise may not be used as capital contribution to the registered capital of the corporate general partner.[103] Regarding decision making, the limited partnership enterprise is the only shareholder of the corporate general partner.[104] Since the partnership enterprise is represented by the corporate general partner, the corporate general partner executes its own shareholder rights.[105] This would cause a conflict of interest when the director of the corporate general partner would have to decide over his own appointment, dismissal and remuneration.[106] Besides, the limited partners could lose any direct influence over the director of the corporate general partner.[107] To avoid such a conflict of interest, appropriate stipulations need to be included in the articles of association of the corporate general partner, and in the partnership agreement.[108] At the same time, the limited partners have to be careful not to lose their liability protection by getting involved in the management of the corporate general partner beyond the permissible scope.[109]

These problems illustrate the complexity of the necessary contractual arrangements, and the overall sophistication of this legal construct. Therefore, it remains questionable whether Chinese authorities would regard such an investment structure as permissible. Information on each partner of the FILPE must be submitted to SAMR during the registration process, and any change to a registered item needs to be registered likewise,[110] thereby creating the possibility that SAMR may refuse to register such a FILPE. In addition, the limited partners could potentially be subject to unlimited liability by later piercing of the corporate veil.

---

[99]Freudenberg (2014), p. 208.

[100]See for detailed references on the legal history of his investment structure in Germany, Lüke (2016), para. 2.464.

[101]Lüke (2016), para. 2.464.

[102]Ibid, para. 2.465.

[103]Ibid, para. 2.465.

[104]Ibid, para. 2.472.

[105]Ibid, para. 2.472.

[106]Ibid, paras. 2.473–2.483.

[107]Ibid, paras. 2.473–2.483.

[108]Ibid, paras. 2.473–2.483.

[109]See analysis in Sect. 8.3.2.1.

[110]Art. 12 Para. 2 No 3 and Art. 18 FIPE Provisions.

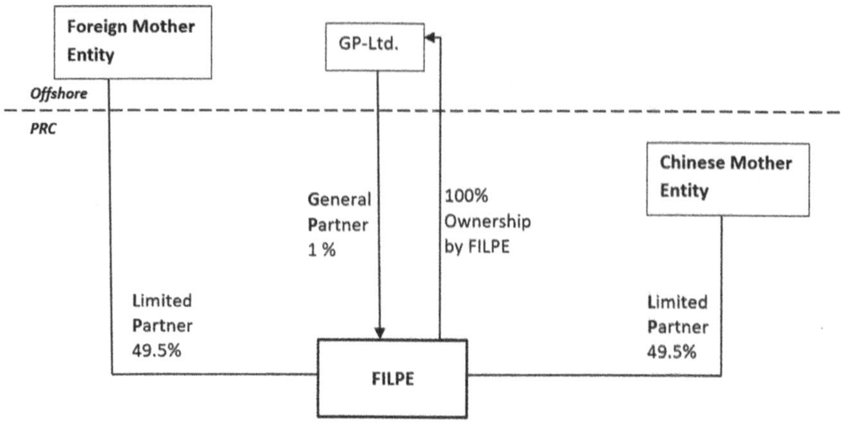

Fig. 5.6 Investment structure of FILPE owning the corporate general partner (offshore structure)

Should this investment construct be utilised, two structuring options are available, relating to the place of incorporation of the corporate general partner. Establishing the corporate general partner as an offshore entity outside of China, as shown in Fig. 5.6, would require the FILPE to make an outbound investment to acquire one hundred per cent of the corporate general partner. The 'Administrative Measures for Outbound Investment'[111] stipulate in Article 2 that any 'enterprise' duly established within the territory of China is entitled to conduct outbound investments. The term 'enterprise' includes partnership enterprises,[112] so that a FILPE in general is eligible to make outbound investments. However, it would have to undergo the registration and approval process for outbound investments and Round-Trip Investments,[113] and it remains to be seen how authorities will react in the light of this particular investment structure.

Establishing the corporate general partner as an onshore entity, as shown in Fig. 5.7, raises the question if this subsidiary of the FILPE would be a domestic limited liability company or a foreign-invested enterprise. In addition, the issues of business scope (in case of a foreign-invested enterprise) of the corporate general partner and re-investment restrictions of the FILPE would likewise apply.[114] Such a re-investment also needs to be registered with the relevant authorities,[115] making it subject to their discretion if this investment structure is eventually approved.

[111] Administrative Measures for Outbound Investment (境外投资管理办法), promulgated by the Ministry of Commerce on 6 September 2014 with effect as of 6 October 2014.

[112] See Sect. 4.1.3.2.

[113] See Sect. 5.3.2.2.1.

[114] See Sect. 4.2.4.1.

[115] Art. 8 FIE Reinvestment Provisions.

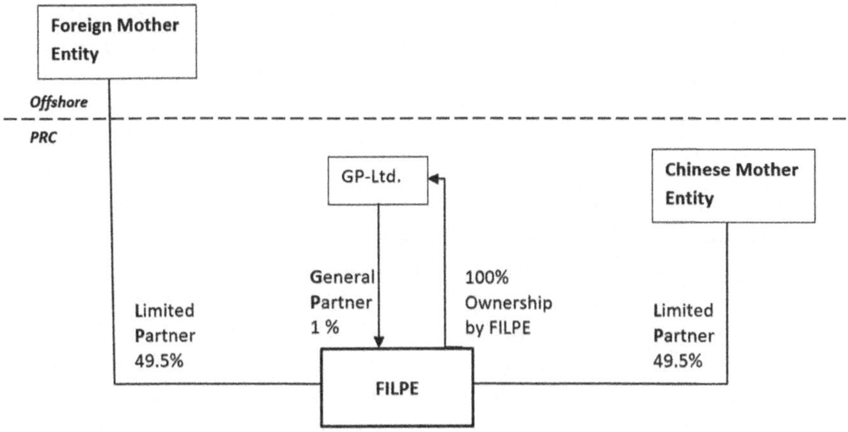

Fig. 5.7 Investment structure of FILPE owning the corporate general partner (onshore structure)

5.3.3 FILPE for Private Equity and Venture Capital Investments

The introduction of the FILPE was especially intended for and anticipated by the foreign private equity and venture capital investment community.[116] The contours of private equity and venture capital can be a little amorphous.[117] In this book, the term private equity (PE) refers to an asset class consisting of pools of actively managed capital organised to invest in equity securities of privately held and certain public companies, with venture capital (VC) being a variation thereof with a focus on early-stage investments in start-up companies.[118]

Within three decades, China has created the fastest developing and the world's second largest VC market in terms of annual VC investments.[119] China's private equity sector has evolved to become a significant element of the country's increasingly multi-layered capital markets.[120] While foreign private equity firms played a leading role in fostering this development, structuring onshore private equity funds has always been a challenge.[121] The high thresholds and cumbersome establishment process for a FIVCE have been outlined above.[122] An alternative structure was sometimes used by utilising a domestic limited partnership enterprise that was

[116]Shen (2015), p. 56; Wang and Yong (2010), p. 16; for an overview of the development of China's domestic Private Equity and Venture Capital Industry, see: Zhang (2017), pp. 235–237.

[117]Zhang (2011), p. 844.

[118]Lin (2011), p. 201; Zhang (2011), p. 844.

[119]Lin (2017), pp. 162–163.

[120]Zhang (2011), p. 883.

[121]Zhang (2017), p. 235; Zhang (2015), p. 20; Zhang (2011), p. 841.

[122]See Sect. 3.2.3.2.

managed by a foreign private equity firm.[123] The general partner would either be a WFOE set up by the foreign private equity firm, or a WFOE that would manage the fund without having a direct equity interest in the fund.[124] The former structuring option would operate in a legal grey-area, and in the latter option, the foreign private equity firm would risk to lose control over the domestic fund.[125] Nevertheless, foreign private equity firms managed to invest in a wide range of industries and regions in China over the years.[126] Key target industries are biotechnology and healthcare, mechanical engineering, food and drinks, internet, retail, reals estate, agriculture and forestry, chemical engineering, and financial services.[127] Geographically, investments are no longer limited to the highly developed coastal areas, but are expanding into the vast inland and western provinces of China.[128] A typical private equity investment in China is a non-controlling stake of 15–40 per cent in an operating company, due to the numerous restrictions on foreign investments.[129]

With the introduction of the FILPE, foreign private equity and venture capital funds were hoping directly to invest in, and manage, an onshore fund structure in the form of a limited partnership enterprise.[130] In international practice, the limited partnership is the most common structure for private equity funds.[131] Among newly raised VC funds in China, the limited partnership enterprise has also become the most popular enterprise form.[132] It offers a good mechanism for combining capital and expertise, which are the two core elements for private equity investments.[133] This structure is illustrated in Fig. 5.8. The general partner exercises control over the day-to-day management of the fund, and is responsible for choosing portfolio companies in which to invest,[134] while the Chinese or foreign limited partners provide capital to the fund.[135] Foreign private equity firms expected finally to be able to operate on a level playing field with domestic RMB funds, which have grown to become formidable competitors to the international players.[136] However, a private equity fund in the form of a FILPE is also subject to foreign investment restrictions, as is expressly set out in Article 62 FIPE Provisions, stating that 'the domestic investment of a foreign-invested partnership enterprise with investment as

[123]Zhang and Du (2014), p. II-5.1.5.

[124]Ibid, p. II-5.1.5-6.

[125]Ibid, p. II-5.1.6.

[126]Zhang (2011), p. 858.

[127]Ibid, p. 858.

[128]Ibid, p. 858.

[129]Ibid, p. 858.

[130]Wang and Yong (2010), pp. 15–16.

[131]Zhang and Du (2014), p. II-5.1.5; Zhang (2011), p. 869; Liu (2008), p. 83.

[132]Lin (2017), p. 184.

[133]Weng and Xia (2007), p. 97.

[134]Lin (2011), p. 201.

[135]Ibid, p. 201.

[136]Zhang (2011), pp. 874–875; Wang and Yong (2010), p. 16.

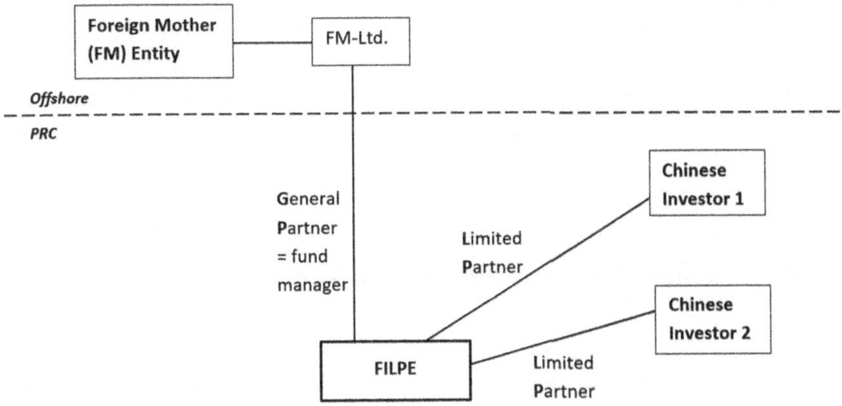

Fig. 5.8 Investment structure of FILPE as Fund Structure

its core business shall be made in compliance with the laws, administrative regulations and rules of the State governing investment of foreign enterprises'. For a private equity fund, this especially refers to the FIE Reinvestment Provisions besides the Guidance Catalogue. According to Article 14 FIPE Measures, foreign-currency funded private equity funds are currently still required to apply for the QFLP program.[137] This limits their ability to attract local as well as foreign investors, and to convert foreign currency at will.

Furthermore, the number of limited partners in a FILPE is capped at 49, narrowing the scope of investors that can participate in one private equity fund.[138] Notwithstanding these restrains, shortly after the FIPE Legislation took effect, in February 2010, US private equity firm Carlyle teamed up with Shanghai conglomerate Fosun Group to establish a 100 million USD jointly held private equity fund based in China and denominated in RMB.[139] Reportedly, this has been the first business licence granted to a FILPE with primary business in private equity investment.[140] Consequently, commentators expect that new RMB funds will most likely adopt the FILPE structure in the future.[141]

The investment structure of a FILPE as an investment vehicle for private equity and venture capital funds is—in principle—very similar to the structure of the FILPE with separate owners of the general partner and limited partner that is analysed in the following chapters. However, for a detailed analysis of the specialties with regard to

137 See the analysis in Sect. 4.2.4.1.

138 Art. 61 Para. 1 PEL. For an analysis of this limitation, see discussion in Sect. 9.2.1.2.1.

139 Zhang (2011), p. 877.

140 Ibid, p. 877.

141 Mahony (2015), pp. 232–233; Zhang and Du (2014), p. II-5.1.3; Zhang (2011), pp. 875–876.

structure and legal problems in a FILPE in the private equity and venture capital industry, reference is made to a separate research project undertaken by *Lin*.[142]

Naturally, the investment structure could also be the reverse in the sense that a Chinese party is acting as general partner and managing the private equity fund, while all foreign partners act as limited partners who are investing capital in such an onshore fund.

5.3.4 Conclusion on Investment Structures

The different structuring options of the FILPE that have been briefly introduced in this section already give an impression on how flexibly and diversely this investment vehicle can be utilised. In practice, even more varieties and much more complex structures of the FILPE can be expected. Therefore, it remains to be seen how FILPE investment scenarios develop in the future. These alternative structures, should they be legally feasible under China's FDI regime, will often present a combination of the issues that are analysed in the subsequent part with regard to the three elements of a standard corporate form. Therefore, the analysis in this book, while being based on the standard investment structure of a FILPE with separate owners of the general partner and limited partner, provides valuable insights for alternative investment scenarios as well.

References

Armour J, Enriques L, Pargendler M, Ringe W-G (2017a) Beyond the anatomy. In: Kraakman R et al (eds) The anatomy of corporate law, 3rd edn. Oxford University Press, Oxford, pp 267–272

Armour J, Hansmann H, Kraakman R, Pargendler M (2017b) What is corporate law? In: Kraakman R et al (eds) The anatomy of corporate law, 3rd edn. Oxford University Press, Oxford, pp 1–28

Bromberg AR, Ribstein LE (1994a) Bromberg and Ribstein on partnership, vol 1 general partnership. Wolters Kluwer, Boston

Bromberg AR, Ribstein LE (1994b) Bromberg and Ribstein on partnership, vol 3 limited partnership. Wolters Kluwer, Boston

Davies P, Enriques L, Hertig G, Hopt K, Kraakman R (2009) Beyond the anatomy. In: Kraakman R et al (eds) The anatomy of corporate law, 2nd edn. Oxford University Press, Oxford, pp 305–315

Du R (杜瑞孔) (2006) On the advantages of partnership enterprises over limited liability companies (论合伙企业相对有限责任公司的比较优势). Theoretical Observation (理论观察) 2006/6:69–70

Federal Statistical Office (2017) Turnover Tax Statistic 2017 (Umsatzsteuerstatistik 2017). https://www.destatis.de/DE/Themen/Staat/Steuern/Umsatzsteuer/Tabellen/voranmeldungen-rechtsformen.html. Accessed 15 May 2020

[142] Lin (forthcoming); Lin (2018), pp. 43–91.

Fleischer H, Wansleben T (2017) Die GmbH & Co. KG in den Auslandsrechten - Zirkulation eines gesellschaftsrechtlichen Regelungsmodells. GmbH-Rundschau 106:633–643

Foreign Investment Department of the Ministry of Commerce (中华人民共和国商务部外国投资管理司) (2019) Statistics about utilisation of foreign investment in China from Jan to Nov 2019 (2019年1-11月利用外资统计简表). http://www.fdi.gov.cn/1800000121_49_5014_0_7.html. Accessed 15 May 2020

Freudenberg G (2014) Ausgewählte Rechtsfragen der GmbH & Co. KG. In: Dauner-Lieb B, Freudenberg G, Werner GW (eds) Festschrift für Mark K Binz, Familienunternehmen im Fokus von Wirtschaft und Wissenschaft. C. H. Beck, Munich, pp 207–214

Goetzmann W, Köll E (2005) The history of corporate ownership in China: state patronage, company legislation, and the issue of control. In: Morck RK (ed) A history of corporate governance around the world. University of Chicago Press, Chicago, pp 149–181

Haase F (2014) Introduction. In: Haase F (ed) Taxation of international partnerships – 15 years OECD partnership report: past, present and future. IBFD, Amsterdam, pp 3–11

Howson NC (2010) Corporate law in the Shanghai People's Courts, 1992-2008: judicial autonomy in a contemporary authoritarian state. East Asia Law Rev 5:303–442

Howson NC (2015) Return of the prodigal form? Partnerships and partnership law in the People's Republic of China. In: Hillman RW, Loewenstein MJ (eds) Research handbook on partnerships, LLCs and alternative forms of business organizations. Edward Elgar, Cheltenham, pp 390–411

Kirby WC (1995) China unincorporated: company law and business enterprise in twentieth-century China. J Asian Stud 54:43–63

Lin L (2011) The limited partner's derivative action: problems and prospects in the private equity market of China. Hong Kong Law J 41:201–230

Lin L (2013) The private equity limited partnership in China: a critical evaluation of active limited partners. J Corp Law Stud 13:185–217

Lin L (2013–2014) Regulating executive compensation in China: problems and solutions. J Law Commerce 32:207–254

Lin L (2017) Engineering a venture capital market: lessons from China. Columbia J Asian Law 30:160–220

Lin L (2018) Private equity investor protection: conceptualizing the duties of general partners in China. Berkeley Bus Law J 15:43–91

Lin L (forthcoming) The limited partnership in China, legal perspectives on venture capital and private equity. Springer, Berlin

Liu C (2008) Chinese company and securities law: investment vehicles, mergers and acquisitions and corporate finance in China. Kluwer Law, Alphen aan den Rijn

Lüke O (2016) Besondere Erscheinungsformen der GmbH & Co. KG. In: Mueller-Thuns T (ed) Handbuch GmbH & Co. KG: Gesellschaftsrecht – Steuerrecht, vol 21. Schmidt, Cologne, para 2.461–2.558

Mahony T (2015) Foreign investment law in China: regulation, practice and context. Tsinghua University Press, Beijing

Mueller-Thuns T (2016) Einleitung. In: Mueller-Thuns T (ed) Handbuch GmbH & Co. KG: Gesellschaftsrecht – Steuerrecht, vol 21. Schmidt, Cologne, para 1.1–1.46

National Bureau of Statistics of China (中华人民共和国国家统计局) (2019) China Statistical Yearbook 2019 (中国统计年鉴2019). China Statistics Publishing House (中国统计出版社), Beijing, Chapter 11–15

Perkins DH (2005) Comment to the history of corporate ownership in China. In: Morck RK (ed) A history of corporate governance around the world. University of Chicago Press, Chicago, pp 181–184

Qiu D (2014) Permanent establishment: an evolving concept under China's tax treaties (1983-2013). Br Tax Rev 2014:274–306

Raaijmakers T (2004) The reform agenda for partnerships and closely held companies in the Netherlands and the European Union. In: McCahery JA, Raaijmakers T, Vermeulen EPM

(eds) The governance of close corporations and partnerships: US and European perspectives. Oxford University Press, Oxford, pp 399–413
Ratigan JJ (1983) Piercing the veil of the corporate general partner in the hybrid limited partnership: a suggested remedy for inequitable conduct by limited partners. Suffolk Univ Law Rev 17:949–985
Reuters (2015) Made in China: Beijing plans new wave of state firm consolidation. http://uk.reuters.com/article/uk-china-parliament-reform-idUKKBN0M70LL20150311. Accessed 15 May 2020
Reuters (2017) Exclusive: in China, the Party's push for influence inside foreign firms stirs fears. https://www.reuters.com/article/us-china-congress-companies/exclusive-in-china-the-partys-push-for-influence-inside-foreign-firms-stirs-fears-idUSKCN1B40JU. Accessed 15 May 2020
Ribstein LE (1988) An applied theory of limited partnership. Emory Law J 37:835–895
Schäfer C (2017) Gesellschaft. In: Säcker FJ et al (eds) Münchener Kommentar zum Bürgerlichen Gesetzbuch, vol 6, 7th edn. C. H. Beck, Munich, pp 3–667
Schaper M (2013) Hybrid legal forms at the gates – the transition from combined legal forms to hybrid corporations and its consequences for creditor protection. Eur Company Financ Law Rev 10:75–112
Shen W (2015) Corporate law in China – structure, governance and regulation. Sweet&Maxwell, Hong Kong
South China Morning Post (2017) Why economic reforms in China mean a bigger role for the state. http://www.scmpcom/print/comment/insight-opinion/article/2111993/why-economic-reforms-china-mean-bigger-role-state. Accessed 15 May 2020
Teichmann C (2014) Die Auslandsgesellschaft & Co. Zeitschrift für Unternehmens- und Gesellschaftsrecht 43:220–251
The Economist (2017) Unnatural selection – China's state enterprises are not retreating but advancing. https://www.economist.com/news/leaders/21725295-bad-china-and-world-chinas-state-enterprises-are-not-retreating-advancing. Accessed 15 May 2020
Wang X (王翔) (2006) Introduction to the circumstances of the revisions of the partnership enterprise law (合伙企业法修改情况介绍). http://www.npc.gov.cn/npc/xinwen/lfgz/lfdt/2006-08/28/content_352015.htm. Accessed 15 May 2020
Wang A, Yong C (2010) Radical reform or unmet expectations? China Law Pract 24:15–17
Weng J, Xia T (2007) Limited liability partnership: the best structure for funds? China Law Pract 21:97
Wenzel J (2016) Rechtsverhältnisse der Gesellschaft zu Dritten. In: Mueller-Thuns T (ed) Handbuch GmbH & Co. KG: Gesellschaftsrecht – Steuerrecht, vol 21. Schmidt, Cologne, para 5.1–5.39
Wiedemann H (2004) Gesellschaftsrecht – Ein Lehrbuch des Unternehmens- und Verbandsrechts, Band II, Recht der Personengesellschaften. C. H. Beck, Munich
Wolff L-C (ed) (2011) China outbound investments – a guide to law and practice. CCH, Hong Kong
World Bank Group (2012) Enterprise Survey 2012. http://www.enterprisesurveys.org/data/exploreeconomies/2012/china#firm-characteristics. Accessed 15 May 2020
Wu Y, Geu TE (2007–2008) The new PRC limited partnership enterprise law and the limited partnership law of the United States: a selective analytical comparison. UCLA Pac Basin Law J 25:133–178
Yu G (1997) The emerging framework of China's business organizations law. Transnatl Lawyer 10:39–76
Yu D, Feng S, Wei J (2012) FIPs as the new investment vehicle. In: Tring D, Mok S (eds) The legal guide to FDI in China. China Law & Practice, Hong Kong, pp 9–12
Zhang LZ (2011) The legal environment for foreign private equity firms in China. Fordham J Corp Financ Law 16:839–889
Zhang L (2015) China's venture capital market: current legal problems and prospective reforms. Chandos Publishing, Amsterdam
Zhang C (2017) The distorted governance model of venture capital limited partnerships in China: a political perspective. Bus Law Rev 38:234–240

Zhang Y, Du A (2014) Private equity funds in China. In: Moser MJ, Yu F (eds) Doing business in China, vol 1. Juris Publishing, Huntington, p II-5.1.2

Zhu C (朱慈蕴) (2008) The problem resulting from a corporation participating in a partnership as a general partner (公司作为普通合伙人投资合伙企业引发的法律思考). Mod Law Sci (现代法学) 30/5:77–85

Chapter 6
Summary of Part I

The analysis of the history and legal framework of foreign-investments into China has illustrated the remarkable development that the legal system has undergone in the past 40 years.[1] With increasing experience and confidence in dealing with foreign investments, the legal framework for FDI has gradually been liberalised, and has become more transparent and accessible.[2] The FIPE was a blueprint for the fundamental reforms that have been implemented with the FIL on 1 January 2020. Most FIEs were characterised by China's parallel structure of the legal system, with foreign and domestic investments being subject to separate sets of regulations.[3] Since the FIPE was introduced, it has broken through this dual legislative structure. The FIPE Legislation is rooted in the PEL, and thus shares the same legal basis as domestic-invested partnership enterprises.[4] For other FIEs, this unification of the legal system has only been realised with the FIL.[5] Likewise, the FIPE has been characterised by a very progressive and more streamlined administrative regime for the establishment and operation of the FIPE, requiring only registration with SAMR instead of interaction with MOFCOM.[6] The same principle, unified registration with SAMR, has been rolled out for other FIEs with the FIL.[7] However, despite the latest reforms, the foreign investment laws still impose many restrictions on foreign investors. Thus, the FIPE is also subject to China's highly regulated and protective investment policies.[8] Therefore, the FILPE cannot yet be utilised for investments in

[1]See Sect. 3.1.6.3.

[2]Chen (2016), p. 859.

[3]See Sect. 3.1.3.

[4]See Sect. 4.1.5.3.

[5]See Sect. 3.1.5.3.

[6]See Sect. 4.1.8.1.

[7]See Sect. 3.1.6.3.2.

[8]See Sect. 4.1.7.

S. Kuntner, *China's Foreign-Invested Limited Partnership Enterprise*, China-EU Law Series 7, https://doi.org/10.1007/978-3-030-54181-1_6

most of the restricted industries that are subject to the 2019 FDI-Negative List. However, it also has been shown that the regulatory framework of the FILPE provides the flexibility that characterises partnership enterprises across jurisdictions. Since the revision in 2006, the PEL—in contrast to most of China's FDI legislation at that time—formulates many rules as default, rather than mandatory, provision.[9] This gives partners the freedom to contract into their own arrangements in the partnership agreement. By allowing the combination of a limited liability enterprise with a foreign corporate general partner, the Chinese lawmaker provides foreign investors with a wide range of options to develop new investment structures.[10] In practice, the FILPE can therefore be utilised as investment vehicle for different purposes and investment projects.[11]

References

Chen J (2016) Chinese law: context and transformation, Revised and Expanded Edition. Brill, Leiden

Schaper M (2013) Hybrid legal forms at the gates – the transition from combined legal forms to hybrid corporations and its consequences for creditor protection. Eur Company Financ Law Rev 10:75–112

[9]See Sect. 4.1.9.3.

[10]Schaper (2013), p. 82.

[11]See Sect. 5.3.

Part II
FILPE as a 'Standard Corporate Form'

The general legal framework under which the FILPE operates, has been established in the previous part. The analysis now turns to the key efficiency criteria that are utilised as a benchmark to evaluate the FILPE in this book.[1] Does the FILPE with a foreign corporate general partner fulfil (1) legal personality; (2) limited liability; and (3) transferable shares as defining elements of the standard corporate form? The analysis will show to what degree these elements are stipulated by statutory provisions in the FIPE Legislation and the PEL, and where the attributes need to be replicated through contractual provision in the partnership agreement.

[1] See Sect. 1.3.1.3.

Chapter 7
Legal Personality

The first attribute of the standard corporate form touches directly on a number of fundamental and dogmatic principles of Chinese partnership enterprise law. The authors of *The Anatomy of Corporate Law* clarify that the commonly used characterisation of a corporation as 'nexus *of* contracts' can be ambiguous.[1] They consider it more accurate to describe a corporation as a 'nexus *for* contracts', in the sense that a corporation 'serves, fundamentally, as the common counterparty in numerous contracts with suppliers, employees, and customers, coordinating the actions of these multiple persons through exercise of its contractual rights'.[2] Therefore, the first and most important contribution of enterprise organisation law is to permit a corporation to serve this coordinating role by operating as a single contracting party that is distinct from the various individuals who own or manage the corporation.[3] This attribute of the corporation is termed 'legal personality' in *The Anatomy of Corporate Law*.[4] Legal personality requires that the enterprise is embedded in a legal framework that provides three foundational types of rules: (1) entity shielding ensures that the enterprise is capable of owning its own property; (2) delegated management conveys that it can delegate authority to agents; (3) procedural rules must enable the enterprise to sue and be sued in turn under its own name.[5] A clarification is necessary that this concept of legal personality is not synonym with the concept of 'separate legal personality' or 'legal person status' as generally understood in legal literature.[6] While an enterprise form with legal person status—such as the German GmbH—usually fulfils these three rules, the legal person status

[1]Armour et al. (2017), p. 5.

[2]ibid, p. 5.

[3]ibid, p. 5.

[4]ibid, p. 8.

[5]ibid, p. 8.

[6]ibid, p. 8.

S. Kuntner, *China's Foreign-Invested Limited Partnership Enterprise*, China-EU Law Series 7, https://doi.org/10.1007/978-3-030-54181-1_7

is not a prerequisite to obtain 'legal personality' as it is used in this book.[7] An enterprise form that is commonly regarded to lack legal person status, can still enjoy each of the three foundational features described above.[8] Legal personality differs from the other four features of a standard corporate form insofar as the three types of rules that establish legal personality must be provided by law, and could not simply be replicated by contractual provisions between the owners[9] of the corporation, and their suppliers and customers.[10] Enterprise organisation law in this aspect serves a significant role in reducing the costs of doing business.[11]

Commentators have noted that the feature of 'continuity of interest' or 'perpetual life'—the fact that corporations are eternal, as long as they stay in business operation by generating revenue and paying their debts—is not listed as a separate feature of the standard corporate form.[12] However, the permanence of the corporate form is recognised to be encompassed in the attribute of legal personality as understood by *The Anatomy of Corporate Law*.[13]

7.1 Entity Shielding

Entity shielding describes rules that separate the assets of the corporation from the assets of the owners of the corporation, and that protect the corporation's assets from the owner's personal creditors.[14]

> The firm's entitlements of ownership over its designated assets include the rights to use the assets, to sell them, and – of particular importance – to make them available for attachment by its creditors. Conversely, because these assets are conceived as belonging to the firm, rather than the firm's owners, they are unavailable for attachment by the owner's personal creditors.[15]

Entity shielding involves two distinct rules of law. First, a 'priority rule' ensures that the firm's creditors will have 'a claim on the firm's assets that is prior to the

[7]ibid, p. 8. See also, Windbichler (2014), pp. 121–122.

[8]Armour et al. (2017), p. 9.

[9]The term 'owner' is used rather loosely in this book, referring to all of these persons: the partners in a general partnership, as well as the limited partners in a limited partnership, the shareholders of a business corporation, and the members of a cooperative, the beneficial owners of a private trust, the beneficiaries of a non-profit corporation, and the residents of a municipal corporation; Hansmann and Kraakman (2000), p. 392.

[10]Armour et al. (2017), pp. 7–8; Skeel (2003–2004), p. 1528.

[11]Armour et al. (2017), p. 7.

[12]Skeel (2003–2004), p. 1526.

[13]ibid, p. 1526.

[14]Armour et al. (2017), pp. 5–6.

[15]ibid, pp. 5–6.

claims of the personal creditors of the firm's owners'.[16] Second, 'liquidation protection' ensures that neither the individual owners can withdraw their share of firm assets at will, nor the personal creditors of an individual owner can foreclose on the owner's share of firm assets, thus preventing that the firm is partially or completely liquidated as a consequence.[17] In modern enterprise law, either one or both of these rules can be fulfilled. An enterprise form that provides the priority rule and liquidation protection is regarded as having 'strong-form' entity shielding.[18] Enterprise forms that are only characterised by the priority rule, are termed 'weak-form' entity shielding.[19] The entity shielding doctrine is interconnected with two other attributes of the standard corporate form. Strong-form entity shielding isolates the value of the firm from the personal financial affairs of the firm's owners, thus facilitating the attribute of tradability of the firm's shares.[20] Furthermore, entity shielding is the opposite of 'owner shielding', which is provided by the attribute of limited liability.[21] While entity shielding protects the assets of the firm from the creditors of the firm's owners, limited liability protects the assets of the firm's owners from the claims of the firm's creditors.[22]

Lin has shown that, historically, ancient Chinese partnerships, unlike their European counterparts, did not possess entity shielding.[23] This lack of the rule of entity shielding is credited to the legal tradition and social attitudes at that time, such as a deep anti-commercial ideology and a strong demand for imperial control over the economy.[24] As most partnerships were formed between close friends and relatives, the partnership relationship was not simply of a commercial nature, but a combination of business and social relationships.[25] 'There were hardly any partnership contracts specifying the assets of the partnership or the partners, or the associated property rights and obligations.'[26] At that time, the absence of workable accounting methods and bankruptcy concepts, and the dominance of alternative customary rules, social norms, and rights shaped Chinese business practice, and the attitudes about the role of law in it.[27] Altogether, these factors led to the lack of entity shielding in ancient Chinese partnerships.[28] The following analysis will explore whether this deviation from Western legal systems still remains today.

---

[16] ibid, p. 6.
[17] ibid, p. 6.
[18] ibid, p. 6.
[19] ibid, p. 6.
[20] ibid, p. 6.
[21] ibid, p. 9.
[22] ibid, p. 9.
[23] Lin (2013), p. 219.
[24] ibid, p. 219.
[25] ibid, p. 244.
[26] ibid, p. 244.
[27] ibid, p. 249.
[28] ibid, p. 249.

7.1.1 Priority Rule for Firm Creditors over Personal Creditors

The priority rule, also called 'affirmative asset partitioning',[29] stipulates that the firm's assets are, as a default rule of law, automatically made available for the enforcement of contractual liabilities entered into in the name of the firm.[30] 'By thus bonding the firm's contractual commitments, the rule makes these commitments credible.'[31] It provides assurance that the firm will perform its contractual obligations.[32] The priority rule thus contains two components. 'The first is the designation of a separate pool of assets that are associated with the firm, and that are distinct form the personal assets of the firm's owners and managers.'[33] In essence, this is fulfilled by legal entities that differ from individual human beings, and that can own assets in their own name.[34] This requires an analysis whether the FILPE constitutes a separate legal entity that can own assets under its own name. The second component is the actual default rule, stipulating that the claims of the firm's creditors must be satisfied before the firm's assets become available to satisfy any personal creditors of the firm's owners.[35] 'This has the virtue of reducing monitoring costs for firm creditors by giving them, in effect, a security interest in firm assets.'[36]

> What makes affirmative asset partitioning especially important is that the parties could not realistically create it themselves. All of the other attributes theoretically could be replicated through contractual provisions (just as the attributes can be, and often are, altered or eliminated by contract). But it would be nearly impossible to achieve affirmative asset partitioning by contract, due to the huge number of actual and potential parties involved (which would include every creditor of every current or future shareholder of the enterprise). As a result, it is here that the corporate form, as supplied by the state, plays its most important role.[37]

This requires an analysis whether the priority rule is facilitated by the FILPE.

7.1.1.1 Legal Nature and Asset Ownership of the FILPE

The question whether the FILPE can own assets under its own name, is directly related to its legal nature. In most jurisdictions, the legal nature of the partnership

[29]This term was used in Hansmann and Kraakman (2000), pp. 387–440, which explores the centrality of entity shielding to organisational law; Armour et al. (2017), p. 6 fn. 13.

[30]Armour et al. (2017), p. 6.

[31]ibid, p. 6.

[32]Hansmann and Kraakman (2000), p. 392.

[33]ibid, p. 393.

[34]ibid, p. 393.

[35]ibid, p. 394.

[36]Hansmann et al. (2005), p. 11.

[37]Skeel (2003–2004), p. 1528.

enterprise has been subject to considerable controversy.[38] The discussion typically revolves around the question whether the partnership enterprise constitutes a separate entity that is distinct from its members or whether it is only a contractual relationship between the partners that forms a mere aggregate of discrete persons.[39] Consequently, the legal nature is also discussed with regard to the Chinese partnership law framework. International comparison shows that cultural and historical aspects can strongly influence the position which a jurisdiction takes on this issue.[40]

German partnership law is characterised by the 'Gesamthand' element.[41] Traditionally, only the partners were regarded as having legal capacity, not the partnership itself.[42] Therefore, the partnership as a separate entity could not own the partnership assets, but all partners in joint ownership would rather own the partnership assets together, holding them, as it were, 'with one hand'.[43] An opposing opinion evolved during the twentieth century, arguing that an organisation which acts as a partnership towards third parties differs not from a legal person, and can thus bear full legal capacity.[44] The prevailing opinion today is a compromise that denies a partnership the legal person status, but recognises that it has full legal capacity.[45] This applies to non-commercial and commercial partnerships alike.[46] For the GmbH & Co. KG, this is even positively reinforced by Article 124, Paragraph 2, in conjunction with Article 161, Paragraph 2 German HGB, stating that the GmbH & Co. KG 'can acquire rights and enter into obligations, acquire ownership and other rights in real property and sue and be sued in its own name'. This makes the GmbH & Co. KG an independent legal subject with full legal capacity.[47] The dogmatic discussion around the Gesamthand in Germany remains relevant only for the undisclosed partnership under the BGB.[48]

US partnership law likewise struggled for a long time with the question whether a partnership is merely an aggregate of its partners, that is, a confederacy of partners that does not rise to the level of a separate entity, or rather a distinct legal entity that

[38]DeMott (2004), p. 404.

[39]DeMott (2004), p. 404.

[40]Taking the US partnership law as example, the death of the first drafter of the Uniform Partnership Act (see Sect. 4.2.2.2 fn. 663) lead to a change from the entity approach to the aggregate approach, initiated by his successor. See DeMott (2004), p. 278.

[41]Haase (2014), pp. 3, 6. For a full account of the development of the *Gesamthand* in Germany, see Schmidt (2002), pp. 196–206.

[42]Schmidt (2002), pp. 196–206.

[43]Haase (2014), pp. 3, 6.

[44]Schmidt (2002), pp. 181–182.

[45]ibid, pp. 181–182.

[46]ibid, p. 182.

[47]ibid, p. 1363.

[48]ibid, pp. 203–206.

is separate from its partners.[49] The initial 'Uniform Partnership Act'[50] (UPA) of 1914 was silent on the legal nature of the partnership enterprise but showed both entity and aggregate characteristics, depending on the specific topic addressed.[51] For limited partnerships, the predominance of entity characteristics was greater than in general partnerships.[52] Starting with the RUPA in 1997, and subsequently affirmed with the ULPA, this question was finally resolved by an unequivocally statement that 'a limited partnership is an entity distinct from its partners'.[53] However, both laws still retain aspects of the aggregate construct, such as the joint and several liability of the general partners for the obligations of a partnership enterprise.[54] Regarding the ownership of property, RUPA clarified in 1997 that 'property acquired by a partnership is property of the partnership and not of the partners individually'.[55] While ULPA does not contain such an explicit provision, the limited partnership is regarded under ULPA as the owner of the property in numerous respects, which is consistent with the entity theory.[56] International comparison thus illustrates that in Germany and the US, but also in Switzerland, Austria, and the UK the predominant principle is nowadays that of the partnership constituting an entity distinct from its partners.[57]

In China, the nature of the partnership enterprise has also been subject to long-lasting controversy. The PEL itself makes no statement in this regard. The GPCL, which was promulgated 10 years before the PEL, recognises only two types of civil subjects: natural persons and legal persons.[58] While the Individual Partnership is regulated under the chapter of natural persons, the partnership enterprise under the PEL obviously does not fall under this category.[59] One of the defining characteristics of the legal person is the ability independently to bear civil liability with all its assets.[60] Enterprise forms with legal person status in China are the EJV, Legal

[49]Comment to Section 201 (a) RUPA; for a detailed overview with further references see: Bromberg and Ribstein (1994a), pp. 1:28–1:33; Bromberg and Ribstein (1994b/2001), pp. 11:31–11:41.

[50]Uniform Partnership Act, promulgated by the National Conference of Commissioners on Uniform State Laws in 1914, subsequently revised and amended multiple times until it has been replaced in 1997 by the Revised Uniform Partnership Act.

[51]Comment to Section 201 (a) RUPA; Wu and Geu (2007–2008), p. 145. An analysis of different topics is provided in Bromberg and Ribstein (1994a), pp. 1:33–1:61.

[52]Bromberg and Ribstein (1994b/2001), pp. 11:31–11:32.

[53]Section 110 (a) ULPA, and with similar wording for the general partnership, Section 201 (a) RUPA.

[54]Comment to Section 201 (a) RUPA.

[55]Section 203 RUPA.

[56]Exemplary, see Section 406(b)(3) ULPA with a default unanimous consent requirement for the transfer of the limited partnership's property outside the regular course of business.

[57]Raaijmakers (2004), p. 404 fn. 3.

[58]Art. 2 GPCL.

[59]Arts. 30-35 GPCL. Regarding the nature of the Individual Partnership, see Sect. 4.2.1.2.

[60]Art. 37 No 4 GPCL / Art. 60 GRCL.

Person CJV, WFOE, and under Company Law, the Limited Liability Company and Joint Stock Company.[61] In the light of the unlimited joint and several liability of the general partner,[62] the majority of commentators agree that a partnership enterprises does not qualify as a legal person under Chinese law.[63] However, the lawmaker has recognised that a partnership enterprise does fulfil many attributes of a separate legal entity.[64] Article 20 PEL stipulates that the partnership enterprise has the ability to own property under its own name. The scope of the partnership enterprise's property is defined in Article 20 PEL to expand to 'all the capital contributions made by the partners, the proceeds derived, and other property obtained in accordance with the law in the name of the partnership shall be deemed as the property of the partnership'. Furthermore, according to Article 3 Partnership Enterprise Registration Measures, a partnership enterprise may engage in business activities after it has been registered, and has acquired a business licence.[65] Therefore, a partnership enterprise is entitled to conduct business transactions with other market participants in its own name. Accordingly, scholars have argued that partnership enterprises constitute a category of their own, different from both natural and legal persons, but still constituting a distinct legal entity.[66] This approach has now been implemented in the new GRCL. In addition to natural persons and legal persons, Article 2 GRCL recognises 'non-legal-person organisations' as a third type of civil subjects. Chapter 4 of the GRCL is dedicated to its regulation. A non-legal-person organisation is defined in Article 102 GRCL as 'an organisation that does not have legal person qualifications but may engage in civil activities in its own name pursuant to the law'. Moreover, the definition contains a list of non-legal-person organisations that expressly includes partnership enterprises.[67] Non-legal-person organisations enjoy the same legal status in civil activities as natural or legal persons.[68] Accordingly, partnership enterprises are recognised as bearing capacity for civil rights and civil conduct.[69] Their property rights, creditor rights, equity and investment rights, and other civil rights and interests are equally protected.[70] With the addition of the

[61]Art. 2 EJV Implementing Regulations; Art. 14 CJV Implementing Regulations; Art. 8 WFOE Law; Art. 3 Company Law.

[62]Art. 2 Para. 2 PEL. For a detailed analysis, see Sect. 8.2.

[63]Howson (2015), p. 401; Chen (2014), pp. 25, 68; Lu (吕美昂) (2011), p. 81; Epstein and Shen (2009), p. I-6.1.38.

[64]Li (李飞) (ed) (2006), p. 12.

[65]An equivalent regulation is stipulated in Article 4 FIPE Provisions.

[66]Lin and Yeo (2010), p. 104; Bu (2017), p. 192.

[67]Art. 102 Para. 2 GRCL.

[68]Art. 4 GRCL.

[69]This is reiterated in Article 108 GRCL, which stipulates that the general provisions on legal persons (Arts. 57-75 GRCL) shall likewise apply as a reference to the non-legal-person organisations; the capacity for civil rights and capacity for civil conduct of legal persons in regulated in Article 57 GRCL.

[70]Arts. 114, 118, 125-126 GRCL.

non-legal-person organisation as a new type of civil subject, the Chinese lawmaker affirms that a partnership enterprise constitutes a separate legal entity.

7.1.1.2 Assignment of Priorities to the FILPE's Creditors

The second component of the priority rule requires an analysis whether a rule in Chinese partnership law stipulates that the claims of the FILPE's creditors must be satisfied before the FILPE's assets become available to satisfy any personal creditors of the partners. The PEL does not provide an explicit regulation for such a priority, but a conclusion can be drawn from several of its provisions.[71]

Article 41 PEL is a basic provision for asset partitioning in partnership enterprises.[72] It stipulates that a personal creditor of a partner who simultaneously is a debtor of the partnership enterprise, is prohibited from offsetting these claims.[73] A creditor of an individual partner is further prohibited from exercising, in subrogation, management or governance rights or authority of the said partner inside the partnership enterprise.[74] This regulation clarifies that the personal debt of a partner and the debt of the partnership enterprise are to be kept separated.[75] The legal relationships that a partner enters into in his own name are separated from those that are entered into in the name of the partnership enterprise.[76] Personal creditors of the partners hence have no direct access to the assets of the partnership enterprise. Regarding the scenario in which a creditor of the partnership enterprise is also a debtor of an individual partner, the PEL provides no regulation.[77] Given the separate nature of the debts, the same principle as stipulated in Article 41 PEL should apply, and prohibit to offset these claims.[78] Furthermore, Article 42, Paragraph 1 PEL stipulates that a partner's personal creditor is primarily to be satisfied with the partner's personal property. Only if the personal property is not sufficient, a personal creditor can stake a claim in the partner's ownership interest in the partnership enterprise.[79] However, it follows from Articles 38 and 39 PEL that the repayment of the creditors of the partnership enterprise also takes precedence in that scenario.[80]

---

[71] Ye (2002), p. 92.

[72] Howson (2015), p. 403.

[73] Article 41 PEL states that '[i]f a partner has debts unrelated to the partnership, the relevant creditor shall not use his creditor's right against the said partner to offset the debts he owes to the partnership, nor may he exercise, in subrogation, the rights of the said partner in the partnership'.

[74] Art. 41 PEL.

[75] Li (李飞) (ed) (2006), pp. 61–62.

[76] ibid, pp. 61–62.

[77] Ye (2002), pp. 94–95.

[78] ibid, pp. 94–95.

[79] For a detailed analysis, see Sect. 7.1.2.2.

[80] Ma (马强) (1998), p. 235.

The dissolution of a partnership enterprise leads to its liquidation.[81] Article 89 PEL sets out a specific order in which the partnership property shall be distributed in the course of the liquidation process. Following the payment of liquidation fees, wages, social insurance premiums, and statutory compensation of employees and taxes, other debts owed by the partnership enterprise are to be settled.[82] The latter include secured and unsecured debts.[83] Last in this order, the remaining property of the partnership enterprise shall be distributed among the partners.[84] This stipulates the principle of 'first payment [of partnership enterprise debts], post allocation [of partnership enterprise property to partners]'.[85] Consequently, it illustrates that also during the liquidation of the partnership enterprise, priority is granted to the creditors of the partnership enterprise.

The bankruptcy of a partnership enterprise is regulated separately from its liquidation as a result of dissolution. When a partnership enterprise is unable to pay off its due debts, Article 92, Paragraph 1 PEL offers the creditors two cumulative options: they can apply to a People's Court for bankruptcy liquidation, and they can additionally force the general partner to pay off the debts. The procedure for bankruptcy of enterprises in China is regulated in the 'Enterprise Bankruptcy Law'[86] since 2007. Even though the Enterprise Bankruptcy Law and the PEL became effective on the same day, the direct application of the Enterprise Bankruptcy Law is limited to enterprises with legal person status.[87] The lawmaker argued that partnership enterprises are popular enterprise forms for small and medium-sized businesses, and that it would be disproportional to fully apply the Enterprise Bankruptcy Law which has been composed to govern corporations.[88] However, Article 135 has been included in the Enterprise Bankruptcy Law, which states that the procedures set out in the Enterprise Bankruptcy Law shall apply, *mutatis mutandis*, when a non-legal person organisation is subject to bankruptcy liquidation 'as required by other laws'. This provision is a direct reference to Article 92 PEL.[89] If the creditor of a partnership enterprise chooses to start bankruptcy proceedings, the court will apply the relevant procedural rules, including imposing a stay of actions, and possibly appointing an independent administrator to manage the assets of the partnership enterprise.[90] Opting for a bankruptcy proceeding instead of going

---

[81]For an analysis of the dissolution and liquidation of a partnership enterprise, see Sect. 9.2.2.

[82]Art. 89 PEL.

[83]Li (李飞) (ed) (2006), p. 142. For a detailed analysis of secured transaction under Chinese law, see Tu (2010), pp. 183–219.

[84]Art. 89 PEL.

[85]Li (李飞) (ed) (2006), p. 142.

[86]PRC Enterprise Bankruptcy Law (中华人民共和国企业破产法), promulgated by the Standing Committee of the National People's Congress on 27 August 2006 with effect as of 1 June 2007.

[87]Art. 2 Enterprise Bankruptcy Law.

[88]Hong (洪虎) (2006), pp. 354, 357.

[89]Zheng (2010), p. 227; Li (李飞) (ed) (2006), pp. 145–146.

[90]Zheng (2010), p. 227.

after the general partner directly, can be advantageous for the creditor. The administrator will protect the value of the bankruptcy estate, and can reclaim transactions that might negatively affect the total value of the debtor's assets.[91] Reports show that Chinese courts have already dealt with enterprise bankruptcy cases relating to partnership enterprises.[92] For the property of the bankrupt enterprise, the Enterprise Bankruptcy Law stipulates a specific order for its liquidation. Debt that is secured with specific property enjoys priority in being repaid with that specific property.[93] Secured debt is followed by bankruptcy expenses, employees' salaries, medical and social benefits and outstanding taxes, and—lastly—any other unsecured debts.[94] Should the remaining property of the partnership enterprise not be sufficient to pay off all debts, Article 92, Paragraph 2 PEL clarifies that its general partners continue to bear unlimited joint and several liability for these debts. If the general partner is an enterprise with legal person status, as is the case in the underlying scenario of the FILPE with a corporate general partner, and if said general partner is unable to repay the outstanding claims, the creditors may then apply to the court to initiate bankruptcy proceedings against that corporate general partner.[95] Depending on whether the corporate general partner has his main place of business or place of incorporation in China or abroad,[96] the Enterprise Bankruptcy Law or a foreign bankruptcy regime would apply.[97] The Enterprise Bankruptcy Law therefore provides priority for the creditors of the FILPE over the creditors of its partners.

All in all, the analysis illustrates that the PEL offers a basic rule of priority as well as regulations for the dissolution and bankruptcy of the partnership enterprise which ensure that the creditors of the FILPE are satisfied before the FILPE's assets become available to satisfy any personal creditors of its partners. For the FILPE with a corporate general partner, affirmative asset partitioning is thereby ensured.

7.1.2 Liquidation Protection

The analysis of the first rule of entity shielding has shown that the FILPE provides affirmative asset partitioning and assigns a prior claim to the FILPE's assets to its creditors. The second rule—liquidation protection—determines how strong the

[91] Arts. 31-34 Enterprise Bankruptcy Law. Instructive on the enterprise bankruptcy proceeding, see Zheng (2010), pp. 221–266.

[92] Zheng (2010), p. 227.

[93] Art. 110 Enterprise Bankruptcy Law.

[94] Art. 113 Enterprise Bankruptcy Law.

[95] Zheng (2010), p. 227.

[96] Regarding the determination of the governing law of the corporate general partner, see Sect. 8.2.2.2.1.

[97] In contrast, should the general partner be a natural person and Chinese law be applicable, the situation is more complicated as China does not yet have an individual bankruptcy regime (Zheng 2010, p. 227).

entity shielding is with regard to the withdrawal or foreclosure of a partner's share of ownership. Under the rule of liquidation protection, neither an owner nor his personal creditors may demand a pay-out of the owner's ownership interest unilaterally.[98] 'So the liquidation protection rule serves to protect the going concern value of the firm against destruction by individual shareholders or their creditors.'[99] Since the liquidation protection rule revolves around the investor's share of ownership, this first requires an analysis of what is the equivalent to the 'share of ownership' in a FILPE, what legal nature and what scope it has under Chinese law.

7.1.2.1 A Partner's Ownership Interest in the FILPE

In return for the investment in an enterprise, an investor is granted a specific legal status, which can be termed as ownership interest or—as used in *The Anatomy of Corporate Law*—as 'share of ownership'.[100] With regard to FIEs, the Chinese lawmaker has implemented rather unusual concepts in the past, as can be illustrated with the EJV.[101] Unlike limited liability companies in western jurisdictions, the EJV does not issue nominal shares.[102] Instead of holding nominal shares of the company, investors hold an equity interest in the EJV in accordance with their respective capital contribution.[103] Hence, the membership right in the EJV is linked to the equity interest, which is also transferrable in principle.[104]

For the partnership enterprise, the legal nature of the (transferable) ownership interest of a partner has been a controversial subject across jurisdictions, similar to the discussion around the legal nature of the partnership enterprise itself.[105] To describe the ownership interest of a partner, the PEL states that a partner holds a 'share of the property in the partnership enterprise' (合伙企业中的财产份额).[106] However, the PEL fails to define the nature and scope of the ownership interest of a partner further. This lack necessitates an interpretation of the meaning of the phrase 'share of the property in the partnership enterprise'.[107] The meaning and scope of

[98]Hansmann et al. (2005), p. 11.

[99]Armour et al. (2017), p. 6.

[100]Huber (1970), p. 1.

[101]The same principal applies to the WFOE and the limited liability company under the Company Law, Mahony (2015), p. 179.

[102]Ting and Ge (2014), p. 670.

[103]Shen (2015), pp. 35, 125; Mahony (2015), p. 179; Ting and Ge (2014), p. 670. Regarding the EJV, see also Sect. 3.2.1.

[104]Art. 4 Para. 4 EJV Law in conjunction with Art. 20 EJV Implementing Regulations; Arts. 72-74 Company Law.

[105]Regarding the discussion in German partnership enterprise law, see Schmidt (2002), pp. 547–565, 1309–1310. Regarding US partnership enterprise law, see Bromberg and Ribstein (1994a), pp. 3:57–3:62; Bromberg and Ribstein (1994c), pp. 13:15–13:17.

[106]Arts. 23-25, 42 Para. 2, Art. 50 Para. 1, Arts. 57, 72-73 PEL.

[107]Wu and Geu (2007–2008), pp. 150–151.

this phrase has determinative significance for several other legal issues, including the determination of what may be assigned to a third party, and what may be obtained by a creditor of a partner—as contrasted with a creditor of the partnership enterprise.[108] Literature on Chinese partnership enterprise law elaborates on this question only sporadically, but two contrasting interpretations of the phrase become apparent. The first limits the meaning of the phrase to mere financial rights that are separated from the other rights and obligations of a partner.[109] The second understands it as a comprehensive membership right in the partnership enterprise that unites the financial rights and all other rights and obligations of a partner in a single legal position.[110]

In support of the first interpretation, commentators invoke Article 50, Paragraph 1 PEL, which states that when a partner dies, or—in case of a corporate partner—is dissolved, the heir or successor of the share of the property in the partnership enterprise 'shall (...) acquire the status of being a partner in the said partnership'. This language is regarded as indicating a distinction between the status of a partner and having a share of the property in the partnership enterprise.[111] Furthermore, the argumentation is based on a specific understanding of the provisions that regulate the transfer of a partner's share of the property in the partnership enterprise to a third party. Unless otherwise specified in the partnership agreement, the PEL requires the other partners to give approval at two stages during such a transfer process.[112] The first approval permits the transfer of the partner's share of the property in the partnership enterprise to the transferee.[113] A second approval is required for the amendment of the partnership agreement to include the transferee as a new partner.[114] Some commentators conclude that this underlines the distinction between the mere financial right of the partner and the other rights and obligations that are associated with being a partner.[115] With the transfer of the partner's share of the property in the partnership enterprise, the transferee shall only hold a financial right and shall merely obtain the right to apply for admission into the partnership.[116] However, this separation of the rights and obligations of a partner could cause serious detriments for the transferee, and likewise for the partnership enterprise. A scenario can arise where the other partners do not consent to the admission of the transferee to the partnership, even though they had agreed to the transfer of the partner's share of the property in the partnership enterprise before. As a consequence, the transferee would hold the financial right, while the other rights and

[108]ibid, p. 146.

[109]Ye (2002), pp. 107–108, 115–116; Wu and Geu (2007–2008), p. 151.

[110]Li (李飞) (ed) (2006), p. 63.

[111]Wu and Geu (2007–2008), p. 151.

[112]For a detailed analysis of the transfer of a partner's ownership interest in a FILPE, see Sect. 9.4.2.

[113]Art. 22 Para. 1 PEL.

[114]Art. 24 in conjunction with Art. 19 Para. 2 PEL.

[115]Ye (2002), pp. 107–108, 115–116.

[116]ibid, p. 108.

obligations of a partner would still rest with the transferor, who remains a partner in the partnership enterprise. Even those in favour of this interpretation have recognised that neither the PEL nor other laws provide a legal remedy for the transferee to resolve this deadlock situation.[117] Moreover, such a dissociation of partnership rights would not be in the interest of the partnership enterprise. The other partners would have to deal with a partner who still has voting rights, but no longer holds a financial interest in the partnership enterprise. Whether a genuine cooperation could be accomplished with such a partner, is doubtful. This problem of a dissociation does not arise under the second interpretation, which regards the ownership interest of a partner as a comprehensive membership right that is transferred to third parties with all financial and other rights and obligations.

The Chinese controversy around the legal nature of the ownership interest of a partner resembles the course of the equivalent discussion under German partnership enterprise law.[118] For the German partnership enterprise, *Huber* has explained in his ground-breaking analysis that a partner in a partnership enterprise holds a comprehensive membership right which comprises financial rights, decision making rights, and other rights and obligations of a partner.[119] He has identified several rights and obligations of a partner to be inseparable from the membership right, for example extending to voting rights, the share of the partnership enterprise's property, personal liability, participating in the profits and losses, managing rights and authority to represent the partnership enterprise.[120] These rights cannot be separated because of the unique and multifaceted nature of the status as a partner in a partnership enterprise.[121] A partner is a party to the partnership agreement, participates in the decision making of the partnership enterprise, and holds a property share in the enterprise.[122] This corresponds to the complex nature of the partnership enterprise, which constitutes a contractual relationship between the partners, forms an alliance that acts in unison, and owns the property to fulfil the common purpose of the partnership enterprise.[123] A partner's share in the profits and losses, in the capital, and in the partnership assets together do not constitute claims to the partnership enterprise or the other partners *in personam*.[124] Instead, they function as the basis to calculate the claims a partner is entitled to, e.g., his claim to the share of proceeds from the partnership enterprise.[125] Therefore, the legal status of the partner cannot be described as merely a set of contractual rights, property rights and powers to

[117] ibid, p. 108.

[118] Instructive: Schmidt (2002), pp. 1321–1324.

[119] Huber (1970).

[120] ibid, pp. 2–3.

[121] ibid, p. 7.

[122] ibid, p. 7.

[123] ibid, p. 7.

[124] ibid, p. 5.

[125] ibid, p. 5.

represent the partnership enterprise.[126] Rather, it is a unique and unitary legal status that encompasses all of the inseparable rights.[127] A partner can only give up his legal status as a partner by withdrawing from the partnership, or transferring the membership right to another partner or a third party.[128] In contrast, certain rights and obligations of a partner fail to touch on the core of his membership right, and can therefore be separated and made subject to an isolated transfer to a third party.[129] Examples thereof are the right to claim the partner's share of proceeds from the partnership enterprise, or the obligation to pay the capital contribution, which could also be fulfilled by a third party.[130] Notably, every partner's membership right need not include all of these rights and obligations, e.g. a limited partner neither bears unlimited personal liability nor enjoys the same management rights as a general partner. However, at least one of the partners must fulfil these rights, and they can only be fulfilled by a partner, not a third party.[131] *Huber's* findings were later confirmed by the BGH. Meanwhile, German partnership enterprise law recognises the ownership interest of a partner as a comprehensive and transferable membership right.[132] In the opinion of the current author, these principles should likewise be applied to the ownership interest of a partner under the PEL. Treating a partner's share of the property in the partnership enterprise as a comprehensive membership right corresponds to the nature of the partnership enterprise as a separate legal entity. Neither a need nor an advantage exists in setting the core financial rights apart from the other rights and obligations of a partner. Rather, the analysis has shown that the potential dissociation of a partner's rights and obligations can harm the interests of the partners as well as the partnership enterprise. The Chinese lawmaker has clarified that, as a result of the transfer of a partner's share of the property in the partnership enterprise, the transferee obtains a status in the partnership enterprise with the rights and obligations as defined and limited by the rights and obligations that the transferor has held in the partnership enterprise.[133] Should the transfer merely encompass the financial rights of the transferor, the transferee could not succeed to this extensive legal position of the transferor. This underlines that the object of the transfer must be a comprehensive membership right in the partnership enterprise. The fact that the PEL distinguishes the partner's share of the property in the partnership enterprise from the partner's claim for the share of the proceeds in certain provisions, is no contradiction.[134] *Huber* has already pointed out that this is not grounds for separating the ownership interest. Rather, these provisions acknowledge that the claim to

[126]ibid, pp. 7–8.

[127]ibid, p. 8.

[128]ibid, p. 5.

[129]ibid, p. 4.

[130]ibid, p. 4.

[131]ibid, p. 3.

[132]Schmidt (2002), pp. 1309–1310, 1322–1323.

[133]Li (李飞) (ed) (2006), p. 68.

[134]Art. 42 Para. 1 and Art. 74 Para. 1 PEL.

the share of the proceeds does not belong to the core of the membership right, and can therefore be transferred separately, e.g. to pay off a partner's debts.

Those who deny a unified membership right further base their argumentation on the requirement that the other partners will have to give a second consent to the amendment of the partnership agreement, after they have already approved the transfer of the ownership interest.[135] However, this argument has been weakened with the revision of the PEL. Under the 1997 PEL, an amendment of the partnership agreement mandatorily required the consent of all other partners.[136] Under the revised PEL, such an amendment only requires the consent of all partners 'unless otherwise specified in the partnership agreement'.[137] Therefore, a transfer of the ownership interest can be carried out without an explicit second consent of the other partners. The analysis has shown that a dissociation of partnership rights may occur when the partners consent to the transfer of a partner's ownership interest, but refuse to accept the transferee as a new partner to the partnership enterprise. Since both these approvals are default rules under the PEL,[138] the careful planner would link the approvals through a provision in the partnership agreement. The provision could state that whenever the partners agree to the transfer of a partners' ownership interest pursuant to Article 22, Paragraph 1 PEL, this simultaneously stipulates a consent to an amendment of the partnership agreement pursuant to Article 24, in conjunction with Article 19, Paragraph 2, PEL to include the transferee as a new partner. In addition, it would be advisable for the transferee to include a condition precedent in the transfer agreement, stipulating that the transfer of the ownership interest only takes effect when the other partners consent to the amendment of the partnership agreement.

In conclusion, all this strongly suggests that the PEL should be understood as granting partners a comprehensive and inseparable membership right that is the object of a transfer of a partner's share of the property in the partnership enterprise.[139] In order to avoid uncertainties, the default provisions in the PEL can be modified so that the transfer of the ownership interest is carried out as a coherent process. Hence, the liquidation protection rule with regard to a FILPE revolves around the partner's share of the property in the partnership enterprise, which is the equivalent to a share of ownership as understood in *The Anatomy of Corporate Law*.

---

[135] Ye (2002), p. 108.

[136] Art. 14 Para. 2 1997 PEL.

[137] Art. 19 Para. 2 PEL.

[138] Article 22, Paragraph 1 PEL, as well as Article 24 in conjunction with Article 19, Paragraph 2 PEL call for consent of all partners, unless otherwise specified in the partnership agreement.

[139] Others effectively reach the same conclusion. See Lin (2017), pp. 201–202; Wolff (2015), p. 160; Werthwein (2010), p. 50; Weng and Xia (2007), p. 97.

7.1.2.2 Protection from Liquidation

The attribute of liquidation protection makes a distinction between strong-form entity shielding and weak-form entity shielding.[140] In the weaker type of entity shielding, an owner can withdraw his ownership interest at will, thus forcing partial or complete liquidation of the firm.[141] Likewise, creditors of a bankrupt owner have the power to force liquidation of the firm by foreclosing on the owner's interest in the firm.[142] This weak form is predominant in the traditional partnership at will.[143] In strong-form entity shielding, an owner cannot withdraw his ownership interest at will, nor can a personal creditor of an insolvent owner force liquidation of firm assets to satisfy his claims upon exhausting the owner's personal assets.[144] Rather, at most, an owner's creditor could step into the role of possessing an ownership interest in the firm, which generally only offers the power to seek liquidation of the firm when agreed upon by at least a majority of the firm's owners.[145] This strong form is typically found in business corporations like the limited liability company.[146]

For the FILPE, the starting point is Article 21, Paragraph 1 PEL, which stipulates that partners cannot request the division of the property of the partnership enterprise before it is liquidated. This regulation underlines that the partnership enterprise, and not the individual partners, own the property of the FILPE, protecting the ongoing operation of the FILPE from destruction due to the division of partnership property.[147] However, the following exceptions to this principle have been defined in the PEL. The provisions on the voluntary withdrawal of a partner differ depending on whether a period of operation for the partnership enterprise has been specified in the partnership agreement.[148] When a fixed period for the partnership enterprise has been specified, a partner cannot withdraw his share of the property in the partnership enterprise at will. Only under the conditions stipulated in Article 45 PEL, e.g. in the event of a major violation by another partner of an obligation stipulated in the partnership agreement, a partner may withdraw from the FILPE.[149] In addition, the partners can define further conditions for voluntary withdrawal in the partnership agreement.[150] When the partnership agreement does not define a duration for the existence of the partnership enterprise, a partner may—pursuant to Article 46 PEL—withdraw from the partnership enterprise without cause, provided that all other

140 Armour et al. (2017), p. 6; Hansmann and Kraakman (2000), p. 394.

141 Armour et al. (2017), p. 7.

142 Hansmann and Kraakman (2000), pp. 394–395.

143 ibid, p. 394.

144 ibid, p. 394.

145 ibid, p. 394.

146 ibid, p. 394.

147 Li (李飞) (ed) (2006), pp. 33–34.

148 For a detailed analysis of the withdrawal of a partner, see Sect. 9.3.2.

149 Art. 45 No 4 PEL.

150 Art. 45 No 1 PEL in conjunction with Art. 18 No 7 PEL.

partners are notified 30 days in advance. However, an exception applies when the withdrawal has an adverse effect on the execution of the partnership's affairs.[151] In a FILPE with one corporate general partner, his withdrawal would deprive the FILPE of the only partner with executive power, resulting in the mandatory dissolution of the FILPE, and its transformation into a Foreign-Invested General Partnership Enterprise.[152] This would clearly have an adverse effect on the FILPE's conduction of affairs. For that reason, a voluntary withdrawal of the only general partner would not be permissible. The question arises, however, whether the only corporate general partner would also be bound to remain in the FILPE should another partner seriously violate his obligations under the partnership agreement. The PEL does not provide any regulation thereof, but the prevailing opinion among Chinese scholars grants the partner a right to withdraw in these circumstances despite the adverse effect on the execution of partnership affair.[153] In contrast, the withdrawal of a limited partner would not trigger a similar effect, as a limited partner is banned from executing the affairs of the FILPE.[154] Therefore, the voluntary withdrawal of a limited partner is not precluded by Article 46 PEL. Importantly, the voluntary withdrawal of a partner under normal circumstances does not lead to the dissolution of the partnership enterprise.[155] Instead, the withdrawing partner is entitled to request settlement of his share of the property in the partnership enterprise.[156] The settlement can be carried out in accordance with the procedure for liquidation of the partnership enterprise.[157] After deducting unsettled liabilities of the withdrawing partner, his share of the property in the partnership enterprise shall be returned in cash or goods.[158] This settlement can be a significant financial burden on the FILPE because the latter might be forced to sell business assets necessary for its continuing conduct of business in order to generate enough cash to compensate the withdrawing partner.[159] Detailed conditions instigating or permitting withdrawal, as well as details on the settlement process can be further defined in the partnership agreement.[160] However, the PEL does not permit completely to rule out a partner's withdrawal right in the partnership agreement.[161] Conversely, a partner who withdraws from the FILPE in violation of the provision in Articles 45 and 46 PEL has to compensate the partnership enterprise for any losses caused by his conduct.[162]

---

[151] Art. 46 PEL.

[152] Art. 75 PEL.

[153] Ye (2002), p. 123.

[154] Art. 68 PEL. For a detailed analysis, see Sect. 8.3.2.1.

[155] Reasons that cause dissolution of a partnership enterprise are listed in Article 85 PEL.

[156] Art. 51 PEL.

[157] Li (李飞) (ed) (2006), p. 84.

[158] Arts. 51-52 PEL.

[159] Wu and Geu (2007–2008), p. 149.

[160] ibid, p. 152.

[161] Li (李飞) (ed) (2006), p. 74.

[162] Art. 47 PEL.

This leads to the question what effect personal creditors of a bankrupt partner can have on the FILPE. The primary principle is codified in Article 41 PEL, stipulating that a personal creditor of a partner may not exercise, in subrogation, any management or governance rights or authority of the partner within the partnership enterprise. Before a creditor can stake a claim in the partner's share of the property in the partnership enterprise, the PEL provides for interim steps to safeguard the interest of the partnership enterprise.[163] For the enforcement by a personal creditor of a general partner and by a limited partner's creditor, regulations are included in Articles 42 and 74 PEL respectively. As a first condition, the partner's own property, other than his share of the property in the partnership enterprise, must be insufficient to pay off his individual debts.[164] Secondly, the proceeds of the partnership enterprise that are distributed to the partner, are to be used to pay the creditor.[165] Only if this is not sufficient, the creditor may request compulsory enforcement of the partner's share of the property in the partnership enterprise by the People's Court.[166] Thirdly, the compulsory enforcement leads to a sale and transfer of the share of the property in the partnership enterprise. In this process, the other partners are granted a right of first refusal under the same conditions of sale.[167] When a general partner's ownership interest is sold, Article 42, Paragraph 2 PEL requires the remaining partners to consent to its transfer to a third party.[168] This provision reflects the personal nature of a partnership enterprise, which is theoretically defined more by the individual owners than in a corporate enterprise form.[169] For the ownership interest of a limited partner, such consent is not stipulated in Article 74, Paragraph 2 PEL, as it is also not required in the normal course of the transfer of a limited partner's ownership interest.[170] Fourthly and finally, if the ownership interest is not sold to another partner[171] or a third party, the foreclosure on the entire ownership interest of a bankrupt partner causes his withdrawal from the partnership enterprise.[172] The partner's share of the property in the partnership enterprise will be settled and compensated in cash, and be paid to the creditor.[173] Notably, the outlined procedure primarily seems to apply to unsecured creditors.[174] Regarding secured creditors, the

[163] Li (李飞) (ed) (2006), pp. 63–64.

[164] Art. 42 Para. 1 PEL, Art. 74 Para. 1 PEL.

[165] Art. 42 Para. 1 PEL, Art. 74 Para. 1 PEL.

[166] Art. 42 Para. 1 PEL, Art. 74 Para. 1 PEL.

[167] Art. 42 Para. 2 PEL, Art. 74 Para. 2 PEL.

[168] Art. 42 Para. 2 PEL.

[169] Li (李飞) (ed) (2006), p. 65.

[170] Art. 73 PEL.

[171] Notably, the ownership interest of a limited partner can also be purchased by a general partner of the FILPE, see: Li (李飞) (ed) (2006), p. 121.

[172] Art. 42 Para. 2 in conjunction with Art. 48 Para. 1 No 5 PEL; Art. 78 in conjunction with Art. 48 Para. 1 No 5 PEL.

[173] Art. 42 Para. 2 in conjunction with Arts. 51-52 PEL.

[174] Wu and Geu (2007–2008), pp. 156–157.

PEL provides that the pledge of a general partner's and limited partner's ownership interest is generally permissible.[175] With regard to a general partner, such a pledge requires the consent of all other partners.[176] A limited partner may pledge his ownership interest, unless otherwise stipulated in the partnership agreement.[177] In consequence, a secured creditor could cut short the four-step procedure outlined above, and directly enforce foreclosure on the entire ownership interest of the respective partner. This would undermine the already rather weak liquidation protection. A careful planner would thus prohibit limited partners to pledge their ownership interest.

In summary, the question has to be addressed where the liquidation protection of the FILPE with a corporate general partner ranks between the strong-form and weak-form entity shielding. Regarding a partner's withdrawal at will, strong-form entity shielding is provided when a fixed term of operation for the FILPE has been specified. Where the term of the partnership enterprise is not limited, the assessment is more complex. While the general partner would be permitted to withdraw at will in principle, this right is usually precluded when the corporate general partner is the only general partner in the enterprise. Instead, a limited partner does have the right to withdrawal at will. However, the withdrawal does not cause the liquidation of the FILPE. Likewise, a personal creditor of a partner cannot immediately force liquidation of a FILPE. Rather, the creditor is bound to follow a multi-level enforcement process before he can foreclose on the partner's ownership interest. Altogether, the FILPE does not clearly fall under either of the two categories. Its liquidation protection is stronger than in the normal partnership at will, but still weaker than in a regular corporation. Therefore, a careful planner will ensure that the conditions for voluntary withdrawal are defined as narrowly as possible in the partnership agreement, and would preclude limited partners from pledging their ownership interest. In a comparative view, this development is in line with the trend in other jurisdictions no longer to view liquidation as the only or even the best method to accommodate the interests of a partner's personal creditors.[178] Since a reform of the German HGB in 1998, the voluntary withdrawal of a partner and the foreclosure by a personal creditor of a partner no longer causes the liquidation of the partnership enterprise.[179] While the partnership enterprise continues to exist, settlement of the concerned partner's ownership share has to be conducted in a manner similar to the situation under the PEL. In contrast, US Law even offers strong form entity shielding for certain variations of hybrid forms of limited partnership enterprises.[180]

---

[175]For a detailed analysis of the pledge, see Sect. 9.4.3.

[176]Art. 25 PEL.

[177]Art. 72 PEL.

[178]Hansmann et al. (2006), p. 1391.

[179]Art. 131 Para. 3 Nos 3 and 4 HGB; Schmidt (2002), pp. 1448–1449.

[180]Hansmann et al. (2006), p. 1392; Wu and Geu (2007–2008), pp. 157–158.

7.2 Delegated Management

For a firm to serve effectively as a contracting party, there must be rules clarifying to third parties which individuals have authority to buy and sell assets in the name of the enterprise, and to enter into contracts that are bonded by those assets.[181] Two aspects of the governance structure of a firm can be distinguished: the management of a firm concerns the internal decision-making competence, while the authority to represent the firm concerns the external relationships toward third parties.[182] 'While participants in a firm are to a large extent free to specify the delegation of authority by contract amongst themselves, background rules are needed—beyond such contractual agreement—to deal with situations where agents induce third parties to rely on the mere appearance of their authority.'[183] In practice, there is often overlap between the scope of such external authority and the internal division of power.[184] The external authority, unlike the internal management, cannot be based purely on agreement between participants in the firm, but rather must be designated by rules of law to some degree.[185] This is underlined by the provisions in the new GRCL on the non-legal-person organisation, which only regulate the external representation of the organisation when carrying out civil activities, but does not address the internal management.[186] The PEL uses the term 'execution of partnership affairs' when addressing the delegated management.[187] This term refers to both the operation and management of the partnership enterprise, as well as the handling of affairs in its internal and external relations.[188] Article 26, Paragraph 2, and Article 68, Paragraph 1, PEL explicitly recognise the right to 'represent the partnership enterprise in relation with outsiders' as distinct from the power to 'execute the partnership affairs'. However, the PEL does not provide separate regulations on the scope and form of the authority to represent.[189] In general, these aspects are jointly governed by the regulations on the execution of partnership affairs.[190]

[181] Armour et al. (2017), p. 7.

[182] Schmidt (2002), p. 172.

[183] Armour et al. (2017), p. 7.

[184] ibid, p. 11 fn. 40.

[185] ibid, p. 11 fn. 40.

[186] Article 105 GRCL reads: 'A non-legal-person organisation may determine one or several individuals to represent the organisation in carrying out civil activities.'

[187] For example in the title of Section 3 of the PEL and in Article 26 PEL.

[188] Li (李飞) (ed) (2006), p. 39.

[189] Ye (2002), p. 83.

[190] Li (李飞) (ed) (2006), p. 39.

7.2.1 Effect of Authority

Before an analysis of the rules on the authority to represent the FILPE can be undertaken, fundamental principles on the representation of partnership enterprises have to be addressed. In Chinese partnership enterprise law, a substantial dogmatic discussion has developed with regard to the question whether the individual partners or the partnership enterprise is represented by the entrusted partner.[191] This discussion is directly linked to the debate around the legal nature of partnership enterprises, and reflects its organisational side.[192] This issue can be traced back to early discussions on German corporate law. The Agent-Theory, associated with *von Savigny,* regards a firm as incapable of forming an own will, and acting in accordance with it.[193] Agents can only act on the basis of contractual relationships that provide their authority to represent.[194] In the Organ-Theory, associated with *von Gierke*, a firm acts through its organs instead.[195] An organ does not decide and act as a third person for the firm. Rather, the decisions and actions of the organ are regarded as those of the firm. The firm itself makes decisions and takes actions through the organ.[196] For *von Gierke*, this makes the actions of an organ qualitatively different from the actions of a third person who functions as an agent.[197] Codifications in German corporate law have essentially implemented the Organ-Theory.[198] Although the Organ-Theory has evolved in respect of the legal person enterprise form, it can likewise be applied to other enterprise forms with legal personality, such as the German partnership enterprise.[199] In Chinese literature, the prevailing opinion with regard to the 1997 PEL has followed the Agent-Theory instead.[200] The relationship between the entrusted partner and the partnership enterprise is regarded as a mutual, contractual principal-agent relationship between the partners.[201] The entrusted partner is regarded as a representative of the other partners.[202] The will of the partners is regarded as the basis for the authority to represent the partnership enterprise, not the partnership agreement.[203] However, this position has been subject to criticism.[204] To base the actions of the entrusted partner on contractual relationships among the

[191] Ye (2002), pp. 85–86.

[192] Schmidt (2002), p. 250.

[193] ibid, p. 250.

[194] ibid, p. 250.

[195] ibid, p. 251.

[196] ibid, p. 251.

[197] ibid, p. 252.

[198] ibid, pp. 251–252.

[199] ibid, pp. 253–254.

[200] Gao (高富平) et al. (1997), p. 221.

[201] ibid, p. 221.

[202] ibid, pp. 221–222.

[203] ibid, p. 222.

[204] Ye (2002), p. 86.

partners contradicts the nature of the partnership enterprise as a separate legal entity.[205] This is affirmed in the wording of Article 26, Paragraph 2 PEL, which states that the entrusted partner 'represents the partnership enterprise in relation with outsiders'—not the individual partners. Similarly, Article 105 GRCL provides that a non-legal-person organisation may appoint individuals to 'represent the organisation in carrying out civil activities'. The actions of the entrusted partner count in favour and against the partnership enterprise, and acquired rights and earnings become property of the partnership enterprise.[206] These provisions recognise that the partnership enterprise is a legal entity that holds rights and obligations, and as such inevitably has to form a unified will that is put into action. The entrusted partner, as its organ, fulfils this function for the partnership enterprise. This illustrates that the underlying ideas of the Organ-Theory are reflected in China's partnership enterprise law. Thus, the FILPE acts through the entrusted partner, who represents the FILPE as its organ.

7.2.2 Authorised Representatives

The first element of delegated management are rules that specify the individuals who have authority to represent the FILPE to third parties. As a general rule, the PEL provides in Article 26, Paragraphs 1 and 2 that all general partners of the partnership enterprise have the authority to represent the partnership enterprise. A general partner is thus regarded as an organ of the partnership enterprise by law. This deviates materially from enterprises with legal person status, which have to appoint third persons—who may also be shareholders of the legal person—to act as their organ.[207] No person is granted the authority to represent the legal person enterprise by law. These differing legal concepts are especially significant in the light of a peculiar feature of Chinese corporate law. All enterprises with legal person status must appoint a legal representative (法定代表人).[208] The legal representative is the organ with the exclusive statutory authority to represent the legal person in the execution of its rights and obligations.[209] Each legal person in China is only allowed to have one legal representative, but for the daily business operation, the legal representative may entrust another person, e.g. a deputy manager, with the power

---

[205] See Sect. 7.1.1.1.

[206] This follows directly from Article 28, Paragraph 2 PEL, and is re-emphasised in Article 170, Paragraph 1 GRCL.

[207] Schmidt (2002), p. 249.

[208] Art. 11 PRC Regulations on the Administration of Enterprise Legal Person Registration (中华人民共和国企业法人登记管理条例), promulgated by the State Council on 3 June 1988, amended on 19 February 2014, amended on 6 February 2016 and amended on 2 March 2019 (Administrative Regulations for Enterprise Legal Person Registration).

[209] Art. 38 GPCL/ Art. 61 GRCL.

to act as his agent.[210] The name and signature of the legal representative must be registered with the authorities.[211] Given the unlimited authority that is statutorily bestowed upon the legal representative, the owners of a legal person are advised to carefully choose a loyal and trustworthy individual to fulfil this role.[212] According to the Company Law, the legal representative in a limited liability company may be the chairman of the board of directors, an executive director, or a manager.[213] However, for an EJV, the legal representative could only be the chairman of the board of directors.[214] Therefore, the importance of being able to appoint the chairman of the board of directors of an EJV cannot be overemphasised, and it has been a crucial point in the negotiations of any joint venture agreement.[215] In a FILPE, however, the peculiar position of a legal representative does not exist. Therefore, investors do not have to concern themselves with controversial negotiations about the position of the legal representative. In a partnership enterprise with more than one general partner, the general partners may jointly or separately represent the partnership enterprise.[216] Alternatively, the general partners can specify and entrust one or more of the general partners—the so called managing partners—[217] to represent the partnership enterprise towards third parties.[218] In that case, the remaining general partners are barred from representing the enterprise.[219] The entrustment of a managing partner can be withdrawn by a decision of the other general partners.[220]

This book is based on a FILPE with a single corporate general partner, which adds an additional level of complexity to the governance structure. For this scenario, the PEL provides a regulation in Article 26, Paragraph 3: 'If a partner that executes partnership affairs is a legal person or any other organisation, the affairs shall be executed by its representatives.'[221] In legal relations with third parties, the FILPE is represented through the corporate general partner as its organ, which itself is represented by its managing director. While the managing director is an organ of the corporation, he simultaneously acts with the competence of an organ of the partnership enterprise.[222] The knowledge and actions of the managing director are

[210]Werthwein (2010), pp. 34, 38.

[211]Art. 11 Administrative Regulations for Enterprise Legal Person Registration.

[212]Mahony (2015), pp. 272–273, 282.

[213]Art. 13 Company Law.

[214]Art. 34 EJV Implementing Regulations, which supersedes the provisions in the Company Law (see Sect. 3.1.3).

[215]Mahony (2015), p. 270.

[216]Li (李飞) (ed) (2006), p. 59.

[217]Art. 28 Para. 1 PEL.

[218]Art. 26 Para. 2 PEL.

[219]Art. 27 Para. 1 PEL.

[220]Art. 29 Para. 2 PEL.

[221]Art. 26 Para. 3 PEL.

[222]Schmidt (2002), p. 1648.

accredited to both the corporation and the partnership enterprise.[223] The dual role of the managing director in a corporate general partner has to be distinguished from other non-partner individuals who are engaged as management personnel by the FILPE. Such management personnel acts on the basis of an employment contract with the FILPE.[224] Conversely, the managing director of a corporate general partner is employed by its corporation, and does not have a direct contractual relationship with the FILPE. Management personnel employed by the FILPE acts as an agent of the partnership enterprise toward third persons, not as its organ.[225] Therefore, the provisions on agency in the GPCL and GRCL directly apply to such engaged management personnel.[226] The scope of the agent's authority can be further defined by the partners.[227]

Regarding limited partners, the PEL stipulates in Article 67 that the affairs of a limited partnership enterprise shall be executed by its general partners. Article 68 PEL further clarifies that a limited partner is not permitted to represent the partnership enterprise in relations with outsiders.[228] The exclusion of limited partners from the management and representation is one of the core principles of the limited partnership enterprise.[229]

In conclusion, for the FILPE with a single corporate general partner, the PEL clearly stipulates that the managing director of the corporate general partner has the authority to represent the FILPE towards third parties.

7.2.3 Scope of Authority and Protection of Third Parties

The second element of delegated management are rules which protect third parties that rely on the mere appearance of an agent's authority. This touches upon the scope of authority, which again can be distinguished between the internal and external perspective. In principle, the scope of authority to represent the partnership enterprise comprises all judicial and extrajudicial transactions.[230] Through stipulations in the partnership agreement or resolutions by the general partners, the scope of authority can be limited or expanded.[231] However, any limitation of the scope of authority only has an internal effect. Towards bona fide third parties, the scope of

[223] ibid, pp. 1648–1649.

[224] The legal basis for the engagement of management personnel is provided in Article 31, Paragraph 6 PEL, and Article 170, Paragraph 1 GRCL.

[225] Art. 35 Para. 1 PEL.

[226] Arts. 63-70 GPCL / Arts. 161-175 GRCL.

[227] Art. 35 Para. 1 PEL.

[228] See Sect. 8.3.2.1.

[229] Li (李飞) (ed) (2006), p. 108. For a further analysis, see Sect. 8.3.2.1.

[230] Ye (2002), p. 87.

[231] Art. 29 Para. 2 PEL.

authority of a (managing) partner cannot be limited. This is stipulated in Article 37 PEL, which provides that limitations on the rights to represent the partnership enterprise shall not be used against a bona fide third party. The provision is mandatory and shows that the Chinese lawmaker aims to protect the good faith of third parties in commercial transactions.[232] Following the Anglo-American doctrine of *Ultra Vires*, controversy arose among Chinese scholars whether the authority to represent an enterprise is generally limited to its approved business scope.[233] Since a FILPE, like all other enterprises in China, is limited to a specific business scope in its operation, this would be a significant restriction.[234] However, with the 'SPC Interpretation of the Contract Law',[235] the Supreme People's Court has clarified in 1999 that a People's Court shall not invalidate a contract which goes beyond an enterprise's business scope, and thus declared the doctrine of *Ultra Vires* to be inapplicable in China.[236] An exception only applies if an FIE concludes a contract that falls within the category of prohibited or restricted industries in the Guidance Catalogue, or within the FDI Negative List. In this case, a contract can be declared invalid by a People's Court.[237]

The lawmaker has identified three conditions for Article 37 PEL to apply. First, both the partner and the third party must bear full civil capacity, and the underlying transaction must be lawful.[238] Second, circumstances must have presented itself which led the third party to objectively believe that the partner had the authority to represent the partnership enterprise.[239] This would for instance be the case if the partner had represented the partnership enterprise in the past, or if the partner had declared to act in the name of the partnership enterprise.[240] Finally, the third party must act in good faith.[241] The third party is not in good faith should it be aware, or is not aware as a result of gross negligence, that the partner lacks the required authority to represent the partnership enterprise.[242] According to Chinese court rulings, the presumption will be that the third party acts in good faith, and the burden of proof to establish bad faith of the third party falls to the partnership enterprise.[243] If all three conditions are fulfilled, the partnership enterprise is bound to the transaction entered

[232]Li (李飞) (ed) (2006), p. 56.

[233]Kroymann (2009), pp. 135–136.

[234]Regarding a FILPE's business scope, see Sect. 4.1.7.

[235]First Interpretation of Certain Issues Concerning the Application of the 'PRC Contract Law' (适用《中华人民共和国合同法》若干问题的解释(一)), promulgated by the Supreme People's Court on 29 December 1999 and with effect as of the same date.

[236]Art. 10 SPC Interpretation of the Contract Law.

[237]Art. 10 SPC Interpretation of the Contract Law.

[238]Li (李飞) (ed) (2006), p. 57.

[239]ibid, p. 57.

[240]ibid, p. 57.

[241]ibid, p. 57.

[242]ibid, pp. 56–57.

[243]Ye (2002), p. 88.

into with the third party, even though the partner has acted beyond the scope of his authority.[244] Internally, the concerned partner bears civil liability towards the partnership enterprise for any losses suffered due to the transaction.[245] If the third party acts in bad faith, however, the third party and the partner shall bear liability towards the partnership enterprise for their respective fault.[246] Regarding the underlying transaction, the PEL does not make explicit stipulations. The third party that acts in bad faith is no longer worthy of protection.[247] Respective provisions on agency in the GRCL should be applicable to the underlying transaction. Under the application of Article 171, Paragraph 1 GRCL, the partnership enterprise would not be bound to the transaction, unless it chooses to ratify the transaction.[248] Excluded from an entrusted partner's scope of authority are transactions with regard to the relationships among the partners, in particular amendments to the partnership agreement.[249] The reason is that the entrusted partner represents the partnership enterprise as a whole rather than any of the individual partners.[250]

When an employed management personnel of the partnership enterprise acts beyond the scope of his power of agency, the GRCL provide a regulation in Article 170, Paragraph 2. The provision contains a similar regulation as Article 37 PEL, protecting third parties that trust the agent's authority in good faith. It binds the partnership enterprise to the underlying transaction with the bona fide third party. Internally, however, the management personnel must bear liability for any losses caused to the partnership enterprise by exceeding the scope of authority.[251] The protective provision of Article 37 PEL does not apply to transactions between the partnership enterprise and any of its partners, as it is presumed that a partner knows the internal stipulations on partner's authority.[252]

Overall, the regulation in Article 37 PEL and Article 170, Paragraph 2 GRCL provide a sufficient protection of third parties that rely on the mere appearance of an agent's authority as representative of the FILPE.

[244]Gao (高富平) et al. (1997), p. 225.

[245]Art. 98 PEL.

[246]Art. 171 Para. 4 GRCL. Interestingly, Article 66 Para. 4 GPCL stipulated joint liability of the third party and the partner, instead of the fault-based liability of the GRCL.

[247]Li (李飞) (ed) (2006), p. 56.

[248]Regarding the similar solution under German law, see: Schmidt (2002), p. 260.

[249]Ye (2002), p. 87.

[250]ibid, p. 87.

[251]Art. 35 Para. 2 PEL.

[252]Ye (2002), pp. 87–88.

7.3 Procedural Rules for Bringing Lawsuits For and Against the FILPE

The third type of rules that is needed for a firm to serve effectively as a contracting party, must specify the procedures by which the firm and its counterparties can bring lawsuits on the contracts entered into in the name of the firm.[253] These rules make it easier to bring suits as a procedural matter, in particular because they eliminate any need to name the firm's individual owners, or to serve a notice to them.[254] The PEL itself is silent on this question, but a respective regulation is provided in the 'Civil Procedure Law',[255] which was further substantiated by the Supreme People's Court with the 'SPC Interpretation of the Civil Procedure Law'.[256] Together, these provisions stipulate that a partnership enterprise has the ability to sue or be sued in its own name.[257] This emphasises that a Chinese partnership enterprise, such as the FILPE, constitutes a separate legal entity. For the GmbH & Co. KG, a respective stipulation is provided directly in the German HGB.[258] The Chinese Individual Partnership under the GPCL, however, does not have the same ability to sue or be sued in its own name. Instead, all the individual partners have to sue or be sued in a joint action.[259]

With regard to lawsuits, a differentiation should be made whether the partnership enterprise or the individual partners are suing or being sued. If the partnership enterprise is the subject of the civil litigation, it is represented by its managing partner(s).[260] The remaining partners are not party to the litigation, but can be heard as witnesses.[261] If a dispute between the individual partners about the performance of the partnership agreement is resolved in court,[262] only the partners are party to the

[253] Armour et al. (2017), p. 7.

[254] ibid, p. 7.

[255] PRC Civil Procedure Law (中华人民共和国民事诉讼法), adopted at the 4th Session of the 7th National People's Congress on 9 April 1991, amended at the 30th Meeting of the Standing Committee of the 10th National People's Congress on 28 October 2007, amended at the 28th Session of the Standing Committee of the 11th National People's Congress on 31 August 2012, and amended at the 28th Meeting of the Standing Committee of the 12th National People's Congress on 27 June 2017.

[256] Interpretations of the Application of the PRC Civil Procedure Law (适用《中华人民共和国民事诉讼法》的解释), promulgated by the Supreme People's Court on 30 January 2015 and with effect as of 4 February 2015.

[257] Art. 48 Para. 1 Civil Procedure Law in conjunction with Art. 52 Para. 2 SPC Interpretation on the Civil Procedure Law.

[258] Art. 161 Para. 2 in conjunction with Art. 124 Para. 1 HGB.

[259] Art. 52 Para. 1 Civil Procedure Law.

[260] Art. 48 Para. 2 Civil Procedure Law.

[261] Ye (2002), p. 102.

[262] Regarding the priority that is granted to mediation and arbitration for conflicts between the partners, see Sect. 4.1.9.5.

lawsuit, not the partnership enterprise itself.[263] German law further acknowledges the *actio pro socio*, which permits an individual partner—under certain conditions—to assert a claim of the partnership enterprise against another partner, if the partnership enterprise neglects enforcement of said claim.[264] However, Chinese partnership law does not recognise an equivalent right of the individual partners.[265]

7.4 Conclusion

The preceding analysis has shown that the legal framework of the FILPE with a corporate general partner provides the three types of rules which are necessary to establish legal personality. Entity shielding is achieved in a combination of mandatory provisions and strategic modification of default rules. Mandatory rules stipulate that a FILPE constitutes a separate legal entity which can own assets under its own name.[266] They further ensure that the creditors of the FILPE are satisfied before the FILPE's assets become available to satisfy any personal creditors of its partners.[267] Thus, forming affirmative asset partitioning for the FILPE with a corporate general partner. Regarding a partner's ownership interest in the FILPE, modifications in the partnership agreement can ensure that each partner is treated as holding a comprehensive and inseparable membership right in the partnership enterprise.[268] Appropriate stipulations in the partnership agreement can further minimise the partner's rights to withdraw their membership right at will.[269] Mandatory provisions in the PEL ensure that a personal creditor of an insolvent partner cannot directly force liquidation of the FILPE's assets to satisfy his claims against said partner.[270] Thus, a moderate level of entity shielding is provided for the FILPE. Regarding delegated management, the provisions on the authority to represent the FILPE in its external relationships towards third parties are mainly mandatory in nature. The PEL stipulates that the FILPE with a single corporate general partner is represented by the managing director of the corporation, and that a third party's good faith in the authority of the managing director is protected.[271] Mandatory rules further ensure that a FILPE can sue and be sued in its own name.[272] Altogether, the legal framework in China permits the FILPE with a corporate general partner to operate

[263] This follows from the wording of Article 103 Paragraph 2 PEL.

[264] Instructive: Schmidt (2002), pp. 623–644.

[265] Ye (2002), p. 102.

[266] See Sect. 7.1.1.1.

[267] See Sect. 7.1.1.2.

[268] See Sect. 7.1.2.1.

[269] See Sect. 7.1.2.2.

[270] See Sect. 7.1.2.2.

[271] See Sect. 7.2.

[272] See Sect. 7.3.

as a single contracting party that is distinct from the various individuals who own or manage the enterprise—thus fulfilling the attribute of legal personality.

References

Armour J, Hansmann H, Kraakman R, Pargendler M (2017) What is corporate law? In: Kraakman R et al (eds) The anatomy of corporate law, 3rd edn. Oxford University Press, Oxford, pp 1–28

Bromberg AR, Ribstein LE (1994a) Bromberg and Ribstein on partnership, vol 1 General partnership. Wolters Kluwer, Boston

Bromberg AR, Ribstein LE (1994b) Bromberg and Ribstein on partnership, vol 3 Limited partnership. Wolters Kluwer, Boston

Bromberg AR, Ribstein LE (1994c) Bromberg and Ribstein on partnership, vol 4 Limited partnership. Wolters Kluwer, Boston

Bu Y (2017) Einführung in das Recht Chinas, 2nd edn. C. H. Beck, Munich

Chen K (2014) Corporations and partnerships in China. Kluwer Law, Alphen aan den Rijn

DeMott DA (2004) Transatlantic perspectives on partnership law: risk and instability. In: McCahery JA, Raaijmakers T, Vermeulen EPM (eds) The Governance of close corporations and partnerships: US and European perspectives. Oxford University Press, Oxford, pp 275–292

Epstein E, Shen WW (2009) Chinese civil law. In: Moser MJ, Yu F (eds) Doing business in China, vol 1. Juris Publishing, Huntington, p I-6.1.20

Gao F (高富平), Su H (苏号朋), Li Z (刘智慧) (1997) Principles and practice of partnership enterprise law (合伙企业法原理与实务). China Legal Publishing House (中国法制出版社), Beijing

Haase F (2014) Introduction. In: Haase F (ed) Taxation of international partnerships – 15 years OECD partnership report: past, present and future. IBFD, Amsterdam, pp 3–11

Hansmann H, Kraakman R (2000) The essential role of organizational law. Yale Law J 110:387–440

Hansmann H, Kraakman R, Squire R (2005) The new business entities in evolutionary perspective. Univ Illinois Law Rev 2005:5–14

Hansmann H, Kraakman R, Squire R (2006) Law and the rise of the firm. Harv Law Rev 119:1335–1403

Hong H (洪虎) (2006) Report on the circumstances of the revision of the amended draft of the PRC partnership enterprise law – delivered on 24 June 2006 to the 22nd Session of the Standing Committee of the 10th National People's Congress (关于《中华人民共和国合伙企业法(修订草案)》修改情况的汇报—2006年6月24日在第十届全国人民代表大会常务委员会第二十二次会议上). Yearbook of the National People's Congress 2006: (全国人民代表大会年鉴2 0 0 6 年卷), pp 354–357

Howson NC (2015) Return of the prodigal form? Partnerships and partnership law in the People's Republic of China. In: Hillman RW, Loewenstein MJ (eds) Research handbook on partnerships, LLCs and alternative forms of Business Organizations. Edward Elgar, Cheltenham, pp 390–411

Huber U (1970) Vermögensanteil, Kapitalanteil und Gesellschaftsanteil an Personalgesellschaften des Handelsrechts. C. Winter, Heidelberg

Kroymann B (2009) Das Kapitalgesellschaftsrecht der VR China – Analyse der Rahmenbedingungen für ausländische Investoren. Mohr Siebeck, Tübingen

Li F (李飞) (ed) (2006) Interpretation of the PRC Partnership Enterprise Law (中华人民共和国合伙企业法释义). Law Press China (法律出版社), Beijing

Lin L (2013) The evolution of partnerships in China from the perspective of asset partitioning. Stanford J Law 18:215–249

Lin L (2017) Engineering a venture capital market: lessons from China. Columb J Asian Law 30:160–220

Lin L, Yeo HY (2010) Limited partnership – the new business vehicle in China. Butterworth J Int Bank Financ Law 25:104–108

Lu M (吕美昂) (2011) A comparison of the nature of foreign-invested enterprises in China (我国外商投资企业性质的比较). Legal System and Society (法制与社会) 8:81–82

Ma Q (马强) (1998) Study on several issues of partnership theory and practice (合伙理论与实践若干问题研究). Law Soc Dev (法制与社会发展) 1998/5:28-32.

Mahony T (2015) Foreign investment law in China: regulation, practice and context. Tsinghua University Press, Beijing

Raaijmakers T (2004) The reform agenda for partnerships and closely held companies in the Netherlands and the European Union. In: McCahery JA, Raaijmakers T, Vermeulen EPM (eds) The Governance of close corporations and partnerships: US and European perspectives. Oxford University Press, Oxford, pp 399–413

Schmidt K (2002) Gesellschaftsrecht, 4th edn. Heymanns, Cologne

Shen W (2015) Corporate law in China – structure, governance and regulation. Sweet & Maxwell, Hong Kong

Skeel DA (2003–2004) Book review: corporate anatomy lessons. Yale Law J 113:1519–1577

Ting A, Ge X (2014) The current state of play of foreign investment vehicles in China: is partnership a rising star? Bull Int Tax 68:669–677

Tu C (2010) Secured transaction. In: Bu Y (ed) Chinese business law. C. H. Beck, Hart and Nomos, Munich/Oxford, pp 183–219

Weng J, Xia T (2007) Limited liability partnership: the best structure for funds? China Law Pract 21:97

Werthwein S (2010) Corporations and partnerships. In: Bu Y (ed) Chinese business law. C. H. Beck, Hart and Nomos, Munich/Oxford, pp 15–54

Windbichler C (2014) Eine internationale Landkarte der Personengesellschaften (einschließlich juristische Personen und Gesamthand). Zeitschrift für Unternehmens- und Gesellschaftsrecht 43:110–138

Wolff L-C (2015) Mergers & acquisitions in China: law and practice, 5th edn. Wolters Kluwer Law & Business, Hong Kong

Wu Y, Geu TE (2007–2008) The new PRC limited partnership enterprise law and the limited partnership law of the United States: a selective analytical comparison. UCLA Pacific Basin Law J 25:133–178

Ye F (2002) Das chinesische Gesetz über Partnerschaftsunternehmen: Im Vergleich zum deutschen Recht. Lang, Frankfurt a.M

Zheng H (2010) Bankruptcy. In: Bu Y (ed) Chinese business law. C. H. Beck, Hart and Nomos, Munich/Oxford, pp 221–266

Chapter 8
Limited Liability

The second attribute of the standard corporate form is the rule of 'limited liability'. It provides a default term in contracts between a firm and its creditors whereby the creditors are limited to making claims against assets that are owned by the firm itself, and have no claim against assets that the firm's shareholders hold in their own name.[1] The term creditor is used quite broadly to include all persons to whom the firm owes a contractual obligation that has not yet been fulfilled, including employees, suppliers and customers.[2] Limited liability effectively shields the firm's owners from creditors' claims.[3]

> The 'owner shielding' provided by limited liability is the converse of the 'entity shielding' described above as a component of legal personality. Entity shielding protects the assets of the firm from the creditors of the firm's owners, while limited liability protects the assets of the firm's owners form the claim of the firm's creditors. Together, these forms of asset shielding (or 'asset partitioning') ensure that business assets are pledged as security to business creditors, while the personal assets of the business's owners are reserved for the owners' personal creditors.[4]

Notably, the owner shielding established by the rule of limited liability is less fundamental than entity shielding in the sense that the latter would generally be quite impossible to establish without organisational law.[5] Limited liability, on the contrary, could also be achieved by contract—at least in theory.[6] This would require a firm to include provisions in its contracts with all of its creditors, whereby the creditors waive any right to proceed against the owner's personal assets to obtain

[1]Armour et al. (2017b), p. 8.

[2]Hansmann and Kraakman (2000), p. 394.

[3]Armour et al. (2017b), p. 9.

[4]ibid, p. 9.

[5]ibid, p. 9 fn. 33; Hansmann and Kraakman (2000), p. 429.

[6]Posner (2014), p. 539.

S. Kuntner, *China's Foreign-Invested Limited Partnership Enterprise*, China-EU Law Series 7, https://doi.org/10.1007/978-3-030-54181-1_8

satisfaction of the creditor's claims against the firm.[7] This would likely involve high transaction costs, especially if it were to extend to even the smallest trade creditors of the firm.[8] A particular costly obstacle would be to induce creditors who use their own standard-form contracts or invoices to incorporate such a waiver in their contracts with the firm.[9] Therefore, while not indispensable, organisational law also plays an important role in facilitating limited liability for the actual business practice.

Over time, the rule of limited liability has become a nearly universal feature of the corporate form.[10] This development underlines the compelling advantages that limited liability offers.[11] The most obvious advantage lies in giving the owner a maximum degree of control over his exposure to liability risks in an investment.[12] With unlimited liability, the risk of losses borne by owners depends on the way that the business is operated.[13] Therefore, owners will generally prefer to be actively involved in the running of the business to control this risk.[14] The containment of downside losses through limited liability enables owners to diversify their investments.[15] This lowers the aggregated risk of an owner's investment portfolio, reduces the risk premium he will demand, and thereby lowers the firm's cost of equity capital.[16] Furthermore, asset partitioning can increase the value of both personal assets and firm assets as security for debt.[17]

> As creditors of the firm commonly have a comparative advantage in evaluating and monitoring the value of the firm's assets, and an owner's personal creditors are likely to have a comparative advantage in evaluating and monitoring the individual's personal assets, such asset shielding can reduce the overall cost of capital to the firm and its owners.[18]

> A related aspect of asset partitioning is that it permits firms to isolate different lines of business for the purpose of obtaining credit. By separately incorporating, as subsidiaries, distinct ventures or lines of business, the assets associated with each venture can conveniently be pledged as security just to the creditors who deal with that venture. Those creditors are commonly well positioned to assess and keep track of the value of those assets, but may have little ability to monitor the parent firm's other ventures.[19]

---

[7]Hansmann and Kraakman (2000), p. 429.

[8]ibid, p. 429.

[9]ibid, p. 429.

[10]Armour et al. (2017b), pp. 8–9.

[11]For a detailed discussion of these advantages see with further references: Hansmann and Kraakman (2000), pp. 423–427; Ribstein (1988), pp. 840–847.

[12]Hansmann and Kraakman (2000), p. 427.

[13]Armour et al. (2017b), p. 9.

[14]ibid, p. 9.

[15]ibid, p. 9.

[16]ibid, p. 9.

[17]ibid, p. 9.

[18]ibid, p. 9.

[19]Armour et al. (2009), p. 10.

Limited liability further facilitates another element of the standard corporate form that is subject to the following analysis:[20] It enables transferability of ownership because markets for ownership interest are unlikely to form unless traders can separate the value of the firm from the personal financial affairs of the firm's owners.[21] Such a separation is obviously facilitated by limited liability.[22] Of course, all these benefits of limited liability do not come without cost.[23] 'Limited liability of owners reduces the creditors' sources of payment and increases business risk because limited liability owners have less incentive than personally liable owners to act consistently with creditor interest.'[24] Creditors are likely to charge the firm *ex ante* for bearing these risks.[25] A debate has taken place among commentators whether the increase in the cost of credit under limited liability necessarily offsets the decrease in the cost of equity capital.[26] However, business practice shows that the feature of limited liability is a top priority for investors, also when establishing a partnership enterprise. The worst case for a foreign investor occurs when the partnership enterprise encounters difficulties—be it due to internal differences, poor management, or lack of internal trust—, subjecting the partnership enterprise to debts, resulting in its dissolution and leaving the investors exposed.[27] Therefore, investors are generally more likely to adopt the statutory limited partnership form because of liability features than for its provisions on the rights and duties among the partners.[28] Hence, this book assumes that foreign investors who establish a sino-foreign partnership enterprise, are likewise eager to benefit from limited liability.[29]

The central regulation for limited liability in the FILPE is stipulated in Article 2 Paragraph 3 PEL. It provides that a limited partner will not be liable to third parties for the limited partnership enterprise's debts, obligations and liabilities beyond the value of the capital contributions that was subscribed by the limited partner. In contrast, general partners personally bear unlimited joint and several liability for the

---

[20]In addition, limited liability enables delegated management because limited liability can effectively shift some of the burden of monitoring the firm's managers from the firm's owners to its creditors. 'If creditors know that they have recourse only to assets held by the firm, they are more likely than they otherwise would be to scrutinise closely – both before and after extending credit – the likely fortunes of the firm and the behaviour of the firm's managers' (Hansmann and Kraakman 2000, p. 425).

[21]Armour et al. (2009), p. 10; Hansmann and Kraakman (2000), p. 425.

[22]Hansmann and Kraakman (2000), p. 425.

[23]Ribstein (1988), p. 841.

[24]ibid, p. 841.

[25]ibid, p. 841.

[26]ibid, pp. 841–842.

[27]Yu et al. (2012b), pp. 10–11.

[28]Ribstein (1988), p. 840.

[29]It should be emphasised that the analysis of limited liability here specifically means limited liability *in contract*—that is, limited liability to creditors who have contractual claims on the corporation. The compelling reasons for limited liability in contract generally do not extend to limited liability *in tort*. See also, Armour et al. (2017b), p. 9.

debts, obligations and liabilities of the limited partnership enterprise. In this definition, limited liability means that the owner's responsibility for business debts is limited to his investment in the partnership enterprise.[30] The limited liable owner risks no more than the money or other consideration he paid or agreed to pay for his ownership interest.[31] An owner with limited liability can be sued personally, but only to enforce a promise he gave as consideration for his ownership interest.[32] In contrast, unlimited liability means that creditors can collect debts of the partnership enterprise not only from partnership enterprise assets, but also from the personal assets of the partner.[33] The contribution of a general partner therefore includes his guarantee of the debts of the partnership enterprise.[34] As has been outlined, it is the aim of the investor to be shielded from liability entirely. Therefore, a corporation is utilised as the general partner in the underlying scenario of this book to limit the liability of the general partner. 'As a result, the corporate general partner will be liable to the full extent of its assets (unlimited liability) but the owners (shareholders) of the corporation (company) will be protected by the corporation's liability shield.'[35]

Thus, the analysis of limited liability in the FILPE begins with the liability of the partnership enterprise, continues with the liability of the general partner, including a discussion of liability management through a corporate general partner, before addressing the liability of the limited partner. The liability of the general partner and limited partner in special liability scenarios are analysed together at the end of this section.

8.1 Liability of the Partnership Enterprise

A preliminary matter for the liability of the partners is the liability of the FILPE itself. The PEL provides in Article 38 that 'with regard to its debts, a partnership enterprise shall make repayment firstly with all of its property'. The debts of a FILPE encompass all liabilities that result from transactions which have been entered into in the name of the partnership enterprise, as well as tort liabilities, and public-law liabilities including taxes, fees and customs duties.[36] The regulation in Article 38 stipulates a priority rule that these debts are firstly to be settled with the property of the partnership enterprise. Thus, a creditor cannot directly claim payment from a

[30] Ribstein (1988), p. 841.
[31] ibid, p. 841.
[32] ibid, p. 841.
[33] ibid, p. 841.
[34] ibid, p. 841.
[35] Wu and Geu (2007–2008), p. 166.
[36] Gao (高富平) et al. (1997), p. 226.

partner.[37] The partnership enterprise's property consists of all capital contributions by the partners, profits and any other property that has been lawfully obtained in the name of the partnership enterprise.[38] The latter extends to all forms of statutory income, creditor's rights, intellectual property rights and business goodwill of the FILPE.[39] Article 39 PEL clarifies that only if and to the extent that the property of the partnership enterprise is not sufficient to settle its debts, the individual partners bear liability. This leads to the focal point of this analysis, the liabilities that are borne by the partners.

8.2 Liability of the General Partner

8.2.1 The Principle: Unlimited Liability

A general partner's liability is twofold under the PEL. The first is the personal liability of the general partner towards creditors of the partnership enterprise for debts that were entered into in the name of the partnership enterprise. This liability is the focus of the following analysis. The second is the personal liabilities of a general partner towards the partnership enterprise and to the other partners because of his personal wrongdoing or losses he caused. These liabilities are analysed at the end of this section.[40]

The PEL stipulates in Article 39 that 'in the event of a partnership enterprise's failure to pay off its due debts, its partners shall bear unlimited joint and several liability'. The provision in Article 2, Paragraph 3 PEL further clarifies that, in a limited partnership enterprise, the obligation to bear joint and several liability falls to the general partner(s).[41] The regulation in Article 39 PEL establishes a subsidiary liability of the general partner.[42] Only if the partnership enterprise itself is unable to pay off the debts, the creditor can claim personal settlement from a general partner. This marks a deviation from German partnership law that stipulates a primary liability of the general partner in Article 128 HGB. Creditors are allowed to take direct action against the partnership enterprise and all general partners as co-defendants.[43] A general partner who settles debts, is thereby entitled to take recourse against the partnership enterprise.[44] Under the PEL, a creditor is bound to first

---

[37]Li (李飞) (ed) (2006a), p. 58.

[38]Art. 20 PEL.

[39]Li (李新) (2006b), p. 128.

[40]See Sect. 8.4.5.

[41]Circumstances under which a limited partner has to bear unlimited liability, are discussed in Sect. 8.3.2.1.

[42]Ye (2002), p. 91.

[43]Foster and Sule (2010), p. 548.

[44]Art. 110 Para. 1 HGB; Schmidt (2002), pp. 1435–1437.

approach the partnership enterprise to claim payment of its debts instead. By its legal nature, the partner's personal liability stipulated in Article 39 PEL is accessory to the liability of the partnership enterprise.[45] The liability of a partner depends on the existence of a liability of the partnership enterprise towards the creditor. Any alteration of the partnership enterprise's liability entails a matching change in liability of the partner.[46] The PEL declares that the liability of a general partner is joint and several.[47] This means that the liability encompasses both the share of the debt that a respective general partner himself shall bear, and the portion of the debts that other general partners must bear.[48] This provides the creditor with the right to assert a claim over any general partner for payment of the entire debt at stake, provided that the property of the partnership enterprise is not sufficient to pay off its debts.[49] The elected partner cannot object to the creditor seeking payment from another general partner.[50] However, the partner can use all possible defences against a creditor's claim insofar as these defences could be raised by the partnership enterprise itself, e.g. when the limitation period of the claim has expired or the validity of the legal transaction underlying the obligation can be challenged.[51] This principle is derived from the accessory nature of a general partner's personal liability.[52] Unlike in German law, which provides a clarifying provision in Article 129 HGB, this is not expressly codified in the PEL.

The joint and several liability of Article 39 PEL only applies to the relationship between general partners and creditors, including the scenario that a partner himself is a creditor of the partnership enterprise.[53] In contrast, the liability of the partnership enterprise towards creditors under Article 38 PEL, and the liability of the partners under Article 39 PEL, together do not yet add up to a joint and several liability. Because the liability of the partners is accessory to the liability of the partnership enterprise, the element of independence is missing that liabilities must have in order to constitute joint and several liability under Chinese law.[54] Under German law, the liabilities of the partnership enterprise and of the general partners are not treated as joint and several in nature either.[55] The scope of liability that the general partner bears under Article 39 PEL follows directly from the subsidiary and accessory nature of this liability. The scope of the unlimited liability corresponds to the scope of debts

---

[45]Ye (2002), p. 91.

[46]Ma (马强) (1997), p. 57.

[47]Art. 39 in conjunction with Art. 2 Para. 3 PEL.

[48]Li (李飞) (ed) (2006a), p. 60.

[49]ibid, p. 60.

[50]Gao (高富平) et al. (1997), p. 232.

[51]Ye (2002), pp. 90–91.

[52]ibid, p. 91.

[53]ibid, p. 90.

[54]Joint and several liability is regulated in Article 87 GPCL/ Article 178 GRCL. See Ye (2002), p. 91.

[55]Schmidt (2002), pp. 1421–1423.

that the partnership enterprise owes to the creditor, limited to the amount that is left after the partnership enterprise has made repayments with its own property.[56] While a general partner is obliged to bear the entire liability vis-a-vis a creditor, internally, each partner is only liable for a specific part of the partnership enterprise's debts. Article 40 PEL entitles a general partner to take recourse against other general partners if two conditions are fulfilled.

First, the amount of the debts that said partner has paid off, must exceed the proportion he is obliged to pay according to the loss-sharing provision in Article, 33 Paragraph 1 PEL. This regulation establishes that losses are usually shared according to the stipulations in the partnership agreement. In the absence of a clear stipulation, the general partners will consult between themselves on a decision. Should this consultation fail, losses are shared *pro rata* in accordance with each partner's proportion of the capital contributions. If the shares of contributed capital cannot be determined, losses shall be borne equally by all general partners.

Second, the other general partners must not have (fully) paid the proportion of losses that they are obliged to share.[57]

Should personal debts of a general partner and his personal liability for debts of the partnership enterprise occur at the same time, the analysis above has shown that the creditors of the partnership enterprise take precedence.[58] Likewise, it has been illustrated above that a personal creditor of a partner, who is a debtor of the partnership enterprise at the same time, is prohibited from offsetting these claims.[59]

8.2.2 *Shielding the General Partner*

The unlimited and joint personal liability of the general partner is contrary to the foreign investor's interest in constricting his liability for an investment project. As has been described, legal practice in various jurisdictions has created the limited partnership enterprise with a corporate general partner to mitigate liability risks.[60] Therefore, an analysis is provided whether the investor's liability in a FILPE can effectively be limited through the use of a corporate general partner.

8.2.2.1 Legal Person Corporations as General Partner

Only since the reform of the PEL in 2006, legal persons, such as limited liability companies, and other organisations are eligible to be a general and/or limited partner

[56] Ye (2002), p. 92.

[57] Gao (高富平) et al. (1997), p. 235.

[58] See Sect. 7.1.1.2.

[59] See Sect. 7.1.1.2.

[60] See Sect. 1.1.

in a Chinese partnership enterprise.[61] This introduction of the limited partnership with a corporate general partner was in line with developments in many jurisdictions.[62] The GmbH & Co. KG originated in Germany in 1912.[63] Similar hybrid enterprise forms have evolved in the US.[64] In the UK, it is legally permissible for a corporation to act as general partner in a limited partnership enterprise, but this combination has only marginal relevance in business practice.[65] In Italy, the formation of hybrid enterprise forms was not permitted until a law reform in 2004 allowed corporations to act as a general partner.[66] In contrast, Swiss law still prohibits the combination of enterprise forms; any partner in a general partnership, and at least the general partner in a limited partnership, must be a natural person.[67]

> This lack of flexibility in Swiss company law is surprising especially since corporate profits in Switzerland are still subject to double taxation. This demonstrates how strictly Switzerland sticks to the classic dichotomy of limited liability and double taxation in company law on the one side, and organisational flexibility and modest formation costs in partnership law on the other side.[68]

Scholars in Switzerland argue that the potential benefits of hybrid forms would be outweighed by the complexity of adjusting and connecting two enterprise forms.[69] In China, the participation of a corporation in a partnership enterprise has historically not been permitted.[70] Article 22 of the Republic of China Company Law of 1929 and Article 20 of the PRC Interim Provisions on Private Enterprises of 1950 both contained provisions that prohibited legal persons from becoming a partner in a partnership enterprise. Under the GPCL of 1986, only natural persons were allowed to form an Individual Partnership.[71] *ZHU* emphasises that the regulation of the corporate general partner is mainly a question of legal policy, a question of how much control the law wants to exercise over the organisation and solvency of enterprises versus how much freedom the law intends to give the partners to choose their investment structure.[72] A reform of the restrictive policy in China was indicated as early as 1997, when the original draft of the first PEL stipulated that legal persons

[61] See Sect. 4.1.4.3.

[62] Zhu (朱慈蕴) (2008), pp. 77–78.

[63] See Sect. 1.1.

[64] For an account of the development in US partnership law, see Schaper (2013), p. 83; Wu and Geu (2007–2008), pp. 165–167; Johnson (1979), pp. 271–287.

[65] For an account of the development in UK partnership law, see Banks (2017), pp. 4.20–4.21; Schaper (2013), pp. 94–97.

[66] Wiedemann (2004), p. 71.

[67] Schaper (2013), p. 98.

[68] ibid, p. 99.

[69] ibid, p. 99.

[70] Yuantao et al. (1989), p. 57.

[71] See Sect. 4.2.1.2.

[72] Zhu (朱慈蕴) (2008), p. 77.

were eligible to become partners.[73] Commentators have supported the draft by pointing out that legal persons were already permitted to form a Non-Legal Person CJV, and that there was no reason to differentiate between these two types of enterprises in this regard.[74] However, the Law Commission of the NPC took a different view, insisting that insufficient experience had been gained in dealing with hybrid enterprise forms, and therefore decided to prohibit legal persons from becoming a partner under the 1997 PEL.[75] However, the academic discussion around the corporate general partner continued. During the drafting process of the revised PEL, this culminated in strong support for permitting corporate general partners among Chinese scholars.[76] Preventing corporations from becoming a partner was regarded as imposing unreasonable limitations on their ability to do business, and denying equal status for corporations and other market players.[77] Corporations should likewise have the chance to benefit from the flexible and effective organisation structure under the PEL.[78] Partnership enterprises are regarded as the ideal structure to enable large corporations to develop new products and technologies in cooperation with innovative small and medium-sized enterprises.[79] However, scholars have also raised concerns with regard to the use of a corporate general partner, for example regarding the protection of creditors of the partnership enterprise.

> An unscrupulous general partner hoping to evade personal liability may establish a shelf company to function as a corporate general partner of the LPE; in effect, the shelf company is merely a 'dummy' acting as an agent for the individual general partner. For such a variation of the LPE structure, the corporate general partner has no substantial assets to be liquidated in the event of the LPE's bankruptcy and there may in the worst-case scenario be no one actually bearing unlimited liability. It is thus incumbent upon the [creditor] to assess the financial status of the sole corporate general partner before entering into any agreement with such an LPE.[80]

Possible remedies against such an unscrupulous general partner are analysed below.[81] *Lin* and *Yeo* propose that a minimum capital contribution should be imposed on the corporate general partner, or an obligation to maintain a certain percentage of the net worth of the LPE throughout its existence.[82] However, the Chinese lawmaker has provided neither of these safeguards in the PEL. Moreover, *ZHU* focuses on the creditors and minority shareholders of the corporate general

---

[73] Chen (2016), p. 657.

[74] Huang (黄毅诚) (1997), p. 14.

[75] Li (厉以宁) (1997), pp. 17–18.

[76] Julius and Bitter (2005), pp. 62–63.

[77] Zhu (朱慈蕴) (2008), p. 79.

[78] Cao (曹德斌) and Zhang (张小奕) (2017), foreword p. 1; Yan (严义埙) (2006), p. 597.

[79] Yan (严义埙) (2006), p. 597.

[80] Lin and Yeo (2010), p. 106.

[81] See Sect. 8.2.2.3.

[82] Lin and Yeo (2010), p. 106.

partner. When a corporation becomes a general partner in a partnership enterprise, the corporation bears the operational risks of the partnership enterprise in addition to its own operational risks, thus making it more difficult to control the corporation's investment risks for minority shareholders and creditors.[83] Therefore, *ZHU* proposes that a reform of China's corporate law system should be undertaken to protect the interests of all market participants.[84] Minority shareholders of the corporate general partner should be given the right to withdraw from the corporation if they oppose the decision to invest in a LPE.[85] Similarly, creditors of the corporate general partner shall have the right to request immediate repayment of outstanding debts or a personal guarantee of the shareholders of the corporation, when a corporation becomes a general partner.[86] However, a corporation can make a risky investment in virtually all aspects of its business operation. That minority shareholders and creditors are exposed to these risks, is immanent in their relationship to the corporation. Thus, the argument is unconvincing that the decision to become a general partner would differ from other business decisions which carry liability risks for the corporation. Despite these unsubstantiated concerns, academia and practitioners widely agree that, among the many adjustments that the revision of the PEL has provided for the system of partnership enterprise law in China, the admission of the corporate general partner marks an 'undoubtedly tremendous progress in the legislation'.[87] Given the widespread agreement to shield the investor behind the corporate general partner from personal liability, the question could be raised whether it is generally still appropriate that a general partner must bear unlimited liability. However, it is advocated that the joint and several liability of the general partner remains important to situations where the enterprise's own assets fail to constitute a credible bond, and the enterprise's owners, be they individuals or other enterprises, must therefore pledge all of their respective assets in support of the firm's obligations to make the partnership enterprise creditworthy.[88]

Notably, the PEL provides an important exception for the eligibility of corporations to serve as general partner. Article 3 PEL states that 'wholly state-owned companies, state-owned enterprises, listed companies, public welfare institutions and social organisations shall not become a general partner'. This provision likewise concerns foreign-invested as well as solely domestic-invested partnership enterprises.[89] The term 'wholly state-owned company' refers to a limited liability company that is invested in solely by the Chinese state, and under the direct supervision of SASAC.[90] The concept of 'state-owned enterprises' is broader in this regard: it

[83]Zhu (朱慈蕴) (2008), p. 81.

[84]ibid, p. 83.

[85]ibid, p. 83.

[86]ibid, p. 83.

[87]ibid, p. 77.

[88]Hansmann et al. (2005), p. 13.

[89]Art. 6 Para. 2 FIPE Provisions.

[90]Li (李飞) (ed) (2006a), p. 6.

can be understood as including wholly state-owned enterprises, (partially) state-controlled enterprises and (partially) state-controlled limited liability companies.[91] The Chinese lawmaker takes the view that the institutions listed in Article 3 PEL, being primarily financed by state-owned assets and funds raised from the public, should not be exposed to potentially unlimited liability for the debts of the partnership enterprise.[92] These restrictions are criticised by scholars, who argue that the revised Company Law and China's securities law regime provide a sufficient mechanism to protect stakeholders.[93] 'In order to respond to market developments and capitalise on business opportunities, the LPE ought to be allowed the freedom of choice to determine whether to proceed with such an alliance and run the 'risk' (if any).'[94] However, Article 3 PEL does not restrict these entities from becoming a limited partner. Unless subject to restrictions outside the PEL, these entities may invest and participate in a LPE or FILPE as limited partners.[95] *Wu* and *Geu* even argue that the role of a limited partner would be appealing for the government in particular in order to pursue the gradual privatisation of selected SOEs by contributing property other than money to the LPE.[96] 'Such use would allow the government or entities it controls to enjoy limited liability, equity return, and still have some modicum of voice or control as a limited partner under the terms and stipulations contained in the limited partnership agreement.'[97] However, given the strong role that SOEs play in China's economy, the provision in Article 3 PEL *de facto* narrows the scope of application for a partnership enterprise. The regulation of Article 3 PEL is repeated in Article 6, Paragraph 2 FIPE Provisions, and thus likewise applies to a FILPE. From the wording of the provision alone, it could be deduced that these restrictions are not limited to Chinese SOEs, Chinese listed companies, etcetera. However, the rationale of this regulation—to shield publicly funded entities in China—plus the China-specific terminology suggest that the lawmaker had the intention to include Chinese entities, and not necessarily foreign entities that are state-owned.

Besides the provisions in the PEL, the issue remains whether the overall corporate law framework in China allows for such a structure with a legal person as the general partner of a partnership enterprise. From the perspective of a domestic limited liability company that acts as general partner, the Company Law governs this question. According to Article 15 Company Law, a company shall not invest in other enterprises if the company has to bear joint and several liability, 'except where otherwise provided for by law'. The general partner in a partnership enterprise must take joint and several liability for the debts of the partnership enterprise. This

[91] ibid, p. 6.

[92] Zhu (朱慈蕴) (2008), pp. 78–79; Hong (洪虎) (2006), pp. 354, 355.

[93] Lin and Yeo (2010), p. 104.

[94] ibid, p. 104.

[95] Wu and Geu (2007–2008), p. 167.

[96] ibid, 167.

[97] ibid, p. 167.

suggests that a legal person cannot act as the general partner. However, commentators argue that, while Article 3 PEL excludes wholly state-owned companies, state owned enterprises, listed companies, public welfare institutions, and social organisations from becoming general partner, this list fails to include limited liability companies.[98] *Argumentum a contrario*, the PEL is understood as allowing limited liability companies to act as general partner, and therefore provides an exception to Article 15 Company Law, as 'otherwise provided for by law'.[99] In practice, the structure of a limited partnership with a limited liability company as general partner is frequently used in China, especially by PE and VC investors.[100] This indicates that SAMR, as the responsible authority for partnership enterprise registration, does not consider the utilisation of a corporate general partner a problematic issue. The use of a FIE as a corporate general partner would raise additional problems, rooted in the particularities of China's foreign investment regime.[101]

8.2.2.2 Utilising a Foreign Corporation as General Partner

The preceding analysis of use of a corporate general partner in a partnership enterprise has shown that the intermixture of company law and partnership enterprise law can already lead to friction within a domestic legal system. The FIPE Legislation permits investors to go even further by combining laws from different jurisdictions when establishing a FILPE with a foreign corporate general partner.[102] For investors, such a combination of enterprise types from different jurisdictions has the advantage of uniting preferential tax treatment with the corporate governance structure of their home-jurisdiction.[103] Investors can combine company and partnership enterprise law in a way that will avoid the application of rules which are considered as undesirable from their perspective.[104] This process is criticised as 'transnational cherry picking because market actors compose a set of rules from different jurisdictions which is most favourable for their needs'.[105] From the perspective of other stakeholders, 'a transnational combination might amount to a lower level of protection for creditors and workers'.[106] Owing to these concerns, the legitimacy of a foreign corporate general partner is still subject to controversy in

[98] Lin and Yeo (2010), pp. 104–105; Weng and Xia (2007), p. 97.

[99] Werthwein (2010), p. 47.

[100] Lin and Yeo (2010), pp. 104–105; Weng and Xia (2007), p. 97.

[101] See the discussion in Sect. 8.2.2.2.2.

[102] Art. 2 FIPE Measures.

[103] Teichmann (2014), pp. 222–223.

[104] Schaper (2013), p. 103.

[105] ibid, p. 103.

[106] ibid, p. 103.

Germany.[107] Because of European Court of Justice Decisions,[108] a company from another European Union (EU) member state can act as corporate general partner in a German KG, most prominently used in the English Limited & Co. KG and the Luxembourgian S.a.r.l. & Co. KG.[109] The same applies to certain non-EU member states with whom Germany has entered into bilateral investment treaties, the most recognised example being US limited liability companies that serve as corporate general partner.[110] For other non-EU member states, however, the eligibility of such transnational combinations has not yet been fully recognised by courts and legal scholars.[111] Conversely, *Shaper* argues that the transnational combination of legal forms not necessarily results in a regulatory 'race to the bottom', but that regulatory competition should rather be seen as an appropriate tool to determine and fulfil the need of market participants, which includes shareholders as well as creditors.[112] *Teichmann* points out that many of the issues that arise with regard to a foreign corporate general partner similarly occur when a foreign company conducts business in another jurisdiction directly.[113] In the light of this background, the Chinese lawmaker has chosen a rather progressive approach with the FIPE Legislation, expressly permitting the utilisation of foreign corporate general partners. However, these transnational combinations also pose a number of legal questions in the context of the Chinese legal system and the FIPE Legislation. A clarification should be provided of which foreign enterprises qualify as a corporate general partner under the FIPE Legislation, and what consequences the transnational combination of enterprise forms has for the governing law of a FILPE and its corporate general partner.

8.2.2.2.1 Foreign Enterprises That Qualify as Corporate General Partner

Initially, the FILPE Legislation states that 'foreign enterprises' (外国企业) are eligible to establish a FILPE in China.[114] Foreign enterprises can participate in legal transactions, and therefore must be recognised under Chinese law as an enterprise form that bears capacity for civil rights and conduct.

Starting the analysis with the term 'enterprise', the FIPE Legislation makes an interesting distinction when it comes to naming the non-natural person investor in a

[107] For a detailed account of the discussion in Germany, see Schläfke (2013), pp. 62–78.

[108] *European Court of Justice*, Case C-212/97, *Centros* [1999], ECR 1999 I-1459; *European Court of Justice*, Case C-20/00, *Überseering* [2002], ECR 2002 I-9919; *European Court of Justice*, Case C-167/01, *Inspire Art.* [2003], ECR 2003 I-10155.

[109] Schläfke (2013), pp. 68–75.

[110] ibid, pp. 75–76.

[111] Raiser and Veil (2015), pp. 657–658; Schläfke (2013), pp. 76–77.

[112] Schaper (2013), pp. 111–112.

[113] Teichmann (2014), p. 227.

[114] Arts. 2-3 FIPE Measures; Art. 2 Para. 1 FIPE Provisions.

FILPE. The Draft FIPE Measures still used the uniform term 'legal persons and other economic organisations' (法人和其他经济组织) for both the foreign and the Chinese investor.[115] However, the FIPE Measures use the term foreign 'enterprise' (企业) to describe the foreign investor, while the same Article uses the wording Chinese 'legal persons and other organisations' (法人和其他组织) when referring to the Chinese investor.[116] According to China's conflict of law rules, the characterisation of legal terms has to be undertaken in accordance with their meaning under Chinese laws and regulations.[117] In Chinese law, the term 'enterprise' is commonly used as the general expression to refer to any type of business organisation.[118] The lawmaker has thus chosen a very broad term that encompasses a wide variety of foreign enterprise forms. For the underlying research question, the assumption is that a foreign investor will use a foreign enterprise form as general partner which shields him from unlimited liability. Therefore, for the subsequent analysis, the entity that serves as corporate general partner in the FILPE is assumed to be an enterprise type with legal person status which itself fulfils the characteristics of a standard corporate form as established by *Kraakman et al.* Given the broad understanding of 'enterprise' in Chinese law, such a legal person corporation would clearly be included under this term. Regarding the Chinese investor, the wording 'legal persons and other organisations' is equivalent to the phrasing that describes the scope of partners in Article 2, Paragraph 1 PEL. The term 'legal person' is very specific and narrow, whereas the term 'other organisations' is not further defined, leaving room for a much broader understanding of Chinese entities that could serve as a general partner. While the wording differs, the interpretation of both terms shows that a rather wide scope of enterprise types is eligible to act as foreign or Chinese partner.[119]

In order to be recognised under Chinese law, the foreign legal person must have been duly established and properly registered with relevant authorities in the foreign jurisdiction. This requirement is reflected in Article 12, Paragraph 2, Number 3 FIPE Provisions, which stipulates that the application for establishment of the FILPE must contain 'the documents evidencing the establishment of the partners as legal persons'. Therefore, a foreign investor must submit respective documents to SAMR in China.

However, lawful establishment of the legal person in its foreign jurisdiction does not directly result in its recognition as a foreign legal person enterprise in China. Rather, Chinese conflict of laws rules determine whether the foreign legal person is regarded as such under the FIPE Legislation.[120] For legal persons, Article

[115]Art. 2 Draft FIPE Measures.

[116]Art. 2 FIPE Measures.

[117]Art. 8 Foreign-Related Civil Relations Law; Chen (2014), p. 54.

[118]Bu (2017), p. 191. See also the discussion in Sect. 4.1.3.2.

[119]Regarding limitations on who can act as Chinese general partner, see also Sect. 9.2.1.2.1.

[120]This follows from Article 14, Paragraph 1 Foreign-Related Civil Relations Law, which stipulates that the applicable law shall govern the issues of legal capacity, the capacity to act, the

14 Foreign-Related Civil Relations Law provides an explicit conflict of laws provision.[121] In general, the governing law of a legal person is the law of the place of its incorporation.[122] For a foreign corporate general partner, this would be the law of the jurisdiction where the corporate general partner is incorporated. Nevertheless, if the place of incorporation differs from the location of the place of the principal business, the law of the latter place may be the governing law instead. This provision is a middle ground between the place of incorporation and the real seat doctrine and leaves great discretionary power to judges.[123] It exposes an investor to the risk that a legal person incorporated in a foreign jurisdiction, with its place of actual administration in China, effectively does not have any foreign legal status.[124] This alternative application of the real seat doctrine is of great relevance to the FILPE with a foreign corporate general partner. The corporate general partner will usually show a strong presence in China in order to manage the daily business operation of the FILPE. If it is the sole purpose of the corporation to act as general partner in the FILPE, a court could assume that the corporation's place of principal business is located in China. A strong motive for the introduction of this middle ground can be seen in the widely popular use of special offshore investment companies since China joined the WTO in 2001.[125] In order to avoid taxes, facilitate overseas listing and return investments, Chinese investors have employed these offshore companies that are *de facto* pseudo-foreign companies.[126] While they are incorporated in foreign jurisdictions, they do all or most of their business in China.[127] 'Under the incorporation theory, the law of the state in which the corporation is incorporated governs the internal affairs of the company. Accordingly, the pseudo-foreign companies are not obliged to comply with [Chinese laws].'[128] Measures to combat the abuse of pseudo-foreign companies have also been introduced by certain states in the US.[129] Laws in California provide:

> [C]orporations incorporated in another state are subject to certain internal governance rules [of California state law] if they operate substantially in California. A company operates

---

organisational structure, shareholders' rights and obligations, and other related matters of a legal person.

[121]Regarding the conflict of laws regime in China, see Sect. 4.1.9.4.

[122]Article 14, Paragraph 1 Foreign-Related Civil Relations Law uses the expression 'place of registration'. Since the concept of registration has a very broad meaning in Chinese law and includes establishment registration, alteration registration, write-off registration, and registration of branch companies, the SPC Interpretation of the Foreign-Related Civil Relations Law clarified in Article 16 that 'place of registration' refers to the 'place of incorporation' of a legal person (Du 2014, p. 342).

[123]Du (2014), pp. 341–342, 348.

[124]ibid, p. 342.

[125]ibid, p. 336.

[126]ibid, p. 336.

[127]ibid, p. 336.

[128]ibid, p. 337.

[129]ibid, p. 337.

> substantially in California if more than 50% of the average of a corporation's property, payroll, and sales factors are allocated to California and more than one-half of its voting securities are held by persons having addresses in California pursuant to the books of the corporation.[130]

A similar regulation is contained in the laws of New York.[131] In China, no further guidelines are provided that assist judges in deciding when to apply the real seat doctrine instead of the place of incorporation doctrine. Within the EU, the European Court of Justice has prohibited such derogations from the internal affairs doctrine when a company is incorporated in one member state, but does all of its business in another member state.[132] However, under Article 14 Foreign-Related Civil Relations Law, uncertainty remains whether the corporate general partner in a FILPE will be granted foreign or Chinese legal status. It is very difficult for a foreign investor to predict when a Chinese court will resort to the real seat doctrine instead. However, it should be noted that the circumstances around the FIPE Legislation differ from the situation in other jurisdictions. Taking Germany as an example, the use of a foreign corporate general partner in the KG is the result of a gradual development that was driven by legal practitioners rather than the lawmaker. This evolution had been observed with a critical eye before this transnational enterprise structure was partially recognised by courts. Conversely, the FILPE with a foreign corporate general partner is a structure that has been expressly permitted by the Chinese lawmaker. The FIPE Legislation has been enacted for the sole reason to allow the establishing of partnership enterprises by foreign investors, in particular by foreign corporations.[133] With the decision to allow a foreign corporation to serve as general partner, the Chinese lawmaker accepted that such a corporation which manages the FILPE, will conduct a major part of its business in China. Alternatively, the FIPE Legislation could have excluded such an offshore company from managing the FILPE to avoid any ambiguity with regard to its legal status. It remains to be seen whether Chinese courts will find the right balance between facilitating foreign investments and preventing the abuse of investment structures when applying the conflict of laws' provisions.

Besides the Foreign-Related Civil Relations Law, international and bilateral (investment) treaties to which China is party, are an important source of Chinese private international law.[134] The SPC Interpretation of the Foreign-Related Civil Relations Law clarifies in Article 4 that the conflict of laws' provisions in international treaties shall take precedence over the Foreign-Related Civil Relations Law.[135] For the research question of this book, the bilateral treaties with Hong

[130]ibid, pp. 337–338.

[131]ibid, p. 338.

[132]See Sect. 4.1.9.4.

[133]Regarding the legislative motives and history, see Sect. 4.1.5.1.

[134]Huang (2014), p. 7.

[135]The interpretation refers to Article 142, Paragraph 2 GPCL, which states that '[i]f any international treaty concluded or acceded to by the PRC contains provisions differing from those in the

Kong and Germany are of particular interest. Hong Kong is a jurisdiction commonly used by foreign investors who want to rely on an offshore company when structuring their investment into China.[136] The FIPE Provisions clarify in Article 65 that the establishment of a partnership enterprise by an enterprise or individual from the Hong Kong Special Administrative Region and the Macao Special Administrative Region is likewise governed by the FIPE Legislation. A bilateral investment treaty has been entered into between Hong Kong and the PRC in 2003 with the signing of the 'Closer Economic Partnership Arrangement' (CEPA).[137] Under the framework of CEPA, an 'Agreement on Trade in Services'[138] and an 'Investment Agreement'[139] have subsequently been concluded between the PRC and Hong Kong in recent years. Together, these agreements cover the four areas of trade in goods, trade in services, investment, and economic and technical cooperation. CEPA is a liberalisation measure that allows qualified Hong Kong products, companies and residents to enjoy preferential treatment when accessing the Chinese market.[140] Accordingly, for a foreign investor who wants to establish a FILPE, it can be desirable to make the investment through a Hong Kong subsidiary, and under the application of CEPA. However, CEPA defines very specific requirements for when a Hong Kong legal person falls under the scope of the investment treaty. The legal person must be incorporated or established pursuant to the Companies Ordinance or other relevant laws of Hong Kong, and engage in substantive business operations in Hong Kong for at least 3 years.[141] Similar preconditions are required in the Agreement on Trade in Services and the Investment Agreement.[142] Therefore, a foreign investor must ensure that his Hong Kong subsidiary meets these qualified requirements, in order to be recognised as a foreign legal person under Chinese laws. Germany and China have concluded the 'German-Chinese Bilateral Investment

---

civil laws of the PRC, the provisions of the international treaty shall apply, unless the provisions are ones on which the PRC has announced reservations.'

[136]See the table at Du (2014), p. 336. For an introduction, see also Pang (2013), pp. 1–3.

[137]Mainland and Hong Kong Closer Economic Partnership Arrangement (内地与香港关于建立更紧密经贸关系的安排), signed by the governments of the PRC and the Hong Kong Special Administrative Region on 29 June 2003.

[138]Mainland and Hong Kong Closer Economic Partnership Arrangement – Agreement on Trade in Services (内地与香港关于建立更紧密经贸关系的安排–服务贸易协议), signed by the governments of the PRC and the Hong Kong Special Administrative Region on 27 November 2015 and effective as of 1 June 2016.

[139]Mainland and Hong Kong Closer Economic Partnership Arrangement – Investment Agreement (内地与香港关于建立更紧密经贸关系的安排–投资协议) signed by the governments of the PRC and the Hong Kong Special Administrative Region on 28 June 2017 and effective as of 1 January 2018.

[140]For more details, see Wang (2004), pp. 647–666.

[141]Art. 12 Para. 2 CEPA in conjunction with Art. 2 Para. 3 and Art. 3 of Annex 5 to CEPA.

[142]Art. 2 Para. 4 Agreement on Trade in Services in conjunction with Art. 2 Para. 3 and Art. 3 of Annex 3 to the Agreement on Trade in Services; Art. 2 Para. 2 Investment Agreement in conjunction with Art. 1 of Annex 1 to the Investment Agreement.

Treaty'[143] in 2003. The treaty covers every kind of asset invested either directly or indirectly by investors of one contracting party in the territory of the other contracting party, including investments in shares and any other kind of interest in companies.[144] The definition of investor contains conflict of laws' provisions that take precedence over the private internal law codifications in China and Germany.[145] Regarded as Chinese investors are 'economic entities, including companies, corporations, associations, partnerships and other organisations, incorporated and constituted under the laws and regulations of and with their seats in the PRC'.[146] A German investor is 'any juridical person as well as any commercial or other company or association with or without legal personality having its seat in the territory of the Federal Republic of Germany'.[147] In relation to a German legal person, the treaty thus applies the real seat doctrine. A German GmbH that functions as a corporate general partner in a FILPE must have its seat in Germany in order to be recognised as a foreign legal person under the FIPE Legislation. This analysis illustrates that, when planning the investment structure for a FILPE with a foreign corporate general partner, potential bilateral treaties and the conflict of laws' provisions of the involved jurisdictions must be considered thoroughly.

For a foreign corporation to act as general partner in a German limited partnership, German law applies a further requirement.[148] Not only is the legal system that governs the partnership enterprise affected by the participation of a foreign corporate general partner, but also the legal system that governs the corporation.[149] Therefore, the establishment of a transnational enterprise must be lawful under both jurisdictions.[150] This requires that, under its foreign governing law, the respective corporation has the legal capacity to act as general partner in the partnership enterprise of another jurisdiction.[151] Swiss law, for example, only permits natural persons to act as general partner in a partnership enterprise.[152] This raises the question whether Swiss law allows a Swiss legal person enterprise to act as a general partner in a foreign jurisdiction.[153] While some scholars criticise this requirement,[154] the current author

---

[143] Agreement between the Federal Republic of Germany and the PRC on the Encouragement and Reciprocal Protection of Investments, concluded on 1 December 2003 and effective as of 11 November 2005, published at the Federal Law Gazette (Bundesgesetzblatt), 2005 Part II, pp. 732–742.

[144] Art. 1 Para. 1 (b) German-Chinese Bilateral Investment Treaty.

[145] Kindler (2018), pp. 1696–1697; Art. 4 SPC Interpretation of the Foreign-Related Civil Relations Law.

[146] Art. 1 Para. 2 (b) German-Chinese Bilateral Investment Treaty.

[147] Art. 1 Para. 2 (a) German-Chinese Bilateral Investment Treaty.

[148] Lüke (2016), para. 2.497–2.501.

[149] Kindler (2018), p. 1784.

[150] ibid, pp. 1784–1785.

[151] Lüke (2016), para. 2.497.

[152] See Sect. 8.2.2.1.

[153] Teichmann (2014), p. 228.

[154] Kindler (2018), p. 1785.

finds it logical to regard the permissibility of a combined transnational enterprise from the perspective of both the involved jurisdictions. It ensures the lawfulness of the transnational enterprise as a whole, and can provide certainty for the investor. Therefore, this requirement should also be considered under Chinese law.

Regarding the general qualification of a foreign partner, the Draft FIPE Measures featured an entire Article with criteria that would exclude a foreign natural person or enterprise from becoming a partner.[155] Foreign enterprises were required 'to have a good reputation and to have not been punished by the industry associations in their respective countries'.[156] These negative requirements have been evaluated critically by Chinese scholars, especially with reference to the practical difficulties in verifying whether a foreign investor fulfils these criteria.[157] Eventually, these negative requirements have not been adopted in the FIPE Legislation, which now does not stipulate any special qualification requirement for foreign partners. However, industry specific rules may impose special qualification requirements on foreign investors that act as general partner.[158] An example is the private equity industry specific 'Investment Fund Measures',[159] which, in Article 12, stipulate detailed criteria regarding the experience, net-worth and investment amounts that a qualified investor must satisfy.

8.2.2.2.2 FIE as (Foreign) General Partner

From the perspective of foreign investors who already have a presence in China, the question arises whether an FIE such as a WFOE, EJV, HoldCo, FIVCE or a FIE under the Company Law is considered a 'foreign' investor under the FIPE Legislation. This would result in a partnership enterprise established by an FIE being considered a FILPE, and thereby subject to the limitations of the FIPE Legislation.[160] Therefore, we will allow a small excursion into this question. When referring to 'foreign' investors, the FIPE Legislation uses the term '外国'. The word '外国' can be translated as 'overseas' or 'foreign',[161] as opposed to '外资', which means 'foreign-invested', used in various laws and regulations to describe FIEs.[162] This could lead to the conclusion that investments in a partnership enterprise by FIEs—as foreign-invested enterprises—are not governed by the FIPE Legislation. However,

155 Art. 8 Draft FIPE Measures.

156 Art. 8 Para. 3 Draft FIPE Measures.

157 Xu (徐春雷) and Cao (曹秀峰) (2007), pp. 29–30.

158 Paul Hastings (2009), p. 2.

159 Interim Measures for the Supervision and Administration of Private Investment Funds (私募投资基金监督管理暂行办法), promulgated by the China Securities Regulatory Commission on 21 August 2014 with effect as of the same day.

160 The investment restrictions that govern a FILPE are analysed in Sect. 4.1.7.

161 Arts. 2-3 FIPE Measures; Art. 2 Para. 1 FIPE Provisions.

162 Taking the title of the WFOE Law for example, '外资企业法'.

the FIPE Provisions stipulate in Article 63 that an investment in a partnership enterprise by an FIE HoldCo[163] or FIVCE[164] is also subject to the FIPE Provisions. Given the wording of the FIPE Provisions and an *argumentum a contrario* of Article 63,[165] scholars have concluded that a partnership enterprise established by an FIE, would be considered a domestic partnership enterprise governed by the PEL alone, with the exception of those established by an FIE HoldCo or FIVCE. The FIL Implementing Regulations now clarify that investments made by FIEs in China are likewise subject to the FIL and the FIL Implementing Regulations, without stipulating further exceptions.[166] This suggests that a FIE now would also have to be considered a foreign investor under the FIPE Legislaiton.

8.2.2.2.3 The Governing Law: Overlap of Jurisdictions

The analysis so far has shown that the FILPE is governed by Chinese law,[167] and that the foreign corporate general partner is governed by the jurisdiction of its place of incorporation.[168] However, the cross-border combination of a corporation and a partnership enterprise raises new legal issues that emerge because of the interaction between domestic partnership enterprise law and foreign company law. Examples are the practice of synchronising the transfer of ownership in the corporation and the partnership enterprise;[169] the specialties that the execution of partnership affairs through a legal person entail, given that partnership enterprises are structured so that natural persons fulfil this role;[170] deviating information rights of limited partners and shareholders of the corporation; varying minimum capital requirements of the corporation and treatment of unlawful capital distributions.[171] In order to resolve these problems, it is a common approach in several jurisdictions to apply particular provisions that govern domestic limited liability companies also—by analogy—to the issues which arise with regard to the foreign corporate general partner.[172]

On a general level, the question arises which measures Chinese law takes to protect the scope of application of Chinese law in transnational combinations of enterprise forms. In a limited partnership enterprise with a domestic corporate general partner, the entire LPE-structure is subject to Chinese law. With the choice of a foreign corporate general partner, the involvement of the foreign law that

---

[163] See Sect. 3.2.3.

[164] See Sect. 3.2.3.2.

[165] Pissler (2010), p. 129.

[166] Art. 47 FIL Implementing Regulations.

[167] See Sect. 4.1.9.4.

[168] See Sect. 8.2.2.2.1.

[169] See Sect. 9.4.2.7.

[170] See Sect. 7.2.2.

[171] See Sect. 8.2.2.1.

[172] Teichmann (2014), p. 220.

governs the corporate general partner could be regarded by a Chinese court as a decline of the level of protection that Chinese law would otherwise provide. Records have shown that Chinese People's Courts have demonstrated a strong tendency to apply Chinese law in foreign-related cases, even though the conflict of laws' provisions stipulate the application of a foreign law.[173] For a foreign investor who relies on the governance of a foreign law, the forced (selective) application of Chinese law can be a crucial concern. The analysis of China's conflict of laws' provisions helps to understand which legal measures a People's Court can use to enforce the application of Chinese law in foreign-related cases. Three statutory provisions are of critical importance in this regard:

In Article 4, the Foreign-Related Civil Relations Law introduces the doctrine of Mandatory Rules in the field of Chinese private international law for the first time.[174] These are mandatory substantive rules of the forum, which may not be derogated from even if a law of another country is designated as the applicable law.[175] Mandatory Rules are to be applied immediately and directly by Chinese organs exercising international jurisdiction.[176] Because of their mandatory nature, such rules of Chinese law prevail over conflicting rules contained in the Foreign-Related Civil Relations Law and other Chinese statutes.[177] The parties may not exclude the application of Mandatory Rules of Chinese law by agreement.[178] Which rules should be treated as mandatory rules of Chinese law is a long-discussed question in China.[179] The SPC has recognised that the incorporation of Mandatory Rules into the Foreign-Related Civil Relations Law represents a significant legislative development.[180] Nevertheless, as Chinese judges are generally unfamiliar with the notion of mandatory rules, Article 10 of the SPC Interpretation of the Foreign-Related Civil Relations Law provides a definition that consists of a general description and a specific enumeration.[181] According to this definition, Mandatory Rules comprise the provisions in laws or administrative regulations that concern the socio-public interest of the PRC. The enumeration stipulates that Mandatory Rules may include provisions that have bearing on the protection of labourer's rights; the safety of food or public sanitation; the environmental safety; the financial safety, e.g. administration of foreign exchange; antitrust and antidumping; and 'other rules that should be regarded as Mandatory Rules'.[182] Furthermore, Article 11 of the SPC Interpretation of the Foreign-Related Civil Relations Law stipulates that the fabrication of a

[173]Huang et al. (2009), pp. 725–733; Wang (2007), p. 366.

[174]Chen (2014), p. 57.

[175]ibid, p. 57; Du (2014), p. 345.

[176]Chen (2014), p. 57.

[177]Art. 10 SPC Interpretation of the Foreign-Related Civil Relations Law.

[178]Art. 10 SPC Interpretation of the Foreign-Related Civil Relations Law.

[179]Du (2014), p. 345.

[180]Tang et al. (2016), p. 42.

[181]ibid, p. 42.

[182]Art. 10 SPC Interpretation of the Foreign-Related Civil Relations Law.

foreign-relation with the purpose of avoiding the application of Mandatory Rules is unlawful, and leads to the application of Chinese law. These regulations leave Chinese judges with considerable discretion in deciding whether to invoke Mandatory Rules in any specific case.[183] The enumeration enhances the impression that Mandatory Rules primarily refer to provisions that implement government control over foreign investments in China.[184] Consequently, scholars urge that 'judges should be very scrupulous when exercising such power. It would be very unfortunate if the notion of Mandatory Rules were to be employed to thwart the application of all foreign laws which would otherwise apply.'[185]

Apart from the doctrine of Mandatory Rules, there is the doctrine of Ordre Public.

> Ordre Public (public order) is one of the most ancient doctrines in the conflict of laws. In accordance with this doctrine, a foreign law that is otherwise applicable is disregarded if its application would violate some fundamental interest, basic policy, general principle of justice, or prevailing concept of good morals in the forum. (...) Serving as a corrective measure of last resort, the doctrine of Ordre Public is of great necessity in guarding against injurious foreign rules, maintaining the stability of local law, and protecting the public welfare of the forum.[186]

In China, the legal community has consistently adopted an affirmative attitude towards the application of the doctrine of Ordre Public.[187] Chinese scholars have developed a reasonably complete theoretical scheme for the doctrine. Ordre Public has been reflected in relevant legislation as early as 1950, with the most prominent codification in Article 150 GPCL.[188] In the Foreign-Related Civil Relations Law, the Ordre Public is incorporated in Article 5 by stating that 'laws of the PRC shall apply where the application of foreign laws will undermine social and public interests of the PRC'. Notably, in the Ordre Public doctrine, it is not the content of the designated foreign law itself, but the effects of its application that is decisive.[189] 'That is to say, a foreign law that would normally be applicable in a particular situation is not necessarily invalid, *per se,* but should be excluded only under circumstances in which the effect of its application is contrary to China's Ordre Public.'[190] At the core of the Ordre Public doctrine lies the question of what is enclosed in the term 'social and public interest of the PRC'. Neither the law nor the SPC provide a precise definition. The common interpretations vary in the level of detail, but all revolve around similar principles, referring to significant social or governmental interests; fundamental principles of law and morality; substantial political guidelines; unity of the PRC; solidarity among ethnic groups; sovereignty

[183]Tang et al. (2016), p. 43.

[184]Hübner (2014), p. 199.

[185]Tang et al. (2016), p. 43.

[186]Xaio and Huo (2005), p. 653.

[187]ibid, p. 654.

[188]Hübner (2014), p. 105; Xaio and Huo (2005), p. 654.

[189]Chen (2014), p. 60.

[190]Xaio and Huo (2005), p. 659.

and security of the PRC.[191] The doctrine of Ordre Public is therefore applied rather broadly in Chinese judicial practice.[192] Under German law, Ordre Public evolves from the same understanding as in Chinese law.[193] However, the respective provisions in German law are more specific, and require violation of 'fundamental' principles.[194] This provides more guidance in the application of the doctrine. Notably, in German law, Ordre Public primarily protects the constitutional and human rights of the citizen, while the doctrine focuses on issues like sovereignty and security of the state, or on political guidelines, in China.[195] Compared to courts in developed countries, Chinese courts have been known for being more apt to apply the doctrine even when there are better alternatives.[196] Chinese scholars therefore demand that, 'as an exception to the application of foreign law, the Ordre Public reservation should be interpreted restrictively and invoked prudently'.[197] *Hübner* promisingly concludes that the attitude of Chinese courts has changed in recent years, and Ordre Public has merely been used in a few cases to prevent the application of foreign laws.[198] Generally, Ordre Public shows great similarities to the Mandatory Rules, with the doctrines occasionally overlapping.[199] Courts may use either to justify the application of Chinese law.[200] However, there is a difference between Mandatory Rules and Ordre Public in that the latter usually acts in a negative way by criticising an otherwise applicable law, while the former act in a positive way by unilaterally applying a domestic law to the specific case.[201]

The third statutory provision that requires an analysis is the Fallback Clause in Article 10, Paragraph 2 Foreign-Related Civil Relations Law. The provision states that 'in the event that foreign laws are unable to be ascertained or contain no relevant provisions, laws of the PRC shall apply'. Similar provisions are prescribed by conflict statutes in a number of jurisdictions.[202] While the ultimate application of the law of the forum may appear to be a reasonable fallback, its statutory recognition creates a certain disincentive to use all possible means for the ascertainment of foreign law.[203] This is of particular relevance in Chinese law, as Chinese judges' avoidance of applying foreign laws is often explained by their reluctance to explore

191 Hübner (2014), p. 107.

192 Xaio and Huo (2005), p. 672.

193 Hübner (2014), p. 113.

194 ibid, p. 113.

195 ibid, p. 114.

196 Xaio and Huo (2005), p. 672.

197 ibid, p. 676.

198 Hübner (2014), pp. 110–112.

199 Tang et al. (2016), p. 244.

200 ibid, 244.

201 ibid, p. 244.

202 Basedow (2014), p. 95.

203 ibid, p. 95.

them.[204] The regulation in Article 10, Paragraph 2 is further subject to criticism because judges have recourse to Chinese law as well where the law of the foreign country contains no relevant provisions.[205]

> What are relevant provisions? The term opens the door to a narrow interpretation tainted by the perspective of the court, which enables the judge to make use of the fallback provision of the *lex fori* as a kind of general rule. Where that happens, the very purpose of private international law is reduced to absurdity.[206]

This criticism emphasises that a foreign investor must be aware that the concepts of Ordre Public, Mandatory Rules, and the Fallback Clause exist under Chinese law, and that these doctrines are applied by Chinese courts. Where the use of a foreign corporate general partner results in a legal structure that significantly deviates from principles of Chinese law, the risk of being subject to these doctrines may increase.

8.2.2.3 Risk of Piercing the Corporate Veil of Corporate General Partner

However, the use of a corporation as general partner fails to provide fail-safe protection from unlimited liability.[207] The analysis above has outlined that the distinction between the firm and its owners is a pre-condition for limited liability. Limited liability protects the assets of the firm's owners from any claim by the firm's creditors. Under this principle, owners are not liable for the firm's debts beyond their investment in the firm.

> However, rigid, formalistic insistence upon this principle may conflict with other policies and values. Since the liability of shareholders is limited to their investments, the risks of operating an enterprise can be shifted to parties outside the corporation, such as business creditors and tort victims.[208]

Hence, the doctrine of 'piercing the corporate veil' has been developed as the judicial remedy for extraordinary situations, whereby courts disregard the corporate entity when equitable considerations require the imposition of personal liability upon the shareholder of the company.[209] When it applies, a shareholder will be held to be liable for the debts and obligations of the corporation because he uses the corporate form in an abusive and inequitable manner.[210] The veil-piercing doctrine originated in the US, and is today a well-established rule of the corporate law throughout many

[204] Hübner (2014), p. 210.
[205] Basedow (2014), p. 96.
[206] ibid, p. 96.
[207] Wu and Geu (2007–2008), p. 167.
[208] Huang (2012), p. 744.
[209] Ratigan (1983), p. 963.
[210] Wu and Geu (2007–2008), pp. 167–168.

developed jurisdictions.[211] However, due to its being a transplant from the common law system, the veil-piercing doctrine has been viewed with strong reservations in the German legal system, and its application has been gradually constrained by German courts.[212] The way Chinese courts interpret and apply the veil-piercing doctrine is of considerable significance to foreign investors as well as to scholars.[213] Research has shown that the role of the standard corporate form in providing asset partitioning through entity shielding and limited liability is particularly fragile where courts—the arbiters of the partitioning—are willing to permit deviations through veil-piercing.[214]

China formally introduced the veil-piercing doctrine with the reform of the Company Law in 2005. The doctrine has been incorporated in Article 20, Paragraph 3 and Article 63 Company Law. While common law jurisdictions served as a model for China's veil-piercing regime, the codification of the doctrine attracted widespread public and academic attention in China and abroad.[215] Codifying a common law doctrine renowned for its complexity and amorphousness is regarded a bold move by commentators.[216]

> In Anglo-American jurisdictions where the doctrine of veil-piercing originated, its application has to date generally relied on case law instead of statute. This is mainly because it is extremely difficult to codify the doctrine which is often characterised as vague in formulation and unpredictable in application.[217]

However, even prior to the formal adoption of the doctrine, the Chinese judiciary was creative and autonomous enough to apply veil-piercing even without a clear statutory basis.[218] Foreign investors are not excluded from liability due to veil-piercing, e.g. when they have committed irresponsible conduct such as abnormally withdrawing capital out of China.[219] In such cases, affected Chinese parties can often count on the support of Chinese authorities, including MOFCOM, the Ministry of Foreign Affairs, and the Ministry of Justice in recovering economic losses.[220]

The veil-piercing doctrine has been developed in consideration of closed corporations with limited liability. However, the relevance of the doctrine is also recognised with regard to hybrid enterprise forms like the limited partnership enterprise with a corporate general partner.[221] The application of veil-piercing is

---

211 Shen (2015), p. 72; Huang (2012), p. 744.

212 Binz and Sorge (2018), pp. 262–265; instructive: Veil (2008), pp. 3264–3266; Veil (2006), pp. 103–121.

213 Shen (2015), p. 72.

214 Armour et al. (2017a), p. 269.

215 Huang (2012), p. 744.

216 ibid, p. 744.

217 ibid, p. 744.

218 For a detailed account, see Shen (2015), pp. 67–70.

219 Shen (2015), p. 76.

220 ibid, p. 76.

221 Ratigan (1983), p. 949.

discussed for the limited partner that simultaneously controls the corporate general partner by acting as its officer, director and shareholder.[222] In a more general sense, the corporate general partner, which is typically a closed corporation, could be regarded as a prime example for the veil-piercing doctrine. The contradiction of a person of limited liability serving in the position of full, unlimited liability becomes especially apparent when the corporate general partner is undercapitalised.[223] However, such an undercapitalised corporate general partner would be a corporation that is incorporated under the laws of a foreign jurisdiction. Piercing the veil of this foreign corporation would subject its owners to personal liability. This raises the conflict of laws question whether piercing the veil of a foreign corporate general partner is subject to Chinese law or to the laws of its place of incorporation. According to German conflict of laws' provisions, the governing law of the foreign corporation would likewise apply to the piercing of its veil in multi-level investment structures.[224] With regard to Chinese international private law, *Wei* reaches the same conclusion: where an intermediate company is used to avert liability, piercing of the corporate veil of this company would be determined under the law of the place where the intermediate company is incorporated.[225] In a 2011 Decision on piercing the veil of a foreign corporation, the SPC affirmed this conception.[226] However, the SPC did not further substantiate why the foreign law has been declared applicable.[227] Notably, the Chinese court of first instance in this case applied the Chinese Company Law instead.[228] *Du* points out that, in a similar case today, the conflict of laws provision in Article 14, Paragraph 2 Foreign-Related Civil Relations Law, which leaves great discretion to the court in determining the governing law of a corporation, could lead to the application of Chinese law. Likewise, a court could regard China's veil-piercing doctrine as a Mandatory Rule of Chinese law, or apply the Ordre Public reservation in such a case.[229] This illustrates that there is at least some possibility that a Chinese court could apply the veil-piercing doctrine to a foreign corporate general partner. When viewing a multi-level investment structure, a court will give decisive weight to the intent as well as the effect of the actions of the initiator of the intermediate company.[230] Should an intermediate company have been established as a mere mailbox company to evade the mandatory rules of Chinese law and have

---

[222]ibid, p. 965.

[223]Schaper (2013), p. 105; Ratigan (1983), p. 949.

[224]Kindler (2018), p. 1814.

[225]Shen (2015), p. 76.

[226]Hebei Yixing Highway Co Ltd v Jingyu Highway Co Ltd et al, credit agreement dispute (河北冀星高速公路有限公司与京域高速公路有限公司等借款合同纠纷民事裁定书), Supreme People's Court of the PRC, Case No 2011/289 (最高人民法院 (2011) 民申字第289号), judgment date: 24 May 2011, available at http://www.court.gov.cn/wenshu/xiangqing-3290.html, accessed 15 May 2020.

[227]Du (2014), p. 347.

[228]ibid, p. 346.

[229]See Sect. 8.2.2.2.3.

[230]Du (2014), p. 347.

caused harmful results in China, an application of the veil-piercing doctrine appears likely. In the above SPC case, a number of mailbox companies were set up to avoid the Chinese mandatory rules that are applicable to the construction of highways in China.[231]

> It has been confirmed by empirical research that Chinese courts have a growing and stronger tendency to pierce corporate veils compared to the courts in the US, the UK and Australia. The veil-piercing doctrine has been an increasingly popular means of protecting creditors. Correspondingly, the courts have taken a more liberal approach to veil-piercing cases.[232]

Therefore, the analysis turns to the veil-piercing doctrine in the Company Law, with a special focus on two regulations. The central provision of the Chinese veil-piercing doctrine is provided in Article 20, Paragraph 3 Company Law,[233] which establishes a direct liability of the shareholder towards the creditors of the company.[234] The provision stipulates three elements that must be satisfied if the court is to pierce the corporate veil:

> (1) [M]isconduct: it must be established that the principle of separate legal personality and limited liability were abused by the shareholder; (2) intent: the abusive behaviour was intended to evade the debt payment; (3) consequence: the abuse caused serious damage to the creditors' interests.[235]

Among these elements, the misconduct element is the most complicated one.[236] While the law does not further specify what constitutes misconduct, empirical research and scholarly writing suggests that four categories of circumstances can be identified that imply a misconduct. The largest group of veil-piercing cases is formed by commingling of assets, business and personal accounts.[237] This is followed by fraud, e.g. evasion of contractual obligations or statutory restrictions like tax evasion and money laundering.[238] Thirdly, the use of excessive control over the subsidiary by a parent company.[239] The category with the least reported cases is veil-piercing because of undercapitalisation of the corporation,[240] in cases where the corporation fails to meet the minimum registered capital requirement, or falls below the level the corporation is required to maintain after initially meeting the

---

[231]ibid, p. 346.

[232]Shen (2015), p. 74.

[233]Article 20, Paragraph 3 Company Law reads: 'Where the shareholder of a company abuses the independent legal person status of the company or the limited liability of shareholders, evades debts and thus seriously damages the interests of the creditors of the company, the shareholder shall bear joint liability for the debts of the company.'

[234]Werthwein (2010), p. 42.

[235]Huang (2012), pp. 744–745.

[236]For more detail regarding the elements intent and consequence, see Huang (2012), p. 759.

[237]Huang (2012), p. 760.

[238]ibid, p. 760.

[239]ibid, p. 760.

[240]Regarding the undercapitalisation of Chinese corporations, see Shen and Watters (2014–2015), p. 497.

requirement.[241] Since the SPC has not provided a clarifying interpretation of the veil-piercing doctrine yet, a number of issues are subject to controversy.[242] Interpreted literally, Article 20, Paragraph 3 Company Law would only permit creditors in debt cases to bring a veil-piercing claim, but exclude tort, consumer protection, and environmental protection cases.[243] However, Chinese courts are taking a more liberal approach by widening the scope beyond trade creditors to include tort victims as well.[244] While Article 20, Paragraph 3 applies to regular companies, Article 63 Company Law[245] is a veil-piercing regulation specifically designed for one-person limited liability companies, which comprise only one natural person or one legal person as a shareholder.[246] In effect, this provision shifts the burden of proof from the plaintiff creditor to the defendant shareholder of a one-person company, making it much easier to substantiate a veil-piercing argument.[247] Compared to Article 20, Paragraph 3 Company Law, this veil-piercing doctrine is harsher.[248] The motive for this differentiation is that it is regarded much easier to abuse the limitation of liability for the sole shareholder of a one-person company than for one shareholder among several shareholders in a regular company.[249]

> It is important to note that the reversed burden of proof applies only to the issue of commingling. This is because the relationship between Art. 20 para. 3 and Art. 63 is that of a general to specific. In other words, Art. 20 para. 3 applies where Art. 63 is silent with respect to the one-person company. This means that the burden to prove other elements stipulated in Art. 20 para. 3, such as intent and harmful consequences, still rests with the plaintiff.[250]

Depending on the number of shareholders of a foreign corporate general partner, this special provision can thus be of relevance. The overall perception of the veil-piercing doctrine in the Company Law is mixed. *Wang* assesses the regulations as vague and ambiguous, and criticises 'the absence of clear-cut rules to determine the standard for invoking the veil-piercing doctrine'.[251] *Shen* states that, while 'the concept of "piercing the veil" has been commended, significant questions regarding the veil-piercing doctrine are not answered by the Chinese Company Law', and he

[241]Huang (2012), pp. 760–761.

[242]For a detailed account, see: Shen (2015), pp. 71–75.

[243]Shen (2015), p. 74.

[244]Huang (2012), p. 763.

[245]Article 63 Company Law reads: 'If the shareholder of a one-person limited liability company is unable to prove that the property of the one-person limited liability company is independent from his own property, he shall bear joint and several liabilities for the debts of the company.'

[246]Art. 57 Para. 2 Company Law.

[247]Huang (2012), p. 746.

[248]Shen (2015), p. 75.

[249]Werthwein (2010), p. 42.

[250]Huang (2012), p. 746.

[251]Wang (2014), p. 83.

calls for a clarifying judicial interpretation of the SPC.[252] Otherwise, creditors, investors and shareholders will continue to have doubts regarding court decisions to pierce the corporate veil, and foreign investors that establish subsidiaries in China are deprived of a transparent understanding of the governing rules.[253] *Shen* and *Watters* argue that the lack of clear standards under Article 20, Paragraph 3 may be the result of internal controversy between key government agencies regarding the application of the veil-piercing doctrine.[254]

Overall, this analysis illustrates that China's veil-piercing doctrine—if regarded applicable by international private law—can have a significant impact for the owner of a FILPE's foreign corporate general partner, and therefore should be taken into account by foreign investors.

8.3 Liability of the Limited Partner

8.3.1 The Principle: Limited Liability

The name 'limited partner' already indicates the key feature of his liability. The PEL stipulates in Article 2, Paragraph 3 that 'limited partners shall bear liability for the debts of the partnership enterprise to the extent of the capital contributions they have subscribed to'. The personal liability of a limited partner to third parties for the partnership enterprise's debts, obligations and liabilities is limited to the extent that he fulfilled his obligation to pay in full his capital contribution to the partnership enterprise.[255] In effect, this provides a limited partner with a statutory shield that protects him from liabilities of the partnership enterprise.[256] 'In this respect, the limited partner's liability is almost exactly like that of a corporate shareholder.'[257] The liability shield for the limited partner is also a principal feature of the limited partnership enterprise in Germany and the US.[258] One of the default rules of the limited partnership enterprise regime entails that, in return for the limited liability, the limited partner may only play a passive role in the partnership operations, and has no right to engage in partnership affairs such as management and investment decisions.[259] An investor must therefore be cautious about choosing to act as limited

[252]Shen (2015), p. 72.

[253]ibid, p. 72.

[254]Shen and Watters (2014–2015), p. 498.

[255]Art. 65 PEL.

[256]Wu and Geu (2007–2008), p. 158.

[257]Callison and Sullivan (2017), § 23:1.

[258]For German law, Article 161, Paragraph 1 and Article 171, Paragraph 1 HGB; for US law, Section 303 (a) ULPA.

[259]Art. 67 and Art. 68 Para. 1 PEL; Li (李飞) (ed) (2006a), p. 110.

partner because he sacrifices control in exchange for limited liability.[260] This makes the role of a limited partner particularly attractive for investors with substantial financial resources that they do not want to risk in the business, and who intend to be passive, rather than active, business participants.[261] Nonetheless, a limited partner may lower the statutory liability shield and expose himself to personal liability by his own conduct.[262] These liability risks are the subject of the following analysis.

8.3.2 Exceptionally Exposed to Unlimited Liability

8.3.2.1 Statutory Provisions in the PEL: The Active Limited Partner

Pursuant to Article 68 para 1 PEL, a limited partner is precluded from 'executing the partnership affairs or representing the limited partnership enterprise in its relations with other parties'. The execution of partnership affairs refers to the operation and management of the partnership enterprise and the handling of its external and internal affairs, such as the organisation of operations, accounting and financial management.[263] The participation of a limited partner in these management activities generally results in the loss of his liability shield, and exposure to unlimited liability. While this liability-threat should ensure that limited partners be content with a passive role in the partnership enterprise, the realities of China's business practice display a different picture. Examples from China's PE and VC industry indicate that the phenomenon of 'active limited partners' is a common problem in China. Limited partners show a strong desire to control investment funds and to challenge the decisions of general partners.[264] Chinese limited partners tend to request voting rights on investment decisions, and often obtain *de facto* control over the investment fund.[265] In justifying their engagement, some limited partners argue that active involvement 'provides them with an effective and less costly way to supervise the fund and support the general partners with their professional insights'.[266] However, more critical investors emphasise that decision-making by limited partners is likely to be rather inefficient, given the difficulty in reaching an agreement among all partners on every investment decision.[267] *Lin* has systematically identified contributing factors that influence limited partners in pursuing active roles in the

[260]Yu et al. (2012a), p. 11.

[261]Callison and Sullivan (2017), § 23:1.

[262]Wu and Geu (2007–2008), p. 158.

[263]Li (李飞) (ed) (2006a), p. 110.

[264]Zhang (2017), pp. 238–239; Lin (2013), p. 187.

[265]Zhang (2017), pp. 238–239; Lin (2013), p. 193; Zhang and Du (2014), p. II-5.1.9.

[266]Lin (2013), p. 194.

[267]ibid, p. 195.

management of PE and VC limited partnership enterprises.[268] These factors can be summarised in three groups. The first revolves around the principal-agent relationship that is inherent in a limited partnership enterprise.[269] The typical concern of the limited partner to closely control the general partner is especially strong on China's young and vibrant PE and VC markets.[270] The second group comprises shortcomings in China's legal infrastructure.[271] The PEL neglects to stipulate clear fiduciary duties of the general partner, and only provides very limited measures for the limited partner to enforce his rights legally.[272] The third group of factors relates to the specific business environment in China. A majority of limited partners in the PE and VC industry are wealthy individuals and families who are less experienced and less risk-tolerant than institutional investors.[273] In addition to the few qualified investors, only a small number of competent fund managers act as general partners.[274] To this list, *Zhang* adds the dominant role of state-owned capital in China's PE and VC industry and the reluctance of the state to waive its control over fund management.[275] While this analysis focuses on one particular industry, it carries important general implications for a foreign investor in a FILPE as it underlines that the problem of active limited partners in China may require more attention than in other jurisdictions.

Even though a limited partner is excluded from actively managing the limited partnership enterprise, he is still a partner of the partnership enterprise, and thus shall not be deprived of the core rights of a partner.[276] Therefore, exercising core membership rights shall not be deemed to constitute executing partnership affairs.[277] Article 68, Paragraph 2 PEL henceforth provides an enumeration of activities that enable limited partners to supervise the business of the partnership enterprise and to engage in some key decisions without affecting their limited liability. The so called 'safe harbour' list assists limited partners in demarcating the legitimate scope of their participation in the enterprise's activities, and includes eight items.[278] (1) Deciding on a general partner's joining or retiring from the partnership enterprise.[279] Because the general partner executes all affairs of the partnership enterprise, the admission of

---

[268]ibid, pp. 196–201. *Lin* further analyses whether special legal rules in the PEL or contractual provisions in the partnership agreement could help in solving the active-investor problem in China, pp. 201–213.

[269]Lin (2013), pp. 196–197.

[270]ibid, p. 216.

[271]ibid, pp. 197–198.

[272]See in more detail: Lin (2011), pp. 201–230.

[273]Lin (2013), pp. 198–200.

[274]ibid, pp. 200–201.

[275]Zhang (2017), p. 240.

[276]Li (李飞) (ed) (2006a), p. 111.

[277]ibid, p. 111.

[278]Lin (2013), p. 201.

[279]Regarding the joining and withdrawing of partners, see the analysis in Sect. 9.3.1.

a new general partner can have significant impact on the interests of a limited partner.[280] (2) Proposing suggestions concerning the business operation and management of the partnership enterprise. While a limited partner may not be directly involved in the management of the partnership business, he should be able to express his views on the business operation.[281] (3) Participating in selecting an auditing firm for the partnership enterprise. This strengthens the information rights of the limited partners, and helps to prevent collusions between the general partner and the auditing firm. (4) Obtaining the audited accounting reports of the partnership enterprise. Understanding the actual situation of the partnership business is important to put the limited partner in a position to protect his interests.[282] (5) Consulting the accounting books and other financial reports of the partnership enterprise. Having the right to access the records of the enterprise further strengthens the information right of a limited partner about the financial situation of the enterprise.[283] A similar information right is provided under German law in Article 166 HGB. (6) When the interests of a limited partner are infringed, claiming his rights from or filing a lawsuit against a responsible partner. In order to safeguard his own rights, a limited partner must be allowed to enforce these rights against other partners.[284] (7) Urging the managing partners to exercise the rights of the partnership enterprise when they are negligent in doing so, or filing a lawsuit in the name of the limited partner for the benefit of the partnership enterprise in such cases. This provision allows the limited partner to execute his right of supervision, and it is the basis for the limited partner's derivative action.[285] (8) Providing a guarantee for the partnership enterprise in accordance with the law. This is regarded a favourable involvement of the limited partner as it increases the solvency of the enterprise, it is beneficial to the protection of the creditors, and it reduces the current financial burden of the general partners.[286] This concept of a statutory safe harbour list is also used in other jurisdictions. Instead of positively defining the meaning of 'executing partnership affairs', the limited partnership-related statutes in jurisdictions such as US-Delaware, Singapore, New Zealand and Australia merely offer guidelines for admissible actions of limited partners by providing a safe harbour list.[287] However, the safe harbour list in China is shorter than the corresponding lists provided in other jurisdictions.[288] The consequence of violating the safe harbour rule is, generally speaking, that the limited

[280]Li (李飞) (ed) (2006a), p. 111.

[281]ibid, p. 111.

[282]ibid, p. 111.

[283]ibid, p. 112.

[284]ibid, p. 112.

[285]ibid, p. 112. Regarding the derivative action of a limited partner, see Lin (2011), pp. 201–230.

[286]Li (李飞) (ed) (2006a), p. 112.

[287]Lin (2013), pp. 185–186. Regarding the US model-law ULPA, however, the concept of the control rule and safe harbour list has been abolished in 2001. For a detailed analysis, see Bishop (2004), pp. 667–717.

[288]Lin and Yeo (2010), pp. 104–105.

partner will lose the limited liability protection, and will be treated as a general partner.[289] This is regulated in two provisions under Article 76 PEL.

Article 76, Paragraph 1 PEL stipulates that, 'if a third party has reasons to believe that a limited partner is a general partner and carries out transactions therewith, the said limited partner shall bear the same liability for the transaction as a general partner'. This provision protects the interests of the creditors of the limited partnership enterprise.[290] A limited partner who acts like a general partner shall no longer enjoy limited liability, but bear the respective responsibility.[291] This rule is similar to the estoppel rule that applies to limited partnership enterprises under common law,[292] and the authority by estoppel (Rechtsscheinhaftung) that is recognised under German customary law for the liability of a limited partner who acts as a general partner.[293] In order to establish liability under Article 76, Paragraph 1 PEL, the third party bears the burden of proving that (1) the third party reasonably believed that a limited partner was a general partner; (2) he reasonably believed that the alleged general partner carried out the transaction on behalf of the partnership enterprise; (3) he entered into the transaction based on these perceptions.[294] The question is how difficult it is for the third party to discharge this burden of proof. Generally, any limited partner who performs management activities that do not fall under the safe harbour list of Article 68, Paragraph 2 PEL could be viewed as an 'apparent' general partner.[295] The wording of Article 68, Paragraph 2 PEL suggest that the enumeration is exhaustive. *Lin* and *Yeo* criticise this exhaustive approach as being excessively restrictive, suggesting a more flexible, non-exhaustive, list instead that would allow for the later inclusion of other activities originally not envisaged by the lawmakers.[296] They point out that, should market participants come to suspect that a limited partner in China may be unwittingly drawn into situations which require him to bear personal liability for the debts of the enterprise, this could seriously undermine the attractiveness of the limited partnership enterprise for investors.[297] Notably, Article 76, Paragraph 1 PEL does not pick up the phrasing that the limited partner is liable when he 'executes partnership affairs', but rather refers to the limited partner being 'recognised as a general partner'. This difference in wording could be seen as allowing for a more flexible interpretation of the regulation. Certainly, a limited partner can also ensure that his own liability shield

---

[289] Weng and Xia (2007), p. 97.

[290] Li (李飞) (ed) (2006a), p. 123.

[291] ibid, p. 123.

[292] Lin (2013), p. 205. In more detail regarding the estoppel rule in the US, see Bishop (2004), pp. 667–717.

[293] Binz and Sorge (2018), p. 73. Regarding detail on the Rechtsscheinhaftung in German law, see Roth (2020a), § 128 Para. 5; Hopt (2020), § 5 Para. 9–17.

[294] Li (李飞) (ed) (2006a), p. 123.

[295] Lin and Yeo (2010), pp. 104–105.

[296] ibid, pp. 104–105.

[297] ibid, p. 105.

is protected by always making clear to third parties that he does not act as a general partner. The liability risk under Article 76, Paragraph 1 PEL is especially apparent for a limited partner in the FILPE who also acts as the director of the corporate general partner.[298] For a limited partner who performs such a dual function, it is even more critical unequivocally to disclose in business transactions which role he fulfils at the time.

Uncertainty also remains with regard to the extent of the limited partner's liability.[299] The Chinese lawmaker emphasises that the unlimited liability in Article 76 PEL only extends to the specific transaction in question.[300] For any other liability of the partnership enterprise, the liability of the limited partner is still protected.[301] Another issue can arise when the limited partner who violates the safe harbour rule belongs to the group of entities that are statutorily excluded from becoming a general partner, such as SOEs.[302] *Zhang* points out that active limited partners in the PE and VC industry are often state-owned investors.[303] The rationale behind Article 3 PEL can be seen in the lawmakers' will to protect these entities, and especially those who stand behind them, from bearing unlimited liability. Comparing the veil-piercing regulation for one-person limited liability companies in Article 63 Company Law, wholly state-owned companies are recognised to be exempt from this rule.[304] Even though they are solely owned by the Chinese state, and thus are literally one-person companies, they are treated as regular limited liability companies for this purpose.[305] This makes it more difficult for creditors to pierce their corporate veil. Therefore, it remains to be seen whether unlimited liability will be imposed upon SOEs that act as limited partners, and violate the safe harbour rule in the PEL.

While Article 76, Paragraph 1 PEL stipulates the liability of a limited partner towards third parties, his liability towards the partnership enterprise and other partners is established in the second Paragraph of the provision. Article 76, Paragraph 2 PEL provides that 'if a limited partner, without authorisation, carries out a transaction with any third party in the name of the limited partnership enterprise, thereby causing losses to the partnership enterprise or other partners, the said limited partner shall bear liability for these losses'. Article 76, Paragraph 2 PEL is a special provision of Article 98 PEL, which stipulates a similar liability for general partners who are not managing partners, and therefore not authorised to represent the partnership enterprise.[306] The liability under Article 76, Paragraph 2 PEL is

---

298 Regarding the similar discussion under US law, see Ratigan (1983), pp. 949–951.

299 Lin and Yeo (2010), pp. 104–105.

300 Li (李飞) (ed) (2006a), p. 124.

301 ibid, p. 124.

302 See Sect. 8.2.2.1.

303 Zhang (2017), pp. 234–235.

304 Wang (2014), p. 82.

305 ibid, p. 82.

306 Li (李飞) (ed) (2006a), p. 156.

additional to the unlimited liability of Paragraph 1.[307] However, if the limited partner is authorised to conduct the transaction in question by the managing general partner, the limited partner is exempt from liability under Paragraph 2.[308] Conversely, an authorisation from the general partner cannot relieve the limited partner from his liability towards third person creditors under Article 76, Paragraph 1 PEL.[309]

Both provisions of Article 76 PEL concern transactions entered into with third parties. *Zhang* raises the question what liability an active limited partner bears when no direct transaction with a third party is carried out, but the limited partner substantively influences the decisions-making within the partnership enterprise that leads to a loss, such as selecting a specific investment target that eventually causes losses—a scenario that appears to be rather common within China's PE and VC industry.[310] Such a limited partner steps outside the permitted scope of Article 68, Paragraph 2, Number 2 PEL of 'proposing suggestions concerning the business operation and management of the partnership enterprise'. The other partners can hold the active limited partner liable under the general provision of Article 106 PEL, which provides that 'if a person violates the provisions of the PEL, he shall bear civil liability for compensation'. The term 'civil liability for compensation' refers to the civil liability for the damages suffered by the other party in violation of the PEL, or in violation of the partnership agreement.[311]

8.3.2.2 Piercing the Corporate Veil of a Limited Partner

The above analysis of China's veil-piercing doctrine has focused on the corporate general partner of the FILPE. A separate question is whether the statutory liability shield of a limited partner can likewise be pierced under Chinese law in certain cases. The PEL itself does not provide any codification of the veil-piercing doctrine. Under China's civil law system, this would seem to exclude its application to limited partnership enterprises, beyond its use against a corporate general partner.[312] Nevertheless, *Wu* and *Geu* argue that 'there is at least some possibility it could be applied by PRC courts because there is evidence those courts showed a reticent willingness to use [veil-piercing] in the company context before its codification there'.[313] Under US law, the application of veil-piercing has been discussed for the limited partner who simultaneously controls the corporate general partner by acting as its officer, director, and shareholder.[314] Since limited liability is extended to limited partners in

307 ibid, p. 124.

308 ibid, p. 124.

309 ibid, p. 124.

310 Zhang (2017), pp. 238–240.

311 Li (李飞) (ed) (2006a), p. 168.

312 Wu and Geu (2007–2008), p. 168.

313 ibid, p. 168.

314 Ratigan (1983), p. 965.

exchange for the renunciation of control, the rationale for limited liability would cease to exist when a limited partner controls the partnership enterprise through his position as the corporate general partner.[315] However, with the reform of ULPA in 2001, which no longer prohibits a limited partner from controlling the partnership enterprise, this argument cannot be sustained.[316]

Under German law, a similar discussion was held whether, in addition to statutory provisions, a limited partner could be subjected to unlimited liability in certain scenarios.[317] In a landmark Decision (Rektor Fall), the BGH denied veil-piercing of the limited partner in a case where the general partner was *de facto* merely a dummy of the limited partner, who was the actual, sole controller of the partnership enterprise.[318] This decision is in line with the overall restraint in German law in respect of the veil-piercing doctrine.[319] Regarding the liability of a limited partner in a FILPE, it cannot be entirely ruled out that a Chinese court would directly apply the veil-piercing doctrine. However, given the rather narrow safe harbour list in the PEL, cases where the limited partner abuses his liability protection and actively engages in the management and control of the partnership enterprise are likely to be addressed under the application of Article 76 PEL.

8.4 Special Liability Scenarios

For special liability scenarios during the lifecycle of a partnership enterprise, explicit liability provisions are set out in the PEL. These provisions are analysed jointly for the general and limited partner of the FILPE.

8.4.1 Liability During the Establishment of the FILPE

The establishment of a FILPE becomes effective as of the date of the issuance of the business licence.[320] Article 4 FIPE Provisions further clarifies that a FILPE 'may engage in business operation only after it has been registered and has acquired the business licence'. This raises the question what liability the partners bear if business

[315]ibid, p. 949.

[316]ULPA 2001 eliminated the so-called 'control rule', which made a limited partner personally liable for the obligations of the partnership enterprise to varying degrees if the limited partner took part in the management and control of the partnership enterprise's affairs like a general partner. For more detail, see Bishop (2004), pp. 667–717.

[317]Instructive: Binz and Sorge (2018), pp. 264–265; Schmidt (2002), pp. 1552–1553.

[318]Schmidt (2002), pp. 1552–1553.

[319]See Sect. 8.2.2.3.

[320]Art. 17 FIPE Provisions, see also Sect. 4.1.8.3.

has been conducted in the name of the partnership enterprise prior to the issuance of its business licence.

Under German law, the liabilities during the establishment of a GmbH & Co. KG are a very complex matter that has been subject to in-depth analysis by scholars and the judiciary.[321] The German HGB makes a distinction between partnership enterprises that require a commercially organised business operation due to the type and size of their enterprise, and therefore are recognised as a business by legal definition, and those enterprises that are very small or exclusively manage their own assets, and thus are only recognised as a business operation if they voluntarily register as such.[322] For a GmbH & Co. KG that is recognised as a business by legal definition, the registration with the commercial register merely has a declaratory effect. From the moment that such a limited partnership enterprise conducts any business activity, including preparations with regard to its establishment, the GmbH & Co. KG is considered an independent legal entity, and its general partner instantly bears unlimited liability according to the statutory provisions.[323] Regarding the limited partner, Article 176, Paragraph 1 HGB provides that

> where the partnership commences business prior to its registration in the commercial register (...), each limited partner who has agreed to the commencement of business is liable, in the same manner as a general partner, for business debts incurred prior to registration, unless his participation as a limited partner was known to the creditor.

However, the BGH has clarified that, when a transaction is entered into under the full name of the GmbH & Co. KG, and thus under disclosure of its liability structure, a creditor shall be treated as if he should have known that the liability of that partner was limited.[324] *De facto*, a limited partner is therefore only liable to the extent of the capital contribution he subscribed to.[325] However, the situation differs for a GmbH & Co. KG that is voluntarily registered as a business. Here, the registration has a constitutive effect for its recognition as a limited partnership enterprise. Before its registration, such a GmbH & Co. KG only had the legal status of a GbR, which is the most basic type of partnership in which all partners bear unlimited liability.[326] Therefore, the GmbH and the limited partners were *de facto* partners of a Gesellschaft bürgerlichen Rechts, and bear unlimited liability.[327] However, with the registration of the GmbH & Co. KG, all obligations that had been entered into

[321] Binz and Sorge (2018), p. 41.

[322] Art. 1 Para. 2, Art. 2 and Art. 105 Para. 2 HGB. For more detail, see Schmidt (2002), pp. 1629–1630.

[323] Art. 124 Para. 1 in conjunction with Art. 161 Para. 2 HGB and Art. 128 HGB; Binz and Sorge (2018), pp. 33–34.

[324] Binz and Sorge (2018), pp. 70–72.

[325] ibid, p. 34.

[326] ibid, p. 34. Instructive regarding the liability in the German Gesellschaft Bürgerlichen Rechts, see Schmidt (2002), pp. 1787–1806.

[327] Binz and Sorge (2018), pp. 34–36.

under the Gesellschaft bürgerlichen Rechts automatically become obligations of the limited partnership enterprise.[328]

Conversely, the Chinese partnership law regime does not provide such a complex regulation. The FIPE Provisions stipulate that the operation of a FILPE without prior issuance of a business licence shall be ordered to stop operation by the competent authorities, and it will be fined between 5000 and 500,000 RMB.[329] However, the FIPE Legislation and PEL make no further stipulations regarding the liability of the general partner and limited partner. Since the FILPE only comes to existence with the issuance of the business licence, it cannot enter into any obligations before this moment. Unlike the German Gesellschaft bürgerlichen Rechts, the Individual Partnership under the GPCL cannot serve as a fallback enterprise form, as an Individual Partnership can only be formed by natural persons, not by a (foreign) corporate general partner.[330] Consequently, any transactions entered into before the establishment of a FILPE would be regarded as a transaction that the acting partner has entered into in his own name, and for which he bears personal liability.[331] Notably, the Company Law similarly does not provide stipulations for the liability during the establishment of a limited liability company.[332] In 2003, the SPC published draft recommendations on how to address legal issues relating to the establishment of a limited liability company, including questions of liability.[333] A formal position on these questions was subsequently formulated in 2011 with the promulgation of the 'Third SPC Interpretation of the Company Law'.[334] These provisions regulate the liability of the company's promoter: 'a person who, for the purpose of setting up a company, signs the articles of association, contributes capital to or subscribes the shares of the company, and performs the duties relating to incorporation'.[335] While these regulations are directly applicable only to corporations under the Company Law, it is not unlikely that they will serve as a reference for a Chinese court that has to decide on similar questions with regard to a partnership enterprise. Therefore, these provisions are analysed briefly: where a promoter, for the purpose of establishing a company, signs a contract with a third party in his own name, the promoter is in principle personally liable.[336] However, if the company recognises said contract after its incorporation, or if the company has enjoyed the contractual

[328]ibid, p. 34.

[329]Art. 51 Para. 1 FIPE Provisions in conjunction with Art. 36 Partnership Enterprise Registration Measures.

[330]See Sect. 4.2.1.2.

[331]*Ye* reaches the same conclusion (Ye 2002, p. 30).

[332]Feuerstein and Duan (2016), p. 203.

[333]ibid, p. 203.

[334]Third Interpretation of Certain Issues Concerning the Application of the 'PRC Company Law' (适用《中华人民共和国公司法》若干问题的规定(三)), promulgated by the Supreme People's Court on 27 January 2011 and amended on 20 February 2014 with effect as of 1 March 2014.

[335]Art. 1 Third SPC Interpretation of the Company Law.

[336]Art. 2 Para. 1 Third SPC Interpretation of the Company Law.

rights or performed the contractual obligations, the third party can request the company to bear the contractual liabilities.[337] Nonetheless, it is unclear whether the third party retains the option to seek recourse against the promoter in this case.[338] The provisions do not expressly stipulate a joint liability of the promoter and the company. Where a promoter signs a contract with a third party in the name of the company prior to its incorporation, the company shall be liable.[339] A parallel or alternative liability of the promoter is not stipulated in this case. An exemption from the liability of the company is regulated in Article 3, Paragraph 2 of the Third SPC Interpretation of the Company Law. The company can object to a liability claim when there is evidence proving that its promoter has signed the contract with the third party in the name of the company for his own personal interest, and the third party was not acting in good faith. Should the company ultimately not be incorporated, the promoters are severally and jointly liable for the expenses and debts incurred during the incorporation process.[340] These costs shall be shared among the promoters internally, unless the wrongdoing of promoters accounts for the non-incorporation, in which case said promoters shall bear the liability according to their share of responsibility.[341] Regarding tortious liability, Article 5, Paragraph 1 of the Third SPC Interpretation of the Company Law provides that the company shall bear this liability after its incorporation. Should the company not be incorporated, all the promoters shall bear joint and several liability for tortious liability.[342] In that case, the promoters who did not commit the tortious action, can recourse against the promoters who were at fault.[343] Consequently, the SPC provisions provide a differentiated mechanism to regulate the liabilities during the establishment process. However, it remains to be seen whether these provisions are applied to partnership enterprises. After all, the operation of a FILPE before its proper registration and issuance of the business licence entails significant liability risks. Where entering into contracts for the establishment of a FILPE cannot be avoided, a foreign investor should always ensure that proper contractual arrangements among the partners address the associated liability issues.

A separate issue occurs when the foreign corporate general partner has not been properly established before the formation of the FILPE. However, the governing law of the corporate general partner will determine in such a case what sort of liability the shareholder of the corporate general partner will have to bear.[344]

---

[337] Art. 2 Para. 2 Third SPC Interpretation of the Company Law.

[338] Feuerstein and Duan (2016), p. 204.

[339] Art. 3 Para. 1 Third SPC Interpretation of the Company Law.

[340] Art. 4 Para. 1 Third SPC Interpretation of the Company Law.

[341] Art. 4 Paras. 2 and 3 Third SPC Interpretation of the Company Law.

[342] Art. 5 Para. 1 Third SPC Interpretation of the Company Law.

[343] Art. 5 Para. 2 Third SPC Interpretation of the Company Law.

[344] For the liability of a German GmbH before its establishment, see Binz and Sorge (2018), pp. 36–39.

8.4.2 *Liability of Joining and Withdrawing Partners and of Partners That Change Status Between Limited and General Partner*

The conditions and technicalities of joining and withdrawing from a partnership enterprise as well as changing the partner-status are discussed in the following chapter.[345] At this point, the analysis focuses on the liability that a partner has to bear in these scenarios.

When a new general partner joins a FILPE, Article 44, Paragraph 2 PEL provides that 'new partners shall bear unlimited joint and several liability for the debts of the partnership enterprise incurred before he joins the partnership enterprise'. A new limited partner that joins a FILPE likewise bears liability for the debts incurred before he joined the partnership enterprise; however, this liability is limited to the extent of his contributed capital according to Article 77 PEL.[346] These provisions are mandatory rules.[347] Should the partnership agreement stipulate that a joining general partner is exempt from bearing unlimited liability, this would only have internal effect among the partners.[348] Towards a third party creditor, the general partner would still have to bear unlimited liability for debts incurred before he joined, but he would have the right to recourse against the other (general) partners.[349] However, it would be permissible—although not necessarily practical—to conclude a direct agreement with the third party creditor that excludes the liability of a newly joined partner.[350] The regulations under the PEL are very similar to the liability provisions for a joining partner under German law.[351] Partnership laws in France and Japan provide equivalent regulations.[352] US partnership law adopts a radically different approach instead by stipulating that a newly admitted partner does not bear unlimited personal liability for partnership obligations incurred before his admission.[353] The advantage of the US approach is seen in the encouragement—or at least lesser discouragement—of the addition of new general partners which may benefit the capital structure of the limited partnership enterprise during its expansions and growth.[354] However, compelling arguments also support the liability that the PEL imposes on newly added partners for prior debts. First, Art. 44, para 1 PEL provides

---

[345]See Sect. 9.3.

[346]Article 77 PEL reads that '[a] new limited partner shall, with regard to the debts of the partnership enterprise before he joins the partnership enterprise, bear liability to the extent of his subscribed amount of capital contribution.'

[347]Li (李飞) (ed) (2006a), pp. 70; 125–126.

[348]ibid, p. 70.

[349]ibid, p. 70.

[350]Regarding German law, see Roth (2020b), § 130 Para. 9; Roth (2020c), § 173 Para. 10.

[351]Article 130 HGB for the general partner and Article 173 HGB for the limited partner.

[352]Li (李飞) (ed) (2006a), p. 70.

[353]Lin (2010), p. 264; Wu and Geu (2007–2008), p. 165.

[354]Wu and Geu (2007–2008), p. 165.

that 'new partners shall assume the equal rights and bear the same liability as the existing partners'. Accordingly, new general partners shall equally bear unlimited liability for the debts of the partnership enterprise.[355] Second, Article 43, Paragraph 2 PEL stipulates that 'the existing partners shall truthfully inform the new partner of the state of business operations and the financial status of the partnership enterprise' at the time of concluding the admission agreement. This allows the incoming partner to be fully aware of the partnership enterprise's financial situation to make an informed decision regarding the existing risks associated with his investment before deciding to join the partnership enterprise.[356] Third,

> the partner's [capital] contribution, together with the interest and property acquired by a partnership, constitute partnership assets. Under the PEL, the debts of the firm must be paid by the partnership assets first.[357] If the new partner does not have to bear liability for the prior debts of the firm, presumably his contribution will not be exposed to the claims of the firm. This will throw up immense logistical difficulties as it would be impractical and difficult to sever the new admitted partner's contribution from the existing partnership assets.[358]

Under the approach of the PEL, conversely, it is not necessary to determine whether an obligation occurred before or after each general partner joined the partnership enterprise.[359] Fourth, the unlimited liability of the new general partner is consistent with the general accessoriness[360] of the general partner's personal liability to the liability of the partnership enterprise, and thereby comprehensively protects creditor's rights.[361]

Regarding the opposite event, the withdrawal of a general partner, Article 53 PEL stipulates that 'the withdrawing partner shall bear unlimited joint and several liability for the debts of the partnership enterprise that originate from causes that arise prior to his withdrawal'. This regulation is a mandatory provision that the partners cannot deviate from with effect towards third parties.[362] This liability is limited to debts of which the cause has occurred prior to the effective date of the withdrawal.[363] For debts that are incurred after the withdrawal, the withdrawing partner bears no more liability.[364] However, the decisive factor is that the debt has been incurred prior to the withdrawal, the debt need not yet have become due at that point.[365] The regulation under the PEL is similar to the German liability provision on a

[355] Li (李飞) (ed) (2006a), pp. 70, 125.

[356] ibid, p. 70.

[357] See Sect. 7.1.1.2.

[358] Lin (2010), p. 265.

[359] Wu and Geu (2007–2008), p. 165.

[360] See Sect. 8.2.1.

[361] Roth (2020b), § 130 Para. 1.

[362] Li (李飞) (ed) (2006a), p. 87.

[363] ibid, p. 87.

[364] ibid, p. 87.

[365] Ye (2002), p. 128.

withdrawing partner in Article 160, Paragraph 1 HGB. However, German partnership law expressly stipulates a 5-year limitation period for these claims in Article 160, Paragraph 1 HGB. The rationale behind the limitation period is to provide legal certainly for all market participants.[366] With regard to the 1997 PEL, it has been discussed whether such a statute of limitation should apply for the liability of a withdrawing general partner.[367] Article 63 of the 1997 PEL stipulated that, in the event of dissolution of the partnership enterprise, the unlimited liability of the general partner for debts incurred during the existence of the partnership enterprise 'terminates, if the creditor does not make a claim against the debtor within five years'. An argument was made that a withdrawing general partner should not be subjected to greater liability risks than a general partner after liquidation of the partnership enterprise.[368] Thus, the limitation period of 5 years of Article 63 of the 1997 PEL should have likewise applied to the liability of the withdrawing partner.[369] However, the 2006 PEL does no longer provide for a limitation period in the event of the liquidation of the partnership enterprise.[370] The Chinese lawmaker points out that, even though the 2006 PEL abolished the limitation period, this does not mean that a general partner shall bear liability indefinitely.[371] Rather, the rationale behind this reform can be found in the legislator not differentiating between the debts of a partnership enterprise, and the debts of other enterprises and legal subjects.[372] The fixed limitation period of 5 years can be an advantage or disadvantage for general partners in comparison with other debtors, depending on the circumstances.[373] In order to align the liability of general partners with other legal subjects, the 5-year limitation period has been abolished and the general provisions on limitation periods of the GRCL (and GPCL) shall apply.[374] According to the general rule for civil law claims, the statute of limitation is 3 years from the date on which the claimant has become aware, or should have become aware of his claim, with a maximum limitation period of 20 years after the underlying claim has come into existence.[375]

Regarding the liability of a withdrawing limited partner, Art. 81 PEL stipulates that 'a limited partner who has withdrawn from the limited partnership enterprise is liable for debts incurred by the limited partnership enterprise prior to his withdrawal up to the amount of property received from the limited partnership enterprise upon his withdrawal'. Similarly, under German law, a settlement payment to the withdrawing limited partner is regarded as an unlawful repayment of his capital

366 Binz and Sorge (2018), p. 158.

367 Ye (2002), p. 128.

368 ibid, p. 128.

369 ibid, p. 128.

370 Art. 91 PEL. See also the subsequent analysis in Sect. 8.4.3.

371 Li (李飞) (ed) (2006a), pp. 144–145.

372 ibid, pp. 144–145.

373 ibid, pp. 144–145.

374 ibid, pp. 144–145.

375 Art. 188 GRCL. Under Article 135 GPCL, the statute of limitation was 2 years only.

contribution, which results in his liability limited to the amount of the received payment.[376] The liability under Article 81 PEL is also limited to obligations that originated prior to the effective date of the withdrawal.[377] The same limitation periods should apply as with regard to the general partner.

A distinct liability scenario occurs when a partner changes his status within the partnership enterprise. For the conversion of a general partner into a limited partner, Article 84 PEL stipulates that the partner 'shall bear unlimited joint and several liability for the debts of the partnership enterprise incurred during the period when he was a general partner'. The rationale behind this regulation is that a general partner who converts into a limited partner shall not be treated differently from a general partner who withdraws from the partnership enterprise.[378] Hence, the limitation periods outlined above shall likewise apply. In the reverse situation of a limited partner converting into a general partner, Article 83 PEL provides that the partner 'shall bear the unlimited joint and several liability for the debts of the partnership enterprise incurred during the period when he was a limited partner'. Because the conversion from a limited partner into a general partner is equivalent to the admission of a new general partner, these scenarios should be treated equally from a legal standpoint.[379] It is a principle of the PEL that all general partners are treated equally, regardless of whether they were newly admitted or converted into a general partner.[380] In addition, differentiating the liability according to the moment in time when a partner obtains the status of a general partner would cause severe difficulties in the practical operation of a partnership enterprise.[381] German partnership law therefore applies a similar liability regime for the change of partnership status.[382] Both provisions in the PEL on the liability due to the conversion of partners are mandatory rules that cannot be deviated from.[383]

In summary, the analysis of these provisions suggests that two dimensions can be distinguished with regard to a partner's liability: time (before and after a specific event) and status (general or limited partner).[384] Regarding the status dimension, a newly admitted or converted general partner will be jointly and severally liable for the obligations of the partnership enterprise, irrespective of when they were incurred. Likewise, a newly admitted limited partner will be liable for the obligations of the partnership enterprise to the extent of his contribution, irrespective of when these obligations were incurred. Regarding the time dimension, a withdrawing general partner and a general partner who converts into a limited partner are unlimitedly

---

[376]Binz and Sorge (2018), p. 159.

[377]Li (李飞) (ed) (2006a), p. 130.

[378]ibid, p. 134.

[379]ibid, p. 133.

[380]ibid, p. 133.

[381]ibid, p. 133.

[382]Binz and Sorge (2018), pp. 156–159.

[383]Li (李飞) (ed) (2006a), p. 133.

[384]Wu and Geu (2007–2008), p. 164.

liable only for obligations of the partnership enterprise that were incurred before the withdrawal or the conversion. Likewise, a withdrawing limited partner bears liability only for debts incurred prior to his withdrawal.

8.4.3 Liability upon Transfer of a Partner's Ownership Interest

The analysis of the liability upon the transfer of a membership right begins with the limited partner, and then turns to the general partner. This liability issue usually arises when one partner wants to sell his ownership interest in the partnership enterprise to a third party. One option to structure such a transaction is a combination of the withdrawal of the seller from the partnership enterprise and the joining as a new partner of the purchaser.[385] From an economic perspective, the purchaser takes over the position of the seller in the partnership enterprise.[386] From a legal perspective, however, the liability issues in this structure are more complex. In principle, the outlined liability of a withdrawing partner applies to the seller, and the liability of a joining partner applies to the purchaser. Because of the withdrawal, the seller receives a compensation payment from the partnership enterprise.[387] This compensation payment can trigger a liability of the limited partner according to Article 81 PEL.[388] The purchaser for his part would have to make the capital contribution to the partnership enterprise that he has subscribed to in order to avoid a personal liability.[389] In business practice, it is even more common for the purchaser to make a direct payment to the seller.[390] This payment from the purchaser to the seller has two legal effects. It is recognised as fulfilling the obligation of the purchaser to make a capital contribution by the partnership enterprise.[391] At the same time, it is recognised as fulfilling the obligation of the partnership enterprise to make a compensation payment by the seller.[392] Under both approaches, a liability issue arises because the capital contribution would have to be made and to be maintained twice—by the seller and by the purchaser—, while in fact only one capital contribution remains with the partnership enterprise.[393] Therefore, this structuring option can expose the seller to a liability in accordance with Article 81 PEL after his

[385]For a detailed analysis regarding the transfer of a partner's share of the property in the partnership enterprise, see Chap. 9.

[386]Schmidt (2002), pp. 1320–1321.

[387]See Sect. 9.3.2.2.

[388]See Sect. 8.4.2.

[389]Art. 2 Para. 3, Art. 65 PEL. See Sect. 8.3.1.

[390]Schmidt (2002), p. 1590.

[391]Art. 64 Contract Law.

[392]Art. 65 Contract Law.

[393]Schmidt (2002), p. 1590.

withdrawal. To avoid such liability issues, it is a much better option for a limited partner to directly transfer his membership right to a third party, pursuant to the regulation in Article 73 PEL.[394] With the fulfilment of his subscribed capital contribution, the limited partner is released from any further liability. In consequence of a direct transfer from the selling transferor to the purchasing transferee, the membership right of the limited partner remains in the partnership enterprise, only the subject owning the membership right changes.[395] The capital contribution of the transferring limited partner remains in the partnership enterprise, and the transferee legally takes over the membership right with a fully paid up capital contribution of the transferring partner.[396] From the perspective of the partnership enterprise's creditors, the transfer of the membership right has no adverse effect. The capital contribution that has been made by the transferor is still available in the partnership enterprise after the transfer. For the transferor, the advantage of a direct transfer is that he is not subject to any subsequent liability after selling his ownership interest. He would only bear liability in accordance with Article 81 PEL if he receives any repayment of the capital contribution from the partnership enterprise.

For a general partner, however, the liability after the direct transfer of his membership right is effectively the same as in a combination of withdrawal and joining of partners. The reason is the distinct role that the general partner plays in the liability of the partnership enterprise by bearing unlimited personal liability. The identity and the solvency of the general partner is a crucial factor for the creditors of the partnership enterprise. In order to protect the creditor's interests, under German law, the liability provisions on a withdrawing general partner are applied to the transferring general partner, even though the direct transfer of the membership right is technically not a withdrawal.[397] Chinese literature is silent on the liability of a transferring general partner. However, the same considerations with regard to protection of the creditor's interests should apply to the partnership enterprise under Chinese law. Therefore, the transferor continues to bear liability in accordance with Article 53 PEL, whereas the transferee bears the full liability of a joining general partner in accordance with Article 44, Paragraph 2 PEL.[398] This is a significant difference between the liability of a limited partner and general partner. However, this research project revolves around a FILPE with a single corporate general partner. Instead of transferring the membership right in the FILPE, the investor can transfer his ownership interest in the corporate general partner.[399] This transaction structure would allow the investor behind the corporate general partner to effectively limit his liability after selling his ownership interest in the FILPE.

---

[394]See Sect. 9.4.2.3.

[395]Li (李飞) (ed) (2006a), p. 68.

[396]Schmidt (2002), pp. 1590–1592.

[397]Schmidt (1992), pp. 909–910.

[398]See Sect. 8.4.2.

[399]See the analysis in Sect. 9.4.2.7.

8.4.4 Liability upon Dissolution and Liquidation

Under the PEL, as is the case for companies under the Company Law, the liquidation upon dissolution is to be distinguished from the liquidation in case of bankruptcy.[400]

The liquidation of the partnership enterprise upon dissolution results in its deregistration.[401] Among other reasons, dissolution of a partnership enterprise is especially relevant when a FILPE is only formed for a fixed duration of time, or with the purpose to undertake one specific project. Regarding the liability, Article 91 PEL provides that 'after deregistration of a partnership enterprise, the former general partners shall continue to bear unlimited joint and several liability for the debts incurred by the partnership enterprise during the period of its existence'. This liability regulation reflects the principle of a partnership enterprise that a general partner bears unlimited personal liability.[402] Therefore, the solvency and creditworthiness of a partnership enterprise is traditionally determined primarily upon the solvency of its general partner rather than the assets owned by the partnership enterprise itself.[403] Should a general partner be able to dispose of the unlimited liability through deregistration of the partnership enterprise, such a deregistration could easily be abused to avoid paying outstanding debts, thereby severely impairing the credibility of partnership enterprises and possibly affecting the stability of the economic and social order.[404] As a result, German law also stipulates a liability of the general partner beyond the liquidation of the partnership enterprise.[405] As pointed out in the previous sub-section, the 2006 PEL no longer provides a special limitation period for the liability after dissolution. The general limitation periods stipulated in the GRCL/GPCL therefore apply. Notably, the starting point to determine the limitation period has also changed with the 2006 PEL. Under Article 63 of the 1997 PEL, the limitation period was 5 years from the day of the dissolution of the partnership enterprise.[406] This corresponded to the regulation under German law, which also stipulates that the 5-year limitation period generally begins with the registration of the dissolution.[407] However, German scholars have criticised that the dissolution is inappropriate as the starting point for the limitation period as such an early beginning infringes creditor's rights.[408] The PEL reform has also recognised this issue, resulting in the wording of Article 91 PEL now naming the deregistration

---

[400] Werthwein (2010), p. 51.

[401] Art. 90 PEL. Regarding a detailed analysis of the dissolution and liquidation process, see Sect. 9.2.2.

[402] Li (李飞) (ed) (2006a), p. 144.

[403] ibid, p. 144.

[404] ibid, p. 144.

[405] Schmidt (2002), p. 1524.

[406] Ye (2002), p. 140.

[407] Art. 159 Para. 2 HGB.

[408] Schmidt (2002), pp. 1524–1525.

instead of the dissolution of the partnership enterprise as the beginning of the limitation period.

Regarding the liability of the limited partner, no special provisions are provided for its dissolution. Any outstanding (refunded) capital contributions of a limited partner are to be claimed during the liquidation process.[409] By the time of the deregistration of the partnership enterprise, a limited partner shall therefore not bear further liability.[410]

Turning to the liquidation because of bankruptcy, the 2006 PEL provides for the first time—very basic—regulations in respect to the bankruptcy of a partnership enterprise.[411] If the creditor of a partnership enterprise chooses to initiate bankruptcy proceedings, the court will apply the relevant procedural rules, including imposing a stay of action, and possibly appointing an independent administrator to manage the assets of the partnership enterprise.[412] Should the remaining property of the partnership enterprise be insufficient to pay off all debts, Article 92, Paragraph 2 PEL stipulates that 'if a partnership enterprise is declared bankrupt in accordance with the law, its general partners shall continue to bear unlimited joint and several liability for the debts of the partnership enterprise'. This regulation is in contrast with the regular bankruptcy provisions on corporations, which generally exempt shareholders from personal liability after the bankruptcy of an enterprise.[413] The liability provision in the PEL is a reflection of the principle of unlimited personal liability of a general partner.[414] If the general partner is an enterprise with legal person status—as is the case in the underlying scenario of the FILPE with a corporate general partner—, and if said general partner is unable to repay the outstanding claims, the creditors may apply to the court to initiate bankruptcy proceedings against that corporate general partner.[415] Depending on whether the corporate general partner has his main place of business or place of incorporation in China or abroad, the Enterprise Bankruptcy Law or a foreign bankruptcy regime would apply.[416] The liability of a general partner in case of bankruptcy is likewise subject to the limitation periods as provided for in the GRCL/GPCL. Regarding the limited partner, no special liability is stipulated for after bankruptcy of the partnership enterprise. However, the administrator has the right to request contribution of any outstanding (refunded) capital

[409]Art. 87 Paras. 2 and 4 in conjunction with Art. 64 Para. 1 and Art. 2 Para. 3 PEL.

[410]Li (李飞) (ed) (2006a), p. 144.

[411]Wang (王翔) (2006), item 5; regarding a detailed analysis of the bankruptcy process, see Sects. 7.1.1.2 and 9.2.2.2.

[412]Zheng (2010), p. 227.

[413]Li (李飞) (ed) (2006a), p. 147.

[414]ibid, p. 147.

[415]Zheng (2010), p. 227.

[416]In contrast, should the general partner be a natural person and Chinese law be applicable, the situation would be more complicated as China does not yet have an individual bankruptcy regime (Zheng 2010, p. 227).

contributions from a limited partner.[417] Under German partnership law, the bankruptcy of the partnership enterprise likewise leads to the application of bankruptcy proceedings and unlimited liability of the general partners for outstanding debts.[418]

8.4.5 Liabilities for Partner's Personal Conduct

Apart from bearing liability towards the creditors of the partnership enterprise, partners are—in certain cases—also liable towards the partnership enterprise itself and the other partners.[419] These liabilities do not derive from debts that arose in the name of the partnership enterprise but rather originate in the personal conduct of a partner. This refers to a partner conducting partnership affairs without the required unanimous resolution of all partners;[420] a partner who conducts partnership affairs despite not being authorised to do so;[421] a general partner who engages in business that competes with the partnership enterprise;[422] a partner who takes possession of partnership enterprise interest or property, thereby causing losses to the partnership enterprise or its other partners;[423] a partner who is responsible for the conduct of partnership affairs and fails to complete enterprise registration formalities regarding changes of registered matters in time;[424] a partner who breaches the partnership agreement.[425] A limited partner may further have to bear liability if he fails to make his capital contribution in full amount on schedule.[426]

8.5 Conclusion

The analysis has illustrated that the PEL permits to mitigate the effect of unlimited liability of the general partner for the debts of the limited partnership enterprise through use of a corporate general partner.[427] With the FIPE Legislation, the Chinese lawmaker goes even further by expressly permitting the use of a foreign corporation

[417]Zheng (2010), p. 251.

[418]See in more detail, Binz and Sorge (2018), pp. 231–265.

[419]Werthwein (2010), p. 52.

[420]Art. 97 PEL.

[421]Art. 98 PEL.

[422]Art. 99 in conjunction with Art. 32 Para. 1 PEL.

[423]Art. 96 PEL.

[424]Art. 95 Para. 3 in conjunction with Art. 13 PEL.

[425]Art. 103 Para. 1 PEL.

[426]Art. 65 PEL.

[427]See Sect. 8.2.2.1.

as a general partner in a FILPE.[428] In comparison with other jurisdictions, this is a rather progressive approach. However, such a transnational combination of enterprise forms creates a number of complex legal issues. Conflict of laws' provisions and bilateral treaties must be considered in order to determine whether a specific enterprise is eligible to act as foreign corporate general partner in a FILPE.[429] Where the utilisation of a foreign corporate general partner leads to significant deviations from principles of Chinese law, a Chinese court can apply the doctrines of Ordre Public, Mandatory Rules and a Fallback Clause to enforce the application of Chinese laws.[430] In addition, the possibility remains that a Chinese court could apply the veil-piercing doctrine to a foreign corporate general partner, thus resulting in personal liability of the investors.[431] Conversely, a limited partner is generally protected from any liability beyond his capital contribution. Nonetheless, a limited partner may lower this statutory liability shield and expose himself to personal liability by his own conduct.[432] This phenomenon of 'active limited partners' is more common in China than in many other jurisdictions. A limited partner is only allowed to engage with the management of the FILPE as set out in the PEL's safe harbour list. Should a limited partner interfere with the execution of partnership affairs beyond these permitted activities, he shall be treated like a general partner and bear unlimited liability. However, the application of the veil-piercing doctrine to limited partners does not find a foothold in the partnership legislation.[433] Through a number of mandatory rules, it is further ensured that the unlimited personal liability of a general partner continues when he withdraws from the FILPE, when he changes status to a limited partner, or when the FILPE is liquidated.[434] In addition, a number of provision in the PEL stipulate personal liabilities of partners because of their personal conduct.[435] However, when carefully planned, the legal framework in China allows the structuring of a FILPE with a foreign corporate general partner in such a manner that the creditors of the FILPE have no claim against the assets of the investors behind the corporate general partner and the limited partners—thus fulfilling the attribute of limited liability.

[428]See Sect. 8.2.2.2.

[429]See Sect. 8.2.2.1.

[430]See Sect. 8.2.2.2.3.

[431]See Sect. 8.2.2.3.

[432]See Sect. 8.3.2.1.

[433]See Sect. 8.3.2.2.

[434]See Sect. 8.4.1.

[435]See Sect. 8.4.5.

References

Armour J, Hansmann H, Kraakman R (2009) What is corporate law? In: Kraakman R et al (eds) The anatomy of corporate law, 2nd edn. Oxford University Press, Oxford, pp 1–34

Armour J, Enriques L, Pargendler M, Ringe W-G (2017a) Beyond the anatomy. In: Kraakman R et al (eds) The anatomy of corporate law, 3rd edn. Oxford University Press, Oxford, pp 267–272

Armour J, Hansmann H, Kraakman R, Pargendler M (2017b) What is corporate law? In: Kraakman R et al (eds) The anatomy of corporate law, 3rd edn. Oxford University Press, Oxford, pp 1–28

Banks R (2017) Lindley & Banks on partnership, 20th edn. Sweet & Maxwell, London

Basedow J (2014) The application of foreign law – comparative remarks on the practical side of private international law. In: Basedow J, Pissler KB (eds) Private international law in Mainland China, Taiwan and Europe. Mohr Siebeck, Tübingen, pp 85–97

Binz MK, Sorge MH (2018) Die GmbH & Co. KG im Gesellschafts- und Steuerrecht, 12th edn. C. H. Beck, Munich

Bishop CG (2004) The new limited partner liability shield: has the vanquished control rule unwittingly resurrected lingering limited partner estoppel liability as well as full general partner liability. Suffolk Univ Law Rev 37:667–717

Bu Y (2017) Einführung in das Recht Chinas, 2nd edn. C. H. Beck, Munich

Callison JW, Sullivan MA (2017) Partnership law and practice: general and limited partnerships, 2017–2018 Edition. Thomson Reuters, Danvers

Cao D (曹德斌), Zhang X (张小奕) (2017) A practical guide to the new partnership enterprise law (新合伙企业法实用手册). China Industry and Commerce Press (中国工商出版社), Beijing

Chen W (2014) Selected problems of general provisions in private international law: the PRC perspective. In: Basedow J, Pissler KB (eds) Private international law in Mainland China, Taiwan and Europe. Mohr Siebeck, Tübingen, pp 51–63

Chen J (2016) Chinese law: context and transformation, Revised and Expanded Edition. Brill, Leiden

Du T (2014) The new Chinese conflict-of-law rules for legal persons: is the middle way feasible? In: Basedow J, Pissler KB (eds) Private international law in Mainland China, Taiwan and Europe. Mohr Siebeck, Tübingen, pp 331–348

Feuerstein M, Duan X (2016) Haftung in der Kapitalgesellschaft. In: Binding J, Pissler KB (eds) Chinesisches Zivil- und Wirtschaftsrecht Band 2 – Schwerpunkt Wirtschaftsrecht. R&W, Frankfurt a.M., pp 201–218

Foster N, Sule S (2010) German legal system and laws, 4th edn. Oxford University Press, Oxford

Gao F (高富平), Su H (苏号朋), Li Z (刘智慧) (1997) Principles and practice of partnership enterprise law (合伙企业法原理与实务). China Legal Publishing House (中国法制出版社), Beijing

Hansmann H, Kraakman R (2000) The essential role of organizational law. Yale Law J 110:387–440

Hansmann H, Kraakman R, Squire R (2005) The new business entities in evolutionary perspective. Univ Illinois Law Rev 2005:5–14

Hong H (洪虎) (2006) Report on the Circumstances of the Revision of the Amended Draft of the PRC Partnership Enterprise Law – delivered on 24 June 2006 to the 22nd Session of the Standing Committee of the 10th National People's Congress (关于《中华人民共和国合伙企业法(修订草案)》修改情况的汇报—2006年6月24日在第十届全国人民代表大会常务委员会第二十二次会议上). Yearbook of the National People's Congress 2006: (全国人民代表大会年鉴2 0 0 6 年卷), pp 354–357

Hopt KJ (2020) HGB § 5 Kaufmann kraft Eintragung. In: Baumbach A, Hopt KJ (eds) Handelsgesetzbuch, 39th edn. C. H. Beck, Munich, § 5 para 1–18

Huang Y (黄毅诚) (1997) Explanations on the Draft PRC Partnership Enterprise Law – delivered on 23 October 1996 to the 22nd Session of the Standing Committee of the 8th National People's Congress (关于《中华人民共和国合伙企业法(草案)》的说明—1996年10月23日在第八届全国人民代表大会常务委员会第二十二次会议上). Gazette of the Standing Committee of the National People's Congress 1997 No 1 (中华人民共和国全国人民代表大会常务委员会公报1997年1号), pp 12–16

Huang H (2012) Piercing the corporate veil in China: where is it now and where is it heading? Am J Comp Law 60:743–774

Huang J (2014) New perspectives on private international law in the People's Republic of China. In: Basedow J, Pissler KB (eds) Private international law in Mainland China, Taiwan and Europe. Mohr Siebeck, Tübingen, pp 3–15

Huang J, Song L, Li Q, Long W (2009) Chinese judicial practice in private international law: 2006. Chin J Int Law 8:715–740

Hübner PA (2014) Rechtsschutz ausländischer Investoren vor chinesischen Gerichten. De Gruyter, Berlin

Johnson PR (1979) The corporation as managing partner in a limited partnership. North Dakota Law Rev 55:271–287

Julius H, Bitter M (2005) Symposium zum chinesischen Personenhandelsgesellschaftsrecht. Zeitschrift für Chinesisches Recht 12:62–63

Kindler P (2018) Internationales Handels- und Gesellschaftsrecht. In: Säcker FJ et al (eds) Münchener Kommentar zum Bürgerlichen Gesetzbuch, vol 12, 7th edn. C. H. Beck, Munich, pp 1565–1929

Li Y (厉以宁) (1997) Examination Report of the Law Commission of the National People's Congress on the Draft PRC Partnership Enterprise Law, delivered to the 24th Session of the Standing Committee of the 8th National People's Congress on 19 February 1997, (全国人大法律委员会关于《中华人民共和国合伙企业法(草案)》审议结果的报告—1997年2月19日在第八届全国人民代表大会常务委员会第二十四次会议上). Gazette of the Standing Committee of the National People's Congress 1997 No 1 (中华人民共和国全国人民代表大会常务委员会公报1997年1号), pp 17–20

Li F (李飞) (ed) (2006a) Interpretation of the PRC partnership enterprise law (中华人民共和国合伙企业法释义). Law Press China (法律出版社), Beijing

Li X (李新) (2006b) On the disposal of property of the partnership enterprise (论合伙企业财产的处分). Econ Forum (经济论坛) 2006(8):128–129

Lin L (2010) The limited liability partnership in China: a long way ahead. Int Company Commer Law Rev 21:259–265

Lin L (2011) The limited partner's derivative action: problems and prospects in the private equity market of China. Hong Kong Law J 41:201–230

Lin L (2013) The private equity limited partnership in China: a critical evaluation of active limited partners. J Corp Law Stud 13:185–217

Lin L, Yeo HY (2010) Limited partnership – the new business vehicle in China. Butterworth J Int Bank Financ Law 25:104–108

Lüke O (2016) Besondere Erscheinungsformen der GmbH & Co. KG. In: Mueller-Thuns T (ed) Handbuch GmbH & Co. KG: Gesellschaftsrecht – Steuerrecht, vol 21. Schmidt, Cologne, para 2.461–2.558

Ma Q (马强) (1997) Study on issues regarding the settlement of partnership debt (合伙债务清偿问题研究). The Jurist (法学家) 1997(4):55–62

Pang MK (2013) Hong Kong as a base for doing business in Mainland China. Bus Law Today 2013 (6):1–3

Paul Hastings (2009) Draft foreign-invested partnership regulations – new possibilities for global funds in China? https://www.paulhastings.com/docs/default-source/PDFs/1400.pdf. Accessed 15 May 2020

Pissler KB (2010) Die Gründung ausländischer Partnerschaftsunternehmen nach den neuen Registrierungsbestimmungen: Konkretisierungen, Antworten, Einschränkungen und neue Fragen. Zeitschrift für Chinesisches Recht 17:125–131

Posner RA (2014) Economic analysis of law, 9th edn. Wolters Kluwer Law & Business, New York

Raiser T, Veil R (2015) Recht der Kapitalgesellschaften, 6th edn. Verlag Franz Vahlen, Munich

Ratigan JJ (1983) Piercing the veil of the corporate general partner in the hybrid limited partnership: a suggested remedy for inequitable conduct by limited partners. Suffolk Univ Law Rev 17:949–985
Ribstein LE (1988) An applied theory of limited partnership. Emory Law J 37:835–895
Roth M (2020a) HGB § 128 Persönliche Haftung der Gesellschafter. In: Baumbach A, Hopt KJ (eds) Handelsgesetzbuch, 39th edn. C. H. Beck, Munich, § 128 para 1-47
Roth M (2020b) HGB § 130 Haftung des eintretenden Gesellschafters. In: Baumbach A, Hopt KJ (eds) Handelsgesetzbuch, 39th edn. C. H. Beck, Munich, § 130 para 1–9
Roth M (2020c) HGB § 173 Haftung bei Eintritt als Kommanditist. In: Baumbach A, Hopt KJ (eds) Handelsgesetzbuch, 39th edn. C. H. Beck, Munich, § 173 para 1–16
Schaper M (2013) Hybrid legal forms at the gates – the transition from combined legal forms to hybrid corporations and its consequences for creditor protection. Eur Company Financ Law Rev 10:75–112
Schläfke H (2013) Vermögensbindung in der Kapitalgesellschaft & Co. KG als haftungsbeschränkter Personengesellschaft, Baden-Baden
Schmidt K (1992) § 160 HGB Haftung des ausscheidenden Gesellschafters. In: Schlegelberger F, Geßler E (eds) Handelsgesetzbuch Kommentar, vol 3.1, 5th edn. Munich, pp 922–927
Schmidt K (2002) Gesellschaftsrecht, 4th edn. Heymanns, Cologne
Shen W (2015) Corporate law in China – structure, governance and regulation. Sweet&Maxwell, Hong Kong
Shen W, Watters C (2014–2015) Is China creating a new business order? Rationalizing China's extraterritorial attempt to expand the veil-piercing doctrine. Northwest J Int Law Bus 35:469–556
Tang ZS, Xiao Y, Huo Z (2016) Conflict of laws in the People's Republic of China. Edward Elgar, Cheltenham
Teichmann C (2014) Die Auslandsgesellschaft & Co. Zeitschrift für Unternehmens- und Gesellschaftsrecht 43:220–251
Veil R (2006) Existenzvernichtungshaftung. Gesellschaftsrechtliche Vereinigung – VGR 10:103–121
Veil R (2008) Gesellschafterhaftung wegen existenzvernichtenden Eingriffs und materieller Unterkapitalisierung. Neue Juristische Wochenschrift – NJW 61:3264–3266
Wang W (2004) CEPA: a lawful free trade agreement under one country, two customs territories. Law Bus Rev Am 10:647–666
Wang X (王翔) (2006) Introduction to the circumstances of the revisions of the partnership enterprise law (合伙企业法修改情况介绍). http://www.npc.gov.cn/npc/xinwen/lfgz/lfdt/2006-08/28/content_352015.htm. Accessed 15 May 2020
Wang B (2007) Neue Entwicklungen im IPR der VR China. Praxis des internationalen Privat- und Verfahrensrechts 27:363–369
Wang J (2014) Company law in China: regulation of business organizations in a socialist market economy. Edward Elgar, Cheltenham
Weng J, Xia T (2007) Limited liability partnership: the best structure for funds? China Law Pract 21:97
Werthwein S (2010) Corporations and partnerships. In: Bu Y (ed) Chinese business law. C. H. Beck, Hart and Nomos, Munich/Oxford, pp 15–54
Wiedemann H (2004) Gesellschaftsrecht – Ein Lehrbuch des Unternehmens- und Verbandsrechts, Band II, Recht der Personengesellschaften. C. H. Beck, Munich
Wu Y, Geu TE (2007–2008) The new PRC limited partnership enterprise law and the limited partnership law of the United States: a selective analytical comparison. UCLA Pacific Basin Law J 25:133–178
Xiao Y, Huo Z (2005) Ordre public in China's private international law. Am J Comp Law 53:653–678

Xu C (徐春雷), Cao X (曹秀峰) (2007) A study on the administrative registration of foreign-invested partnership enterprises (外商投资合伙企业登记管理问题研究). Study on China's Administration for Industry & Commerce (中国工商管理研究) 2007(12):29–31

Yan Y (严义埙) (2006) Explanations on the revised draft of the PRC partnership enterprise law – delivered on 25 April 2006 to the 21st Session of the Standing Committee of the 10th National People's Congress (关于《中华人民共和国合伙企业法(修订草案)》的说明—2006年4月25日在第十届全国人民代表大会常务委员会第二十一次会议上). Gazette of the Standing Committee of the National People's Congress 2006 No 7 (中华人民共和国全国人民代表大会常务委员会公报2006年7号), pp 595–597

Ye F (2002) Das chinesische Gesetz über Partnerschaftsunternehmen: Im Vergleich zum deutschen Recht. Lang, Frankfurt a.M

Yu D, Feng S, Wei J (2012a) FIPs as the new investment vehicle. In: Tring D, Mok S (eds) The legal guide to FDI in China. China Law & Practice, Hong Kong, pp 9–12

Yu D, Feng S, Wei J (2012b) Foreign invested partnerships: a new vehicle for investments? China Law Pract 26(8):10–13

Yuantao X, Binxue S, Zhang D (1989) Translation of Liufang Fang: Chinese partnership. Law Contemp Probl 52:43–67

Zhang C (2017) The distorted governance model of venture capital limited partnerships in China: a political perspective. Bus Law Rev 38:234–240

Zhang Y, Du A (2014) Private equity funds in China. In: Moser MJ, Yu F (eds) Doing business in China, vol 1. Juris Publishing, Huntington, p II-5.1.2

Zheng H (2010) Bankruptcy. In: Bu Y (ed) Chinese business law. Springer, Munich, pp 221–266

Zhu C (朱慈蕴) (2008) The problem resulting from a corporation participating in a partnership as a general partner (公司作为普通合伙人投资合伙企业引发的法律思考). Mod Law Sci (现代法学) 30(5):77–85

Chapter 9
Transferable Ownership Interest

The third attribute of the standard corporate form is the characteristic of transferable ownership interest, which is named 'transferable shares' in *The Anatomy of Corporate Law*. Full transferability permits the firm to conduct business without interruptions when the identity of its owners changes.[1] This avoids the complications associated with the withdrawal of members that are common among other enterprise forms, including general partnerships.[2] Transferability of shares enhances the liquidity of shareholders' interests, making it easier for shareholders to construct and maintain diversified investment portfolios.[3] Importantly, 'fully transferable shares do not necessarily mean freely tradable shares. Even if shares are transferable, they may not be tradable without restriction in public markets, but rather just transferable among limited groups of individuals or with the approval of the current shareholders or of the corporation.'[4] While free tradability has the advantage of maximising the firm's flexibility in raising capital and increasing the liquidity of the shareholder, negotiated arrangements for sharing control and participation in management can become difficult to maintain.[5] Therefore, all of the jurisdictions analysed in *The Anatomy of Corporate Law* provide for free tradability for at least one type of enterprise, while likewise providing mechanisms for restricting transferability for others.[6]

With regard to terminology, corporations with freely tradable shares are termed 'open' or 'public' corporations, while corporations that have restrictions on the

[1] Armour et al. (2017), p. 10.
[2] Ibid, p. 10.
[3] Ibid, p. 10.
[4] Ibid, p. 10.
[5] Ibid, p. 10.
[6] Ibid, p. 10.

S. Kuntner, *China's Foreign-Invested Limited Partnership Enterprise*, China-EU Law Series 7, https://doi.org/10.1007/978-3-030-54181-1_9

tradability of their shares are termed 'closed' or 'private' corporations.[7] In addition, shares of open corporations may be listed for trading on a stock exchange, which can be referred to as 'listed' or 'publicly traded' corporations in contrast to 'unlisted' corporations.[8] The phenomenon of publicly traded limited partnerships has evolved in the US in the late 1980s.[9] Ownership interest in limited partnerships is traded on the New York Stock Exchange.[10] German law also provides an enterprise form that is a hybrid between a stock corporation and a partnership enterprise. The Kommanditgesellschaft auf Aktien (KGaA) can be traded on the stock exchange, and it is commonly described as a partnership limited by shares. However, it is recognised as a legal person by law, and based on its organisational nature, it is a corporation rather than a partnership enterprise.[11] Conversely, Chinese law does not provide for a partnership enterprise to be listed and traded on the stock exchange.[12] When a firm's shares are held by a small number of individuals whose interpersonal relationships are important to the management of the firm, it is referred to as 'closely held' as opposed to 'widely held'.[13] However, not all companies with freely tradable shares are actually listed on stock exchanges or have widely held share ownership.[14] At the same time, some closed corporations in certain jurisdictions have hundreds or thousands of shareholders, thereby having little in common with a typical closely held corporation.[15] Notably, Chinese reports from the early twentieth century state that it has been regarded as an advantage of the partnership at that time that the ownership interest could only be transferred among the existing partners, and third parties were not allowed to enter the closed circle of partners.[16]

Transferability of shares is closely connected to two other characteristics of a standard corporate form: legal personality and limited liability.[17]

'Transferability of shares is the flipside of the [strong form] liquidation protection that the corporation's legal personality assures to its contractual counterparties. Precisely because counterparties can be confident that the "bundle of contracts" that constitutes the firm will be kept together, there is no need for a rule requiring owners to continue to participate.'[18] In the absence of the legal frame of an enterprise, counterparties would be concerned that an assignment of their contracts

---

[7]Ibid, p. 10.

[8]Ibid, p. 10.

[9]Ribstein (1988), p. 874.

[10]Ibid, pp. 835, 860.

[11]For more detail regarding the KGaA, see Raiser and Veil (2015), pp. 389–411.

[12]See Sect. 3.2.3.3.

[13]Armour et al. (2017), p. 11.

[14]Ibid, p. 11.

[15]Ibid, p. 11.

[16]Yuantao et al. (1989), p. 46.

[17]Armour et al. (2017), p. 11.

[18]Ibid, p. 10.

would reduce the value of their expected performance and hence wish to restrict it.[19] This is the reason why it is common among jurisdictions to provide a default rule prohibiting the assignment of most contracts without prior consent of the other contracting party.[20]

> Legal personality addresses these problems by enabling the simultaneous transfer of all, but no less than all, of a firm's contracts by transferring the corporation's shares. In other words, it permits the free transferability of all of a firm's contracts taken together ('bundle assignability'), while preserving the general default rule that makes individual contracts non-assignable without consent of the contractual counterparty.[21]

The second prerequisite for transferable shares is limited liability, because it facilitates the development of an efficient market in the firm's shares.[22] Without limited liability, a purchaser must be prepared to purchase an interest in the firm as well as to assume a guarantee of its debts, which leads to the purchaser fully investigating the financial structure of the company to assess its insolvency prospects.[23] In such a scenario, the seller is likewise subject to lingering liability, which forces him to guarantee debts of a firm he no longer controls.[24] The seller cannot negate his liability without the consent of the creditors, which is unlikely to be granted unless all debts are paid.[25] In addition, the other owners of the company would insist on the right to block sales to new owners in order to screen the purchasers' credit and managerial skills.[26] This advantage of enabling a market for ownership interest is also recognised to exist in the limited partnership, despite the personal liability of the general partners.[27] However, 'that limited liability facilitates the development of an efficient market in limited partnership interests does not mean that there will actually be such a market; this depends on whether the firm is publicly or closely held'.[28] In the absence of either legal personality or limited liability, the creditworthiness of a firm as whole could change, perhaps fundamentally, should the identity of its shareholders change.[29] In consequence, the value of shares would be difficult to assess for potential purchasers.[30] In addition, transferability of shares constitutes a strategy to resolve agency problems within a company, as it provides shareholders with an option to exit the company.[31] 'It is therefore not surprising that

[19] Ibid, p. 10.
[20] Ibid, p. 10.
[21] Ibid, p. 10.
[22] Ribstein (1988), p. 864.
[23] Ibid, p. 844.
[24] Ibid, p. 844.
[25] Ibid, pp. 844–845.
[26] Ibid, p. 845.
[27] Ibid, p. 864.
[28] Ibid, p. 864 fn. 93.
[29] Armour et al. (2017), p. 11.
[30] Ibid, p. 11.
[31] Enriques (2004), pp. 1015–1016.

strong-form legal personality, limited liability, and transferable shares tend to go together, and are all features of the standard corporate form everywhere. This contrasts with the conventional general partnership, which lacks all of these features.'[32] Regarding limited partnership enterprises, however, the following analysis will show whether the FILPE with a foreign corporate general partner can be structured in such a way that the feature of transferable ownership interest is fulfilled.

In general, the transfer of ownership interest is only one of various ways in which a membership right in an enterprise can be acquired and lost.[33] For the acquisition of a membership right, three categories can be differentiated: (1) participation in the establishment of the enterprise; (2) subsequently joining the enterprise; and (3) legal succession.[34] Likewise, three categories of losing the membership right can be distinguished: (1) dissolution of the enterprise; (2) withdrawal or exclusion from the enterprise; and (3) legal succession.[35] In both regards, legal succession includes succession by inheritance and succession by assignment.[36] For corporations, legal succession is the standard method of transferring its shares.[37] For partnership enterprises, however, many jurisdictions have struggled to grasp the legal transfer of ownership interest. It is understood either as a combination of the withdrawal of the transferor and the joining of the transferee, or as a direct legal succession of the ownership interest from the transferor to the transferee.[38] For a comprehensive analysis of this issue with regard to Chinese law, the different methods of acquiring and losing an ownership interest in the FILPE are considered in this section—beginning with a summary of the findings with regard to the ownership interest in a FILPE.

9.1 The Ownership Interest in a FILPE

Some of the essential legal issues around the transferability of ownership interest in a FILPE are also preliminary questions with regard to its legal personality, and therefore have been analysed in the preceding analysis above. These findings are briefly summarised to define the foundation for the following analysis. A FILPE is recognised under Chinese law as a separate legal entity in the form of a non-legal-person organisation.[39] The property of the FILPE is owned by the partnership

[32]Armour et al. (2017), p. 11.

[33]Schmidt (2002), pp. 551–552.

[34]Ibid, p. 551.

[35]Ibid, p. 552.

[36]Ibid, p. 551.

[37]Ibid, p. 551.

[38]With regard to German law, see Schmidt (2002), pp. 1320–1325.

[39]See Sect. 7.1.1.1.

enterprise, not by the individual partners.[40] The equivalent to the 'share of ownership' in a corporation is the ownership interest in a FILPE, which is termed as 'share of the property in the partnership enterprise' in the PEL. Dogmatically, strong arguments support the understanding of ownership interest of a partner as a comprehensive and inseparable membership right in the partnership enterprise that unites the financial rights and all other core rights and obligations of a partner in a single legal position which can be transferred to a third party.[41] This understanding corresponds with the nature of the FILPE as a separate legal entity. However, the following analysis will also address how the same result, a unified transfer of all a partner's rights and obligations, can be ensured through contractual arrangements. The consequences that a transfer of the ownership interest has for the FILPE, and its creditors and partners, have already been touched upon in the above analysis of the legal personality and limited liability. These findings will also be integrated into the following analysis.

9.2 Establishment and Dissolution of a FILPE

With few exceptions, the establishment and the dissolution of a FILPE are subject to the same regulations. Therefore, they are analysed together.

9.2.1 Establishment

9.2.1.1 Establishing a FILPE

The preconditions for establishing a FILPE are stipulated in Article 14 PEL. The registration process of a FILPE is governed by Article 6 FIPE Provisions, and subsequently by the Partnership Enterprise Registration Measures. These regulations have already been analysed above.[42] The formation of a partnership enterprise requires the participation of a minimum of two partners.[43] With respect to a limited partnership enterprise, at least one of the partners must become a general partner and at least one other partner must act as limited partner.[44] In order to qualify as a FILPE, at least one of the partners must be a foreign enterprise or individual.[45] The establishment of the FILPE takes effect on the date on which the business licence

[40] Art. 20 PEL.

[41] For a detailed explanation, see Sect. 7.1.2.1.

[42] See Sect. 4.1.8.

[43] Art. 14 Para. 1 PEL.

[44] Art. 2 Para. 3 PEL.

[45] Art. 2 FIPE Provisions.

for the FIPE is issued by SAMR.[46] From that moment on, the investors become the founding partners of the FILPE.

9.2.1.2 Permitted Partners in a FILPE

In principle, the scope of potential partners in a FILPE is defined in Article 2 FIPE Provisions. Regarding foreign partners, it extends to foreign enterprises and individuals; regarding Chinese partners, it encompasses Chinese natural persons, legal persons, and other Chinese organisations. Several aspects with regard to these potential partners have already been addressed in the previous analysis. Conflict of laws' provisions must be considered to determine whether a foreign enterprise qualifies as corporate general partner under the FIPE Legislation.[47] Chinese wholly state-owned companies, state-owned enterprises, listed companies, public welfare institutions and social organisations are barred from acting as general partner in a FILPE.[48] However, two aspects regarding the scope of partners still require further analysis: the upper limit on the number of limited partners in a FILPE, and the innovation of Chinese natural persons being allowed to invest together with foreign investors. While these aspects are analysed in regard to the establishment of the FILPE, they are likewise important for joining partners, and the question to whom an ownership interest in a FILPE can be transferred.

9.2.1.2.1 Restricted Number of Partners in a Limited Partnership Enterprise

Art. 61, para 1 PEL provides that a limited partnership enterprise is to be established by between two and fifty partners, with at least one partner acting as a general partner. This caps the number of limited partners at a maximum of 49. Notably, no similar limitation exists for the number of partners in a general partnership enterprise. This is explained with the nature of the general partnership enterprise.[49] Because all the partners bear unlimited liability and represent and operate the partnership enterprise jointly together, the required coordination between the partners practically makes it impossible to have a large number of general partners.[50] The PEL therefore does not have to stipulate a maximum number of partners for the general partnership enterprise.[51] The limited partnership differs insofar as the role of the limited partner is very similar to that of a passive investor. This allows to multiply the number of partners without causing interruptions of the normal business

[46] Art. 17 FIPE Provisions. See also Sect. 4.1.8.3.

[47] See analysis in Sect. 8.2.2.2.1.

[48] See analysis in Sect. 8.2.2.1.

[49] Li (李飞) (ed) (2006), p. 99.

[50] Ibid, p. 99.

[51] Ibid, p. 99.

operation of the limited partnership enterprise.[52] In certain jurisdictions, therefore, limited partnership enterprises can have tens of thousands of limited partners.[53] The original draft of the 2006 revision of the PEL likewise did not impose any restrictions on the total number of limited partners.[54] However, during the deliberation of the draft law, members of the SCNP raised concerns about the fact that a partnership enterprise is defined by the personal element of the interaction of its partners.[55] If the number of partners is so large that they cannot know each other personally, it is feared that this personal characteristic of the partnership enterprise perishes.[56] Furthermore, a limited partnership enterprise that invites a large number of investors to raise funds is *de facto* similar to the public offering of securities.[57] Without proper regulation, the limited partnership enterprise could be abused for illegal fundraising activities.[58] The limited partnership system in China is relatively new, and no sufficient experience has been gained in the country to encourage investors to become a limited partner, and to implement effective measures to protect investors from such abuses.[59] Experience in German law, which does not cap the number of partners, shows that limited partnership enterprises with a large number of limited partners cause various legal problems.[60] They are therefore classified as a separate category of limited partnership enterprises in Germany, the so called 'Publikumspersonengesellschaften'. The special issues associated with these enterprises are subject to numerous court decisions and controversies among legal scholars.[61] In Germany, these complications are also accredited to the fact that the laws governing partnership enterprises were originally drafted to govern small and medium size enterprises with few partners who have a personal relationship among themselves.[62] Therefore, the upper level of limited partners under the PEL can be understood as a precautionary measure by the Chinese lawmaker.[63] The 'magic number' of fifty partners corresponds with the regulation in Article 24 Company Law, which stipulates that a Chinese limited liability company may at most have fifty shareholders. Notably, the EJV Law and CJV Law made no stipulations in this regard; the limitation of the Company Law likewise applied for these enterprise forms.[64] While the limitation to fifty partners in Article 61, Paragraph 1 PEL is a

[52]Ibid, p. 99.

[53]Ibid, p. 99.

[54]Chen (2016), p. 658.

[55]Li (李飞) (ed) (2006), pp. 99–100.

[56]Ibid, pp. 99–100.

[57]Ibid, p. 100.

[58]Hong (洪虎) (2006), pp. 602, 603.

[59]Li (李飞) (ed) (2006), p. 100.

[60]Julius and Bitter (2005), p. 63.

[61]Instructive: Schmidt (2002), pp. 1665–1688.

[62]Julius and Bitter (2005), p. 63.

[63]Li (李飞) (ed) (2006), p. 100.

[64]See Sect. 3.1.3.

mandatory provision, it simultaneously provides that this restriction applies 'unless otherwise specified by law'. The lawmaker thus allows for the further development of the limited partnership enterprise as investment vehicle, and leaves room to gradually open it to a larger number of investors in specific industries or sectors.[65] While some commentators have criticised the cap on the number of partners as significantly restricting the fundraising capabilities of the limited partnership enterprise in China,[66] the reasoning of the lawmaker for this restraint seems rather sensible.

9.2.1.2.2 Chinese Individuals Investing Together with Foreign Investors

The FIPE Provisions allow foreign enterprises or foreign individuals to establish a partnership enterprise together with Chinese individuals.[67] This is a significant change as regards former foreign investment rules, as Chinese individuals had not been allowed directly to invest in an EJV or CJV together with a foreign investor up to that point.[68] Only Chinese enterprises or other economic organisations were allowed to do so. As an often-used workaround, Chinese individuals would first establish a company, e.g., a one-person limited liability company, which could subsequently form an EJV or CJV together with a foreign investor. Commentators have regarded the opening up of the investment options for Chinese individuals as a sign of increasing confidence of the Chinese government in the abilities of its citizens to make independent investment decisions.[69] This change of policy is particularly interesting as the FIPE Provisions apparently contravene Article 18, Paragraph 1 of the Constitution of the PRC, which may permit foreign enterprises and individuals to invest in China and enter into economic cooperation with 'Chinese enterprises and other Chinese economic organisations', but fails to include Chinese individuals in this provision. However, commentators have pointed out that, in the Chinese legal system, conflicts with the constitution should not be viewed strictly dogmatically, as long as the actual practice is tolerated and regarded with favour by the leadership of the CPC.[70] Examples of joint ventures between Chinese individuals and foreign investors can be found as early as 1984, and have even been stipulated in local government regulations in Beijing in 2004.[71] Compared to the EJV and CJV, the scope of potential partners in a FILPE was therefore broader.[72] However, with the promulgation of the FIL Implementing Regulations, it has been clarified that

[65] Li (李飞) (ed) (2006), p. 100.
[66] Zhang (2015), p. 48.
[67] Art. 2 FIPE Provisions.
[68] Jiao and Kasteleijn (2011), p. 52.
[69] Ibid, p. 52; Liu (2010), p. 39.
[70] von Senger (2006), pp. 54–55.
[71] Ibid, p. 53; Li (2007), p. 35ff.
[72] Lu (吕美昂) (2011), pp. 81–82.

foreign investors are now expressly permitted to make investments in China jointly with Chinese individuals, irrespective of the enterprise form.[73] The PEL further clarifies in Article 14, Paragraph 1 that 'a natural person shall have the full capacity for civil conduct'. With regard to Chinese natural persons, this is regulated in Articles 9–15 GPCL/Articles 13–25 GRCL. Regarding a foreign natural person, the Foreign-Related Civil Relations Law stipulates in Article 12, Paragraph 1 that the capacity for civil conduct shall be governed by the laws of his habitual residence. In case the foreign natural person engages in civil activities for which he has no capacity under the laws of his habitual residence, but he has capacity for such civil conduct in accordance with Chinese law, Article 12, Paragraph 2 provides that the latter shall prevail. This could be relevant when, for example, a nineteen year-old natural person becomes a partner in a FILPE, but the laws of his habitual residence only grant full capacity for civil conduct from the age of twenty rather than eighteen as in China.[74]

9.2.2 *Dissolution and Liquidation*

The dissolution of a partnership enterprise is the termination of the partnership agreement between the partners due to reasons stipulated by law or upon agreement by the partners.[75] The dissolution halts the business activities of the partnership enterprise and leads to its liquidation, at the end of which the membership rights of all partners cease to exist.[76] For the dissolution and liquidation of a FILPE, Article 7 FIPE Measures declares applicable the respective provisions of the PEL. In the PEL, the fourth Chapter (Articles 85–92) is reserved to regulate the dissolution and liquidation of the partnership enterprise. Details regarding the procedure and filing requirements with the relevant authorities are provided in the chapter on 'cancelation of registration' in the FIPE Provisions (Articles 31–34). It reflects the relevant chapter in the Partnership Enterprise Registration Measures (Articles 21–24) in most regards. The following sub-sections analyse the reasons behind dissolution of a FILPE and the liquidation process.

9.2.2.1 Reasons for Dissolution

The PEL stipulates a number of grounds upon which the partnership enterprise must be dissolved. The main provision is the list of seven grounds in Article 85 PEL, plus the additional cause in Article 75 PEL that exclusively applies to limited partnership

[73] Art. 3 FIL Implementing Regulations.

[74] Xu (徐春雷) and Cao (曹秀峰) (2007), pp. 29–30.

[75] Li (李飞) (ed) (2006), p. 135.

[76] Ibid, p. 135.

enterprises. These grounds for dissolution can be divided into two categories. One comprises the arbitrary grounds, that is, the dissolution is based on the partners' decision. The first three items of Article 85 PEL fall within this category. The second category are the statutorily prescribed grounds, that is, laws and administrative regulations forcing the dissolution of the partnership enterprise. The last four items of Article 85 PEL and the regulation in Article 75 PEL belong to this category. Each of these reasons for dissolution will be analysed briefly.

Article 85, Number 1 PEL provides for dissolution when the intended term of operation of the partnership enterprise, as determined in the partnership agreement, expires, and the partners 'decide not to continue the business operation'. To define a specific term of operation for the partnership enterprise is not uncommon in China.[77] One of the reasons is that the conditions under which a partner may withdraw from a partnership enterprise differ depending on whether a term has been specified.[78] Article 7, Paragraph 2 FIPE Provisions stipulates that if a term is specified in the partnership agreement, this information must be registered with the relevant authorities. The partnership enterprise shall be dissolved if the partners decide not to continue its business operation. Among Chinese scholars, it has been disputed how to proceed with the partnership enterprise if only a minority of the partners decides against continuing the business operation.[79] While some argued that this should still cause the dissolution, others argued that the partnership enterprise shall remain in existence but those partners who oppose continuing the business operation shall have the right to withdraw from the partnership enterprise.[80] The wording of Article 85, Number 1 PEL does not require a unanimous decision by all partners, in contrast to the provision in Article 85, Number 3 PEL. A list of matters that generally require the consent of all partners is provided in Article 31 PEL. This list does not include the question at hand. Consequently, the general stipulations in Article 30, Paragraph 1 PEL on voting among the partners applies. Unless otherwise stipulated in the partnership agreement, each partner has one vote, with the question whether to discontinue the partnership operation being subject to a majority of more than half of all the partners.[81] When only a minority of partners opposes the continuation of the partnership enterprise, this does not cause its liquidation. The question whether these partners shall have a right to withdraw from the partnership enterprise, will be addressed in the subsequent analysis.[82] To avoid any ambiguities, it would be advisable to specify the voting mechanisms for Article 85, Number 1 PEL in the partnership agreement.

Article 85, Number 2 PEL provides for dissolution if 'any cause for dissolution that is specified in the partnership agreement arises'. This provision is an expression

---

[77] Ibid, p. 30.

[78] Arts. 45–46 PEL. See also Sects. 7.1.2.2 and 9.3.2.1.1.

[79] Ye (2002), pp. 137–138.

[80] Ibid, pp. 137–138.

[81] Art. 30 Para. 1 PEL.

[82] See Sect. 9.3.2.1.1.

of the party autonomy that characterises partnership enterprises. Partners are free to define reasons for dissolution in the partnership agreement, as long as they do not violate any laws or regulations.[83] An example of such circumstances could be the death of a partner.[84] However, considering the interest of an investor to ensure continuance of the partnership enterprise, stipulating any circumstance that causes its dissolution should be considered carefully.

Article 85, Number 3 PEL codifies the dissolution when 'all the partners decide to dissolve' the partnership enterprise. A partnership enterprise is established based on the willingness of all partners to do so; naturally, it can also be dissolved based on such will among the partners.[85] This is irrespective of whether the partnership was formed with a fixed term.[86] However, the provision explicitly requires that all the partners consent to the dissolution. In general, the decision to dissolve the partnership enterprise can also be formed by implication, e.g. through discontinuance of the business operation.[87] To avoid ambiguity, it would be advisable to stipulate certain formal requirements in the partnership agreement for such a fundamental decision. Notably, an EJV and WFOE can also be dissolved by a shareholder resolution in accordance with Article 180, Number 2 Company Law. However, MOFCOM has often denied the required approval for a voluntary dissolution, and was only willing to approve a compulsory dissolution in accordance with Article 180, Number 3–5 Company Law.[88] This has made it more difficult for a foreign investor effectively to de-invest from an EJV and WFOE, compared to a FILPE.[89] It remains to be seen if, in the light of the latest reforms, the de-investments from an FIE that is directly governed by the Company Law will become easier.

Article 85, Number 4 stipulates dissolution is required in the event that 'the number of partners does not meet the statutory minimum requirement for 30 days'. A limited partnership enterprise must have at least two partners, of whom at least one must be a general partner.[90] Because of the death, withdrawal or exclusion of partners, the number of remaining partners can drop below two partners. In this event, the remaining general partner has thirty days to find new partners, or otherwise must dissolve the partnership enterprise. *Lin* criticises this regulation for generating uncertainties for the continuity of a limited partnership enterprise.[91] She points out that Singaporean law allows a limited partnership enterprise with

[83]Li (李飞) (ed) (2006), p. 136.

[84]Ye (2002), p. 138.

[85]Li (李飞) (ed) (2006), p. 136.

[86]Gao (高富平) et al. (1997), p. 268.

[87]Ye (2002), p. 139.

[88]Shen and Weidlich (2016), p. 182.

[89]For a detailed analysis of the MOFCOM approval-requirements with regard to FIEs, see Sect. 9.2.2.2.

[90]Art. 14 Para. 1, Art. 61 PEL When a FILPE loses all of its foreign partners, this does not automatically cause dissolution of the FILPE. The consequences are analysed below in Sect. 9.3.4.

[91]Lin and Yeo (2010), p. 106.

only one partner—who must be a general partner—to remain in operation, which ensures business stability and economic efficiency.[92] However, the PEL does not order the immediate dissolution but allows an interim period of thirty days for the remaining general partner to find new investors, whereas under German partnership law, a partnership enterprise is terminated immediately, and without liquidation, if only one partner remains.[93]

Article 75 PEL is a special provision applicable to limited partnership enterprises that complements the regulation in Article 85, Number 4 PEL. It provides that a limited partnership enterprise shall be dissolved 'when it only has limited partners'. The combination of unlimited and limited liability of partners is a defining characteristic of the limited partnership enterprise relied on by its creditors.[94] Article 61, Paragraph 2 PEL therefore stipulates that a limited partnership enterprise must have at least one general partner, and cannot consist of limited partners alone. However, a limited partnership enterprise without any general partners does not fulfil this basic criterion, and should no longer exist as a partnership enterprise.[95] Notably, while Article 85, Number 4 PEL grants a transition period of thirty days to regain the minimum number of partners, Article 75 PEL does not stipulate a similar time frame. Based on the wording, the dissolution of the limited partnership enterprise appears to be effective immediately. Conversely, German partnership law does not expressly codify the consequences when the only general partner leaves the partnership enterprise.[96] However, German courts have decided that the remaining limited partners have up to three months to find a new general partner.[97] Otherwise, the limited partnership enterprise is dissolved, and transformed into a general partnership enterprise if its business operation is carried on.[98] *Lin* criticises the regulation in Article 75 PEL, pointing out that, in the PE industry, limited partnership enterprises make long-term investments in a number of companies.[99] Forcing a limited partnership enterprise to be dissolved would create unnecessary costs and adversely affect the operation of the investee's portfolio companies, which largely rely on the funding and management of the PE fund.[100] Therefore, a limited partnership enterprise with only limited partners should be allowed to continue operating as a limited partnership enterprise over a grace period so as to explore possible options and attract incoming general partners.[101]

---

[92]Ibid, p. 106.

[93]Schmidt (2002), pp. 1304–1305.

[94]Li (李飞) (ed) (2006), p. 121.

[95]Ibid, p. 122.

[96]Binz and Sorge (2018), p. 160.

[97]Ibid, p. 161.

[98]Ibid, p. 161.

[99]Lin (2017), p. 203.

[100]Ibid, p. 203.

[101]Ibid, p. 203.

Article 85, Number 5 PEL prescribes dissolution when 'the objectives of the partnership, as specified in the partnership agreement, have been achieved or it is impossible to achieve them'. The objective of the partnership enterprise describes the goal that it aims to pursue.[102] The objective is one of the mandatory items that must be specified in the partnership agreement.[103] When the purpose of the partnership enterprise has been achieved, or it has become impossible to achieve, there is no need for the partnership enterprise to continue to exist.[104] The impossibility to achieve the objective can result from factual reasons or legal reasons.[105] However, it is not clear how the impossibility is to be determined. *Lin* points out that this regulation can therefore be used as a strong sword, e.g. in a conflict between a limited partner and the managing general partner.[106] If the limited partner can prove that the partnership enterprise cannot reasonably carry on because of the alleged wrongdoing of the general partner, the partnership enterprise is at risk of dissolution.[107] Because of the ambiguity that is inherent in determining when the objective of a partnership enterprise can no longer be achieved, the German lawmaker opted not to include this in the list of mandatory causes for dissolution.[108] This underlines the importance of carefully drafting the wording when specifying the objective of a FILPE in the partnership agreement.

Article 85, Number 6 PEL calls for dissolution when the partnership enterprise 'in accordance with the law is revoked of its business licence, or it is ordered to close down or is cancelled'. This addresses the scenario when a partnership enterprise is subject to administrative punishment by the competent authorities for violating laws or regulations, and has therefore been deprived of its right to continue business operations.[109] Such a partnership enterprise is regarded as having lost the qualification as an independent legal entity, and therefore should be dissolved.[110] Relevant provisions that provide for administrative punishments are scattered throughout industry specific laws and regulations.

Finally, Article 85, Number 7 PEL is a catch-all clause that stipulates dissolution for 'other reasons specified by laws or administrative regulations'. In order to ensure the economic and social development of China, other laws and administrative regulations may directly stipulate the dissolution of the partnership enterprise

[102]See Sect. 4.1.9.3 fn. 439.

[103]Art. 18 No 2 PEL.

[104]Li (李飞) (ed) (2006), p. 136.

[105]Gao (高富平) et al. (1997), p. 269.

[106]Lin (2011), p. 219.

[107]Ibid, p. 219.

[108]Schmidt (2002), p. 1512.

[109]Li (李飞) (ed) (2006), p. 136.

[110]Ibid, p. 136.

under certain circumstances.[111] This regulation has the purpose of harmonising the PEL with other laws and regulations.[112]

9.2.2.2 Liquidation as Consequences of Dissolution

The occurrence of one of the reasons for dissolution does not mean that the partnership enterprise will immediately be terminated and disappear.[113] Upon dissolution, the partnership enterprise is subject to liquidation by liquidators.[114] Liquidation describes the legal process during which the debts of the partnership enterprise are cleared, its remaining assets are distributed, and application for the cancellation of its registration is submitted to the relevant authorities.[115] Liquidation is a mandatory procedure for the termination of a partnership enterprise.[116] The purpose of liquidation is to protect the interest of the partners and the creditors of the partnership enterprise.[117] During its liquidation of the partnership enterprise, the partnership enterprise undergoes certain changes in nature and function.[118] The partnership enterprise still holds the qualification as an independent civil subject, but its rights and capabilities are subject to certain restrictions.[119] The scope of activities that the partnership enterprise can engage in is limited to matters related to its liquidation; it may no longer engage in its normal business operation.[120] If the partnership enterprise were to enter into new contracts and establish new rights and obligations towards third parties, this would undermine the actual purpose of the liquidation, and thereby not be 'conducive to the stability of China's social and economic order'.[121]

After the dissolution, the liquidator functions as the executor who is legally responsible for carrying out the liquidation procedure.[122] As a default rule, the PEL provides in Article 86, Paragraph 2 that all partners shall serve as liquidators. This would include the limited partners as well. However, by a voting majority of at least half of the partners, one or several of the partners, or a third person, may be entrusted to act as liquidators.[123] The timeframe to appoint a liquidator is fifteen days

[111]Ibid, pp. 136–137.
[112]Ibid, p. 137.
[113]Ibid, p. 141.
[114]Art. 86 Para. 1 PEL.
[115]Li (李飞) (ed) (2006), p. 137.
[116]Ibid, p. 137.
[117]Ibid, p. 137.
[118]Ibid, p. 135.
[119]Ibid, p. 141.
[120]Art. 88 Para. 3 PEL.
[121]Li (李飞) (ed) (2006), p. 141.
[122]Ibid, p. 137.
[123]Art. 86 Para. 2 PEL.

after the cause for dissolution has occurred.[124] If no liquidator has been appointed at that point, the partners or creditors may apply to the People's Court for the appointment of liquidators.[125] Article 86, Paragraph 2 PEL is a default provision.[126] The partners can stipulate a regulation for determining the liquidator already in the partnership agreement.[127] The names of the appointed liquidators of a FILPE shall be filed on record with SAMR within ten days of their designation.[128] The PEL does not provide stipulations for the dismissal of a liquidator. According to Chinese scholars, a liquidator can be dismissed through the appointment of a new liquidator by a majority vote of the other partners.[129] Liquidators exercise their duties as representatives of the partnership enterprise: they participate in civil litigation, arbitration and other matters on behalf of the partnership enterprise.[130] If more than one liquidator have been appointed, they can only represent the partnership enterprise jointly, that is, each liquidator cannot exercise his powers alone.[131] The core duties of the liquidator are stipulated in Article 87 PEL: (1) clearing the property of the partnership enterprise, preparing separate statements of assets and liabilities of the partnership enterprise, and an inventory of its property; (2) handling the outstanding business affairs of the partnership enterprise. This refers to rounding off contractual matters that have been entered into but not yet performed by the partnership enterprise.[132] The liquidator may decide to continue or to terminate the contractual relationships, depending on the circumstances.[133] However, an exceptional right to terminate a contract because of the liquidation is not granted under Chinese law. If the termination constitutes a breach of contract, the partnership enterprise must bear the corresponding liabilities, and pay damages and compensation from the property of the partnership enterprise.[134] In handling the outstanding business affairs, the liquidator thus must balance the aim to complete liquidation as soon as possible against protecting the legitimate interest of all creditors of the partnership enterprise.[135] Furthermore, the liquidator shall (3) pay any outstanding taxes; (4) settle creditor's rights and debts; (5) distribute the residual property of the partnership enterprise after paying off all debts according to the regulation in Article 89 PEL;[136] (6) represent the partnership enterprise in litigation and arbitration. An

[124] Art. 86 Para. 2 PEL.

[125] Art. 86 Para. 3 PEL.

[126] Li (李飞) (ed) (2006), p. 142.

[127] Ibid, p. 142.

[128] Art. 31 FIPE Provisions.

[129] Li (李飞) (ed) (2006), p. 142.

[130] Ibid, p. 138.

[131] Ibid, pp. 137, 143.

[132] Ibid, p. 139.

[133] Ibid, p. 139.

[134] Ibid, p. 139.

[135] Ibid, p. 139.

[136] For a detailed analysis, see Sect. 7.1.1.2.

additional responsibility of the liquidator is codified in Article 88 PEL. Within ten days of being appointed as liquidator, he shall notify the creditors of the partnership enterprise of the dissolution, and publish a corresponding announcement in a newspaper within sixty days.[137] Notably, under German law, the dissolution of the partnership enterprise must already be registered with the local court to fulfil the obligation to inform creditors and the public,[138] while the PEL does not provide for the dissolution to be registered with SAMR. For a creditor to declare his rights, the PEL stipulates a timeframe of thirty days from notice, or forty five days from the public announcement if he did not receive a notice.[139] When declaring his rights to the liquidator, a creditor shall specify the circumstances of the concerned right, particularly the date, nature, amount and maturity date of the right, and provide sufficient evidence such as contracts, debits, and other documents.[140] The liquidator on his part shall register all creditor's rights that have been adequately substantiated.[141]

Upon completion of the liquidation, the liquidator shall prepare a liquidation report that summarises the liquidation process with reports about the assets of the partnership enterprise before dissolution, the settled partnership affairs, creditor rights and debts, and the final distribution of the remaining assets.[142] The liquidation report shall verify that the rights of the creditors and partners were rightfully observed and satisfied during the liquidation process.[143] Given the significance of the liquidation report, Article 90 PEL stipulates two instances of supervision: the liquidation report must be confirmed by all partners (signed and sealed) and approved by SAMR. In order to ensure a timely liquidation, the lawmaker does not grant each creditor the right to review the liquidation report.[144] The revision and approval through SAMR shall therefore serve as a safeguard for the creditor's rights.[145] In order to protect the rights and interest of the creditors and partners during the liquidation process, the PEL also provides corresponding administrative measures. Article 100 PEL grants SAMR the right to order the liquidator to submit the liquidation report or to correct false statements in the report, and any expenses and losses resulting thereof shall be borne by the liquidator.[146] Articles 101 and 102 PEL stipulate that if the liquidator infringes on the rights and interests of

[137] Art. 88 Para. 1 PEL. The newspaper shall be a local newspaper of the place of registration of the partnership enterprise (Li (李飞) (ed) 2006, p. 140).

[138] Art. 143 Para. 1 HGB; Schmidt (2002), pp. 1509–1510.

[139] Art. 88 Para. 1 PEL.

[140] Art. 88 Para. 2 PEL; Li (李飞) (ed) (2006), p. 140.

[141] Art. 88 Para. 2 PEL.

[142] Art. 90 PEL; Li (李飞) (ed) (2006), p. 143.

[143] Ibid, p. 143.

[144] Ibid, p. 143.

[145] Ibid, p. 143.

[146] Article 56 FIPE Provisions restates the provisions of Article 100 PEL.

creditors, the partnership enterprise or other partners, he shall bear the civil liability for damages and losses.

After the liquidation report has been signed by all partners, the liquidator must submit the liquidation report to SAMR within fifteen days to apply for cancellation of the FILPE's registration.[147] The SAMR responsible for the cancellation of the registration is the SAMR that originally registered the FILPE.[148] The documents that need to be submitted for cancelling the registration are listed in Article 33 FIPE Provision. With the cancellation of the enterprise registration by SAMR, the FILPE is terminated.[149] The liability that the general partner bears in accordance with Article 91 PEL after a FILPE has been de-registered and terminated has already been analysed in the previous chapter.[150]

In one important aspect for foreign investors, the liquidation of a FILPE is less bureaucratic than the liquidation of other FIEs. In contrast to domestic corporations, the dissolution and liquidation of an EJV, CJV, and WFOE required prior approval from MOFCOM—in certain cases.[151] The circumstances under which a prior MOFCOM approval is required, are stipulated in the 'Circular on Deregistration after Dissolution of FIEs'.[152] Taking an EJV as example, dissolution due to the following causes triggers the requirement for MOFCOM approval: inability to continue its business operation due to incurrence of severe losses, or severe losses caused by force majeure such as natural disasters; failing to reach the business objective of the EJV, and lack of a development prospect; any other reason for dissolution specified in the joint venture contract or articles of association.[153] Under what circumstances MOFCOM may approve or deny the required approval is not further regulated.[154] This leaves great discretionary power to the local authorities, who will usually try to keep a foreign investment within their jurisdiction.[155] It has not been uncommon that MOFCOM would try to postpone the liquidation and require the foreign investor to undertake restructuring measures for the EJV.[156] Reportedly, the dissolution and liquidation of a FIE has therefore taken up to several years.[157] Therefore, this approval requirement can significantly limit the freedom of

[147] Art. 90 PEL, Art. 7 FIPE Measures.

[148] Art. 32 FIPE Provisions.

[149] Art. 34 FIPE Provisions.

[150] See analysis in Sect. 8.4.3.

[151] Shen and Weidlich (2016), p. 181.

[152] Circular on certain issues regarding the deregistration after dissolution of Foreign-Invested Enterprises (外商投资企业解散注销登记管理有关问题的通知), promulgated jointly by the State Administration for Industry and Commerce and the Ministry of Commerce on 20 November 2008 with effect as of the same day.

[153] Art. 2 Para. 1 Circular On Deregistration After Dissolution of FIEs in conjunction with Art. 90 Para. 1 Nos 2, 4–6 EJV Implementing Regulations.

[154] Shen and Weidlich (2016), p. 182.

[155] Ibid, p. 182.

[156] Ibid, p. 182.

[157] Ibid, p. 185.

foreign investors to strategically de-invest from an FIE when the investment turns out to be unprofitable. Because of the absence of such approval requirement for a FILPE, de-investment should be easier and faster. In the light of the implementation of the FIL, it remains to be seen what requirements are applied to the de-investments from an FIE that is directly governed by the Company Law.

A different form of liquidation is the bankruptcy liquidation that is regulated in a separate provision of the PEL. When a partnership enterprise is unable to pay off its due debts, Article 92, Paragraph 1 PEL provides its creditors the option to apply to a People's Court for bankruptcy liquidation.[158] The liability of partners after bankruptcy liquidation was analysed in the previous chapter.[159]

9.2.2.3 Converting to a Non-Partnership Enterprise Form

Related to the topic of dissolution is the question whether a FILPE can be directly converted into a corporation or other non-partnership enterprise form.[160] A practical need for such a conversion is especially recognised in the PE industry where it is not uncommon for a fund to convert to a corporate enterprise form when the fund is expanding its business.[161] The law in Delaware provides specific rules on the conversion from a partnership enterprise into a corporation,[162] whereas the PEL does not contain any regulations in this regard. In China, PE funds must therefore go through the dissolution process and re-establish themselves as a limited liability company in order to 'convert' to a corporation.[163] In view of the complexity and cost of such a conversion process, commentators suggest that the Chinese lawmaker should issue appropriate rules for conversions in order to further encourage the PE and VC industries.[164]

9.3 Joining, Withdrawal and Exclusion

Following the establishment of a FILPE, the composition of its members can change. New partners may join the partnership enterprise, and existing partners may withdraw or may be excluded from it. Because of China's unique classification of foreign-invested and domestic-invested partnership enterprises, additional

158 See analysis in Sect. 7.1.1.2.

159 See Sect. 8.4.4.

160 Regarding the conversion of a limited partnership enterprise to a general partnership enterprise, see Sect. 9.3.3.

161 Lin (2017), p. 202.

162 Ibid, p. 202.

163 Ibid, p. 202.

164 Ibid, p. 202.

regulations need to be regarded when the membership structure of a FILPE changes. Regarding changes of the membership composition within the corporate general partner of a FILPE, these are regulated by the governing law of the corporation and not part of the following analysis.[165] However, it might be advisable to include provisions in the partnership agreement of the FILPE to respond to changes of the membership structure of the corporate general partner.[166]

9.3.1 Joining a FILPE

Besides participating in the establishment of a partnership enterprise, entering into it at a later stage is another way of becoming a partner. Two modes of entering into a FILPE can be distinguished: the first is joining the existing FILPE as a new partner, the second is obtaining the ownership interest of another partner through legal succession. Joining the FILPE—which is the subject of this sub-section—is different from legal succession insofar as the group of partners is enlarged because of the additional partner who joins the partnership enterprise.[167] Allowing a joining partner to enter the partnership enterprise is therefore a common method of raising new investment capital.[168] The provisions in the FIPE Legislation on joining partners are rather straight forward, and allow for the general partner and limited partner to be analysed together.

9.3.1.1 Joining an Existing FILPE

The key regulations for joining an existing FILPE are stipulated in the PEL. Two requirements for the joining of a new partner are established in Article 43, Paragraph 1 PEL. The first condition is the consent of—generally—all partners to the admission of a new partner. The requirement of unanimous consent reflects the personal nature of a partnership enterprise.[169] Because the partners depend on each other and share (unlimited) liability, all partners shall have the right to participate in the decision on admitting a new partner.[170] Under the 1997 PEL, the unanimous consent was still a mandatory requirement.[171] Any deviating regulation in the partnership

[165] Regarding a German GmbH, see exemplary Binz and Sorge (2018), pp. 119–122, 126–127, 129–131, 156.

[166] This especially applies to an investment structure where all limited partners are also owners of the corporate general partner of the FILPE. See Sect. 5.3.2.2.1.

[167] Legal succession of the ownership interest in a FILPE is analysed in Sect. 9.4.

[168] Meyer (2016), p. 217.

[169] Li (李飞) (ed) (2006), p. 66.

[170] Ibid, p. 66.

[171] Art. 44 Para. 1 1997 PEL.

agreement would have been regarded as invalid.[172] With the revision of the PEL in 2006, this requirement was relaxed 'if the partners have agreed otherwise in the partnership agreement'.[173] This reform reflects the party autonomy of the partners, and it is an appropriate liberalisation as the personal bond and dependency is less strong in a limited partnership enterprise—which was not provided for under the 1997 PEL—than in a general partnership enterprise.[174] German law likewise leaves partners the discretion to regulate such an approval requirement in the partnership agreement.[175] As a special provision for limited partnership enterprises, Article 63, Number 5 PEL requires that the conditions and procedure for joining a FILPE must be specified in the partnership agreement. In the light of the difficulties it can cause to obtain unanimous consent from all partners, a foreign investor should therefore consider including a less rigid regulation in the partnership agreement.

The second condition is the conclusion of a written entering agreement between the joining partner and the other partners.[176] The agreement shall determine the rights and obligations of the joining partner, including his capital contribution, and accordingly adjust the rights and obligations of the other partners to avoid disputes in the future.[177] Dogmatically, the entering agreement does not constitute a re-establishment of the partnership enterprise, but is rather regarded as a mere extension of, or amendment to the original partnership agreement.[178] The form of the entering agreement must be made in writing.[179] The requirement to conclude such an agreement with a joining partner is mandatory, and any contravening provision in the partnership agreement is invalid.[180] This is however different for the transfer of ownership interest by legal succession, as will be analysed further below.[181] When concluding the entering agreement, Article 43, Paragraph 2 PEL stipulates the obligation of the existing partners to 'truthfully inform the new partner of the state of business operations and the financial status of the partnership enterprise'. This provision shall protect the joining partner who will bear (unlimited) liability after becoming a partner.[182] Before joining, he shall gain a comprehensive understanding of the financial and business status of the partnership enterprise.[183] The other partners must provide true and accurate facts, and shall not conceal

[172]Gao (高富平) et al. (1997), p. 240.

[173]Art. 43 Para. 1 PEL.

[174]Li (李飞) (ed) (2006), p. 66.

[175]Schmidt (2002), p. 1316.

[176]Art. 43 Para. 1 PEL.

[177]Li (李飞) (ed) (2006), p. 68.

[178]Ye (2002), p. 120.

[179]Art. 43 Para. 1 PEL.

[180]Li (李飞) (ed) (2006), p. 68.

[181]See Sect. 9.4.

[182]Li (李飞) (ed) (2006), p. 68.

[183]Ibid, p. 68.

relevant information.[184] Otherwise, the partners may be subject to civil liabilities should their false information cause losses to the joining partner.[185]

The legal consequences of joining a partnership enterprise are regulated in Article 44 PEL. The addition of a new partner leaves the identity of the partnership enterprise unchanged.[186] The joining partner, once accepted into the partnership enterprise, 'shall enjoy the equal rights and bear the same liability as the other partners.'[187] With becoming a member of the partnership enterprise, the new partner also obtains a share of the property in the partnership enterprise. The assignment of a new share of the property in the partnership enterprise results in the depreciation of the value rights that are associated with the other partner's membership rights. This legal consequence is unique and characteristic for the partnership enterprise. It is analysed in detail below, together with the consequences of the withdrawal of a partner.[188] The equal treatment of the new partner underlines that a partnership enterprise is established on the basis of equal consultation among partners.[189] However, the new partner joins after the initial establishment and a partnership enterprise is also characterised by party autonomy.[190] The joining partner may make his joining subject to conditions regarding the rights and obligations that he is willing to bear. Likewise, the other partners may want to impose restrictions on the rights and obligations of subsequently joining partners. Therefore, if the parties have modified the rights and obligations of the joining partner in the entering agreement, such provisions shall have prevailing effect.[191] The liability that a joining partner bears for the debts of the partnership enterprise is regulated in Article 44, Paragraph 2 PEL for the general partner, and in Article 77 PEL for the limited partner. These provisions have already been analysed in the previous section.[192]

The joining of a new partner must be registered with the competent authorities. Article 26, Paragraph 1 FIPE Provisions stipulates that the FILPE shall apply to the original registration authority for an amendment of the enterprise registration. The documents that must be submitted are listed in Article 26, Paragraph 1 in conjunction with Article 12 FIPE Provisions. Under Chinese law, this registration merely has a declaratory effect, and is not a precondition for the effectiveness of the joining. However, the FIPE Legislation stipulates a penalty of up to 20,000 RMB for failure to perform the appropriate registration.[193]

---

[184] Ibid, p. 68.

[185] Ibid, p. 68.

[186] Ye (2002), p. 130.

[187] Art. 44 Para. 1 PEL.

[188] See Sect. 9.3.2.2.

[189] Li (李飞) (ed) (2006), p. 69.

[190] Ibid, p. 69.

[191] Art. 44 Para. 1 PEL.

[192] See Sect. 8.4.2.

[193] Article 53 FIPE Provisions refers to Article 38 Partnership Enterprise Registration Measures, which reiterates the content of Article 95 Para. 2 PEL.

The described process of joining is the typical form of adding additional members to a partnership enterprise.[194] In a corporation, additional members are instead added by issuing new shares as a result of an increase of capital.[195] For an EJV, an increase of capital required a decision by the board of directors, obtaining approval from MOFCOM, and going through a change of company registration with SAMR.[196] Moreover, the joint venture contract and the articles of association of the EJV had to be updated to reflect the capital increase and the addition of a new party to the joint venture. These amendments only became effective upon receiving a further approval from MOFCOM.[197] Increasing the number of members in an EJV was therefore a much more bureaucratic and cumbersome process than in a FILPE.

9.3.1.2 Joining a Domestic-Invested Partnership Enterprise

A special variation of a joining partner occurs when a foreign investor joins a domestic-invested partnership enterprise. In addition to the provisions that have been analysed, the joining of a foreign investor causes the status of the domestic-invested partnership enterprise to change into a foreign-invested partnership enterprise. Considering the highly regulated and restrictive foreign investment regime in China, it is not self-evident that a foreign investor is allowed to join a domestic-invested partnership enterprise. However, the legal basis is provided in Article 12 FIPE Measures, which stipulates that 'in the event that a foreign enterprise or individual becomes a new partner of a partnership enterprise established in the territory of China by a Chinese natural person, legal person or other organisation, the partnership enterprise shall apply to the enterprise registration authority for change of its registration'. Article 63 FIPE Provisions further clarifies that these regulations shall apply as a reference regulation when a foreign investor joins a domestic-invested partnership enterprise. Article 65 FIPE Provisions emphasises the same for when an investor from Hong Kong, Macao or Taiwan joins a partnership enterprise 'already established by Mainland natural persons, legal persons or other organisations'.

Similarly to the establishment of a FILPE, only registration with SAMR is required when a foreign investor joins a domestic-invested partnership enterprise.[198] However, the general investment restrictions on the establishment of a FIPE likewise apply to such an investment structure.[199] In certain industries and sectors, foreign investors will therefore not be allowed to join a domestic-invested partnership

[194]Schmidt (2002), p. 551.

[195]Ibid, p. 551.

[196]Art. 21 EJV Implementing Regulations.

[197]Art. 14 EJV Implementing Regulations.

[198]Wolff (2015), pp. 159–160.

[199]Ibid, pp. 159–160.

enterprise.[200] With the joining of a foreign investor, the partnership enterprise will be regarded as a foreign-invested partnership enterprise, and thus be subject to the additional conditions that are analysed in this research project.

9.3.2 Withdrawing from a FILPE

Withdrawal refers to a partner leaving the enterprise, e.g. because he voluntarily withdraws or is excluded, with the result that the withdrawing partner loses his position as a partner and his ownership interest in the enterprise. The withdrawal is the complement to a new partner joining the enterprise. While a joining partner has to make a capital contribution, the withdrawal leads to compensation payments.[201]

Withdrawal is the alternative to remaining in the partnership enterprise until it is dissolved and liquidated. With the withdrawal, the group of partners decreases. This is one of the key differences with the transfer of ownership interest through legal succession. The analysis will show that the PEL provides a diversified and complex regime on the withdrawal of a partner. The reason is that the withdrawal of a partner is the archetypical mechanism of losing the membership right in a partnership enterprise.[202] Conversely, corporations are developed with a focus on the free tradability of shares.[203] A shareholder who wants to exit a corporation must therefore transfer his ownership interest to another shareholder or to a third party. Legal mechanisms like the exclusion of a shareholder by the other shareholders of a corporation are only gradually developing.[204] With regard to a corporate type FIE, the EJV Law, the EJV Implementing Regulations or the Company Law do not provide any stipulations on a withdrawal of shareholders. This constitutes a structural difference between the partnership enterprise and corporate type joint ventures.

For a partnership enterprise, the reasons for and consequences of the withdrawal of a partner are regulated in Articles 45–54 PEL. Of relevance for a FILPE, the PEL requires in Article 63, Number 5 PEL that the partnership agreement of a limited partnership enterprise must make stipulations with regard to 'conditions and procedure for joining and withdrawing from the limited partnership enterprise and the relevant liabilities'. Certain aspects of the withdrawal of a partner have already been addressed in the analysis of the FILPE's legal personality and liquidation protection.[205] A more thorough analysis is undertaken here, because of the importance that the withdrawal has for partners and for the partnership enterprise. In business practice, BOT-projects in the infrastructure sector are structured from the beginning

---

[200] Regarding these restrictions, see Sect. 4.1.7.

[201] Schmidt (2002), p. 1447.

[202] Ibid, p. 552.

[203] Ibid, p. 552.

[204] Ibid, p. 552.

[205] See Sect. 7.1.2.2.

so that some investors will withdraw from the enterprise after the project has been built.[206] In other sectors, such as the PE industry, investment returns are generally only realised several years after the establishment of the PE fund.[207] An early withdrawal of partners may endanger the realisation of a fund's investment goals or even directly result in the dissolution of the partnership enterprise.[208] For partners that hold a minority ownership interest in the partnership enterprise, the withdrawal right can also serve as an important governance measure in conflicts with other partners.[209] A partnership enterprise is therefore very likely to experience the withdrawal of a partner during its lifecycle.[210] In each jurisdiction, partnership legislation must strike a balance in the inevitable trade-offs between stability for the partnership enterprise and the autonomy of partners to decide on how long they want to remain invested in a certain enterprise.[211] The analysis now begins with the different causes that can lead to a partner's withdrawal and is then followed by an analysis of the consequences that a withdrawal causes.

9.3.2.1 Reasons for Withdrawal

Under the PEL, three types of withdrawals can be differentiated: (1) in a voluntary withdrawal, the partner chooses to withdraw from the partnership enterprise based on his subjective will; (2) in a statutory withdrawal, a situation arises for which the law prescribes that the partner must mandatorily withdraw from the partnership enterprise; (3) the exclusion of a partner refers to the decision of the other partners that the withdrawing partner must leave the partnership enterprise.

9.3.2.1.1 Voluntary Withdrawal

For the right to voluntarily withdraw, the PEL draws a distinction between partnership enterprises that have been formed for a fixed period and those that have been established with an indefinite term. A similar distinction is provided under German partnership law with Article 132 HGB granting an ordinary right to withdraw only for a partnership enterprise that has been established for an indefinite term. In addition, an extraordinary right to withdraw is recognised for partnership enterprises with or without a fixed term. While this right is not explicitly provided in the law, it has been stipulated by the judiciary as the lesser right for situations in which a partner may demand the dissolution of the partnership enterprise according to Article

[206] See Sect. 3.2.2.

[207] Li (李飞) (ed) (2006), p. 103.

[208] Ibid, p. 103.

[209] Lin (2011), p. 220; Hansmann et al. (2005), p. 13.

[210] Li (李飞) (ed) (2006), p. 71.

[211] DeMott (2004), p. 275.

133 HGB and Article 161, Paragraph 2 HGB.[212] Conversely, the PEL provides explicit regulations for the voluntary withdrawal from a partnership enterprise with a fixed or an indefinite term. These regulations likewise apply to general partners and limited partners.

The right to withdraw from a partnership enterprise with a fixed term is codified in Article 45 PEL. This regulation only permits a voluntary withdrawal under special circumstances.

> If the partnership agreement stipulates a fixed duration for the partnership enterprise, this means that each partner promised to cooperate with the other partners until the expiration of the set period. A partner's withdrawal before the fixed period constitutes a breach of his promise, at the same time affects the expectations of the other partners regarding the continuity of operation and may cause losses to the partnership enterprise or other partners. Therefore, the partner's voluntary withdrawal from a partnership enterprise with a fixed term is subject to certain restrictions.[213]

The circumstances under which a voluntary withdrawal is permissible, are listed in Article 45, Number 1–4 PEL. The first circumstance is 'the occurrence of a reason for withdrawal as prescribed in the partnership agreement'.[214] This reflects the partner's autonomy to stipulate grounds for an early withdrawal in the partnership agreement. The second circumstance is 'the unanimous consent of all partners to the withdrawal.'[215] Same as the previous cause, the consent of all partners is an expression of the party autonomy. Where the partners can self-impose a fixed term for the partnership enterprise, they can also agree to allow an early withdrawal of one of the partners. A withdrawal based on an agreement between the withdrawing partner and the other partners is not uncommon in business practice.[216] It allows for agreement on the conditions and compensation of the withdrawal, and often avoids lengthy disputes among the partners.[217] However, under Article 45, Number 2 PEL, it is expressly stipulated that such an agreement cannot be based on a majority decision by the other partners, but instead requires the unanimous consent of all partners. The third circumstance that allows an early withdrawal is 'the occurrence of any cause under which it is difficult for the partner to remain in the partnership enterprise'.[218] This provision is rather vague and needs to be interpreted. The lawmaker explains that the withdrawing partner must have subjective reasons that do not allow him to continue to be engaged in the partnership enterprise, and these subjective reasons must be objectively determinable.[219] Taking the relocation of a partner to a different city or a foreign country as an example, this shall not count

---

[212] Binz and Sorge (2018), pp. 124–125; Schmidt (2002), pp. 1457–1458.

[213] Li (李飞) (ed) (2006), p. 71.

[214] Art. 45 No 1 PEL.

[215] Art. 45 No 2 PEL.

[216] Schmidt (2002), pp. 1459–1460.

[217] Ibid, pp. 1459–1460.

[218] Art. 45 No 3 PEL.

[219] Li (李飞) (ed) (2006), p. 72.

as a sufficient justification for the partner not to remain in the partnership enterprise.[220] It has been concluded above that Article 85, Number 1 PEL provides for the dissolution of a partnership enterprise if the partners decide not to continue the business operation beyond its fixed term.[221] The question remains whether the partners who oppose a continuance of the partnership enterprise, but who are in the minority among the partners, shall have a right to withdraw from the partnership enterprise. Since the partners had initially agreed to form the partnership enterprise only for a limited time period, a partner's intention to adhere to this plan is a plausible subjective cause that should permit the partner to withdraw. In addition, with the renunciation of the fixed term, the minority partners can also withdraw from the partnership enterprise under the terms of Article 46 PEL for the withdrawal from a partnership enterprise with an indefinite term. The fourth and final circumstance is that 'other partners have been seriously in breach of their obligations as stipulated in the partnership agreement'.[222] A partner's violation of the duties of the partnership agreement can have a detrimental effect on the mutual trust among the partners.[223] This can deprive the other partners of the common basis for participating in the partnership enterprise, and thus shall entitle them to withdraw from it.[224] However, the PEL does not further specify when a violation of the partnership agreement is 'serious' enough to constitute such a withdrawal right for the other partners. Under German law, the reference to Article 133, Paragraph 2 HGB provides more certainty by requiring a minimum degree of intent of the partner in violation: a partner shall have the right to withdraw when 'another partner intentionally or by reason of gross negligence violates a material obligation set forth in the partnership agreement, or if the fulfilment of such an obligation becomes impossible'. Overall, it is important to note that the occurrence of the circumstances of Article 45 PEL does not mean that the affected partner must withdraw from the partnership enterprise.[225] The provision merely grants the affected partner the right to withdraw, and he can elect whether to execute this right or to remain in the partnership enterprise.[226]

The right to withdraw from a partnership enterprise with an indefinite term is codified in Article 46 PEL. This provision allows a partner to voluntarily withdraw if 'his withdrawal does not cause an adverse influence on the execution of the partnership affairs and the other partners are notified 30 days in advance'. The question when the withdrawal of a partner negatively impacts on the operation of a FILPE has already been analysed above.[227] This provision is similar to the ordinary right to withdraw under the German HGB. However, Article 132 HGB stipulates that

[220]Ibid, p. 72.

[221]See Sect. 9.2.2.1.

[222]Art. 45 No 4 PEL.

[223]Li (李飞) (ed) (2006), p. 72.

[224]Ibid, p. 72.

[225]Ye (2002), p. 123.

[226]Ibid, p. 123.

[227]See Sect. 7.1.2.2.

the notice of termination only takes effect as of the close of a fiscal year, and that it must be given at least six months before that date. In comparison, the termination period of thirty days under the PEL is significantly shorter. While the shorter termination period grants more flexibility to partners, a longer period provides more stability for the partnership enterprise.

While Articles 45 and 46 PEL lay down the rules for an orderly voluntary withdrawal, Article 47 PEL stipulates that the partner withdrawing in violation of these provisions has to compensate the losses caused to the partnership enterprise. Ultimately, Article 47 PEL grants a statutory right to withdraw from the partnership enterprise at any time against the payment of compensation.[228] This regulation takes into account the practical circumstance that a partner who is determined to end his engagement in a partnership enterprise, effectively cannot be prevented from doing so.[229] Because of the strong personal relationship and trust among the partners that characterises a partnership enterprise, it is impossible to force an unwilling partner to cooperate.[230] Therefore, the withdrawal of such a partner shall be effective after all.[231] However, since the wrongful withdrawal of a partner will most certainly affect the partnership enterprise and the other partners, the withdrawing partner is bound to bear its partnership liabilities.[232]

9.3.2.1.2 Statutory Withdrawal

Contrary to the voluntary withdrawal of a partner, the rules for statutory withdrawal in the PEL are of a mandatory nature.[233] If a partner fulfils the circumstances or conditions for which a statutory withdrawal is prescribed by law, said partner automatically loses his status as a partner, and must withdraw from the partnership enterprise.[234] Statutory withdrawal does not depend on the subjective intention of the partner, and is therefore also called involuntary withdrawal.[235] A regulation in the partnership agreement that exempts partners from the statutory withdrawal would be invalid.[236] The key provision is Article 48 PEL, which stipulates five situations that result in the statutory withdrawal of a partner. Under German law, a similar regulation is provided in Article 131, Paragraph 3 HGB, which stipulates six

228 Werthwein (2010), p. 49.

229 Li (李飞) (ed) (2006), p. 74.

230 Ibid, p. 74.

231 Ibid, p. 74.

232 Ibid, p. 74.

233 Ye (2002), p. 124.

234 Li (李飞) (ed) (2006), p. 75.

235 Ibid, p. 75. Other terms that are used are 'natural withdrawal' or 'rightful withdrawal' (Wu and Geu 2007–2008, p. 152).

236 Ye (2002), p. 124.

causes for a statutory withdrawal. The general regulation in Article 48 PEL is further modified by Articles 78 and 79 PEL with regard to limited partners.

The first cause for statutory withdrawal is that 'the partner in his capacity as a natural person dies or is legally declared dead'.[237] According to Chinese law, a natural person's capacity to perform civil acts begins at birth and ends at death.[238] If a natural person partner dies, he loses his capacity to perform civil acts, and no longer has a legal personality.[239] Consequently, he loses his qualification as a partner in the partnership enterprise.[240] However, Article 50, Paragraph 1 PEL provides that, instead of the withdrawal of the deceased general partner, his legal successor shall be entitled to inherit his share of the property in the partnership enterprise, and to take over the role of the deceased partner, if such is stipulated in the partnership agreement or all partners consent to continuing the partnership enterprise with the heir as his legal successor. Regarding the death of a limited partner, Article 80 PEL likewise provides for the legal successor to remain as a limited partner in the partnership enterprise. These regulations shall protect the interests of the deceased partner and his legal successors as well as those of the partnership enterprise.[241] The deceased partner might have substantially contributed to the establishment and development of the partnership enterprise's business.[242] Permitting the legal successor to remain in the partnership enterprise allows him to participate in the long term economic success of the business that the deceased partner has helped to build.[243] For the partnership enterprise, this regulation can be beneficial as it ensures the continuity of the partnership enterprise, and allows to avoid the financial burden of paying compensation to the legal successor in consequence of his withdrawal.[244] The legal succession because of inheritance is analysed in further detail below.[245]

However, despite the regulations in Article 80 and Article 50, Paragraph 1 PEL, a withdrawal of the deceased partner may still occur. Regarding the general partner, Article 50, Paragraph 2 PEL stipulates circumstances under which the withdrawal of the deceased general partner is carried out, and the successor of the deceased partner is compensated for the share of the property in the partnership enterprise.[246] This shall apply in three scenarios. (1) 'The successor is not willing to become a

[237]Art. 48 Para. 1 No 1 PEL.

[238]Art. 9 GPCL/Art. 13 GRCL.

[239]Li (李飞) (ed) (2006), p. 75.

[240]The same shall apply when a partner is legally declared dead. Regarding the regulations for declaring a person legally dead, see Articles 23–25 GPCL/Articles 46–53 GRCL; Li (李飞) (ed) (2006), p. 75.

[241]Li (李飞) (ed) (2006), pp. 81, 128–129.

[242]Ibid, p. 81.

[243]Ibid, p. 81.

[244]Ibid, p. 129.

[245]See Sect. 9.4.1.

[246]Li (李飞) (ed) (2006), p. 75.

partner.'[247] Becoming a partner is a right of the successor rather than an obligation.[248] Therefore, the law respects the party autonomy of the legal successor when he chooses to forfeit this right. The PEL does not regulate how much time the successor has to waive his right to become a partner. The lawmaker suggests that the other partners shall set a reasonable deadline; if the successor does not decline within this deadline, it shall be regarded as consent to become a partner.[249] (2) 'The successor does not have the qualification to be a partner, as is required by law or the partnership agreement.'[250] If the successor does not fulfil a mandatorily required qualification, he naturally cannot become a partner.[251] This exception is most likely to apply to professional service firms, such as law firms and accountancy firms that have been established in the form of a FISGPE. (3) 'The partnership agreement stipulates other circumstances under which a successor cannot become a partner.'[252] This regulation is a consideration of the partner's party autonomy that allows them to exclude heirs based on specific criteria,[253] examples would be minimum or maximum age requirements. When a successor of a general partner does not bear the full capacity for civil conduct, Article 50, Paragraph 3 PEL provides that, instead of withdrawing from the partnership enterprise, the successor may become a limited partner. This regulation is identical to that in Article 48, Paragraph 2 PEL, which is analysed in detail below.[254] Regarding the limited partner, the legal successor of the deceased limited partner may also decide not to take over the position of a limited partner.[255] In that situation, the deceased limited partner withdraws from the partnership enterprise, and his legal successor must be compensated. Under German law, the death of a partner likewise leads to his withdrawal.[256] With respect to a general partner, the partnership agreement can stipulate that the partnership enterprise shall be continued with his legal successor. Although, the successor may request within three months for his role to be transformed into that of a limited partner.[257] Should the other partners not agree to this transformation, the successor can immediately withdraw from the partnership enterprise, and is entitled to receive compensation.[258] Conversely, Chinese law only allows such a transition when the successor does not bear full capacity of civil conduct. In respect to the death of a limited partner, the GmbH & Co. KG is continued with the successor, unless otherwise stipulated in the

[247] Art. 50 Para. 2 No 1 PEL.

[248] Li (李飞) (ed) (2006), p. 75.

[249] Ye (2002), p. 120.

[250] Art. 50 Para. 2 No 2 PEL.

[251] Li (李飞) (ed) (2006), p. 75.

[252] Art. 50 Para. 2 No 3 PEL.

[253] Li (李飞) (ed) (2006), p. 75.

[254] See Sect. 9.3.2.1.2.

[255] Li (李飞) (ed) (2006), p. 129.

[256] Art. 131 Para. 3 No 1 HGB.

[257] Art. 139 Para. 1 HGB.

[258] Binz and Sorge (2018), p. 120.

partnership agreement.[259] In case of such a stipulation, the limited partnership enterprise is continued by the remaining partners, while the successor of the deceased partner withdraws from the partnership enterprise and is compensated.[260]

The second cause for statutory withdrawal is that the partner 'loses the ability to pay off his personal debts'.[261] A general partner assumes unlimited and joint liability for the debts of the partnership enterprise with all his personal property. When a general partner loses the ability to pay off his personal debt, he no longer provides adequate security, and thereby make retaining him in the partnership enterprise detrimental to the protection of the enterprise's creditors.[262] At the same time, if the partner is not able to pay off his debts, his share of the property in the partnership enterprise will eventually be utilised to satisfy his personal creditors.[263] The withdrawal with the subsequent compensation of the partner achieves the same result, but in an orderly manner. Unfortunately, the law does not specify when a partner has 'lost the ability to pay off his personal debts'. Since China does not yet have a personal bankruptcy regime,[264] this cannot provide any guidance. However, Article 48, Paragraph 1, Number 5 PEL addresses the situation of a partner's ownership interest being compulsorily enforced by the People's Court. The prevailing opinion within Chinese literature requires for the application of Article 48, Paragraph 1, Number 2 PEL that the partner is *de facto* not able to pay off his personal debts.[265] This shall be assessed objectively without consideration of the subjective opinion of the partner.[266] The assessment shall take into consideration the partner's personal wealth and assets, but also his overall creditworthiness.[267] The vagueness of this provision presumably makes its application in practice difficult. The stipulation of more detailed requirements in the partnership agreement can therefore help to avoid ambiguities. The provisions on statutory withdrawal under German partnership law are rather clear in comparison, and based on specific criteria with regard to the partner's solvency.[268] Regarding a limited partner, his liability only extends to the amount of capital subscribed. An exposure of the personal solvency of a limited partner therefore generally has no effect on the normal operation of the partnership enterprise, or on the protection of its creditors.[269] A withdrawal of a limited partner

---

[259] Art. 177 HGB.

[260] Binz and Sorge (2018), p. 120.

[261] Art. 48 Para. 1 No 2 PEL.

[262] Li (李飞) (ed) (2006), p. 76.

[263] Ibid, p. 76.

[264] Zheng (2010), p. 227.

[265] Ye (2002), p. 124.

[266] Ibid, p. 124.

[267] Ibid, p. 124; Li (李飞) (ed) (2006), p. 76.

[268] The provisions in Article 131, Paragraph 3, Nos 2 and 4 HGB are addressed in the subsequent analysis.

[269] Li (李飞) (ed) (2006), p. 127.

who is not able to pay of his personal debts is therefore not necessary.[270] This has been recognised by the Chinese lawmaker in Article 78 PEL, which stipulates that the regulation in Article 48, Paragraph 1, Number 2 PEL is not applicable to limited partners.

The third cause for statutory withdrawal is that 'the partner, as a legal person or other organisation, has its business licence revoked, is ordered to close down, is dissolved or is declared bankrupt'.[271] If a partner, in the capacity of a legal person or other organisation, is subject to one of these circumstances, it means that the partner has lost his legal personality, which is equivalent to the death of a natural person partner, and therefore shall have the same consequence of withdrawal from the partnership enterprise.[272] In comparison, German law explicitly recognises the bankruptcy of a partner as grounds for statutory withdrawal.[273] For the dissolution of a corporate general partner, however, German law does not make any stipulations. It will therefore be discussed whether the provision in Article 131, Paragraph 3, Number 1 HGB on the death of a natural person shall be applied analogously.[274] The regulation in the PEL is more comprehensive in this regard. The bankruptcy of a foreign corporate general partner raises additional questions, regarding the interaction of insolvency regimes from different jurisdictions.[275]

The fourth cause for statutory withdrawal is that 'the partner no longer possesses the qualifications which a partner shall possess as specified by law or the partnership agreement'.[276] This regulation is largely identical to that in Article 50, Paragraph 2, Number 2 PEL. If a specific qualification of a partner is required by law or the partnership agreement, this constitutes a foundation of the partnership enterprise.[277] Should the partner lose this qualification, this foundation no longer exists, necessitating his withdrawal from the partnership enterprise.[278] This regulation was newly added with the reform of the PEL in 2006, and mainly applies to professional service firms that have been established in the form of a FISGPE.

The fifth cause for statutory withdrawal is that 'all the partner's shares of the property in the partnership enterprise are compulsorily enforced by the People's Court'.[279] However, the PEL provides for interim steps before a creditor can force the withdrawal of a limited partner. These steps have already been addressed above

[270] Ibid, p. 127.

[271] Art. 48 Para. 1 No 3 PEL.

[272] Li (李飞) (ed) (2006), p. 76.

[273] Art. 131 Para. 3 No 2 HGB.

[274] For an overview of this discussion, see: Schmidt (2002), pp. 1451–1452.

[275] For a detailed analysis of the cross-border insolvency regime in China, see: Hu (2018), pp. 523–551.

[276] Art. 48 Para. 1 No 4 PEL.

[277] Li (李飞) (ed) (2006), p. 76.

[278] Ibid, p. 76.

[279] Art. 48 Para. 1 No 5 PEL.

under the analysis of the liquidation protection in the FILPE.[280] This interim procedure protects the continuity of the partnership enterprise. Under German law, the compulsory enforcement of the partner's ownership interest by a personal creditor likewise causes the partner's withdrawal if the creditor follows the prescribed procedure.[281]

A cause that eventually can lead to a statutory withdrawal is stipulated in Article 48, Paragraph 2 PEL. This provision regulates the consequences when 'a partner is legally recognised as a person without capacity for civil conduct or with only limited capacity for civil conduct'. In this case, however, the withdrawal is only the final consequence. In principle, if a partner is a natural person, he shall have the full capacity for civil conduct.[282] Therefore, the 1997 PEL stipulated that if a partner loses his capacity for civil conduct, he must withdraw from the partnership enterprise.[283] However, this regulation caused difficulties in practice, as a partner would sometimes make a substantial capital contribution or play a central role in the business success of the partnership enterprise, but would eventually lose his capacity for civil conduct for some reason.[284] Forcing such a partner to withdraw would deprive him of participating in the long-term economic success of the partnership enterprise.[285] Furthermore, the compensation payments to the withdrawing partner could place a significant financial burden on the partnership enterprise. With the reform of the PEL in 2006, the limited partnership enterprise was introduced. A limited partner does not participate in the management of the partnership enterprise, and he does not represent the enterprise towards third parties. Therefore, his ability to exercise his full capacity for civil conduct will not materially affect the operation of the partnership enterprise, and is of less significance.[286] Drawing lessons from foreign partnership legislation, the amended PEL in Article 48, Paragraph 2 provides a more flexible approach.[287] If all the other partners agree, the general partner without full capacity for civil conduct may change his status into that of a limited partner, and a general partnership enterprise consequently shall transform into a limited partnership enterprise. Only if the other partners fail to reach such a unanimous agreement must the general partner withdraw from the partnership enterprise. Regarding a limited partner who loses his capacity for civil conduct, Article 79 PEL provides a special regulation. For the establishment of a limited partnership enterprise, a limited partner must also have the full capacity for civil conduct, as the conclusion of the partnership agreement by the limited partner must be legally

[280] See Sect. 7.1.2.2.

[281] Art. 131 Para. 3 No 4, Art. 135, Art. 166 Para. 2 HGB.

[282] Art. 14 Para. 1 PEL. See also the analysis in Sect. 9.2.1.2.2.

[283] Art. 49 Para. 2 1997 PEL.

[284] Li (李飞) (ed) (2006), p. 77.

[285] Ibid, p. 77.

[286] Ibid, p. 128.

[287] Ibid, p. 77.

effective.[288] A natural person that does not have full capacity for civil conduct does not possess the full capacity to enter into such a contract, and therefore cannot participate in the establishment of a limited partnership enterprise.[289] However, for the reasons outlined above, the capacity for civil conduct of a limited partner is not as crucial for the operation of a partnership enterprise as that of a general partner. Therefore, Article 79 PEL stipulates that the other partners cannot request a limited partner, who later on loses his full capacity for civil conduct, to withdraw from the partnership enterprise. It should be noted that Article 79 PEL merely precludes *ad hoc* votes on the withdrawal of such a partner. If the partnership agreement stipulates that a limited partner without the full capacity for civil conduct must withdraw from the partnership enterprise, this would be a valid cause to exclude the partner from the partnership enterprise under Article 49, Paragraph 1, Number 4 PEL.[290]

The question of when the statutory withdrawal of a partner becomes effective, is regulated in Article 48, Paragraph 3 PEL. The determination of the moment of effectiveness is of the upmost importance, as it directly affects the rights and obligations of the withdrawing partner, the partnership enterprise, and third parties.[291] The calculation of the withdrawing partner's compensation, as well as his legal liability refer to the moment of effectiveness of his withdrawal.[292] The statutory withdrawal is based on objective circumstances rather than the partner's subjective intention.[293] Article 48, Paragraph 3 therefore stipulates that 'the withdrawal shall become effective from the date when the cause for withdrawing actually arises'. The specific time of occurrence of the circumstances is thus taken as the relevant time for the effectiveness of the withdrawal.

9.3.2.1.3 Exclusion of a Partner

The exclusion of a partner can be regarded as the counterpart to the voluntary withdrawal of a partner.[294] A partner generally has the right to choose not to cooperate any longer with the other partners, and can voluntarily withdraw from the partnership enterprise.[295] Conversely, the other partners have the right to choose not to cooperate with a certain partner any longer, and can exclude this partner from the partnership enterprise.[296] Nevertheless, the exclusion of a partner is the act of

---

[288] Ibid, p. 128.

[289] Ibid, p. 128.

[290] Ibid, p. 128.

[291] Ibid, p. 78.

[292] Ibid, p. 78.

[293] Ibid, p. 78.

[294] Binz and Sorge (2018), p. 125.

[295] Li (李飞) (ed) (2006), p. 79.

[296] Ibid, p. 79.

forcing a partner to be deprived of his membership right.[297] The exclusion is vulnerable to a majority of partners joining together to exclude a small number of partners, thus violating the interests and rights of minority partners.[298] Because the exclusion is such a delicate measure, and affects the core of a partner's membership rights, it must be treated with caution. Therefore, the PEL in Article 49 regulates the reasons for, and the process of an exclusion. Only when there is a statutory cause, a partner may be excluded subject to a unanimous resolution by all other partners.[299] The requirement of a unanimous decision by the other partners is a mandatory stipulation.[300] A deviating provision in the partnership agreement, e.g. stipulating a majority vote, would be invalid.[301] Under German law, the exclusion of a partner statutorily requires that the other partners obtain a court ruling that excludes the partner in question.[302] However, if the partnership agreement—as is common business practice—stipulates that the court ruling shall be replaced by a decision of the partners, such an exclusion by partner resolution is also valid.[303] The decision does not have to be unanimous, but can be a simple decision by the majority of the partners.[304] In comparison, the PEL places more stringent requirements on the consent of the other partners. However, the PEL is silent on whether the other partners are obligated to participate in the exclusion of the said partner. *Ye* argues in favour of such an obligation, as the regulation in Article 49 PEL would otherwise have no effect.[305] In addition, such an exclusion would objectively be in the interest of the partnership enterprise considering a partner who fulfils the circumstances listed in Article 49, Paragraph 1 PEL is detrimental to the partnership enterprise.[306] Under German law, such an obligation of the other partners is acknowledged as a result of the partner's fiduciary duty.[307]

In contrast to the rules on statutory withdrawal, the regulation in Article 49 PEL does not automatically lead to the exclusion of a partner who fulfils the requirements. The PEL gives the other partners the right to exclude said partner, but they can still choose not to execute this right.[308] The provision in Article 49 PEL likewise applies to general partners and limited partners.[309] Under German law, the other partners can

[297] Ibid, p. 79.

[298] Ibid, p. 79.

[299] Art. 49 Para. 1 PEL.

[300] Ye (2002), p. 126.

[301] Ibid, p. 126.

[302] Art. 140, Art. 161 Para. 2 HGB. For details regarding the court ruling, see Schmidt (2002), pp. 1461–1468.

[303] Binz and Sorge (2018), p. 128; Schmidt (2002), p. 1461.

[304] Schmidt (2002), p. 1469.

[305] Ye (2002), p. 125.

[306] Ibid, p. 125.

[307] Binz and Sorge (2018), p. 129.

[308] Ye (2002), p. 125.

[309] Art. 60 PEL.

exclude a partner when the said partner fulfils the circumstances that would entitle the other partners to demand the dissolution of the partnership enterprise according to Article 133 HGB.[310] The exclusion of the partner would then be the lesser evil compared to the dissolution of the entire partnership enterprise. However, German law requires that an 'important reason' must have occurred to justify an exclusion of a partner.[311] Continuing the co-operation with the partner in question must be unacceptable for the other partners.[312] Any less restrictive measures, such as an amendment of the partnership agreement or the withdrawal of the partner's right to execute partnership affairs, must take precedence.[313] The exclusion of a partner can only be the last resort to resolve a conflict among partners.[314] Conversely, the PEL in Article 49, Paragraph 1 PEL lists statutory causes that can lead to the exclusion of a partner.

The first statutory cause is that the partner 'fails to fulfil the obligation to make his capital contribution'.[315] All partners commit to making a capital contribution as stipulated in the partnership agreement. These capital contributions are the funding of the partnership enterprise, and only if all partners fulfil their obligation, the partnership enterprise can be set up and operate normally.[316] If a partner fails to make his capital contribution, this shows that he is not willing to cooperate with the other partners, and thereby usually loses their trust.[317] The other partners should therefore be allowed to exclude such a partner from the partnership enterprise.

The second circumstance is that the partner 'causes losses to the partnership enterprise due to intentional or gross negligent actions'.[318] Such intentional or gross negligent actions of a partner constitute a financial risk to the other partners.[319] Unlike in a case where a partner causes losses due to general negligence, the gross negligent or intentional nature of his action can also affect the trust and willingness of the other partners to continue to cooperate with such a partner.[320] Therefore, they should be able to exclude the partner from the partnership enterprise.

The third cause is that the partner has 'conducted irregular actions in executing the partnership affairs'.[321] A smooth operation of the partnership enterprise requires that all partners comply with the provisions of the PEL and the stipulations in the partnership agreement with regard to performing partnership affairs, so that the

---

[310] Art. 140 Para. 1, Art. 161 Para. 2 HGB. Regarding Article 133 HGB, see Sect. 9.3.2.1.1.

[311] Binz and Sorge (2018), p. 128; Schmidt (2002), p. 1462.

[312] Binz and Sorge (2018), p. 128; Schmidt (2002), p. 1462.

[313] Binz and Sorge (2018), p. 128; Schmidt (2002), p. 1462.

[314] Binz and Sorge (2018), p. 128; Schmidt (2002), p. 1462.

[315] Art. 49 Para. 1 No1 PEL.

[316] Li (李飞) (ed) (2006), p. 79.

[317] Ibid, p. 79.

[318] Art. 49 Para. 1 No 2 PEL.

[319] Li (李飞) (ed) (2006), p. 79.

[320] Ibid, p. 79.

[321] Art. 49 Para. 1 No 3 PEL.

interest of the partnership enterprise are maintained.[322] With regard to the general partner, Article 32 PEL makes stipulations for the orderly execution of the partnership affairs, e.g. not engaging in competing business to that of the partnership enterprise. However, the limited partner is obliged to abstain from any engagement in the execution of the partnership affairs.[323] If a partner improperly acts in the execution of the partnership affairs, this can affect the successful operation, and may damage the interests of the partnership enterprise and the other partners.[324] In addition to possible penalties,[325] the other partners should be able to exclude such a partner from the partnership enterprise.

The fourth reason that can be grounds for the exclusion of a partner is that 'circumstances arise that are specified in the partnership agreement'.[326] The option to stipulate further circumstances in the partnership agreement is an expression of the partner's party autonomy.[327] Under German law, it is highly controversial whether causes for exclusion can be prescribed in the partnership agreement that are below the threshold of an 'important reason' as stipulated in Article 133 HGB, and thus would leave the exclusion to the discretion of the other partners.[328] This question has practical relevance especially for family-owned partnership enterprises, e.g. partners wanting to reserve the right to exclude the heir of a deceased partner if he turns out 'not to fit in' with the other partners.[329] Another example are co-operation partners of the partnership enterprise that are made partners to intensify the business co-operation but shall be excluded when the co-operation comes to an end.[330] Judgments of the BGH have greatly limited the partner's discretion for exclusions without an important reason.[331] The Court argues that a limited partner who must constantly fear that he may be excluded from the partnership enterprise may not fully exercise his control and supervision rights to avoid upsetting the other partners.[332] This can lead to despotism by the other partners, which would constitute a violation of their fiduciary duties.[333] An exclusion without an important reason would further violate the principle of mutual trust and co-operation that characterises the

[322]Li (李飞) (ed) (2006), p. 80.

[323]See Sect. 8.3.2.1.

[324]Li (李飞) (ed) (2006), p. 80.

[325]For example, Article 99 PEL for a general partner who enters into competition with the partnership enterprise, or the liability provisions for a limited partner who engages in the execution of partnership affairs.

[326]Art. 49 Para. 1 No 4 PEL.

[327]Li (李飞) (ed) (2006), p. 80.

[328]Binz and Sorge (2018), pp. 131–143; Schmidt (2002), pp. 1470–1474.

[329]Binz and Sorge (2018), p. 132.

[330]Ibid, p. 132.

[331]Ibid, p. 140.

[332]Ibid, p. 140.

[333]Ibid, p. 140.

partnership enterprise.[334] Therefore, the BGH upholds that a stipulation of causes for exclusion in the partnership agreement should not result in a partner being exposed to the arbitrariness of the other partners.[335] While the PEL explicitly provides reasons for exclusion in the partnership agreement, these should likewise be drafted with caution to balance the interests and rights of minority and majority partners.

The procedure of an orderly exclusion is further specified in Article 49, Paragraph 2 PEL. The due process has the function of properly protecting the rights of the partner who is to be excluded.[336] Said partner must therefore be notified in writing of the resolution on his exclusion. The exclusion becomes effective from the date that the partner receives this notice.[337] From that date on, the partner is regarded as having withdrawn from the partnership enterprise. The partner who is subject to the exclusion is reduced to a passive role while the other partners decide over his exclusion. In order to prevent any abuse of the exclusion mechanism and to protect the lawful rights and interest of the partner, Article 49, Paragraph 3 PEL stipulates remedial measures that the affected partner may employ. 'If the excluded partner opposes the resolution on his exclusion, he may file a lawsuit with the People's Court within 30 days from the date of the receipt of the notice on his exclusion.'[338] Under Chinese law, the partner carries the burden of proof when he claims that the resolution on his exclusion is formally or substantively unlawful.[339] Should the People's Court decide that the exclusion was invalid, the partner will resume the position of a partner with all the rights and obligations of a partner from the date the judgment enters into force.[340] In addition, the wrongfully excluded partner may request indemnity from the other partner(s) for any losses he suffered as consequence of the exclusion.[341] The limitation period of thirty days for bringing such a lawsuit is rather short to avoid a negative effect on the stability and normal operation of the partnership enterprise.[342] Beyond this period, the excluded partner can no longer appeal to the court against the resolution of his exclusion.[343] The regulation in Article 49, Paragraph 3 PEL is a mandatory provision; a stipulation in the

[334]Ibid, p. 140.

[335]Ibid, p. 140.

[336]Li (李飞) (ed) (2006), p. 80.

[337]The provisions on the effectiveness of an 'expression of intention' in Articles 137–142 GRCL apply, the notice therefore becomes effective when the partner becomes aware of its contents. This is also the case when a letter reaches the partner's general sphere of control, e.g. his mailbox (Weidlich and Shen 2015, pp. 102–103).

[338]Art. 49 Para. 3 PEL.

[339]Ye (2002), p. 126.

[340]Li (李飞) (ed) (2006), p. 80; Gao (高富平) et al. (1997), p. 251.

[341]Li (李飞) (ed) (2006), p. 80; Gao (高富平) et al. (1997), p. 251.

[342]Li (李飞) (ed) (2006), p. 80.

[343]Ibid, p. 80.

partnership agreement that limits or excludes the partner's right to bring such a lawsuit is considered invalid.[344]

9.3.2.2 Consequences of Withdrawal

The different reasons for withdrawal that have been analysed all lead to the same consequences, stipulated in Articles 51 to 54 PEL. Most importantly, the withdrawal of a partner does not trigger the dissolution of the partnership enterprise.[345] This entity approach adopted by the PEL helps to facilitate the continuity of the partnership enterprise.[346] Moreover, the identity of the partnership enterprise does not change due to the withdrawal of a partner, unless only one partner remains after the withdrawal.[347] The partnership enterprise continues to exist with the remaining partners.[348] Since a reform of the HGB in 1998, German law likewise ensures the continuity of the partnership enterprise after the withdrawal of a partner.[349] This has strengthened the independence of the partnership enterprise from its members.[350] Under Chinese law, the withdrawing partner upon withdrawal loses all the rights and obligations that are granted to a partner under the partnership agreement and the PEL.[351] The previous analysis has shown that the assets of a partnership enterprise are not owned by the individual partners but by the partnership enterprise.[352] The partner's share of the property in the partnership enterprise is a value right that the partner holds as part of his membership right.[353] The overall value of the partnership enterprise is divided among the partners, which allows the determination of the value of each partner's membership right.[354] With the withdrawal of a partner, he loses this value right together with his membership of the partnership enterprise. The question arises what happens to the value associated with the withdrawing partner's share of the property in the partnership enterprise. German law contains an explicit regulation that the value right of the withdrawing partner is added to the value rights of the other partners.[355] This addition occurs automatically; no additional transfer is

[344] Ye (2002), p. 126.

[345] Reasons that cause dissolution of a partnership enterprise are conclusively listed in Article 85 PEL.

[346] Lin (2017), p. 183.

[347] See the analysis in Sect. 9.2.2.1.

[348] Ye (2002), p. 127.

[349] Binz and Sorge (2018), p. 124; Schmidt (2002), pp. 1448–1449.

[350] Windbichler (2014), p. 126.

[351] Ye (2002), p. 127.

[352] Art. 20 PEL. See Sect. 9.2.2.1.

[353] Schmidt (2002), p. 207.

[354] Ibid, p. 207.

[355] Art. 738 Para. 1 BGB; Art. 105 Para. 3 HGB.

necessary.[356] While the PEL does not contain such an explicit provision, the legal effect of the withdrawal must be the same. The withdrawing partner receives a compensation payment from the partnership enterprise for the forfeiture of his value right. The value of his membership right is then absorbed by the partnership enterprise, which is effectively an attribution to the value rights of the remaining partners. However, the joining of a new partner in the partnership enterprise leads to the contrary effect—the value rights of the original partners are depreciated to create a value right for the joining partner.[357] Therefore, the joining partner usually has to make a capital contribution to the partnership enterprise.[358] Because of the capital contribution, the overall assets of the partnership enterprise increase, and the value of the original partner's membership right does not incur an actual loss.[359] This principle of attributing and depreciating the value rights of the individual partners is a result of the principle that the partnership enterprise remains the owner of its assets, regardless of any change among the partners.[360] This ensures a continuity of the partnership enterprise's assets that is in accordance with that of a corporation's assets.[361]

Upon the withdrawal, new rights and obligations of the withdrawing partner are also established.[362] A core aspect is the partner's right, stipulated in Articles 51 and 52 PEL, to receive a compensation payment after settling his share of the property in the partnership enterprise with the other partners. In the absence of a contrary agreement, the withdrawing partner will essentially receive a return on his share of the property in the partnership enterprise minus any liabilities owed to the partnership enterprise.[363] This compensation payment can have disastrous financial consequences for the partnership enterprise because it might be forced to sell business assets necessary for its continuing business operation in order to generate enough funds to pay the withdrawing partner.[364] The regulations in the PEL and possible adjustments in the partnership agreement for the determination of the compensation payment are therefore of great importance for the continuance of the partnership enterprise. The regulations in Articles 51 and 52 PEL set out the following principles for the settlement with a withdrawing partner.

The first principle is that the provisions on the settlement and compensation apply regardless of the reason for the withdrawal.[365] It is a principle of fair and just treatment of all partners that any withdrawing partner shall have the right to

[356] Schmidt (2002), p. 1319.
[357] Ibid, pp. 207–208.
[358] Ibid, p. 208.
[359] Ibid, p. 208.
[360] Ibid, p. 208.
[361] Ibid, pp. 1319–1320.
[362] Ye (2002), p. 128.
[363] Art. 51 Para. 1 PEL.
[364] Wu and Geu (2007–2008), p. 149.
[365] Li (李飞) (ed) (2006), p. 83.

participate in the settlement process.[366] If the withdrawing partner has died or has been declared dead, settlement shall be carried out with his heirs.[367]

The second principle refers to the valuation date to which the calculation of the compensation payment refers. During the operation of a partnership enterprise, the value of its assets is constantly fluctuating due to varying business activities and changing market prices. The determination of the valuation date can therefore have a significant impact on the amount of the compensation payment. The PEL stipulates in Article 51, Paragraph 1 that the calculation shall be based on the financial status of the partnership enterprise 'at the time of the withdrawal', thus referring to the effectiveness of the withdrawal.[368] A statutory withdrawal becomes effective at the date when the cause for withdrawing actually arises, and an exclusion of a partner becomes effective from the date when the partner receives the notice of his exclusion.[369] Regarding the voluntary withdrawal, the PEL does not make an explicit stipulation which leaves the question to be decided by the partners.[370] To avoid disputes over this matter, a regulation on the effectiveness of a voluntary withdrawal should be included in the partnership agreement. However, it is important to note that a withdrawal is a matter that occurs within the partnership enterprise, and that is difficult to recognise for any third party.[371] Only with the registration of the withdrawal of the partner with the competent authorities can a third party take note of this change within the partnership enterprise.[372] Like the joining of a new partner, a withdrawal or exclusion of a partner must be registered with the relevant authorities within fifteen days of the partner withdrawing from the partnership enterprise.[373] Therefore, between the effectiveness of the withdrawal and the date of the official registration, the withdrawing partner cannot use his withdrawal against a bona fide third party.[374]

The third principle is that the settlement with the withdrawing partner must be carried out 'based on the financial status of the partnership enterprise'. The value of the partnership enterprise must therefore be reflected in the amount of the compensation payment. However, the question on what basis the value of the partnership enterprise is calculated, is not regulated in the PEL, and is subject to controversy among Chinese scholars. Since the valuation of a partnership enterprise is a difficult undertaking, the issue of which method of valuation is best suited to provide an outcome that balances the interests of the withdrawing partner and the other partners

[366]Ibid, p. 83.

[367]Ibid, p. 84.

[368]Ibid, p. 84.

[369]Art. 48 Para. 3; Art. 49 Para. 2 PEL.

[370]Li (李飞) (ed) (2006), p. 84.

[371]Ibid, p. 78.

[372]Ibid, p. 78.

[373]Art. 18–19 FIPE Provisions, Art. 13 PEL.

[374]Li (李飞) (ed) (2006), p. 78; Ye (2002), p. 124.

has likewise been a matter of controversy under German law.[375] Some Chinese scholars argue that the book value (Buchwert) of the partnership enterprise at the time of the withdrawal should form the basis for the calculation of the compensation.[376] The book value captures the value of all assets of the partnership enterprise as are carried on its balance sheet.[377] Because the withdrawal of a partner under the PEL does not lead to the dissolution of the partnership enterprise, these scholars argue that the withdrawing partner shall not be entitled to the same compensation as he would be after the liquidation of the partnership enterprise.[378] Utilising the book value is also appealing from a practical perspective, as it can be determined rather easily based on the balance sheet of the partnership enterprise. However, other scholars argue that for the affected partner, a withdrawal is not different from the liquidation of the partnership enterprise, and that he should therefore be treated accordingly.[379] This understanding is shared by German law, which explicitly states that the withdrawing partner shall be compensated with the same amount that he would receive in case of a liquidation of the partnership enterprise.[380] The book value approach has two major shortcomings: it does not take into account hidden assets, which are assets that are carried on the books at a substantially reduced value that is considerably less than market value;[381] it does not consider the goodwill of a partnership enterprise, which are its reputation, patronage and other intangible assets that enable the partnership enterprise to earn income in excess of the income that would be expected from the enterprise viewed as a mere collection of assets.[382] Especially in a partnership enterprise that has been in business for a long time, the hidden assets and the goodwill can be of significant value. Partners who have been members in the partnership enterprise for a long time will have contributed—to some degree—to the establishment of the hidden assets and the goodwill, and a withdrawing partner therefore should also benefit from these values.[383] The calculation of the compensation should thus be based on an overall valuation of the partnership enterprise that takes into account the hidden assets and the goodwill. This is achieved by the so called capitalised value approach (Ertragswertverfahren), which is also the predominantly used valuation method in Germany.[384] Because an overall evaluation is much more complex in practice than the book value method, it is usually conducted by officially recognised experts in Germany.[385] Fundamentally, the

[375]Instructively: Schmidt (2002), pp. 1477–1478.

[376]Gao (高富平) et al. (1997), p. 256.

[377]Garner (2009), p. 207.

[378]Gao (高富平) et al. (1997), p. 256.

[379]Ye (2002), p. 127.

[380]Art. 738 Para. 2 BGB; Art. 105 Para. 3 HGB.

[381]Garner (2009), p. 134.

[382]Ibid, p. 763.

[383]Ye (2002), p. 127.

[384]Binz and Sorge (2018), p. 144; Schmidt (2002), pp. 1477–1478.

[385]Schmidt (2002), pp. 1477–1478.

compensation claim of a withdrawing partner in China is in substance equivalent to that in Germany.[386]

The withdrawing partner is entitled to a proportion of the overall value of the partnership enterprise. For the determination of that proportion, reference can be made to Article 89 PEL, which regulates the distribution of the remaining profits after liquidation, and again refers to Article 33, Paragraph 1 PEL.[387] Accordingly, the proportion shall be determined by a provision in the partnership agreement, in absence thereof through consultation among the partners, and in case of failure of consultation *pro rata* in accordance with the partner's capital contribution; should all this fail, as a last resort, an equal proportion will be assigned to all partners.

The principle formulated in Article 51, Para 1 PEL is further complemented by the stipulation in Article 52 PEL that 'the method for returning the withdrawing partner's share of the property in the partnership enterprise shall be specified in the partnership agreement or determined by all the partners; it may be returned either in currency or in physical items'. When a partner fulfils his obligation to make a capital contribution, he may do so in the form of currency, but also with material items, intellectual property rights, land use rights, other property rights, or—if he is a general partner—in the form of labour services.[388] If a partner has made his capital contribution in kind, he may want to reclaim what he has contributed.[389] The Chinese lawmaker therefore decided to stipulate more than one method for settling the withdrawing partner's claim.[390] Instead, the PEL adopts a flexible approach that allows the partners to decide on the appropriate method.[391] While currency is the most often used method in practice, others may be chosen in specific cases.[392] While Article 52 PEL mentions the method of returning currency and physical items, this enumeration is not exclusive, and partners have the autonomy to determine any method they deem fit, e.g. the return of property rights to the withdrawing partner.[393] However, two limitations apply. If a capital contribution has been made in the form of labour services, this can naturally not be returned as such, and therefore the withdrawing partner shall be compensated with currency.[394] If the partner has made a capital contribution in kind, and this item or right is an essential prerequisite for the continuing business operation of the partnership enterprise, this item shall not be returned to the withdrawing partner.[395] In this case, the partner is compensated with currency instead. However, it remains unclear under what circumstances an item or

386 Ye (2002), p. 135.

387 Li (李飞) (ed) (2006), p. 84.

388 Arts. 16, 64 PEL.

389 Li (李飞) (ed) (2006), p. 85.

390 Ibid, p. 86.

391 Ibid, p. 86.

392 Ibid, p. 86.

393 Ibid, p. 86.

394 Ibid, pp. 85–86.

395 Ibid, p. 86; Ye (2002), p. 128.

right is so crucial to the partnership enterprise that it cannot be returned. Under German law, the withdrawing partner has a claim to get back any items that he allowed to be used by the partnership enterprise.[396] However, this does not apply to items or rights that have been the partner's capital contribution.[397] Any capital contribution made in kind remains with the partnership enterprise.[398] This regulation under German law is thus stricter, but also clearer than the approach under the PEL.

It has been shown that the PEL stipulates the time of the withdrawal as the decisive time for calculating the compensation settlement. However, the law does not provide any regulation as to the time frame within which the other partners are to conclude the settlement with the withdrawing partner, or a time limit on when the compensation payment must be made.[399] Leaving these aspects unregulated can result in disputes if the settlement process is prolonged. It is therefore advisable to stipulate time limits for the calculation of the execution of the settlement in the partnership agreement.[400]

The fourth principle with regard to the consequences of the withdrawal is stipulated in the second sentence of Article 51, Paragraph 1 PEL: 'if the withdrawing partner bears compensation liability for losses he caused to the partnership enterprise, this amount of compensation shall be deducted from this settlement claim'. A liability of the withdrawing partner towards the partnership enterprise can arise because the partner's personal conduct violates regulations in the PEL or the partnership agreement.[401] Deducting these liabilities from the compensation payment is a very practical and functional approach.[402] Claiming the payment of outstanding liabilities after the withdrawal has been settled, would increase the burden on both the withdrawing partner and the partnership enterprise.[403]

The fifth principle is stipulated in Article 51, Paragraph 2 PEL: 'if there is outstanding business of the partnership enterprise at the time of withdrawal, the settlement thereof shall be carried out after such business has been concluded'. In effect, this is an exception to the principle that the settlement shall be calculated based on the financial status at the time of the withdrawal.[404] This regulation shall ensure that the withdrawing partner also participates in the business affairs that are still outstanding at that time.[405] In this context, outstanding business shall refer to business that has already been established through a legal transaction, but has not yet

[396] Art. 738 Para. 1 BGB; Art. 105 Para. 3 HGB.
[397] Schmidt (2002), p. 1475.
[398] Ibid, p. 1475.
[399] Ye (2002), p. 127.
[400] Ibid, p. 127.
[401] See Sect. 8.4.5.
[402] Li (李飞) (ed) (2006), p. 84.
[403] Ibid, p. 84.
[404] Ibid, p. 85.
[405] Ibid, p. 85.

been concluded.[406] The outstanding business shall be settled separately from the overall compensation claim, based on its actual outcome.[407] However, the PEL does not regulate how the withdrawing partner can obtain the necessary information with regard to the completion of the outstanding business. Following his withdrawal from the partnership enterprise, he does no longer possess the information rights of a partner. Conversely, German law does explicitly entitle the partner to request adequate information after his withdrawal.[408] With regard to a FILPE, this issue should therefore be regulated in the partnership agreement. A similar provision to Article 51, Paragraph 2 PEL is also stipulated under German partnership law.[409] However, the concept of separately settling the outstanding business has been criticised harshly as outdated and no longer appropriate.[410] The modern valuation methods, like the capitalised value approach, consider the overall value of a partnership enterprise, including its goodwill, and thus already take into account the outstanding business of the partnership enterprise.[411] Therefore, these business transactions shall not be considered a second time under a separate claim.[412] This criticism is likewise relevant to the PEL should the capitalised value approach be applied. In that case, the application of Article 51, Paragraph 2 PEL should be excluded in the partnership agreement.

An additional supplementary regulation for the settlement with a withdrawing general partner is provided in Article 54 PEL: 'if at the time of withdrawal the property of a partnership enterprise is less than its debts, the withdrawing partner shall share the losses in accordance with the provision in Article 33, Paragraph 1 PEL'. This regulation reiterates the principle that the general partners in a partnership enterprise share the profits as well as the losses of the partnership enterprise, and are liable for the latter with their entire property.[413] If the partnership enterprise runs at a loss at the time of withdrawal, the withdrawing partner must settle his share of these losses.[414] With regard to how the losses are shared, the same principle applies, codified in Article 33, Paragraph 1 PEL, as to how the profits are shared among the partners. Similar to the provision in Article 54 PEL, a general partner in Germany is also obliged to settle his share of the partnership debts at the time of his withdrawal.[415]

The previous analysis has shown that the settlement with and compensation of the withdrawing partner entails a multitude of complex issues that can lead to problems

---

[406] Ye (2002), p. 128.

[407] Ibid, p. 128.

[408] Art. 161 Para. 2, Art. 105 Para. 3 HGB, Art. 740 Para. 2 BGB.

[409] Art. 161 Para. 2, Art. 105 Para. 3 HGB, Art. 740 Para. 1 BGB.

[410] Schmidt (2002), p. 1478.

[411] Ibid, p. 1478.

[412] Ibid, p. 1478.

[413] Li (李飞) (ed) (2006), p. 87.

[414] Ibid, p. 87.

[415] Art. 739 BGB; Art. 105 Para. 3 HGB.

and disputes. Therefore, it appears reasonable to include a comprehensive provision for settlement with a withdrawing partner in the partnership agreement. In Germany, it is common to find clauses that regulate the amount of the compensation payment, the basis of its calculation (book value approach vs capitalised value approach; exclusion of profits from outstanding business transactions) and the terms of its payment (payable in instalments over several years).[416] So called ‘compensation clauses’ fulfil different purposes: preventing expensive legal disputes; ensuring the continuity of the partnership enterprise by limiting the amount of the compensation payment, and thus indirectly making it less attractive for partners to voluntarily withdraw; providing transparency and thus helping to make an investment calculable.[417] A compensation clause must balance the conflicting interests of two parties: the withdrawing partner has the interest to receive a high compensation payment, while it is in the interest of the other partners to keep the payment low and to maintain the continuity of the partnership enterprise. The lawfulness of compensation clauses is therefore a subject of academic discussion and court judgments in Germany. The core question is how much the settlement payment granted under the compensation clause can differ from the amount that the law would award to a withdrawing partner. This issue touches upon a fundamental question of party autonomy in the partnership enterprise.[418] While the compensation clause is concluded among the founding partners of the partnership enterprise, it also takes effect for the legal successors of the founding partners and partners who join the partnership enterprise later.[419] Therefore, the effect of the clause can be described as supra-individual.[420] While the principle of party autonomy allows to agree on a compensation clause without restrictions, its supra-individual effect requires that limits are set in exceptional cases.[421] The BGH established that a compensation clause shall be (partially) unlawful when it *de facto* excludes or limits the withdrawal right. This shall be the case when the disparity between the compensation payment in the clause, and the amount granted by law is so substantial that it typically would prevent a partner from exercising his right to withdraw. The BGH has recognised this for instance when the value granted under the compensation clause was 20 per cent less than the value granted by law; when varying compensation amounts were stipulated for different partners without any cause; or when the payment of the compensation was delayed for an unreasonable amount of time.[422] Evaluation of these clauses was conducted by the BGH on a case-by-case basis, which is why a significant level of legal uncertainty remains in Germany as to when a compensation clause is unlawful. In respect to the FILPE, it remains to be seen how Chinese courts

[416]Schmidt (2002), p. 1482.

[417]Binz and Sorge (2018), p. 145; Schmidt (2002), p. 1483.

[418]Schmidt (2002), p. 1484.

[419]Ibid, p. 1484.

[420]Ibid, p. 1484.

[421]Ibid, p. 1484.

[422]Ibid, pp. 1484–1488.

will evaluate compensation clauses. However, it is a rather safe prediction that a clause which strikes a reasonable balance between the interests of the partners is more likely to be considered lawful.

A further consequence of the withdrawal is that the withdrawing partner continues to bear liabilities under certain circumstances. The relevant regulations in Articles 53 and 81 PEL have been analysed above.[423]

9.3.3 Withdrawal of All Limited Partners

The analysis has shown that the withdrawal of all general partners of a FILPE leads to its dissolution,[424] while the withdrawal of all limited partners does not have the same effect. Instead, Article 75 PEL stipulates that 'when a limited partnership enterprise only consists of general partners, it shall be transformed into a general partnership enterprise'. The PEL thus stipulates a statutory transformation of the enterprise that does not require any consent from the remaining general partners. However, the partnership enterprise must comply with the conditions for establishment of the type of partnership enterprise to which it intends to change, and a registration must be made with SAMR with submission of the relevant documents.[425] The transformation does not affect the liability of the general partners, as they continue to bear the same unlimited liability under a FIGPE as they had to share under the FILPE.

9.3.4 Withdrawal of All Foreign Partners

As a result of the withdrawal of partners, a FILPE may be left with only Chinese investors as partners, and thus no longer fulfil the requirement of a foreign-invested partnership enterprise, which is to have at least one foreign enterprise or individual as partner.[426] However, this does not lead to the dissolution of the FILPE. Instead, Article 27 FIPE Provisions stipulates that the FILPE can be transformed into a domestic-invested partnership enterprise 'if all the foreign partners withdraw form a foreign-invested partnership enterprise but the partnership enterprise continues to exist'. Thus, this presents the opposite scenario to a foreign investor joining a domestic-invested partnership enterprise.[427] The transformation from a FILPE into a domestic-invested limited partnership enterprise is a statutory transformation that

[423]See Sect. 8.4.2.

[424]Art. 75 PEL. See Sect. 9.2.2.1.

[425]Arts. 18–19, 23 FIPE Provisions, Art. 13 PEL.

[426]Art. 2 FIPE Measures.

[427]See Sect. 9.3.1.2.

must be registered with the competent authorities.[428] The liabilities of the general partners and limited partners are not affected by the transformation as foreign and domestic partners are subject to the same liability regulations.

9.3.5 Conversion of Partner Status

While strictly speaking not a withdrawal, the question arises what effect the conversion of a partner's status from general partner to limited partner and vice versa has on the partnership enterprise. Article 63, Paragraph 6 PEL stipulates that the partnership agreement of a limited partnership enterprise must contain regulations on the procedure for such a conversion. The rights and obligations of a general partner and a limited partner differ significantly in aspects such as liability and execution of partnership affairs.[429] The conversion of a partner from one to the other thus inevitably has an effect on the partnership enterprise and the other partners.[430] The PEL therefore stipulates in Article 82 that such a conversation 'shall be subject to the consent of all the partners, unless stipulated otherwise in the partnership agreement'. This leaves discretion to the partners in deciding on the threshold for consent to such a conversion. The liability that a former general partner and a former limited partner continue to bear after the conversion has already been analysed.[431] Regarding the partnership enterprise as a whole, the conversion does not have additional consequences, as long as the minimum number of general partners and limited partners is still fulfilled after the conversion.

9.4 Legal Succession Because of Inheritance and Transfer

The analysis of the legal succession turns to the core of the attribute of transferable ownership interest, the question whether a FILPE can conduct business without interruptions when the identity of its owners changes by means of a legal succession. The transfer of ownership interest through legal succession differs from the withdrawal of a partner and the joining of a new partner insofar as the share of the property in the partnership enterprise—and the membership right with it—remains in the partnership enterprise. Therefore, the membership right of the assignor is not dissolved, and no new membership right of the assignee needs to be established. Instead, the assignee of the ownership interest legally succeeds into the rights and

[428] Art. 8 FIPE Measures, Art. 27 FIPE Provisions, Arts. 18–19 Partnership Enterprise Registration Measures.

[429] Li (李飞) (ed) (2006), p. 132.

[430] Ibid, p. 132.

[431] See Sect. 8.4.2.

obligations that the assignor has held as a partner. Two types of legal succession can be differentiated in this regard: legal succession because of inheritance and legal succession because of transfer.

9.4.1 Legal Succession Because of Inheritance

The circumstances under which a deceased partner withdraws from a partnership enterprise have been analysed above. The consequence would be a compensation settlement between the partnership enterprise and the legal successors of the deceased partner. As an alternative to the withdrawal, the PEL provides in Articles 50 and 80 that the partnership enterprise can be continued with the legal successor of the deceased partner. Regarding the death of a general partner, Article 50, Paragraph 1 PEL provides that the legal successor shall 'acquire the status of a partner' in the partnership enterprise from the deceased general partner, if this is approved in the partnership agreement or all other partners have given their consent. Regarding the death of a limited partner, Article 80 PEL stipulates that the legal successor may 'acquire the status of a limited partner in the partnership enterprise'.[432] Both provisions stipulate a direct legal succession of the membership right in the partnership enterprise from the deceased partner to his legal successor.[433] The lawmaker clarifies that the rights and obligations which the legal successor holds as a partner, are defined and limited by the rights and obligations of the deceased partner.[434] The membership right in the partnership enterprise remains the same.[435] Ultimately, only the subject holding the membership right changes as a result of the legal succession.[436] Because of the special role and authority of a general partner, his legal successor does not automatically become a general partner. The transfer of the membership right is conditional to the approval of the other partners, either expressed in advance in a so-called entry clause in the partnership agreement or given by a unanimous vote in favour of the transfer.[437] From the perspective of ensuring the continuity of the partnership enterprise, it is advisable already to regulate such consent in an entry clause in the partnership agreement. Because the limited partner is not involved in the execution of the partnership affairs and does not bear personal liability, the legal succession of his membership right does not require the approval of the other partners. Consequently, the legal successor becomes a

[432]The same shall apply for the successor in title to a legal person or other organisation that has been terminated (Art. 80 PEL).

[433]Li (李飞) (ed) (2006), pp. 81, 129.

[434]Ibid, p. 68.

[435]Ibid, p. 68.

[436]Ibid, p. 68.

[437]Art. 50 Para. 1 PEL.

partner with effect from the date of the inheritance.[438] However, the legal successor also has the right to reject a transfer of the membership right, and opt for a withdrawal and settlement instead. Continuing as a partner in the partnership enterprise is a right of the legal successor rather than an obligation.[439] Should the deceased partner have more than one legal successor, his membership right is split among all successors in proportion to their inheritance.[440] Each successor thereby becomes a partner in the partnership enterprise, holding a proportion of the deceased partner's share of the property in the partnership enterprise.[441] With regard to a general partner, the other partners can require that only one legal successor becomes a partner who holds the entire membership right, to avoid having to deal with a large number of general partners. With regard to the limited partner, however, the PEL in Article 80 does not leave room to stipulate such a condition. Because of the transfer of the membership right to the legal successor, the partnership agreement must be updated with his name.[442] Yet, an additional written entry agreement between the partnership enterprise and the legal successor, as prescribed in Article 43, Paragraph 1 PEL for the joining of a new partner, is not required in case of a legal succession.[443]

The effect of the legal succession because of inheritance is the same in Germany as in China. The membership right is directly transferred from the deceased partner to the legal successor.[444] Regarding the limited partner, the transfer of the membership right occurs automatically.[445] No further declaration of the legal successor or the other partners is required.[446] The same applies to the successor of a general partner, if the partnership agreement includes a succession clause (Nachfolgeklausel) which stipulates that in the event of the death of a partner, his membership right is passed on to his legal successor.[447] Such an automatic transfer of the membership right without the consent of the legal successor is alien to Chinese law. Alternatively, partners under German law can stipulate an entry clause (Eintrittsklausel) that gives a legal successor only the right to become a partner in the partnership enterprise.[448] The successor subsequently has to make an explicit declaration, and conclude an entry agreement with the partnership enterprise.[449] While the entry clause is similar to the regulative approach under Chinese law, the PEL does not require to conclude a

[438] Art. 50 Para. 1 PEL.

[439] Li (李飞) (ed) (2006), p. 75.

[440] Ibid, p. 129.

[441] Ibid, p. 129.

[442] Art. 13, 24 PEL, Arts. 18–19 FIPE Provisions.

[443] Li (李飞) (ed) (2006), p. 68.

[444] Schmidt (2002), p. 1338.

[445] Art. 177 HGB.

[446] Roth (2020), § 177 Para. 3.

[447] Schmidt (2002), pp. 1338–1343.

[448] Ibid, pp. 1346–1350.

[449] Ibid, pp. 1346–1350.

special agreement. Under German law, it is further permissible to stipulate specific requirements that a successor of the deceased general or limited partner must fulfil, in order to be allowed to become a partner.[450] A common form is that only one of several children of the deceased partner shall be allowed to become a partner. Under Chinese law, the PEL only permits such a stipulation with regard to the successor of a general partner.

9.4.2 Legal Succession Because of Transfer

In business practice, a partner may want to sell his ownership interest in the FILPE to another partner or a third party for various reasons.[451] For a limited partner who wants to de-invest from a FILPE, the transfer of his ownership interest is the most favourable method from a liability perspective.[452] Such an acquisition of ownership interest falls under the scope of M&A transactions, which have only gradually been permitted by the Chinese lawmaker since 1997. Initially only allowing the transfer of equity interest in FIEs between foreign investors, it was not until 2003 that foreign investors were permitted to acquire equity interest in a domestic-invested Chinese enterprise.[453] Regarding partnership enterprises, the transfer of a partner's ownership interest is regulated in Articles 22–24 and 73 PEL, and Article 26 FIPE Provisions. The previous analysis has shown that the object of a transfer of the partner's share of the property in the partnership enterprise is the comprehensive and inseparable membership right of a partner.[454] The analysis here focuses on how such a transfer is carried out and its effect on the partnership enterprise and the parties involved. Depending on whether a limited partner or a general partner transfers his membership right and whether a partner transfers it to another partner or a third party, certain additional requirements are stipulated for such a transfer.

9.4.2.1 Applicable Regulations

Legally, the common dogmatic basis for all these scenarios is the transfer of the membership right in the partnership enterprise from the transferor to the transferee. Under German law, the transfer of a membership right is not expressly codified in the provisions governing the partnership enterprise, because the German lawmaker did not consider the transfer of the membership rights when the HGB was drafted.[455]

[450] Ibid, pp. 1343–1346.

[451] Li (李飞) (ed) (2006), p. 35.

[452] Weng and Xia (2007), p. 97. For more details, see Sect. 8.4.3.

[453] See Sect. 3.1.4.

[454] See Sect. 7.1.2.1.

[455] Schmidt (2002), p. 563.

However, jurisprudence has dogmatically regarded the transfer of a membership right as a 'transfer of other rights', to which the regulations on the transfer of claims in the BGB are applied respectively.[456] German civil law thus provides a systematic and solid legal framework for the transfer of the membership right in a partnership enterprise, whereas civil law matters are still regulated only rudimentarily in China.[457] The transfer of contractual rights and obligations was first regulated in the 1986 GPCL. Under Article 91 GPCL, if a party to a contract transfers all or part of its contractual rights or obligations to a third party, 'he shall obtain the other party's consent and may not seek profits therefrom'. Among the two restrictions that this regulation imposes, the latter—prohibiting to seek profits form the transaction—is particularly remarkable. The background to this regulation can be found in the concern at the time of the promulgation of the GPCL that speculative transactions could destabilise China's economy.[458] Nowadays, the sale and purchase of rights and obligations is an important component of daily business activities in China's economy, as in all other developed economies. The transfer of the membership right in a FILPE would also be conducted with the goal of making a profit in most cases. Therefore, the legal effect of this regulation is not entirely clear and subject to controversy among commentators.[459] The aim of making profit is uniformly regarded as a legitimate goal of commercial transactions.[460] The prohibition shall only cover those contracts that have been entered into by one party with the intention of transferring the contracts while the transferring party has never been able to fulfil the underlying contractual obligations by itself.[461] In all other cases, the realisation of a reasonable profit is regarded as permissible.[462] Moreover, the assignment of contractual rights and obligations was regulated in the 1999 Contract Law, but without the prohibition of 'profit-seeking'.[463] Regarding the relationship between the GPCL and the Contract Law, *Zhang* points out that the Contract Law takes precedence under the doctrine of newer law taking precedence over older law.[464] However, the GPCL have been revised in 2009 in order to bring the law in line with the evolved realities of the Chinese socialist market economy. Notably, Article 91 GPCL remained unchanged during this reform. However, the Contract Law is also the more special law, which is equally grounds for taking precedence over a more general law.[465] The 2017 GRCL do not provide any regulation on the transfer of rights and obligations. Thus, it remains to be seen if and how this will be regulated

[456] Art. 413 BGB; Schmidt (2002), pp. 1321–1323.

[457] Binding and Zhang (2015), p. 82.

[458] Ibid, p. 84.

[459] Ibid, p. 84.

[460] Ibid, p. 84.

[461] Ibid, p. 84.

[462] Ibid, p. 84.

[463] Arts. 79–90 Contract Law.

[464] Art. 92 Legislation Law; Zhang (2006), p. 235.

[465] Art. 92 Legislation Law; Zhang (2006), p. 235.

in subsequent sections of the comprehensive Civil Code that shall be enacted in the near future.[466] Regarding the membership right in a partnership enterprise, the analysis has shown that a membership right fulfils regular contractual elements, but also goes beyond a contract for the mutual exchange of specific performances.[467] The provisions on the transfer in the PEL reflect this unique nature of the membership right, as is expressed in the differentiated requirements when consent from the other partners must be obtained. Nevertheless, the prohibition of 'profit-seeking' has completely been abolished in the PEL. According to the doctrine of the more special law, the PEL likewise takes precedence over Article 91 GPCL in this regard.[468] Realising a profit with the transfer of a membership right in a FILPE therefore does not affect the lawfulness and effectiveness of such a transfer, which is governed by the regulations in the PEL and the FIPE Legislation.

9.4.2.2 Transfer of General Partner's Membership Right to a Third Party

The transfer of a general partner's share of the property in the partnership enterprise to a third party is regulated in Article 22, Paragraph 1, and Articles 23 and 24 PEL. A partner can transfer the whole or a part of his share of the property in the partnership enterprise.[469] By default, the membership right of a general partner is not freely transferable. Consent needs to be obtained from all other partners. This requirement reflects the personal element of the partnership enterprise that is especially strong with regard to a general partner, who not only bears unlimited liability but also participates in the management of the partnership enterprise.[470] The legitimate interest of the other partners must be protected in the transfer of a membership right.[471] They must be secured against the threat of exchanging a desired general partner for an undesirable general partner.[472] Under the 1997 PEL, the consent of all other partners was still a statutory prerequisite for the transfer to a third party.[473] With the revision of the PEL, this has been changed to a default rule that requires unanimous consent only 'unless otherwise specified in the partnership agreement'.[474] This provides partners with full flexibility in stipulating which partners under what circumstances shall decide on the transfer of a general partner's

---

[466] At the time of writing of this book, the new Civil Code has not yet been promulgated by the NPC and therefore cannot be considered in the analysis.

[467] See Sects. 4.1.9.1 and 7.1.2.1.

[468] Art. 92 Legislation Law.

[469] Art. 22 Para. 1 PEL.

[470] Li (李飞) (ed) (2006), p. 35.

[471] Schmidt (2002), pp. 1322–1323.

[472] Ibid, pp. 1322–1323.

[473] Art. 21 Para. 1 1997 PEL.

[474] Art. 22 Para. 1 PEL.

membership right. The transfer can be made subject to only the consent of the other general partners, the consent of a majority decision among all partners, or even an exemption from any consent. In family-owned partnership enterprises, it is further common to limit the circle of potential transferees to family members of the general partner.[475] However, if the partnership agreement makes no further stipulations and the transfer is subject to the consent of all other partners, a transfer in violation of this requirement is deemed to be invalid.[476] Under German partnership law, the consent of all other partners to the transfer is likewise required, unless otherwise stipulated in the partnership agreement.[477] Regarding the Chinese EJV and CJV, however, the consent of all other parties to the joint venture was a statutory requirement for a valid transfer.[478] The FILPE therefore offers more flexibility with regard to the transferability of its ownership interest.

The second condition for a transfer is stipulated in Article 23 PEL, requiring that the other partners are granted a right of first refusal to purchase the ownership interest of the transferor under equivalent terms and conditions. The admission of a third party as a new general partner can lead to conflicts among the partners because the general partner participates in the execution of partnership affairs, and partners may have different opinions with regard to the strategy of the partnership enterprise.[479] In order to maintain the personal relationship among the partners and to safeguard the stability of the partnership enterprise, it is common in many jurisdictions to provide existing partners with such a pre-emptive right.[480] Other partners who want to exercise the right of first refusal need to be aware of two restrictions. Firstly, priority to another partner over a third party is only granted if the partner's offer is made 'under equal conditions'.[481] If the offer of the third party contains a higher purchase price than that of the other partner, the latter cannot invoke any priority.[482] Secondly, the right of first refusal is subject to a time constraint in practice. The other partners can only exercise their right of first refusal before the transaction with the third party has been concluded.[483] Thereafter, the priority right is forfeited.[484] The PEL makes no further stipulations on how much time must be granted to the other partners to execute their right of first refusal. However, the purpose of the regulation is to provide the other partners with an actual chance to purchase the ownership interest in question. This requires that a reasonable

[475]Schmidt (2002), p. 1323.

[476]Ye (2002), p. 108.

[477]Schmidt (2002), p. 1323.

[478]Art. 4 Para. 4 EJV Law, Art. 20 EJV Implementing Regulations, Art. 10 CJV Law, and Art. 23 CJV Implementing Regulations.

[479]Li (李飞) (ed) (2006), p. 36.

[480]Ibid, p. 36.

[481]Art. 23 PEL.

[482]Li (李飞) (ed) (2006), p. 36.

[483]Ibid, p. 36.

[484]Ibid, p. 36.

amount of time is granted to the other partners to execute their right of first refusal. Partners can also specify a minimum amount of time in the partnership agreement. Notably, the wording of Article 23 PEL does not limit the circle of partners who can exercise the priority right to other general partners alone. The term 'partner' may therefore reasonably be interpreted to include both general and limited partners.[485] A limited partner who executes the right of first refusal would thereby change his status into that of a general partner.[486] However, the right of first refusal is bound to the membership right in the partnership enterprise, and cannot be transferred as a singular right to a third party.[487] Under the 1997 PEL, the right of first refusal was a statutory element of the transfer process.[488] Since the revision of the PEL, the other partners only enjoy this right 'unless otherwise specified in the partnership agreement'.[489] By changing this regulation into a default provision, the Chinese lawmaker has further facilitated the free transferability of the partner's share of the property in the partnership enterprise. In comparison, a statutory right of first refusal for the EJV is granted to the other joint venture parties that effectively cannot be evaded.[490] This is one of the reasons why it is difficult for investors to exit from an EJV.[491] However, German partnership law does not codify a right of first refusal at all. Such a right would have to be stipulated by the partners in the partnership agreement.

The transfer of the membership right further requires that the partnership agreement be amended to include the name of the transferee as the new partner. This is a crucial step in the transfer process, as Article 24 PEL stipulates that the transferee 'becomes a partner of the partnership enterprise when an amendment is made to the partnership agreement'. Because the transferee begins to bear the rights and obligations of a partner from that moment on, it is essential that he keeps track of the amendment process.[492] It can also be advisable for the transferee to include a condition precedent in the transfer agreement, stipulating that the transfer of the ownership interest only takes effect when the other partners consent to the amendment of the partnership agreement. The stipulations for an amendment to the partnership agreement in Article 19, Paragraph 2 PEL require 'the consent of all partners, unless otherwise specified in the partnership agreement'. The unanimous approval requirement had been a statutory precondition under the 1997 PEL, but was changed to a default provision with the reform of the PEL. It has already been pointed out that when partners consent to the transfer of a membership right, this

[485] Wu and Geu (2007–2008), p. 149.

[486] Regarding the requirements and consequences of such a transfer, see Sect. 9.3.5.

[487] Gao (高富平) et al. (1997), p. 188.

[488] Art. 22 1997 PEL.

[489] Art. 23 PEL.

[490] Art. 20 Para. 2 EJV Implementing Regulations; Mahony (2015), p. 183. Notably, no right of first refusal has been stipulated for the CJV, which reflects its more flexible structure in comparison to the EJV.

[491] Mahony (2015), p. 183.

[492] Li (李飞) (ed) (2006), p. 37.

should be followed by a consent to amend the partnership agreement.[493] A careful drafter can therefore include a provision in the partnership agreement that the consent to the transfer of the ownership interest according to Article 22, Paragraph 2 PEL concurrently stipulates consent to the amendment of the partnership agreement according to Article 19, Paragraph 2 PEL. Such a regulation can prevent contradictory voting behaviour of the partners.

When a new partner joins the partnership enterprise pursuant to Article 43 PEL, the law requires the conclusion of a written entering agreement. This agreement is dogmatically regarded as an extension of, or amendment to the original partnership agreement.[494] This is necessary because the addition of a new partner usually entails a new capital contribution that causes the other partner's share of the property in the partnership enterprise to shift.[495] When a membership right is transferred from a partner to a third party, this does not affect the capital structure of the partnership enterprise, and the other partner's shares of ownership interest. In effect, only the subject who owns the membership right is changing.[496] Therefore, no additional entering agreement needs to be concluded.[497] Only the name of the transferring partner in the partnership agreement needs to be changed to the name of the transferee, as stipulated in Article 24 PEL.

9.4.2.3 Transfer of Limited Partner's Membership Right to a Third Party

The transfer of a limited partner's membership right to a third party is regulated in Article 73 PEL. A limited partner is not involved in the management of the partnership enterprise, and he does not bear any liability beyond the capital contribution he has subscribed to. Therefore, the personal identity of the limited partner does not have the same significance as that of the general partner.[498] The PEL thus stipulates fewer restrictions on the transfer of a limited partner's membership right than it does on the general partner. The only statutory requirement is that the transferring partner 'notifies the other partners [about the transfer] thirty days in advance'.[499] This notification period shall give the other partners time to prevent potential adverse effects on the operation of the partnership enterprise.[500] However, Article 73 PEL neither requires the transferor to obtain consent from the other partners, nor does it grant the other partners a right of first refusal. However, the

[493]See Sect. 7.1.2.1.

[494]See Sect. 9.3.1.1.

[495]Li (李飞) (ed) (2006), p. 68.

[496]Ibid, p. 68.

[497]Ibid, p. 68.

[498]Ibid, p. 119.

[499]Art. 73 PEL.

[500]Li (李飞) (ed) (2006), p. 119.

provision states that the limited partner may transfer his membership right to a third party 'in accordance with the terms of the partnership agreement'.[501] Therefore, the lawmaker leaves it up to the partners to define the transfer procedure.[502] The partnership agreement may require the unanimous consent of all partners, or all general partners, or request that the transferee fulfils certain qualifications, or grant the other partners a right of first refusal.[503] These options are an expression of the strong party autonomy that the Chinese lawmaker has allowed for the partnership enterprise. The partners themselves can determine whether the ownership interest of a limited partner shall be freely transferable or subject to certain restrictions. *Ribstein* pleads for the ownership interest of a limited partner to be freely transferable as any constrains will harm the tradability, and thereby the development of an efficient market in the ownership interests of enterprises.[504] Under German law, the partners must stipulate in the partnership agreement that the membership right of a limited partner is (freely) transferable while they are also free to add certain requirements or restrictions. Similarly, with regard to the transfer of a general partner's ownership interest, the transferee obtains the status of a limited partner with the amendment of the partnership agreement pursuant to Article 24 PEL. Reference can be made to the above analysis.

9.4.2.4 Transfer of a Partner's Membership Right to Another Partner

The transfer of a general partner's membership right to another partner is regulated in Article 22, Paragraph 2 PEL. Because such a transfer is an internal process among the existing partners, the PEL imposes fewer requirements.[505] No consent from other partners needs to be obtained, and no right of first refusal is granted to the other partners. The transferring partner is only obliged to notify the other partners about the transfer.[506] Unlike the thirty-day notification period stipulated in Article 73 PEL, the law makes no further stipulations in Article 22, Para 2 PEL regarding the timeline or formal requirements of the notice. Absent a special provision for limited partners, the same provision applies to the transfer of a limited partner's membership right to another partner.

Notably, practical experience with regard to the EJV has shown that the transfer of equity interest to the joint venture parties was far more common than a transfer to a third party.[507] However, this can be accredited to the statutory restrictions in the

[501] Art. 73 PEL.

[502] Ibid, p. 119.

[503] Ibid, p. 119.

[504] Ribstein (1988), p. 893.

[505] Li (李飞) (ed) (2006), p. 35.

[506] Art. 22 Para. 2 PEL.

[507] Kroymann (2009), p. 163.

EJV legislation that made a transfer to a third party so difficult.[508] For a FILPE, however, transfer of membership rights to third parties may become more common.

9.4.2.5 Filing Requirements

The transfer of the membership right to a third party and the exchange of the name of the transferor for the name of the transferee in the partnership agreement constitute changes in the registration items of a FILPE. These changes require that the FILPE applies to the local SAMR for a change of registration within fifteen days of the decision to amend the partnership agreement.[509] Article 26, Paragraph 2 FIPE Provisions further stipulates that the transfer agreement between the transferor and transferee shall be submitted to the local SAMR. These filing requirements are in stark contrast to the rigid approval requirements that used to apply to the transfer of ownership interest in an EJV.[510] A transfer of equity interest in an EJV had to be approved by MOFCOM, which would issue an amended FIE approval certificate.[511] The equity transfer agreement, the agreement to revise the original joint venture contract, and the articles of association of the EJV only became effective at the date of issuance of the amended FIE approval certificate.[512] This is a special characteristic of Chinese corporate law that could cause severe difficulties in M&A transactions, as the date when the transaction became effective could not be defined by the parties, but was determined unilaterally by MOFCOM. With regard to the transfer of ownership interest in a FILPE, the parties maintain more control over the M&A process, as the transfer of the membership right becomes effective upon the conclusion of the written transfer agreement. The transferee becomes a partner upon the amendment of the partnership agreement.[513] The amendment of the partnership agreement becomes effective after all partners have signed it or affixed their seals thereto.[514] The filing of the amended partnership agreement with SAMR is thus not a precondition for its effectiveness, but can be relevant for the liability of the transferring partner towards a bona fide third party.[515] This illustrates that the transfer of ownership interest in a FILPE is less bureaucratic than it was in an EJV.

[508] Mahony (2015), p. 183.

[509] Arts. 18–19, Art. 26 Para. 1, Art. 53 FIPE Provisions.

[510] The same requirement applies with regard to CJVs and WFOEs.

[511] Art. 7 Para. 1 FIE Changes in Equity Provisions.

[512] Art. 20 FIE Changes in Equity Provisions.

[513] Art. 24 PEL.

[514] Art. 19 Para. 1 PEL.

[515] See Sect. 9.3.2.2.

9.4.2.6 Effect of the Transfer

With the amendment of the partnership agreement, the transferee becomes a partner of the partnership enterprise.[516] As a partner, the rights and obligations of the transferee are defined and limited by the rights and obligations that the transferor held in the partnership enterprise.[517] This includes the liability for debts of the partnership enterprise.[518] However, the transferor exits the partnership enterprise with the transfer, if he has transferred his entire ownership interest. Should he only have transferred a part of his ownership interest, he continues to be a partner with his remaining ownership interest.[519] Whether the transferor continues to bear liabilities after transferring his membership right depends on whether he is a general partner or a limited partner.[520]

For the partnership enterprise, the transfer of a partner's ownership interest generally has no substantial consequences. The ownership interest remains in the partnership enterprise, only the subject owning the membership right changes.[521] However, the statutory requirements of a FILPE must still be fulfilled after such a transfer. This means that at least one partner must be a foreign investor, and at least one partner must be a general partner and another must be a limited partner. Should these requirements no longer be fulfilled, this would cause the transformation of the enterprise form of the FILPE or even its dissolution.[522]

9.4.2.7 Offshore Transfer of the Corporate General Partner

In the introduction to this chapter, it was observed that limited liability is one of the prerequisites for transferable shares.[523] *The Anatomy of Corporate Law* differentiates further, and points out that limited liability is not mandatorily essential for transferable shares.[524] 'So long as shareholder liability for a firm's debts is *pro rata* rather than joint and several, free tradability of shares is feasible with unlimited personal shareholder liability for corporate debts.'[525] However, the analysis under limited liability of the FILPE has shown that the general partner who transfers his membership right to a third party continues to bear 'unlimited joint and several liability for the debts of the partnership enterprise' in accordance with Article

516 Art. 24 PEL.

517 Li (李飞) (ed) (2006), p. 68; Gao (高富平) et al. (1997), p. 188.

518 See Sect. 8.4.3.

519 Ye (2002), p. 108.

520 See Sect. 8.4.3.

521 Li (李飞) (ed) (2006), p. 68.

522 See Sects. 9.3.2.2 and 9.3.3.

523 See introduction to Sect. 9.

524 Armour et al. (2009), p. 10.

525 Ibid, p. 10.

53 PEL. Because this research project revolves around a FILPE with a single foreign corporate general partner, the question arises whether it would be an option for the foreign investor to transfer his ownership interest in the corporate general partner instead of transferring the corporation's membership right in the FILPE. This transaction structure would allow the investor behind the corporate general partner to shield himself effectively from any liability after de-investing from the FILPE.[526]

A similar investment structure has been frequently used by foreign investors with regard to EJVs, CJVs, and WFOEs.[527] In order to avoid the restrictions and approval requirements for a direct transfer of ownership interest in a joint venture or WFOE, it was common for foreign investors to use an intermediary offshore holding company to transfer the ownership interest in the actual on-shore investment in China.[528] These offshore holding companies were typically established in Hong Kong, or in one of the so-called tax havens such as the British Virgin Islands or Cayman Island.[529]

> Thus, instead of investing directly in the joint venture or WFOE from an entity in the investor's home country, a two-tier structure [was] utilised under which the ultimate investor establishe[d] an intermediary holding company in the desired jurisdiction. In turn, the holding company [made] the actual PRC on-shore investment and all payment flows [were] channelled through this entity. If the investor subsequently wishe[d] to exit the venture it need[ed] only sell its shares in the offshore holding company, a transaction that [was] not subject to PRC approval requirements, thus avoiding the need to obtain MOFCOM approval (since the investor on record ha[d] not changed).[530]

When a foreign corporate general partner in a FILPE is utilised effectively to limit the liability of the investor behind the general partner, this can be compared to the offshore holding company in this two-tier investment structure. However, the above analysis of the veil-piercing regime has illustrated that the Chinese lawmaker does not hesitate to take measures when the use of specific investment structure harms the interests of third parties.[531] In this sense, China's tax authority has promulgated 'Tax Circular 698'[532] in an effort to avoid the loss of tax revenue resulting from the use of foreign holding companies.[533] The regulation permits the tax authority to deny the corporate veil of an offshore holding company if a transaction is regarded as constituting an abuse of the corporate form with the sole aim to avoid certain tax

---

[526]See Sect. 8.4.3.

[527]Mahony (2015), p. 183.

[528]Ibid, p. 183.

[529]Ibid, pp. 183–184.

[530]Ibid, p. 184.

[531]See Sect. 8.2.2.3.

[532]Circular on Strengthening the Management of Enterprise Income Tax Colletion of Proceeds from Equity Transfers by Non-Resident Enterprises (加强非居民企业股权转让所得企业所得税管理的通知), promulgated by the State Administration of Taxation on 10 December 2009, amended on 12 December 2013, amended on 3 February 2015 and amended on 17 October 2017.

[533]For a detailed discussion on Tax Circular 698, see Shen (2015), pp. 75–87.

liabilities, 'without a reasonable business purpose'.[534] This provision effectively creates 'a new regime in which the corporate veil can be pierced outside the conventional veil-piercing framework under the Company Law. (...) As a result, a capital gain tax (in the form of the enterprise income tax under Chinese Tax Law) will be levied on such a transaction.'[535] *Shen* criticises that the condition

> without a reasonable business purpose is a black or white approach, which may oversimplify the complexity of commercial transactions. A typical transnational company has a high degree of discretion over its financial structure so that it can devise optimal routes for internal transactions within the firm through its chains of affiliates. To form intermediary entities in convenient jurisdictions is a critically important part of this overall discretion, which is generally protected by basic modern company law principles. Setting up an intermediate entity in a convenient jurisdiction is often specifically for the purpose of reducing tax liability. A transnational company has a natural right to adopt such techniques so as to take advantage of the limitations of the tax treaty system and hence reduce its cost of capital, making it gain a substantial competitive advantage. Arguably, these are important and reasonable business objectives and strategies.[536]

The corporate general partner in a FILPE is not only set up to avoid taxes but primarily to shield the investor from unlimited liability. However, it remains unclear whether this would be regarded as a 'reasonable business objective' by Chinese tax authorities. Therefore, a foreign investor should be aware of the possible tax liabilities that are imposed on an offshore transfer of the corporate general partner under Tax Circular 698.

A further issue to consider is that the foreign corporate general partner of the FILPE is governed by the law of its place of incorporation. A transfer of ownership interest must therefore be legal under the applicable foreign law. In an investment structure where all limited partners are also owners of the corporate general partner of the FILPE,[537] it should be ensured that the membership right in the FILPE can only be transferred together with the ownership interest in the corporate general partner and vice versa.[538] Respective provisions must be included in the partnership agreement of the FILPE, and in the articles of association of the corporate general partner.[539] Therefore, the foreign law that governs the corporate general partner must permit such a restriction of the transferability of ownership interest.

[534] Art. 6 Tax Circular 698.

[535] Shen (2015), p. 78.

[536] Ibid, pp. 80–81.

[537] See Sect. 5.3.2.2.1.

[538] Teichmann (2014), p. 240.

[539] Ibid, p. 240.

9.4.2.8 Acquiring Ownership Interest in a Domestic-Invested Partnership Enterprise

Besides acquiring the ownership interest in a FILPE, a foreign investor can also acquire the ownership interest in a domestic-invested partnership enterprise from a Chinese investor.[540] In addition to the provisions that have been analysed, the joining of a foreign investor causes the status of the domestic-invested partnership enterprise to change into a foreign-invested partnership enterprise. With regard to a corporation, the M&A Provisions apply when a foreign investors purchases equity in a domestic-invested Chinese corporation, thereby transforming it into an FIE.[541] This raises the question whether the M&A Provisions likewise apply to the acquisition of an ownership interest in a domestic-invested partnership enterprise. Accordingly, such a transaction could be subject to MOFCOM revision and approval under the M&A Provisions.[542] However, the wording of the M&A Provisions make reference to corporations alone, like limited liability companies and joint stock companies, e.g. when using terms like 'equity interest' and 'subscribing to increased capital'. These are terms that are not associated with a partnership enterprise. To summarise the domestic-invested target companies, the term 'domestic companies' (境内公司) is used. The expression 'company' (公司) in Chinese Company Law exclusively refers to limited liability companies and joint stock companies.[543] Nevertheless, Article 63 FIPE Provisions expressly states that the regulations of the FIPE Provisions shall apply to the purchase of an ownership interest in a domestic-invested partnership enterprise by a foreign investor.[544] Because the content of the M&A Provisions—a foreign investor buying into a domestic-invested enterprise—is directly regulated in the PEL and the FIPE Provisions, the M&A Provisions are not applicable. However, the general investment restrictions on the establishment of a FIPE naturally have to be adhered to.[545] Of importance to a foreign investor is that the domestic-invested enterprise which is the target of the foreign investor's interest, is not infrequently in fact a state-owned enterprise, or holds state-owned assets.[546] In such circumstances, an extensive set of rules governing the disposal of state-owned assets applies and a lengthy and rather complex approval process needs to be undertaken.[547]

---

[540] Meyer (2016), p. 219.

[541] Art. 2 M&A Provisions.

[542] Art. 6 M&A Provisions.

[543] Art. 2 Company Law; Du (2014), p. 335; Werthwein (2010), p. 17; Bu (2017), p. 191. Additionally, see Sect. 4.1.3.2.

[544] Art. 63 FIPE Provisions. Additionally, see Sect. 9.3.1.2.

[545] Wolff (2015), pp. 159–160.

[546] Mahony (2015), p. 59.

[547] Ibid, pp. 59–61.

9.4.3 Pledge of Ownership Interest

Strictly speaking, the pledge of ownership interest does not directly constitute a legal succession. However, it is a form of disposal over the ownership interest that can lead to its transfer. Therefore, it appears appropriate to analyse the pledge at this point. In China, security rights are widely used in domestic transactions.[548] A pledge falls under the category of 'so-called real security rights – a legal term originating from the continental European legal system – by which the fulfilment of the claim is secured by the encumbered property, i.e. by immovable and movable properties as well as certain property rights'.[549] Pledges had already been recognised in Article 89, Paragraph 2 GPCL. With the promulgation of the 'Securities Law'[550] in 1995, more detailed rules on the pledge were introduced.[551] Most recently, the 'Property Law'[552] of 2007 has modified and partly revised existing regulations on real security rights, including pledges.[553] In case of any inconsistencies between the provisions, the Property Law shall take precedence over the Securities Law.[554] Chinese law distinguishes between the pledge of movable properties and the pledge of rights.[555] This distinction corresponds to the concept under German civil law.[556] Rights that may be subject to a pledge are listed under Article 223 Property Law. One of the listed rights is 'share of equity', which is a terminology used in China primarily with regard to corporations.[557] It is unclear whether this term also includes a partner's share of the property in the partnership enterprise. However, the enumeration ends with 'other property rights which may be pledged as provided for by laws and administrative regulations'.[558] In turn, the PEL in Article 25 stipulates the procedure for the pledge of a partner's share of the property in the partnership enterprise. Similarly to the transfer of the partner's share of the property in the partnership enterprise, the pledge must also revolve around a comprehensive and inseparable membership right of the partner.[559] The provisions of the Property Law on the

548Tu (2010), p. 191.

549Ibid, p. 183.

550PRC Security Law (中华人民共和国担保法), adopted at the 14th Session of the Standing Committee of the 8th National People's Congress on 30 June 1995 and effective from 1 October 1995.

551Arts. 63–81 Securities Law.

552PRC Property Law (中华人民共和国物权法), adopted at the 5th Session of the 10th National People's Congress on 16 March 2007 and effective from 1 October 2007.

553Tu (2010), p. 184.

554Art. 178 Property Law.

555Arts. 208–222 Property Law, Arts. 223–229 Property Law.

556Arts. 1204–1259 BGB, Arts. 127–1296 BGB.

557Art. 223 Para. 4 Property Law.

558Art. 223 Para. 7 Property Law.

559See Sect. 7.1.2.1. Regarding the discussion what constitutes the objective of a pledge under German partnership law, see Schmidt (2002), p. 1327.

pledge of rights are therefore applicable to the pledge of a membership right in a partnership enterprise.[560] The provisions with regard to the pledge of movable properties still apply subsidiarily to the pledge of rights.[561] Overall, the pledge of a membership right in a partnership enterprise is governed by the provision in the PEL and the regulations in the Property Law.

'The pledge is a possessory right, i.e. the creation of a pledge requires the physical possession of the pledged property to be transferred to the pledgee.'[562] However, a pledge does not involve the transfer of title on the pledged property.[563] The creation of a pledge on rights requires an effective pledge contract between the pledger and the pledgee, and the delivery of any relevant certificate of the right to be pledged or the registration of the pledge.[564] Article 223 Property Law stipulates that a right may be pledged if the debtor 'is entitled to dispose of the right'. This leads to the respective provisions in the PEL. With regard to the membership right of a general partner, Article 25 PEL stipulates that such a pledge 'shall be subject to the consent of all the other partners'. This mandatory requirement to obtain consent follows from the distinct role that the general partner plays in managing the partnership enterprise, and bearing unlimited liability for its debts.[565] Eventually, a pledge can result in the transfer of the membership right to a third party which subsequently will act as general partner.[566] Therefore, the other partners shall have the right to keep information on the debt and pledge so that they can reach an informed decision on whether they want to accept the risks that a pledge might entail for the partnership enterprise.[567] Should the other partners refuse to consent, Article 25 PEL stipulates that 'an unauthorised pledge shall be invalid and, if losses are caused to a bona fide third party, the said partner shall bear the liability for compensation'. This provision is more streamlined than the preceding regulation in the 1997 PEL, which had stipulated alternative consequences for an unauthorised pledge: either the pledge was regarded as invalid, or the action of the partner was to be regarded as his withdrawal from the partnership enterprise.[568] The choice of which consequence applied rested on the other partners.[569] Under the PEL, the other partners effectively maintain control over each pledge of a general partner's membership right. Regarding a limited partner, however, Article 72 PEL stipulates that he may pledge his membership right 'unless otherwise specified in the partnership agreement'. This default provision reflects that the exchange of a limited partner has a less significant

---

[560] Li (李飞) (ed) (2006), p. 117.
[561] Art. 229 Property Law.
[562] Tu (2010), p. 211.
[563] Ibid, p. 211.
[564] Ibid, p. 212.
[565] Li (李飞) (ed) (2006), p. 38.
[566] Ibid, p. 38.
[567] Ibid, p. 38.
[568] Art. 24 Para. 2 1997 PEL.
[569] Ye (2002), p. 111.

effect on the operation of a partnership enterprise than that of a general partner.[570] However, the analysis of the liquidation protection of the FILPE suggested that it may be more advisable to exclude the right to pledge a limited partner's membership right in the partnership agreement.[571]

Being a possessory right, the pledge requires that a relevant certificate of the right to be pledged is delivered to the pledgee, or that the pledge of the right is registered.[572] A commercial paper that can be delivered, as is required for the pledge of a bill of lading, bond or promissory note,[573] does not exist for the membership right in a partnership enterprise, or for shares in a limited liability company. Article 226, Paragraph 1 Property Law stipulates that besides a joint stock company, for 'other kinds of shares that are pledged, the interest of the pledge is established at the time when the pledge is registered with SAMR. It seems reasonable to assume that such a registration is also the prerequisite for a valid pledge of a membership right in a partnership enterprise. However, the PEL, the Partnership Enterprise Registration Measures and the FIPE Legislation all include no stipulation on whether and how such a pledge is to be registered with SAMR.

Regarding the effect of the pledge, the pledgee does not become a partner in the partnership enterprise.[574] This is emphasised in Article 41 PEL, which states that a personal creditor or a partner may not exercise, in subrogation, any management or governance rights or authority of the partner inside the partnership enterprise. Therefore, the pledgee does also not bear any liability for the debts of the partnership enterprise. The legal position of the pledgee is reduced to holding a pledge. When the principal debtor or the pledger pays off the debts he guaranteed, the pledgee shall return the pledged property.[575] For a membership right in a partnership enterprise, this would lead to the de-registration of the pledge with SAMR. Conversely, the enforcement of the pledge is triggered upon the default of the principal debtor on the secured claim, or the occurrence of a contractually stipulated circumstance.[576] As a result, the pledgee may either acquire the pledged right at market price, and subsequently offset the purchase price against the secured claim, or seek payments received from an auction or private sale of the pledged right at market price.[577] Effectively, this leads to a transfer of the membership right from the partner who pledged his membership right to the pledger, a third party or another partner. The consent of the other partners to the pledge thereby constitutes the consent that is otherwise required for the transfer of a membership right.[578] For a third party to

---

570 Li (李飞) (ed) (2006), p. 118.

571 See Sect. 7.1.2.2.

572 Tu (2010), p. 212.

573 Art. 224 Property Law.

574 Ye (2002), p. 110.

575 Art. 219 Para. 1 Property Law.

576 Art. 219 Para. 2 Property Law.

577 Art. 219 Paras. 2 and 3 Property Law.

578 See Sect. 9.4.2.2.

become a partner, the partnership agreement also needs to be changed. In order to ensure that the consent that is required for this amendment is granted, stipulations should be made in the partnership agreement.[579]

In comparison, the pledge of equity interest in an EJV was permitted with the FIE Changes in Equity Provisions.[580] As noted above, these provisions did not apply to the FILPE.[581] While many prerequisites were similar to the pledge of a membership right in a FILPE, the pledge of equity interest in an EJV required approval by MOFCOM.[582] In addition, the later enforcement of such a pledge needed to be approved by MOFCOM again.[583]

Overall, the analysis shows that the partners have control over whether they want to permit the pledge of a membership right, which entails the risk of having to accept a third party as a new partner. Where partners opt to permit the pledge, it is significantly less bureaucratic than was the case for a pledge of ownership interest in an EJV.

9.5 Conclusion

The attribute of transferable ownership interest shall ensure that the business operation of the FILPE is not interrupted when the identity of its owners changes. For the transfer of a membership right from one partner to another partner or to a third party, the analysis has shown that the PEL facilitates the tradability of a membership right in the FILPE.[584] As a consequence of such a transfer of the membership right, only the subject who owns the membership right changes. The identity of the FILPE, its capital structure and the other partners' share of ownership interest are not affected. By default, the transfer of a general partner's membership right is subject to the other partner's consent and their right of first refusal.[585] In terms of the categories in *The Anatomy of Corporate Law*, this would classify as a 'closed' or 'private' enterprise. However, the partnership agreement can also waive these measures so that a general partner's membership right becomes 'freely tradable'. However, a limited partner's membership right is freely tradable by default, unless otherwise stipulated in the partnership agreement.[586] Comparing this with the EJV and CJV, the consent of all other joint venture parties was a statutory condition for a valid transfer of ownership interest. Likewise, the other joint venture parties had a statutory right of first refusal.

[579] See Sect. 9.4.2.2.

[580] Art. 6 FIE Changes in Equity Provisions.

[581] See Sect. 9.4.2.1.

[582] Mahony (2015), p. 44.

[583] Ibid, pp. 44–45.

[584] See Sect. 9.4.2.

[585] See Sect. 9.4.2.2.

[586] See Sect. 9.4.2.3.

Applying the same standard, the EJV thus fell under the category of 'closed' or 'private' enterprises.[587] Regarding the categories of 'widely' and 'closely' held enterprises, the FILPE does not fall clearly under either.[588] Historically, the partnership enterprise in China has been used for very small groups of investors alone. In comparison to the widely held partnership enterprises in Germany, which have several hundred limited partners, the number of fifty partners is still rather low.[589] The transfer of a membership right in a FILPE becomes effective with the conclusion of the written transfer agreement, and only needs to be filed with SAMR.[590] In comparison, a transfer of ownership in an EJV used to be subject to a rigid approval process with MOFCOM. From a liability perspective, a limited partner is exempted from any subsequent liability after a transfer,[591] whereas a general partner continues to bear liabilities. An investor behind a corporate general partner may therefore favour a transfer of ownership in the corporation rather than transferring the corporation's ownership interest in the FILPE.[592] However, China's tax law regime provides special veil-piercing provisions for such offshore-transactions that need to be considered by a foreign investor.

Compared to the transfer of a membership right, a withdrawal of a partner can pose a greater threat to the continuance of a FILPE's business operation.[593] Compensation must be paid to the withdrawing partner. However, the withdrawal does not trigger the dissolution of the FILPE, and does not change its identity. The FILPE continues to exist with the remaining partners. This entity approach adopted by the PEL helps to facilitate the continuity of the FILPE. In order to constrain the consequences of a withdrawal, the reasons that permit a voluntary withdrawal and an exclusion should be defined as narrowly as possible in the partnership agreement.[594] Therein, a balance must be struck between the stability of the partnership enterprise and the autonomy of the partners to decide how long they want to remain invested in the FILPE. While the prerequisite for a statutory withdrawal may not be altered,[595] the conditions of the compensation payment should be stipulated in the partnership agreement. A comprehensive 'compensation clause' allows the parties to define the amount of compensation, the basis for its calculation, and the terms of its payment.[596]

The pledge of a membership right in a FILPE is less bureaucratic than that was for an ownership interest in an EJV, as MOFCOM approval was required for the

---

[587] See Sect. 9.4.2.2.

[588] See Sect. 9.2.1.2.1.

[589] Binz and Sorge (2018), p. 266.

[590] See Sect. 9.4.2.6.

[591] See Sect. 8.4.3.

[592] See Sect. 9.4.2.7.

[593] See Sect. 9.3.2.2.

[594] See Sects. 9.3.2.1.1 and 9.3.2.1.3.

[595] See Sect. 9.3.2.1.2.

[596] See Sect. 9.3.2.2.

latter.[597] However, a pledge can result in the withdrawal of the partner who eventually obtains the membership right in the FILPE. Therefore, it should be considered whether a pledge of the membership right should be precluded in the partnership agreement.

The dissolution of a FILPE is settled in an organised liquidation process.[598] The partnership enterprise is not immediately terminated. The reasons that can lead to dissolution should be defined as precisely and narrowly as possible in the partnership agreement. While the dissolution of an EJV required MOFCOM approval, this is not necessary for a FILPE. The PEL thus provides more freedom to foreign investors to strategically de-invest from the FILPE when the investment turns out to be unprofitable.

Overall, the regulations in the PEL that affect the attribution of transferable ownership interest are to a large degree default provisions. This leaves it to the discretion of the foreign investor to structure a FILPE in such a way that the transfer, withdrawal or pledge of the membership rights affects the continuity of its business operation as little as possible. Together with the discussed adjustments to the attributes of legal personality and limited liability, the legal framework in China thus allows for the development of a market for ownership interests in FILPEs.

References

Armour J, Hansmann H, Kraakman R (2009) What is corporate law? In: Kraakman R et al (eds) The anatomy of corporate law, 2nd edn. Oxford University Press, Oxford, pp 1–34

Armour J, Hansmann H, Kraakman R, Pargendler M (2017) What is corporate law? In: Kraakman R et al (eds) The anatomy of corporate law, 3rd edn. Oxford University Press, Oxford, pp 1–28

Binding J, Zhang H (2015) Die Allgemeinen Grundsätze des Zivilrechts. In: Binding J, Pissler KB, Xu L (eds) Chinesisches Zivil- und Wirtschaftsrecht. R&W, Frankfurt a.M., pp 27–92

Binz MK, Sorge MH (2018) Die GmbH & Co. KG im Gesellschafts- und Steuerrecht, 12th edn. C. H. Beck, Munich

Bu Y (2017) Einführung in das Recht Chinas, 2nd edn. C. H. Beck, Munich

Chen J (2016) Chinese law: context and transformation, revised and expanded edition. Brill, Leiden and Boston

DeMott DA (2004) Transatlantic perspectives on partnership law: risk and instability. In: McCahery JA, Raaijmakers T, Vermeulen EPM (eds) The governance of close corporations and partnerships: US and European perspectives. Oxford University Press, Oxford, pp 275–292

Du T (2014) The new Chinese conflict-of-law rules for legal persons: is the middle way feasible? In: Basedow J, Pissler KB (eds) Private international law in Mainland China, Taiwan and Europe. Mohr Siebeck, Tübingen, pp 331–348

Enriques L (2004) Book review: the comparative anatomy of corporate law. Am J Comp Law 52:1011–1036

Gao F (高富平), Su H (苏号朋), Li Z (刘智慧) (1997) Principles and practice of partnership enterprise law (合伙企业法原理与实务). China Legal Publishing House (中国法制出版社), Beijing

---

[597] See Sect. 9.4.3.

[598] See Sect. 9.2.2.

Garner B (ed) (2009) Black's law dictionary, 9th edn. Thomson West, St. Paul-Minn
Hansmann H, Kraakman R, Squire R (2005) The new business entities in evolutionary perspective. Univ Ill Law Rev 2005:5–14
Hong H (洪虎) (2006) Examination Report on the Draft Revision of the PRC Partnership Enterprise Law – delivered on 22 August 2006 to the 23rd Session of the Standing Committee of the 10th National People's Congress (关于《中华人民共和国合伙企业法(修订草案)》审议结果的报告—2006年8月22日在第十届全国人民代表大会常务委员会第二十三次会议上). Gazette of the Standing Committee of the National People's Congress 2006 No 7 (中华人民共和国全国人民代表大会常务委员会公报2006年7号), pp 602–604
Hu D (2018) Cross-border insolvency regime in China: finding the most pragmatic interim solution for globalized companies under localized practices. Am Bankruptcy Law J 92:523–551
Jiao L, Kasteleijn B (2011) Foreign acquisitions and joint ventures in China. In: Campbell D (ed) Mergers and acquisitions in North America, Latin America, Asia and the Pacific: selected issues and jurisdictions. Wolters Kluwer Law & Business, Alphen aan den Rijn, pp 29–62
Julius H, Bitter M (2005) Symposium zum chinesischen Personenhandelsgesellschaftsrecht. Zeitschrift für Chinesisches Recht 12:62–63
Kroymann B (2009) Das Kapitalgesellschaftsrecht der VR China – Analyse der Rahmenbedingungen für ausländische Investoren. Mohr Siebeck, Tübingen
Li F (李飞) (ed) (2006) Interpretation of the PRC partnership enterprise law (中华人民共和国合伙企业法释义). Law Press China (法律出版社), Beijing
Li S (2007) The legal environment and risks for foreign investment in China. Springer, Berlin
Lin L (2011) The limited partner's derivative action: problems and prospects in the private equity market of China. Hong Kong Law J 41:201–230
Lin L (2017) Engineering a venture capital market: lessons from China. Columbia J Asian Law 30:160–220
Lin L, Yeo HY (2010) Limited partnership – the new business vehicle in China. Butterworth J Int Bank Financ Law 25:104–108
Liu X (2010) Partnerschaftsunternehmen als neues Vehikel für Auslandsinvestitionen in China. Zeitschrift für Chinesisches Recht 17:37–40
Lu M (吕美昂) (2011) A comparison of the nature of foreign-invested enterprises in China (我国外商投资企业性质的比较). Leg Syst Soc (法制与社会) 8:81–82
Mahony T (2015) Foreign investment law in China: regulation, practice and context. Tsinghua University Press, Beijing
Meyer P (2016) Besteuerung und steuerliche Gestaltung deutscher Direktinvestitionen in China. Springer Gabler, Wiesbaden
Raiser T, Veil R (2015) Recht der Kapitalgesellschaften, 6th edn. Verlag Franz Vahlen, Munich
Ribstein LE (1988) An applied theory of limited partnership. Emory Law J 37:835–895
Roth M (2020) HGB § 177 Tod des Kommanditisten Kommanditist. In: Baumbach A, Hopt KJ (eds) Handelsgesetzbuch, 39th edn. C. H. Beck, Munich, § 177 para 1–7
Schmidt K (2002) Gesellschaftsrecht, 4th edn. Heymanns, Cologne
Shen W (2015) Corporate law in China – structure, governance and regulation. Sweet&Maxwell, Hong Kong
Shen E, Weidlich T (2016) Gründung, Organisationsstruktur und Liquidation von FIE. In: Binding J, Pissler KB (eds) Chinesisches Zivil- und Wirtschaftsrecht Band 2 – Schwerpunkt Wirtschaftsrecht. R&W, Frankfurt a.M., pp 163–185
Teichmann C (2014) Die Auslandsgesellschaft & Co. Zeitschrift für Unternehmens- und Gesellschaftsrecht 43:220–251
Tu C (2010) Secured transaction. In: Bu Y (ed) Chinese business law. C. H. Beck, Hart and Nomos, Munich/Oxford, pp 183–219
von Senger H (2006) Von der Vergleichung des Rechts zur Vergleichung der Gesellschaftsführung. Zeitschrift für Europarecht, internationales Privatrecht und Rechtsvergleichung 47:43–62
Weidlich T, Shen Y (2015) Vertragliche Schuldverhältnisse. In: Binding J, Pissler KB, Xu L (eds) Chinesisches Zivil- und Wirtschaftsrecht. R&W, Frankfurt a.M., pp 93–162

Weng J, Xia T (2007) Limited liability partnership: the best structure for funds? China Law Pract 21:97

Werthwein S (2010) Corporations and partnerships. In: Bu Y (ed) Chinese business law. C. H. Beck, Hart and Nomos, Munich/Oxford, pp 15–54

Windbichler C (2014) Eine internationale Landkarte der Personengesellschaften (einschließlich juristische Personen und Gesamthand). Zeitschrift für Unternehmens- und Gesellschaftsrecht 43:110–138

Wolff L-C (2015) Mergers & acquisitions in China: law and practice, 5th edn. Wolters Kluwer Law & Business, Hong Kong

Wu Y, Geu TE (2007–2008) The new PRC limited partnership enterprise law and the limited partnership law of the United States: a selective analytical comparison. UCLA Pac Basin Law J 25:133–178

Xu C (徐春雷), Cao X (曹秀峰) (2007) A study on the administrative registration of foreign-invested partnership enterprises (外商投资合伙企业登记管理问题研究). Study on China's Administration for Industry & Commerce (中国工商管理研究) 2007/12:29–31

Ye F (2002) Das chinesische Gesetz über Partnerschaftsunternehmen: Im Vergleich zum deutschen Recht. Lang, Frankfurt a.M

Yuantao X, Binxue S, Zhang D (1989) Translation of Liufang Fang: Chinese Partnership. Law Contemp Problems 52:43–67

Zhang M (2006) Chinese contract law – theory and practice. Martinus Nijhoff Publishers, Leiden

Zhang L (2015) China's venture capital market: current legal problems and prospective reforms. Chandos Publishing, Amsterdam

Zheng H (2010) Bankruptcy. In: Bu Y (ed) Chinese business law. C. H. Beck, Hart and Nomos, Munich/Oxford, pp 221–266

Chapter 10
Summary of Part II

The preceding analysis has illustrated that the interlocking of statutory rules and appropriate governance provisions in the partnership agreement allows the creation of a FILPE with a foreign corporate general partner that satisfies the features of a standard corporate form. The attribute of legal personality is mainly facilitated by mandatory rules. The latter stipulate that a FILPE constitutes a separate legal entity that can own assets under its own name.[1] Mandatory provisions form affirmative asset partitioning for the FILPE, and establish the authority to represent the FILPE in its external relationships.[2] The feature of limited liability requires more elaborate contractual structuring efforts. By permitting the use of a foreign corporate general partner, Chinese law *de facto* allows to limit the liability of the investor behind the general partner.[3] In order to protect the investor from veil-piercing and to make this hybrid enterprise form coherent, particular attention must be paid to drafting appropriate provisions in the partnership agreement.[4] However, the limited liability of the limited partner is mandatorily stipulated in the PEL.[5] The attribute of transferable ownership interest is largely subject to default provisions. While the PEL permits the transferability of a membership right, the specifics are all left to default provisions.[6] This allows the establishment of a FILPE as a 'freely tradable' or a 'closed' enterprise form. The withdrawal of a partner cannot be ruled out completely, but appropriate provisions in the partnership agreement allow for mitigation of the negative effects of a withdrawal as much as possible.[7] Strikingly, the analysis has

[1]See Sect. 7.1.1.1.

[2]See Sect. 7.1.1.2.

[3]See Sect. 8.2.2.2.

[4]See Sect. 8.2.2.3.

[5]See Sect. 8.3.

[6]See Sect. 9.4.2.

[7]See Sect. 9.3.2.2.

S. Kuntner, *China's Foreign-Invested Limited Partnership Enterprise*, China-EU Law Series 7, https://doi.org/10.1007/978-3-030-54181-1_10

also shown how strongly these three attributes of the standard corporate form are interrelated and interdependent. When a FILPE with a foreign corporate general partner is structured so that it facilitates legal personality, limited liability, and transferable ownership interest, it creates an enterprise form that provides foreign investors with a level of protection and familiarity that is common in international business practice.

Part III
Conclusion

Chapter 11
Summary of the Book

The research question of this book is whether the FILPE with a foreign corporate general partner as an enterprise form does fulfil legal personality, limited liability and transferable ownership interest as three important characteristics of a standard corporate form. In the previous two parts, a detailed analysis of the specific legal issues that arise with regard to this research question has been conducted in the light of the overall legal framework under which a FILPE operates. Instead of recapitulating the findings of the prior analysis, this conclusion provides a more abstract summary of the results in six points.

Firstly, the legal framework of the FILPE was a novelty in China's FIE legislation. The legal frameworks for the EJV, CJV, and WFOE were regulated separately from the general domestic legal system that governs corporations, thus leading to a parallel legal structure of foreign-invested and domestic-invested corporations.[1] However, the FILPE is legally based in the same law as the domestic partnership enterprise, and governed by administrative legislation that also falls under the same law. For a significant part, the same provisions therefore apply to domestic-invested and foreign-invested partnership enterprises.[2] For other FIEs, such a unified legal framework has only been established recently with the promulgation of the new FIL.[3]

Secondly, investments in a FILPE are subject to the same governmental policies of guidance and restriction that have characterised China's FDI regime for the past decades. Despite the latest reforms of the Guidance Catalogue, certain industries and sectors are still prohibited for foreign investments.[4] In comparison to joint ventures, a FILPE is banned from even more investment areas. When planning an FDI project,

[1]See Sect. 3.1.3.

[2]See Sect. 4.1.5.3.

[3]See Sect. 3.1.5.3.

[4]See Sect. 3.1.6.3.3.

S. Kuntner, *China's Foreign-Invested Limited Partnership Enterprise*, China-EU Law Series 7, https://doi.org/10.1007/978-3-030-54181-1_11

a foreign investor must therefore analyse the Guidance Catalogue and industry-specific investment restrictions to determine whether the choice of a FILPE is permitted for the particular project.[5]

Thirdly, the establishment and subsequent changes of a FILPE have always been subject to registration with only SAMR.[6] This has been regarded as a ground-breaking innovation as the FILPE was the first type of FIE to be released from having to obtain MOFCOM approval, and undergo the rigid two-tier administrative procedure. This unified administrative approach of the FIPE can be regarded as the blueprint for the new unified registration with SAMR that was implemented for all FIEs with the new FIL.

Fourthly, in an international comparison the FIPE Legislation also stands out as particularly progressive by statutorily permitting the use of foreign corporations as general partner in a FILPE.[7] This allows foreign investors to combine an enterprise form from their home jurisdiction—or a particularly tax-friendly jurisdiction—with the Chinese FILPE. However, the analysis has shown that conflicts between law and regulations from different jurisdictions need to be considered when structuring such an investment.

Fifthly, the interaction of mandatory rules and default provisions allows a FILPE to be structured with a foreign corporate general partner so that it fulfils the attributes of legal personality, limited liability, and transferable ownership interest.[8] This gives foreign investors the assurance that this investment vehicle—in key aspects—provides the functionality and security that the investor relies on in his home jurisdiction. However, as these three main features are not statutorily provided for by law, their formation requires sophisticated and comprehensive contractual drafting of the partnership agreement.

Ultimately, the FILPE is the type of FIE that offers the most flexibility when structuring an investment vehicle in China.[9] This flexibility requires more effort in drafting the partnership agreement and dealing with the loopholes and uncertainties that the rather young enterprise form of the FILPE still contains. However, a foreign investor who wants to make an investment in China needs to consider the most fitting enterprise form for his individual commercial needs. For the business and investment situations that require the kind of flexibility which only a partnership enterprise can provide, the use of a FILPE with a foreign corporate general partner can be highly attractive.

[5]See Sect. 4.1.7.

[6]See Sect. 4.1.8.1.

[7]See Sect. 8.2.2.2.

[8]See Chap. 10.

[9]See Sect. 5.3.

Table of Cases

I. Supreme People's Court of the PRC (中华人民共和国最高人民法院)

Su Qi et al. vs. Li Zhanfei et al., application for retrial of civil ruling on dispute over recognition of equity interest and profit distribution (苏琪与府谷县老高川乡恒益煤矿、李占飞、李维斌、李旺荣股权确认及分配利润纠纷申请再审民事裁定书), Supreme People's Court of the PRC, case no 2014/20 (最高人民法院(2014)民申字第20号) , judgement date: 26 January 2014, available at <http://www.court.gov.cn/wenshu/xiangqing-2539.html>, accessed 15 May 2020.

Hebei Yixing Highway Co. Ltd. v. Jingyu Highway Co. Ltd. et al., credit agreement dispute (河北冀星高速公路有限公司与京域高速公路有限公司等借款合同纠纷民事裁定书), Supreme People's Court of the PRC, case no 2011/289(最高人民法院(2011)民申字第289号), judgement date: 24 May 2011, available at <http://www.court.gov.cn/wenshu/xiangqing-3290.html>, accessed 15 May 2020.

II. European Court of Justice

European Court of Justice, Case C-167/01, Inspire Art [2003], ECR 2003 I-10155.

European Court of Justice, Case C-20/00, Überseering [2002], ECR 2002 I-9919.

European Court of Justice, Case C-212/97, Centros [1999], ECR 1999 I-1459.

III. Bavarian Higher Regional Court (BayObLG)

Bavarian Higher Regional Court (BayObLG), 16.02.1912, in: Deutsche Juristen-Zeitung vol 18 (1913), pp. 647–648.

S. Kuntner, *China's Foreign-Invested Limited Partnership Enterprise*, China-EU Law Series 7, https://doi.org/10.1007/978-3-030-54181-1

Table of Legislation

The cited legislation is grouped by jurisdictions, within a jurisdiction legislation is organised in alphabetical order of the abbreviated form of the legislation's name that is being used in the book.

I. People's Republic of China

13th Five-Year Plan	13th Five-Year Plan for National Economic and Social Development (国民经济和社会发展第十三个五年规划纲要), adopted at the 4th Session of the 12th National People's Congress on 16 March 2016.
1950 Interim Provisions on Private Enterprises	Interim Provisions on Private Enterprises (私营企业暂行条例), promulgated by the Administrative Council on 30 December 1950 and repealed on 25 July 1986.
1997 Partnership Enterprise Law (1997 PEL)	PRC Partnership Enterprise Law (中华人民共和国合伙企业法), adopted at the 24th Session of the Standing Committee of the 8th National People's Congress on 23 February 1997 and effective from 1 August 1997.
1997 Partnership Enterprise Registration Measures	PRC Administrative Measures for Partnership Enterprise Registration (中华人民共和国合伙企业登记管理办法), promulgated by the State Council on 19 November 1997 and effective as of the same date.
2014 Foreign Investment Measures	Administrative Measures for the Verification and Record-filing of Foreign Investment Projects (外商投资项目核准和备案管理办法), promulgated by the National Development and Reform Commission on 17 May 2014 and amended on 27 December 2014; substituting the Interim Administrative Measures for the Verification of Foreign Investment Projects (外商投资项目核准暂行管理办法), promulgated by the National Development and Reform Commission on 9 October 2004.
2015 Draft Foreign Investment Law (2015 Draft FIL)	PRC Foreign Investment Law (Draft for Comments) 中华人民共和国外国投资法 (草案征求意见稿), promulgated by the Ministry of Commerce on 19 January 2015.

(continued)

S. Kuntner, *China's Foreign-Invested Limited Partnership Enterprise*, China-EU Law Series 7, https://doi.org/10.1007/978-3-030-54181-1

2016 Draft Guidance Catalogue	Notice on Soliciting Public Opinions on the Revised Draft Catalogue of Industries for Guiding Foreign Investment (《外商投资产业指导目录》修订稿公开征求意见的公告), promulgated jointly by the National Development and Reform Commission and the Ministry of Commerce on 7 December 2016.
2016 Government Verification Catalogue	Catalogue of Investment Projects Subject to Government Verification—2016 Version (政府核准的投资项目目录—2016年本), promulgated by the State Council on 12 December 2016, substituting the Catalogue of Investment Projects Subject to Government Verification—2014 Version (政府核准的投资项目目录—2014年本), promulgated by the State Council on 31 October 2014; the Catalogue of Investment Projects Subject to Government Verification—2013 Version (政府核准的投资项目目录—2013年本), promulgated by the State Council on 2 December 2013 and the Catalogue of Investment Projects Subject to Government Verification—2004 Version (政府核准的投资项目目录—2004年本), promulgated by the State Council on 16 July 2004.
2018 Draft Foreign Investment Law (2018 Draft FIL)	Notice on Soliciting Public Opinions on the Foreign Investment Law (Draft) (外商投资法(草案)征求意见), issued by the Standing Committee of the National People's Congress on 21 December 2018.
2018 Master Negative List	Circular on the publication of the Market Access Negative List (2018 Version) (印发市场准入负面清单草案(试点版)的通知), promulgated jointly by the National Development and Reform Commission and the Ministry of Commerce on 21 December 2018 and effective as of the same date.
2019 Master Negative List	Circular on the publication of the Market Access Negative List (2018 Version) (印发市场准入负面清单草案(试点版)的通知), promulgated jointly by the National Development and Reform Commission and the Ministry of Commerce on 24 October 2019 and effective as of the same date.
Administrative Licensing Law	PRC Administrative Licensing Law (中华人民共和国行政许可法), adopted at the 4th Session of the Standing Committee of the 10th National People's Congress on 27 August 2003 and amended at the 10th Session of the Standing Committee of the 13th National People's Congress on 23 April 2019 and effective as of the same date.
Administrative Reconsideration Law	PRC Administrative Reconsideration Law (中华人民共和国行政复议法), adopted at the 9th Session of the Standing Committee of the 9th National People's Congress on 29 April 1999, amended at the 10th Session of the Standing Committee of the 11th National People's Congress on 27 August 2009 and amended at the 29th Session of the Standing Committee of the 12th National People's Congress on 1 September 2017 and with effect as of 1 January 2018.
Administrative Regulations for Enterprise Legal Person Registration	PRC Regulations on the Administration of Enterprise Legal Person Registration (中华人民共和国企业法人登记管理条例), promulgated by the State Council on 3 June 1988, amended on 19 February 2014, amended on 6 February 2016 and amended on 2 March 2019.

(continued)

Administrative Procedure Law	PRC Administrative Procedure Law (中华人民共和国行政诉讼法), adopted at the 2nd Session of the 7th National People's Congress on 4 April 1989, amended at the 11th Session of the Standing Committee of the 12th National People's Congress on 1 November 2014 and amended at the 28th Session of the 12th National People's Congress on 27 June 2017 and effective as of 1 July 2017.
Anti-monopoly Law	PRC Anti-monopoly Law (中华人民共和国反垄断法), adopted at the 29th Session of the Standing Committee of the 10th National People's Congress on 30 August 2007 and effective as of 1 August 2008.
Arbitration Law	PRC Arbitration Law (中华人民共和国仲裁法), adopted at the 9th Session of the Standing Committee of the 8th National People's Congress on 31 August 1994, amended on 27 August 2009 and effective as of the same date.
Catalogue for Guiding FDI to Central and Western China	Catalogue of Priority Industries for Foreign Investment in Central and Western China (中西部地区外商投资优势产业目录), promulgated jointly by the National Development and Reform Commission and the Ministry of Commerce on 16 June 2000; amended on 23 December 2008, amended on 9 May 2013 and amended on 17 February 2017 and repealed on 30 July 2019.
Catalogue for Guiding Industrial Restructuring	Catalogue for Guiding Industrial Restructuring (产业结构调整指导目录), promulgated by the National Development and Reform Commission on 27 March 2011, amended on 16 February 2013 and amended on 30 October 2019 with effect as of 1 January 2020.
Catalogue of Encouraged Hi-tech Products for Foreign Investment	Catalogue of Encouraged Hi-tech Products for Foreign Investment (鼓励外商投资高新技术产品目录), promulgated jointly by the Ministry of Commerce and Ministry of Science and Technology on 2 June 2003 and amended on 31 December 2006.
Catalogue of Encouraged Industries for Foreign Investment	Catalogue of Industries for Encouraging Foreign Investment (2019 Version) (鼓励外商投资产业目录(2019年版)), promulgated jointly by the National Development and Reform Commission and the Ministry of Commerce on 30 June 2019 with effect as of 30 July 2019.
Circular On Deregistration after Dissolution of FIEs	Circular on certain issues regarding the deregistration after dissolution of Foreign-Invested Enterprises (外商投资企业解散注销登记管理有关问题的通知), promulgated jointly by the State Administration for Industry and Commerce and the Ministry of Commerce on 20 November 2008 with effect as of the same day.
Civil Procedure Law	PRC Civil Procedure Law (中华人民共和国民事诉讼法), adopted at the 4th Session of the 7th National People's Congress on 9 April 1991; amended at the 30th Meeting of the Standing Committee of the 10th National People's Congress on 28 October 2007, amended at the 28th Session of the Standing Committee of the 11th National People's Congress on 31 August 2012, and amended at the 28th Meeting of the Standing Committee of the 12th National People's Congress on 27 June 2017.

(continued)

CJV Implementing Regulations	PRC Sino-Foreign Cooperative Joint Venture Law Detailed Implementing Regulations (中华人民共和国中外合作经营企业法实施细则), promulgated by the State Council on 4 September 1995, amended on 19 February 2014, amended on 1 March 2017 and repealed on 1 January 2020.
CJV Law	PRC Sino-Foreign Cooperative Joint Venture Law (中华人民共和国中外合作经营企业法), adopted at the 1st Session of the 7th National People's Congress on 13 April 1988; amended at the 18th Session of the Standing Committee of the 9th National People's Congress on 31 October 2000, amended at the 22nd Session of the Standing Committee of the 12th National People's Congress on 3 September 2016, amended at the 30th Session of the Standing Committee of the 12th National People's Congress on 4 November 2017 and repealed on 1 January 2020.
Company Law	PRC Company Law (中华人民共和国公司法), adopted at the 5th Session of the Standing Committee of the 8th National People's Congress on 29 December 1993; amended at the 13th Session of the Standing Committee of the 9th National People's Congress on 25 December 1999; amended at the 11th Session of the Standing Committee of the 10th National People's Congress on 28 August 2004; amended at the 18th Session of the Standing Committee of the 10th National People's Congress on 27 October 2005; amended at the 6th Session of the Standing Committee of the 12th National People's Congress on 28 December 2013; and amended at the 6th Session of the Standing Committee of the 13th National People's Congress on 26 October 2018 and effective as of the same date.
Constitution of the PRC (Constitution)	Constitution of the PRC (中华人民共和国宪法), adopted at the 5th Session of the 5th National People's Congress on 4 December 1982, amended at the 1st Session of the 7th National People's Congress on 12 April 1988, amended at the 1st Session of the 8th National People's Congress on 29 March 1993, amended at the 2nd Session of the 9th National People's Congress on 15 March 1999, amended at the 2nd Session of the 10th National People's Congress on 14 March 2004, and amended at the 1st Session of the 13th National People's Congress on 11 March 2018.
Contract Law	PRC Contract Law (中华人民共和国合同法), adopted at the 2nd Session of the 9th National People's Congress on 15 March 1999 and effective as of 1 October 1999.
Decision to Revise FIE Laws	Decision to Revise Four Laws including the PRC Wholly Foreign-Owned Enterprise Law (修改《中华人民共和国外资企业法》等四部法律的决定), adopted at the 22nd Session of the Standing Committee of the 12th National People's Congress on 3 September 2016 and effective as of 1 October 2016.
Draft Civil Code	PRC Civil Code (Draft) (中华人民共和国民法典 (草案)), issued by the NPC in November and December 2019.
Draft FIE Administration Measures	Interim Measures for the Administration of the Establishment and Change of Foreign-invested Enterprises (Draft for Comments) (《外商投资企业设立及变更备案管理暂行办法》(征求意见稿)), promulgated by the Ministry of Commerce on 3 September 2016.

(continued)

Draft FIL Implementing Regulations	PRC Foreign Investment Law Implementing Regulations (Draft for Comments) (中华人民共和国外商投资法实施条例(征求意见稿)), promulgated by the Ministry of Justice on 1 November 2019.
Draft FIPE Measures	Draft Administrative Measures for Foreign-Invested Partnership Enterprises (外商投资合伙企业管理办法(送审稿)), promulgated by the Ministry of Commerce on 23 January 2007, <http://www.mofcom.gov.cn/aarticle/bh/200703/20070304413083.html>, accessed 15 May 2020.
EJV Implementing Regulations	PRC Sino-Foreign Equity Joint Venture Law Implementing Regulations (中华人民共和国中外合资经营企业法实施条例), promulgated by the State Council on 20 September 1983; amended on 21 December 1987; amended on 22 July 2001; amended on 29 February 2014; amended on 2 March 2019 and repealed on 1 January 2020.
EJV Law	PRC Sino-Foreign Equity Joint Venture Law (中华人民共和国中外合资经营企业法), adopted by the 2nd Session of the 5th National People's Congress on 1 July 1979; amended at the 3rd Session of the 7th National People's Congress on 4 April 1990, amended at the 4th Session of the 9th National People's Congress on 15 March 2001, amended at the 22nd Session of the Standing Committee of the 12th National People's Congress on 3 September 2016 and repealed on 1 January 2020.
Enterprise Bankruptcy Law	PRC Enterprise Bankruptcy Law (中华人民共和国企业破产法), promulgated by the Standing Committee of the National People's Congress on 27 August 2006 with effect as of 1 June 2007.
Enterprise Income Tax Law	PRC Law on Enterprise Income Tax (中华人民共和国企业所得税法), adopted at the 5th Session of the 10th National People's Congress on 16 March 2007, amended at the 26th session of the Standing Committee of the 12th National People's Congress on 24 February 2017, amended at the 7th Session of the Standing Committee of the 13th National People's Congress on 29 December 2018 with effect as of the same day.
Enterprise Income Tax Law Implementing Regulations	PRC Law on Enterprise Income Tax Implementing Regulations (中华人民共和国企业所得税法实施条例), promulgated by the State Council on 6 December 2007, amended on 23 April 2019 with effect as of the same day.
Enterprise Information Regulations	Interim Regulations on the Disclosure of Enterprise Information (企业信息公示暂行条例), promulgated by the State Council 7 August 2014 and effective as of 1 October 2014.
Enterprise Name Administrative Provisions	Administrative Provisions for the Enterprise Name Registration (企业名称登记管理规定), promulgated on 22 July 1991 and amended on 9 November 2012 with effect as of 1 January 2013.
Explanations on Draft FIPE Measures	Explanations on the Draft Administrative Measures for Foreign-Invested Partnership Enterprises (外商投资合伙企业管理办法(送审稿)起草说明), promulgated by the Ministry of Commerce on 23 January 2007, <http://www.mofcom.gov.cn/aarticle/bh/200703/20070304413077.html>, accessed 15 May 2020.
Explanatory Notes on the 2015 Draft Foreign Investment Law (Explanatory Notes on 2015 Draft FIL)	Explanatory Notes on the PRC Foreign Investment Law (Draft for Comments) (中华人民共和国外国投资法 (草案征求意见稿)的说明), promulgated by the Ministry of Commerce on 19 January 2015.

(continued)

Explanatory Notes on the CJV Implementing Regulations	Explanatory Notes on the Implementation of the "PRC Sino-Foreign Cooperative Joint Venture Law Detailed Implementing Regulations" (关于执行《中华人民共和国中外合作经营企业法实施细则》若干条款的说明), promulgated by the Ministry of Foreign Trade and Economic Cooperation on 22 October 1996.
FDI Encouragement Provisions	Provisions of the State Council for the Encouragement of Foreign Investment (国务院关于鼓励外商投资的规定), promulgated by the State Council on 11 October 1986.
FICLS Provisions	Interim Provisions on Certain Issues Concerning the Establishment of Foreign-invested Companies Limited by Shares (关于设立外商投资股份有限公司若干问题的暂行规定), promulgated by the Ministry of Foreign Trade and Economic Cooperation on 1 October 1995, amended on 28 October 2015 and repealed on 1 January 2020.
FIE Administration Circular	Circular on Issues Related to Strengthening the Administration over the Approval, Registration, Foreign Exchange, and Taxation Pertaining to Foreign-Invested Enterprises (关于加强外商投资企业审批、登记、外汇及税收管理有关问题的通知), promulgated jointly by the State Administration for Industry and Commerce; State Administration of Foreign Exchange; Ministry of Foreign Trade and Economic Cooperation and State Administration of Taxation on 30 December 2002 and effective as of 1 January 2003.
FIE Administration Measures	Interim Measures for the Administration of the Establishment and Change of Foreign-invested Enterprises (外商投资企业设立及变更备案管理暂行办法), promulgated by the Ministry of Commerce on 8 October 2016, revised on 30 July 2017, revised on 29 June 2018 and repealed on 1 January 2020.
FIE Changes in Equity Provisions	Certain Provisions on Change of the Equity Interests of the Investors of a Foreign-Invested Enterprise (外商投资企业投资者股权变更的若干规定), promulgated by the Ministry of Foreign Trade and Economic Cooperation and the State Administration for Industry and Commerce on 28 May 1997 and repealed on 1 January 2020.
FIE HoldCo Provisions	Interim Provisions on Foreign Investor's Establishment of Companies with Investment Nature (关于外商投资举办投资性公司的暂行规定), promulgated by the Ministry of Foreign Trade and Economic Cooperation on 4 April 1995 and repealed by the Provisions on the Establishment of Investment Companies by Foreign Investors (关于外商投资举办投资性公司的规定), promulgated by the Ministry of Commerce on 17 November 2004, amended on 26 May 2006 and amended on 28 October 2015 with effect as of the same date.
FIE Mergers and Divisions Provisions	Provisions on Merger and Division of Foreign-Invested Enterprises (关于外商投资企业合并与分立的规定), promulgated by the Ministry of Foreign Trade and Economic Cooperation and the State Administration for Industry and Commerce on 23 September 1999, amended on 22 September 2001 and amended on 28 October 2015.

(continued)

FIE Reinvestment Provisions	Interim Provisions on Investment Made by Foreign-Invested Enterprises in China (关于外商投资企业境内投资的暂行规定), promulgated by the Ministry of Foreign Trade and Economic Cooperation and the State Administration for Industry and Commerce on 25 July 2000, amended on 26 May 2006 and amended on 28 October 2015.
FIL Implementing Regulations	PRC Foreign Investment Law Implementing Regulations (中华人民共和国外商投资法实施条例), promulgated by the State Council on 26 December 2019 and effective as of 1 January 2020.
FIPE Business Licence Circular	Circular on Usage of Business Licence for Foreign Investment Partnership Enterprise and Business Licence for Branches of Foreign Investment Partnership Enterprise (启用《外商投资合伙企业营业执照》和《外商投资合伙企业分支机构营业执照》的通知), promulgated by the State Administration for Industry and Commerce on 12 February 2010 and repealed on 14 July 2014.
FIPE Implementation Circular	Circular on Implementing the Measures for the Administration of the Establishment of Partnership Enterprises by Foreign Enterprises or Individuals in China (《外国企业或者个人在中国境内设立合伙企业管理办法》贯彻实施工作的通知), promulgated by the State Administration for Industry and Commerce on 10 February 2010 and repealed on 31 May 2016.
FIPE Measures	Measures for the Administration of the Establishment of Partnership Enterprises by Foreign Enterprises or Individuals in the Territory of China (外国企业或者个人在中国境内设立合伙企业管理办法), promulgated by the State Council on 25 November 2009 and effective as of 1 March 2010.
FIPE Provisions	Administrative Provisions for the Registration of Foreign-Invested Partnership Enterprises (外商投资合伙企业登记管理规定), promulgated by the State Administration of Industry and Commerce on 29 January 2010 with effect from 1 March 2010, amended on 20 February 2014 and amended on 8 August 2019.
FIVCE Provisions	Interim Provisions on Establishing Foreign Venture Capital Investment Enterprises (设立外商投资创业投资企业的暂行规定), promulgated jointly by the Ministry of Foreign Trade and Economic Cooperation, the Ministry of Science and Technology and the State Administration of Industry and Commerce on 28 August 2001; later replaced by the Administrative Provisions for Foreign-Invested Venture Capital Investment Enterprises (外商投资创业投资企业管理规定), promulgated on 30 January 2003 and amended on 28 October 2015.
Foreign Investment Law (FIL)	PRC Foreign Investment Law (中华人民共和国外商投资法), adopted at the 2nd Session of the 13th National People's Congress on 15 March 2019 and with effect as of 1 January 2020.
Foreign-Related Civil Relations Law	PRC Law on the Application of Laws to Foreign-Related Civil Relations (中华人民共和国涉外民事关系法律适用法), adopted at the 17th Session of the Standing Committee of the 11th National People's Congress on 28 October 2010 and effective as of 1 April 2011.

(continued)

FOREX Circular	Circular on the Administration of Foreign Exchange Involved in Offshore Investment, Financing and Round-Trip Investment Conducted by Domestic Residents Through Special Purpose Vehicles (境内居民通过境外特殊目的公司融资及返程投资外汇管理有关问题的通知), promulgated by the State Administration of Foreign Exchange on 4 July 2014 with effect as of the same day.
FTZ Negative List	Special Management Measures on the Entry of Foreign Investment into the China (Shanghai) Pilot Free Trade Zone (2013 Negative List) (中国(上海)自由贸易试验区外商投资准入特别管理措施(负面清单) (2013年修订)), promulgated by the Shanghai Municipal People's Government on 29 September 2013, repealed by the Special Management Measures on the Entry of Foreign Investment into the China (Shanghai) Pilot Free Trade Zone (2014 Negative List) (中国(上海)自由贸易试验区外商投资准入特别管理措施(负面清单) (2014年修订)), promulgated by the Shanghai Municipal People's Government on 30 June 2014, and substituted by the Special Management Measures for the Market Entry of Foreign Investment into Pilot Free Trade Zones (Negative List) (自由贸易试验区外商投资准入特别管理措施(负面清单)), promulgated by the General Office of the State Council on 8 April 2015, amended on 5 June 2017; amended jointly by the National Development and Reform Commission and the Ministry of Commerce on 30 June 2018 and amended on 30 June 2019 with effect as of 30 July 2019.
General Principles of Civil Law (GPCL)	PRC General Principles of the Civil Law (中华人民共和国民法通则), adopted at the 4th Session of the 6th National People's Congress on 12 April 1986, amended at the 10th Session of the Standing Committee of the 11th National People's Congress on August 27, 2009 and effective from the same date.
General Rules of Civil Law (GRCL)	PRC General Rules of Civil Law (中华人民共和国民法总则), adopted at the 5th Session of the 12th National People's Congress 15 on March 2017 and with effect as 1 October 2017.
Guidance Catalogue	Catalogue of Industries for Guiding Foreign Investment (外商投资产业指导目录), promulgated jointly by the National Development and Reform Commission and Ministry of Commerce on 20 June 1995, amended on 31 December 1997, amended on 3 November 2002, amended on 30 November 2004, amended on 31 October 2007, amended on 24 December 2011, amended on 10 March 2015, amended on 28 June 2017, amended on 28 June 2018 and most recently amended on 30 June 2019 with effect as of 30 July 2019.
Guidance Provisions	Interim Provisions Guiding Foreign Investment (指导外商投资方向暂行规定), promulgated jointly by the State Planning Commission; State Economic and Trade Commission and Ministry of Foreign Trade and Economic Cooperation on 20 June 1995; subsequently repealed by the Provisions on Guiding the Direction of Foreign Investment (指导外商投资方向规定), promulgated by the State Council on 11 February 2002 and effective as of 1 April 2002.

(continued)

Implementing Measures for Interim Regulations on Private Enterprises	Implementing Measures for PRC Interim Regulations on Private Enterprises (中华人民共和国私营企业暂行条例施行办法), promulgated by the State Administration of Industry and Commerce on 16 January 1989; amended on 17 December 1996 and amended on 3 December 1998.
Implementing Measures for Interim Regulations on Private Enterprises	Measures for Implementing the Interim Regulations on Private Enterprises (私营企业暂行条例施行办法), promulgated by the Finance and Economic Commission of the Administrative Council on 30 March 1951 and repealed on 25 July 1986.
Individual Income Tax Law	PRC Law on Individual Income Tax (中华人民共和国个人所得税法), adopted at the 3rd Session of the 5th National People's Congress on 10 September 1980, amended at the 4th Session of the Standing Committee of the 8th National People's Congress on 31 October 1993, amended at the 11th Session of the Standing Committee of the 9th National People's Congress on 30 August 1999, amended at the 18th Session of the Standing Committee of the 10th National People's Congress on 27 October 2005, amended at the 28th Session of the Standing Committee of the 10th National People's Congress on 29 June 2007, amended at the 31st Session of the Standing Committee of the 10th National People's Congress on 29 December 2007, amended at the 21st Session of the Standing Committee of the 11th National People's Congress on 30 June 2011 and amended at the 5th Session of the Standing Committee of the 13th National People's Congress on 31 August 2018 and with effect as of 1 January 2019.
Institutional Reform Plan	Decision on the Institutional Reform Plan of the State Council (关于国务院机构改革方案的决定), adopted at the 1st Session of the 13th National People's Congress on 17 March 2018 and effective as of the same day.
Interim Provisions on the Merger of State-Owned and Private-Owned Industrial Enterprises	Interim Provisions on the Merger of State-Owned and Private-Owned Industrial Enterprises (公私合营工业企业暂行条例), promulgated by the Administrative Council on 5 September 1954 and repealed on 25 July 1986.
Interim Regulations on Private Enterprises	PRC Interim Regulations on Private Enterprises (中华人民共和国私营企业暂行条例), promulgated by the State Council on 26 June 1988 and repealed on 19 March 2018.
Interpretation of the Opinions on Applying the Company Law	Interpretation of Key Provisions of the "Implementing Opinions on Certain Issues Concerning the Application of the Law in the Administration of the Examination, Approval and Registration of Foreign-Invested Enterprises" (《关于外商投资的公司审批登记管理法律适用若干问题的执行意见》重点条款解读), promulgated by the State Administration for Industry and Commerce on 22 September 2006.
Investment Fund Measures	Interim Measures for the Supervision and Administration of Private Investment Funds (私募投资基金监督管理暂行办法), promulgated by the China Securities Regulatory Commission on 21 August 2014 with effect as of the same day.
Law Firm Measures	Measures for the Administration of Law Firms (律师事务所管理办法), promulgated by the Ministry of Justice on 18 July 2008, amended on 30 November 2012, amended on 6 September 2016, and amended on 5 December 2018 with effect as of 15 January 2019.

(continued)

Lawyers Law	PRC Law on Lawyers (中华人民共和国律师法), adopted at the 19th Session of the Standing Committee of the 9th National People's Congress on 15 May 1996; amended at the 25th Session of the Standing Committee of the 9th National People's Congress on 29 December 2001, amended at the 30th Session of the Standing Committee of the 10th National People's Congress on 28 October 2007, amended at the 29th Session of the Standing Committee of the 11th National People's Congress on 26 October 2012, and amended at the 29th Session of the Standing Committee of the 12th National People's Congress on 1 September 2017 and with effect as of 1 January 2018.
Legislation Law	PRC Legislation Law (中华人民共和国立法法), adopted at the 3rd Session of the 9th National People's Congress on 15 March 2000; amended at the 3rd Session of the 12th National People's Congress on 15 March 2015.
M&A Provisions	Interim Provisions on Mergers with and Acquisitions of Domestic Enterprises by Foreign Investors (关于外国投资者并购境内企业暂行规定), promulgated jointly by the Ministry of Foreign Trade and Economic Cooperation, the State Taxation Administration, the State Administration for Industry and Commerce, and the State Administration of Foreign Exchange on 2 January 2003; later repealed by the Provisions on Mergers with and Acquisitions of Domestic Enterprises by Foreign Investors (关于外国投资者并购境内企业的规定), promulgated jointly by the Ministry of Commerce, State-Owned Assets Supervision and Administration Commission of the State Council, State Administration of Taxation, State Administration of Industry and Commerce, China Securities Regulatory Commission and State Administration of Foreign Exchange on 8 August 2006 and amended on 22 June 2009.
Made in China 2025 Circular	Circular on the publication of "Made in China 2025" (印发《中国制造2025》的通知), promulgated by the State Council on 8 May 2015.
Market Access Negative List Opinion	Opinions on Implementing the System of Negative List for Market Access (实行市场准入负面清单制度的意见), promulgated by the State Council on 2 October 2015 and effective as of the same date.
Measures for Authorisation of FIE Registration	Administrative Measures on the Authorisation over the Registration of Foreign Invested Enterprises (外商投资企业授权登记管理办法), promulgated by the State Administration of Industry and Commerce on 12 December and amended on 29 April 2016.
NDRC Circular No 111	Circular on Proper Implementation of the Catalogue of Investment Projects Subject to Government Verification - 2016 Version - Regarding Foreign Investments (做好贯彻落实《政府核准的投资项目目录(2016年本)》有关外资工作的通知), promulgated by the National Development and Reform Commission on 14 January 2017 and effective as of the same date.
Notice No 22	Notice No 22 of 2016 (公告2016年第22号), promulgated jointly by the National Development and Reform Commission and the Ministry of Commerce on 8 October 2016 and effective as of the same date.

(continued)

Notice on Registration of FIEs	Notice on Effectively Completing the Registration of Foreign Invested Enterprises for the Implementation of the Foreign Investment Law (贯彻落实《外商投资法》做好外商投资企业登记注册工作的通知), promulgated by the State Administration for Market Regulation on 31 December 2019 and effective as of 1 January 2020.
Opinion of the SPC on the Implementation of the GPCL	Opinions on Certain Issues Concerning the Implementation of the "General Principles of Civil Law of the PRC" (Trial) (贯彻执行《中华人民共和国法通则》若干问题的意见 (试行)), promulgated by the Supreme People's Court on 26 January 1988 and revised on 18 December 2008 with effect as of 24 December 2008.
Opinions on Applying the Company Law	Implementing Opinions on Certain Issues Concerning the Application of the Law in the Administration of the Examination, Approval and Registration of Foreign-Invested Enterprises (关于外商投资的公司审批登记管理法律适用若干问题的执行意见), promulgated jointly by the State Administration for Industry and Commerce; Ministry of Commerce; General Administration of Customs and State Administration of Foreign Exchange on 24 April 2006.
Partnership Enterprise Administrative Circular	Circular on Proper Registration of Partnership Enterprise (做好合伙企业登记管理工作的通知), promulgated by the State Administration for Industry and Commerce on 29 May 2007 and effective as of the same date.
Partnership Enterprise Law (PEL)	PRC Partnership Enterprise Law (中华人民共和国合伙企业法), adopted at the 24th Session of the Standing Committee of the 8th National People's Congress on 23 February 1997; amended at the 23rd Session of the Standing Committee of the 10th National People's Congress on 27 August 2006 and effective from 1 June 2007.
Partnership Enterprise Registration Measures	PRC Administrative Measures for Partnership Enterprise Registration (中华人民共和国合伙企业登记管理办法), promulgated by the State Council on 19 November 1997, amended on 9 May 2007, amended on 19 February 2014 and amended on 2 March 2019.
Pilot Master Negative List Circular	Circular on the publication of the Draft Market Access Negative List (Pilot Edition) (印发市场准入负面清单草案(试点版)的通知), promulgated jointly by the National Development and Reform Commission and the Ministry of Commerce on 2 March 2016.
Property Law	PRC Property Law (中华人民共和国物权法), adopted at the 5th Session of the 10th National People's Congress on 16 March 2007 and effective from 1 October 2007.
QFLP Shanghai Pilot Measures	Implementation Measures on Pilot Program of Foreign-Invested Equity Investment Enterprises in Shanghai (本市开展外商投资股权投资企业试点工作的实施办法), jointly promulgated by the Shanghai Financial Services Office, Shanghai Municipal Commission of Commerce and Shanghai Administration for Industry and Commerce on 24 December 2010 with effect as of 24 January 2011.

(continued)

Record-Filing Administration Circular	Circular on Proper Registration for Foreign-Invested Enterprises after the Implementation of Record-Filing Administration (关于做好外商投资企业实行备案管理后有关登记注册工作的通知), promulgated by the State Administration of Industry and Commerce on 30 September 2016 and effective as of 1 October 2016.
Regulations on Guangdong SEZ	Regulations on Special Economic Zones in Guangdong Province (广东省经济特区条例), promulgated by the Standing Committee of the Guangdong Province People's Congress on 15 April 1980 and approved at the 15th Session of the Standing Committee of the 5th National People's Congress on 26 August 1980 and effective as of the same date.
Regulations on the Administration of Company Registration	Regulations on the Administration of Company Registration (中华人民共和国公司登记管理条例), promulgated by the State Council on 24 June 1994, amended on 18 December 2005, amended on 19 February 2014 and amended on 6 February 2016.
Regulations on the Zhongguancun Science and Technology Park	Regulations on the Zhongguancun Science and Technology Park (中关村科技园区条例), promulgated by the Standing Committee of the Beijing Municipal People's Congress on 8 December 2000 and repealed on 23 December 2010.
Reporting Measures	Foreign Investment Information Reporting Measures (外商投资信息报告办法), jointly promulgated by the Ministry of Commerce and the State Administration for Market Regulation on 30 December 2019 and effective as of 1 January 2020.
Reporting Notice	Notice No. 62 on Matters Relating to Foreign Investment Information Reporting (公告2019年第62号——关于外商投资信息报告有关事项的公告), promulgated by the Ministry of Commerce on 31 December 2019 and effective as of 1 January 2020.
SAFE Circular 19	Circular on Reforming the Administrative Approach Regarding the Settlement of the Foreign Exchange Capitals of Foreign-Invested Enterprises (改革外商投资企业外汇资本金结汇管理方式的通知), promulgated by the State Administration of Foreign Exchange on 30 March 2015 and amended on 30 December 2019.
SAFE Circular 37	Administrative Measures for Outbound Investment (境外投资管理办法), promulgated by the Ministry of Commerce on 6 September 2014 with effect as of 6 October 2014.
SAFE Circular 142	Circular on the Relevant Operating Issues concerning the Improvement of the Administration of Payment and Settlement of Foreign Currency Capital of Foreign-Invested Enterprises (完善外商投资企业外汇资本金支付结汇管理有关业务操作问题的通知), promulgated by the General Affairs Department of the State Administration of Foreign Exchange on 29 August 2008 and repealed with effect as of 1 June 2015.
Securities Law	PRC Security Law (中华人民共和国担保法), adopted at the 14th Session of the Standing Committee of the 8th National People's Congress on 30 June 1995 and effective from 1 October 1995.
Shanghai FTZ Authorisation Decision	Decision Authorising the State Council to Temporarily Adjust Administrative Approvals under Relevant Laws Within the China (Shanghai) Pilot Free Trade Zone (授权国务院在中国(上海)自由贸易试验区暂时调整有关法律规定的行政审批的决定), adopted at the 4th Session of the Standing Committee of the 12th National People's Congress on 30 August 2013, effective as of 1 October 2013 and repealed with effect as of 1 October 2016 by Art. 4 para. 3 of the Decision to Revise FIE Laws.

(continued)

Shanghai FTZ Confirmation Plan	Plan for the Comprehensive Deepening of the Reform and Liberalisation of the China (Shanghai) Pilot Free Trade Zone (全面深化中国(上海)自由贸易试验区改革开放方案的通知), promulgated by the State Council on 30 March 2017 with effect as of the same day.
Shanghai FTZ General Plan	General Plan for the China (Shanghai) Pilot Free Trade Zone (中国(上海)自由贸易试验区总体方案), promulgated by the State Council on 18 September 2013.
Shenzhen Partnership Regulations	Regulations of the Shenzhen Special Economic Zone on Partnerships (深圳经济特区合伙条例), promulgated by the Standing Committee of the Shenzhen Municipal People's Congress on 20 April 1994 and effective as of 1 May 1994; repealed on 27 April 2012.
SPC Interpretation of the Civil Procedure Law	Interpretations of the Application of the PRC Civil Procedure Law (适用《中华人民共和国民事诉讼法》的解释), promulgated by the Supreme People's Court on 30 January 2015 and with effect as of 4 February 2015.
SPC Interpretation of the Contract Law	First Interpretation of Certain Issues Concerning the Application of the "PRC Contract Law" (适用《中华人民共和国合同法》若干问题的解释(一)), promulgated by the Supreme People's Court on 29 December 1999 and with effect as of the same date.
SPC Interpretation of the Foreign Investment Law	Interpretation of Certain Issues Concerning the Application of the "PRC Foreign Investment Law" (适用《中华人民共和国外商投资法》若干问题的解释), promulgated by the Supreme People's Court on 26 December 2019 and with effect as of 1 January 2020.
SPC Interpretation of the Foreign-Related Civil Relations Law	First Interpretation of Certain Issues Concerning the Application of the "PRC Law on the Application of Laws to Foreign-Related Civil Relations" (适用《中华人民共和国涉外民事关系法律适用法》若干问题的解释(一)), promulgated by the Supreme People's Court on 28 December 2012 and with effect as of 7 January 2013.
State Council Circular No 5	Circular on Several Measures for the Active Use of Foreign Capital in Opening Up to the Outside World (扩大对外开放积极利用外资若干措施的通知), promulgated by the State Council on 12 January 2017 and effective as of the same date.
State Council Circular No 19	Circular on Several Measures for the Active and Effective Use of Foreign Capital to Promote Quality Economic Development (积极有效利用外资推动经济高质量发展若干措施的通知), promulgated by the State Council on 10 June 2018 and effective as of the same date.
Tax Circular 91	Circular Concerning Collecting Individual Income Tax from Investors of Sole Proprietorship Enterprises and Partnership Enterprises (关于个人独资企业和合伙企业投资者征收个人所得税的规定的通知), jointly promulgated by the Ministry of Finance and State Administration of Taxation on 19 September 2000, amended on 10 April 2006, amended on 3 June 2008 and amended on 29 July 2011.
Tax Circular 159	Circular on Issues Concerning Income Tax for Partners of Partnership Enterprises (关于合伙企业合伙人所得税问题的通知), promulgated jointly by the Ministry of Finance and State Administration of Taxation on 23 December 2008 and effective as of 1 January 2008.

(continued)

Tax Circular 698	Circular on Strengthening the Management of Enterprise Income Tax Collection of Proceeds from Equity Transfers by Non-Resident Enterprises (加强非居民企业股权转让所得企业所得税管理的通知), promulgated by the State Administration of Taxation on 10 December 2009, amended on 12 December 2013, amended on 3 February 2015 and amended on 17 October 2017.
Third SPC Interpretation of the Company Law	Third Interpretation of Certain Issues Concerning the Application of the "PRC Company Law" (适用《中华人民共和国公司法》若干问题的规定(三)), promulgated by the Supreme People's Court on 27 January 2011 and amended on 20 February 2014 with effect as of 1 March 2014.
WFOE Implementing Regulations	PRC Wholly Foreign-Owned Enterprise Law Detailed Implementing Regulations (中华人民共和国外资企业法实施细则), approved by the State Council on 28 October 1990 and promulgated by the Ministry of Foreign Economic Relations and Trade on 12 December 1990; amended on 12 April 2001, amended on 19 February 2014 and repealed on 1 January 2020.
WFOE Law	PRC Wholly Foreign-Owned Enterprise Law (中华人民共和国外资企业法), adopted at the 4th Session of the 6th National People's Congress on 12 April 1986; amended at the 18th Session of the Standing Committee of the 9th National People's Congress on 31 October 2000, amended at the 22nd Session of the Standing Committee of the 12th National People's Congress on 3 September 2016 and repealed on 1 January 2020.

II. Federal Republic of Germany

German Civil Code (BGB)	German Civil Code (Bürgerliches Gestzbuch), adopted by the German Reichstag on 18 August 1896; last amended by the German Bundestag on 19 March 2020.
German Commercial Code (HGB)	German Commercial Code (Handelsgesetzbuch), adopted by the German Reichstag on 10 May 1897; last amended by the German Bundestag on 12 December 2019.
German Partnership Enterprise Law	German Partnership Enterprise Law (Partnerschaftsgesellschaftsgesetz), promulgated on 30 July 1994; last amended on 22 December 2015.

III. United States of America

RUPA	Revised Uniform Partnership Act, promulgated by the National Conference of Commissioners on Uniform State Laws in 1997 as a replacement for the 1914 Uniform Partnership Act ("UPA"), later amended in 2011 and 2013.
ULPA	Uniform Limited Partnership Act (2001), promulgated by the National Conference of Commissioners on Uniform State Laws in 2001, amended in 2011 and 2013.
UPA	Uniform Partnership Act, promulgated by the National Conference of Commissioners on Uniform State Laws in 1914, subsequently revised and amended multiple times until it has been replaced in 1997 by the Revised Uniform Partnership Act.

IV. International Governmental Organisation and Bilateral Agreements

Agreement on Trade in Services	Mainland and Hong Kong Closer Economic Partnership Arrangement—Agreement on Trade in Services (内地与香港关于建立更紧密经贸关系的安排–服务贸易协议), signed by the governments of the PRC and the Hong Kong Special Administrative Region on 27 November 2015 and effective as of 1 June 2016.
Closer Economic Partnership Arrangement (CEPA)	Mainland and Hong Kong Closer Economic Partnership Arrangement (内地与香港关于建立更紧密经贸关系的安排), signed by the governments of the PRC and the Hong Kong Special Administrative Region on 29 June 2003.
German-Chinese Bilateral Investment Treaty	Agreement between the Federal Republic of Germany and the PRC on the Encouragement and Reciprocal Protection of Investments, concluded on 1 December 2003 and effective as of 11 November 2005, published at the Federal Law Gazette (Bundesgesetzblatt), 2005 Part II, pp. 732–742.
Investment Agreement	Mainland and Hong Kong Closer Economic Partnership Arrangement—Investment Agreement (内地与香港关于建立更紧密经贸关系的安排–投资协议) signed by the governments of the PRC and the Hong Kong Special Administrative Region on 28 June 2017 and effective as of 1 January 2018.
New York Convention	Convention on the Recognition and Enforcement of Foreign Arbitral Awards, promulgated by the Secretary-General of the United Nations and effective as of 7 June 1959.

The manufacturer's authorised representative in the EU is Springer
Nature Customer Service Centre GmbH, Europaplatz 3, 69115 Heidelberg,
Germany. If you have any concerns regarding our products, please
contact ProductSafety@springernature.com

Printed and bound by CPI Group (UK) Ltd, Croydon, CR0 4YY
30/09/2026
02225325-0015